CAMBRIDGE
UNIVERSITY PRESS

Biology

for Cambridge International AS & A Level

COURSEBOOK

Mary Jones, Richard Fosbery, Dennis Taylor & Jennifer Gregory

CAMBRIDGE
UNIVERSITY PRESS

University Printing House, Cambridge CB2 8BS, United Kingdom

One Liberty Plaza, 20th Floor, New York, NY 10006, USA

477 Williamstown Road, Port Melbourne, VIC 3207, Australia

314–321, 3rd Floor, Plot 3, Splendor Forum, Jasola District Centre, New Delhi – 110025, India

79 Anson Road, #06–04/06, Singapore 079906

Cambridge University Press is part of the University of Cambridge.

It furthers the University's mission by disseminating knowledge in the pursuit of education, learning and research at the highest international levels of excellence.

www.cambridge.org
Information on this title: www.cambridge.org/9781108859028

© Cambridge University Press 2020

First edition 2003
Second edition 2007
Third edition 2012
Fourth edition 2014
Fifth edition 2020

20 19 18 17 16 15 14 13 12 11 10 9 8 7 6 5 4 3 2 1

Printed in Dubai by Oriental Press

A catalogue record for this publication is available from the British Library

ISBN 978-1-108-85902-8 Coursebook Paperback with Digital Access (2 Years)
ISBN 978-1-108-79651-4 Digital Coursebook (2 Years)
ISBN 978-1-108-79653-8 Coursebook eBook

Additional resources for this publication at www.cambridge.org/9781108859028

DEDICATED TEACHER AWARDS

Teachers play an important part in shaping futures. Our Dedicated Teacher Awards recognise the hard work that teachers put in every day.

Thank you to everyone who nominated this year; we have been inspired and moved by all of your stories. Well done to all our nominees for your dedication to learning and for inspiring the next generation of thinkers, leaders and innovators.

Congratulations to our incredible winner and finalists

WINNER

Ahmed Saya
rdoba School for A-Level,
Pakistan

Sharon Kong Foong
Sunway College,
Malaysia

Abhinandan Bhattacharya
JBCN International School Oshiwara,
India

Anthony Chelliah
Gateway College,
Sri Lanka

Candice Green
St Augustine's College,
Australia

Jimrey Buntas Dapin
University of San Jose-Recoletos,
Philippines

For more information about our dedicated teachers and their stories, go to

dedicatedteacher.cambridge.org

CAMBRIDGE
UNIVERSITY PRESS

Brighter Thinking
Better Learning

Building Brighter Futures **Together**

> # Contents

Introduction   vii

How to use this series   ix

How to use this book   xi

1 Cell structure

1.1	Cells are the basic units of life	3
1.2	Cell biology and microscopy	4
1.3	Plant and animal cells as seen with a light microscope	4
1.4	Measuring size and calculating magnification	11
1.5	Electron microscopy	14
1.6	Plant and animal cells as seen with an electron microscope	17
1.7	Bacteria	32
1.8	Comparing prokaryotic cells with eukaryotic cells	34
1.9	Viruses	34

2 Biological molecules

2.1	Biochemistry	45
2.2	The building blocks of life	45
2.3	Monomers, polymers and macromolecules	45
2.4	Carbohydrates	46
2.5	Lipids	53
2.6	Proteins	57
2.7	Water	66

3 Enzymes

3.1	What is an enzyme?	75
3.2	Mode of action of enzymes	76
3.3	Investigating the progress of an enzyme-catalysed reaction	79
3.4	Factors that affect enzyme action	81
3.5	Comparing enzyme affinities	84
3.6	Enzyme inhibitors	85
3.7	Immobilising enzymes	87

4 Cell membranes and transport

4.1	The importance of membranes	98
4.2	Structure of membranes	98
4.3	Roles of the molecules found in membranes	101
4.4	Cell signalling	102
4.5	Movement of substances across membranes	104

5 The mitotic cell cycle

5.1	Growth and reproduction	124
5.2	Chromosomes	125
5.3	The cell cycle	126
5.4	Mitosis	127
5.5	The role of telomeres	132
5.6	The role of stem cells	133
5.7	Cancers	134

6 Nucleic acids and protein synthesis

6.1	The molecule of life	144
6.2	The structure of DNA and RNA	144
6.3	DNA replication	149
6.4	The genetic code	150
6.5	Protein synthesis	151
6.6	Gene mutations	153

7 Transport in plants

7.1	The transport needs of plants	163
7.2	Vascular system: xylem and phloem	163
7.3	Structure of stems, roots and leaves and the distribution of xylem and phloem	164
7.4	The transport of water	170
7.5	Transport of assimilates	180

8 Transport in mammals

8.1	Transport systems in animals	194
8.2	The mammalian circulatory system	194
8.3	Blood vessels	195

8.4	Tissue fluid	200
8.5	Blood	202
8.6	The heart	209

9 Gas exchange

9.1	Gas exchange	224
9.2	Lungs	225
9.3	Trachea, bronchi and bronchioles	226
9.4	Warming and cleaning the air	226
9.5	Alveoli	228

10 Infectious disease

| 10.1 | Infectious diseases | 238 |
| 10.2 | Antibiotics | 253 |

11 Immunity

11.1	Defence against disease	267
11.2	Cells of the immune system	268
11.3	Active and passive immunity	277

P1 Practical skills for AS Level

P1.1	Practical skills	292
P1.2	Experiments	292
P1.3	Variables and making measurements	292
P1.4	Recording quantitative results	298
P1.5	Displaying data	299
P1.6	Making conclusions	301
P1.7	Describing data	301
P1.8	Making calculations from data	301
P1.9	Identifying sources of error and suggesting improvements	303
P1.10	Drawings	304

12 Energy and respiration

12.1	The need for energy in living organisms	312
12.2	Aerobic respiration	313
12.3	Mitochondrial structure and function	319
12.4	Respiration without oxygen	320
12.5	Respiratory substrates	322

13 Photosynthesis

13.1	An energy transfer process	332
13.2	Structure and function of chloroplasts	333
13.3	The light-dependent stage of photosynthesis	337
13.4	The light-independent stage of photosynthesis	339
13.5	Limiting factors in photosynthesis	340

14 Homeostasis

14.1	Homeostasis	349
14.2	The structure of the kidney	352
14.3	Control of water content	360
14.4	The control of blood glucose	364
14.5	Homeostasis in plants	371

15 Control and coordination

15.1	Hormonal communication	388
15.2	Nervous communication	389
15.3	Muscle contraction	406
15.4	Control and coordination in plants	413

16 Inheritance

16.1	Gametes and reproduction	428
16.2	The production of genetic variation	433
16.3	Genetics	435
16.4	Monohybrid inheritance and genetic diagrams	437
16.5	Dihybrid inheritance	441
16.6	The chi-squared (χ^2) test	449
16.7	Genes, proteins and phenotype	451
16.8	Control of gene expression	453

17 Selection and evolution

17.1	Variation	465
17.2	Natural selection	469
17.3	Genetic drift and the founder effect	474
17.4	The Hardy–Weinberg principle	476
17.5	Artificial selection	478
17.6	Evolution	482
17.7	Identifying evolutionary relationships	486

18 Classification, biodiversity and conservation

18.1	Classification	497
18.2	Biodiversity	507
18.3	Maintaining biodiversity	521
18.4	Protecting endangered species	524
18.5	Controlling alien species	530
18.6	International conservation organisations	531

19 Genetic technology

19.1	Genetic engineering	544
19.2	Tools for the gene technologist	545
19.3	Gene editing	552
19.4	Separating and amplifying DNA	555
19.5	Analysing and storing genetic information	560
19.6	Genetic technology and medicine	564
19.7	Genetic technology and agriculture	570

P2 Practical skills for A Level

P2.1	Practical skills	582
P2.2	Planning an investigation	582
P2.3	Constructing a hypothesis	582
P2.4	Identifying variables	583
P2.5	Describing the sequence of steps	586
P2.6	Risk assessment	586
P2.7	Recording and displaying results	587
P2.8	Analysis, conclusions and evaluation	587
P2.9	Evaluating evidence	600
P2.10	Conclusions and discussion	600

Appendix 1: Amino acid R groups — 608

Appendix 2: DNA and RNA triplet codes — 609

Glossary — 611

Index — 631

Acknowledgements — 643

〉 Introduction

This is the fifth edition of the Cambridge International AS & A Level Biology Coursebook, and it provides everything that you need to support your course for Cambridge AS & A Level Biology (9700). It provides full coverage of the syllabus for examinations from 2022 onwards.

The chapters are arranged in the same sequence as the topics in the syllabus. Chapters 1 to P1 cover the AS material, and Chapters 12 to P2 cover the material needed for A Level. The various features that you will find in these chapters are explained on the next two pages.

Many questions will test a deeper understanding of the facts and concepts that you will learn during your course. It is therefore not enough just to learn words and diagrams that you can repeat in your examinations; you need to ensure that you really understand each concept fully. Trying to answer the questions that you will find within each chapter, and at the end of each chapter, should help you to do this.

Although you will study your biology as a series of different topics, it is very important to appreciate that all of these topics link up with each other. You need to make links between different areas of the syllabus to answer some questions. For example, you might be asked a question that involves bringing together knowledge about protein synthesis, infectious disease and transport in mammals. In particular, you will find that certain key concepts come up again and again. These include:

- Cells as units of life

- Biochemical processes

- DNA, the molecule of heredity

- Natural selection

- Organisms in their environment

- Observation and experiment.

As you work through your course, make sure that you keep reflecting on the work that you did earlier and how it relates to the current topic that you are studying. Some of the reflection questions at the ends of the chapters suggest particular links that you could think about. They also ask you to think about *how* you learn, which may help you to make the very best use of your time and abilities as your course progresses. You can also use the self-evaluation checklists at the end of each chapter to decide how well you have understood each topic in the syllabus, and whether or not you need to do more work on each one.

Practical skills are an important part of your biology course. You will develop these skills as you do experiments and other practical work related to the topics you are studying. Chapters P1 (for AS Level) and P2 (for A Level) explain what these skills are and what you need to be able to do.

You may like to look at two other books in this series – the Workbook and the Practical Workbook. The Workbook provides clear guidance on many of the skills that you need to develop as you work through the course – such as constructing and analysing graphs, and planning experiments – with exercises for you to try. The Practical Workbook is full of detailed explanations of how to carry out all the practicals required in the syllabus, and many others too, that will help you to become more confident in practical work.

This is an exciting time to be studying biology, with new discoveries and technologies constantly finding their way into the news. We very much hope that you will enjoy your biology course, and that this book will help you not only to prepare for your examinations but also to develop a life-long interest in this subject.

> How to use this series

This suite of resources supports students and teachers following the Cambridge International AS & A Level Biology syllabus (9700). All of the books in the series work together to help students develop the necessary knowledge and scientific skills required for this subject. With clear language and style, they are designed for international learners.

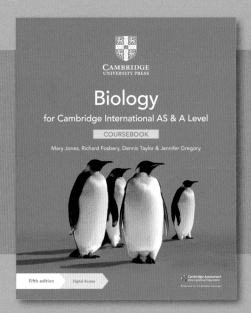

The coursebook provides comprehensive support for the full Cambridge International AS & A Level Biology syllabus (9700). It clearly explains facts, concepts and practical techniques, and uses real-world examples of scientific principles. Two chapters provide full guidance to help students develop investigative skills. Questions within each chapter help them to develop their understanding, while exam-style questions provide essential practice.

The workbook contains over 100 exercises and exam-style questions, carefully constructed to help learners develop the skills that they need as they progress through their Biology course. The exercises also help students develop understanding of the meaning of various command words used in questions, and provide practice in responding appropriately to these.

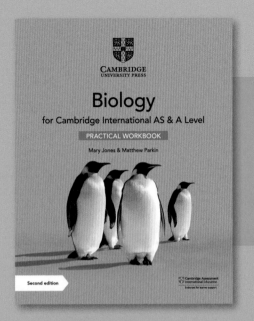

This write-in book provides students with a wealth of hands-on practical work, giving them full guidance and support that will help them to develop all of the essential investigative skills. These skills include planning investigations, selecting and handling apparatus, creating hypotheses, recording and displaying results, and analysing and evaluating data.

The teacher's resource supports and enhances the questions and practical activities in the coursebook. This resource includes detailed lesson ideas, as well as answers and exemplar data for all questions and activities in the coursebook and workbook. The practical teacher's guide, included with this resource, provides support for the practical activities and experiments in the practical workbook.

Teaching notes for each topic area include a suggested teaching plan, ideas for active learning and formative assessment, links to resources, ideas for lesson starters and plenaries, differentiation, lists of common misconceptions and suggestions for homework activities. Answers are included for every question and exercise in the coursebook, workbook and practical workbook. Detailed support is provided for preparing and carrying out for all the investigations in the practical workbook, including tips for getting things to work well, and a set of sample results that can be used if students cannot do the experiment, or fail to collect results.

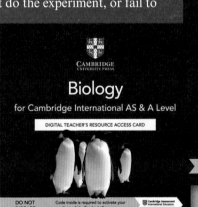

> How to use this book

Throughout this book, you will notice lots of different features that will help your learning. These are explained below.

LEARNING INTENTIONS

These set the scene for each chapter, help with navigation through the coursebook and indicate the important concepts in each topic.

BEFORE YOU START

This contains questions and activities on subject knowledge you will need before starting this chapter.

SCIENCE IN CONTEXT

This feature presents real-world examples and applications of the content in a chapter, encouraging you to look further into topics. There are discussion questions at the end which look at some of the benefits and problems of these applications.

PRACTICAL ACTIVITY

This book does not contain detailed instructions for doing particular experiments, but you will find background information about the practical work you need to do in these boxes. There are also two chapters, P1 and P2, which provide detailed information about the practical skills you need to develop during the course.

Questions

Appearing throughout the text, questions give you a chance to check that you have understood the topic you have just read about. You can find the answers to these questions in the digital version of the Coursebook.

KEY WORDS

Key vocabulary is highlighted in the text when it is first introduced. Definitions are then given in the margin, which explain the meanings of these words and phrases.

You will also find definitions of these words in the Glossary at the back of this book.

COMMAND WORDS

Command words that appear in the syllabus and might be used in exams are highlighted in the exam-style questions when they are first introduced. In the margin, you will find the Cambridge International definition. You will also find these definitions in the Glossary at the back of the book with some further explanation on the meaning of these words.*

*The information in this section is taken from the Cambridge International syllabus (9700) for examination from 2022. You should always refer to the appropriate syllabus document for the year of your examination to confirm the details and for more information. The syllabus document is available on the Cambridge International website at www.cambridgeinternational.org.

WORKED EXAMPLE

Wherever you need to know how to use a formula to carry out a calculation, there are worked examples boxes to show you how to do this.

REFLECTION

These activities ask you to look back on the topics covered in the chapter and test how well you understand these topics and encourage you to reflect on your learning.

IMPORTANT

Important equations, facts and tips are given in these boxes.

EXAM-STYLE QUESTIONS

Questions at the end of each chapter provide more demanding exam-style questions, some of which may require use of knowledge from previous chapters. Some questions are taken from past papers. Where this is the case, they include references to the relevant past paper. All other questions are written by the authors. Answers to these questions can be found in the digital version of the Coursebook.

SUMMARY

There is a summary of key points at the end of each chapter.

SELF-EVALUATION

The summary checklists are followed by 'I can' statements which match the Learning intentions at the beginning of the chapter. You might find it helpful to rate how confident you are for each of these statements when you are revising. You should revisit any topics that you rated 'Needs more work' or 'Almost there'.

I can	See section	Needs more work	Almost there	Ready to move on

These boxes tell you where information in the book is extension content, and is not part of the syllabus.

Chapter 1

Cell structure

LEARNING INTENTIONS

In this chapter you will learn how to:

- explain that cells are the basic units of life
- use the units of measurement relevant to microscopy
- recognise the common structures found in cells as seen with a light microscope and outline their structures and functions
- compare the key structural features of animal and plant cells
- use a light microscope and make temporary preparations to observe cells
- recognise, draw and measure cell structures from temporary preparations and micrographs
- calculate magnifications of images and actual sizes of specimens using drawings or micrographs
- explain the use of the electron microscope to study cells with reference to the increased resolution of electron microscopes
- recognise the common structures found in cells as seen with an electron microscope and outline their structures and functions
- outline briefly the role of ATP in cells
- describe the structure of bacteria and compare the structure of prokaryotic cells with eukaryotic cells
- describe the structure of viruses.

BEFORE YOU START

- Make a list of structures that could be found in a cell.

- Try to write down the functions of the structures you have listed.

- Which structures are found in plant cells and which are found in animal cells?

- Are there any cells that are not animal or plant cells?

THINKING OUTSIDE THE BOX

Progress in science often depends on people thinking 'outside the box' – original thinkers who are often ignored or even ridiculed when they first put forward their radical new ideas. One such individual, who battled constantly throughout her career to get her ideas accepted, was the American biologist Lynn Margulis (1938–2011; Figure 1.1). Her greatest achievement was to use evidence from microbiology to help firmly establish an idea that had been around since the mid-19th century – that new organisms can be created from combinations of existing organisms. Importantly, the existing organisms are not necessarily closely related. The organisms form a symbiotic partnership (they live together in a partnership in which both partners benefit). Margulis imagined that one organism engulfed ('ate') another. Normally the engulfed organism would be digested and killed, but sometimes the organism engulfed may survive and even be of benefit to the organism in which it finds itself. This type of symbiosis is known as endosymbiosis ('endo' means inside). A completely new type of organism is created, representing a dramatic evolutionary change.

The best-known example of Margulis' ideas is her suggestion that mitochondria and chloroplasts were originally free-living bacteria (prokaryotes). She suggested that these bacteria invaded the ancestors of modern eukaryotic cells, which are much larger and more complex cells than bacteria, and entered into a symbiotic relationship with the cells. This idea has been confirmed as true by later work. Margulis saw such symbiotic unions as a major driving cause of evolutionary change. Throughout her life, she continued to challenge the

Figure 1.1: Lynn Margulis: 'My work more than didn't fit in. It crossed the boundaries that people had spent their lives building up. It hits some 30 sub-fields of biology, even geology.'

traditional view, first put forward by Charles Darwin, that evolution occurs mainly as a result of competition between species.

Questions for discussion

- Can you think of any ideas people have had which were controversial at the time but are now accepted? Try to think of scientific examples. You may also like to consider why the ideas were controversial.

- Can you think of any scientific ideas people have now which are controversial and not accepted by everybody?

1.1 Cells are the basic units of life

Towards the middle of the 19th century, scientists made a fundamental breakthrough in our understanding of how life 'works'. They realised that the basic unit of life is the cell.

The origins of this idea go back to the early days of microscopy when an English scientist, Robert Hooke, decided to examine thin slices of plant material. He chose cork as one of his examples. Looking down the microscope, he made a drawing to show the regular appearance of the structure, as you can see in Figure 1.2. In 1665 he published a book containing this drawing.

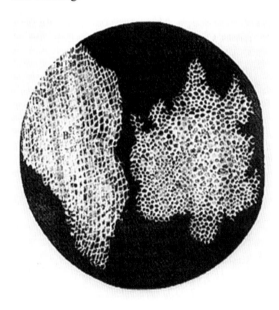

Figure 1.2: Drawing of cork cells published by Robert Hooke in 1665.

If you examine the drawing you will see the regular structures that Hooke called 'cells'. Each cell appeared to be an empty box surrounded by a wall. Hooke had discovered and described, without realising it, the fundamental unit of all living things.

Although we now know that the cells of cork are dead, Hooke and other scientists made further observations of cells in *living* materials. However, it was not until almost 200 years later that a general cell theory emerged from the work of two German scientists. In 1838 Schleiden, a botanist, suggested that all plants are made of cells. A year later Schwann, a zoologist, suggested the same for

animals. It was soon also realised that all cells come from pre-existing cells by the process of cell division. This raises the obvious question of where the original cell came from. There are many hypotheses, but we still have no definite answers to this question.

Why cells?

A cell can be thought of as a bag in which the chemistry of life occurs. The activity going on inside the cell is therefore separated from the environment outside the cell. The bag, or cell, is surrounded by a thin membrane. The membrane is an essential feature of all cells because it controls exchange between the cell and its environment. It can act as a barrier, but it can also control movement of materials across the membrane in both directions. The membrane is therefore described as partially permeable. If it were freely permeable, life could not exist, because the chemicals of the cell would simply mix with the surrounding chemicals by diffusion and the inside of the cell would be the same as the outside.

Two types of cell

During the 20th century, scientists studying the cells of bacteria and of more complex organisms such as plants and animals began to realise that there were two fundamentally different kinds of cells. Some cells were very simple, but some were much larger and more complex. The complex cells contained a nucleus (plural: nuclei) surrounded by two membranes. The genetic material, DNA, was in the nucleus. In the simple cells the DNA was not surrounded by membranes, but apparently free in the cytoplasm.

KEY WORDS
cell: the basic unit of all living organisms; it is surrounded by a cell surface membrane and contains genetic material (DNA) and cytoplasm containing **organelles**
organelle: a functionally and structurally distinct part of a cell, e.g. a ribosome or mitochondrion
nucleus (plural: **nuclei**): a relatively large organelle found in eukaryotic cells, but absent from prokaryotic cells; the nucleus contains the cell's DNA and therefore controls the activities of the cell; it is surrounded by two membranes which together form the nuclear envelope

Organisms made of cells with membrane-bound nuclei are now known as eukaryotes, while the simpler cells lacking membrane-bound nuclei are known as prokaryotes ('eu' means true, 'karyon' means nucleus, 'pro' means before). Eukaryotes are thought to have evolved from prokaryotes more than two billion years ago. Prokaryotes include bacteria. Eukaryotes include animals, plants, fungi and some other organisms.

> ### KEY WORDS
>
> eukaryote: an organism whose cells contain a nucleus and other membrane-bound organelles
>
> prokaryote: an organism whose cells do not contain a nucleus or any other membrane-bound organelles

1.2 Cell biology and microscopy

The study of cells has given rise to an important branch of biology known as cell biology. Cell biologists study cells using many different methods, including the use of various types of microscope.

There are two fundamentally different types of microscope: the light microscope and the electron microscope. Both use a form of radiation in order to see the specimen being examined. The light microscope uses light as a source of radiation, while the electron microscope uses electrons, for reasons which are discussed later.

Units of measurement

In order to measure objects in the microscopic world, we need to use very small units of measurement, which are unfamiliar to most people. Before studying light and electron microscopy further, you need to become familiar with these units.

According to international agreement, the International System of Units (SI units) should be used. In this system, the basic unit of length is the metre (symbol, m). More units are created by going a thousand times larger or smaller. Standard prefixes are used for the units. For example, the prefix 'kilo' means 1000 times. Thus, 1 kilometre = 1000 metres. The units of length relevant to cell studies are shown in Table 1.1.

The smallest structure visible with the human eye is about 50–100 μm in diameter (roughly the diameter of the sharp end of a pin). The cells in your body vary in size from about 5 μm to 40 μm. It is difficult to imagine how small these cells are, especially when they are clearly visible using a microscope. An average bacterial cell is about 1 μm across. One of the smallest structures you will study in this book is the ribosome, which is only about 25 nm in diameter! You could line up about 20 000 ribosomes across the full stop at the end of this sentence.

1.3 Plant and animal cells as seen with a light microscope

Microscopes that use light as a source of radiation are called light microscopes. Figure 1.3 shows how the light microscope works.

> Note: the structure of a light microscope is extension content, and is not part of the syllabus.

Fraction of a metre	Unit	Symbol
one thousandth = 0.001 = 1/1000 = 10^{-3}	millimetre	mm
one millionth = 0.000 001 = 1/1000 000 = 10^{-6}	micrometre	μm
one thousand millionth = 0.000 000 001 = 1/1000 000 000 = 10^{-9}	nanometre	nm

Table 1.1: Units of measurement relevant to cell studies: 1 micrometre is a thousandth of a millimetre; 1 nanometre is a thousandth of a micrometre.

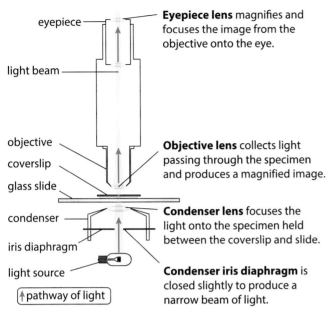

eyepiece

Eyepiece lens magnifies and focuses the image from the objective onto the eye.

light beam

objective

Objective lens collects light passing through the specimen and produces a magnified image.

coverslip

glass slide

condenser

Condenser lens focuses the light onto the specimen held between the coverslip and slide.

iris diaphragm

light source

Condenser iris diaphragm is closed slightly to produce a narrow beam of light.

pathway of light

Figure 1.3: How the light microscope works. The coverslip is a thin sheet of glass used to cover the specimen. It protects specimens from drying out and also prevents the objective lens from touching the specimen.

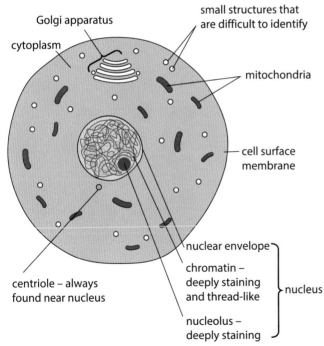

Golgi apparatus

cytoplasm

small structures that are difficult to identify

mitochondria

cell surface membrane

centriole – always found near nucleus

nuclear envelope

chromatin – deeply staining and thread-like

nucleus

nucleolus – deeply staining

Figure 1.4: Structure of a generalised animal cell (diameter about 20 μm) as seen with a very high quality light microscope.

Figure 1.4 is a drawing showing the structure of a generalised animal cell and Figure 1.5 is a drawing showing the structure of a generalised plant cell, both as seen with a light microscope. (A generalised cell shows all the structures that may commonly be found in a cell.) Figures 1.6 and 1.7 are photomicrographs. A photomicrograph is a photograph of a specimen as seen with a light microscope. Figure 1.6 shows some human cells. Figure 1.7 shows a plant cell taken from a leaf. Both figures show cells magnified 400 times, which is equivalent to using the high-power objective lens on a light microscope. See also Figures 1.8a and 1.8b for labelled drawings of these figures.

Many of the cell contents are colourless and transparent so they need to be stained with coloured dyes to be seen. The human cells in Figure 1.6 have been stained. The chromatin in the nuclei is particularly heavily stained. The plant cells in Figure 1.5 have not been stained because the chloroplasts contain the green pigment chlorophyll and are easily visible without staining.

Question

1 Using Figures 1.4 and 1.5, name the structures that:

a animal and plant cells have in common

b are found only in plant cells

c are found only in animal cells.

Features that animal and plant cells have in common

Cell surface membrane

All cells, including those of both eukaryotes and prokaryotes, are surrounded by a very thin cell surface membrane. This is also sometimes referred to as the plasma membrane. As mentioned before, it is partially permeable and controls the exchange of materials between the cell and its environment.

Nucleus

All eukaryotic cells contain a nucleus. The nucleus is a relatively large structure. It stains intensely and

> **KEY WORD**
>
> cell surface membrane: a very thin membrane (about 7 nm diameter) surrounding all cells; it is partially permeable and controls the exchange of materials between the cell and its environment

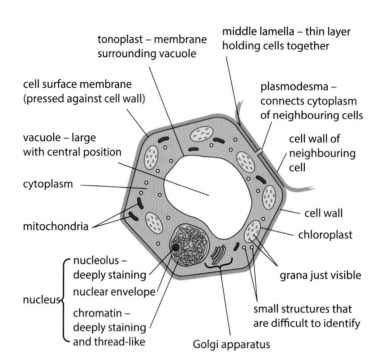

tonoplast – membrane surrounding vacuole

middle lamella – thin layer holding cells together

cell surface membrane (pressed against cell wall)

plasmodesma – connects cytoplasm of neighbouring cells

vacuole – large with central position

cell wall of neighbouring cell

cytoplasm

mitochondria

cell wall

chloroplast

nucleolus – deeply staining

nuclear envelope

nucleus

chromatin – deeply staining and thread-like

grana just visible

small structures that are difficult to identify

Golgi apparatus

Figure 1.5: Structure of a generalised plant cell (diameter about 40 μm) as seen with a very high quality light microscope.

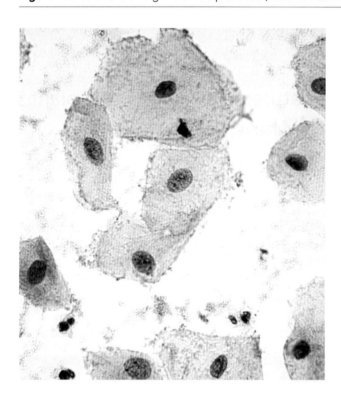

Figure 1.6: Cells from the lining of the human cheek (×400). Each cell shows a centrally placed nucleus, which is typical of animal cells. The cells are part of a tissue known as squamous (flattened) epithelium.

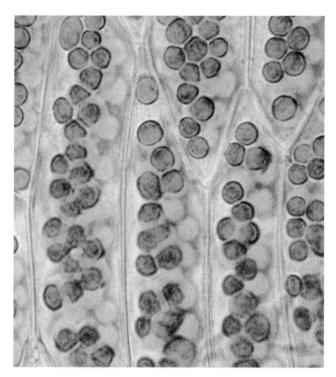

Figure 1.7: Cells in a moss leaf (×400). Many green chloroplasts are visible inside each cell. The grana are just visible as black grains inside the chloroplasts ('grana' means grains). Cell walls are also clearly visible (animal cells lack cell walls).

is therefore very easy to see when looking down the microscope. The deeply staining material in the nucleus is called chromatin ('chroma' means colour). Chromatin is a mass of coiled threads. The threads are seen to collect together to form chromosomes during nuclear division (Chapter 5, Section 5.2, Chromosomes). Chromatin contains DNA (deoxyribonucleic acid), the molecule which contains the instructions (genes) that control the activities of the cell (Chapter 6).

Inside the nucleus an even more deeply staining area is visible, the nucleolus. This is made of loops of DNA from several chromosomes. The number of nucleoli is variable, one to five being common in mammals. One of the main functions of nucleoli is to make ribosomes.

Cytoplasm

All the living material inside the cell is called protoplasm. It is also useful to have a term for all the living material outside the nucleus; it is called cytoplasm. Therefore, cytoplasm + nucleus = protoplasm.

Cytoplasm is an aqueous (watery) material, varying from a fluid to a jelly-like consistency. Using a light microscope, many small structures can be seen within it. These have been likened to small organs and are therefore known as organelles (meaning 'little organs'). An organelle can be defined as a functionally and structurally distinct part of a cell. Organelles are often, but not always, surrounded by one or two membranes so that their activities can be separated from the surrounding cytoplasm. Organising cell activities in separate compartments is essential for a structure as complex as an animal or plant cell to work efficiently.

Mitochondria (singular: mitochondrion)

The most numerous organelles seen with the light microscope are usually mitochondria (singular: mitochondrion). Mitochondria are only just visible using a light microscope. Videos of living cells, taken with the aid of a light microscope, have shown that mitochondria can move about, change shape and divide. They are specialised to carry out aerobic respiration.

Golgi apparatus

The use of special stains containing silver resulted in the Golgi apparatus being discovered in 1898 by Camillo Golgi. The Golgi apparatus collects and processes molecules within the cell, particularly proteins.

Note: you do not need to learn this structure. It is sometimes called the Golgi body or Golgi complex.

KEY WORDS

chromatin: the material of which chromosomes are made, consisting of DNA, proteins and small amounts of RNA; visible as patches or fibres within the nucleus when stained

chromosome: in the nucleus of the cells of eukaryotes, a structure made of tightly coiled chromatin (DNA, proteins and RNA) visible during cell division; the term 'circular DNA' is now also commonly used for the circular strand of DNA present in a prokaryotic cell

nucleolus: a small structure, one or more of which is found inside the nucleus; the nucleolus is usually visible as a densely stained body; its function is to manufacture ribosomes using the information in its own DNA

protoplasm: all the living material inside a cell (cytoplasm plus nucleus)

cytoplasm: the contents of a cell, excluding the nucleus

mitochondrion (plural: mitochondria): the organelle in eukaryotes in which aerobic respiration takes place

cell wall: a wall surrounding prokaryote, plant and fungal cells; the wall contains a strengthening material which protects the cell from mechanical damage, supports it and prevents it from bursting by osmosis if the cell is surrounded by a solution with a higher water potential

Differences between animal and plant cells

One of the structures commonly found in animal cells which is absent from plant cells is the centriole. Plant cells also differ from animal cells in possessing cell walls, large permanent vacuoles and chloroplasts.

Centrioles

Under the light microscope the centriole appears as a small structure close to the nucleus (Figure 1.4). Centrioles are discussed later in this chapter.

Cell walls and plasmodesmata

With a light microscope, individual plant cells are more easily seen than animal cells. This is because they are usually larger and, unlike animal cells, are surrounded by a cell wall. Note that the cell wall is an extra structure which is outside the cell surface membrane. The wall is relatively rigid because it contains fibres of cellulose, a polysaccharide which strengthens the wall. The cell wall gives the cell a definite shape. It prevents the cell from bursting when water enters by osmosis, allowing large pressures to develop inside the cell (Chapter 4, Section 4.5, Movement of substances across membranes). Cell walls may be reinforced with extra cellulose or with a hard material called lignin for extra strength (Chapter 7). Cell walls are freely permeable, allowing free movement of molecules and ions through to the cell surface membrane.

Plant cells are linked to neighbouring cells by means of pores containing fine strands of cytoplasm. These structures are called **plasmodesmata** (singular: **plasmodesma**). They are lined with the cell surface membrane. Movement through the pores is thought to be controlled by the structure of the pores.

Vacuoles

Vacuoles are sac-like structures which are surrounded by a single membrane. Although animal cells may possess small vacuoles such as phagocytic vacuoles (Chapter 4, Section 4.5, Movement of substances across membranes), which are temporary structures, mature plant cells often possess a large, permanent, central vacuole. The plant vacuole is surrounded by a membrane, the **tonoplast**, which controls exchange between the vacuole and the cytoplasm. The fluid in the vacuole is a solution of pigments, enzymes, sugars and other organic compounds (including some waste products), mineral salts, oxygen and carbon dioxide.

In plants, vacuoles help to regulate the osmotic properties of cells (the flow of water inwards and outwards) as well as having a wide range of other functions. For example, the pigments which colour the petals of certain flowers and the parts of some vegetables, such as the red pigment of beetroots, may be found in vacuoles.

Chloroplasts

Chloroplasts are organelles specialised for the process of **photosynthesis**. They are found in the green parts of the plant, mainly in the leaves. They are relatively large organelles and so are easily seen with a light microscope. It is even possible to see tiny 'grains' or **grana** (singular: **granum**) inside the chloroplasts using a light microscope (Figure 1.7). These are the parts of the chloroplast that contain chlorophyll, the green pigment which absorbs light during the process of photosynthesis. Chloroplasts are discussed further in Chapter 13 (Section 13.2, Structure and function of chloroplasts).

KEY WORDS

plasmodesma (plural: **plasmodesmata**): a pore-like structure found in plant cell walls; plasmodesmata of neighbouring plant cells line up to form tube-like pores through the cell walls, allowing the controlled passage of materials from one cell to the other; the pores contain ER and are lined with the cell surface membrane

vacuole: an organelle found in eukaryotic cells; a large, permanent central vacuole is a typical feature of plant cells, where it has a variety of functions, including storage of biochemicals such as salts, sugars and waste products; temporary vacuoles, such as phagocytic vacuoles (also known as phagocytic vesicles), may form in animal cells

tonoplast: the partially permeable membrane that surrounds plant vacuoles

chloroplast: an organelle, bounded by an envelope (i.e. two membranes), in which photosynthesis takes place in eukaryotes

photosynthesis: the production of organic substances from inorganic ones, using energy from light

grana (singular: **granum**): stacks of membranes inside a chloroplast

IMPORTANT

- You can think of a plant cell as being very similar to an animal cell but with extra structures.
- Plant cells are often larger than animal cells, although cell size varies enormously.
- Do not confuse the cell wall with the cell surface membrane. Cell walls are relatively thick and physically strong, whereas cell surface membranes are very thin. Cell walls are freely permeable, whereas cell surface membranes are partially permeable. All cells have a cell surface membrane, but animal cells do not have a cell wall.
- Vacuoles are not confined to plant cells; animal cells may have small vacuoles, such as phagocytic vacuoles, although these are not usually permanent structures.

PRACTICAL ACTIVITY 1.1

Making temporary slides

A common method of examining material with a light microscope is to cut thin slices of the material called 'sections'. The advantage of cutting sections is that they are thin enough to allow light to pass through the section. The section is laid ('mounted') on a glass slide and covered with a coverslip to protect it. Light passing through the section produces an image which can then be magnified using the objective and eyepiece lenses of the microscope.

Biological material may be examined live or in a preserved state. Prepared slides contain material that has been killed and preserved in a life-like condition.

Temporary slides are quicker and easier to prepare and are often used to examine fresh material containing living cells. In both cases the sections are typically stained before being mounted on the glass slide.

Temporary preparations of fresh material are useful for quick preliminary investigations. Sometimes macerated (chopped up) material can be used, as when examining the structure of wood (xylem). A number of temporary stains are commonly used. For example, iodine in potassium iodide solution is useful for plant specimens. It stains starch blue-black and will also colour nuclei and cell walls a pale yellow. A dilute solution of methylene blue can be used to stain animal cells such as cheek cells.

Viewing specimens yourself with a microscope will help you to understand and remember structures. Your understanding can be reinforced by making a pencil drawing on good quality plain paper. Remember always to draw what you see, and not what you think you should see.

Procedure

Place the biological specimen on a clean glass slide and add one or two drops of stain. Carefully lower a cover over the specimen to protect the microscope lens and to help prevent the specimen from drying out. Adding a drop of glycerine and mixing it with the stain can also help prevent drying out.

- Suitable animal material: human cheek cells obtained by gently scraping the lining of the cheek with a finger nail
- Suitable plant material: onion epidermal cells, lettuce epidermal cells, *Chlorella* cells, moss slip leaves

(See Practical Investigation 1.1 in the Practical Workbook for additional information.)

PRACTICAL ACTIVITY 1.2

Biological drawing

To reinforce your learning, you will find it useful to make labelled drawings of some of your temporary and permanent slides, as well as labelled drawings of photomicrographs.

Practical Activity 7.1 in Chapter 7 provides general guidance on biological drawing. Read the relevant sections of Practical Activity 7.1 before answering the question below, which is relevant to this chapter. Figures 1.8a and b show examples of good drawing and labelling technique based on Figures 1.6 and 1.7. Note that it is acceptable to draw only a representative portion of the cell contents of Figure 1.7, but add a label explaining this.

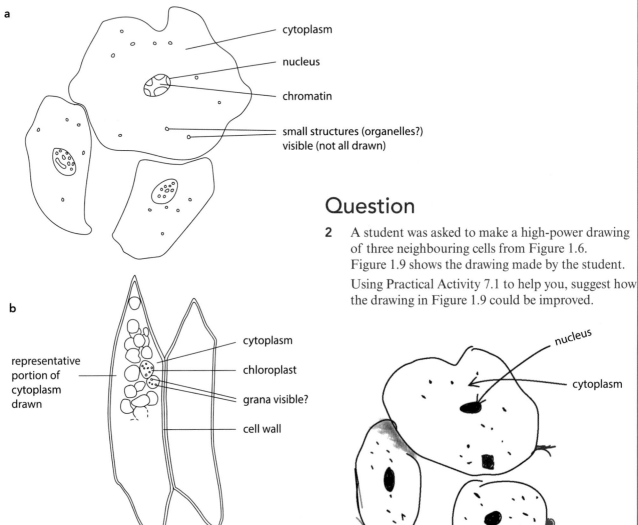

a

cytoplasm

nucleus

chromatin

small structures (organelles?) visible (not all drawn)

b

representative portion of cytoplasm drawn

cytoplasm

chloroplast

grana visible?

cell wall

Figure 1.8: Examples of good drawing technique: **a** high-power drawing of three neighbouring animal cells from Figure 1.6; **b** high-power drawing of two neighbouring plant cells from Figure 1.7.

Question

2 A student was asked to make a high-power drawing of three neighbouring cells from Figure 1.6. Figure 1.9 shows the drawing made by the student.

Using Practical Activity 7.1 to help you, suggest how the drawing in Figure 1.9 could be improved.

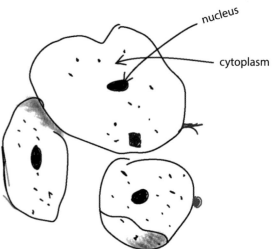

nucleus

cytoplasm

Figure 1.9: A student's high-power drawing of three neighbouring cells from Figure 1.6.

(See Practical Investigation 1.1 in the Practical Workbook for additional information.)

1.4 Measuring size and calculating magnification

Magnification is the number of times larger an image of an object is than the real size of the object.

$$\text{magnification} = \frac{\text{observed size of the image}}{\text{actual size}}$$

or

$$M = \frac{I}{A}$$

M = magnification

I = observed size of the image (what you can measure with a ruler)

A = actual size (the real size – for example, the size of a cell before it is magnified).

If you know two of the values M, I and A, you can work out the third one. For example, if the observed size of the image and the magnification are known, you can work out the actual size $A = \dfrac{I}{M}$. If you write the formula in a triangle as shown below and cover up the value you want to find, it should be obvious how to do the right calculation.

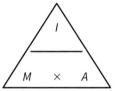

Measuring cell size

Cells and organelles can be measured with a microscope by means of an **eyepiece graticule**. This is a transparent scale. It usually has 100 divisions (see Figure 1.10a). The eyepiece graticule is placed in the microscope eyepiece so that it can be seen at the same time as the object to be measured, as shown in Figure 1.10b. Figure 1.10b shows the scale over one of a group of six human cheek epithelial cells (like those shown in Figure 1.6). The cell selected lies between 40 and 60 on the scale. We therefore say it measures 20 eyepiece units in diameter (the difference between 60 and 40). We will not know the actual size of the eyepiece units until the eyepiece graticule is calibrated.

> **KEY WORDS**
>
> **magnification:** the number of times larger an image of an object is than the real size of the object; magnification = image size ÷ actual (real) size of the object
>
> **eyepiece graticule:** small scale that is placed in a microscope eyepiece

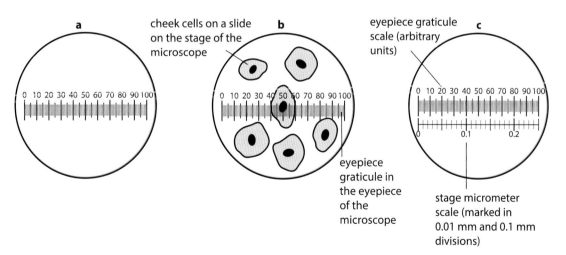

Figure 1.10: Microscopical measurement. Three fields of view seen using a high-power (×40) objective lens: **a** an eyepiece graticule scale; **b** superimposed images of human cheek epithelial cells and the eyepiece graticule scale; **c** superimposed images of the eyepiece graticule scale and the stage micrometer scale.

To calibrate the eyepiece graticule, a miniature transparent ruler called a **stage micrometer** is placed on the microscope stage and is brought into focus. This scale may be etched onto a glass slide or printed on a transparent film. It commonly has subdivisions of 0.1 and 0.01 mm. The images of the stage micrometer and the eyepiece graticule can then be superimposed (placed on top of one another) as shown in Figure 1.10c.

Calculating magnification

Figure 1.11 shows **micrographs** of two sections through the same plant cell. The difference in appearance of the two micrographs is explained in the next section.

If we know the actual (real) length of a cell in such a micrograph, we can calculate its magnification, M, using the formula:

$$M = \frac{I}{A}$$

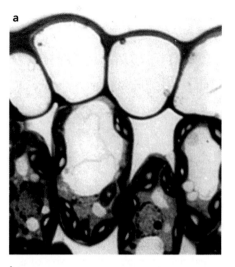

a

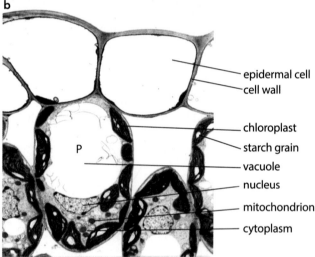

b

- epidermal cell
- cell wall

- chloroplast
- starch grain
- vacuole
- nucleus
- mitochondrion
- cytoplasm

P

Figure 1.11: Micrographs of two sections of the same plant cells, as seen **a** with a light microscope, and **b** with an electron microscope. Both are shown at the same magnification (about ×750).

KEY WORDS

stage micrometer: very small, accurately drawn scale of known dimensions, engraved on a microscope slide

micrograph: a picture taken with the aid of a microscope; a photomicrograph (or light micrograph) is taken using a light microscope; an electron micrograph is taken using an electron microscope

---

WORKED EXAMPLE

1   In the eyepiece graticule shown in Figure 1.10, 100 units measure 0.25 mm. Hence, the value of each eyepiece unit is:

$$\frac{0.25}{100} = 0.0025 \text{ mm}$$

Or, converting mm to μm:

$$\frac{0.25 \times 1000}{100} = 2.5 \text{ μm}$$

The diameter of the cell shown superimposed on the scale in Figure 1.8b measures 20 eyepiece units and so its actual diameter is:

$$20 \times 2.5 \text{ μm} = 50 \text{ μm}$$

This diameter is greater than that of many human cells because the cell is a flattened epithelial cell.

WORKED EXAMPLE

2 Suppose we want to know the magnification of the plant cell labelled P in Figure 1.11b. The real length of the cell is 80 μm.

Step 1 Measure the length in mm of the cell in the micrograph using a ruler. You should find that it is about 50 mm.

Step 2 Convert mm to μm. (It is easier if we first convert all measurements to the same units – in this case micrometres, μm.)

So: 1 mm = 1000 μm

50 mm = 50 × 1000 μm

= 50 000 μm

Step 3 Use the equation to calculate the magnification.

$$\text{magnification, } M = \frac{\text{image size, } l}{\text{actual size, } A}$$

$$= \frac{50\,000\,\mu m}{80\,\mu m}$$

$$= \times 625$$

The multiplication sign (×) in front of the number 625 means 'times'. We say that the magnification is 'times 625'.

Question

3 **a** Calculate the magnification of the drawing of the animal cell in Figure 1.4.

b Calculate the actual (real) length of the chloroplast labelled **X** in Figure 1.34.

WORKED EXAMPLE

3 Figure 1.12 shows a lymphocyte with a scale bar. We can use this scale bar to calculate the magnification.

6 μm

Figure 1.12: A lymphocyte.

Step 1 Measure the scale bar. Here, it is 36 mm.

Step 2 Convert mm to μm:

36 mm = 36 × 1000 μm = 36 000 μm

Step 3 The scale bar represents 6 μm. This is the actual size, A. Use the equation to calculate the magnification:

$$\text{magnification, } M = \frac{\text{image size, } l}{\text{actual size, } A}$$

$$= \frac{36\,000\,\mu m}{6\,\mu m}$$

$$= \times 6000$$

Calculating the real size of an object from its magnification

To calculate the real or actual size of an object, we can use the same magnification equation.

WORKED EXAMPLE

4 Figure 1.20 shows parts of three plant cells magnified ×5600. Suppose we want to know the actual length of the labelled chloroplast in this electron micrograph.

Step 1 Measure the observed length of the image of the chloroplast (I), in mm, using a ruler. The maximum length is 25 mm.

Step 2 Convert mm to μm:
25 mm = 25 × 1000 μm = 25 000 μm

Step 3 Use the equation to calculate the actual length:

$$\text{actual size, } A = \frac{\text{image size, } I}{\text{magnification, } M}$$
$$= \frac{25\,000 \ \mu m}{5600}$$
$$= 4.5 \ \mu m \text{ (to one decimal place)}$$

1.5 Electron microscopy

Before studying what cells look like with an electron microscope, you need to understand the difference between magnification and resolution.

Magnification and resolution

Look again at Figure 1.11. Figure 1.11a is a light micrograph. Figure 1.11b is an electron micrograph. Both micrographs are of the same cells and both have the same magnification. However, you can see that Figure 1.11b, the electron micrograph, is much clearer. This is because it has greater resolution. **Resolution** can be defined as the ability to distinguish between two

separate points. If the two points cannot be resolved, they will be seen as one point. In practice, resolution is the amount of detail that can be seen – the greater the resolution, the greater the detail.

The maximum resolution of a light microscope is 200 nm. The reason for this is explained in the next section, 'The electromagnetic spectrum'. A resolution of 200 nm means that, if two points or objects are closer together than 200 nm, they cannot be distinguished as separate.

You might imagine that you could see more detail in Figure 1.11a by magnifying it (simply making it larger). In practice you would be able to see what is already there more easily, but you would not see any more detail. The image would just get more and more blurred as magnification increased. The resolution would not be greater.

The electromagnetic spectrum

How is resolution linked with the nature of light? One of the properties of light is that it travels in waves. The lengths of the waves of visible light vary, ranging from about 400 nm to about 700 nm. The human eye can distinguish between these different wavelengths, and in the brain the differences are converted to colour differences. Waves that are 400 nm in length are seen as violet. Waves that are 700 nm in length are seen as red.

Visible light is a form of electromagnetic radiation. The range of different wavelengths of electromagnetic radiation is called the electromagnetic spectrum. Visible light is only one part of this spectrum. Figure 1.13 shows some of the parts of the electromagnetic spectrum. The longer the waves, the lower their frequency. (All the waves travel at the same speed, so imagine them passing a post: shorter waves pass at higher frequency.) In theory, there is no limit to how short or how long the waves can be. Wavelength changes with energy: the greater the energy, the shorter the wavelength.

KEY WORD

resolution: the ability to distinguish between two objects very close together; the higher the resolution of an image, the greater the detail that can be seen

---

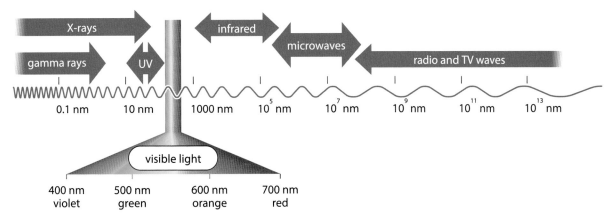

Figure 1.13: Diagram of the electromagnetic spectrum. The numbers indicate the wavelengths of the different types of electromagnetic radiation. Note the waves vary from very short to very long. Visible light is part of the spectrum. The double-headed arrow labelled UV is ultraviolet light.

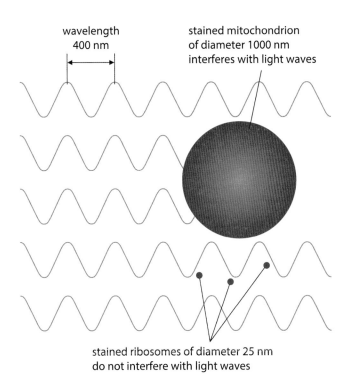

Figure 1.14: A mitochondrion and some ribosomes in the path of light waves of 400 nm length.

Now look at Figure 1.14. It shows a mitochondrion and some very small cell organelles called ribosomes. It also shows some wavy blue lines that represent light of 400 nm wavelength. This is the shortest visible wavelength. The mitochondrion is large enough to interfere with the light waves. However, the ribosomes are far too small to have any effect on the light waves.

The general rule when viewing specimens is that the limit of resolution is about one half the wavelength of the radiation used to view the specimen. In other words, if an object is any smaller than half the wavelength of the radiation used to view it, it cannot be seen separately from nearby objects. This means that the best resolution that can be obtained using a microscope that uses visible light (a light microscope) is 200 nm, since the shortest wavelength of visible light is 400 nm (violet light). Ribosomes are approximately 25 nm in diameter and can therefore never be seen using a light microscope.

If an object is transparent, it will allow light waves to pass through it and therefore will still not be visible. This is why many biological structures have to be stained before they can be seen.

Question

4 Explain why ribosomes are not visible using a light microscope.

The electron microscope

So how can we look at things smaller than 200 nm? The only solution to this problem is to use radiation of a shorter wavelength than visible light. If you study Figure 1.13, you will see that ultraviolet light or X-rays look like possible candidates. A much better solution, though, is to use electrons. Electrons are negatively charged particles which orbit the nucleus of an atom. When a metal becomes very hot, some of its electrons gain so much energy that they escape from their orbits, similar to a rocket escaping from Earth's gravity. Free electrons behave like electromagnetic radiation. They have a very short wavelength: the greater the energy, the shorter the wavelength. Electrons are a very suitable form of radiation for microscopy for two major reasons. First, their wavelength is extremely short (at least as short as that of X-rays). Second, unlike X-rays, they are negatively charged, so they can be focused easily using electromagnets (a magnet can be made to alter the path of the beam, the equivalent of a glass lens bending light).

Using an electron microscope, a resolution of 0.5 nm can be obtained, 400 times better than a light microscope.

Transmission and scanning electron microscopes

Two types of electron microscope are now in common use. The transmission electron microscope (TEM) was the type originally developed. The beam of electrons is passed through the specimen before being viewed. Only those electrons that are transmitted (pass through the specimen) are seen. This allows us to see thin sections of specimens, and thus to see inside cells. In the scanning electron microscope (SEM), the electron beam is used to scan the surfaces of structures and only the reflected beam is observed.

An example of a scanning electron micrograph is shown in Figure 1.15. The advantage of this microscope is that surface structures can be seen. Because much of the specimen is in focus at the same time, a three-dimensional appearance is achieved. A disadvantage of the SEM is that it cannot achieve the same resolution as a TEM. Using an SEM, resolution is between 3 nm and 20 nm.

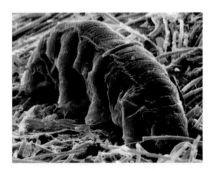

Figure 1.15: Scanning electron micrograph (SEM) of a tardigrade. Tardigrades or water bears, are about 0.5 mm long, with four pairs of legs. They are common in soil and can survive extreme environmental conditions (×86).

Viewing specimens with the electron microscope

Figure 1.16 shows how a TEM works and Figure 1.17 shows one in use.

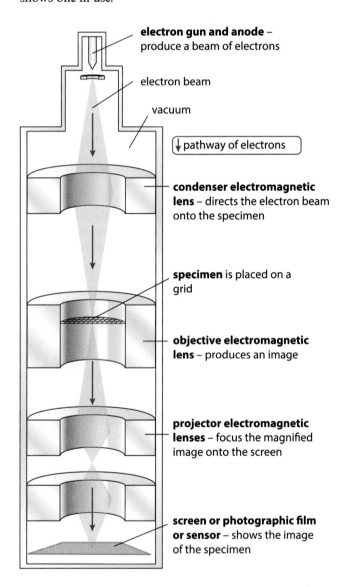

Figure 1.16: How a TEM works.

Note: the structure of an electron microscope is extension content, and is not part of the syllabus.

It is not possible to see an electron beam, so to make the image visible the electron beam has to be projected onto a fluorescent screen. The areas hit by electrons

Figure 1.17: A TEM in use.

The electron beam, and therefore the specimen and the fluorescent screen, must be in a vacuum. If the electrons collided with air molecules, they would scatter, making it impossible to achieve a sharp picture. Also, water boils at room temperature in a vacuum, so all specimens must be dehydrated before being placed in the microscope. This means that only dead material or non-living can be examined. Great efforts are therefore made to try to preserve material in a life-like state when preparing it for electron microscopy.

1.6 Plant and animal cells as seen with an electron microscope

The fine (detailed) structure of a cell as revealed by the electron microscope is called ultrastructure and is shown in Figures 1.18–1.21.

shine brightly, giving overall a black and white picture. The stains used to improve the contrast of biological specimens for electron microscopy contain heavy metal atoms, which stop the passage of electrons. The resulting picture is like an X-ray photograph, with the more densely stained parts of the specimen appearing blacker. 'False-colour' images can be created by colouring the standard black and white image using a computer.

Question

5   Copy and complete Table 1.2, which compares light microscopes with electron microscopes. Some boxes have been filled in for you.

Feature	Light microscope	Electron microscope
source of radiation		
wavelength of radiation used		about 0.005 nm
maximum resolution		0.5 nm in practice
lenses	glass	
specimen		non-living or dead
stains	coloured dyes	
image	coloured	

Table 1.2: Comparison of light microscopes and electron microscopes.

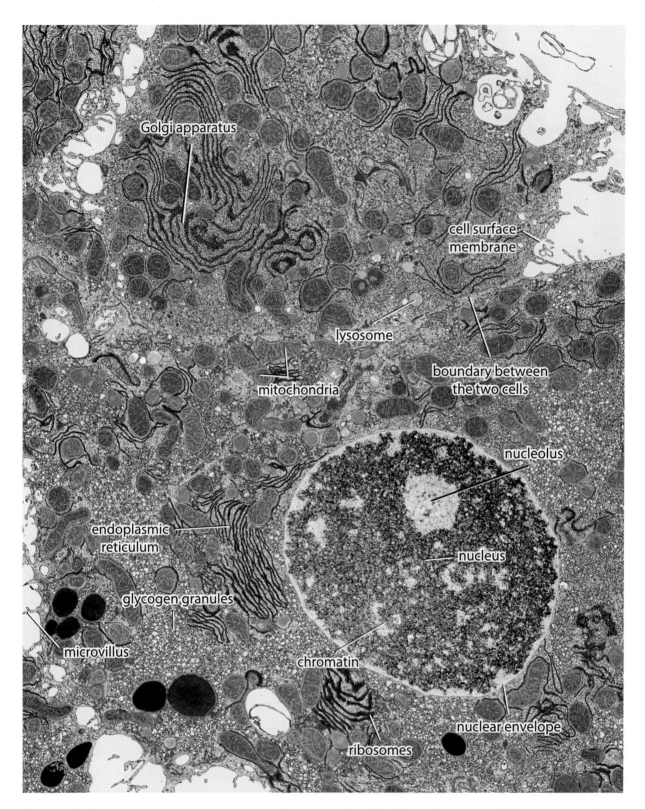

Figure 1.18: Parts of two representative animal cells as seen with a TEM. The cells are liver cells from a rat (×9600). The nucleus is clearly visible in one of the cells. The boundary between the two cells is difficult to see because the cell surface membranes are so thin.

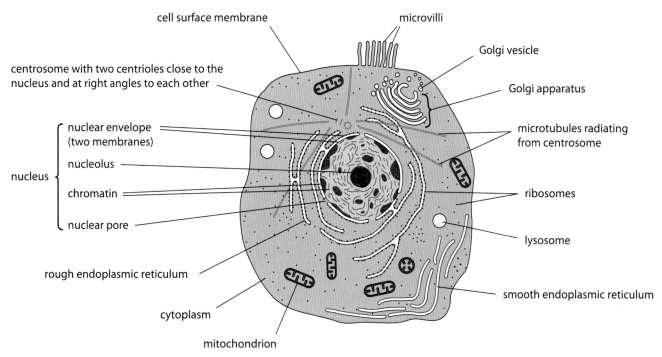

Figure 1.19: Ultrastructure of a typical animal cell as seen with an electron microscope. This drawing is based on many micrographs of animal cells. In reality, the endoplasmic reticulum is more extensive than shown here, and free ribosomes may be more extensive. Glycogen granules are sometimes present in the cytoplasm.

Question

6   Compare Figure 1.19 with Figure 1.4. Name the structures in an animal cell that can be seen with the electron microscope but not with the light microscope.

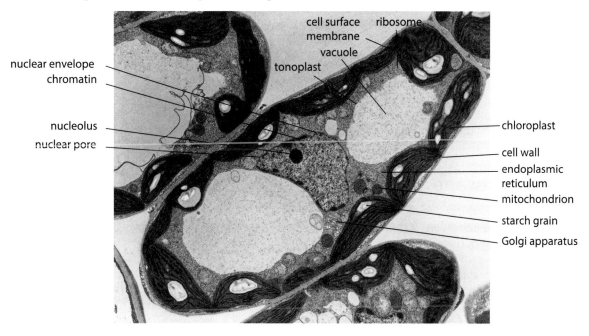

Figure 1.20: Representative plant cells as seen with a TEM. The cells are palisade cells from a soya bean leaf. The boundaries between the cells can clearly be seen due to the presence of cell walls (×5600).

Question

7   Compare Figure 1.21 with Figure 1.5. Name the structures in a plant cell that can be seen with the electron microscope but not with the light microscope.

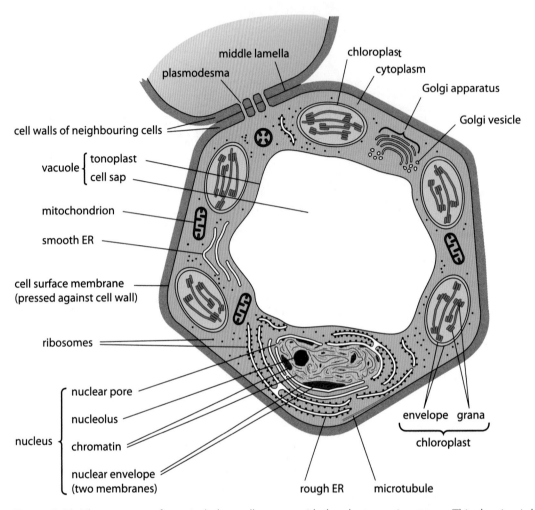

Figure 1.21: Ultrastructure of a typical plant cell as seen with the electron microscope. This drawing is based on many micrographs of plant cells. In reality, the ER is more extensive than shown. Free ribosomes may also be more extensive.

Cell surface membrane

The cell surface membrane is extremely thin (about 7 nm). However, at very high magnifications it can be seen to have three layers – two dark (heavily stained) layers surrounding a narrow, pale interior (Figure 1.22). The membrane is partially permeable and controls exchange between the cell and its environment. Membrane structure is discussed further in Chapter 4.

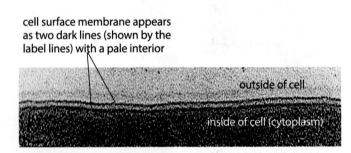

cell surface membrane appears as two dark lines (shown by the label lines) with a pale interior

Figure 1.22: Cell surface membrane (×250 000). At this magnification the membrane appears as two dark lines at the edge of the cell.

Microvilli

Microvilli (singular: microvillus) are finger-like extensions of the cell surface membrane. They are typical of certain animal cells, such as epithelial cells. Epithelial cells cover the surfaces of structures. The microvilli greatly increase the surface area of the cell surface membrane, as shown in Figure 1.19. This is useful, for example, for reabsorption in the proximal convoluted tubules of the kidney and for absorption of digested food into cells lining the gut.

KEY WORDS

microvilli (singular: microvillus): small, finger-like extensions of a cell which increase the surface area of the cell for more efficient absorption or secretion

Question

8   a   Using the magnification given, determine the actual maximum diameter of the nucleus shown in Figure 1.23.

b   The diameter you have calculated for the nucleus shown in Figure 1.23 is not necessarily the maximum diameter of this nucleus. Explain why this is the case.

IMPORTANT

Use modelling clay to make a spherical shape (a ball), like a nucleus. Try cutting it into two at different places and looking at the sizes of the cut surfaces. This represents the process of sectioning material for examination using a microscope.

Nucleus

The nucleus (Figure 1.23) is the largest cell organelle.

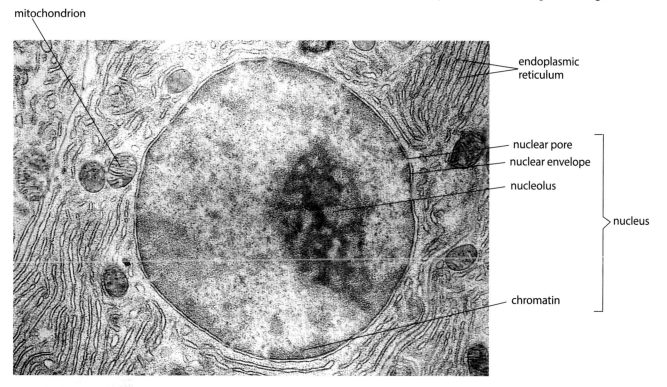

Figure 1.23: Transmission electron micrograph (TEM) of a nucleus. This is the nucleus of a cell from the pancreas of a bat (×11000). The circular nucleus is surrounded by a double-layered nuclear envelope containing nuclear pores. The nucleolus is more darkly stained. Rough ER is visible in the surrounding cytoplasm.

The nuclear envelope

The nucleus is surrounded by two membranes, forming the **nuclear envelope**. The outer membrane of the nuclear envelope is continuous with the endoplasmic reticulum (Figures 1.19 and 1.21).

The nuclear envelope has many small pores called **nuclear pores**. These allow and control exchange between the nucleus and the cytoplasm. Examples of substances leaving the nucleus through the pores are messenger RNA (mRNA), transfer RNA (tRNA) and ribosomes for protein synthesis. Examples of substances entering through the nuclear pores are proteins (to help make ribosomes), nucleotides, ATP (adenosine triphosphate) and some hormones such as thyroid hormone T3.

Chromosomes and chromatin

The nucleus contains the chromosomes. Chromosomes contain DNA, the genetic material. DNA is organised into functional units called genes. Genes control the activities of the cell and inheritance; thus the nucleus controls the cell's activities.

The DNA molecules are so long (a human cell contains about two metres of DNA) that they have to be folded up into a more compact shape to prevent the strands becoming tangled. This is achieved by combining with proteins, particularly with proteins known as histones. The combination of DNA and proteins is known as chromatin. Chromatin also contains some RNA. Thus, chromosomes are made of chromatin (Chapter 5, Section 5.2, Chromosomes).

When a cell is about to divide, the nucleus divides first so that each new cell will have its own nucleus (Chapters 5 and 16).

Also within the nucleus is a structure called the nucleolus.

Nucleolus

The nucleolus appears as a darkly stained, rounded structure in the nucleus (Figure 1.23). As mentioned earlier, one or more may be present, although one is most common. Its function is to make ribosomes using the information in its own DNA. It contains a core of DNA from one or more chromosomes which contain the genes that code for ribosomal RNA (rRNA), the form of RNA used in the manufacture of ribosomes. It also contains genes for making tRNA. Around the core are less dense regions where the ribosomal subunits are assembled, combining the rRNA with ribosomal proteins imported from the cytoplasm. The more ribosomes a cell makes, the larger its nucleolus.

The different parts of the nucleolus only come together during the manufacture of ribosomes. They separate when, as during nuclear division, ribosome synthesis ceases. The nucleolus as a structure then disappears.

Endoplasmic reticulum

When cells were first seen with the electron microscope, biologists were amazed to see so much detailed structure. The existence of much of this had not been suspected. This was particularly true of the **endoplasmic reticulum (ER)** (Figures 1.23, 1.24 and 1.28). The membranes of the ER form flattened compartments called sacs or

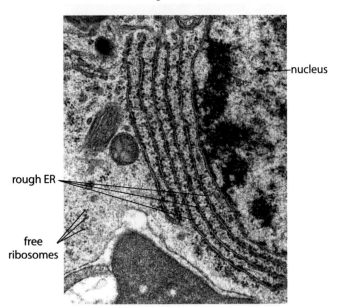

Figure 1.24: TEM of rough ER covered with ribosomes (black dots) (×17 000). Some free ribosomes can also be seen in the cytoplasm on the left.

KEY WORDS

nuclear envelope: the two membranes, situated close together, that surround the nucleus; the envelope is perforated with nuclear pores

nuclear pores: pores found in the nuclear envelope which control the exchange of materials, e.g. mRNA, between the nucleus and the cytoplasm

endoplasmic reticulum (ER): a network of flattened sacs running through the cytoplasm of eukaryotic cells; molecules, particularly proteins, can be transported through the cell inside the sacs separate from the rest of the cytoplasm; ER is continuous with the outer membrane of the nuclear envelope

cisternae. Processes can take place inside the cisternae separated from the cytoplasm. Molecules, particularly proteins, can be transported through the ER separate from the rest of the cytoplasm. The ER is continuous with the outer membrane of the nuclear envelope (Figures 1.19 and 1.21).

Rough endoplasmic reticulum

There are two types of ER: rough ER (RER) and smooth ER (SER). RER is so called because it is covered with many tiny organelles called ribosomes (described later). These are just visible as black dots in Figures 1.23 and 1.24. Ribosomes are the sites of protein synthesis (Chapter 6). They can be found free in the cytoplasm as well as on the RER.

Smooth endoplasmic reticulum

SER has a smooth appearance because it lacks ribosomes. It has a completely different function to RER. It makes lipids and steroids, such as cholesterol and the reproductive hormones oestrogen and testosterone. SER is also a major storage site for calcium ions. This explains why it is abundant in muscle cells, where calcium ions are involved in muscle contraction (Chapter 15, Section 15.3, Muscle contraction). In the liver, SER is involved in drug metabolism.

Ribosomes

Ribosomes are very small and are not visible with a light microscope. At very high magnifications using an electron microscope they can be seen to consist of two subunits: a large and a small subunit. The sizes of structures this small are often quoted in S units (Svedberg units). S units are a measure of how rapidly substances sediment in a high speed centrifuge (an ultracentrifuge). The faster they sediment, the higher the S number. Eukaryotic ribosomes are 80S ribosomes. The ribosomes of prokaryotes are 70S ribosomes, so are slightly smaller. Mitochondria and chloroplasts contain 70S ribosomes, revealing their prokaryotic origins (see the sections on mitochondria and chloroplasts).

Ribosomes are made of roughly equal amounts by mass of ribosomal RNA (rRNA) and protein. Their three-dimensional structure has now been worked out (Figure 1.25). Ribosomes allow all the interacting molecules involved in protein synthesis, such as

mRNA, tRNA, amino acids and regulatory proteins, to gather together in one place (Chapter 6, Section 6.5, Protein synthesis).

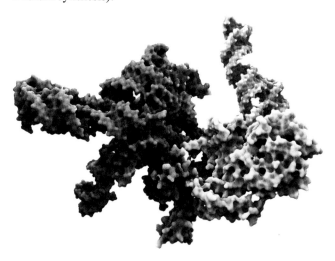

Figure 1.25: Structure of the human 80S ribosome.

Golgi apparatus

The **Golgi apparatus** is a stack of flattened sacs called cisternae (Figure 1.26). More than one Golgi apparatus may be present in a cell. The stack is constantly being formed at one end from vesicles which bud off from the ER, and are broken down again at the other end to form **Golgi vesicles**. The stack of sacs together with the associated vesicles is referred to as the Golgi apparatus or Golgi complex.

KEY WORDS

ribosome: a tiny organelle found in large numbers in all cells; prokaryotic ribosomes are about 20 nm in diameter while eukaryotic ribosomes are about 25 nm in diameter

Golgi apparatus (Golgi body, Golgi complex): an organelle found in eukaryotic cells; the Golgi apparatus consists of a stack of flattened sacs, constantly forming at one end and breaking up into Golgi vesicles at the other end

Golgi vesicles: carry their contents to other parts of the cell, often to the cell surface membrane for secretion; the Golgi apparatus chemically modifies the molecules it transports, e.g. sugars may be added to proteins to make glycoproteins

---

The Golgi apparatus collects and processes molecules, particularly proteins from the RER. It contains hundreds of enzymes for this purpose. After processing, the molecules can be transported in Golgi vesicles to other parts of the cell or out of the cell. Releasing molecules from the cell is called secretion and the pathway followed by the molecules is called the secretory pathway. These are some examples of the functions of the Golgi apparatus

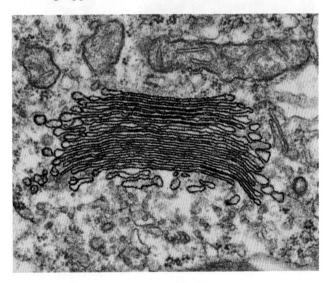

Figure 1.26: TEM of a Golgi apparatus. A central stack of saucer-shaped sacs can be seen budding off small Golgi vesicles (green). These may form secretory vesicles whose contents can be released at the cell surface by exocytosis (Chapter 4).

- Golgi vesicles are used to make lysosomes.

- Sugars are added to proteins to make molecules known as glycoproteins.

- Sugars are added to lipids to make glycolipids. Glycoproteins and glycolipids are important components of membranes (Chapter 4, Section 4.2, Structure of membranes) and are important molecules in cell signalling (Chapter 4, Section 4.4, Cell signalling).

- During plant cell division, Golgi enzymes are involved in the synthesis of new cell walls.

- In the gut and the gas exchange system, cells called goblet cells release a substance called mucin from the Golgi apparatus (Chapter 9, Section 9.4, Warming and cleaning the air). Mucin is one of the main components of mucus.

Lysosomes

Lysosomes are simple sacs, surrounded by a single membrane. In animal cells they are usually 0.1–0.5 µm in diameter (Figure 1.27). In plant cells the large central vacuole may act as a lysosome, although lysosomes similar to those in animal cells are also seen in the cytoplasm.

KEY WORD

lysosome: a spherical organelle found in eukaryotic cells; it contains digestive (hydrolytic) enzymes and has a variety of destructive functions, such as removal of old cell organelles

---

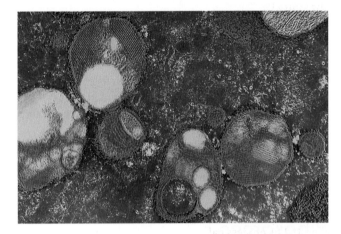

Figure 1.27: Lysosomes (orange) in a mouse kidney cell (×55 000). They contain cell structures in the process of digestion. Cytoplasm is coloured blue here.

Lysosomes contain digestive enzymes. The enzymes are called hydrolases because they carry out hydrolysis reactions. These enzymes must be kept separate from the rest of the cell to prevent damage. Lysosomes are responsible for the breakdown (digestion) of unwanted substances and structures such as old organelles or even whole cells. Hydrolysis works fastest in an acid environment so the contents of lysosomes are acidic, pH 4–5 compared with 6.5–7.0 in the surrounding cytoplasm. Among the 60+ enzymes contained in lysosomes are proteases, lipases and nucleases which break down proteins, lipids and nucleic acids respectively. The enzymes are synthesised on RER and delivered to lysosomes via the Golgi apparatus.

The activities of lysosomes can be split into the four categories discussed below.

Getting rid of unwanted cell components

Lysosomes can engulf and destroy unwanted cell components, such as molecules or organelles, that are located inside the cell.

Endocytosis

Endocytosis is described in more detail in Chapter 4 (Section 4.5, Movement of substances across membranes). Material may be taken into the cell by endocytosis, for example when white blood cells engulf bacteria. Lysosomes may fuse with the endocytic vacuoles formed and release their enzymes to digest the contents.

Exocytosis

Lysosomal enzymes may be released from the cell for extracellular digestion. An example is the replacement of cartilage by bone during development. The heads of sperms contain a special lysosome, the acrosome, for digesting a path through the layers of cells surrounding the egg just before fertilisation.

Self-digestion

The contents of lysosomes are sometimes released into the cytoplasm. This results in the whole cell being digested (a process called autolysis). This may be part of normal development, as when a tadpole tail is reabsorbed during metamorphosis or when a uterus is restored to its normal size after pregnancy. It also occurs after the death of an individual as membranes lose their partial permeability.

Mitochondria

Structure

The structure of the mitochondrion (plural: mitochondria) as seen with the electron microscope is visible in Figures 1.18, 1.28 and 12.10. Mitochondria are usually about 1 µm in diameter and can be various shapes, often sausage-shaped as in Figure 1.28. They are surrounded by two membranes (an envelope). The inner membrane is folded to form finger-like cristae (singular: crista) which project into the interior of the mitochondrion which is called the matrix. The space between the two membranes is called the intermembrane space.

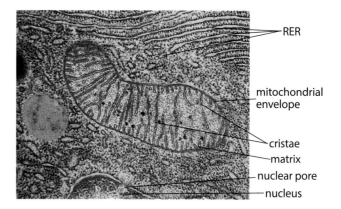

Figure 1.28: Mitochondrion (orange) with its double membrane (envelope); the inner membrane is folded to form cristae (×20 000). Mitochondria are the sites of aerobic cell respiration. Note also the RER.

The number of mitochondria in a cell is very variable. As they are responsible for aerobic respiration, it is not surprising that cells with a high demand for energy, such as liver and muscle cells, contain large numbers of mitochondria. A liver cell may contain as many as 2000 mitochondria. If you exercise regularly, your muscles will make more mitochondria.

Functions of mitochondria and the role of ATP

The main function of mitochondria is to carry out aerobic respiration, although they do have other functions, such as the synthesis of lipids. During respiration, a series of reactions takes place in which energy is released from energy-rich molecules such as sugars and fats. Most of the energy is transferred to molecules of **ATP** (**adenosine triphosphate**). This is the energy-carrying molecule found in all living cells. It is known as the universal energy carrier.

> ### KEY WORDS
>
> **cristae** (singular: **crista**): folds of the inner membrane of the mitochondrial envelope on which are found stalked particles of ATP synthase and electron transport chains associated with aerobic respiration
>
> **ATP** (**adenosine triphosphate**): the molecule that is the universal energy currency in all living cells; the purpose of respiration is to make ATP

The reactions of respiration take place in solution in the matrix and in the inner membrane (cristae). The matrix contains enzymes in solution, including those of the Krebs cycle. Electron carriers are found in the cristae. For more detail, see Chapter 12 (Section 12.2).

Once made, ATP leaves the mitochondrion and, as it is a small, soluble molecule, it can spread rapidly to all parts of the cell where energy is needed. Its energy is released by breaking the molecule down to **ADP (adenosine diphosphate)**. This is a hydrolysis reaction. The ADP can then be recycled in a mitochondrion for conversion back to ATP during aerobic respiration.

The endosymbiont theory

> **Note:** The endosymbiont theory is extension content, and is not part of the syllabus.

In the 1960s, it was discovered that mitochondria and chloroplasts contain ribosomes which are slightly smaller than those in the cytoplasm and are the same size as those found in bacteria. Cytoplasmic ribosomes are 80S, while those of bacteria, mitochondria and chloroplasts are 70S. It was also discovered in the 1960s that mitochondria and chloroplasts contain small, circular DNA molecules, also like those found in bacteria. It was later proved that mitochondria and chloroplasts are, in effect, ancient bacteria which now live inside the larger cells of animals and plants (see 'Thinking outside the box' at the beginning of this chapter). This is known as the endosymbiont theory. 'Endo' means 'inside' and a 'symbiont' is an organism which lives in a mutually beneficial relationship with another organism. The DNA and ribosomes of mitochondria and chloroplasts are still active and responsible for the coding and synthesis of certain vital proteins, but mitochondria and chloroplasts can no longer live independently. Mitochondrial ribosomes are just visible as tiny dark orange dots in the mitochondrial matrix in Figure 1.28.

Microtubules and microtubule organising centres (MTOCs)

Microtubules are long, rigid, hollow tubes found in the cytoplasm. They are very small, about 25 nm in diameter. Together with actin filaments and intermediate filaments (not discussed in this book), they make up the cytoskeleton, an essential structural component of cells which helps to determine cell shape.

Microtubules are made of a protein called tubulin. Tubulin has two forms, α-tubulin (alpha-tubulin) and β-tubulin (beta-tubulin). α- and β-tubulin molecules combine to form dimers (double molecules). These dimers are then joined end to end to form long 'protofilaments'. This is an example of polymerisation, the process by which giant molecules are made by joining together many identical subunits. Thirteen protofilaments line up alongside each other in a ring to form a cylinder with a hollow centre. This cylinder is the microtubule. Figure 1.29a shows the helical pattern formed by neighbouring α- and β-tubulin molecules.

Apart from their mechanical function of support, microtubules have a number of other functions.

- Secretory vesicles and other organelles and cell components can be moved along the outside surfaces of the microtubules, forming an intracellular transport system, as in the movement of Golgi vesicles during exocytosis.
- During nuclear division (Chapter 5), a spindle made of microtubules is used for the separation of chromatids or chromosomes.
- Microtubules form part of the structure of centrioles.
- Microtubules form an essential part of the mechanism involved in the beating movements of cilia and flagella.

The assembly of microtubules from tubulin molecules is controlled by special locations in cells called microtubule organising centres (MTOCs). These are discussed further in the following section on centrioles. Because of their simple construction, microtubules can be formed and broken down very easily at the MTOCs, according to need.

KEY WORDS

ADP (adenosine diphosphate): the molecule that is converted to ATP by addition of phosphate (a reaction known as phosphorylation) during cell respiration; the enzyme responsible is ATP synthase; the reaction requires energy

microtubules: tiny tubes made of a protein called tubulin and found in most eukaryotic cells; microtubules have a large variety of functions, including cell support and determining cell shape; the 'spindle' on which chromatids and chromosomes separate during nuclear division is made of microtubules

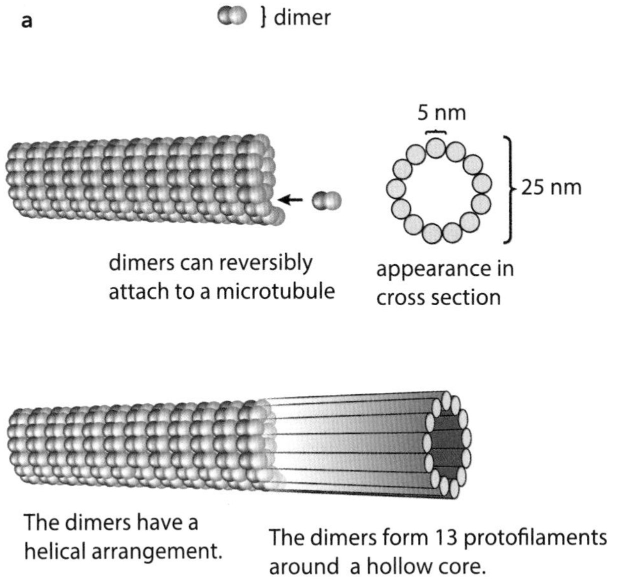

a

⬤⬤ } dimer

5 nm

25 nm

dimers can reversibly
attach to a microtubule

appearance in
cross section

The dimers have a
helical arrangement.

The dimers form 13 protofilaments
around a hollow core.

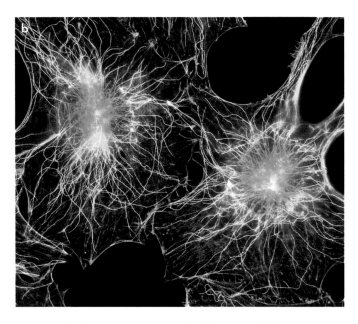

Figure 1.29: a The structure of a microtubule and **b** the arrangement of microtubules in two cells. The microtubules are coloured yellow.

Centrioles and centrosomes

Note: Centrosomes are extension content, and are not part of the syllabus.

The extra resolution of the electron microscope reveals that just outside the nucleus of animal cells there are really *two* **centrioles** and not one as it appears under the light microscope (compare Figures 1.4 and 1.19).

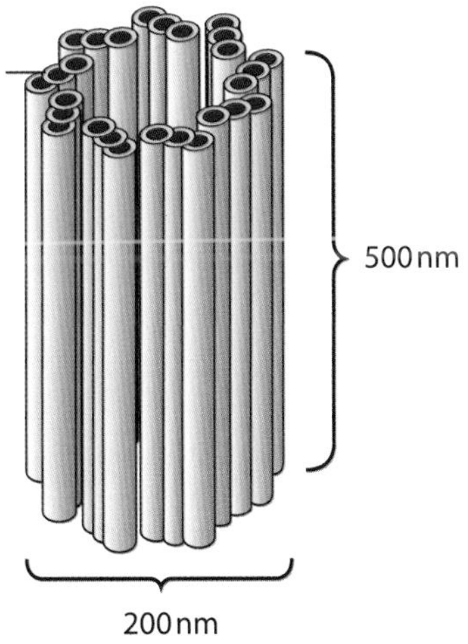

triplet of microtubules (one complete microtubule and two partial microtubules)

500 nm

200 nm

Figure 1.30: The structure of a centriole. It consists of nine groups of microtubules. Each group is made up of three microtubules, a triplet.

They lie close together and at right angles to each other in a region known as the **centrosome**. Centrioles and the centrosome are absent from most plant cells.

A centriole is a hollow cylinder about 500 nm long, formed from a ring of short microtubules. Each centriole contains nine triplets of microtubules (Figures 1.30 and 1.31).

Until recently, it was believed that centrioles acted as MTOCs for the assembly of the microtubules that make up the spindle during nuclear division (Chapter 5). It is now known that this is done by the centrosome, but does not involve the centrioles. However, centrioles are needed for the production of cilia. Centrioles are found at the bases of cilia and flagella, where they are known as basal bodies. The centrioles act as MTOCs. The microtubules that extend from the basal bodies into the cilia and flagella are essential for the beating movements of these organelles.

KEY WORDS

centriole: one of two small, cylindrical structures, made from microtubules, found just outside the nucleus in animal cells, in a region known as the centrosome; they are also found at the bases of cilia and flagella

centrosome: the main microtubule organising centre (MTOC) in animal cells

Figure 1.31: Centrioles in transverse and longitudinal section (TS and LS) (×86 000). The one on the left is seen in TS and clearly shows the nine triplets of microtubules which make up the structure.

KEY WORDS

cilia (singular: **cilium**): whip-like structures projecting from the surface of many animal cells and the cells of many unicellular organisms; they beat, causing locomotion or the movement of fluid across the cell surface

flagella (singular: **flagellum**): whip-like structures projecting from the surface of some animal cells and the cells of many unicellular organisms; they beat, causing locomotion or the movement of fluid across the cell surface; they are identical in structure to cilia, but longer

Note: the structure of flagella is extension content, and not part of the syllabus.

Cilia and flagella

Cilia (singular: **cilium**) and **flagella** (singular: **flagellum**) have identical structures. They are whip-like, beating extensions of many eukaryotic cells. Each is surrounded by an extension of the cell surface membrane. They were given different names before their structures were discovered: flagella are long and found usually one or two per cell, whereas cilia are short and often numerous.

Structure

Cilia and flagella are extremely complicated structures, composed of over 600 different polypeptides. This complexity results in very fine control of how they beat.

The structure of a cilium is shown in Figure 1.32. Cilia have two central microtubules and a ring of nine microtubule doublets (MTDs) around the outside. This is referred to as a '9 + 2' structure. Each MTD contains an A and a B microtubule (Figure 1.32a). The wall of the A microtubule is a complete ring of 13 protofilaments and the B microtubule attached is an incomplete ring with only 10 protofilaments (see Figure 1.32a). Figure 1.32a shows that each A microtubule has inner and outer arms. These are made of the protein dynein. They connect with the B microtubules of neighbouring MTDs during beating. If you imagine the microtubule in three dimensions, there are two rows of several hundred dynein arms along the outside of each A microtubule. The whole cylindrical structure inside the cell surface membrane is called the axoneme.

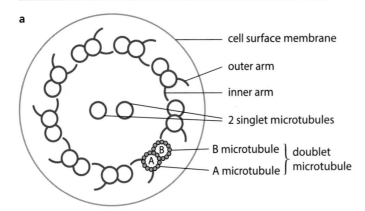

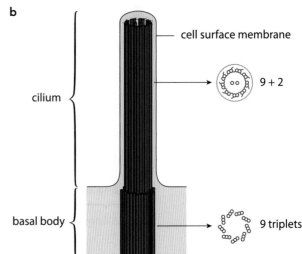

Figure 1.32: The structure of a cilium. **a** A cilium seen in TS. Note the '9 + 2' arrangement of microtubules. **b** A cilium. TSs of the cilium (9 + 2) and basal body (9 triplets) are also shown.

At the base of each cilium and flagellum is a structure called the basal body which is identical in structure to the centriole. We now know that centrioles replicate themselves to produce these basal bodies, and that cilia and flagella grow from basal bodies. Figure 1.33 is a scanning electron micrograph of cilia in the respiratory tract.

Figure 1.33: Scanning electron micrograph of cilia in the respiratory tract

Beating mechanism

The beating motion of cilia and flagella is caused by the dynein (protein) arms making contact with, and moving along, neighbouring microtubules. This produces the force needed for cilia to beat. As neighbouring MTDs slide past each other, the sliding motion is converted into bending by other parts of the cilium.

Functions

If the cell is attached to something so that it cannot move, fluid will move past the cell. If the cell is not attached, the cell will swim through the fluid. Single-celled organisms can therefore use the action of cilia and flagella for locomotion. You will easily be able to find videos of such motion on the internet. In vertebrates, beating cilia are found on some epithelial cells, such as those lining the airways (Chapter 9). Here more than 10 million cilia may be found per mm². They maintain a flow of mucus which removes debris such as dust and bacteria from the respiratory tract.

Question

9   In vertebrates, beating cilia are also found on the epithelial cells of the oviduct (the tube connecting the ovary to the uterus). Suggest what function cilia have in the oviduct.

Chloroplasts

The structure of the chloroplast as seen with the electron microscope is shown in Figures 1.20, 1.21 and 1.34. You can also see a higher-resolution micrograph in Figure 13.4. Chloroplasts tend to have an elongated shape and a diameter of about 3–10 μm (compare 1 μm diameter for mitochondria). Like mitochondria, they are surrounded by two membranes, which form the chloroplast envelope.

The main function of chloroplasts is to carry out photosynthesis. During the first stage of photosynthesis (the light-dependent stage), light energy is absorbed by photosynthetic pigments, particularly chlorophyll. The pigments are found on the membranes of the chloroplast.

The membrane system consists of fluid-filled sacs called **thylakoids**, which spread out like sheets in three dimensions. In places, the thylakoids form flat, disc-like structures that stack up like piles of coins, forming structures called grana (from their appearance in the light microscope; 'grana' means grains).

KEY WORD

thylakoid: a flattened, membrane-bound, fluid-filled sac which is the site of the light-dependent reactions of photosynthesis in a chloroplast

The second stage of photosynthesis (the light-independent stage) uses the energy and reducing power generated during the first stage to convert carbon dioxide into sugars. This takes place in the stroma. The sugars made may be stored in the form of starch grains in the stroma (Figures 1.20 and 13.3 and 13.4).

Lipid droplets are also seen in the stroma. They appear as black spheres in electron micrographs (Figure 1.34). They are reserves of lipid for making membranes or are formed from the breakdown of internal membranes as the chloroplast ages.

Like mitochondria, chloroplasts have their own protein synthesising machinery, including 70S ribosomes and circular DNA. In electron micrographs, the ribosomes can just be seen as small black dots in the stroma (Figure 13.4).

As with mitochondria, it has been shown that chloroplasts originated as endosymbiotic bacteria, in this case photosynthetic blue-green bacteria. The endosymbiont theory is discussed in more detail in the earlier section on mitochondria.

Cell walls

Structure

The first walls formed by plant cells are known as primary walls. They are relatively rigid. The primary wall consists of parallel fibres of the polysaccharide cellulose running through a matrix of other polysaccharides such as pectins and hemicelluloses. Cellulose fibres are inelastic and have high tensile strength, meaning they are difficult to break by pulling on each end. This makes it difficult to stretch the wall, for example when water enters the cell by osmosis. The structure of cellulose is described in Chapter 2.

In most cells extra layers of cellulose are added to the first layer of the primary wall, forming a secondary wall. In a given layer the cellulose fibres are parallel, but the fibres of different layers run in different directions forming a cross-ply structure which is stronger as a result (see Figure 2.10).

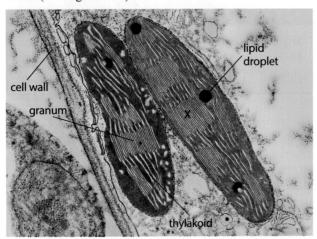

Figure 1.34: Two chloroplasts (×16 000). Thylakoids (yellow) run through the stroma (dark green) and are stacked in places to form grana. Black circles among the thylakoids are lipid droplets. See also Figures 13.3 and 13.4. Chloroplast **X** is referred to in Question 3b.

Some cell walls become even stronger and more rigid by the addition of lignin. Xylem vessel elements and sclerenchyma are examples (Chapter 7). Lignin adds compressional strength to tensile strength (it prevents buckling). It is what gives wood (secondary xylem) its strength and is needed for support in shrubs and trees.

Functions

Some of the main functions of cell walls are summarised below.

- Mechanical strength and support for individual cells and the plant as a whole. Lignification is one means of support. Turgid tissues are another means of support that is dependent on strong cell walls.

- Cell walls prevent cells from bursting by osmosis if cells are surrounded by a solution with a higher water potential (Chapter 2).

- Different orientations of the layers of cellulose fibres help determine the shapes of cells as they grow.

- The system of interconnected cell walls in a plant is called the apoplast. It is a major transport route for water, inorganic ions and other materials (Chapter 7).

- Living connections through neighbouring cell walls, the plasmodesmata, help form another transport pathway through the plant known as the symplast (Chapter 7).

- The cell walls of the root endodermis are impregnated with suberin, a waterproof substance that forms a barrier to the movement of water, thus helping in the control of water and mineral ion uptake by the plant (Chapter 7).

- Epidermal cells often have a waterproof layer of waxy cutin, the cuticle, on their outer walls. This helps reduce water loss by evaporation.

Vacuoles

As we have seen, animal cell vacuoles are relatively small and include phagocytic vacuoles, food vacuoles and autophagic vacuoles.

Unlike animal cells, plant cells typically have a large central vacuole (Figure 1.20). Some examples of the functions of the large central vacuole of plants are listed below. It is useful to try to remember one or two of these examples.

Support

The solution in the vacuole is relatively concentrated. Water therefore enters the vacuole by osmosis, inflating the vacuole and causing a build-up of pressure. A fully inflated cell is described as turgid. Turgid tissues help to support the stems of plants that lack wood (wilting demonstrates the importance of this).

Lysosomal activity

Plant vacuoles may contain hydrolases and act as lysosomes.

Secondary metabolites

Plants contain a wide range of chemicals known as secondary metabolites which, although not essential for growth and development, contribute to survival in various ways. These are often stored in vacuoles. Examples of their functions are:

- Anthocyanins are pigments that are responsible for most of the red, purple, pink and blue colours of flowers and fruits. They attract pollinators and seed dispersers.

- Certain alkaloids and tannins deter herbivores from eating the plant.

- Latex, a milky fluid, can accumulate in vacuoles, for example in rubber trees. The latex of the opium poppy contains alkaloids such as morphine from which opium and heroin are obtained.

Food reserves

Food reserves, such as sucrose in sugar beet, or mineral salts, may be stored in the vacuole. Protein-storing vacuoles are common in seeds.

Waste products

Waste products, such as crystals of calcium oxalate, may be stored in vacuoles.

Growth in size

Osmotic uptake of water into the vacuole is responsible for most of the increase in volume of plant cells during growth. The vacuole occupies up to a third of the total cell volume.

PRACTICAL ACTIVITY 1.3

Work in groups of ten. Each group should make one copy of the following table on stiff card.

START	Photosynthesis occurs in this organelle
Chloroplast	Chromosomes are found in this structure in eukaryotic cells
Nucleus	These are found on rough endoplasmic reticulum (RER)
Ribosomes	This structure contains cellulose as a strengthening material
Cell wall	Makes ribosomes
Nucleolus	Site of ATP synthesis in aerobic respiration
Mitochondrion	Makes lysosomes
Golgi apparatus	Has a '9 + 2' arrangement of microtubules
Cilium	Mainly contains digestive enzymes
Lysosome	END

Cut up the card so that each piece of card has one term and one description (one row of the table). There are therefore ten cards.

Shuffle the cards and take one each. The student with the **START** card reads out the description and the student who has the correct matching term reads out **THE** correct term from their card. They then read out the description on their card. This continues until it reaches the **END** card. Your teacher will help if you get stuck.

The cards can be reshuffled and the activity repeated to see if you can do it faster the second time.

1.7 Bacteria

You will recall that there are two fundamental types of cell: prokaryotes and eukaryotes. The plant and animal cells you have studied so far are eukaryotic cells. Bacteria are prokaryotes and their cells are much simpler than those of eukaryotes. Prokaryotic cells are generally about 1000 times smaller in volume and lack a nucleus that is surrounded by a double membrane. Prokaryotes are thought to have been the first living organisms on Earth. The earliest known fossil prokaryotes are about 3.5 billion years old (the Earth was formed about 4.5 billion years ago). Most biologists believe that eukaryotes evolved from prokaryotes about 2 billion years ago. There are two groups of prokaryotes, known as Bacteria and Archaea. (The classification of living organisms is discussed in Chapter 18.) We consider only Bacteria in this book.

Structure of bacteria

Figure 1.35 shows the structure of a typical **bacterium** (plural: **bacteria**). The left side of the diagram shows the structures that are always present. The right side of the diagram shows the structures which are sometimes found in bacteria.

KEY WORD

bacteria (singular: **bacterium**): a group of single-celled prokaryotic microorganisms; they have a number of characteristics, such as the ability to form spores, which distinguish them from the other group of prokaryotes known as Archaea

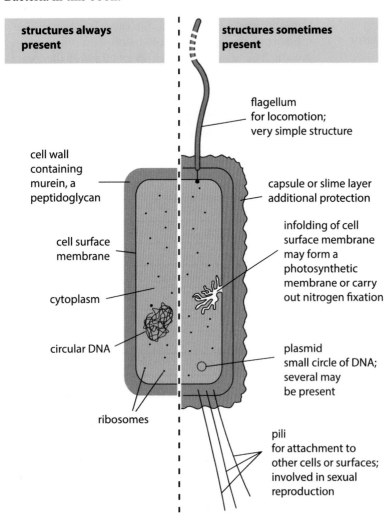

structures always present	structures sometimes present

flagellum
for locomotion;
very simple structure

cell wall containing murein, a peptidoglycan

capsule or slime layer additional protection

cell surface membrane

infolding of cell surface membrane may form a photosynthetic membrane or carry out nitrogen fixation

cytoplasm

circular DNA

plasmid small circle of DNA; several may be present

ribosomes

pili
for attachment to other cells or surfaces; involved in sexual reproduction

Figure 1.35: Diagram of a bacterium. Cells are generally about 1–5 µm in diameter.

Cell wall

Bacterial cell walls contain a strengthening material called **peptidoglycan**. The cell wall protects the bacterium and is essential for its survival. It prevents the cell from swelling up and bursting if water enters the cell by osmosis.

> **KEY WORD**
>
> **peptidoglycan:** a polysaccharide combined with amino acids; it is also known as murein; it makes the bacterial cell wall more rigid

Cell surface membrane

Like all cells, bacterial cells are surrounded by a cell surface membrane.

Cytoplasm

The cytoplasm does not contain any double membrane-bound organelles (such as mitochondria).

Circular DNA

The DNA molecule in bacteria is circular. It is found in a region called the nucleoid, which also contains proteins and small amounts of RNA. It is not surrounded by a double membrane, unlike the nucleus of eukaryotes. There may be more than one copy of the DNA molecule in a given cell.

Ribosomes

Bacterial ribosomes are 70S ribosomes, slightly smaller than the 80S ribosomes of eukaryotes.

Flagellum

Some bacteria are able to swim because they have one or more flagella. Bacterial flagella have a much simpler structure than eukaryotic flagella. The bacterial flagellum is a simple hollow cylinder made of identical protein molecules. It is a rigid structure, so it does not bend, unlike the flagella in eukaryotes. It is wave-shaped and works by rotating at its base like a propeller to push the bacterium through its liquid environment. As a result, the bacterium moves forward with a corkscrew-shaped motion.

Infolding of cell surface membrane

In some bacteria, the cell surface membrane folds into the cell forming an extra surface on which certain biochemical reactions can take place. In blue–green bacteria, for example, the infolded membrane contains photosynthetic pigments which allow photosynthesis to take place. In some bacteria, nitrogen fixation takes place on the infolded membrane. Nitrogen fixation is the ability to convert nitrogen in the air to nitrogen-containing compounds, such as ammonia, inside the cell. All life depends on nitrogen fixation. Eukaryotes cannot carry out nitrogen fixation.

Capsule

Some bacteria are surrounded by an extra layer outside the cell wall. This may take the form of a capsule or a slime layer. A capsule is a definite structure, made mostly of polysaccharides. A slime layer is more diffuse and is easily washed off. Both help to protect the bacterium from drying out and may have other protective functions. For example, a capsule helps protect some bacteria from antibiotics. Some capsules prevent white blood cells known as phagocytes from engulfing disease-causing bacteria.

Plasmid

A **plasmid** is a small circle of DNA separate from the main DNA of the cell. It contains only a few genes. Many plasmids may be present in a given cell. The genes have various useful functions. Commonly, plasmids contain genes that give resistance to particular antibiotics, such as penicillin. Plasmids can copy themselves independently of the chromosomal DNA and can spread rapidly from one bacterium to another. Plasmid DNA is not associated with protein and is referred to as 'naked' DNA.

> **KEY WORD**
>
> **plasmid:** a small circular piece of DNA in a bacterium (not its main chromosome); plasmids often contain genes that provide resistance to antibiotics

Pili (singular: pilus)

Pili are fine protein rods. They vary in length and stiffness. One to several hundred may be present on the outside of the cell. They are used for attachment and interactions with other cells or surfaces. They allow the transfer of genes, including plasmids, from one bacterium to another during conjugation.

1.8 Comparing prokaryotic cells with eukaryotic cells

Table 1.3 compares prokaryotic cells with eukaryotic cells.

Prokaryotes	Eukaryotes
Prokaryotes are thought to have evolved about 3.5 billion years ago.	Eukaryotes are thought to have evolved about 1.5 billion years ago.
Their typical diameter is 1–5 μm.	Cells are up to 40 μm diameter and up to 1000 times the volume of prokaryotic cells.
DNA is circular and free in the cytoplasm; it is not surrounded by a double membrane.	DNA is not circular and is contained in a nucleus. The nucleus is surrounded by a double membrane (the nuclear envelope).
70S ribosomes are present (smaller than those of eukaryotes).	80S ribosomes are present (larger than those of prokaryotes).
Very few types of cell organelle are present. No separate membrane-bound organelles are present.	Many types of cell organelle are present. • Some organelles are surrounded by a single membrane (e.g. lysosomes, Golgi apparatus, vacuoles, ER). • Some are surrounded by an envelope of two membranes (e.g. nucleus, mitochondrion, chloroplast). • Some have no membrane (e.g. ribosomes, centrioles, microtubules).
The cell wall contains peptidoglycan (a polysaccharide combined with amino acids).	A cell wall is sometimes present (e.g. in plants and fungi); it contains cellulose or lignin in plants, and chitin (a nitrogen-containing polysaccharide similar to cellulose) in fungi.
Flagella are simple and lack microtubules; they project outside the cell surface membrane so they are extracellular (outside the cell).	Flagella (and cilia) are complex with a '9 + 2' arrangement of microtubules; they are surrounded by the cell surface membrane so they are intracellular (inside the cell).
Cell division occurs by binary fission (the cell splits into two); it does not involve a spindle (see Chapter 6).	Cell division takes place by mitosis or meiosis and involves a spindle (see Chapter 6).
Some carry out nitrogen fixation.	None carries out nitrogen fixation.

Table 1.3: Comparing prokaryotic cells and eukaryotic cells.

Question

10 List the structural features that prokaryotic and eukaryotic cells have in common. Briefly explain why each of the structures you have listed is essential.

1.9 Viruses

In 1852, a Russian scientist discovered that certain diseases could be transmitted by agents that, unlike bacteria, could pass through very fine filters. This was the first evidence for the existence of viruses. **Viruses** are tiny 'particles' which are much smaller than bacteria and are on the boundary between what we think of as living and non-living. Unlike prokaryotes and eukaryotes, viruses do not have a cell structure. In other words, they

KEY WORD

virus: a very small (20–300 nm) infectious particle which can replicate only inside living cells; it consists of a molecule of DNA or RNA (the genome) surrounded by a protein coat; an outer lipid envelope may also be present

are not surrounded by a partially permeable membrane containing cytoplasm with ribosomes. They are much simpler in structure. They consist only of the following:

- a self-replicating molecule of DNA or RNA (the genome or complete genetic instructions)

- a protective coat of protein molecules called a capsid

- (some viruses only) a membrane-like outer layer, called the envelope, that is made of **phospholipids**. (The structure of phospholipids is described in Chapter 2.) Proteins may project from the envelope.

Figure 1.36 shows the structure of a virus with an envelope. Viruses typically have a very symmetrical shape. The protein coat (or capsid) is made up of separate protein molecules, each of which is called a capsomere.

Viruses range in size from about 20 nm to 300 nm (about 50 times smaller on average than bacteria).

All viruses are parasitic because they can only reproduce by infecting and taking over living cells. The virus DNA or RNA takes over the protein synthesising machinery of the host cell, which then helps to make new virus particles.

a
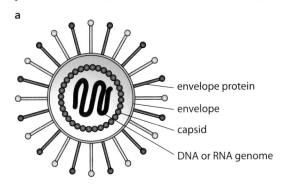

envelope protein

envelope

capsid

DNA or RNA genome

b
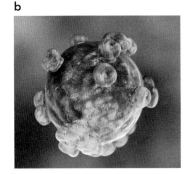

c
Zika virus
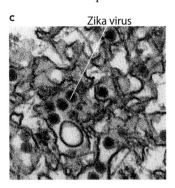

Figure 1.36: **a** The structure of a virus with an envelope; **b** model of a Zika virus. The virus is an RNA virus. Its capsid has an outer envelope; **c** electron micrograph of a cell infected by Zika virus. The virus particles are the darkly stained roughly spherical structures. Each virus particle is about 40 nm in diameter.

REFLECTION

Think about everything you know about cells. What answers would you give to the following questions?

- What is a cell?

- Why are all living things made of cells?

Look back at the differences between eukaryotic and prokaryotic cells.

- Write down a list of criteria to compare the success of prokaryotic and eukaryotic cells.

- Suggest why trying to compare the success of prokaryotic and eukaryotic cells may be a meaningless exercise. (Tip: think about the meaning of the word 'success'.)

Personal reflection questions

Changing from studying at GCSE to studying at AS Level is a big jump. Has anything surprised you about the change? Are you confident about

being able to adapt the way you work? If not, what particular concerns do you have?

You have studied cells in Chapter 1 and learnt a lot about their structure and function. The Reflection activity gives you a chance to use this information to think again about cells from a slightly different point of view.

How did the Reflection activity improve your understanding of what you have studied in Chapter 1?

Final reflection

Discuss with a friend which, if any, parts of Chapter 1 you need to:

- read through again to make sure you really understand

- seek more guidance on, even after going over it again.

SUMMARY

The basic unit of life is the cell. The simplest cells are prokaryotic cells, which are thought to have evolved before, and given rise to, the much more complex and much larger eukaryotic cells.

Cells can be seen clearly only with the aid of microscopes. The light microscope uses light as a source of radiation, whereas the electron microscope uses electrons. The electron microscope has greater resolution (allows more detail to be seen) than the light microscope because electrons have a shorter wavelength than light.

With a light microscope, cells may be measured using an eyepiece graticule and a stage micrometer. Using the formula $A = \dfrac{I}{M}$ the actual size of an object (A) or its magnification (M) can be found if its observed (image) size (I) is measured and A or M, as appropriate, is known.

All cells are surrounded by a partially permeable cell surface membrane that controls exchange between the cell and its environment. All cells contain genetic material in the form of DNA, and ribosomes for protein synthesis.

All eukaryotic cells possess a nucleus containing DNA. The DNA is linear (not circular) and bound to proteins and RNA to form chromatin.

The cytoplasm of eukaryotic cells contains many organelles, some of which are surrounded by one or two membranes. Organelles of eukaryotic cells include endoplasmic reticulum (ER), 80S ribosomes, Golgi apparatus, lysosomes and mitochondria. Animal cells also contain a centrosome and centrioles and may contain cilia. Plant cells have a cell wall containing cellulose. They may contain chloroplasts and often have a large central vacuole.

Prokaryotic cells lack a true nucleus and have smaller (70S) ribosomes than eukaryotic cells. They also lack membrane-bound organelles. Their DNA is circular and lies free in the cytoplasm.

Viruses do not have a cellular structure. They are extremely small and simple. They consist of a molecule of DNA or RNA, a protein coat and sometimes an outer envelope.

EXAM-STYLE QUESTIONS

1 Which **one** of the following cell structures can be seen with a light microscope?

   A mitochondrion   **C** rough ER

   B ribosome   **D** smooth ER   [1]

2 What property of electrons allows high resolution to be achieved by electron microscopes?

   a Electrons are negatively charged.

   b Electrons can be focused using electromagnets.

   c Electrons have a very short wavelength.

   d Electrons travel at the speed of light.   [1]

3 Which **one** of the following structures is found in animal cells but not in plant cells?

   A cell surface membrane

   B centriole

   C chloroplast

   D Golgi apparatus   [1]

CONTINUED

4 List **ten** structures you could find in an electron micrograph of an animal cell which would be absent from the cell of a bacterium. [10]

5 Distinguish between the following pairs of terms:

   a magnification and resolution [3]

   b light microscope and electron microscope [2]

   c nucleus and nucleolus [4]

   d chromatin and chromosome [3]

   e membrane and envelope [3]

   f smooth ER and rough ER [4]

   g prokaryote and eukaryote [4]

   h cell wall and cell surface membrane [4]

   i capsid and cell wall [4]

   j capsid and capsomere [3]

[Total: 34]

6 List:

   a **three** organelles each lacking a boundary membrane [3]

   b **three** organelles each surrounded by a single membrane [3]

   c **three** organelles each surrounded by two membranes (an envelope). [3]

[Total: 9]

7 **Identify** each cell structure or organelle from its description below.

   a manufactures lysosomes

   b manufactures ribosomes

   c site of protein synthesis

   d can bud off vesicles which form the Golgi apparatus

   e can transport newly synthesised protein round the cell

   f manufactures ATP in animal and plant cells

   g controls the activity of the cell because it contains the DNA

   h carries out photosynthesis

   i can act as a starting point for the growth of spindle microtubules during cell division

   j contains chromatin

   k partially permeable barrier only about 7 nm thick

   l organelle about 25 nm in diameter

   m organelle with a '9 + 2' arrangement of microtubules [13]

COMMAND WORD

Identify: name / select / recognise.

8 The transmission electron micrograph shows parts of two palisade cells from a leaf.

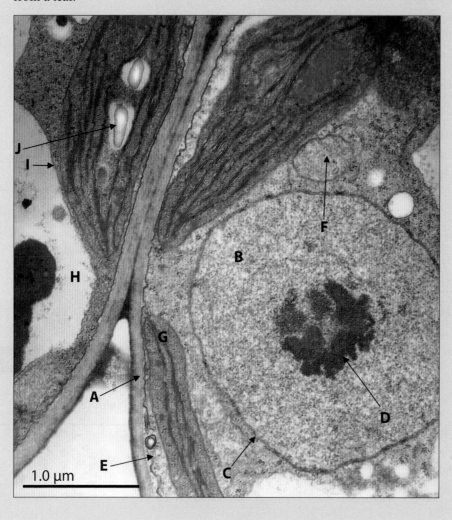

CONTINUED

Copy the table. Identify the labelled structures **A–J** and write a brief statement about their functions.

Label	Name of structure	Function	
A			[3]
B			[3]
C			[2]
D			[2]
E			[3]
F			[3]
G			[3]
H			[2]
I			[2]
J			[2]

[Total: 25]

CONTINUED

9 The electron micrograph shows part of a secretory cell from the pancreas. You are not expected to have seen a micrograph of this type of cell before. The cell contains many secretory vesicles. These are Golgi vesicles. They appear as small, roughly circular structures with black circular contents. The magnification is ×8000.

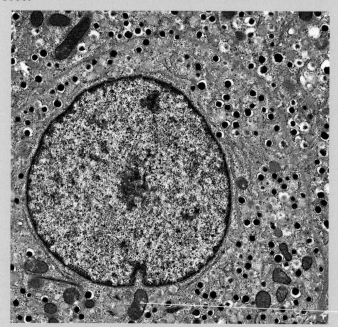

mitochondrion

COMMAND WORDS

Calculate: work out from given facts, figures or information.

Give: produce an answer from a given source or recall/memory.

Suggest: apply knowledge and understanding to situations where there is a range of valid responses in order to make proposals / put forward considerations.

a Copy the table. **Calculate** the actual sizes of the structures listed in the table. Use a ruler with mm divisions to help you. Show your measurements and calculations. When you have your answers, complete the table with the required information. **Give** your answers in micrometres.

Structure	Observed diameter (measured with ruler)	Actual size
maximum diameter of a Golgi vesicle		
maximum diameter of nucleus		
maximum length of the labelled mitochondrion		

[9]

b Make a fully labelled drawing of representative parts of the cell. You do not have to draw everything, but enough to show the structures of the main organelles. Use a full page of plain paper and a sharp pencil. Use Figures 1.18 and 1.19 in this book and the simplified diagram in **d** below to help you identify the structures. [14]

c The mitochondria in pancreatic cells are mostly sausage-shaped in three dimensions. **Suggest** why some of the mitochondria in the electron micrograph here appear roughly circular. [1]

IMPORTANT

Use modelling clay to make a sausage shape to represent a mitochondrion (or use a real sausage). Try cutting the sausage with a knife at different angles. This represents the process of sectioning material for examination using a microscope. The cut surfaces will reveal the variation you can expect to see in sections.

CONTINUED

d   The figure is a diagram based on an electron micrograph of a secretory cell
from the pancreas. This type of cell is specialised for secreting (exporting)
proteins. Some of the proteins are digestive enzymes of the pancreatic juice.
The cell is very active, requiring a lot of energy. The arrows **A**, **B**, **C** and **D**
show the route taken by the protein molecules.

Note that arrow **A** is shown magnified in a separate diagram.

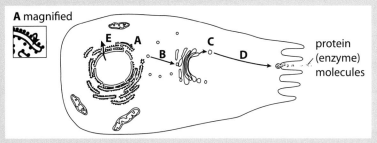

i   Describe briefly what is happening at each of the stages **A**, **B**, **C** and **D**.   **[8]**

ii   Arrow **E** shows the path of a molecule or structure leaving the nucleus
through the nuclear envelope. Name **one** molecule or structure which
leaves the nucleus by route **E**.   **[1]**

iii   The molecule or structure you named in **ii** passes through the nuclear
envelope. Name the structure in the nuclear envelope through which the
molecule or structure passes.   **[1]**

iv   Name the molecule which leaves the mitochondrion in order to provide
energy for the cell.   **[1]**

[Total: 35]

10   One technique used to investigate the activity of cell organelles is called
differential centrifugation. In this technique, a tissue is homogenised
(ground in a blender), placed in tubes and spun in a centrifuge. This makes
organelles sediment (settle) to the bottom of the tubes. The larger the
organelles, the faster they sediment. By repeating the process at faster and
faster speeds, the organelles can be separated from each other according to
size. Some liver tissue was treated in this way to separate ribosomes, nuclei
and mitochondria. The centrifuge was spun at 1000 g, 10 000 g or 100 000 g
(g is gravitational force).

a   State in which of the three sediments (1000 g, 10 000 g or 100 000 g) you
would expect to find the following:

i   ribosomes

ii   nuclei

iii   mitochondria   **[1]**

b   Liver tissue contains many lysosomes. Suggest why this makes it difficult
to study mitochondria using the differential centrifugation technique.   **[4]**

[Total: 5]

COMMAND WORDS

Describe: state the
points of a topic / give
characteristics and
main features.

State: express in clear
terms.

SELF-EVALUATION CHECKLIST

After studying this chapter, complete a table like this:

I can	See section...	Needs more work	Almost there	Ready to move on
explain that cells are the basic units of life	1.1			
use the units of measurement relevant to microscopy	1.2			
recognise the common structures found in cells as seen with a light microscope and outline their structures and functions	1.3			
compare the key structural features of animal and plant cells	1.3			
use a light microscope and make temporary preparations to observe cells	1.3			
recognise, draw and measure cell structures from temporary preparations and micrographs	1.3, 1.4			
calculate magnifications of images and actual sizes of specimens using drawings or micrographs	1.4			
explain the use of the electron microscope to study cells with reference to the increased resolution of electron microscopes	1.5			
recognise the common structures found in cells as seen with an electron microscope and outline their structures and functions	1.6			
outline briefly the role of ATP in cells	1.6			
describe the structure of bacteria and compare the structure of prokaryotic cells with eukaryotic cells	1.7, 1.8			
describe the structure of viruses	1.9			

> Chapter 2

Biological molecules

LEARNING INTENTIONS

In this chapter you will learn how to:

- describe how large biological molecules are made from smaller molecules
- describe the structure of carbohydrates, lipids and proteins and how their structure relates to their functions
- describe and carry out biochemical tests to identify carbohydrates, lipids and proteins
- explain some key properties of water that make life possible.

BEFORE YOU START

It is useful to remind yourself of how atoms join together to make molecules. The best way to do this is to draw or make models of some simple molecules. You want to show how the carbon, hydrogen, oxygen and nitrogen atoms are joined together with covalent bonds. Carbon has four bonds, nitrogen three, oxygen two and hydrogen one. The bonds should be arranged with the correct orientation (see Figures 2.11, 2.16, 2.23 and 2.27 to help you).

If you can, use model kits. Otherwise, coloured balls of modelling clay (or coloured jelly beans) can be used to represent atoms. Use black for carbon, white for hydrogen, red for oxygen and blue for

nitrogen. Join the balls or jelly beans with short sticks such as toothpicks, matchsticks or straws. The sticks represent covalent bonds.

Try making models of or drawing these molecules:

- methane, CH_4
- water, H_2O
- ethanol, C_2H_5OH
- a hydrocarbon, e.g. C_3H_8
- ammonia, NH_3
- ethanoic acid, CH_3COOH.

THE PROTEIN-FOLDING PROBLEM – FROM DEEP BLUE TO ALPHAZERO AND BEYOND

In 1962, two Cambridge scientists, John Kendrew and Max Perutz, received the Nobel Prize for Chemistry for their work on the three-dimensional structure of the proteins myoglobin and haemoglobin. The work was a vital step in understanding how proteins function. Thirty-five years later, in 1997, a world chess champion, Garry Kasparov, was beaten at chess for the first time by the computer Deep Blue. So what is the connection between these two events?

The answer lies in the applications of artificial intelligence (AI). The IBM computer Deep Blue was an important milestone on the road to developing AI. One of the most exciting recent computers to be developed is AlphaZero, the creation of another British scientist, Demis Hassabis. AlphaZero has taught itself to be the best chess player ever. It took only four hours starting from scratch, using the technique known as 'reinforcement learning' – learning by trial and error by playing millions of games against itself.

How can a computer like this be of use to humans? There are many problems in the world, such as climate change, which are too complex for the human brain to analyse fully. AI may help. Some of the problems that AI is beginning to tackle relate to biological molecules.

For example, Demis Hassabis has suggested that, in the future, AlphaZero and computers like it may be able to design more effective drugs and medicines. One of the key problems in biology is the so-called 'protein-folding problem'. This is the problem of trying to discover the rules of how proteins fold into the precise three-dimensional shapes essential for their functions. Ideally, knowing the primary structure of a protein and its chemical environment (e.g. pH and temperature) would enable scientists to predict how the protein will fold up. The work has vital applications. For example,

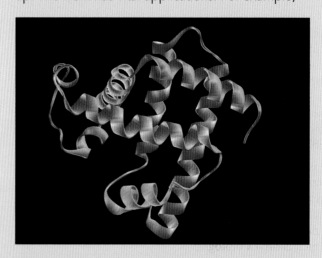

Figure 2.1: The protein-folding problem.

CONTINUED

many diseases and disorders including Alzheimer's, Parkinson's and cystic fibrosis are caused by faulty protein folding. In December 2018, the computer AlphaFold won an international contest to predict protein structure more accurately than previous attempts.

Around 60 years after the pioneering work of Kendrew and Perutz, scientists are getting closer

to the goal of predicting how proteins will fold, but it seems only AI can provide all the answers (Figure 2.1).

Questions for discussion

Can you think of any potential problems with AI? Do you think the benefits outweigh these problems, or not?

2.1 Biochemistry

Biochemistry looks at the chemical reactions of biological molecules. The sum total of all the biochemical reactions in the body is known as metabolism. You may think biochemistry is a complicated subject, but it has an underlying simplicity. For example, only 20 common amino acids are used to make proteins, whereas theoretically there could be millions. Having a limited variety of molecules makes it easier to control metabolism.

Another feature of biochemistry is the close link between the structures of molecules and their functions. This will become clear in this chapter and in Chapter 3.

2.2 The building blocks of life

The four most common elements in living organisms are, in order of abundance, hydrogen, carbon, oxygen and nitrogen. They account for more than 99% of the atoms found in all living things. Carbon is particularly important because carbon atoms can join together to form long chains or ring structures. They can be thought of as the basic skeletons of organic molecules (molecules that contain carbon). Other atoms, with different functions, are attached to the carbon skeletons.

It is believed that, before life evolved, there was a period of chemical evolution in which simple carbon-based biological molecules evolved from even simpler molecules. The simple biological molecules are relatively limited in variety. They act as the building blocks for larger, complex biological molecules (Figure 2.2).

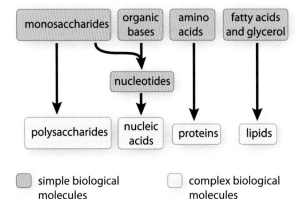

Figure 2.2: The building blocks of life are simple biological molecules which join together to form larger more complex molecules.

2.3 Monomers, polymers and macromolecules

A **macromolecule** is a giant molecule. There are three types of macromolecule in living organisms:

- polysaccharides
- proteins (polypeptides)
- nucleic acids (polynucleotides).

KEY WORD

macromolecule: a large molecule such as a polysaccharide, protein or nucleic acid

The words polysaccharides, polypeptides and polynucleotides all contain the term *poly*. 'Poly' means many. Macromolecules are described as **polymers** because they are made up of many repeating subunits that are similar or identical to each other. The subunits are called **monomers** ('mono' means one). Monomers are joined together by covalent bonds. These are bonds in which the atoms are joined by sharing electrons. Covalent bonds are relatively strong bonds. Examples you will learn about in this chapter are the glycosidic bond, the ester bond and the peptide bond.

Making biological polymers from monomers is relatively simple because the same reaction is repeated many times. The reaction involves joining together two monomers by the *removal* of a water molecule. This type of reaction is called a **condensation reaction**. The opposite reaction (*adding* water) can be used to break down the polymer again. Adding water to split a molecule is called **hydrolysis**. You will meet many examples of condensation and hydrolysis in this chapter.

The monomers from which polysaccharides, proteins and nucleic acids are made are monosaccharides, amino

acids and nucleotides respectively (Figure 2.2.) Figure 2.2 also shows the role of organic bases (not monomers) in nucleotides and the role of fatty acids and glycerol in the formation of lipids (not polymers).

Cellulose and rubber are examples of naturally occurring polymers. There are many examples of industrially produced polymers, such as polyester, polythene, PVC (polyvinyl chloride) and nylon. All these are made up of carbon-based monomers and contain thousands of carbon atoms joined end to end.

Let's now look at some of the small biological molecules (monosaccharides, fatty acids and amino acids) and the larger molecules (carbohydrates, lipids and proteins) made from them. Organic bases, nucleotides and nucleic acids are discussed in Chapter 6.

2.4 Carbohydrates

All carbohydrates contain the elements carbon, hydrogen and oxygen. The 'hydrate' part of the name refers to water; the hydrogen and oxygen atoms are present in the ratio of 2 : 1 as in water. The general formula for a carbohydrate can be written as $C_x(H_2O)_y$.

Carbohydrates are divided into three main groups: monosaccharides, disaccharides and polysaccharides. The word 'saccharide' means a sugar or sweet substance.

Monosaccharides

Monosaccharides are sugars. Sugars dissolve easily in water to form sweet-tasting solutions. Monosaccharides consist of a single sugar molecule ('mono' means one, 'saccharide' means sugar). They have the general formula $(CH_2O)_n$. The main types of monosaccharides (when classified according to the number of carbon atoms in each molecule) are trioses (3C), pentoses (5C) and hexoses (6C). The names of all sugars end with -ose. Common hexoses are glucose, fructose and galactose. Two common pentoses are ribose and deoxyribose.

Molecular and structural formulae

The molecular formula for a hexose can be written as $C_6H_{12}O_6$. It means there are 6 carbon atoms, 12 hydrogen atoms and 6 oxygen atoms in the molecule. It is useful to show the arrangements of the atoms using a diagram known as the structural formula. Figure 2.3 shows the structural formula of glucose, the most common monosaccharide. Glucose is a hexose.

KEY WORDS

polymer: a giant molecule made from many similar repeating subunits joined together in a chain; the subunits are much smaller and simpler molecules known as monomers; examples of biological polymers are polysaccharides, proteins and nucleic acids

monomer: a relatively simple molecule which is used as a basic building block for the synthesis of a polymer; many monomers are joined together by covalent bonds to make the polymer, usually by condensation reactions; common examples of monomers are monosaccharides, amino acids and nucleotides

condensation reaction: a chemical reaction involving the joining together of two molecules by removal of a water molecule

hydrolysis: a chemical reaction in which a chemical bond is broken by the addition of a water molecule; commonly used to break down complex molecules into simpler molecules

monosaccharide: a molecule consisting of a single sugar unit and with the general formula $(CH_2O)_n$.

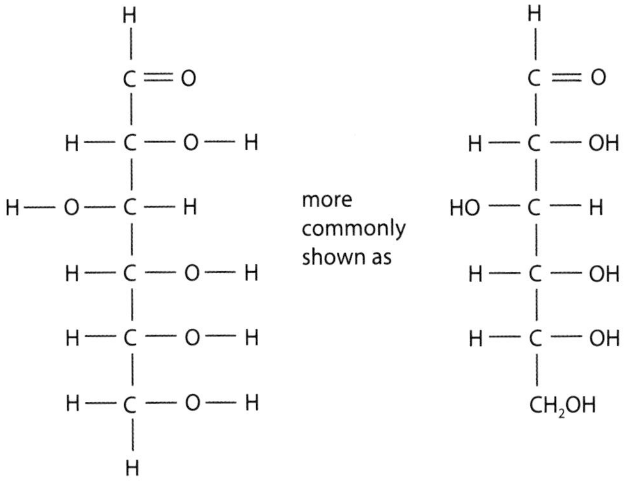

Figure 2.3: Structural formula of glucose. –OH is known as a hydroxyl group. There are five in glucose.

Ring structures

One important aspect of the structure of pentoses and hexoses is that the chain of carbon atoms is long enough to close up on itself to form a more stable ring structure. When glucose forms such a ring, carbon atom number 1 joins to the oxygen on carbon atom number 5

(Figure 2.4). The ring therefore contains oxygen, and carbon atom number 6 is not part of the ring.

You will see from Figure 2.4 that the hydroxyl group, –OH, on carbon atom 1 may be above or below the plane of the ring. The form of glucose where it is below the ring is known as α-glucose (alpha-glucose) and the form where it is above the ring is β-glucose (beta-glucose). Two forms of the same chemical are known as isomers, and the extra variety provided by the existence of α- and β-isomers has important biological consequences, as you will see in the structures of starch, glycogen and cellulose.

Question

1   The formula for a hexose is $C_6H_{12}O_6$ or $(CH_2O)_6$. What would be the formula of:

   a   a triose?

   b   a pentose?

Functions of monosaccharides in living organisms

Monosaccharides have two major functions. First, they are commonly used as a source of energy in respiration. This is due to the large number of carbon–hydrogen bonds. These bonds can be broken to release

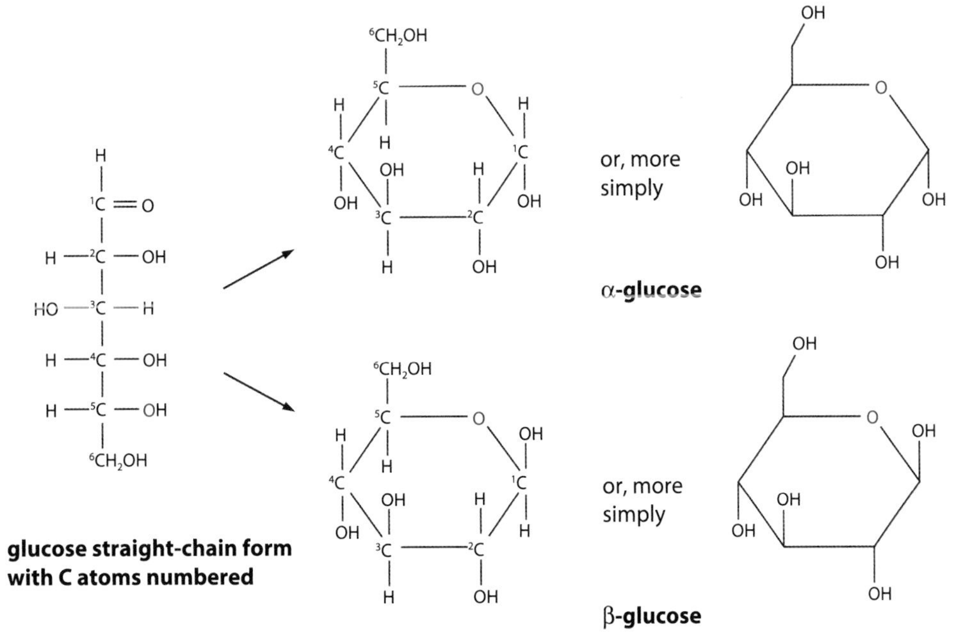

Figure 2.4: Structural formulae for the straight-chain and ring forms of glucose. Chemists often leave out the C and H atoms from the structural formula for simplicity.

a lot of energy, which is transferred to help make ATP (adenosine triphosphate) from ADP (adenosine diphosphate) plus phosphate during the process of respiration. The most important monosaccharide in energy metabolism is glucose.

Second, monosaccharides are important as building blocks for larger molecules. For example, glucose is used to make the polysaccharides starch, glycogen and cellulose. Ribose (a pentose) is one of the molecules used to make RNA (ribonucleic acid) and ATP. Deoxyribose (also a pentose) is one of the molecules used to make DNA (Chapter 6).

Disaccharides and the glycosidic bond

Disaccharides, like monosaccharides, are sugars. They are formed by two monosaccharides joining together ('di' means two). The three most common disaccharides are maltose (glucose + glucose), sucrose (glucose + fructose) and lactose (glucose + galactose). Sucrose is the transport sugar in plants and the sugar commonly

> **KEY WORD**
>
> **disaccharide:** a sugar molecule consisting of two monosaccharides joined together by a glycosidic bond

bought in shops. Lactose is the sugar found in milk and is therefore an important constituent of the diet of young mammals.

The process of joining two monosaccharides is an example of a condensation reaction (Figure 2.5; see also Section 2.3, Monomers, polymers and macromolecules). The reverse process (splitting a disaccharide into two monomers) is also shown in Figure 2.5 and is an example of a hydrolysis reaction. Notice that fructose has a different ring structure from glucose.

For each condensation reaction, two hydroxyl (–OH) groups line up alongside each other. One combines with a hydrogen atom from the other to form a water molecule. This allows an oxygen 'bridge' to form between the two molecules, holding them together

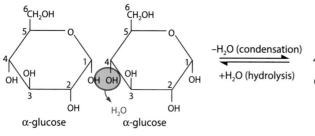
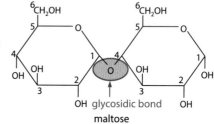

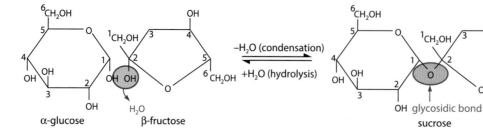

Figure 2.5: Formation of a disaccharide from two monosaccharides by condensation. **a** Maltose is formed from two α-glucose molecules. This can be repeated many times to form a polysaccharide. Note that in this example the glycosidic bond is formed between carbon atoms 1 and 4 of neighbouring glucose molecules. **b** Sucrose is made from an α-glucose and a β-fructose molecule.

and forming a disaccharide. The bridge is called a **glycosidic bond**.

In theory, any two –OH groups can line up and, since monosaccharides have many –OH groups, there are a large number of possible disaccharides. The shape of the enzyme controlling the reaction determines which –OH groups come alongside each other. Only a few of the possible disaccharides are common in nature.

The addition of water in hydrolysis takes place during the digestion of disaccharides and polysaccharides, when they are broken down to monosaccharides.

> **KEY WORD**
>
> glycosidic bond: a C–O–C link between two sugar molecules, formed by a condensation reaction; it is a covalent bond

PRACTICAL ACTIVITY 2.1

Testing for the presence of sugars

1 Reducing sugars

Reducing sugars are so called because they can carry out a type of chemical reaction known as reduction. In the process they are oxidised. The reducing sugars include all monosaccharides and some disaccharides. The only common non-reducing sugar is sucrose.

The ability of some sugars to carry out reduction is the basis of **Benedict's test** for the presence of sugar. The test uses Benedict's reagent which is copper(II) sulfate in an alkaline solution. It has a distinctive blue colour. Reducing sugars reduce the soluble blue copper sulfate to insoluble brick-red copper oxide, containing copper(I). The copper oxide is seen as a brick-red precipitate.

$$\text{reducing sugar} + Cu^{2+} \rightarrow \text{oxidised sugar} + Cu^{+}$$

blue   red-brown

Procedure

Add Benedict's reagent to the solution you are testing and heat it in a water bath. If a reducing sugar is present, the solution will gradually turn through green, yellow and orange to red-brown as the insoluble copper(I) oxide forms a precipitate.

> **KEY WORD**
>
> Benedict's test: a test for the presence of reducing sugars; the unknown substance is heated with Benedict's reagent, and a change from a clear blue solution to the production of a yellow, red or brown precipitate indicates the presence of reducing sugars such as glucose

As long as you use excess Benedict's reagent (more than enough to react with all of the sugar present), the intensity of the red colour is related to the concentration of the reducing sugar. The test can therefore be used as a semi-quantitative test. You can estimate the concentration of a reducing sugar solution using colour standards made by comparing the colour against the colours obtained in tests done with reducing sugar solutions of known concentration. You could also measure the time taken for the first colour change.

Alternatively, you can use a colorimeter to measure small differences in colour more precisely.

2 Non-reducing sugars

Some disaccharides, such as sucrose, are not reducing sugars, so you would get a negative result from Benedict's test. In such a case, you should then carry out the test for a non-reducing sugar.

In the non-reducing sugars test, the disaccharide is first broken down into its two monosaccharide constituents. The chemical reaction is hydrolysis and can be brought about by adding hydrochloric acid. The constituent monosaccharides will be reducing sugars and their presence can be tested for using Benedict's test after the acid has been neutralised.

Procedure

Carry out Benedict's test on the solution. If you get a negative result, start again with a fresh sample of the solution. Heat the solution with hydrochloric acid. If a non-reducing sugar is present, it will break down to monosaccharides. Benedict's reagent needs alkaline conditions to work, so you need to neutralise the test solution now by adding an alkali such as sodium

CONTINUED

hydroxide. Add Benedict's reagent and heat as before and look for the colour change. If the solution now goes red, a non-reducing sugar is present. If both a reducing sugar and a non-reducing sugar are present, the precipitate will be heavier than the one obtained

in the Benedict's test. If there is still no colour change, then there is no sugar of any kind present.

(See Practical Investigation 2.1 in the Practical Workbook for additional information.)

Question

2 a   Why do you need to use excess Benedict's reagent to find the concentration of a sugar solution?

b   Outline how you could use the Benedict's test to estimate the concentration of a solution of a reducing sugar.

Polysaccharides

Polysaccharides are polymers made by joining many monosaccharide molecules by condensation. Each successive monosaccharide is added by means of a glycosidic bond, as in disaccharides. The final molecule may be several thousand monosaccharide units long, forming a macromolecule. The most important polysaccharides are starch, glycogen and cellulose, all of which are polymers of glucose. Polysaccharides are not sugars.

Starch and glycogen

Since glucose is the main source of energy for cells, it is important for living organisms to store glucose in an appropriate form. If glucose itself accumulated in cells, it would dissolve and make the contents of the cell too concentrated. This would seriously affect the osmotic properties of the cell (Chapter 4, Section 4.5, Movement of substances across membranes). Glucose is also a reactive molecule and would interfere with normal cell chemistry. These problems are avoided when glucose is converted by condensation reactions to a storage polysaccharide. The storage polysaccharide is a convenient, compact, inert (unreactive) and insoluble molecule. The storage polysaccharide in plants is starch; in animals, it is glycogen. When needed, glucose is quickly made available again by enzyme-controlled hydrolysis reactions.

Starch is a mixture of two substances – amylose and amylopectin. Amylose is made by condensations between α-glucose molecules (Figure 2.5a). In this way, a long, unbranching chain of several thousand 1,4 linked glucose molecules is built up. ('1,4 linked' means

they are linked between carbon atoms 1 and 4 of successive glucose units.) The chains are curved (Figure 2.6) and coil up into helical structures like springs, so the final molecule is compact.

Amylopectin is also made of many 1,4 linked α-glucose molecules, but the chains are shorter than in amylose and also contain 1,6 linkages. These start branches out to the sides of the chain (Figure 2.7).

Mixtures of amylose and amylopectin molecules build up into relatively large starch grains. Starch grains are commonly found in chloroplasts and in storage organs, such as potato tubers and the seeds of cereals and legumes (Figure 2.8). Starch grains are easily seen with a

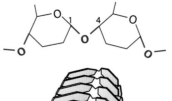

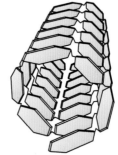

Figure 2.6: Arrangement of α-glucose units in amylose. The 1,4 linkages cause the chain to turn and coil. The glycosidic bonds are shown in red and the hydroxyl groups are omitted.

KEY WORDS

polysaccharide: a polymer whose subunits are monosaccharides joined together by glycosidic bonds

glycogen: a polysaccharide made of many glucose molecules linked together, that acts as a glucose store in liver and muscle cells

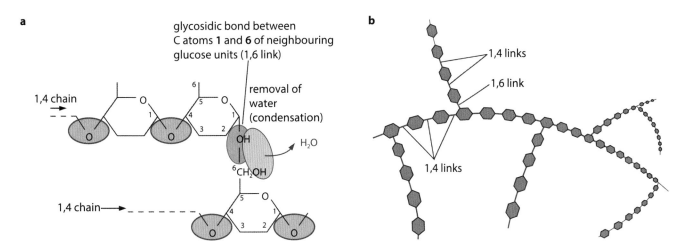

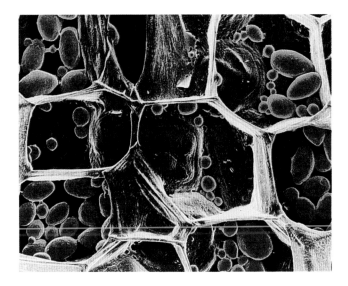

Figure 2.7: Branching structure of amylopectin and glycogen. **a** Formation of a 1,6 link, making a branchpoint; **b** overall structure of an amylopectin or glycogen molecule. Amylopectin and glycogen differ only in the amount of branching of their glucose chains; glycogen is more branched than amylopectin.

light microscope, especially if stained. Rubbing a freshly cut potato tuber on a glass slide and staining with iodine–potassium iodide solution (Practical Activity 2.2) is a quick method of preparing a specimen for viewing.

Figure 2.8: False-colour scanning electron micrograph of a slice through a raw potato showing cells containing starch grains or starch-containing organelles (coloured red) (×260).

Starch is never found in animal cells. Glycogen is the storage carbohydrate in animals. It has molecules very like those of amylopectin because it is made of chains of 1,4 linked α-glucose with 1,6 linkages making branch points (Figure 2.7b). Glycogen molecules clump together to form

granules, which are visible in liver cells (see Figure 1.18) and muscle cells, where they form an energy reserve.

Questions

3   What type of chemical reaction happens when glucose is formed from starch or glycogen?

4   List **five** ways in which the molecular structures of glycogen and amylopectin are similar.

PRACTICAL ACTIVITY 2.2

Testing for the presence of starch

Starch molecules tend to curl up into long spirals. The hole that runs down the middle of this spiral is just the right size for iodine molecules to fit into. To test for starch, you use 'iodine solution'. (Iodine doesn't dissolve in water; iodine solution is actually iodine in potassium iodide solution.) The starch–iodine complex that forms has a strong blue-black colour.

Procedure

Iodine solution is orange-brown. Add a drop of iodine solution to the solid or liquid substance to be tested. A blue-black colour is quickly produced if starch is present.

(See Practical Investigation 2.1 in the Practical Workbook for additional information.)

Cellulose

Cellulose is the most abundant organic molecule on the planet. This is due to its presence in plant cell walls and its slow rate of breakdown in nature. It has a structural role because it is a mechanically strong molecule, unlike starch and glycogen. The only difference is that cellulose is a polymer of β-glucose, and starch and glycogen are polymers of α-glucose.

> **KEY WORD**
>
> **cellulose:** a polysaccharide made from beta-glucose subunits; used as a strengthening material in plant cell walls

Remember that the –OH group on carbon atom 1 projects above the ring in the β-isomer of glucose (Figure 2.4). In order to form a glycosidic bond with carbon atom 4, where the –OH group is below the ring, one glucose molecule must be upside down (rotated 180°) relative to the other. Thus successive glucose units are linked at 180° to each other (Figure 2.9).

This arrangement of β-glucose molecules results in a strong molecule because the hydrogen atoms of –OH groups are weakly attracted to oxygen atoms in the same cellulose molecule (the oxygen of the glucose ring) and also to oxygen atoms of –OH groups in neighbouring molecules. These hydrogen bonds are individually weak, but there are so many of them (due to the large number of –OH groups) that collectively they provide enormous strength. Between 60 and 70 cellulose molecules become tightly cross-linked by hydrogen bonding to form bundles called microfibrils. Microfibrils are in turn held together by hydrogen bonding in bundles called fibres.

A cell wall typically has several layers of fibres, running in different directions to increase strength (Figure 2.10). Cellulose makes up about 20–40% of the average cell wall; other molecules help to cross-link the cellulose fibres, and some form a glue-like matrix around the fibres, which further increases strength.

Cellulose fibres have a very high tensile strength, almost equal to that of steel. This means that, if pulled at both ends, they are very difficult to stretch or break. The high tensile strength of the cellulose fibres makes it possible for a cell to withstand the large pressures that develop within it as a result of osmosis (Chapter 4, Section 4.5, Movement of substances across membranes). Without the wall, the cell would burst when in a dilute solution. These pressures help provide support for the plant by making tissues rigid, and are responsible for cell expansion during growth. The arrangement of fibres around the cell helps to determine the shape of the cell as it grows.

Despite their strength, cellulose fibres are freely permeable, allowing water and solutes to reach or leave the cell surface membrane.

Question

5   Make a table to show **three** ways in which the molecular structures of amylose and cellulose differ.

Dipoles and hydrogen bonds

When atoms in molecules are held together by covalent bonds, they share electrons with each other. Each shared pair of electrons forms one covalent bond. For example, in a water molecule, two hydrogen atoms each share a pair of electrons with an oxygen atom, forming a molecule with the formula H_2O.

a

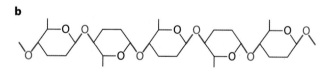

β-glucose (only the relevant –OH groups are shown)

b

Figure 2.9: a Two β-glucose molecules lined up to form a 1,4 link. Note that one glucose molecule must be rotated 180° relative to the other. **b** Arrangement of β-glucose units in cellulose: glycosidic bonds are shown in red and hydroxyl groups are omitted.

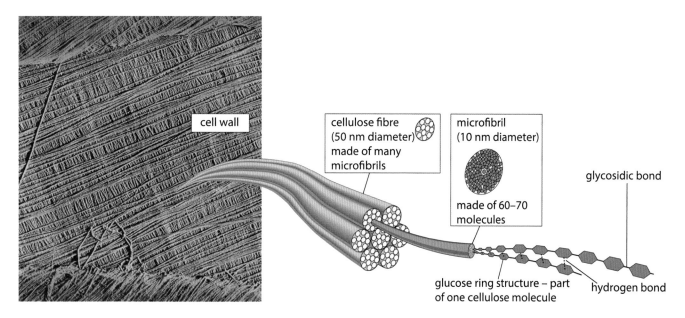

Figure 2.10: Structure of cellulose.

However, the electrons are not shared absolutely equally. In water, the oxygen atom gets slightly more than its fair share, and so has a small negative charge, written δ− (delta minus). The hydrogen atoms get slightly less than their fair share, and so have a small positive charge, written δ+ (delta plus).

This unequal distribution of charge is called a dipole:

$$\delta+ H \diagdown O^{\delta-} \diagup H\,\delta+$$

In water, the negatively charged oxygen of one molecule is attracted to a positively charged hydrogen of another, and this attraction is called a **hydrogen bond**. The hydrogen bond is traditionally shown as a dotted or dashed line in diagrams:

$$>C = O \underset{\delta-}{} - - - - \underset{\delta+}{} H - N<$$

It is much weaker than a covalent bond, but still has a very significant effect. You will find out how

hydrogen bonds affect the properties of water in Section 2.7, Water.

Dipoles occur in many different molecules, particularly where there is an –OH, –CO or –NH group. Hydrogen bonds can form between these groups, because the negatively charged part of one group is attracted to the positively charged part of another. These bonds are very important in the structure and properties of carbohydrates and proteins.

Molecules that have groups with dipoles, such as sugars, are said to be polar. Polar molecules are attracted to water molecules because the water molecules also have dipoles. Such molecules are hydrophilic (water-loving), and tend to be soluble in water. Molecules which do not have dipoles are said to be non-polar. They are not attracted to water, and so, are hydrophobic (water-hating). Such properties make possible the formation of cell membranes (Chapter 4).

KEY WORD

hydrogen bond: a relatively weak bond formed by the attraction between a group with a small positive charge on a hydrogen atom ($H^{\delta+}$) and another group carrying a small negative charge ($^{\delta-}$), e.g. between two $-O^{\delta-} H^{\delta+}$ groups

2.5 Lipids

Lipids are a very varied group of chemicals. They are all organic molecules which are insoluble in water. Most lipids are formed by fatty acids combining with an alcohol. The most familiar lipids are fats and oils. Fats are solid at room temperature and oils are liquid at room temperature, but chemically they are very similar.

Fatty acids

Fatty acids are a series of acids, some of which are found in lipids. They contain the acidic group –COOH, known as a carboxyl group. The carboxyl group forms the 'head' of the fatty acid molecule. The common fatty acids have long hydrocarbon tails attached to the carboxyl group (Figure 2.11). As the name suggests, the hydrocarbon tail consists of a chain of carbon atoms combined with hydrogen. The chain is often 15 or 17 carbon atoms long.

The tails of some fatty acids have double bonds between neighbouring carbon atoms, like this: –C=C–. Such fatty acids are described as unsaturated because they do not contain the maximum possible amount of hydrogen. They form unsaturated lipids. Double bonds make fatty acids and lipids melt more easily – for example, most oils are unsaturated. If there is more than one double bond, the fatty acid or lipid is described as polyunsaturated; if there is only one, it is monounsaturated.

Animal lipids are often saturated (no double bonds) and occur as fats, whereas plant lipids are often unsaturated and occur as oils, such as olive oil and sunflower oil.

Alcohols and esters

Alcohols are a series of organic molecules which contain a hydroxyl group, –OH, attached to a carbon atom. Glycerol is an alcohol with three hydroxyl groups (Figure 2.12).

The reaction between an acid and an alcohol produces a chemical known as an ester. The chemical link between the acid and the alcohol is called an **ester bond** or an **ester linkage**.

$$-\overset{|}{\underset{|}{C}}-COOH \ + \ HO-\overset{|}{\underset{|}{C}}- \ \longrightarrow \ -\overset{|}{\underset{|}{C}}-COOC-\ + \ H_2O$$

acid   alcohol   ester

> ### KEY WORD
>
> **ester bond / ester linkage:** a chemical bond, represented as –COO– , formed when an acid reacts with an alcohol

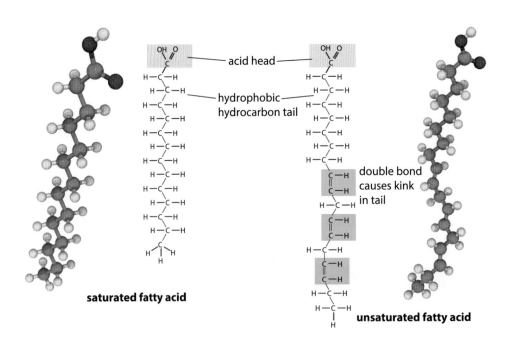

Figure 2.11: Structure of a saturated and an unsaturated fatty acid. Photographs of models are shown to the sides of the structures. In the models, hydrogen is white, carbon is grey and oxygen is red.

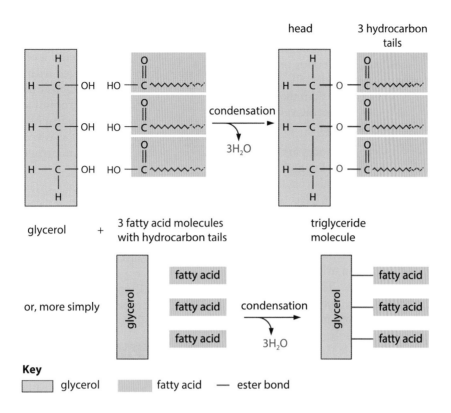

Key

☐ glycerol ▨ fatty acid — ester bond

Figure 2.12: Formation of a triglyceride from glycerol and three fatty acid molecules.

The –COOH group on the acid reacts with the –OH group on the alcohol to form the ester bond, –COO– . This is a condensation reaction because water is formed as a product. The resulting ester can be converted back to acid and alcohol by the reverse reaction of adding water, a reaction known as hydrolysis.

Triglycerides

The most common lipids are **triglycerides** (Figure 2.13). These are fats and oils. A glyceride is an ester formed by a fatty acid combining with the alcohol glycerol. As you have seen, glycerol has three hydroxyl groups. Each one is able to undergo a condensation reaction with a fatty acid. When a triglyceride is made, as shown in Figure 2.12, the final molecule contains three fatty acid tails and three ester bonds ('tri' means three). The tails can vary in length, depending on the fatty acids used.

Triglycerides are insoluble in water but are soluble in certain organic solvents such as ethanol. This is because the hydrocarbon tails are non-polar: they have no uneven distribution of electrical charge.

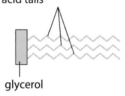

Figure 2.13: Diagrammatic representation of a triglyceride molecule.

Consequently, they are hydrophobic and do not mix freely with water molecules. Figure 2.13 shows a simplified diagram of a triglyceride.

> ### KEY WORD
>
> **triglyceride:** a type of lipid formed when three fatty acid molecules combine with glycerol, an alcohol with three hydroxyl (–OH) groups

Functions of triglycerides

Triglycerides make excellent energy stores because they are even richer in carbon–hydrogen bonds than carbohydrates. A given mass of triglyceride will therefore yield more energy on oxidation than the same mass of carbohydrate (it has a higher calorific value), an important advantage for a storage product.

Triglycerides are stored in a number of places in the human body, particularly just below the skin and around the kidneys. Below the skin they also act as an insulator against loss of heat. Blubber, a triglyceride found in sea mammals such as whales, has a similar function, as well as providing buoyancy.

An unusual role for triglycerides is as a metabolic source of water. When oxidised in respiration, triglycerides are converted to carbon dioxide and water. The water may be of importance in very dry habitats. For example, the desert kangaroo rat (Figure 2.14) never drinks water and survives on metabolic water from the triglyceride-containing foods it eats.

Figure 2.14: The desert kangaroo rat uses metabolism of food to provide the water it needs.

Phospholipids

Phospholipids are a special type of lipid. Each molecule has the unusual property of having one end which is soluble in water. This is because one of the three fatty acid molecules is replaced by a phosphate group, which is polar and can therefore dissolve in water. The phosphate group is hydrophilic and makes the head of a phospholipid molecule hydrophilic.

The two remaining hydrocarbon tails are still hydrophobic (Figure 2.15). This allows phospholipids to form a membrane around a cell; two rows of phospholipids are arranged with their hydrophilic heads in the watery solutions on either side of the membrane and their hydrophobic tails forming a layer that is impermeable to hydrophilic substances. The biological significance of this will become apparent when you study membrane structure (Chapter 4).

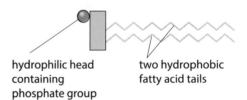

hydrophilic head containing phosphate group

two hydrophobic fatty acid tails

Figure 2.15: Diagrammatic representation of a phospholipid molecule. Compare this with Figure 2.13.

PRACTICAL ACTIVITY 2.3

Testing for the presence of lipids

Lipids are insoluble in water, but soluble in ethanol (alcohol). This fact is made use of in the emulsion test for lipids.

Procedure

The substance that is thought to contain lipids is shaken vigorously with some absolute ethanol (ethanol with little or no water in it). This allows any lipids in the substance to dissolve in the ethanol. The ethanol is then poured into a tube containing water. If lipid is present, a cloudy white suspension is formed.

Further information

If there is no lipid present, the ethanol just mixes into the water. Light can pass straight through this mixture, so it looks completely transparent. But if there is lipid dissolved in the ethanol, it cannot remain dissolved when mixed with the water. The lipid molecules form tiny droplets throughout the liquid. This kind of mixture is called an emulsion. The droplets reflect and scatter light, making the liquid look white and cloudy.

(See Practical Investigation 2.1 in the Practical Workbook for additional information.)

2.6 Proteins

Proteins are an extremely important class of macromolecule in living organisms. More than 50% of the dry mass of most cells is protein. Proteins have many important functions:

- all enzymes are proteins

- proteins are essential components of cell membranes – their functions in membranes are discussed in Chapter 4

- some hormones are proteins – for example, insulin and glucagon

- the oxygen-carrying pigments haemoglobin and myoglobin are proteins

- antibodies, which attack and destroy invading microorganisms, are proteins

- collagen is a protein that adds strength to many animal tissues – for example, bone and the walls of arteries

- hair, nails and the surface layers of skin contain the protein keratin

- actin and myosin are the proteins responsible for muscle contraction

- proteins may be storage products – for example, casein in milk and ovalbumin in egg white.

Despite their tremendous range of functions, all proteins are made from the same basic monomers. These are amino acids.

Amino acids

Figure 2.16 shows the general structure of all amino acids and the structure of glycine, the simplest amino acid. All amino acids have a central carbon atom which is bonded to an amino group, $-NH_2$, and a carboxylic acid group, $-COOH$. These two groups give amino acids their name. The third component that is always bonded to the carbon atom is a hydrogen atom. So, the only way in which amino acids differ from each other is in the fourth group of atoms bonded to the central carbon. This is called the R group.

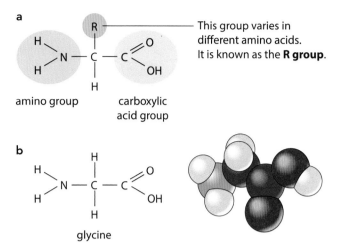

Figure 2.16: a The general structure of an amino acid; **b** structure of the simplest amino acid, glycine, in which the R group is H, hydrogen.

The R groups for the 20 different amino acids which occur in the proteins of living organisms are shown in Appendix 1. You do not need to remember these. Appendix 1 also shows the three-letter abbreviations for the names of the amino acids. Many other amino acids have been synthesised in laboratories.

The peptide bond

Figure 2.17 shows how two amino acids can join together. One loses a hydroxyl (–OH) group from its carboxylic acid group, while the other loses a hydrogen atom from its amino group. This leaves a carbon atom of the first amino acid free to bond with the nitrogen atom of the second. The link is called a **peptide bond**. The oxygen and two hydrogen atoms removed from the amino acids form a water molecule. You have seen condensation reactions like this in the formation of glycosidic bonds (Figure 2.5) and in the synthesis of triglycerides (Figure 2.12).

> **KEY WORD**
>
> **peptide bond:** the covalent bond joining neighbouring amino acids together in proteins; it is a C–N link between two amino acid molecules, formed by a condensation reaction

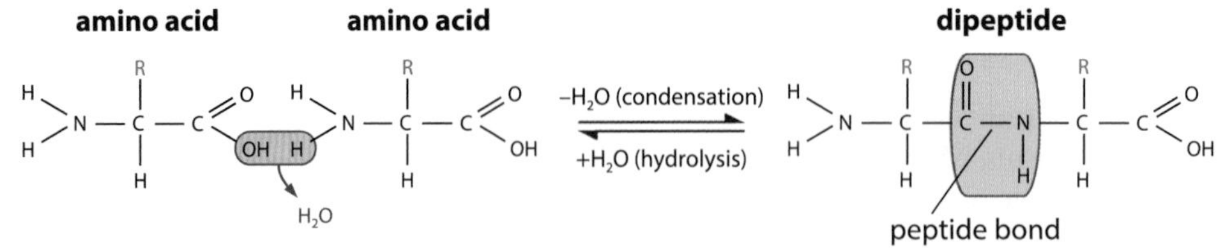

Figure 2.17: Amino acids link together by the loss of a molecule of water to form a peptide bond.

The new molecule is made up of two linked amino acids and is called a dipeptide. A molecule made up of many amino acids linked together by peptide bonds is called a **polypeptide**. A polypeptide is another example of a polymer and a macromolecule, like a polysaccharide. A protein may have just one polypeptide chain or it may have two or more chains.

In living cells, protein synthesis takes place at ribosomes (Chapter 6).

Proteins can be broken down to amino acids by breaking the peptide bonds. This is a hydrolysis reaction, involving the addition of water (Figure 2.17). It happens naturally in the stomach and small intestine during digestion of proteins in food. The amino acids released are absorbed into the blood.

Primary structure

A polypeptide or protein molecule may contain several hundred amino acids linked into a long chain. The particular amino acids contained in the chain, and the sequence in which they are joined, is called the **primary structure** of the protein (Figure 2.18).

KEY WORDS

polypeptide: a long chain of amino acids formed by condensation reactions between the individual amino acids; proteins are made of one or more polypeptide chains; *see* peptide bond

primary structure: the sequence of amino acids in a polypeptide or protein

secondary structure: the structure of a protein molecule resulting from the regular coiling or folding of the chain of amino acids (an α-helix or β-pleated sheet)

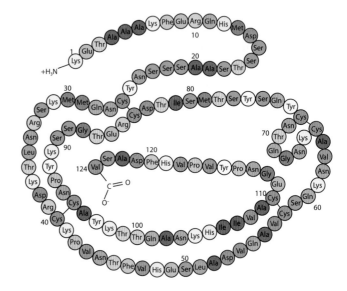

Figure 2.18: The primary structure of ribonuclease. Ribonuclease is an enzyme found in pancreatic juice, which hydrolyses (digests) RNA (Chapter 6). Notice that at one end of the amino acid chain there is an amino group ($-NH_3^+$), while at the other end there is a carboxyl group ($-COO^-$). These are known as the amino and carboxyl ends or the N and C terminals respectively. Note the three-letter abbreviations for the amino acids. These are explained in Appendix 1.

There are an enormous number of different possible primary structures. A change in a single amino acid in a chain made up of thousands may completely alter the properties of the polypeptide or protein.

Secondary structure

The amino acids in a polypeptide chain may have an effect on each other even if they are not next to each other in the primary sequence of amino acids. This is because the polypeptide chain can bend back on itself. A polypeptide chain, or part of it, often coils into a corkscrew shape forming a **secondary structure** called an α-helix (Figure 2.19a). This secondary structure is due to hydrogen bonding between the oxygen of the C=O group of one amino acid and the hydrogen of the –NH group of the amino acid four places ahead of it. Each amino acid has an –NH and a C=O group, and Figure 2.19a shows that all these groups are involved in hydrogen bonding in the α-helix, holding the structure firmly in shape. Hydrogen bonding is a result of the polar characteristics of the C=O and –NH groups.

Sometimes hydrogen bonding can result in a much looser, straighter shape than the α-helix, which is called a β-pleated sheet (Figure 2.19b). Although hydrogen bonds are strong enough to hold the α-helix and β-pleated sheet structures in shape, they are easily broken by high temperatures and pH changes. As you will see, this has important consequences for living organisms.

KEY WORDS

α-helix: a helical structure formed by a polypeptide chain, held in place by hydrogen bonds; an α-helix is an example of secondary structure in a protein

β-pleated sheet: a loose, sheet-like structure formed by hydrogen bonding between parallel polypeptide chains; a β-pleated sheet is an example of secondary structure in a protein

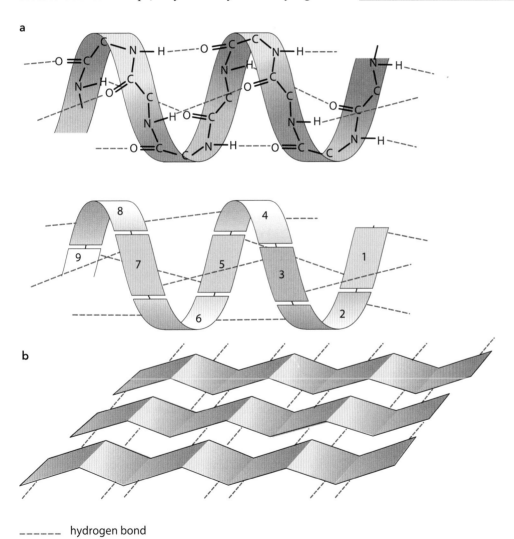

a

b

------ hydrogen bond

Figure 2.19: Protein secondary structure. **a** Structure of the α-helix. The R groups are not shown. **b** Another common secondary structure is the β-pleated sheet. Both of these structures are held in shape by hydrogen bonds between the amino acids.

Figure 2.20: Secondary and tertiary structure of lysozyme. α-helices are shown as blue coils, β-pleated sheets as green arrows, and random coils as red ribbons. The black zig-zags are disulfide bonds.

Some proteins or parts of proteins show no regular arrangement at all. It all depends on which R groups are present and what attractions occur between amino acids in the chain.

In diagrams of protein structure, α-helices can be represented as coils or cylinders: β-pleated sheets as arrows, and random coils as ribbons (Figures 2.20 and 2.21).

Tertiary structure

In many proteins, the secondary structure itself is coiled or folded. Figures 2.20 and 2.21 show the complex way in which secondary structure coils or folds to form the **tertiary structure** of a protein. The figures show different ways in which the structures can be represented by diagrams. At first sight, the lysozyme and myoglobin molecules in these figures look like disorganised tangles, but this is not so. The shape of the molecules is very precise, and the molecules are held in these exact shapes by bonds between amino acids in different parts of the chain.

KEY WORD

tertiary structure: the compact structure of a protein molecule resulting from the three-dimensional coiling of the chain of amino acids

---

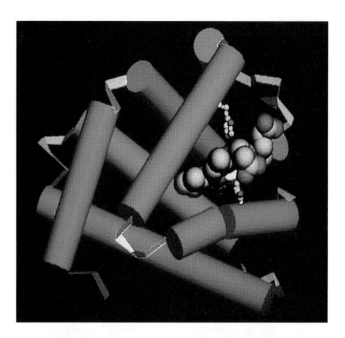

Figure 2.21: A computer graphic showing the secondary and tertiary structures of a myoglobin molecule. Myoglobin is the substance which makes meat look red. It is found in muscle, where it acts as an oxygen-storing molecule. The blue cylinders are α-helices and are linked by sections of polypeptide chain which are random coils (shown in red). At the centre right is an iron-containing haem group.

Figure 2.22 shows the four types of bond that help to keep folded proteins in their precise shapes.

- Hydrogen bonds can form between a wide variety of R groups. Hydrogen bonds are weak in isolation but many together can form a strong structure.

- Disulfide bonds form between two cysteine molecules. Cysteine molecules contain sulfur atoms. The disulfide bond forms when the sulfur atoms of neighbouring cysteines join together with a covalent bond. This is a strong bond. (Can you spot the four disulfide bonds in ribonuclease in Figure 2.18?)

- Ionic bonds form between R groups containing amino and carboxyl groups. (Which amino acids have R groups containing amino or carboxyl groups?)

- Hydrophobic interactions occur between R groups that are non-polar. Such R groups are hydrophobic so tend to avoid water if possible. If the protein is in a typical watery environment inside the cell, then the hydrophobic R groups will tend to come together, excluding water. The overall shape of many proteins is affected by such hydrophobic interactions.

a Hydrogen bonds form between strongly polar groups –
for example, –NH–, –CO– and –OH groups.

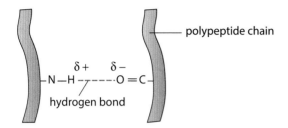

b Disulfide bonds form between cysteine molecules. They are
strong covalent bonds. They can be broken by reducing agents.

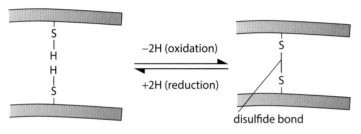

−2H (oxidation)

+2H (reduction)

disulfide bond

c Ionic bonds form between ionised amino (NH_3^+) groups and
ionised carboxylic acid (COO^-) groups. They can be broken by
pH changes.

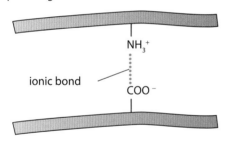

NH_3^+

ionic bond

COO^-

d Weak hydrophobic interactions occur between non-polar
R groups. Although the interactions are weak, the groups tend
to stay together because they are repelled by the watery
environment around them.

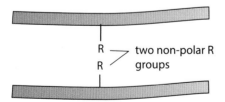

R
R

two non-polar R
groups

Figure 2.22: The four types of bond which are important in
protein tertiary structure: **a** hydrogen bonds, which are also
important in secondary structure; **b** disulfide bonds; **c** ionic
bonds; **d** hydrophobic interactions.

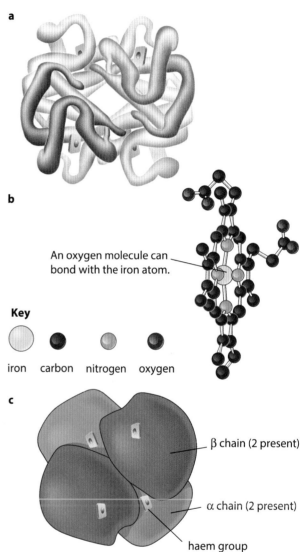

a

b

An oxygen molecule can
bond with the iron atom.

Key

iron   carbon   nitrogen   oxygen

c

β chain (2 present)

α chain (2 present)

haem group

Figure 2.23: Haemoglobin. **a** Each haemoglobin
molecule contains four polypeptide chains. The two
α chains are shown in purple and blue, and the two
β chains in brown and orange. Each polypeptide
chain contains a haem group, shown in yellow and
red. **b** The haem group contains an iron atom, which
can bond reversibly with an oxygen molecule. **c** The
complete haemoglobin molecule is nearly spherical.

The R groups are typically orientated towards the centre of the proteins, facing away from the outside watery environment, with the hydrophilic R groups surrounding them and pointing outwards and in contact with the watery environment.

Quaternary structure

Many protein molecules are made up of two or more polypeptide chains. The overall structure formed by the different polypeptide chains is called the **quaternary structure** of the protein. **Haemoglobin** is an example of a protein with a quaternary structure. A molecule of haemoglobin has four polypeptide chains (Figure 2.23).

The polypeptide chains in quaternary structures are held together by the same four types of bond as in tertiary structures.

Globular and fibrous proteins

A protein whose molecules curl up into a ball shape, such as myoglobin or haemoglobin, is known as a **globular protein**. Globular proteins usually curl up so that their non-polar, hydrophobic R groups point into the centre of the molecule, away from their watery surroundings. Water molecules are excluded from the centre of the folded protein molecule. The polar, hydrophilic R groups remain on the outside of the molecule. Globular proteins, therefore, are usually soluble, because water molecules cluster around their outward-pointing hydrophilic R groups (Figure 2.24).

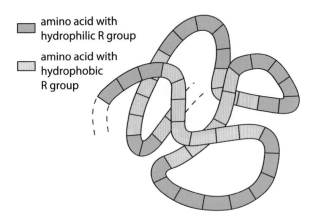

☐ amino acid with hydrophilic R group

☐ amino acid with hydrophobic R group

Figure 2.24: A section through part of a globular protein molecule. The polypeptide chain coils up with hydrophilic R groups outside and hydrophobic R groups inside. This arrangement makes the molecule soluble.

Many globular proteins have roles in metabolic reactions. Their precise shape is the key to their functioning. Enzymes, for example, are globular proteins.

Many other protein molecules do not curl up into a ball, but form long strands. These are known as fibrous proteins. Fibrous proteins are not usually soluble in water and most have structural roles. For example, the fibrous protein keratin forms hair, nails and the outer layers of skin, making these structures waterproof. Another example of a fibrous protein is collagen.

Haemoglobin – a globular protein

Haemoglobin is the oxygen-carrying pigment found in red blood cells. It is a globular protein. You have seen that it is made up of four polypeptide chains, so it has a quaternary structure. Each chain is a protein known as globin. Globin is related to myoglobin and so has a very similar tertiary structure (Figures 2.21 and 2.23). There are many types of globin – two types are used to make haemoglobin, and these are known as α-globin (alpha-globin) and β-globin (beta-globin). Two of the haemoglobin chains, called α chains, are made from α-globin, and the other two chains, called β chains, are made from β-globin.

The haemoglobin molecule is nearly spherical (Figure 2.23). The four polypeptide chains pack closely together. Their hydrophobic R groups point in towards the centre of the molecule, and their hydrophilic ones point outwards.

The interactions between the hydrophobic R groups inside the molecule are important in holding it in its correct three-dimensional shape. The outward-pointing hydrophilic R groups on the surface of the molecule are

KEY WORDS

quaternary structure: the three-dimensional arrangement of two or more polypeptides, or of a polypeptide and a non-protein component such as haem, in a protein molecule

haemoglobin: the red pigment found in red blood cells, whose molecules contain four iron atoms within a globular protein made up of four polypeptides; it combines reversibly with oxygen

globular protein: a protein whose molecules are folded into a relatively spherical shape, often has physiological roles and is often water-soluble and metabolically active, e.g. insulin, haemoglobin and enzymes

important in maintaining its solubility. In the genetic condition known as **sickle cell anaemia**, one amino acid on the surface of the β chain is replaced with a different amino acid. The correct amino acid is glutamic acid, which is polar. The substitute is valine, which is non-polar. Having a non-polar R group on the outside of the molecule makes the haemoglobin much less soluble, and causes the unpleasant and dangerous symptoms associated with sickle cell anaemia (Figure 2.25).

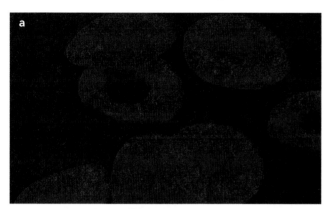

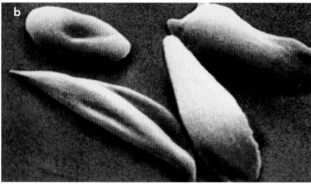

Figure 2.25: a Scanning electron micrograph of human red blood cells (×3300). Each cell contains about 250 million haemoglobin molecules. **b** Scanning electron micrograph of red blood cells from a person with sickle cell anaemia. You can see a normal cell and three sickled cells (×3300).

Each of the four polypeptide chains of haemoglobin contains a haem group (Figure 2.23b). A group like this, which is an important and permanent part of a protein molecule, but is not made of amino acids, is called a prosthetic group.

Each haem group contains an iron atom. One oxygen molecule (O_2) can bind with each iron atom. So a complete haemoglobin molecule, with four haem groups, can carry four oxygen molecules (eight oxygen atoms) at a time.

It is the haem group which is responsible for the colour of haemoglobin. This colour changes depending on whether or not the iron atoms are combined with oxygen. If they are, the molecule is known as oxyhaemoglobin and is bright red. If not, the colour is a darker, more bluish red.

Collagen – a fibrous protein

Collagen is the most common protein found in animals, making up 25% of the total protein in mammals. It is an insoluble **fibrous protein** (Figure 2.26) found in skin, tendons, cartilage, bones, teeth and the walls of blood vessels. It is an important structural protein in almost all animals.

> ### KEY WORDS
>
> **sickle cell anaemia:** a genetic disease caused by a faulty gene coding for haemoglobin, in which haemoglobin tends to precipitate when oxygen concentrations are low
>
> **collagen:** the main structural protein of animals; known as 'white fibres', the fundamental unit of the fibre consists of three helical polypeptide chains wound around each other, forming a 'triple helix' with high tensile strength
>
> **fibrous protein:** a protein whose molecules have a relatively long, thin structure that is generally insoluble and metabolically inactive, and whose function is usually structural, e.g. keratin and collagen

A collagen molecule consists of three polypeptide chains, each in the shape of a helix (Figure 2.26b). (This is not an α-helix – it is not as tightly wound.) These three helical polypeptides are wound around each other, forming a three-stranded 'rope' or 'triple helix'. The three strands are held together by hydrogen bonds and some covalent bonds. Almost every third amino acid in each polypeptide is glycine, the smallest amino acid. Glycine is found on the insides of the strands and its small size allows the three strands to lie close together and so form a tight coil. Any other amino acid would be too large.

Each complete, three-stranded molecule of collagen interacts with other collagen molecules running parallel to it. Covalent bonds form between the R groups of amino acids lying next to each other. These cross-links hold many collagen molecules side by side, forming fibrils. The ends of the parallel molecules are staggered;

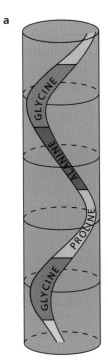

a

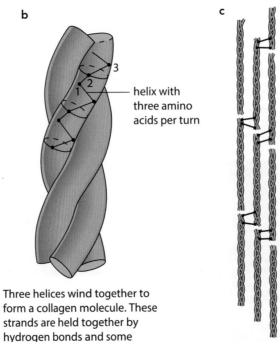

b

helix with three amino acids per turn

Three helices wind together to form a collagen molecule. These strands are held together by hydrogen bonds and some covalent bonds.

The polypeptides which make up a collagen molecule are in the shape of a stretched-out helix. Every third amino acid is glycine.

c

Many of these triple helices lie side by side, linked to each other by covalent cross-links between the side chains of amino acids near the ends of the polypeptides. Notice that these cross-links are out of step with each other; this gives collagen greater strength.

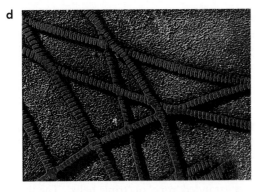

d

A scanning electron micrograph of collagen fibrils (× 17 000). Each fibril is made up of many triple helices lying parallel with one another. The banded appearance is caused by the regular way in which these helices are arranged, with the staggered gaps between the molecules (shown in **c**) appearing darker.

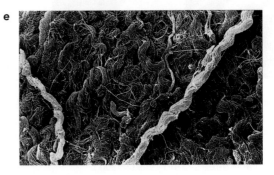

e

A scanning electron micrograph of human collagen fibres (×2000). Each fibre is made up of many fibrils lying side by side. These fibres are large enough to be seen with an ordinary light microscope.

Figure 2.26: Collagen. The diagrams and photographs begin with the very small and work up to the not-so-small. Thus, three polypeptide chains like the one shown in **a** make up a collagen molecule, shown in **b**; many collagen molecules make up a fibril, shown in **c** and **d**; many fibrils make up a fibre, shown in **e**.

if they were not, there would be a weak spot running right across the collagen fibril. Finally, many fibrils lie alongside each other, forming strong bundles called fibres. Note that many collagen molecules make up one collagen fibre.

The advantage of collagen is that it is flexible but at the same time has tremendous tensile strength. High tensile strength means it can withstand large pulling forces without stretching or breaking. The human Achilles tendon, which is almost pure collagen fibres, can withstand a pulling force of 300 N per mm² of

cross-sectional area, about one-quarter the tensile strength of mild steel.

Collagen fibres are lined up in different structures according to the forces they must withstand. In tendons, they line up in parallel bundles along the length of the tendon, in the direction of tension. In skin, they may form layers, with the fibres running in different directions in the different layers, like cellulose in cell walls. In this way, they resist tensile (pulling) forces from many directions.

PRACTICAL ACTIVITY 2.4

Testing for the presence of proteins

All proteins have peptide bonds, containing nitrogen atoms. The nitrogen forms a purple complex with copper(II) ions and this forms the basis of the biuret test.

The reagent used for this test is called biuret reagent. You can use it as two separate solutions: a dilute solution of potassium hydroxide or sodium hydroxide, and a dilute solution of copper(II) sulfate. Alternatively, you can use a ready-made biuret reagent that contains both the copper(II) sulfate

solution and the hydroxide ready mixed. To stop the copper ions reacting with the hydroxide ions and forming a precipitate, this ready-mixed reagent also contains sodium potassium tartrate or sodium citrate.

Procedure

The biuret reagent is added to the solution to be tested. No heating is required. A purple colour indicates that protein is present. The colour develops slowly over several minutes.

(See Practical Investigation 2.1 in the Practical Workbook for additional information.)

Questions

6   State **three** similarities and **three** differences between cellulose and collagen.

7   Copy Table 2.1. Fill in the blanks in the second column of the table using the words below:

hydrophilic   haemoglobin   ionic bond

hydrophobic   disaccharide   disulfide bond

Try with a partner to make a similar table with different statements based on the topics in this chapter. Try it out on other students.

8   'The protein-folding problem' box at the beginning of this chapter discussed how scientists are trying to predict the final shapes of proteins from a knowledge of their primary structures. What information about amino acids and proteins would be relevant to feed into a computer program trying to make such predictions?

KEY WORD

biuret test: a test for the presence of amine groups and thus for the presence of protein; biuret reagent is added to the unknown substance, and a change from pale blue to purple indicates the presence of protein

Description	Word/term
term for water-hating	
broken by a reduction reaction	
formed by a condensation reaction	
characteristic of globular proteins	
has two alpha chains and two beta chains	
can be broken by pH changes	

Table 2.1: Table for Question 7.

2.7 Water

Water is arguably the most important biochemical of all. Without water, life would not exist on this planet. It is important for two reasons. First, it is a major component of cells, typically forming between 70% and 95% of the mass of the cell. You are about 60% water. Second, it provides an environment for those organisms that live in water. Three-quarters of the planet is covered in water.

Although it is a simple molecule, water has some surprising properties. For example, such a small molecule would exist as a gas at normal Earth temperatures were it not for its special property of hydrogen bonding to other water molecules, discussed earlier. Also, because water is a liquid, it provides a medium for molecules and ions to mix in, and hence a medium in which life can evolve.

The hydrogen bonding of water molecules makes it more difficult to separate the molecules and thus affects the physical properties of water. For example, the energy needed to break the hydrogen bonds makes it relatively difficult to convert water from a liquid to a gas. It is more difficult than for similar compounds which lack hydrogen bonds, such as hydrogen sulfide (H_2S), which is a gas at normal air temperatures.

Water as a solvent

Water is an excellent solvent for ions and polar molecules (molecules with an uneven charge distribution, such as sugars and glycerol). This is because the water molecules are attracted to the ions and polar molecules and therefore collect around them and separate them (Figure 2.27). This is what happens when a chemical dissolves in water. Once a chemical is in solution, its molecules or ions are free to move about and react with other chemicals. Most processes in living organisms take place in solution in this way. The fact that molecules and ions dissolve in water also makes it ideal as a transport medium, for example, in the blood and lymphatic systems in animals, and in xylem and phloem in plants.

By contrast, non-polar molecules such as lipids are insoluble in water and, if surrounded by water, tend to be pushed together by the water, since the water molecules are attracted to each other. This is important, for example, in hydrophobic interactions in protein structure and in membrane structure (Chapter 4), and it increases the stability of proteins and membranes.

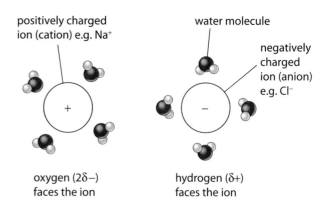

oxygen ($2\delta-$) faces the ion

hydrogen ($\delta+$) faces the ion

Figure 2.27: Distribution of water molecules around ions in a solution. Note which atoms of the water molecules face the ions.

High specific heat capacity

The heat capacity of a substance is the amount of heat required to raise its temperature by a given amount. The specific heat capacity of water is the amount of heat energy required to raise the temperature of 1 kg of water by 1 °C.

Water has a relatively high specific heat capacity. In order for the temperature of a liquid to be raised, the molecules must gain energy and consequently move about more rapidly. The hydrogen bonds that tend to make water molecules stick to each other make it more difficult for the molecules to move about freely. The bonds must be broken to allow free movement. This explains why more energy is needed to raise the temperature of water than would be the case if there were no hydrogen bonds. Hydrogen bonding, in effect, allows water to store more energy for a given temperature rise than would otherwise be possible.

The high specific heat capacity of water has important biological implications because it makes water more resistant to changes in temperature. This means that the temperature within cells and within the bodies of organisms (which have a high proportion of water) tends to be more constant than that of the air around them. As a result, biochemical reactions operate at relatively constant rates and are less likely to be adversely affected by extremes of temperature. It also means that large bodies of water such as lakes and oceans are slow to change temperature as air temperature changes. As a result, lakes and oceans provide stable habitats for aquatic organisms.

High latent heat of vaporisation

The latent heat of vaporisation is a measure of the heat energy needed to vaporise a liquid (cause it to evaporate), changing it from a liquid to a gas. In the case of water, it involves the change from liquid water to water vapour.

Water has a relatively high latent heat of vaporisation. This is a consequence of its high specific heat capacity. The fact that water molecules tend to stick to each other by hydrogen bonds means that relatively large amounts of energy are needed for vaporisation to occur, because hydrogen bonds have to be broken before molecules can escape as a gas. The energy transferred to water molecules during vaporisation results in a corresponding loss of energy from their surroundings, which therefore cool down. This is biologically important because it means that living organisms can use evaporation as a cooling mechanism, as in sweating or panting in mammals. A large amount of heat energy can be lost for relatively little loss of water, reducing the risk of dehydration.

It can also be important in cooling leaves during transpiration.

The reverse is true when water changes from liquid to solid ice. This time the water molecules must lose a relatively large amount of energy, making it less likely that water will freeze. This is an advantage for aquatic organisms. It also makes it less likely that the bodies of living organisms, which have a high water content, will freeze.

Question

9   State the property of water that allows each of the following (**a**, **b** and **c**) to take place. Explain the importance of **a**, **b** and **c**:

   a   the cooling of skin during sweating

   b   the transport of glucose and ions in a mammal

   c   much smaller temperature fluctuations in lakes and oceans than in terrestrial (land-based) habitats.

REFLECTION

- Explain the importance of simple biochemical molecules such as sugars, amino acids, organic bases, fatty acids and glycerol in the evolution of life.

- Water and carbon are important for life. How would you justify this statement?

Personal reflection questions

While studying this chapter, what activities have been particularly useful in improving your understanding of biochemistry? What does this show you about the way you like to learn?

Final reflection

Discuss with a friend which, if any, parts of Chapter 2 you need to:

- read through again to make sure you really understand

- seek more guidance on, even after going over it again.

SUMMARY

The larger biological molecules are made from smaller molecules. The smaller molecules are joined together by condensation reactions. Condensation involves removal of water. The reverse process, adding water, is called hydrolysis and is used to break the large molecules back down into smaller molecules. Polysaccharides are made from monosaccharides, proteins (polypeptides) from amino acids, lipids from fatty acids and glycerol. Polysaccharides and proteins are formed from repeating identical or similar subunits called monomers. They are, therefore, polymers. These build up into giant molecules called macromolecules.

Carbohydrates have the general formula $C_x(H_2O)_y$ and include monosaccharides, disaccharides and polysaccharides. Monosaccharides are joined together by glycosidic bonds to make disaccharides and polysaccharides. Monosaccharides (e.g. glucose) and disaccharides (e.g. sucrose) are very water-soluble and are known as sugars. They are important energy sources in cells and also important building blocks for larger molecules like polysaccharides.

Monosaccharides may have straight-chain or ring structures and may exist in different isomeric forms such as α-glucose and β-glucose.

Benedict's reagent can be used to test for reducing and non-reducing sugars. The test is semi-quantitative.

Polysaccharides include starch, glycogen and cellulose. Starch is an energy storage compound in plants. Starch is made up of two types of molecule, amylose and amylopectin, both made from α-glucose. Amylose is an unbranching molecule, whereas amylopectin has a branching structure.

'Iodine solution' can be used to test for starch.

Glycogen is an energy storage compound in animals. It is made from α-glucose. Its structure is similar to that of amylopectin but with more branching. Cellulose is a polymer of β-glucose molecules. The molecules are grouped together by hydrogen bonding to form mechanically strong fibres with high tensile strength that are found in plant cell walls.

Lipids are a diverse group of chemicals, the most common of which are triglycerides (fats and oils). Triglycerides are made by condensation between three fatty acid molecules and glycerol. Ester bonds join the fatty acids to the glycerol. Triglycerides are hydrophobic and do not mix with water. They act as energy storage compounds, as well as having other functions such as insulation and buoyancy in marine mammals. Phospholipids have a hydrophilic phosphate head and two hydrophobic fatty acid tails. This is important in the formation of membranes.

The emulsion test can be used to test for lipids.

Proteins are long chains of amino acids which fold into precise shapes. Amino acids are joined together by peptide bonds.

Proteins have up to four levels of structure known as primary, secondary, tertiary and quaternary structures. The primary structure is the sequence of amino acids in a protein. This largely determines the way that it folds and hence its three-dimensional shape and function.

Secondary structure is a result of hydrogen bonding between the amino acids. Examples of secondary structure are the α-helix and the β-pleated sheet. Further folding of proteins produces the tertiary structure. Often, a protein is made from more than one polypeptide chain. The association between the different chains is the quaternary structure of the protein. Tertiary and quaternary structures are very precise and are held in place by hydrogen bonds, disulfide bonds (which are covalent), ionic bonds and hydrophobic interactions.

CONTINUED

Proteins may be globular or fibrous. A molecule of a globular protein – for example, haemoglobin – is roughly spherical. Most globular proteins are soluble and have physiological roles. Haemoglobin contains a non-protein (prosthetic) group, the haem group, which contains iron. This combines with oxygen. Molecules of a fibrous protein – for example, collagen – form long strands. Fibrous proteins are usually insoluble and have a structural role. Collagen has high tensile strength and is the most common animal protein, being found in a wide range of tissues.

Biuret reagent can be used to test for proteins.

Hydrogen bonding between water molecules gives water unusual properties.

Water is liquid at most temperatures on the Earth's surface. It has a high specific heat capacity, which makes liquid water relatively resistant to changes in temperature. Water acts as a solvent for ions and polar molecules, and causes non-polar molecules to group together. Water has a relatively high latent heat of vaporisation, meaning that evaporation has a strong cooling effect.

EXAM-STYLE QUESTIONS

1 Which term describes both collagen and haemoglobin?

   A enzymes

   B fibrous proteins

   C globular proteins

   D macromolecules [1]

2 What type of chemical reaction is involved in the formation of disulfide bonds?

   A condensation

   B hydrolysis

   C oxidation

   D reduction [1]

3 Which diagram best represents the arrangement of water molecules around sodium (Na^+) and chloride (Cl^-) ions in solution? [1]

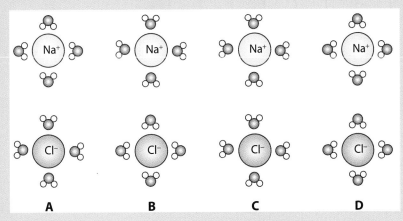

4 Copy and complete the following table. Place a tick or a cross in each box as appropriate.

	Globlular protein (e.g. haemoglobin)	Fibrous protein (e.g. collagen)	Monosaccharide	Disaccharide	Glycogen	Starch	Cellulose	Lipid
monomer								
polymer								
macromolecule								
polysaccharide								
contains subunits that form branched chains								
contains amino acids								
made from organic acids and glycerol								
contains glycosidic bonds								
contains peptide bonds								
one of its main functions is to act as an energy store								
usually insoluble in water								
usually has a structural function								
can form helical or partly helical structures								
contains only carbon, hydrogen and oxygen								

1 mark for each correct column   [8]

5 Copy the table and complete both columns. The table shows some functions of proteins, with examples of proteins that carry out these functions.

Function	Example
structural	1 2
enzyme	
	insulin
	haemoglobin and myoglobin
defence	
	actin and myosin
storage	

[8]

CONTINUED

6   State **three** characteristics of monosaccharides.   [3]

7   The diagram shows a disaccharide called lactose. The carbon atoms are numbered. You are not expected to have seen this structure before. Lactose is a reducing sugar found in milk. It is made from a reaction between the two monosaccharides glucose and galactose.

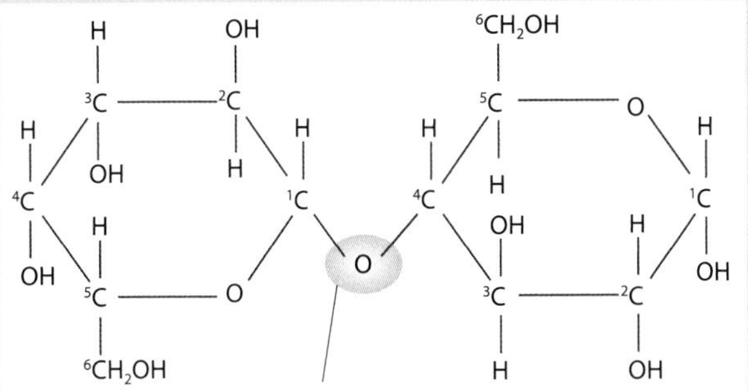

X

a   Suggest **two** functions that lactose could have.   [2]

b   What is the name given to the reaction between two monosaccharides that results in the formation of lactose?   [1]

c   Identify the bond labelled **X** in the diagram.   [1]

d   Draw diagrams to show the structures of separate molecules of glucose and galactose.   [2]

e   Using the information in the diagram, is the alpha or beta form of glucose used to make lactose? **Explain** your answer.   [2]

f   Like lactose, sucrose is a disaccharide. If you were given a solution of lactose and a solution of sucrose, state briefly how you could distinguish between them.   [2]

[Total: 10]

COMMAND WORD

Explain: set out purposes or reasons / make the relationships between things evident / provide why and/or how and support with relevant evidence.

8   a   This diagram shows the structures of three amino acids.

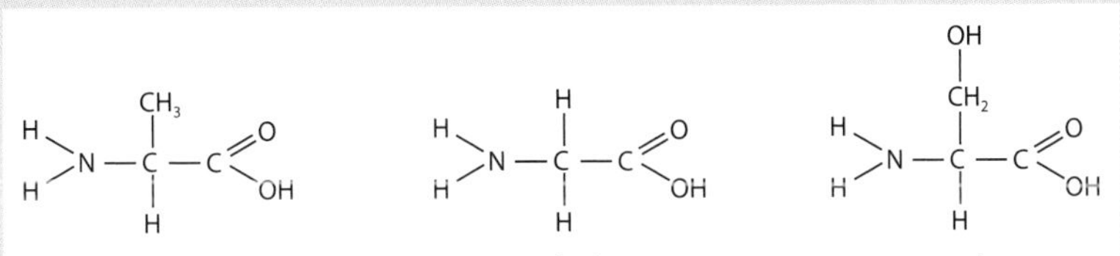

alanine   glycine   serine

i   Draw a diagram to show the structure of the tripeptide with the following sequence: alanine–glycine–serine.   [3]

ii   What is the name given to the sequence of amino acids in a protein?   [1]

iii   What substance, apart from the tripeptide, would be formed when the three amino acids combine?   [1]

iv   Draw a ring around an atom or group of atoms making up an R group that could hydrogen bond with a neighbouring R group.   [1]

CONTINUED

    v Draw a ring around and label the peptide bond(s) you have drawn in the diagram. [1]

    vi Draw a ring around a group of atoms which could hydrogen bond with a –CO– group in an alpha helix (α-helix). Label this group **A**. [1]

  b State three features that α-helices and beta sheets (β-sheets) have in common. [3]

  c A protein can be described as a polymer. State the meaning of the term *polymer*. [2]

  d X and Y represent two different amino acids.

    i Write down the sequences of all the possible tripeptides that could be made with just these two amino acids. [1]

    ii From your answer to **d i**, what is the formula for calculating the number of different tripeptides that can be formed from two different amino acids? [1]

[Total: 15]

9 Copy diagrams A and B.

          A   B

  a Identify with labels which one represents a lipid and which a phospholipid. [1]

  b **i** For molecule **A**, indicate on the diagram where hydrolysis would take place if the molecule was digested. [2]

    ii Name the products of digestion. [2]

  c Each molecule has a head with tails attached. For molecule **B**, label the head to identify its chemical nature. [1]

  d **i** Which of the two molecules is water-soluble? [1]

    ii Explain your answer to **d i**. [1]

  e State **one** function of each molecule. [2]

[Total: 10]

10 a Copy and complete the table to summarise some differences between collagen and haemoglobin. [5]

	Collagen	Haemoglobin
1		
2		
3		
4		
5		

CONTINUED

Use the following to guide you.

Row 1 State whether globular or fibrous.

Row 2 State whether entirely helical or partly helical.

Row 3 State the type of helix.

Row 4 State whether a prosthetic group is present or not.

Row 5 State whether soluble in water or not.

b State **one** way in which the structure of haemoglobin is related to its function. [2]

c Haemoglobin possesses a quaternary structure. What does this mean? [1]

d Name the **five** elements found in haemoglobin. [2]

[Total: 10]

SELF-EVALUATION CHECKLIST

After studying this chapter, complete a table like this:

I can	See section...	Needs more work	Almost there	Ready to move on
describe how large biological molecules are made from smaller molecules	2.2, 2.3			
describe the structure of carbohydrates, lipids and proteins and how their structure relates to their functions	2.4, 2.5, 2.6			
describe and carry out biochemical tests to identify carbohydrates, lipids and proteins	2.4, 2.5, 2.6			
explain some key properties of water that make life possible	2.7			

> Chapter 3
Enzymes

LEARNING INTENTIONS

In this chapter you will learn how to:

- state what enzymes are
- explain the mode of action of enzymes
- investigate the progress of enzyme-controlled reactions
- outline the use of a colorimeter for measuring the progress of enzyme-catalysed reactions
- investigate and explain the effect of temperature, pH, enzyme concentration and substrate concentration on the rate of enzyme-catalysed reactions
- use V_{max} and K_m to compare the affinity of different enzymes for their substrates
- explain the effects of reversible inhibitors, both competitive and non-competitive, on enzyme activity
- state the advantages of using immobilised enzymes.

BEFORE YOU START

- Enzymes are catalysts. Check your understanding of the term *catalyst* by stating two important properties of catalysts.

- Enzymes are proteins. You studied proteins in Chapter 2. Discuss what properties of proteins might make them suitable to act as catalysts in living cells.

THE BEST MEANS OF DEFENCE IS ATTACK

If you are a beetle and you are about to be eaten by a predator such as a spider or a frog, how do you escape? The bombardier beetle has evolved a spectacular and successful strategy (Figure 3.1). It makes use of the very high speeds of enzyme-controlled reactions. When threatened by a predator, the beetle uses the tip of its abdomen to squirt a boiling hot chemical spray at its attacker.

The release of the spray is accompanied by a loud popping sound. The beetle can swivel the tip of its abdomen to spray accurately in almost any direction. With the predator reeling from this surprise attack, the beetle escapes.

How are enzymes involved? Inside the beetle's abdomen is a chemical mixing chamber into which hydrogen peroxide and hydroquinone are released. The chamber contains two enzymes, catalase and peroxidase. These enzymes speed up the reactions they catalyse by several million times. Hydrogen peroxide is broken down into oxygen and water and the oxygen is used to oxidise the hydroquinone

into quinone. The reactions are violent and release a great deal of heat, vaporising about 20% of the resulting liquid. Within a fraction of a second, a boiling, stinking mixture of gas and liquid is explosively released through an outlet valve.

Question for discussion

It could be argued that carrying out research into the defence mechanism of the bombadier beetle is a waste of time and money. Can you justify the research?

Figure 3.1: a A bombardier beetle sprays a boiling chemical spray at an annoying pair of forceps; **b** abdominal organs generating the spray.

3.1 What is an enzyme?

An **enzyme** is a biological catalyst. It is biological because all enzymes are proteins. It is a catalyst because it speeds up a chemical reaction but remains unchanged at the end of the reaction.

The following points are also important.

- Enzymes are globular proteins. They fold up into precise shapes.

- Almost all metabolic reactions which take place in living organisms are catalysed by enzymes; enzymes are therefore essential for life.

- Many enzyme names end in –ase; for example, amylase and ATPase.

Question

1   A student investigated the effect of several different catalysts on the rate of decomposition of hydrogen peroxide to water and oxygen. The speed of the reaction was judged by how 'fizzy' or frothy the contents of the tube became when the catalyst was added (oxygen is a product of the reaction and forms bubbles).

KEY WORD

enzyme: a protein produced by a living organism that acts as a biological catalyst in a chemical reaction by reducing activation energy

The student used iron filings and manganese dioxide as inorganic catalysts. They also used a commercial preparation of the enzyme catalase and pieces of liver and pieces of potato tuber, both of which contain catalase. Catalase catalyses the decomposition of hydrogen peroxide.

Results showed:

- catalase, liver and potato were much more efficient than the inorganic catalysts
- pure catalase was more efficient than the liver and potato
- liver was more efficient than potato
- ground-up liver was more efficient than pieces of liver.

Try to explain the student's results.

Intracellular and extracellular enzymes

Not all enzymes work inside cells. Those that do are described as intracellular. Enzymes that are secreted by cells and catalyse reactions outside cells are described as extracellular. Digestive enzymes in the gut are extracellular enzymes. Some organisms secrete enzymes outside their bodies. Fungi, for example, often do this in order to digest the food on which they are growing.

3.2 Mode of action of enzymes

The lock-and-key hypothesis and the induced-fit hypothesis

Like all globular proteins, enzyme molecules are coiled into a precise three-dimensional shape. Hydrophilic R groups (side-chains) on the outside of the molecule make them soluble in the water in the cytoplasm.

Enzyme molecules have a special feature called an active site (Figure 3.2). The active site of an enzyme is a region to which another molecule (or molecules) can bind. This molecule is the substrate of the enzyme. The shape of the active site allows the substrate to fit perfectly. The idea that the enzyme has a particular shape into which the substrate fits exactly is known as

the lock-and-key hypothesis. The substrate is the key whose shape fits the lock of the enzyme. The substrate is held in place by temporary bonds which form between the substrate and some of the R groups of the enzyme's amino acids. This combined structure is termed the enzyme–substrate complex.

Each enzyme will act on only one type of substrate molecule. This is because the shape of the active site will only allow one shape of molecule to fit. The enzyme is said to be specific for this substrate. You can also describe the enzyme as showing specificity.

In 1959 the lock-and-key hypothesis was modified in the light of evidence that enzyme molecules are more flexible than is suggested by a rigid lock and key. The modern hypothesis for enzyme action is known as the induced-fit hypothesis. It is basically the same as the lock-and-key hypothesis, but adds the idea that the enzyme, and sometimes the substrate, can change shape slightly as the substrate molecule enters the enzyme, in order to ensure a perfect fit. This makes the catalysis even more efficient.

An enzyme may catalyse a reaction in which the substrate molecule is split into two or more molecules, as shown in Figure 3.2. Alternatively, it may catalyse the joining together of two molecules, as when making a dipeptide from two amino acids. A simplified diagram is shown in Figure 3.3. This diagram also shows the enzyme–product complex which is briefly formed before release of the product. When the reaction is complete, the product or products leave the active site. The enzyme is unchanged by this process, so it is now available to receive another substrate molecule.

KEY WORDS

active site: an area on an enzyme molecule where the substrate can bind

lock-and-key hypothesis: a hypothesis for enzyme action; the substrate is a complementary shape to the active site of the enzyme, and fits exactly into the site; the enzyme shows specificity for the substrate

induced-fit hypothesis: a hypothesis for enzyme action; the substrate is a complementary shape to the active site of the enzyme, but not an exact fit – the enzyme, or sometimes the substrate, can change shape slightly to ensure a perfect fit, but it is still described as showing specificity

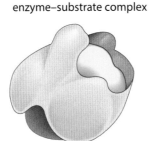
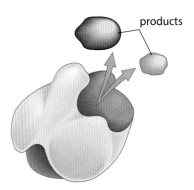

a An enzyme has a cleft in its surface, called the active site. The substrate molecule has a complementary shape.

b Random movement of enzyme and substrate brings the substrate into the active site. An enzyme–substrate complex is temporarily formed. The R groups of the amino acids in the active site interact with the substrate.

c The interaction of the substrate with the active site breaks the substrate apart. An enzyme–product complex is briefly formed, before the two product molecules leave the active site, leaving the enzyme molecule unchanged and ready to bind with another substrate molecule.

Figure 3.2: How an enzyme catalyses the breakdown of a substrate molecule into two product molecules.

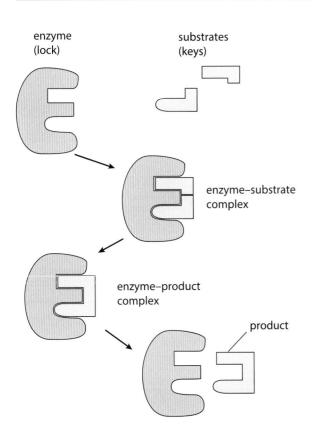

Figure 3.3: A simplified diagram of enzyme function. Note that in this example the enzyme is catalysing the joining together of two molecules.

The rate of the overall reaction can be very high. A molecule of the enzyme catalase, for example, can bind with hydrogen peroxide molecules, split them into water and oxygen, and release the products at a rate of 10 million molecules per second.

The example of lysozyme

The interaction between the substrate and the active site, including the slight change in shape of the enzyme (induced fit) which results from the binding of the substrate, is clearly shown by the enzyme lysozyme. Lysozyme is found in tears, saliva and other secretions. It acts as a natural defence against bacteria. It does this by breaking the polysaccharide chains that form the cell walls of the bacteria. The tertiary structure of the enzyme has already been shown in Figure 2.20. Figure 3.4 shows how the polysaccharide chains in the bacterial cell wall are broken down in the active site of lysozyme.

Enzymes reduce activation energy

Enzymes increase the rate at which chemical reactions occur. Without enzymes, most of the reactions that occur in living cells would occur so slowly that life could not exist.

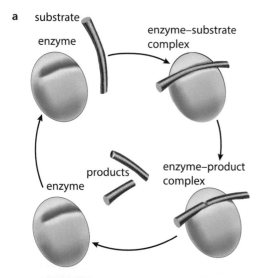

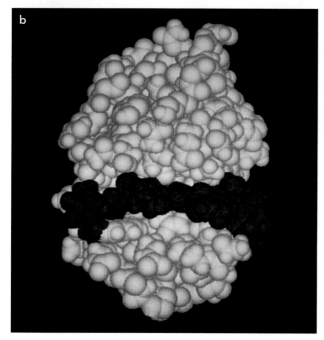

Figure 3.4: Lysozyme breaking a polysaccharide chain. This is a hydrolysis reaction. **a** Diagram showing the formation of enzyme–substrate and enzyme–product complexes, and release of the products. **b** Space-filling model showing the substrate in the active site of the enzyme. The substrate is a polysaccharide chain which slides neatly into the groove (active site) and is split by the enzyme. Many such chains give the bacterial cell wall rigidity. When the chains are broken, the wall loses its rigidity and the bacterial cell explodes as a result of osmosis.

In many chemical reactions, the substrate is not converted to a product unless some energy is added. This energy is called **activation energy** (Figure 3.5a).

One way of providing the extra energy needed is to heat the substances. For example, in the Benedict's test for reducing sugar you need to heat the Benedict's reagent and sugar solution together before they will react.

Enzymes avoid this problem because they decrease the activation energy of the reactions they catalyse (Figure 3.5b). They do this by holding the substrate or substrates in such a way that their molecules can react more easily. As a result, reactions catalysed by enzymes take place rapidly at a much lower temperature than they otherwise would.

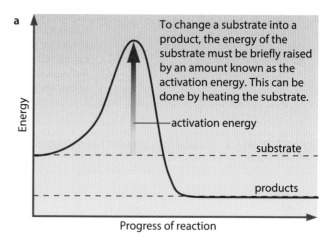

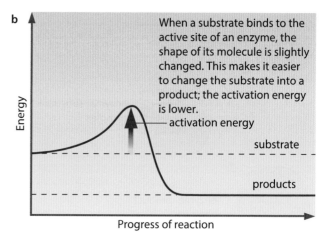

Figure 3.5: Activation energy: **a** without enzyme; **b** with enzyme.

KEY WORD

activation energy: the energy that must be provided to make a reaction take place; enzymes reduce the activation energy required for a substrate to change into a product

3.3 Investigating the progress of an enzyme-catalysed reaction

Measuring the rate of formation of a product

You may be able to carry out an investigation into the progress of an enzyme-controlled reaction by measuring the rate at which the product is formed from the substrate.

Figure 3.6 shows the results of such an investigation using the enzyme catalase. This enzyme is found in the tissues of most living things and catalyses the breakdown of hydrogen peroxide into water and oxygen. (Hydrogen peroxide is sometimes produced inside cells. It is toxic (poisonous), so it must be got rid of quickly.) The oxygen that is released can be collected and measured, so it is an easy reaction to follow.

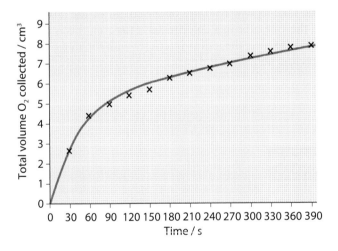

Figure 3.6: The course of an enzyme-catalysed reaction. Catalase was added to hydrogen peroxide at time 0. The gas released was collected in a gas syringe, the volume being read at 30 s intervals.

The reaction begins very quickly. As soon as the enzyme and substrate are mixed, bubbles of oxygen are released. A large volume of oxygen is collected in the first minute of the reaction. As the reaction continues, however, the rate at which oxygen is released gradually slows down. The reaction gets slower and slower, until it eventually stops completely.

The explanation for the course of the reaction is quite straightforward. When the enzyme and substrate are first mixed, there are a large number of substrate molecules. At any moment, almost every enzyme molecule has a substrate molecule in its active site. The rate at which the reaction occurs depends on:

- how many enzyme molecules there are
- the speed at which the enzyme can convert the substrate into product, release it, and then bind with another substrate molecule.

However, as more and more substrate is converted into product, there are fewer and fewer substrate molecules to bind with enzymes. Enzyme molecules may be 'waiting' for substrate molecules to hit their active sites. As fewer and fewer substrate molecules are left, the reaction gets slower and slower, until it eventually stops.

The curve of a graph such as the one in Figure 3.6 is therefore steepest at the beginning of the reaction: the rate of an enzyme-controlled reaction is always fastest at the beginning. This rate is called the initial rate of reaction. You can measure the initial rate of the reaction by calculating the slope of a tangent to the curve, as close to time 0 as possible (see Figure P1.9 for advice on how to do this). An easier way of doing it is simply to read off the graph the amount of oxygen given off in the first 30 seconds. In this case, the rate of oxygen production in the first 30 seconds is $2.7\,cm^3$ of oxygen per 30 seconds, or $5.4\,cm^3$ per minute.

Question

2   Why is it better to calculate the initial rate of reaction from a curve such as the one in Figure 3.6 than simply by measuring how much oxygen is given off in 30 seconds?

Using a colorimeter to measure the progress of an enzyme-controlled reaction

If the method used for measuring the progress of an enzyme-controlled reaction involves a colour change, a **colorimeter** can be used to measure the colour change

---

KEY WORD

colorimeter: an instrument that measures the colour of a solution by measuring the absorption of different wavelengths of light

---

PRACTICAL ACTIVITY 3.1

Measuring the rate of disappearance of a substrate

Sometimes it is easier to measure the rate of disappearance of a substrate than the rate of appearance of a product. A good example of this is using the enzyme amylase. Amylase breaks down starch to the reducing sugar maltose, a hydrolysis reaction. Starch reacts with iodine solution to produce a blue-black colour. During the reaction, small samples can be taken at known times to test for starch using iodine solution. As the starch is converted to maltose, the concentration of starch

in the reaction mixture decreases. The colour of the samples tested will, therefore, change from blue-black to brown to pale brown and finally remain colourless. You can time how long it takes for the starch to disappear completely, that is, how long before the iodine test gives a colourless result. Alternatively, a suitable end-point can be chosen, such as the time taken to reach a pale brown colour in the iodine test.

(See Practical Investigation 3.3 in the Practical Workbook for additional information.)

quantitatively. This will provide numbers that can be plotted on a graph. A colorimeter is an instrument that measures the colour of a solution by measuring the absorption of different wavelengths of light. The greater the absorption, the greater the concentration of the substance causing the colour. Figure 3.7a shows the main components of a colorimeter.

In the amylase/starch experiment described in Practical Activity 3.1 you can measure the intensity of the blue-black colour obtained in the iodine test using a colorimeter. The colour acts as a measure of the amount of starch still remaining. Figure 3.7b shows a typical range of colours.

If you do this over a period of time, you can plot a curve of 'amount of starch remaining' against 'time'. You can then calculate the initial reaction rate in the same way as for the catalase/hydrogen peroxide reaction described previously.

It is even easier to observe the course of this reaction if you mix starch, iodine solution and amylase in a tube, and take regular readings of the colour of the mixture in this one tube in a colorimeter. However, this is not ideal, because the iodine interferes with the rate of the reaction and slows it down.

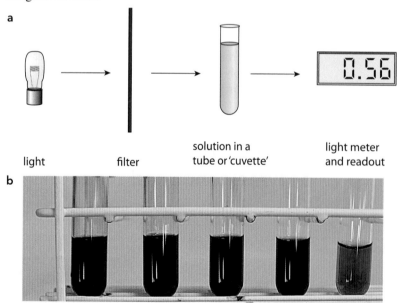

a

light   filter   solution in a tube or 'cuvette'   light meter and readout

0.56

b

Figure 3.7: a Diagram showing how a colorimeter works. b Photograph of a range of colours obtained with the iodine test during the course of an experiment investigating the digestion of starch by amylase. The tubes show increasing time for digestion of the starch from left to right.

Question

3 a In the breakdown of starch by amylase, if you were to plot the amount of starch remaining against time, draw the curve you would expect to obtain.

   b How could you use this curve to calculate the initial reaction rate?

3.4 Factors that affect enzyme action

The effect of temperature on the rate of enzyme activity

Figure 3.8 shows the effect of temperature on the rate of activity of a typical enzyme. At low temperatures, the reaction takes place only very slowly. This is because molecules are moving relatively slowly. In other words, their kinetic energy is relatively low. Substrate molecules will not often collide with the active site of the enzyme. As temperature rises, the kinetic energy of the molecules increases and so the enzyme and substrate molecules move faster. Collisions happen more frequently, so that substrate molecules enter the active site more often. Also, when substrate and enzyme molecules collide, they do so with more energy. This makes it easier for bonds to be formed or broken so that the reaction can occur.

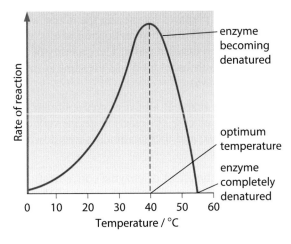

Figure 3.8: The effect of temperature on the rate of an enzyme-controlled reaction.

As temperature continues to increase, kinetic energy increases so the speed of movement of the substrate and enzyme molecules also continues to increase.

However, above a certain temperature, the enzyme molecule vibrates so much that some of the bonds holding the enzyme molecule in its precise shape begin to break. This is especially true for hydrogen bonds. The enzyme's active site begins to lose its shape and therefore its activity: it is said to be denatured. At first, the substrate molecule fits less well into the active site of the enzyme, so the rate of the reaction begins to slow down. Eventually the substrate no longer fits at all and the reaction stops (the rate becomes zero).

The temperature at which an enzyme catalyses a reaction at the maximum rate is called the optimum temperature. Most human enzymes have an optimum temperature of around 40 °C. By keeping our body temperatures at about 37 °C, we ensure that enzyme-catalysed reactions occur at close to their maximum rate.

Enzymes from other organisms may have different optimum temperatures. Some enzymes, such as those found in bacteria which live in hot springs (Figure 3.9), have much higher optimum temperatures. Some plant enzymes have lower optimum temperatures, depending on their habitat.

Figure 3.9: Not all enzymes have an optimum temperature of 40 °C. Bacteria and algae living in hot springs such as this one in Yellowstone National Park, USA, are able to tolerate very high temperatures. Enzymes from such organisms are useful in various commercial applications, such as biological washing powders.

The effect of pH on the rate of enzyme activity

Figure 3.10 shows the effect of pH on the rate of activity of a typical enzyme. Most enzymes work fastest at a pH of somewhere around 7, that is, in fairly neutral conditions. Some, however, have a different optimum pH. For example, pepsin, an enzyme found in the acidic conditions of the stomach, has an optimum pH of about 1.5. Pepsin is a protease, an enzyme that catalyses the digestion of proteins.

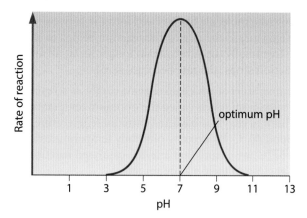

Figure 3.10: The effect of pH on the rate of an enzyme-controlled reaction. The optimum pH depends on the enzyme: in this case, the optimum pH is 7.

pH is a measure of the concentration of hydrogen ions in a solution. The lower the pH, the higher the hydrogen ion concentration. Hydrogen ions are positively charged, so they are attracted to negatively charged ions and repelled by positively charged ions. Hydrogen ions can therefore interact with any charged R groups on the amino acids of enzyme molecules. This may break the ionic bonding between the R groups (Chapter 2), which affects the three-dimensional structure of the enzyme molecule. The shape of the active site may change and therefore reduce the chances of the substrate molecule fitting into it. A pH which is different from the optimum pH can cause denaturation of an enzyme.

When investigating pH, you can use buffer solutions (Chapter P1, Section P1.3, Variables and making measurements). Buffer solutions each have a particular pH and maintain that pH even if the reaction taking place would otherwise cause the pH to change. You add a measured volume of the buffer to your reaction mixture.

Questions

4   How could you carry out an experiment to determine the effect of temperature on the rate of breakdown of hydrogen peroxide by catalase?

5   Proteases are used in biological washing powders.

   a   How does a protease remove a blood stain from clothes?

   b   Most biological washing powders are recommended for use at low washing temperatures. Why is this?

   c   Washing powder manufacturers have produced proteases which can work at temperatures higher than 40 °C. Why is this useful?

6   Trypsin is a protease secreted in pancreatic juice, which acts in the duodenum. If you add trypsin to a suspension of milk powder in water, the enzyme digests the protein in the milk, so that the suspension becomes clear.

   How could you carry out an investigation into the effect of pH on the rate of activity of trypsin? (A suspension of 4 g of milk powder in 100 cm³ of water will become clear in a few minutes if an equal volume of a 0.5% trypsin solution is added to it.)

The effect of enzyme concentration on the rate of enzyme activity

Figure 3.11a shows the results of an investigation using the enzyme catalase and its substrate hydrogen peroxide. The catalase is present in an extract made from celery. Different concentrations of catalase solution were added to hydrogen peroxide solutions. The different concentrations were prepared by varying the initial volume of celery extract and then making up to a standard volume with distilled water. The quantity of hydrogen peroxide (substrate) used was the same at the start of all five reactions.

You can see that the shape of all five curves is similar (Figure 3.11a). In each case, the reaction begins very quickly (a steep curve) and then gradually slows down (the curve levels off).

In order to look at the effect of enzyme concentration on reaction rate, you must compare the rates of these five reactions. It is best to look at the rate right at the beginning of the reaction. This is because, once the reaction is under way, the amount of substrate in each reaction begins to vary, because substrate is converted to product at different rates in each of the five reactions. It is only at the very beginning that you can be sure that the substrate concentration is the same

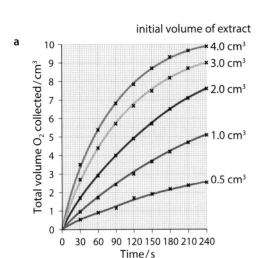

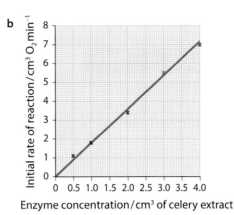

Figure 3.11: The effect of enzyme concentration on the rate of an enzyme-catalysed reaction. **a** Different volumes of celery extract, which contains catalase, were added to the same volume of hydrogen peroxide. Water was added to make the total volume of the mixture the same in each case. **b** The rate of reaction in the first 30 s was calculated for each enzyme concentration.

in each tube. By calculating the initial rates you can be sure that differences in reaction rate are caused only by differences in enzyme concentration and not by substrate concentration.

To work out the initial rate for each enzyme concentration, you can calculate the slope of the curve 30 seconds after the beginning of the reaction, as explained in Chapter P1 (Section P1.3, Variables and making measurements). Ideally, you should do this for an even earlier stage of the reaction, but in practice this is impossible. You can then plot a second graph, Figure 3.11b, showing the initial rate of reaction against enzyme concentration.

This graph shows that the initial rate of reaction increases linearly. In these conditions, reaction rate is directly proportional to the enzyme concentration. This is just what common sense says should happen. The more enzyme present, the more active sites will be available for the substrate to slot into. As long as there is plenty of substrate available, the initial rate of a reaction increases linearly with enzyme concentration.

The effect of substrate concentration on the rate of enzyme activity

Figure 3.12 shows the results of an investigation using the enzyme catalase and its substrate hydrogen peroxide. The volume of hydrogen peroxide was varied and the

volume of catalase was kept constant. As in the previous experiment, curves of oxygen released against time were plotted for each reaction, and the initial rate of reaction calculated for the first 30 seconds. These initial rates of reaction were then plotted against substrate concentration.

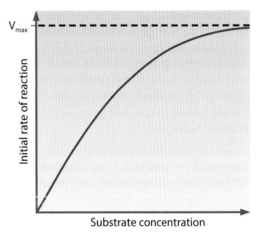

Figure 3.12: The effect of substrate concentration on the rate of an enzyme-catalysed reaction.

As substrate concentration increases, the initial rate of reaction also increases. This is what you would expect: the more substrate molecules there are, the more often one will enter an active site. However, if you go on increasing substrate concentration, keeping the enzyme concentration constant, there comes a point when every enzyme active site is full. If more substrate is added, the enzyme simply cannot work faster; substrate molecules are effectively 'queuing up' for an active site to become vacant. The enzyme is working at its maximum possible rate, known as V_{max}. V stands for velocity (speed), max stands for maximum.

> **KEY WORD**
>
> V_{max}: the theoretical maximum rate of an enzyme-controlled reaction, obtained when all the active sites of the enzyme are occupied

Question

7 Sketch the shape that the graph in Figure 3.11b would have if excess hydrogen peroxide were not available.

3.5 Comparing enzyme affinities

Affinity is a measure of the strength of attraction between two things. A high affinity means there is a strong attraction. When applied to enzymes, affinity is a measure of the strength of attraction between the enzyme and its substrate. The greater the affinity of an enzyme for its substrate, the faster it works. Another way of thinking about this is to say that the higher the affinity, the more likely it is that the product will be formed when a substrate molecule enters the active site. If the affinity is low, the substrate may leave the active site before a reaction takes place.

There is enormous variation in the speed at which different enzymes work. A typical enzyme molecule can convert around 1000 substrate molecules into product per second. The enzyme carbonic anhydrase (Chapter 8, Section 8.5, Blood) is one of the fastest enzymes known. It can remove 600 000 molecules of carbon dioxide from respiring tissue per second. This is roughly 10^7 times as fast as the reaction would occur without the enzyme. It has presumably evolved such a high efficiency because a build-up of carbon dioxide in tissues would become lethal very quickly.

In the previous section, you saw that a useful indicator of the efficiency of an enzyme is its V_{max}. This tells you the maximum speed at which an enzyme works. Remember, V stands for velocity, which means speed.

At V_{max} all the enzyme molecules are bound to substrate molecules – the enzyme is saturated with substrate. All the active sites are full. V_{max} can be measured in the way described in Figure 3.11b. The initial rate of the reaction is measured at different substrate concentrations while keeping the enzyme concentration constant. As substrate concentration is increased, reaction rate rises until the reaction reaches its maximum rate, V_{max}.

Question

8 For each substrate concentration tested, the rate should be measured as soon as possible. Explain why.

The initial rate for each substrate concentration is plotted against substrate concentration, producing a curve like those shown in Figures 3.12 and 3.13. Unfortunately, this type of curve never completely flattens out in practice, as shown by the dashed line on both figures. It only does so in theory at infinite substrate concentration. You cannot, therefore, read off the value of V_{max} from the graphs in Figure 3.12 and 3.13. (Note that V_{max} is at the end of the dashed line in the figures.) There is a mathematical way out of this problem. From the data in such graphs, it is possible to calculate $\frac{1}{2}V_{max}$. You do not need to understand how to do this. $\frac{1}{2}V_{max}$ is exactly half the maximum velocity. It is just as useful as V_{max} as an indicator of how fast an enzyme works. You can plot $\frac{1}{2}V_{max}$ on a graph like Figures 3.12 and 3.13, and from that find the substrate concentration that will result in $\frac{1}{2}V_{max}$. This is the substrate concentration at which half the enzyme's active sites are occupied by substrate. Figure 3.13 shows a graph with $\frac{1}{2}V_{max}$ added. You will

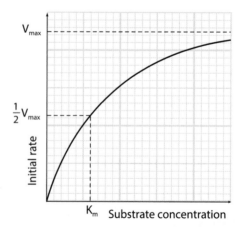

Figure 3.13: A graph showing the effect of substrate concentration on initial rate of an enzyme reaction, with V_{max}, $\frac{1}{2}V_{max}$ and K_m values shown.

Enzyme	Substrate	V_{max}/arbitrary units	K_m/µmol dm^{-3}
carbonic anhydrase	carbon dioxide	600 000	8000
penicillinase	penicillin	2000	50
chymotrypsin	protein	100	5000
lysozyme	acetylglucosamine	0.5	6

Table 3.1: V_{max} and K_m values for four enzymes. Note that the unit for K_m is a concentration.

see that the substrate concentration which causes $\frac{1}{2}V_{max}$ is labelled K_m. K_m is known as the **Michaelis–Menten constant**. The Michaelis–Menten constant of an enzyme is the substrate concentration at which the enzyme works at half its maximum rate. It is used as a measure of the affinity of the enzyme for its substrate.

> **KEY WORD**
>
> **Michaelis–Menten constant (K_m):** the substrate concentration at which an enzyme works at half its maximum rate ($\frac{1}{2}V_{max}$), used as a measure of the efficiency of an enzyme; the lower the value of K_m, the more efficient the enzyme

If you think about it, the higher the affinity of an enzyme for its substrate, the lower the substrate concentration needed before $\frac{1}{2}V_{max}$ is reached. The lower the substrate concentration, the lower the value of K_m (see Figure 3.13). So the higher the affinity of an enzyme for its substrate, the lower its K_m will be.

Questions

9 Which of the four enzymes in Table 3.1:
   a works fastest?
   b has the highest affinity for its substrate? Briefly explain your answer.

10 Figure 3.14 shows the results of two experiments. The aim of the experiments was to compare the affinity of two different enzymes for their substrates. Enzyme **A** had a higher affinity for its substrate than enzyme **B**. The two curves plot the results obtained for enzyme **A** and enzyme **B**.
   a Copy Figure 3.14 and:
      i label the axes appropriately
      ii label appropriately one curve enzyme **A** and one curve enzyme **B**.

b i Which enzyme had the higher Michaelis–Menten constant?
   ii Which enzyme had the higher V_{max}?
   iii Which enzyme required the greater concentration of substrate to achieve V_{max}?
   iv Which enzyme required the greater concentration of substrate to saturate its active sites?

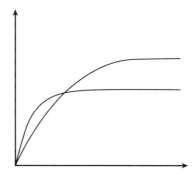

Figure 3.14: Comparison of affinity of two different enzymes for their substrates.

3.6 Enzyme inhibitors

Competitive, reversible inhibition

As you have seen, the active site of an enzyme fits its substrate perfectly. It is possible, however, for a molecule which is similar in shape to the substrate to enter an enzyme's active site. This would then inhibit the enzyme's function.

If an inhibitor molecule binds only briefly to the site and comes out again, there is competition between it and the substrate for the site. If there is much more of the substrate present than the inhibitor, substrate molecules can easily 'win' the competition, and so the enzyme's function is more or less unaffected. However, if the concentration of the inhibitor rises or that of the substrate falls, it becomes less and less likely that the substrate will collide with an empty active site. The enzyme's function is then inhibited. This is known as competitive inhibition (Figure 3.15a). It is said to be reversible (not permanent) because it can be reversed by increasing the concentration of the substrate. This is how you can tell the difference between competitive and non-competitive inhibition (Figure 3.15).

a Competitive inhibition

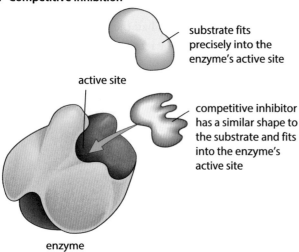

b Non-competitive inhibition

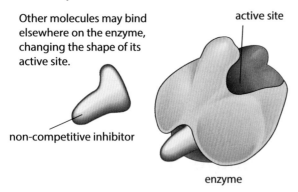

Figure 3.15: Enzyme inhibition: **a** competitive inhibition; **b** non-competitive inhibition. Both these types of inhibition are reversible.

An example of competitive inhibition occurs in the treatment of a person who has drunk ethylene glycol. Ethylene glycol is used as antifreeze, and is sometimes drunk accidentally. Ethylene glycol is rapidly converted in the body to oxalic acid, which can cause irreversible kidney

damage. However, the active site of the enzyme which converts ethylene glycol to oxalic acid will also accept ethanol. If the poisoned person is given a large dose of ethanol, the ethanol acts as a competitive inhibitor, slowing down the action of the enzyme on ethylene glycol for long enough to allow the ethylene glycol to be excreted.

Non-competitive, reversible inhibition

A different kind of reversible inhibition is possible which is non-competitive. In this type of inhibition, the inhibitor molecule binds to another part of the enzyme, not the active site. While the inhibitor is bound to the enzyme, it can seriously affect the normal arrangement of hydrogen bonds and hydrophobic interactions holding the enzyme molecule in its three-dimensional shape. The resulting distortion changes the shape of the active site and therefore inhibits the ability of the substrate to enter the active site. While the inhibitor is attached to the enzyme, the enzyme's function is blocked. The substrate molecule and the inhibitor are not competing for the active site, so this is an example of non-competitive inhibition (Figure 3.15b). Increasing the substrate concentration has no effect on the inhibition, unlike the case with competitive inhibition.

Inhibition of an enzyme can be harmful or even fatal but, in many situations, inhibition is essential. For example, metabolic reactions must be controlled so that no enzyme can be allowed to work without stopping at some point, otherwise more and more product would constantly be being made.

KEY WORDS

competitive inhibition: when a substance reduces the rate of activity of an enzyme by competing with the substrate molecules for the enzyme's active site; increasing substrate concentration reduces the degree of inhibition; increasing inhibitor concentration increases the degree of inhibition

non-competitive inhibition: when a substance reduces the rate of activity of an enzyme, but increasing the concentration of the substrate does not reduce the degree of inhibition; many non-competitive inhibitors bind to areas of the enzyme molecule other than the active site itself

One way of controlling metabolic reactions is to use the end product of a chain of reactions as a non-competitive, reversible inhibitor (Figure 3.16). The end product inhibits the enzyme at the beginning of the chain of reactions (enzyme 1 in Figure 3.16). The enzyme is gradually slowed down as the amount of end product increases. However, the end product can lose its attachment to the enzyme (the reaction is reversible) so, if it gets used somewhere else, the enzyme returns to its active state and makes more end product. This way of regulating the amount of end product formed is called end product inhibition.

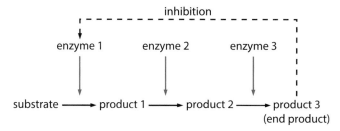

Figure 3.16: End product inhibition. As levels of product 3 rise, there is increasing inhibition of enzyme 1. So, less product 1 is made and therefore less product 2 and 3. Falling levels of product 3 allow increased function of enzyme 1 so products 1, 2 and 3 rise again and the cycle continues. This end product inhibition finely controls levels of product 3 between narrow upper and lower limits, and is an example of a feedback mechanism.

3.7 Immobilising enzymes

Enzymes have an enormous range of commercial applications – for example, in medicine, food technology and industrial processes. Enzymes are expensive. No company wants to have to keep buying them over and over again if it can recycle them in some way. One of the best ways of keeping costs down is to use **immobilised enzymes**. Immobilised enzymes are fixed in some way to prevent them from diffusing freely in a solution.

KEY WORD

immobilised enzymes: enzymes that have been fixed to a surface or trapped inside beads of agar gel

The enzyme lactase can be immobilised using alginate beads (Figure 3.17 in Practical Activity 3.2). The substrate of lactase is the disaccharide sugar lactose. Milk is allowed to run through a column of lactase-containing beads (Figure 3.18). The lactase hydrolyses the lactose in the milk to glucose and galactose. The milk is therefore lactose-free, and can be used to make lactose-free dairy products for people who cannot digest lactose.

You can see that enzyme immobilisation has several obvious advantages compared with just mixing up the enzyme with its substrate. If you just mixed lactase with milk, you would have a very difficult job to get the lactase back again. Not only would you lose the lactase, but you would also have milk contaminated with the enzyme. Using immobilised enzymes means that you can keep and re-use the enzymes, and that the product is enzyme-free.

Another advantage of this process is that the immobilised enzymes are more tolerant of temperature changes and pH changes than enzymes in solution. This may be partly because their molecules are held firmly in shape by the alginate in which they are embedded, and so do not denature so easily. It may also be because the parts of the molecules that are embedded in the beads are not fully exposed to the temperature or pH changes.

Questions

11 a Outline an investigation you could carry out to compare the temperature at which the enzyme lactase is completely denatured within ten minutes

    i   when free in solution

    ii when immobilised in alginate beads.

  b Outline an experiment you could carry out to investigate how long it takes the enzyme lactase to denature at 90 °C

    i   when free in solution

    ii when immobilised in alginate beads.

  c Outline how you would determine the optimum pH of the enzyme lactase

    i   when free in solution

    ii when immobilised in alginate beads.

12 Summarise the advantages of using immobilised enzymes rather than enzyme solutions.

PRACTICAL ACTIVITY 3.2

Immobilising enzymes

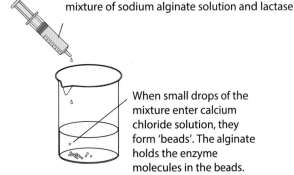

mixture of sodium alginate solution and lactase

When small drops of the mixture enter calcium chloride solution, they form 'beads'. The alginate holds the enzyme molecules in the beads.

Figure 3.17: Immobilising enzyme in alginate.

Figure 3.17 shows one way in which enzymes can be immobilised. The enzyme is mixed with a solution of sodium alginate. Little droplets of this mixture are then added to a solution of calcium chloride. The sodium alginate and calcium chloride instantly react to form jelly, which turns each droplet into a little bead. The jelly bead contains the enzyme. The enzyme is held in the bead, or immobilised.

These beads can be packed gently into a column. A liquid containing the enzyme's substrate can be allowed to trickle steadily over them (Figure 3.18).

As the substrate runs over the surface of the beads, the enzymes in the beads catalyse a reaction that converts the substrate into product. The product continues to trickle down the column, emerging from the bottom, where it can be collected and purified.

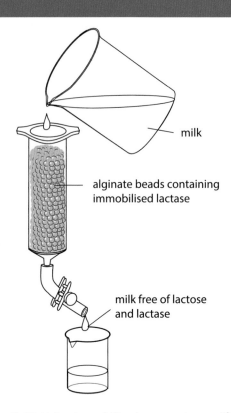

milk

alginate beads containing immobilised lactase

milk free of lactose and lactase

Figure 3.18: Using immobilised enzyme to modify milk.

(See Practical Investigation 3.5 in the Practical Workbook for additional information.)

REFLECTION

If you were designing a new enzyme to solve a complex biological or chemical problem, what characteristics and features would it be useful to be able to control? Try to think of both structural and functional features. Can you think of any new uses for enzymes, such as substances it would be useful to be able to break down using enzymes?

Personal reflection question

If you were the teacher, what comments would you make about your performance in this activity?

Final reflection

Discuss with a friend which, if any, parts of Chapter 3 you need to:

*   read through again to make sure you really understand
*   seek more guidance on, even after going over it again.

SUMMARY

Enzymes are globular proteins which catalyse metabolic reactions. Each enzyme has an active site with a flexible structure which can change shape slightly to fit precisely the substrate molecule. This is called the induced-fit hypothesis.

Enzymes may be involved in reactions which break down molecules or join molecules together. They work by lowering the activation energy of the reactions they catalyse.

The course of an enzyme reaction can be followed by measuring the rate at which a product is formed or the rate at which a substrate disappears. A progress curve, with time on the x-axis, can be plotted. The curve is steepest at the beginning of the reaction, when substrate concentration is at its highest. This rate is called the initial rate of reaction.

Temperature, pH, enzyme concentration and substrate concentration all affect the rate of activity of enzymes.

Each enzyme has an optimum temperature at which it works fastest. As temperature increases above the optimum temperature, the enzyme gradually denatures (loses its precise tertiary structure).

Each enzyme has an optimum pH. Some enzymes operate within a narrow pH range; some have a broad pH range.

The greater the concentration of the enzyme, the faster the rate of reaction, provided there are enough substrate molecules present. The greater the concentration of the substrate, the faster the rate of reaction, provided enough enzyme molecules are present. During enzyme reactions, rates slow down as substrate molecules are used up.

The efficiency of an enzyme can be measured by finding the value known as the Michaelis–Menten constant, K_m. To do this, the maximum rate of reaction, V_{max}, must first be determined. Determination of V_{max} involves finding the initial rates of reactions at different substrate concentrations while ensuring that enzyme concentration remains constant.

Enzymes are affected by the presence of inhibitors, which slow down or stop their activity. Competitive inhibitors have a similar shape to the normal substrate molecules. They compete with the substrate for the active site of the enzyme. Competitive inhibition is reversible because the inhibitor can enter and leave the active site.

Reversible non-competitive inhibitors bind at a site elsewhere on the enzyme, causing a change in shape of the active site.

Enzymes can be immobilised – for example, by trapping them in jelly (alginate) beads. This is commercially useful because the enzyme can be re-used and the product is separate from (uncontaminated by) the enzyme. Immobilisation often makes enzymes more stable.

EXAM-STYLE QUESTIONS

1 The diagram shows an enzyme and two inhibitors of the enzyme, **X** and **Y**. Which of the following describes the two inhibitors?

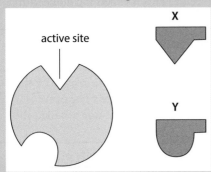

 A **X** and **Y** are competitive inhibitors.

 B **X** and **Y** are non-competitive inhibitors.

 C **X** is a competitive inhibitor and **Y** is a non-competitive inhibitor.

 D **X** is a non-competitive inhibitor and **Y** is a competitive inhibitor.   [1]

2 In a reaction controlled by an enzyme, which of the following graphs shows the effect of substrate concentration on the rate of the reaction, assuming the reaction is allowed to go to completion?

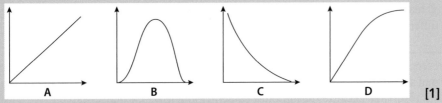

[1]

3 The graph shows the progress of the digestion of starch by the enzyme salivary amylase. Why does the reaction slow down?

 A There is end-product inhibition by maltose.

 B The salivary amylase is becoming denatured.

 C The salivary amylase is gradually becoming saturated with starch.

 D There are fewer and fewer substrate molecules left to bind with the salivary amylase.

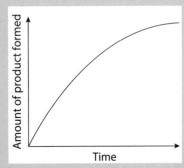

[1]

4 An enzyme with a high affinity for its substrate has a:

 A high K_m C high V_{max}

 B low K_m D low V_{max} [1]

CONTINUED

5 If methylene blue dye is added to a suspension of yeast cells, any living cells remain colourless. However, any dead cells are stained blue. This fact was used to carry out an investigation into the rate at which yeast cells were killed at two different temperatures (at high temperatures the yeast enzymes will be denatured). The results are shown in the diagram.

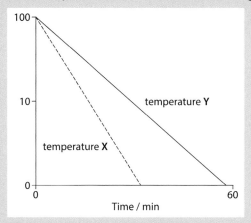

Which of the following is correct?

	The higher temperature is	The vertical axis (y-axis) should be labelled
A	X	% coloured cells
B	Y	% coloured cells
C	X	% colourless cells
D	Y	% colourless cells

[1]

6 Copy the graph in Question 3 and draw a line from which the initial rate of reaction could be calculated. [1]

7 The graph shows the effect of changes in pH on the activity of the enzyme lysozyme.

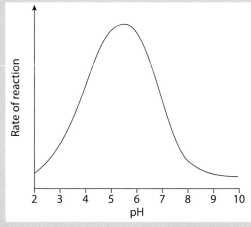

a Describe the effect of pH on this enzyme. [2]

b Explain why pH affects the activity of the enzyme. [4]

[Total: 6]

CONTINUED

8 The graph shows the effect of temperature on the rate of reaction of an enzyme.

   a What is indicated by **X**? [1]

   b What temperature would **X** be for a mammalian enzyme? [1]

   c Explain what is happening in region **A**. [3]

   d Explain what is happening in region **B**. [3]

   e Enzymes are effective because they lower the activation energy of the reactions they catalyse.

     Explain what is meant by 'activation energy'. [2]

[Total: 10]

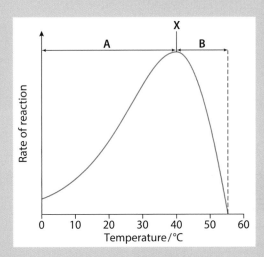

9 The reaction shown occurs during aerobic respiration. The reaction is catalysed by the enzyme succinate dehydrogenase.

```
COOH                              COOH
 |                                 |
CH₂    succinate dehydrogenase    CH
 |          ──────────────►       ||
CH₂                               CH
 |                                 |
COOH                              COOH
succinic acid                    fumaric acid
```

   a Name the substrate in this reaction. [1]

   b The molecule malonic acid, which is shown below, inhibits the reaction shown. It does not bind permanently to the enzyme. Describe how malonic acid inhibits the enzyme succinate dehydrogenase. [3]

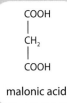

```
COOH
 |
CH₂
 |
COOH
```
malonic acid

CONTINUED

   c Heavy metals such as lead and mercury bind permanently to –SH groups of amino acids present in enzymes. These –SH groups could be in the active site or elsewhere in the enzyme.

     i Name the amino acid which contains –SH groups. **[1]**

     ii Explain the function of –SH groups in proteins and why binding of heavy metals to these groups might inhibit the activity of an enzyme. **[4]**

                                   [Total: 9]

10 You are provided with three solutions, **A**, **B** and **C**. One solution contains the enzyme amylase, one contains starch and one contains glucose. Starch is the substrate of the enzyme. The product is the sugar maltose. You are provided with only one reagent, Benedict's solution, and the usual laboratory apparatus.

   a Outline the procedure you would follow to identify the three solutions. **[6]**

   b What type of reaction is catalysed by the enzyme? **[1]**

                                   [Total: 7]

> **COMMAND WORD**
>
> **Outline:** set out the main points.

11 The activity of the enzyme amylase can be measured at a particular temperature by placing a sample into a Petri dish containing starch–agar ('a starch–agar plate'). Starch–agar is a jelly containing starch. One or more 'wells' (small holes) are cut in the agar jelly with a cork borer, and a sample of the enzyme is placed in each well. The enzyme molecules then diffuse through the agar and gradually digest any starch in their path. At the end of the experiment, iodine solution is poured over the plate. Most of the plate will turn blue-black as iodine reacts with starch, but a clear 'halo' (circle) will be seen around the well where starch has been digested. Measuring the size of the halo can give an indication of the activity of the enzyme.

A student decided to investigate the rate at which a mammalian amylase is denatured at 60 °C. They heated different samples of the enzyme in a water bath at 60 °C for 0, 1, 5, 10 and 30 minutes. They then allowed the samples to cool down to room temperature and placed samples of equal volume in the wells of five starch–agar plates, one plate for each heating period. They then incubated the plates in an oven at 40 °C for 24 hours.

The results of the student's experiment are shown below. A diagram of one dish is shown, and the real size of one halo from each dish is also shown.

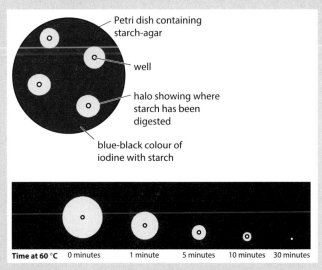

CONTINUED

a   Why did the student cut four wells in each dish rather than just one?   [1]

b   One dish contained samples from amylase which was not heated
    (0 minutes). This is a control dish.
    Explain the purpose of this control.   [1]

c   Explain why the starch–agar plates were incubated at 40 °C and not
    room temperature.   [1]

d   Describe what was happening in the dishes during the 24 hours of
    incubation.   [4]

e   Why was it important to add the same volume of amylase solution to
    each well?   [1]

f   Measure the diameter in mm of the representative halo from each dish.
    Record the results in a suitable table.   [4]

g   Only one halo from each dish is shown in the diagrams. In practice,
    there was some variation in the diameters of the four halos in each
    dish. How would you allow for this when processing your data?   [1]

h   Plot a graph to show the effect of length of time at 60 °C on the activity
    of the enzyme.   [5]

i   Describe and explain your results.   [4]

j   Another student discovered that amylases from fungi and bacteria are
    more resistant to high temperatures than mammalian amylases. Using
    starch–agar plates as a method for measuring the activity of an amylase
    at 40 °C, outline an experiment that the student could perform to discover
    which type of amylase (mammalian, fungal or bacterial) is most resistant
    to heat. Note that temperatures up to 120 °C can be obtained by using an
    autoclave (pressure cooker).   [5]

k   Enzymes are used in many industrial processes where resistance to high
    temperatures is an advantage. State **three** other variables apart from
    temperature which should be controlled in an industrial process
    involving enzymes.   [3]

[Total: 30]

12 Two inhibitors of the same enzyme, inhibitor **A** and inhibitor **B**, were
    investigated to discover if they were competitive or non-competitive. In
    order to do this, the rate of reaction of the enzyme was measured at different
    concentrations of substrate without inhibitor, with inhibitor **A** and with
    inhibitor **B**. Graphs of the data were plotted as shown. The graphs showed
    that one inhibitor was competitive and the other non-competitive.

CONTINUED

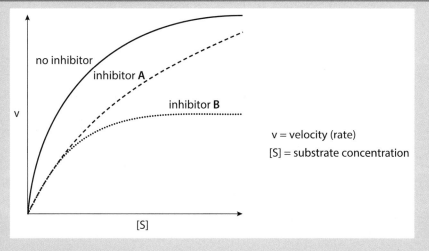

v = velocity (rate)

[S] = substrate concentration

Copy the graphs.

a Label the graph for 'no inhibitor' to show the position of V_{max}, $\frac{1}{2}V_{max}$ and K_m. [3]

b State the effect that inhibitor **A** had on V_{max} and K_m of the enzyme. [2]

c State the effect that inhibitor **B** had on V_{max} and K_m of the enzyme. [2]

d Which inhibitor is competitive and which is non-competitive? Explain your answer. [4]

[Total: 11]

SELF-EVALUATION CHECKLIST

After studying this chapter, complete a table like this:

I can	See section...	Needs more work	Almost there	Ready to move on
state what enzymes are	3.1			
explain the mode of action of enzymes	3.2			
investigate the progress of enzyme-controlled reactions	3.3			
outline the use of a colorimeter for measuring the progress of enzyme-catalysed reactions	3.3			
investigate and explain the effect of temperature, pH, enzyme concentration and substrate concentration on the rate of enzyme-catalysed reactions	3.4			
use V_{max} and K_m to compare the affinity of different enzymes for their substrates	3.5			
explain the effects of reversible inhibitors, both competitive and non-competitive, on enzyme activity	3.6			
state the advantages of using immobilised enzymes	3.7			

Cell membranes and transport

BEFORE YOU START

- Why are *all* cells (prokaryotes and eukaryotes) surrounded by a cell surface membrane (Chapter 1)?

- What is the meaning of 'partially permeable' when applied to membranes (Chapter 1)?

- Why are phospholipids important in membrane structure (Chapter 2)?

- State **two** examples where the surface area of membranes has been increased by folding. For each example, state why the increased surface area is an advantage (Chapter 1).

- Give an example of a cell organelle that is surrounded by **a** a single membrane and **b** two membranes (an envelope) (Chapter 1).

DELIVERY BAGS

Liposomes are artificially prepared membrane-bound compartments (vesicles) (Figure 4.1). They can be prepared by breaking biological membranes into pieces, some of which re-seal themselves into balls resembling empty cells, though much smaller than cells on average.

Like intact cells, liposomes are surrounded by a phospholipid bilayer and the interior is usually aqueous. They were first described in 1961. Since then they have been used as artificial models of cells and, more importantly, for medical applications. In particular, they have been used to deliver drugs.

To do this, the liposome is made while in a solution of the drug, so the drug is inside the liposome. The liposome is then introduced into the body and, when it reaches a target cell, such as a cancer cell or other diseased cell, it fuses with that cell's surface membrane, delivering the drug inside the cell. Precise targeting can be achieved by inserting the correct recognition molecule – for example, an antigen or antibody – into the liposome membrane. Other targeting methods also exist.

In 2013 it was discovered that liposomes could provide a safe way to deliver the powerful anti-cancer drug staurosporine. Although this drug had been available since 1977, it had not been used because it kills any cells, including healthy ones, that it comes into contact with. This is because it interferes with several cell-signalling pathways.* The drug is added to liposomes and then disguising agents are added to the outer surfaces of the liposomes. These hide the drug from the immune system and allow it to target cancer cells only.

Liposomes have many other uses. For example, they are used in the cosmetics industry to deliver

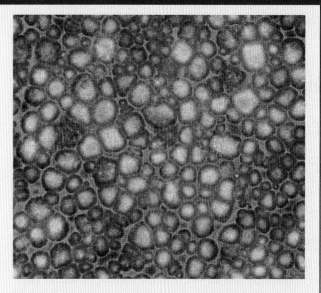

Figure 4.1: Liposomes.

skin care products such as aloe vera, collagen, elastin and vitamins A and E when rubbed on skin. Liposome delivery of food supplements by mouth has also been tried with some success – absorption rates can be much higher than with traditional tablets.

Questions for discussion

Some of the trials with staurosporine have involved experiments on mice.

- What are the arguments for and against medical research on non-human animals?

- What rights do you think test animals should have?

* Staurosporine is a protein kinase inhibitor. The role of protein kinases in cell signalling is described in Chapter 14 (Section 14.4, The control of blood glucose).

4.1 The importance of membranes

In Chapter 1 you saw that all living cells are surrounded by a very thin membrane, the cell surface membrane. This controls the exchange of materials such as nutrients and waste products between the cell and its environment. Inside cells, regulation of transport across the membranes of organelles is also vital. Membranes have other important functions. For example, they enable cells to receive hormone messages and in chloroplasts they contain the light-absorbing pigments needed for photosynthesis. It is important to study the structure of membranes to understand how these functions are achieved.

4.2 Structure of membranes

Phospholipids

Understanding the structure of membranes depends on understanding the structure of phospholipids (see Chapters 1 and 2). Phospholipids help to form the membranes that surround cells and organelles.

Figure 4.2a shows what happens if phospholipid molecules are spread out over the surface of water. They form a single layer with their heads in the water, because the heads are polar (hydrophilic). Their tails project out of the water, because they are non-polar (hydrophobic). The term *polar* refers to an uneven distribution of charge. The significance of this is explained in Chapter 2 (Section 2.5, Lipids).

If the phospholipids are mixed with water, they form either:

- ball-like structures called micelles (Figure 4.2b), or
- sheet-like structures called bilayers (Figure 4.2c).

In a micelle, all the hydrophilic heads face outwards into the water. They shield the hydrophobic tails from the water. In the middle of the ball, the tails point in

towards each other, creating a hydrophobic environment inside the micelle, as shown in Figure 4.2a. In bilayers, the hydrophobic tails are also shielded from the water by the hydrophilic heads, as shown in Figure 4.2c.

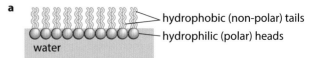

a
hydrophobic (non-polar) tails
hydrophilic (polar) heads
water

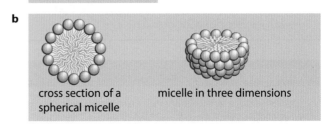

b
cross section of a spherical micelle
micelle in three dimensions

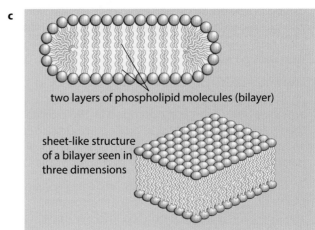

c
two layers of phospholipid molecules (bilayer)

sheet-like structure of a bilayer seen in three dimensions

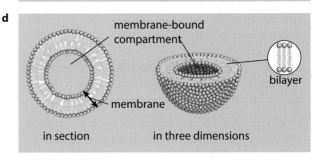

d
membrane-bound compartment
bilayer
membrane
in section
in three dimensions

Figure 4.2: Phospholipids in water: **a** spread as a single layer of molecules (a monolayer) on the surface of water; **b** forming micelles surrounded by water; **c** forming bilayers; **d** bilayers forming membrane-bound compartments.

It is now known that the phospholipid bilayer is the basic structure of membranes, as shown in Figure 4.2d. 'Bilayer' means two layers, as shown in Figures 4.2c and d. The bilayer, or membrane, is about 7 nm wide (see Figure 1.22).

Membranes also contain proteins. The proteins can be seen in certain electron micrographs, such as Figure 4.3.

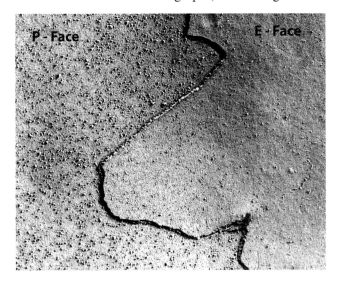

Figure 4.3: Scanning electron micrograph of a cell surface membrane. The membrane has been prepared by freeze-fracturing, which has split open the bilayer. The 'P-face' in the picture is the phospholipid layer nearest the inside of the cell and shows the many protein particles embedded in the membrane. The 'E-face' is part of the outer phospholipid layer (×50 000).

The fluid mosaic model of membrane structure

In 1972 two scientists, Singer and Nicolson, used all the available evidence to put forward a hypothesis for membrane structure. They called their model the **fluid mosaic model**. It is described as 'fluid' because both the phospholipids and the proteins can move about by diffusion. The phospholipid bilayer has the sort of fluidity you associate with olive oil. The phospholipid molecules move sideways in their layers. Some of the protein molecules also move about within the phospholipid bilayer, like icebergs in the sea. Others remain fixed to structures inside or outside the cell. The word 'mosaic' describes the pattern produced by

the scattered protein molecules when the surface of the membrane is viewed from above.

Figures 4.4 and 4.5 are diagrams of what scientists imagine a membrane might look like if you could see the individual molecules.

KEY WORD

fluid mosaic model: the currently accepted model of membrane structure, proposed by Singer and Nicolson in 1972, in which protein molecules are free to move about in a fluid bilayer of phospholipid molecules

Features of the fluid mosaic model

The membrane is a double layer (bilayer) of phospholipid molecules. The individual phospholipid molecules move about by diffusion within their layers.

The phospholipid tails point inwards, facing each other and forming a non-polar hydrophobic interior. The phospholipid heads face outwards into the aqueous (water-containing) medium that surrounds the membranes.

Some of the phospholipid tails are saturated and some are unsaturated. (Remember, unsaturated tails contain double bonds.) The more unsaturated they are, the more fluid the membrane. This is because the unsaturated fatty acid tails are bent (see Figure 2.11) and therefore fit together more loosely. Fluidity is also affected by tail length: the longer the tail, the less fluid the membrane. As temperature decreases, membranes become less fluid, but some organisms which cannot regulate their own temperature, such as bacteria and yeasts, respond by increasing the proportion of unsaturated fatty acids in their membranes.

Proteins may be found in the inner layer, the outer layer or, most commonly, spanning the whole membrane, in which case they are known as transmembrane proteins.

The proteins have hydrophobic (non-polar) and hydrophilic (polar) regions. They stay in the membrane because the hydrophobic regions, made from hydrophobic amino acids, are next to the hydrophobic fatty acid tails and are repelled by the watery environment either side of the membrane. The hydrophilic regions, made from hydrophilic amino acids, are repelled by the hydrophobic interior of the membrane and therefore face into the aqueous environment inside or outside the cell, or line hydrophilic pores which pass through the membrane (see Figure 4.5).

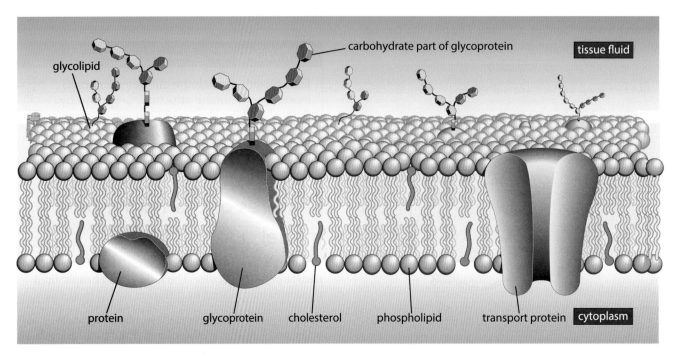

Figure 4.4: An artist's impression of the fluid mosaic model of membrane structure.

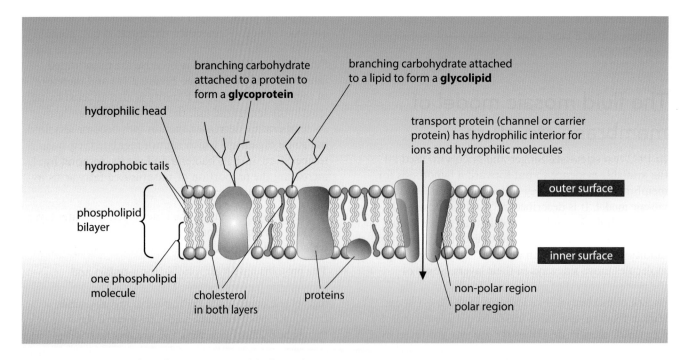

Figure 4.5: Diagram of the fluid mosaic model of membrane structure.

Most of the protein molecules float like icebergs in the phospholipid layers, although some are fixed to structures inside or outside the cell and do not move about.

Many proteins and lipids have short, branching carbohydrate chains, forming glycoproteins and glycolipids. The carbohydrate chains face outside the membrane.

Molecules of cholesterol are also found in the membrane.

4.3 Roles of the molecules found in membranes

You have seen that cell membranes contain several different types of molecule. There are three types of lipid: phospholipids, cholesterol and glycolipids. There are also proteins and glycoproteins. Each of these has a particular role to play in the overall structure and function of the membrane.

Phospholipids

As explained:

* phospholipids form a bilayer, which is the basic structure of the membrane

* fluidity of the membrane is affected by the length of the fatty acid tails and how saturated or unsaturated they are.

Because the tails of phospholipids are non-polar (hydrophobic), it is difficult for polar molecules or ions to pass through membranes. Membranes therefore act as a barrier to most water-soluble substances. This means that water-soluble molecules such as sugars, amino acids and proteins cannot leak out of the cell, and unwanted water-soluble molecules cannot enter the cell.

Some phospholipids can be modified to act as signalling molecules (see Section 4.4, Cell signalling).

Cholesterol

Cholesterol is a relatively small molecule. Like phospholipids, cholesterol molecules have hydrophilic heads and hydrophobic tails. They fit between the phospholipid molecules with their heads at the membrane surface. Cell surface membranes in animal cells contain almost as much cholesterol as phospholipid. Cholesterol is much less common in plant

cell membranes and is absent from prokaryotes. In these organisms, compounds very similar to cholesterol serve the same function.

Cholesterol is important for the mechanical stability of membranes. It strengthens membranes by getting in between the phospholipid molecules and reducing fluidity. Without cholesterol, membranes quickly break and cells burst open.

The hydrophobic regions of cholesterol molecules help to prevent ions or polar molecules from passing through the membrane. This is particularly important in the myelin sheath, which surrounds nerve cells. The myelin sheath is made up of many layers of cell surface membrane. Leakage of ions would slow down nerve impulses.

At low temperatures the phospholipid tails tend to pack closer together, but cholesterol prevents this from happening too much. Maintaining the correct fluidity of the membrane means cells can survive colder temperatures.

Glycolipids, glycoproteins and proteins

Probably all the protein molecules and many of the lipid molecules on the outer surfaces of cell surface membranes have short carbohydrate chains attached to them. These 'combination' molecules are known as glycoproteins and glycolipids. Some of the functions of glycolipids and proteins, including glycoproteins, are summarised below.

Receptor molecules

The carbohydrate chains help the glycoproteins and glycolipids to act as receptor molecules. The function of receptor molecules is to bind with particular substances at the cell surface. Different cells have different receptors, depending on their function.

KEY WORD
cholesterol: a small, lipid-related molecule with a hydrophilic head and a hydrophobic tail which is an essential constituent of membranes; it is particularly common in animal cells and gives flexibility and stability to the membrane as well as reducing fluidity

One group of receptors are called 'signalling receptors', because they are part of a signalling system that coordinates the activities of cells. Signalling receptors recognise messenger molecules like hormones and neurotransmitters. (Neurotransmitters are discussed in Chapter 15, Section 15.2, Nervous communication.) When the messenger molecule binds to the signalling receptor, a series of chemical reactions is started inside the cell. An example of a signalling receptor is the glucagon receptor in liver cells (see Figure 14.26). Only cells that have glucagon receptors are affected by glucagon. Signalling is discussed further in Section 4.4, Cell signalling.

Cell-to-cell recognition

Some glycolipids and glycoproteins act as cell markers or antigens, allowing cells to recognise each other. The carbohydrate chains bind to complementary sites on other cells. Cell–cell recognition is important in growth and development and for immune responses. Each type of cell has its own type of antigen, rather like countries with different flags. For example, the ABO blood group antigens are glycolipids and glycoproteins which have small differences in their carbohydrate chains.

Transport proteins

Many proteins act as transport proteins. These provide hydrophilic channels or passageways for ions and polar molecules to pass through the membrane. Each transport protein is specific for a particular kind of ion or molecule. There are two types of transport protein: channel proteins and carrier proteins. Their roles are described in Section 4.5, Movement of substances across membranes.

Enzymes

Some membrane proteins are enzymes – for example, the digestive enzymes found in the cell surface membranes of the cells lining the small intestine. These catalyse the hydrolysis of molecules such as disaccharides.

Cytoskeleton

Some proteins on the inside of the cell surface membrane are attached to a system of protein filaments inside the cell known as the cytoskeleton. These proteins help to maintain and decide the shape of the cell. They may also be involved in changes of shape when cells move.

Other roles

Proteins also play important roles in the membranes of organelles. For example, in the membranes of mitochondria and chloroplasts they are involved in the processes of respiration and photosynthesis. (You will find out much more about this if you continue your biology course to A Level.)

Question

1 Prepare a table to summarise briefly the major functions of phospholipids, cholesterol, glycolipids, glycoproteins and proteins in cell surface membranes.

4.4 Cell signalling

Cell signalling is an important area of research in modern biology, with wide applications. It is important because it helps to explain how living organisms control and coordinate their bodies. In this chapter you will consider a few basic principles of signalling, especially the importance of membranes. Many features of cell signalling are shared between all living organisms.

> ### KEY WORD
>
> cell signalling: the molecular mechanisms by which cells detect and respond to external stimuli, including communication between cells

What is signalling? Basically, signalling is getting a message from one place to another.

Why do living organisms need signalling? All cells and organisms must be able to respond appropriately to their environments. This is made possible by means of signalling pathways which coordinate the activities of cells, even if they are large distances apart in the same body.

Signalling pathways can be electrical (e.g. the nervous system) or chemical (e.g. the hormone system in animals). They involve a wide range of molecules such as neurotransmitters and hormones. In this chapter you will concentrate on signalling pathways involving chemicals.

The first part of the pathway typically involves the following three main stages.

- A stimulus causes cells to secrete a specific chemical. The chemical is called a ligand. (The word ligand comes from the Latin word 'ligare', meaning to bind: you will see below that ligands bind to receptors.) The hormone glucagon is an example of a ligand. It is a specific chemical secreted by certain cells in the pancreas in response to a drop in blood sugar levels (the stimulus) (see Chapter 14, Section 14.4, The control of blood glucose).

- The ligand is transported to the target cells. Signalling molecules are usually relatively small for easy transport. In the case of hormones, the transport system is the blood system.

- The ligand binds to cell surface receptors on the target cells. The receptors are protein molecules located in the cell surface membrane.

The cell surface receptor is a specific shape and recognises the ligand. Only cells with this receptor can recognise the ligand. The ligand brings about a change in the shape of the receptor. The receptor spans the membrane, so the message is passed to the inside of the cell. Changing the shape of the receptor allows it to interact with the next component of the signalling pathway, so the message gets transmitted. Conversion of the original signal to a message that is then transmitted is called transduction.

> ## KEY WORDS
>
> ligand: a biological molecule which binds specifically to another molecule, such as a cell surface membrane receptor, during cell signalling
>
> transduction: occurs during cell signalling and is the process of converting a signal from one method of transmission to another

The next component in the signalling pathway is often a 'G protein', which acts as a switch to bring about the release of a 'second messenger'. The second messenger is a small molecule which diffuses through the cell relaying the message. (G proteins are so-called because the switch mechanism involves binding to GTP (guanine triphosphate) molecules. GTP is similar to ATP, but with guanine in place of adenine.)

The stimulation of one receptor molecule results in many second messenger molecules being made in response. This represents an amplification (magnification) of the original signal, a key feature of signalling. The second messenger typically activates an enzyme, which in turn activates further enzymes, increasing the amplification at each stage. Finally, enzymes are produced which bring about the required change in cell metabolism.

The sequence of events triggered by the G protein is called a signalling cascade. Figure 4.6 is a diagram of a simplified cell-signalling pathway involving a second messenger. Examples of such a pathway involving the hormones glucagon and adrenaline are discussed in Chapter 14 (see Figure 14.26).

Apart from second messengers, there are three other basic ways in which a receptor can alter the activity of a cell:

- opening an ion channel, resulting in a change of membrane potential (e.g. nicotine-accepting acetylcholine receptors, Chapter 15)

- acting directly as a membrane-bound enzyme (e.g. glucagon receptor, Chapter 14)

- acting as an intracellular receptor when the initial signal passes straight through the cell surface membrane (e.g. the oestrogen receptor is in the nucleus and directly controls gene expression when combined with oestrogen).

Figure 4.7 summarises some typical signalling systems.

Some signalling molecules are hydrophobic. Examples include the steroid hormones (e.g. oestrogen). Figure 4.7 shows a hydrophobic signal molecule entering the cell. Hydrophobic signalling molecules can diffuse directly across the cell surface membrane and bind to receptors in the cytoplasm or nucleus.

Question

2   Why does the cell surface membrane not provide a barrier to the entry of hydrophobic molecules into the cell?

Direct cell-to-cell contact is another mechanism of signalling. This occurs, for example, when lymphocytes detect foreign antigens on other cells.

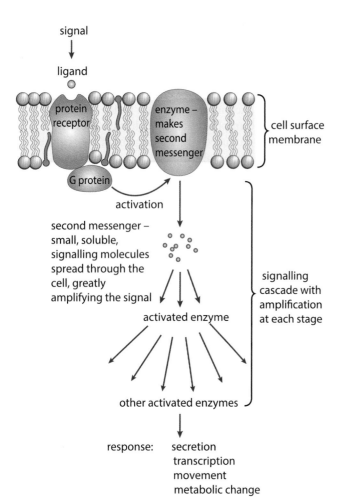

Figure 4.6: A simplified cell-signalling pathway involving a ligand and a second messenger.

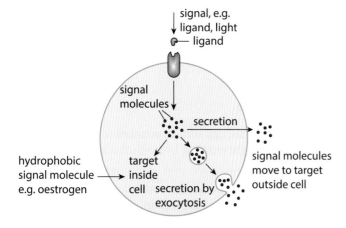

Figure 4.7: A few of the possible signalling pathways commonly found in cells.

4.5 Movement of substances across membranes

You have seen that a phospholipid bilayer around cells makes a very effective barrier, particularly against the movement of water-soluble molecules and ions. Such a barrier prevents the aqueous contents of the cell from escaping. However, some exchange between the cell and its environment is essential. There are five basic mechanisms by which this exchange is achieved:

- diffusion
- facilitated diffusion
- osmosis
- active transport
- bulk transport.

Question

3   Suggest **three** reasons why exchange between the cell and its environment is essential.

Diffusion

If you open a bottle of perfume in a room, it is not long before molecules of scent spread to all parts of the room (and are detected when they fit into membrane receptors in your nose). This will happen, even in still air, by the process of diffusion. **Diffusion** can be defined as the net movement of a substance from a region of its higher concentration to a region of its lower concentration as a result of random motion of its molecules or ions. The molecules or ions move down a concentration gradient. The random movement is caused by the natural kinetic energy (energy of movement) of the molecules or ions. As a result of diffusion, molecules or ions tend to reach an equilibrium situation where they are evenly spread

> KEY WORD
>
> **diffusion:** the net movement of molecules or ions from a region of higher concentration to a region of lower concentration down a concentration gradient, as a result of the random movements of particles

out within a given volume of space. Diffusion can be demonstrated easily using non-living materials such as glucose and Visking tubing (Practical Activity 4.1) or plant tissue (Practical Activity 4.2).

Some molecules or ions are able to pass through living cell membranes by diffusion. For example, the respiratory gases – oxygen and carbon dioxide – cross membranes by diffusion. They are uncharged and non-polar, and so can cross through the phospholipid bilayer between the phospholipid molecules. Water molecules, despite being very polar, can diffuse rapidly across the phospholipid bilayer because they are small enough.

PRACTICAL ACTIVITY 4.1

Demonstrating diffusion using Visking tubing

Visking tubing (also known as dialysis tubing) is a partially permeable, non-living membrane made from cellulose. It has molecular-sized pores which are small enough to prevent the passage of large molecules, such as starch and sucrose, but will allow the passage by diffusion of smaller molecules, such as glucose.

This can be demonstrated by filling a length of Visking tubing (about 15 cm) with a mixture of starch and glucose solutions. If the tubing is suspended in a test tube (or boiling tube) of water for a period of time, the presence of starch and glucose outside the tubing can be tested for at intervals to monitor whether diffusion out of the tubing has occurred. The results should indicate that glucose, but not starch, diffuses out of the tubing.

This experiment can be made more quantitative. It would be interesting, for example, to try to estimate the concentration of glucose outside the Visking tubing at different time intervals by setting up separate tubes, one for each planned time interval, and using a semi-quantitative Benedict's test each time. A colorimeter would be useful for this. Alternatively, a set of colour standards could be prepared. A graph could be drawn showing how the rate of diffusion changes with the concentration gradient between the inside and outside of the tubing.

You could design experiments in which sucrose and sucrase (an enzyme that breaks down sucrose) are added to the Visking tubing. You could also design experiments involving amylase, which breaks down starch.

(See Practical Investigation 4.2 in the Practical Workbook for additional information.)

PRACTICAL ACTIVITY 4.2

Demonstrating diffusion using plant tissue

Temporary staining of living plant cells – for example, adding iodine solution to epidermal cells to stain the nuclei and cytoplasm – shows that diffusion through cell surface membranes is possible. An experiment showing how the permeability of membranes is affected by environmental factors such as chemicals and temperature can be performed with beetroot.

Pieces of beetroot can be placed into water at different temperatures or into different alcohol concentrations. Any damage to the cell membranes results in the red pigment, which is normally contained within the large central vacuole, leaking out of the cells by diffusion. Changes in the colour of the surrounding solution can be monitored

qualitatively or quantitatively. As in the experiment in Practical Activity 4.1, a colorimeter or a set of colour standards could be used. Alternatively, you could simply put the tubes in order and make up a colour scale (e.g. from 0 to 10), using water as 0 and the darkest solution as 10. There is an opportunity to design your own experiment.

What you are seeing is diffusion of the red dye from a region of high concentration in the vacuoles to a region of low concentration in the solution outside the pieces of beetroot. Diffusion is normally prevented by the partially permeable nature of the cell membranes.

(See Practical Investigation 4.8 in the Practical Workbook for additional information.)

Hydrophobic molecules can cross membranes because the interior of the membrane is hydrophobic.

The rate at which a substance diffuses across a membrane depends on a number of factors, including:

- steepness of the concentration gradient
- temperature
- the nature of the molecules or ions
- surface area.

The 'steepness' of the concentration gradient

The steeper the concentration gradient of a substance across a membrane, the faster the rate of diffusion of that substance. The steepness of the gradient is the difference in the concentration of the substance on the two sides of the membrane. If there are more molecules of the substance on one side of the membrane than on the other, there will be a net movement of molecules from where there are more to where there are fewer. Notice that it is a net movement. This means that although molecules move in both directions, more will move one way than the other depending on the gradient.

Temperature

At high temperatures, molecules and ions have much more kinetic energy than at low temperatures. They move faster, so diffusion is faster.

The nature of the molecules or ions

Large molecules require more energy to get them moving than small ones do, so large molecules tend to diffuse more slowly than small molecules. Non-polar molecules, such as glycerol, alcohol and steroid hormones, diffuse much more easily through cell membranes than polar ones, because they are soluble in the non-polar phospholipid tails.

The surface area across which diffusion is taking place

The greater the area of a surface, the more molecules or ions can cross it at any one moment, and therefore the faster diffusion can occur. The surface area of cell membranes can be increased by folding, as in microvilli in the cells lining the intestine or the cristae inside mitochondria.

An important factor is that the larger the cell, the smaller its surface area in relation to its volume. This is easily seen by studying Figure 4.8 in Question 4. To make the relevant calculations easier, cells are shown as cubes rather than spheres, but the principle remains the same: volume increases much more rapidly than surface area as size increases (see also Practical Activity 4.3). This has important implications for cells.

Question

4   Figure 4.8 shows three cubes.

Calculate the surface area, volume and surface area : volume ratio of each of the cubes.

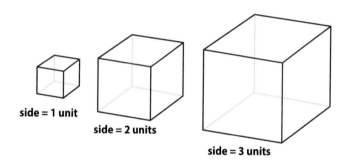

side = 1 unit

side = 2 units

side = 3 units

Figure 4.8: Diagram of three cubes.

The surface area : volume ratio decreases as the size of any three-dimensional (3D) object increases.

> **IMPORTANT**
>
> The surface area : volume ratio decreases as the size of any three-dimensional (3D) object increases.

Cells rely on diffusion because it is the main method by which molecules move about inside cells. This results in a limit on the size of cells, because the time taken to travel any distance by diffusion increases much faster than the distance does. Diffusion is, therefore, only effective over very short distances. An amino acid molecule, for example, can travel a few micrometres in several seconds, but would take several hours to diffuse 10 000 micrometres (a centimetre). Most eukaryotic cells are no larger than about 50 micrometres in diameter; prokaryotic cells are even smaller. An aerobic cell would quickly run out of oxygen and die if it were too large.

Question

5 The fact that surface area : volume ratio decreases with increasing size is also true for whole organisms. Explain the relevance of this for transport systems within organisms.

PRACTICAL ACTIVITY 4.3

Investigating the effect of size on diffusion

The effect of size on diffusion can be investigated by timing the diffusion of ions through blocks of agar of different sizes.

Solid agar is prepared in suitable containers such as ice cube trays. If the agar is made up with very dilute sodium hydroxide solution and Universal indicator, it will be coloured purple. Cubes of the required dimensions (e.g., sides of 2 cm × 2 cm, 1 cm × 1 cm, 0.5 cm × 0.5 cm) can be cut from the agar, placed in a container and covered with a diffusion solution such as dilute hydrochloric acid. (The acid should have a higher molarity than the sodium hydroxide so that its diffusion can be monitored by a change in colour of the indicator. Alternatively, the agar can be made up with Universal indicator only, although its colour will be affected by the pH of the water used.)

Either the time taken for the acid to completely change the colour of the indicator in the agar blocks, or the distance travelled into the block by the acid in a given time (e.g. 5 minutes), can be measured. The times can be converted to rates.

Finally, the rate of diffusion (rate of colour change) can be plotted against the surface area : volume ratio.

Using the same techniques, you may be able to design further experiments. For example, you could investigate the effect of the steepness of the concentration gradient on the rate of diffusion.

(See Practical Investigations 4.3 and 4.4 in the Practical Workbook for additional information.)

Facilitated diffusion

Large polar molecules, such as glucose and amino acids, cannot diffuse through the phospholipid bilayer. Nor can ions such as sodium (Na^+) or chloride (Cl^-). These can only cross the membrane with the help of certain protein molecules. Diffusion that needs help in this way is called **facilitated diffusion**. 'Facilitated' means made easy or made possible; the proteins facilitate the diffusion.

There are two types of transport protein involved, namely **channel proteins** and **carrier proteins**. Each channel protein or carrier protein is highly specific, allowing only one type of molecule or ion to pass through it.

Channel proteins

Channel proteins have water-filled pores as part of their structure. The pores allow charged substances, usually ions, to diffuse through the membrane. Most channel proteins are 'gated'. This means that part of the protein molecule on the inside surface of the membrane can move to close or open the pore, like

a gate. This allows control of ion exchange. Two examples are the gated proteins found in nerve cell surface membranes. One type allows entry of sodium ions (Na^+), which happens during the production of an action potential (Chapter 15, Section 15.2,

---

KEY WORDS

facilitated diffusion: the diffusion of a substance through a transport protein (channel protein or carrier protein) in a cell membrane; the protein provides hydrophilic areas that allow the molecule or ion to pass through the membrane, which would otherwise be less permeable to it

channel protein: a membrane protein of fixed shape which has a water-filled pore through which selected hydrophilic ions or molecules can pass by facilitating diffusion or active transport

carrier protein: a membrane protein which changes shape to allow the passage into or out of the cell of specific ions or molecules by facilitated diffusion or active transport

---

Nervous communication). Another type allows exit of potassium ions (K^+) during the recovery phase, known as repolarisation. Some channels occur in a single protein; others are formed by several proteins combined. Some gated channel proteins require energy (in the form of ATP) to operate the gate.

Carrier proteins

Whereas channel proteins have a fixed shape, carrier proteins can flip between two shapes (Figure 4.9). As a result, the binding site is alternately open to one side of the membrane, then the other. This allows the molecule or ion to cross the membrane. Some carrier proteins change shape spontaneously. These are the ones that allow facilitated diffusion. Some carrier proteins, known as pumps, require energy and are involved in active transport (discussed later in this chapter).

Rate of diffusion through channel and carrier proteins

If molecules are diffusing across a membrane, the direction of movement depends on their relative concentration on each side of the membrane. They move down a concentration gradient from a higher to a lower concentration. However, the rate at which facilitated diffusion takes place is also affected by how many channel or carrier protein molecules there are in the membrane and, in the case of channel proteins, on whether they are open or not.

Osmosis

Osmosis is a special type of diffusion involving only water molecules. In the explanations that follow, remember that:

$$solute + solvent = solution$$

In a sugar solution, for example, the solute is sugar and the solvent is water.

> ### KEY WORD
>
> **osmosis:** the net diffusion of water molecules from a region of higher water potential to a region of lower water potential, through a partially permeable membrane

In Figure 4.10 there are two solutions separated by a partially permeable membrane. This is a membrane that allows only certain molecules through, just like membranes in living cells. In Figure 4.10a, solution **B** has a higher concentration of solute molecules than solution **A**. Solution **B** is described as more concentrated than solution **A**, and solution **A** is more dilute than solution **B**.

First, imagine what would happen if the membrane was not present. Both solute molecules and water molecules are free to move anywhere within the solutions. As they move randomly, both water molecules

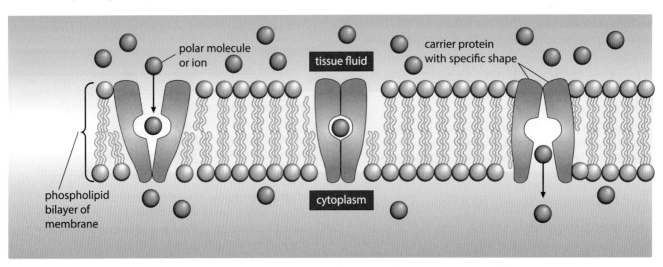

Figure 4.9: Changes in the shape of a carrier protein during facilitated diffusion. In this example, there is a net diffusion of molecules or ions into the cell down a concentration gradient.

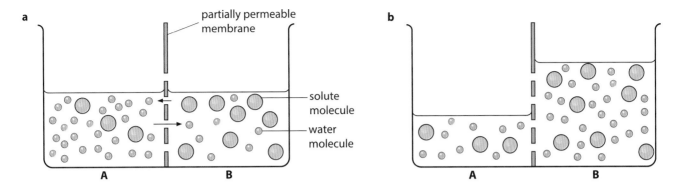

Figure 4.10: Two solutions separated by a partially permeable membrane. **a** Before osmosis. The solute molecules are too large to pass through the pores in the membrane, but the water molecules are small enough. **b** As the arrows in **a** show, more water molecules move from **A** to **B** than from **B** to **A**, so the net movement is from **A** to **B**, raising the level of solution in **B** and lowering it in **A**.

and solute molecules will tend to spread themselves evenly throughout the space available, by diffusion. At equilibrium, the concentration of the solution would be the same in **A** and **B**.

Now consider the situation where a partially permeable membrane *is* present, as in Figure 4.10. The solute molecules are too large to get through the membrane. Only water molecules can pass through. The solute molecules move about randomly, but as they hit the membrane they simply bounce back. The numbers of solute molecules each side of the membrane stay the same. The water molecules also move about randomly, but they are able to move both from **A** to **B** and from **B** to **A**. Over time, the water molecules will tend to spread themselves out more evenly between **A** and **B**.

This means that **A** will end up with fewer water molecules, so that the solution becomes more concentrated with solute. **B** will end up with more water molecules, so that it becomes more dilute. The volume of liquid in **B** will increase because it now contains the same number of solute molecules but has more water molecules. The solutions in **A** and **B** will have the same concentration.

The net diffusion of water molecules from a region of higher water potential to a region of lower water potential, through a partially permeable membrane, is called osmosis.

Water potential

The term **water potential** is very useful when considering osmosis. The Greek letter psi, ψ, can be used to mean water potential.

You can think of water potential as being the tendency of water to move from one place to another. Water *always* moves from a region of higher water potential to a region of lower water potential. So water always moves down a water potential gradient. For example, when water falls down a waterfall, it is moving from a higher water potential to a lower water potential.

Water will move until the water potential is the same throughout the system, at which point you can say that equilibrium has been reached.

With reference to osmosis, water potential depends on two factors:

- the concentration of the solution
- how much pressure is applied to it.

For example, a solution containing a lot of water (a dilute solution) has a higher water potential than a solution containing relatively little water (a concentrated solution). In Figure 4.10a, solution **A** has a higher water potential than solution **B**, because solution **A** is more dilute than solution **B**. This is why the net movement of water is from **A** to **B**. (high water potential to low water potential)

a

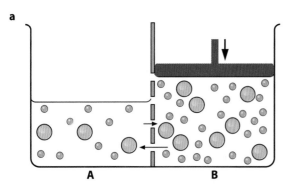

b

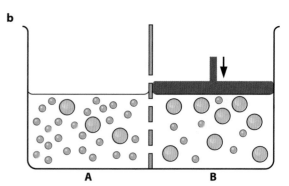

Figure 4.11: a Applying pressure to a solution increases the tendency of water to move out of it, so in this figure the pressure increases the water potential of the solution in **B**. **b** Water has moved from **B** to **A** as a result of the pressure. The equilibrium situation is shown. The pressure applied has returned the solutions to the situation shown in Figure 4.10a.

Now look again at Figure 4.10b. What would happen if you could now press down very hard on side **B**, as shown in Figure 4.11a?

Applying pressure to solution **B** makes it possible to 'squeeze' some of the water back into solution **A**. By increasing the pressure on solution **B**, you are increasing the tendency for water to move out of it – that is, you are increasing its water potential, until it is higher than the water potential in **A**. Pressure on a solution increases its water potential.

Measuring water potential

Water potential can be measured in pressure units called kiloPascals (abbreviated to kPa). As you have seen, the water potential of pure water will always be higher than the water potential of a solution (assuming there is no extra pressure applied to the solution). For reasons that you do not need to consider here, the water potential of pure water is set at 0 kPa. Since all solutions have a lower water potential than pure water, the water potential of all solutions must be less than zero. In other words their water potentials must be negative and the units will be –kPa. A dilute solution will have a less negative value than a concentrated solution. For example, a solution with a water potential of -10 kPa has a higher water potential than a solution with a water potential of -20 kPa.

Question

6   a   In Figure 4.10b, the system has come into equilibrium, so there is no net movement of water molecules. What can you say about the water potentials of the two solutions **A** and **B**?

b   i   In Figure 4.11b, the solutions **A** and **B** are at equilibrium. Which solution, **A** or **B**, is more concentrated?

ii   Why does water not move from the more dilute solution to the more concentrated solution?

Osmosis in animal cells

Figure 4.12 shows the effect of osmosis on an animal cell. A convenient type of animal cell to study in practical work is the red blood cell. A slide of fresh blood viewed with a microscope will show large numbers of red blood cells. Different samples of blood can be mixed with solutions of different water potential. Figure 4.12a shows that, if the water potential of the solution surrounding the cell is too high, the cell swells and bursts. If it is too low, the cell shrinks (Figure 4.12c). This shows one reason why it is important to maintain a constant water potential inside the bodies of animals.

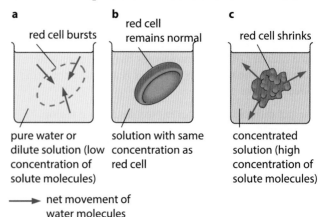

Figure 4.12: Movement of water into or out of red blood cells by osmosis in solutions of different concentration.

Question

7   In Figure 4.12:

   a   which solution has the highest water potential?

   b   in which solution is the water potential of the red cell the same as that of the solution?

Osmosis in plant cells

Unlike animal cells, plant cells are surrounded by cell walls, which are very strong and rigid. Imagine a plant cell being placed in pure water or a dilute solution (Figure 4.13a). The water or solution has a higher water potential than the plant cell, and water therefore enters the cell through its partially permeable cell surface membrane by osmosis. Just like in the animal cell, the volume of the cell increases, but in the plant cell the wall resists the expansion of the **protoplast**, which is the living part of the cell inside the cell wall surrounded by the cell surface membrane. Pressure rapidly starts to build up inside the cell. This pressure increases the water potential of the cell until the water potential inside the cell equals the water potential outside the cell, and equilibrium is reached (Figure 4.13b). The cell wall is so inelastic that the pressure builds up quickly and it takes very little water to enter the cell to achieve equilibrium. The cell wall prevents the cell from bursting, unlike the situation when an animal cell is placed in pure water or a dilute solution. When a plant cell is fully inflated with water, it is described as turgid.

Figure 4.13c shows the situation when a plant cell is placed in a solution of lower water potential. An example would be a concentrated sucrose solution. In such a solution, water will leave the cell by osmosis. As it does so, the protoplast gradually shrinks until it is exerting no pressure at all on the cell wall. Both the solute molecules and the water molecules of the external solution can continue to pass through the freely permeable cell wall, and so the external solution remains in contact with the shrinking protoplast.

As the protoplast continues to shrink, it begins to pull away from the cell wall (Figures 4.14 and 4.15). This process is called **plasmolysis**, and a cell in which it has happened is said to be plasmolysed (Figures 4.13c, 4.14 and 4.15). The point at which plasmolysis is about to occur is referred to as **incipient plasmolysis**. This is the point when the protoplast no longer exerts any pressure on the cell wall. Eventually, as with the animal cell, an equilibrium is reached when the water potential of the cell has decreased until it equals that of the external solution.

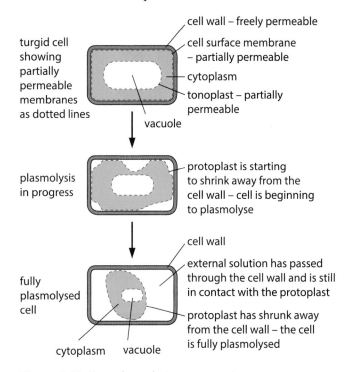

Figure 4.14: How plasmolysis occurs.

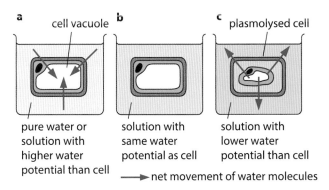

Figure 4.13: Osmotic changes in a plant cell in solutions of different water potential.

KEY WORDS

protoplast: the living contents of a plant cell, including the cell surface membrane but excluding the cell wall

plasmolysis: the loss of water from a plant or prokaryote cell to the point where the protoplast shrinks away from the cell wall

incipient plasmolysis: the point at which plasmolysis is about to occur when a plant cell or a prokaryote cell is losing water; at this point the protoplast is exerting no pressure on the cell wall

The changes described can easily be observed with a light microscope using strips of epidermis peeled from rhubarb petioles or from the swollen storage leaves of onion bulbs (Figure 4.15). The epidermal strips could be placed in a range of sucrose solutions of different concentration to find out which cause plasmolysis (Practical Activity 4.4).

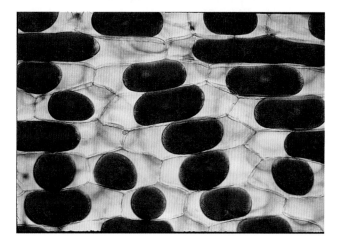

Figure 4.15: Light micrograph of red onion cells that have plasmolysed (×100).

Questions

8   Figures 4.14 and 4.15 show a phenomenon called plasmolysis. Why can plasmolysis not take place in an animal cell?

9   Inflating a balloon can mimic water entering a cell by osmosis.

   a   What does the skin of the balloon represent?

   b   What will happen if inflation continues (animal cell)?

   c   What will happen if the balloon is inside a strong box (plant cell)?

10   Two neighbouring plant cells are shown in Figure 4.16. Cell A has a higher water potential than cell B. (Remember, the closer the water potential is to zero, the higher it is.)

   a   In which direction would there be net movement of water molecules?

   b   Explain what is meant by 'net movement'.

   c   Explain your answer to **a**.

   d   Explain what would happen if both cells were placed in:

      i   pure water

      ii   a sucrose solution with a lower water potential than either cell.

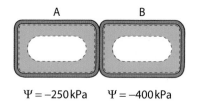

Figure 4.16 Water potential in two neighbouring plant cells.

PRACTICAL ACTIVITY 4.4

Investigating osmosis in plant cells

Observing osmosis in plant cells

Epidermal strips are useful material for observing plasmolysis. Coloured sap makes observation easier. Suitable sources are the inner surfaces of the fleshy storage leaves of red onion bulbs, rhubarb petioles and red cabbage leaves.

The strips of epidermis may be placed in a range of molarities of sucrose solution (up to 1.0 mol dm^{-3}) or sodium chloride solutions of up to 3%. Small pieces of the strips can then be placed on glass slides, mounted in the relevant solution, and observed with a microscope. Plasmolysis may take several minutes, if it occurs.

Determining the water potential of a plant tissue

The principle in this experiment is to find a solution of known water potential which will cause neither a gain nor a loss in water of the plant tissue being examined. Samples of the tissue – for example, potato chips of standard size – are allowed to come into equilibrium with a range of solutions of different water potentials. Sucrose solutions may be used. Changes in either mass or volume are recorded. Length of chips can be used as a measure of volume if chips are all the same dimensions. Plotting a graph of the results allows the solution that causes no change in mass or volume to be determined. This solution will have the same water potential as the plant tissue.

(See Practical Investigations 4.5, 4.6 and 4.7 in the Practical Workbook for additional information.)

11 In an experiment to determine the water potential of fresh beetroot tissue, a student cut 12 rectangular 'chips' of tissue approximately 2 mm thick, 5 mm wide and 50 mm long, taken from the middle of a large beetroot. Two chips were immersed in each of six covered Petri dishes, one containing water and the others containing solutions of sucrose of different molarity, up to a maximum of 1 mol dm^{-3}. The lengths of the chips were then measured accurately against graph paper seen through the bottoms of the dishes. Mean percentage changes in length of the chips were then measured after six hours.

   a Why was it important to use fresh beetroot tissue in this experiment?

   b Why would it have been important to immerse the beetroot chips as soon as possible after they were cut?

   c Suggest why length was measured rather than volume.

   d Why were at least two chips added to each dish?

   e Why were the dishes covered when left?

   f Suggest **one** advantage of measuring change in length rather than change in mass of the chips in this experiment.

   g Suggest **one** advantage of measuring change in mass rather than change in length.

Active transport

Certain ions, such as potassium and chloride ions, are often found to be 10–20 times more concentrated inside cells than outside. In other words, a concentration gradient exists, with a lower concentration outside and a higher concentration inside the cell. The ions inside the cell originally came from the external solution. Therefore diffusion cannot be responsible for the gradient because, as you have seen, ions diffuse from high concentration to low concentration. The ions must therefore build up *against* a concentration gradient.

The process responsible is called **active transport**. It is achieved by carrier proteins called pumps, each of which is specific for a particular type of molecule or ion. However, unlike facilitated diffusion, active transport requires energy because movement occurs up a concentration gradient rather than down. The energy is most often supplied by the molecule ATP (adenosine triphosphate) which is produced during respiration inside the cell. The energy is used to make the carrier protein change its shape, transferring the molecules or ions across the membrane in the process (Figure 4.17).

An example of a carrier protein used for active transport is the **sodium–potassium pump** (**Na$^+$–K$^+$ pump**) (Figure 4.18). Such pumps are found in the cell surface membranes of all animal cells. In most cells, they run

> **KEY WORDS**
>
> **active transport:** the movement of molecules or ions through transport proteins across a cell membrane, against their concentration gradient, using energy from ATP
>
> **sodium–potassium pump (Na$^+$–K$^+$ pump):** a membrane protein (or proteins) that moves sodium ions out of a cell and potassium ions into it, using ATP

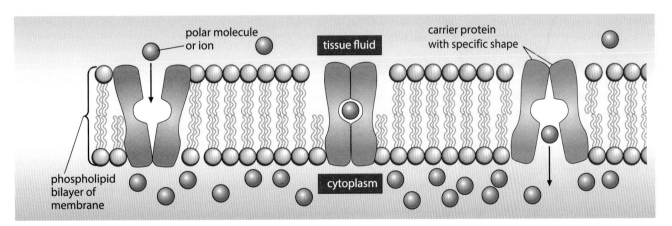

Figure 4.17: Changes in the shape of a carrier protein during active transport. Here, molecules or ions are being pumped into the cell *against* a concentration gradient. (Compare Figure 4.9.)

all the time, and it is estimated that on average they use 30% of a cell's energy (70% in nerve cells).

The role of the sodium–potassium pump is to pump three sodium ions out of the cell at the same time as allowing two potassium ions into the cell for each ATP molecule used. Sodium and potassium ions are both positively charged, so the net result is that the inside of the cell becomes more negative than the outside. A potential difference (p.d.) is created across the membrane. The significance of this in nerve cells is discussed in Chapter 15 (Section 15.2, Nervous communication).

In Figure 4.18 you can see that the pump has a receptor site for ATP on its inner surface (coloured red in the diagram). The receptor site acts as an ATPase enzyme in bringing about the hydrolysis of ATP to ADP (adenosine diphosphate) and phosphate to release energy.

Active transport can therefore be defined as the energy-consuming transport of molecules or ions across a membrane against a concentration gradient (from a lower to a higher concentration). The energy is provided by ATP from cell respiration. Active transport can occur either into or out of the cell.

Active transport is important in reabsorption in the kidneys, where certain useful molecules and ions have to be reabsorbed into the blood after filtration into the kidney tubules. It is also involved in the absorption of some products of digestion from the gut. In plants, active transport is used to load sugar from the photosynthesising cells of leaves into the phloem tissue for transport around the plant (Chapter 7, Section 7.5, Transport of assimilates), and to load inorganic ions from the soil into root hairs.

Endocytosis and exocytosis

So far you have been looking at ways in which individual molecules or ions cross membranes. Sometimes cells need to transport materials across their cell surface membranes on a much larger scale than is possible using the mechanisms studied so far. The materials include large molecules such as proteins or polysaccharides, parts of cells or even whole cells. As a result, mechanisms have evolved for the bulk transport of large quantities of materials into and out of cells.

Bulk transport of materials into cells is called endocytosis. Bulk transport out of cells is called exocytosis. These processes require energy.

Endocytosis

In endocytosis the cell surface membrane engulfs material to form a small sac (also known as a vesicle or a vacuole). Endocytosis takes two forms.

> **KEY WORDS**
>
> endocytosis: the bulk movement of liquids (pinocytosis) or solids (phagocytosis) into a cell, by the infolding of the cell surface membrane to form vesicles containing the substance; endocytosis is an active process requiring ATP
>
> exocytosis: the bulk movement of liquids or solids out of a cell, by the fusion of vesicles containing the substance with the cell surface membrane; exocytosis is an active process requiring ATP

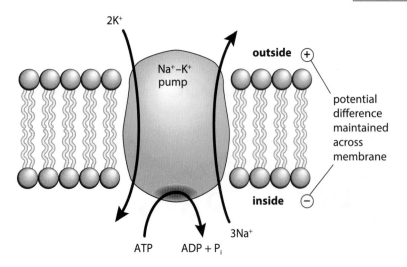

Figure 4.18: The sodium–potassium pump (Na⁺–K⁺ pump).

- Phagocytosis or 'cell eating' – this is the bulk uptake of solid material. Cells specialising in this are called **phagocytes**. The process is called phagocytosis and the vacuoles are called phagocytic vacuoles. An example is the engulfing of bacteria by white blood cells (Figure 4.19).

- Pinocytosis or 'cell drinking' – this is the bulk uptake of liquid. The vacuoles or vesicles formed are often extremely small, in which case the process is called micropinocytosis.

> **KEY WORD**
>
> **phagocyte:** a type of cell that ingests (eats) and destroys pathogens or damaged body cells by the process of phagocytosis; some phagocytes are white blood cells

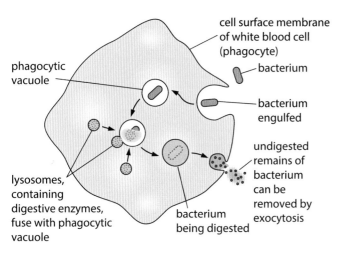

Figure 4.19: Stages in phagocytosis of a bacterium by a white blood cell.

Exocytosis

Exocytosis is the reverse of endocytosis and is the process by which materials are removed from cells (Figure 4.20). It happens, for example, in the secretion of digestive enzymes from cells of the pancreas (Figure 4.21). Secretory vesicles from the Golgi apparatus carry the enzymes to the cell surface and release their contents. Plant cells use exocytosis to get their cell wall building materials to the outside of the cell surface membrane.

Question

12 There are more mitochondria than average in pancreatic acinar cells. Suggest a reason for this. (See Figure 4.21 and also Exam-style Question 9 in Chapter 1.)

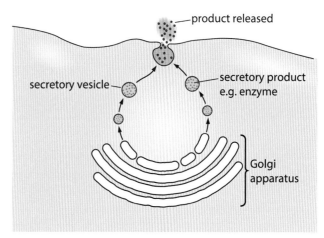

Figure 4.20: Exocytosis in a secretory cell. If the product being secreted is a protein, the Golgi apparatus is often involved in chemically modifying the protein before it is secreted, as in the secretion of digestive enzymes by the pancreas.

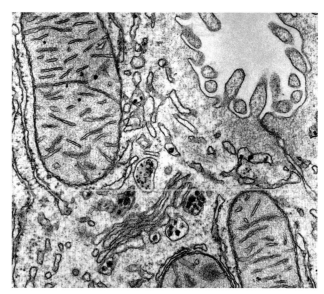

Figure 4.21: Transmission electron micrograph (TEM) of a pancreatic acinar cell secreting protein. The outside of the cell is coloured green. Golgi vesicles (secretory vesicles) with darkly stained contents can be seen making their way from the Golgi apparatus to the cell surface membrane. Mitochondria are coloured blue.

REFLECTION

The following exercise will help you to consider some of the connections that can be made between the many new biological terms you have studied in the first four chapters of this book.

For each pair of terms below, find a suitable word or term that links the pair. Also try to explain the connection between the pairs. For example:

mitochondrion – ATP: The missing term could be 'cell respiration' because cell respiration takes place in mitochondria and the product of cell respiration is ATP.

β-glucose – cell wall

monomer – protein

Michaelis–Menten constant – affinity

centrosome – microtubule

animal storage product – 1,4 and 1,6 linkages

nm – mm

Golgi apparatus – hydrolytic enzymes

ribosome – amino acid

amino acid – protein

α-glucose – plant storage product

monomer – polymer

microtubule – 9 + 2

induced fit – lock and key

peptidoglycan – cellulose

pinocytosis – endocytic vacuole

fatty acid – triglyceride

ligand – G protein

nucleolus – protein synthesis

The following grid shows some more terms that can be linked in some way. For example:

- hydrogen bond can be linked in some way with water and also with protein.

- fluid mosaic model can be linked with four terms.

A short line between two terms shows that they can be linked. Try to explain links.

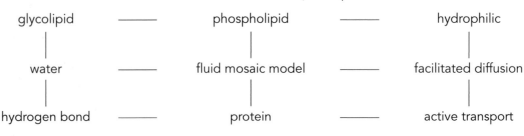

glycolipid ——— phospholipid ——— hydrophilic

water ——— fluid mosaic model ——— facilitated diffusion

hydrogen bond ——— protein ——— active transport

Personal reflection question

In what ways do you think you need to improve based on your performance in this activity?

Final reflection

Discuss with a friend which, if any, parts of Chapter 4 you need to:

- read through again to make sure you really understand

- seek more guidance on, even after going over it again.

SUMMARY

The basic structure of a membrane is a 7 nm thick phospholipid bilayer containing protein molecules. The structure is described as a fluid mosaic.

Phospholipid bilayers are a barrier to most water-soluble substances because the interior of the membrane is hydrophobic.

Cholesterol is also needed for membrane fluidity and stability.

Some proteins are transport proteins, transporting molecules or ions across the membrane. They may be either channel proteins or carrier proteins. Channel proteins have a fixed shape; carrier proteins change shape. Some proteins act as enzymes.

Glycolipids and glycoproteins form receptors – for example, for hormones or neurotransmitters. Glycolipids and glycoproteins also form cell–cell recognition markers.

Membranes play an important role in cell signalling, the means by which cells communicate with each other.

The cell surface membrane controls exchange between the cell and its environment. Some chemical reactions take place on membranes inside cell organelles, as in photosynthesis and respiration.

Diffusion is the net movement of molecules or ions from a region of their higher concentration to one of lower concentration. Oxygen, carbon dioxide and water cross membranes by diffusion. Diffusion of ions and polar molecules through membranes is allowed by transport proteins. This process is called facilitated diffusion.

Water moves from regions of higher water potential to regions of lower water potential. When water moves from regions of higher water potential to regions of lower water potential through a partially permeable membrane, such as the cell surface membrane, this diffusion is called osmosis.

Adding solute lowers the water potential. Adding pressure to a solution increases the water potential.

In dilute solutions, animal cells burst as water moves into the cytoplasm from the solution. In dilute solutions, a plant cell does not burst, because the cell wall provides resistance to prevent it expanding. In concentrated solutions, animal cells shrink, while in plant cells the protoplast shrinks away from the cell wall in a process known as plasmolysis.

Some ions and molecules move across membranes by active transport, against the concentration gradient. This needs a carrier protein and ATP to provide energy. Exocytosis and endocytosis involve the formation of vacuoles to move larger quantities of materials respectively out of, or into, cells by bulk transport. There are two types of endocytosis, namely phagocytosis (cell eating) and pinocytosis (cell drinking).

EXAM-STYLE QUESTIONS

1 What are the most abundant molecules in the cell surface membranes of plant cells?

A cholesterol

B glycolipids

C phospholipids

D proteins [1]

CONTINUED

2 Where are the carbohydrate portions of glycolipids and glycoproteins located in cell surface membranes?

A the inside and outside surfaces of the membrane

B the inside surface of the membrane

C the interior of the membrane

D the outside surface of the membrane [1]

3 In a signalling pathway, which of the following types of protein acts as a switch to release a second messenger?

A enzyme

B glycoprotein

C G protein

D receptor [1]

4 One role of cholesterol in membranes is:

A cell recognition

B cell-signalling receptor

C controlling fluidity

D hydrophilic channel [1]

5 a Describe fully what will occur if a plant cell is placed in a solution that has a higher water potential than the cell. Use the following terms in your answer:

> cell wall, freely permeable, partially permeable, cell surface membrane, vacuole, tonoplast, cytoplasm, water potential, turgid, osmosis, protoplast, equilibrium

[12]

b Describe fully what will occur if a plant cell is placed in a solution that has a lower water potential than the cell. Use the following terms in your answer:

> cell wall, freely permeable, partially permeable, cell surface membrane, vacuole, tonoplast, cytoplasm, water potential, incipient plasmolysis, plasmolysed, osmosis, protoplast, equilibrium

[13]

[Total: 25]

6 The diagram below shows part of a membrane containing a channel protein.

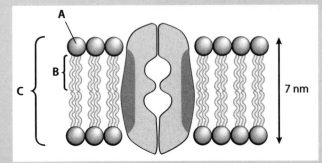

a Identify the parts labelled A, B and C. [3]

CONTINUED

    b For each of the following, state whether the component is hydrophilic or hydrophobic:

        i A

        ii B

        iii darkly shaded part of protein

        iv lightly shaded part of protein   **[2]**

    c Explain how ions would move through the channel protein.   **[3]**

    d State **two** features that the channel proteins and carrier proteins of membranes have in common, apart from being proteins.   **[2]**

    e State **one** structural difference between channel and carrier proteins.   **[1]**

    f Calculate the magnification of the drawing. Show your working.   **[4]**

                  [Total: 15]

7 Copy the table below and place a tick or cross in each box as appropriate.

Process	Uses energy in the form of ATP	Uses proteins	Specific	Controllable by cell
diffusion				
osmosis				
facilitated diffusion				
active transport				
endocytosis and exocytosis				

                  [20]

8 Copy and complete the table below to compare cell walls with cell membranes.

Feature	Cell wall	Cell membrane
is the thickness normally measured in nm or µm?		
cell location		
permeability		
fluid or rigid		

                  [4]

COMMAND WORD

Compare: identify / comment on similarities and/or differences.

CONTINUED

9 A plant tissue was placed in pure water at time zero. The rate of entry of water into the tissue was measured as the change in water potential with time. The graph shows the results of this investigation.

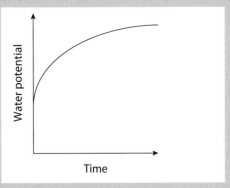

Describe and explain the results obtained. [8]

10 The rate of movement of molecules or ions across a cell surface membrane is affected by the relative concentrations of the molecules or ions on either side of the membrane. The graph below shows the effect of concentration difference (the steepness of the concentration gradient) on three transport processes: diffusion, facilitated diffusion and active transport.

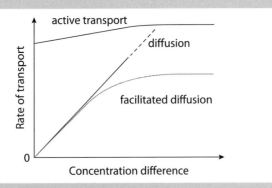

a **With reference to the graphs**, state what the **three** transport processes have in common. [1]

b Describe the rates of transport observed when the concentration difference is zero. [2]

c Explain the rates of transport observed when the concentration difference is zero. [2]

d i Which **one** of the processes would stop if a respiratory inhibitor was added? [1]

 ii Explain your answer. [2]

e Suggest an explanation for the difference between the graphs for diffusion and facilitated diffusion. [5]

[Total: 13]

CONTINUED

11 When a cell gains or loses water, its volume changes. The graph shows changes in the water potential (ψ) of a plant cell as its volume changes as a result of gaining or losing water. (Note that 80% relative cell volume means the cell or protoplast has shrunk to 80% of the volume it was at 100% relative cell volume.)

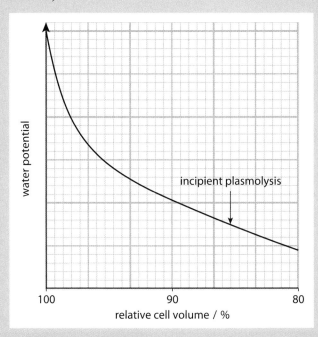

a What is a protoplast? [1]

b i State the relative cell volume when the cell is at maximum turgidity. [1]

   ii Describe what happens inside the cell as relative cell volume increases. [5]

c The graph shows the point of incipient plasmolysis.

   i State the relative cell volume at incipient plasmolysis. [1]

   ii State what is meant by the term *incipient plasmolysis*. [1]

   iii Describe what is happening to the cell between the point of incipient plasmolysis and the point where it has shrunk to a relative volume of 80%. [3]

[Total: 12]

CONTINUED

12 The diagram shows the concentration in mmol dm^{-3} of two different ions inside a human red blood cell and in the plasma outside the cell.

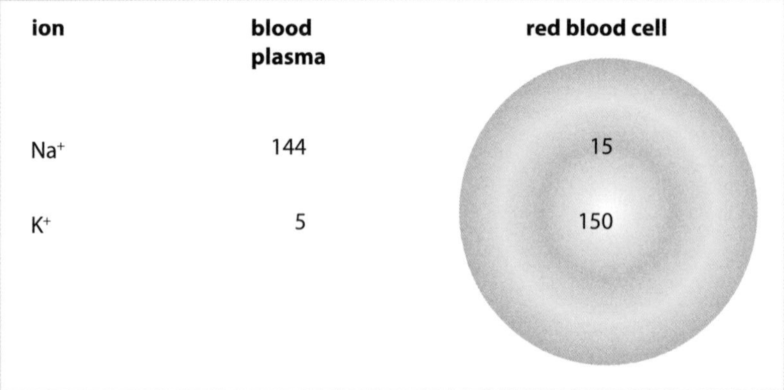

ion	blood plasma	red blood cell
Na$^+$	144	15
K$^+$	5	150

a Explain why these concentrations could not have occurred as a result of diffusion. [1]

b Explain how these concentrations could have been achieved. [2]

c If respiration of red blood cells is inhibited, the concentrations of potassium ions and sodium ions inside the cells gradually change until they come into equilibrium with the plasma. Explain this observation. [4]

[Total: 7]

SELF-EVALUATION CHECKLIST

After studying this chapter, complete a table like this:

I can	See section...	Needs more work	Almost there	Ready to move on
describe the structure of phospholipids and the fluid mosaic model of membrane structure	4.2			
describe the arrangement of the molecules in cell surface membranes	4.2			
describe the roles of the molecules found in cell surface membranes	4.3			
outline the process of cell signalling	4.4			
explain how substances enter and leave cells across cell surface membranes	4.5			
carry out practical investigations into diffusion and osmosis	4.5			
illustrate the principle that surface area : volume ratios decrease with increasing size	4.5			
explain the movement of water between cells and solutions in terms of water potential	4.5			

> Chapter 5
The mitotic cell cycle

LEARNING INTENTIONS

In this chapter you will learn how to:

- describe the structure of chromosomes
- outline the cell cycle – the cycle of events by which body cells grow to a certain size and then divide into two
- describe the behaviour of chromosomes during mitosis and the associated behaviour of the nuclear envelope, the cell surface membrane and the spindle
- identify stages of mitosis in photomicrographs, diagrams and microscope slides
- explain the importance of mitosis
- outline the role of telomeres
- outline the role of stem cells
- explain how uncontrolled cell division can lead to cancer.

BEFORE YOU START

During growth of multicellular organisms, the nucleus divides before the cell divides so that each new cell contains an identical nucleus. With a partner, discuss briefly why this is important. Then carry out the following exercise.

- Make a list of **four** structural features of the nucleus of eukaryotes.

- For each feature, outline its function (or an example of its function).

WHY GROW OLD?

Is it useful to prolong human life? The forerunners of modern chemists, the alchemists, thought so (Figure 5.1). They had two main aims:

- to discover how to transform 'base' metals (e.g. lead) into 'noble' metals (e.g. gold and silver)

- to discover the elixir of life, which would give eternal youth.

By the early 20th century, scientists had relegated these aims to impossible dreams. Now, however, humans are once again challenging the idea that the process of ageing is inevitable.

Why do organisms grow old and die? Interest in the process of ageing was rekindled with the discovery of telomeres in 1978. Telomeres are protective sequences of nucleotides found at the ends of chromosomes, which become shorter every time a cell divides. A gradual degeneration of the organism occurs, resulting in ageing.

Some cells are able to replenish their telomeres using the enzyme telomerase. It is thought that cancer cells can do this and so remain immortal (will never die). It may therefore be possible to prevent the ageing of normal cells by keeping the enzyme telomerase active.

Figure 5.1: A 19th-century oil painting showing an alchemist at work.

Question for discussion

If the ageing process could be slowed or prevented, this would raise some important moral and ethical issues. Try to identify and discuss some of these issues.

5.1 Growth and reproduction

All living organisms grow and reproduce. Living organisms are made of cells, so this means that cells must be able to grow and reproduce. Cells reproduce by dividing and passing on copies of their genes to 'daughter' cells. The process must be very precisely controlled so that no vital genetic information is lost.

In Chapter 6 you will learn how DNA can copy itself accurately. In this chapter you will learn how whole cells can do the same.

In Chapter 1 you saw that one of the most easily recognised structures in eukaryotic cells is the nucleus. The importance of the nucleus has been obvious ever since it was realised that the nucleus always divides before a cell divides. Each of the two daughter cells therefore contains its own nucleus. This is important because the nucleus controls the cell's activities. It does this because it contains the genetic material, DNA, which acts as a set of instructions, or code, for life (Chapter 6).

All the cells in the bodies of multicellular organisms are genetically identical, apart from the reproductive cells known as gametes. This is because they all come from one cell, the zygote. This is the cell formed when one gamete from your mother and one gamete from your father fused. When the zygote starts the process of growth, it divides into two cells with identical nuclei. This involves a type of nuclear division called mitosis. This process of nuclear division followed by cell division continues to be repeated in a cycle called the mitotic cell cycle to produce all the cells of your body, about 30 trillion in an average human.

You will study the process of mitosis and the mitotic cell cycle in this chapter.

5.2 Chromosomes

Just before a eukaryotic cell divides, a number of threadlike structures called chromosomes gradually become visible in the nucleus. They are easily seen, because they stain intensely with particular stains.

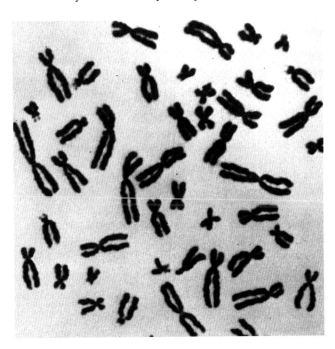

Figure 5.2: Photograph of a set of chromosomes in a human male, just before cell division. Each chromosome is composed of two chromatids held together at the centromere. Note the different sizes of the chromosomes and the different positions of the centromeres.

Before their function was known, they were called chromosomes because 'chromo' means coloured and 'somes' means bodies.

The number of chromosomes is characteristic of the species. For example, in human cells there are 46 chromosomes; in fruit fly cells there are only 8 chromosomes. Figure 5.2 is a photograph of a set of chromosomes in the nucleus of a human cell.

The structure of chromosomes

Before studying nuclear division, you need to understand a little about the structure of chromosomes. Figure 5.3 is a simplified diagram of the structure of a chromosome just before cell division.

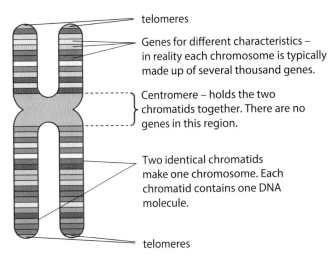

telomeres

Genes for different characteristics – in reality each chromosome is typically made up of several thousand genes.

Centromere – holds the two chromatids together. There are no genes in this region.

Two identical chromatids make one chromosome. Each chromatid contains one DNA molecule.

telomeres

Figure 5.3: Simplified diagram of the structure of a chromosome.

You can see that the chromosome at this stage is a double structure. It is made of two identical structures called **chromatids**, joined together. The two identical chromatids of one chromosome are known as sister chromatids. There are two chromatids because, during the period between nuclear divisions, known as interphase, each DNA molecule in a nucleus makes an identical copy of itself (Chapter 6, Section 6.3, DNA

> ### KEY WORD
>
> **chromatid:** one of two identical parts of a chromosome, held together by a centromere, formed during interphase by the replication of the DNA strand

replication). Each chromatid contains one of these DNA copies. The sister chromatids are held together by a narrow region called the centromere, to form a single chromosome. The centromere could be anywhere along the length of the chromosome, but the position is characteristic for a particular chromosome.

DNA is the molecule of inheritance and is made up of a series of genes. Each gene is one unit of inheritance. The two DNA molecules, one in each of the sister chromatids, are identical. This means the genes on the chromatids are also identical. The fact that there are two identical chromatids is the key to precise nuclear division. When cells divide, one chromatid goes into one daughter cell and one goes into the other daughter cell, making the daughter cells genetically identical.

So much information is stored in DNA that it needs to be a very long molecule. Although the molecule is only 2 nm wide, the total length of DNA in the 46 chromosomes of an adult human cell is about 1.8 metres. This has to be packed into a nucleus which is only 6 μm in diameter. This is the equivalent of trying to get an 18 km length of string into a ball which is only 6 cm in diameter! A precise scaffolding made of protein molecules prevents the DNA from getting tangled up into knots. The DNA is wound around the outside of these protein molecules. The combination of DNA and proteins is called chromatin. Chromosomes are made of chromatin. Chemically speaking, most of the proteins are basic (the opposite of acidic) and are of a type known as histones. Because they are basic, they can interact easily with DNA, which is acidic.

Chromosomes also possess two more features essential for successful nuclear division: centromeres and telomeres. Centromeres are visible in Figures 5.2 and 5.3. Telomeres are visible if chromosomes are stained appropriately (Figure 5.4). Centromeres are discussed with mitosis in Section 5.4 and the role of telomeres is discussed in Section 5.5.

Question

1   The primary structure of histone protein molecules is highly conserved during evolution, meaning there are extremely few changes over time (far fewer than is usual for proteins).

   a   State what is meant by the primary structure of a protein.

   b   What does the fact that histone molecules are highly conserved suggest about their functioning?

Histones help to package DNA into a smaller space. The packing ratio is a useful measure of the degree of compactness achieved. If a 10 cm long piece of string was packed into a 5 cm long tube, the packing ratio would be 2 (2 cm of string per cm of tube). The same idea can be applied to the problem of packing DNA into chromosomes.

   c   Chromosomes vary in length. A chromosome 10 μm long was estimated to contain 8.7 cm of DNA. What is the packing ratio of DNA in this chromosome? Show your working.

   d   There are 46 chromosomes in an adult human cell. Their average length is about 6 μm. The total length of DNA in the 46 chromosomes is about 1.8 m. What is the approximate overall packing ratio for DNA in human chromosomes? Show your working.

   e   Explain briefly how histone proteins contribute to reducing the packing ratio for DNA.

5.3 The cell cycle

Mitosis is nuclear division that produces two genetically identical daughter nuclei, each containing the same number of chromosomes as the parent nucleus. Mitosis is part of a precisely controlled process called the **cell cycle**.

The cell cycle is the sequence of events that takes place between one cell division and the next. It has three phases: interphase, nuclear division and cell division. These are shown in Figure 5.5.

During interphase, the cell grows to its normal size after cell division and carries out its normal functions. At some point during interphase, a signal may be received that the cell should divide again. If this happens, the DNA in the nucleus replicates so that each chromosome consists of two identical chromatids. This phase of the cell cycle is called the S phase – S stands for synthesis (of DNA). This is a relatively short phase. The gap after cell division and before the S phase is called the

> ### KEY WORDS
>
> **mitosis:** the division of a nucleus into two so that the two daughter cells have exactly the same number and type of chromosomes as the parent cell
>
> **cell cycle:** the sequence of events that takes place from one cell division until the next; it is made up of interphase, mitosis and cytokinesis

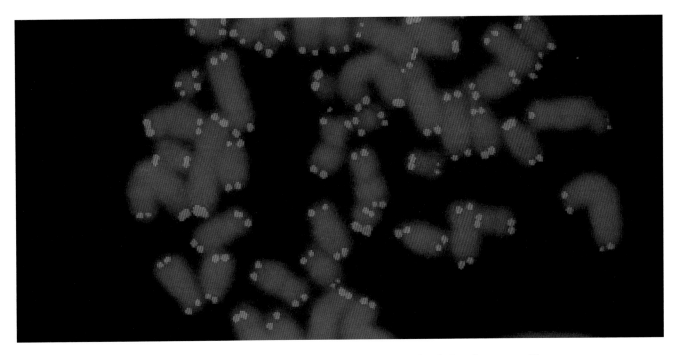

Figure 5.4: Fluorescent staining of human chromosome telomeres as seen with a light microscope. Chromosomes appear blue and telomeres appear pink (×4000).

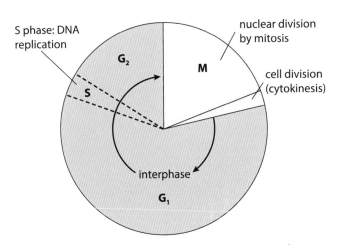

Figure 5.5: The mitotic cell cycle. DNA replication takes place during interphase, the period between cell division and the next nuclear division: **S** = synthesis (of DNA); **G** = gap; **M** = mitosis.

G_1 phase (G for gap). The gap after the S phase and before cell division is called the G_2 phase. Interphase therefore consists of G_1, S and G_2. During G_1, cells make the RNA, enzymes and other proteins needed for growth. At the end of G_1, the cell becomes committed to dividing or not dividing.

During G_2, the cell continues to grow and the new DNA that was made during the S phase is checked. Any errors are usually repaired. Preparations are also made to begin the process of division. For example, there is a sharp increase in production of the protein tubulin which is needed to make microtubules for the mitotic spindle.

Nuclear division follows interphase. Nuclear division is referred to as the M phase (M for mitosis). Growth stops temporarily during mitosis. After the M phase, when the nucleus has divided into two, the whole cell divides to create two genetically identical cells. In animal cells, cell division involves constriction of the cytoplasm between the two new nuclei, a process called cytokinesis. In plant cells, it involves the formation of a new cell wall between the two new nuclei.

The length of the cell cycle is very variable, depending on environmental conditions and cell type. On average, root tip cells of onions divide once every 20 hours; epithelial cells in the human intestine every 10 hours.

5.4 Mitosis

The process of mitosis is best described by annotated diagrams as shown in Figure 5.6. Although in reality the process is continuous, it is usual to divide it into four main stages for convenience, like four snapshots from a film. The four stages are called prophase, metaphase, anaphase and telophase.

Most nuclei contain many chromosomes, but the diagrams in Figure 5.6 show a cell containing only four chromosomes for convenience. Colours are used to show whether the chromosomes are from the female or male parent. An animal cell is used as an example. Note that during late prophase the nuclear envelope 'disappears'. In fact, it breaks up into small vesicles which cannot be seen with a light microscope. It reassembles during telophase, as shown in Figure 5.6. As a result, diagrams of metaphase and anaphase do not show the nuclear envelope. At the end of telophase, after the nucleus has divided, the cell divides by constriction of the cytoplasm, a process called cytokinesis. As the cell changes shape, the surface area of the cell increases as the two new cells form, so new cell surface membrane has to be made.

The behaviour of chromosomes in plant cells is identical to that in animal cells. However, plant cells differ in two ways:

* plant cells do not contain centrosomes

* after nuclear division of a plant cell, a new cell wall must form between the daughter nuclei.

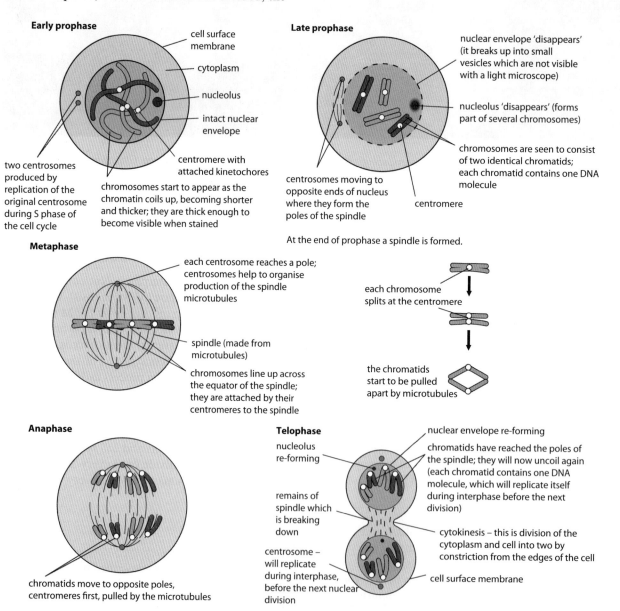

Figure 5.6: Mitosis and cytokinesis in an animal cell.

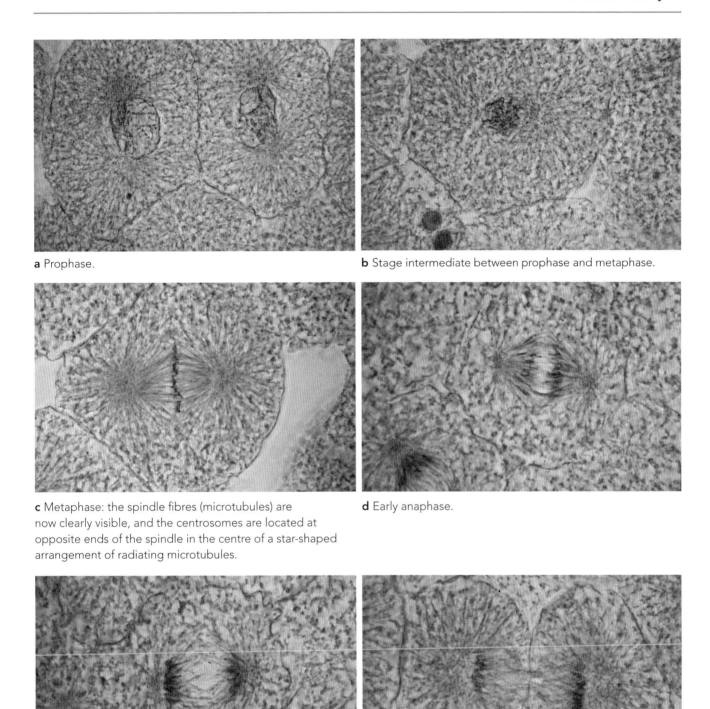

a Prophase.

b Stage intermediate between prophase and metaphase.

c Metaphase: the spindle fibres (microtubules) are now clearly visible, and the centrosomes are located at opposite ends of the spindle in the centre of a star-shaped arrangement of radiating microtubules.

d Early anaphase.

e Anaphase.

f Telophase and cell division (cytokinesis).

Figure 5.7: Stages of mitosis and cell division in an animal cell (whitefish) (×900). Chromosomes are stained darkly.

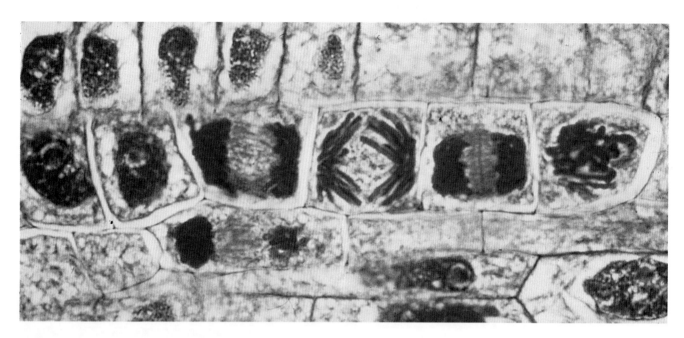

Figure 5.8: Longitudinal section (LS) of onion root tip showing stages of mitosis and cell division typical of plant cells (×400). Try to identify the stages based on information given in Figure 5.7.

It is the behaviour of the chromosomes, though, that is of particular interest. Figure 5.7 (animal) and Figure 5.8 (plant) show photographs of mitosis as seen with a light microscope.

Centrosomes, centrioles and centromeres

Centrosomes are located at the poles of the spindle, one at each pole. (The poles are the two ends of the spindle. The spindle gets its name from the fact that it is similar in shape to some spindles used in spinning – Sleeping Beauty pricked her finger on a spindle in the well-known fairy tale.) As noted in Chapter 1, the centrosome is an organelle found in animal cells that acts as a microtubule organising centre (MTOC). Centrosomes are responsible for making the spindle, which is made of microtubules. The spindle is needed for separation of the chromatids. Each centrosome consists of a pair of centrioles surrounded by a large number of proteins. It is these proteins that control production of the microtubules, not the centrioles. Plant mitosis occurs without centrosomes.

The centromere holds the chromatids together (see Figures 5.2 and 5.3), but is also involved in the separation of chromatids during mitosis. During mitosis the centromere is the site of attachment of spindle microtubules. Each metaphase chromosome has two **kinetochores** at its centromere, one on each chromatid (Figure 5.9).

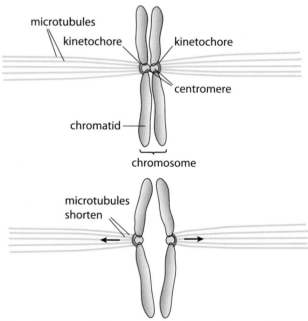

Figure 5.9: Role of the centromere, kinetochores and microtubules during mitosis

KEY WORD

kinetochore: a protein structure found at the centromere of a chromatid to which microtubules attach during nuclear division

The kinetochores are made of protein molecules which connect the centromere to the spindle microtubules. Bundles of microtubules called spindle fibres extend from the kinetochores to the poles of the spindle during mitosis. Construction of kinetochores begins before nuclear division starts (during the S phase of the cell cycle) and they are lost again afterwards.

The microtubules attached to the kinetochore pull the kinetochore towards the pole of the spindle. The rest of the chromatid drags behind, giving the characteristic > or < shape of chromatids during anaphase (Figures 5.6–5.8). The pulling action is achieved by shortening of the microtubules, both from the pole end and from the kinetochore end.

Question

2   How can the microtubules be shortened? (Refer back to Chapter 1.)

Importance of mitosis

Growth of multicellular organisms

The two daughter cells formed after mitosis have the same number of chromosomes as the parent cell and are genetically identical (that is, they are clones). This allows growth of multicellular organisms from unicellular zygotes. Growth may occur over the entire body, as in animals, or be confined to certain regions, as in the meristems (growing points) of plants.

Replacement of damaged or dead cells and repair of tissues by cell replacement

This is possible using mitosis followed by cell division. Cells are constantly dying and being replaced by identical cells. In the human body, for example, cell replacement is particularly rapid in the skin and in the lining of the gut. Some animals are able to regenerate whole parts of the body; for example, starfish can regenerate new arms.

Asexual reproduction

Mitosis is the basis of **asexual reproduction**, the production of new individuals of a species by a single parent organism. The offspring are genetically identical to the parents. Asexual reproduction can take many forms.

> **KEY WORD**
>
> **asexual reproduction**: the production of new individuals of a species by a single parent organism

For a unicellular organism such as *Amoeba*, cell division inevitably results in reproduction. For multicellular organisms, new individuals may be produced which bud off from the parent in various ways (Figure 5.10). Budding is particularly common in plants. It is most commonly a form of vegetative propagation in which a bud on part of the stem simply grows a new plant. The new plant eventually becomes detached from the parent and lives independently. The bud may be part of the stem of an overwintering structure such as a bulb or tuber. The ability to generate whole organisms from single cells or small groups of cells is important in biotechnology and genetic engineering, and it is the basis of cloning.

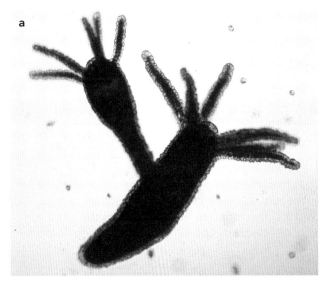

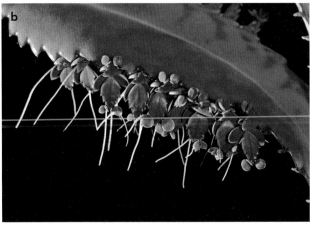

Figure 5.10: a Asexual reproduction by budding in *Hydra* (×60). *Hydra* lives in fresh water, catching its prey with the aid of its tentacles. The bud growing from its side is genetically identical to the parent and will eventually break free and live independently. **b** Asexual reproduction in *Kalanchoe pinnata*. The plant produces genetically identical new individuals along the edges of its leaves.

Immune response

The cloning of B- and T-lymphocytes during the immune response is dependent on mitosis (Chapter 11, Section 11.2, Cells of the immune system).

Questions

3   Outline how mitosis allows asexual reproduction to take place.

4   Human cells contain 46 chromosomes. In the mitotic cell cycle of a human cell:

   a   how many chromatids are present as the cell enters mitosis?

   b   how many DNA molecules are present?

   c   how many kinetochores are present?

d   how many chromatids are present in the nucleus of each daughter cell after mitosis and cell division?

e   how many chromatids are present in the nucleus of a cell after replication of DNA?

5   Draw a simple diagram of a cell which contains only one pair of chromosomes:

   a   at metaphase of mitosis

   b   at anaphase of mitosis.

6   State **two** functions of centromeres during nuclear division.

7   Thin sections of adult mouse liver were prepared and the cells stained to show up the chromosomes. In a sample of 75 000 cells examined, 9 were found to be in the process of mitosis. Calculate the length of the cell cycle in days in mouse liver cells, assuming that mitosis lasts one hour.

PRACTICAL ACTIVITY 5.1

Investigating mitosis using a root tip squash

Growth in plants is confined to regions known as meristems. A convenient example to study is the root tip meristem. This lies just behind the protective root cap. In this meristem there is a zone of cell division containing small cells in the process of mitosis.

You may be able to study commercially prepared permanent slides of root tips. You can also make your own temporary slides. Cutting thin sections of plant material is tricky, but this is not needed if the squash technique is used. This involves staining the root tip, then gently squashing it. This spreads the cells out into a thin sheet in which individual dividing cells can be clearly seen.

Procedure

The root tips of garlic, onion, broad bean and sunflower provide suitable material. Bulbs or seeds can be grown suspended by a pin over water for a period of a week or two. The tips of the roots (about 1 cm) are removed and placed in a suitable stain such as warm, acidified acetic orcein. This stains chromosomes a deep purple. The stained root tip can be squashed into a sheet of cells on a glass slide, using a blunt instrument such as the end of the handle of a mounted needle.

You should be able to see and draw cells similar to those shown in Figure 5.8 (but note that Figure 5.8 shows a longitudinal section of a root tip, not a squash). You could also use Figure 5.8 to make some annotated drawings of the different stages of mitosis.

(See Practical Investigation 5.1 in the Practical Workbook for additional information.)

5.5 The role of telomeres

You have seen that DNA is replicated (copied) during the S phase of the cell cycle. The copying enzyme cannot run to the end of a strand of DNA and complete the replication – it stops a little short of the end. (It is not possible to understand the reason for this without a detailed knowledge of replication.) If part of the DNA is not copied, that piece of information is lost. At each subsequent division, another small section of information from the end of the DNA strand would be lost. Eventually, the loss of vital genes would result in cell death.

The main function of **telomeres** is to ensure that the ends of the molecule are included in the replication and not left out when DNA is replicated. Telomeres are found at the ends of chromosomes (see Figure 5.11 and also Figure 5.4). They have been compared with the plastic tips on the ends of shoe laces. Telomeres are made of DNA with short base sequences that are repeated many times ('multiple repeat sequences').

Telomeres work by making the DNA a bit longer. They have no useful information, but allow the copying enzyme to complete copying all the meaningful DNA. As long as extra bases are added to the telomere during each cell cycle to replace those that are not copied, no vital information will be lost from the non-telomere DNA and the cell will be able to continue dividing successfully. The enzyme that performs the role of adding bases to telomeres is called telomerase. The main function of telomeres is therefore to prevent the loss of genes during cell division and to allow continued replication of a cell.

Some cells do not 'top up' their telomeres at each division. These tend to be fully differentiated (specialised) cells. With each division, their telomeres get a little shorter until the vital DNA is no longer protected and the cell dies. This could be one of the mechanisms of ageing, by which humans grow old and die. This, of course, suggests that by somehow preventing the loss of telomeres scientists might be able to slow down or even prevent the process of ageing (see 'Why grow old?' at the beginning of the chapter).

5.6 The role of stem cells

A **stem cell** is a cell that can divide an unlimited number of times (by mitosis). When it divides, each new cell has the potential to remain a stem cell or to develop (differentiate) into a specialised cell such as a blood cell or a muscle cell.

The power of a stem cell to produce different types of cell is variable and is referred to as its potency. Stem cells that can produce any type of cell are described as totipotent. The zygote formed by the fusion of a sperm with an egg at fertilisation is totipotent, as are all the cells up to the 16-cell stage of development in humans. After that, some cells become specialised to form the placenta, while others lose this ability but can form all the cells that will lead to the development of the embryo and later the adult. These embryonic stem cells are described as pluripotent.

As tissues, organs and systems develop, cells become more and more specialised. There are more than 200 different types of cell in an adult human body.

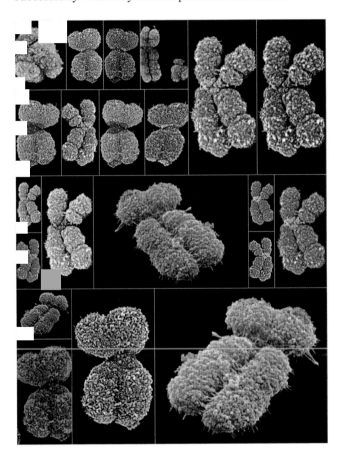

Figure 5.11: Coloured scanning electron micrographs of human chromosomes showing the location of telomeres at the ends of the chromosomes. Chromatids and centromeres are also clearly visible. Telomeres contain short repeated sequences of DNA. As cells replicate and age, the telomeres gradually get shorter. Stem cells are an exception.

KEY WORDS

telomere: repetitive sequence of DNA at the end of a chromosome that protects genes from the chromosome shortening that happens at each cell division

stem cell: a relatively unspecialised cell that retains the ability to divide an unlimited number of times, and which has the potential to become a specialised cell (such as a blood cell or muscle cell)

Question

8 As a result of mitosis, all 200+ different types of cell contain the same set of genes as the zygote. Genes control the activities of cells. What does this suggest about the mechanism by which cells become different?

The more 'committed' cells become to particular roles, the more they lose the ability to divide until, in the adult, most cells do not divide. However, for growth and repair it is essential that small populations of stem cells remain which can produce new cells. Adult stem cells have already lost some of the potency associated with embryonic stem cells and are no longer pluripotent. They are only able to produce a few types of cell and may be described as multipotent. For example, the stem cells found in bone marrow are of this type. They can replicate any number of times, but can produce only blood cells, such as red blood cells, monocytes, neutrophils and lymphocytes. Mature blood cells have a relatively short lifespan, so the existence of these stem cells is essential. For example, around 250 billion red blood cells and 20 billion white blood cells are lost and must be replaced each day.

In the adult, stem cells are found throughout the body – for example, in the bone marrow, skin, gut, heart and brain. Research into stem cells has opened up some exciting medical applications. Stem cell therapy is the introduction of new adult stem cells into damaged tissue to treat disease or injury. Bone marrow transplantation is an example of this therapy that has progressed beyond the experimental stage into routine medical practice. It is used to treat blood and bone marrow diseases, and blood cancers such as leukaemia. In the future, it is hoped to be able to treat conditions such as diabetes, muscle and nerve damage, and brain disorders such as Parkinson's and Huntington's diseases. Experiments with growing new tissues, or even organs, from isolated stem cells in the laboratory have also been conducted.

5.7 Cancers

In high-income countries, cancers cause roughly one in four deaths. Globally, cancers account for about one in six deaths (9.6 million people in 2018). This makes cancers second only to cardiovascular disease as a cause of death. There are more than 200 different forms of cancer, and the medical profession no longer thinks of cancers as a single disease.

Cancers illustrate the importance of controlling cell division precisely, because cancers are a result of uncontrolled mitosis. Cancerous cells divide repeatedly and form a tumour, which is an irregular mass of cells. Figure 5.12 shows a tumour in the lung of a patient who died of lung cancer compared to a healthy lung (from a patient who died from some other cause). Worldwide, lung cancer kills more people than any other cancer. Cancer cells usually show abnormal changes in shape (Figure 5.13).

Cancers start when changes occur in the genes that control cell division. A change in any gene is called a **mutation**. The term for a mutated gene that causes cancer is an *oncogene*, from the Greek word 'onkos' meaning bulk or mass. Mutations causing cancer can be inherited but most of the mutations that cause cancers occur over the course of the lifetime of an individual. Mutations are not unusual events, and most of the time they do not lead to cancer. Most mutated cells are affected in some way that results in their early death or their destruction by the body's immune system. Most cells can be replaced, so mutation usually has no harmful effect on the body. Unfortunately, cancer cells manage to escape both cell death and destruction so, although the mutation may originally occur in only one cell, it is passed on to all that cell's descendants. By the time it is detected, a typical tumour usually contains about a billion cancer cells. Any agent, such as asbestos, that causes cancer is called a **carcinogen** and is described as carcinogenic.

Although you do not need to know about different types of tumour, you may be interested to know that not all tumours are cancerous. Some tumours do not spread from their site of origin – these are known as

> ### KEY WORDS
>
> **cancers:** a group of diseases that result from a breakdown in the usual control mechanisms that regulate cell division; certain cells divide uncontrollably and form tumours, from which cells may break away and form secondary tumours in other areas of the body (metastasis)
>
> **mutation:** a random change in the base sequence (structure) of DNA (a gene mutation), or in the structure and/or number of chromosomes (a chromosome mutation)
>
> **carcinogen:** a substance or environmental factor that can cause cancer

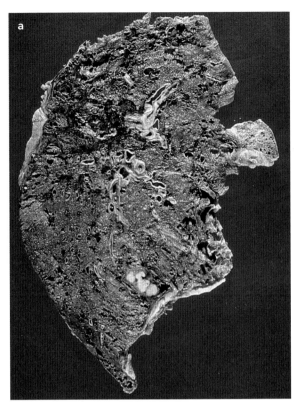

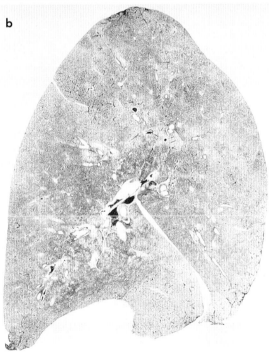

Figure 5.12: a Lung of a patient who died of lung cancer, showing rounded deposits of tumour (white area at bottom of picture). Black tarry deposits throughout the lung show the patient was a heavy smoker. **b** Section of a healthy human lung. No black tar deposits are visible.

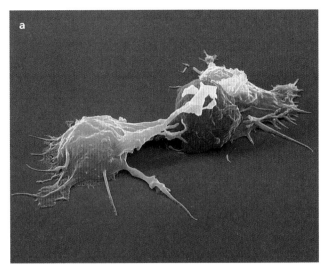

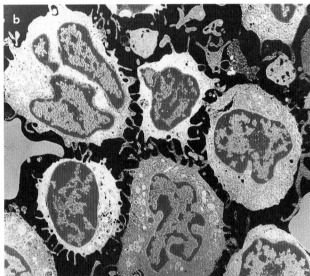

Figure 5.13: a False-colour scanning electron micrograph of a cancer cell (red) and white blood cells (orange and yellow). White blood cells gather at cancer sites as an immune response. They are beginning to flow around the cancer cell, which they will kill using toxic chemicals (×4500). **b** False-colour transmission electron micrograph (TEM) of abnormal white blood cells isolated from the blood of a person with hairy-cell leukaemia. The white blood cells are covered with characteristic hair-like cytoplasmic projections. Leukaemia is a disease in which the bone marrow and other blood-forming organs produce too many of certain types of white blood cells. These immature or abnormal cells suppress the normal production of white and red blood cells, and increase the patient's susceptibility to infection (×6400).

benign tumours; warts are a good example. It is only tumours that spread through the body, invading and destroying other tissues, that cause cancer. These are known as malignant tumours. Malignant tumours interfere with the normal functioning of the area where they have started to grow. They may block the intestines, lungs or blood vessels. Cells can break off and spread through the blood and lymphatic system to other parts of the body to form secondary growths. The spread of cancers in this way is called metastasis. It is the most dangerous characteristic of cancer because

it can be very hard to find the secondary cancers and remove them.

The steps involved in the development of cancer are shown in Figure 5.14.

Question

9   Research is being carried out into ways of inactivating the enzyme telomerase in cancer cells. Explain the reason for this.

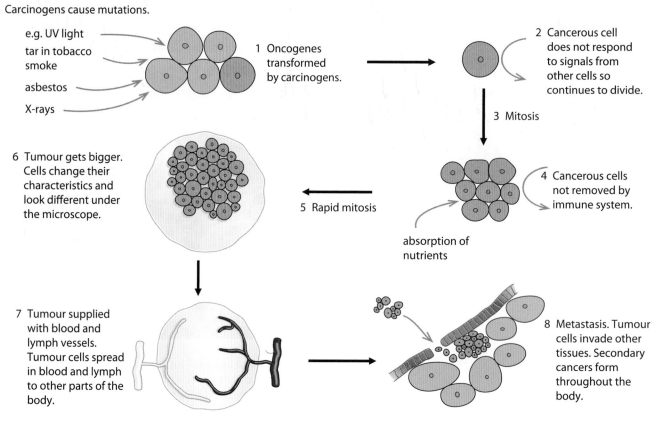

Figure 5.14: Stages in the development of cancer.

REFLECTION

Make a set of two pairs of chromosomes (one short pair, one long pair so they can easily be distinguished) as in Figure 5.6 late prophase. Use pipe-cleaners or Pop or Poppit beads which can be joined together to represent chromatids. Use two different colours if possible (to represent their origins from male and female parents), though this is not essential.

Use these model chromosomes to test your understanding of the stages of mitosis. It is useful to draw a large spindle on a large sheet of paper on which the model chromosomes can be moved appropriately.

CONTINUED

Personal reflection question

What did you enjoy about this activity? What parts of it did you particularly like or dislike? Why? Will it help you to remember the process of mitosis?

Final reflection

Discuss with a friend which, if any, parts of Chapter 5 you need to:

- read through again to make sure you really understand
- seek more guidance on, even after going over it again.

SUMMARY

Chromosomes are made of chromatin. Chromatin consists mainly of DNA wrapped around basic protein molecules called histones.
During nuclear division chromosomes become visible and are seen to consist of two chromatids held together by a centromere. Each chromatid contains one DNA molecule.
Growth of a multicellular organism is a result of cells dividing to produce genetically identical daughter cells.
During cell division, the nucleus divides first, followed by division of the whole cell. Division of a nucleus to produce two genetically identical nuclei is achieved by the process of mitosis. Mitosis is divided into four phases: prophase, metaphase, anaphase and telophase.
Mitosis is used in growth, repair, asexual reproduction and cloning of cells during an immune response.
The period from one cell division to the next is called the cell cycle. It has four phases: G_1 is the first growth phase after cell division; S phase is when the DNA replicates; G_2 is a second growth phase; M phase is when nuclear division takes place (followed by cell division).
The ends of chromosomes are capped with special regions of DNA known as telomeres. Telomeres are needed to prevent the loss of genes from the ends of chromosomes during replication of DNA.
Many specialised cells lose the ability to divide, but certain cells known as stem cells retain this ability. Stem cells are essential for growth from zygote to adult and for cell replacement and tissue repair in the adult.
The behaviour of chromosomes during mitosis can be observed in stained preparations of root tips, either in section or in squashes of whole root tips.
Cancers are tumours resulting from repeated and uncontrolled mitosis. They are thought to start as the result of mutation.

EXAM-STYLE QUESTIONS

1   During prophase of mitosis, chromosomes consist of two chromatids. At which stage of the cell cycle is the second chromatid made?

   A cytokinesis

   B G_1

   C G_2

   D S   [1]

2   Growth of cells and their division are balanced during the cell cycle. Which column shows the consequences that would follow from the two errors shown in the table?   [1]

Error	Consequence			
	A	B	C	D
speeding up the growth rate without speeding up the cell cycle	larger and larger cells	larger and larger cells	smaller and smaller cells	smaller and smaller cells
speeding up the cell cycle without speeding up the growth rate	larger and larger cells	smaller and smaller cells	larger and larger cells	smaller and smaller cells

3   A cell with four chromosomes undergoes a cell cycle including mitosis. Which diagram correctly shows the changes in chromatid number during interphase?

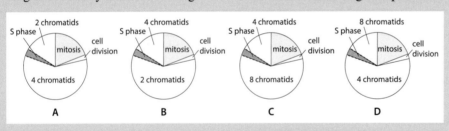

                                                                              [1]

4   Cell potency refers to the varying ability of stem cells to:

   A create more copies of themselves

   B differentiate into different cell types

   C produce different types of blood cells

   D stimulate growth of tissues   [1]

5   Stem cells found in bone marrow are:

   A multipotent

   B omnipotent

   C pluripotent

   D totipotent   [1]

6   Distinguish between the following terms: centrosome, centriole and centromere.   [6]

7 The diagram shows three cells (labelled **A**, **B** and **C**) from a root tip which has been stained to show chromosomes.

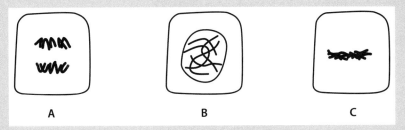

a   Identify the stage of mitosis shown by each cell. [3]

b   Describe what is happening at each stage. [3]

[Total: 6]

8 a   Diagram **A** shows a plant cell dividing by mitosis. Only two chromosomes are shown for simplicity.

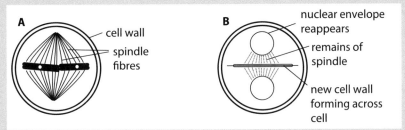

i   What stage of mitosis is shown in diagram **A**? [1]

ii   Draw prophase for the same cell. [1]

b   Diagram **B** shows the same cell at telophase. The cell is beginning to divide and a new cell wall is forming, spreading out from the middle of the cell. Copy the diagram and add drawings of the chromosomes as they would appear at this stage. [1]

c   Diagram **C** shows chromosomes in the nucleus of an animal cell.

Draw a diagram to show what the nucleus would look like in anaphase of mitosis. [3]

[Total: 6]

9 In Chapter 1 it was noted that microtubules are tiny tubes made by protein subunits joining together. The protein is called tubulin. Colchicine is a natural chemical which binds to tubulin molecules, preventing the formation of microtubules.

a Why should the binding of colchicine to tubulin molecules interfere with the formation of microtubules? [2]

b What structure or structures involved in mitosis are made of microtubules? [2]

c When cells treated with colchicine are observed, the dividing cells are all seen to be in the same stage of mitosis. Suggest, with reasons, the identity of this stage. [3]

[Total: 7]

10 Which of the following statements are true and which are false?

A Centrosomes are replicated before M phase of the cell cycle begins.

B Sister chromatids contain identical DNA.

C The microtubules attached to a given kinetochore extend to both poles of the spindle.

D Microtubule polymerisation and depolymerisation is a feature of the S phase of the cell cycle.

E Kinetochores are found in the centrosomes.

F Telomeres are the sites of attachment of microtubules during mitosis.

G Sister chromatids remain paired as they line up on the spindle at metaphase.

[1 mark each]

[Total: 7]

11 a Cancer has been described as a genetic disease. Explain why. [2]

b Define the term *carcinogen*. [1]

c The diagram on the next page shows the number of people suffering from cancer worldwide, separated into different age categories. It also shows changes between the years 1990 and 2016.

i State the age category in which cancer is most common. [1]

ii Suggest why this age group has the greatest number of cancer cases. [3]

COMMAND WORD

Define: give the precise meaning.

CONTINUED

iii **Comment** on the overall changes shown between 1990 and 2016. **[5]**

[Total: 12]

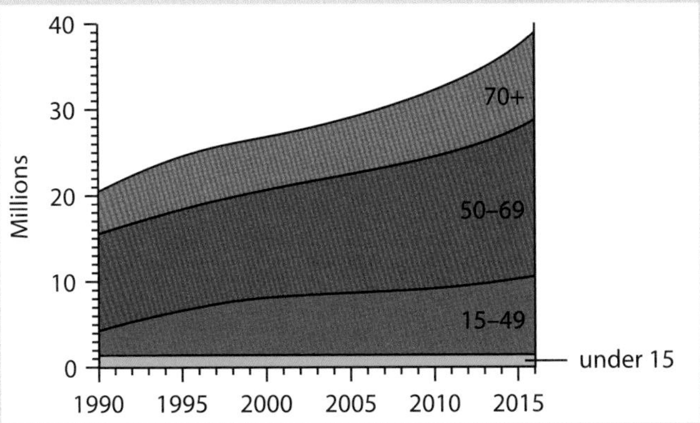

COMMAND WORD

Comment: give an informed opinion.

SELF-EVALUATION CHECKLIST

After studying this chapter, complete a table like this:

I can	See section...	Needs more work	Almost there	Ready to move on
describe the structure of chromosomes	5.2			
outline the cell cycle – the cycle of events by which body cells grow to a certain size and then divide into two	5.3			
describe the behaviour of chromosomes during mitosis and the associated behaviour of the nuclear envelope, the cell surface membrane and the spindle	5.4			
identify stages of mitosis in photomicrographs, diagrams and microscope slides	5.4			
explain the importance of mitosis	5.4			
outline the role of telomeres	5.5			
outline the role of stem cells	5.6			
explain how uncontrolled cell division can lead to cancer	5.7			

Chapter 6

Nucleic acids and protein synthesis

LEARNING INTENTIONS

In this chapter you will learn how to:

- describe the structure of nucleotides, including ATP
- describe briefly the structures of the bases found in DNA and RNA (adenine, guanine, thymine, cytosine and uracil)
- describe the structure of DNA
- describe the structure of RNA, using messenger RNA as an example
- describe the semi-conservative replication of DNA
- explain how the sequence of amino acids in a polypeptide is coded for by a sequence of nucleotides in DNA (a gene)
- describe the principle of the universal genetic code in which DNA bases code for amino acids plus start and stop signals
- explain the roles of DNA and RNA in the transcription and translation stages of protein synthesis
- explain the modification of RNA after transcription and the nature of introns and exons
- explain the nature, types and effects of gene mutations.

BEFORE YOU START

- Where is DNA found in cells?

- Why is DNA sometimes called 'the molecule of life'?

- It can be argued that the discovery of the structure of DNA is one of the most important discoveries ever made by humans. How would you justify this statement?

EDITING HUMANS

The nucleic acid DNA controls growth and development, but it sometimes carries mutations (changes) that can be harmful. There is a long list of human genetic diseases, such as cystic fibrosis and haemophilia, caused by 'faulty' DNA. A dream of the medical profession is to be able to safely correct the faults by the process of gene editing. Gene-editing tools act like molecular scissors, cutting DNA so that a new gene can be inserted or a problem gene can be removed.

Much research has been carried out on animals and tests have also been done on human cells in the laboratory, but in 2017 Brian Madeux, a 44 year old American, became the first human to receive treatment that acts inside the body. Brian suffers from Hunter syndrome. This rare inherited condition causes mucopolysaccharides to build up in body tissues and shortens life expectancy. It is caused by lack of a lysosomal enzyme. The new treatment consisted of introducing into the blood system billions of harmless virus particles which were thereby circulated to vital organs. The viruses carried the DNA for a gene-editing tool and also carried copies of the correct gene. Other sufferers of the syndrome have now received similar treatment and some have begun to show signs of improvement. The technique is still being developed.

Scientists in China currently lead the world in gene-editing techniques. Large-scale trials are underway tackling diseases such as cancer and HIV. The gene-editing tool most commonly used, and used by the Chinese, is known as CRISPR-Cas9. This was invented in 2013 by the American scientist Jennifer Doudna (Figure 6.1).

Figure 6.1: Jennifer Doudna, inventor of the gene editing tool CRISPR-Cas9 which has revolutionised the speed and cost of editing genes.

Despite optimism about future progress, there are strong ethical and moral issues. In 2018 the UK's Nuffield Council on Bioethics agreed that changing the DNA of a human embryo could be 'morally permissible' if it were in the child's best interests, but work on human embryos is still illegal in the UK and many other countries. There are fears about the safety of the treatment as well as issues such as the fact that changes to DNA are permanent, and any long-term effects, which could be passed on to future generations, are unknown.

Question for discussion

Discuss the moral and ethical issues relating to gene editing in human embryos.

6.1 The molecule of life

If you wanted to design a molecule that could act as the genetic material in living things, it would have to have two key features:

- the ability to store information – the information needed is a set of instructions for controlling the behaviour of cells

- the ability to copy itself accurately – whenever a cell divides it must pass on exact copies of the 'genetic molecule' to each of its daughter cells so no information is lost.

Until the mid 1940s, biologists assumed that such a molecule must be a protein. Only proteins were thought to be complex enough to be able to carry the huge number of instructions which would be necessary to make such a complicated structure as a living organism. But during the 1940s and 1950s, evidence came to light that proved beyond doubt that the genetic molecule was not a protein at all, but DNA.

6.2 The structure of DNA and RNA

DNA stands for deoxyribonucleic acid, and RNA stands for ribonucleic acid. As you saw in Chapter 2, DNA and RNA are macromolecules (giant molecules). Together they are known as nucleic acids because they were originally found in the nucleus. Proteins and polysaccharides are also macromolecules. You also saw in Chapter 2 that macromolecules are polymers, made up of many similar, smaller molecules (monomers) joined together to form a long chain. The monomers from which DNA and RNA molecules are made are **nucleotides**. DNA and RNA are therefore **polynucleotides**.

> ### KEY WORDS
>
> **nucleotide:** a molecule consisting of a nitrogen-containing base, a pentose sugar and a phosphate group
>
> **polynucleotide:** a chain of nucleotides joined together by phosphodiester bonds

Nucleotides

Nucleotides are made up of three smaller components. These are:

- a nitrogen-containing base

- a pentose sugar

- a phosphate group.

Figure 6.2 shows the structure of a nucleotide and how its three components fit together.

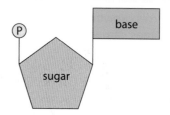

Figure 6.2: Structure of a nucleotide. A nucleotide is made of a nitrogen-containing base, a pentose sugar and a phosphate group P.

Nitrogen-containing base

There are four different nitrogen-containing bases found in DNA and four in RNA. In DNA the bases are: adenine, guanine, thymine and cytosine. In RNA thymine is replaced by a similar base called uracil. The bases are often referred to by their first letters: A, G, T, C and U.

Two of the bases, adenine and guanine, are related to the chemical purine and are referred to as purines. The other three bases, thymine, cytosine and uracil, are related to the chemical pyrimidine and are referred to as pyrimidines. Purine has two rings in its structure; pyrimidine has one ring.

Pentose sugar

You saw in Chapter 2 that sugars with five carbon atoms are called pentoses. Two pentoses are found in nucleic acids, ribose and deoxyribose.

A nucleic acid containing ribose is called a ribonucleic acid (RNA). One containing deoxyribose is called a deoxyribonucleic acid (DNA). As the name suggests, deoxyribose is almost the same as ribose except that it has one fewer oxygen atoms in its molecule.

Phosphate group

The phosphate group gives nucleic acids their acid nature.

Question

1   Look at the structure of the nucleotide in Figure 6.2. By identifying the sugar and the base with labels in each case, draw a nucleotide that could be found:

   a   only in DNA

   b   only in RNA.

The structure of ATP

Although ATP (adenosine triphosphate) is not part of DNA or RNA, you will look at its structure here because it is also a nucleotide.

The structure of ATP is shown in Figure 6.3. Its three components are adenine, ribose and phosphate. Adenine plus ribose forms a sugar–base called adenosine. Adenosine can be combined with one, two or three phosphate groups to give, in turn, adenosine monophosphate (AMP), adenosine diphosphate (ADP) or adenosine triphosphate (ATP).

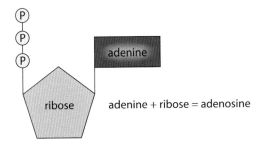

Figure 6.3: Structure of ATP, adenosine triphosphate.

Do not confuse adenine with adenosine, which is part of the name of ATP (adenosine triphosphate); adenosine is adenine with a sugar joined to it. And do not confuse thymine with thiamine; thiamine is a vitamin.

Dinucleotides and polynucleotides

Two nucleotides can be joined together by a condensation reaction (the same type of reaction used to join one amino acid to another, or one sugar to another).

Question

2   Name the bond formed when:

   a   two amino acids join by condensation

   b   two sugars join by condensation.

The molecule formed by joining two nucleotides is called a **dinucleotide** (Figure 6.4a). The bond formed is called a **phosphodiester bond**. The term *diester* is used because the phosphate group involved now has two ester bonds, one to each of the sugars it is connected to. The process can be repeated up to several million times to make a polynucleotide which has the form of a long, unbranching strand of nucleotides as shown in Figure 6.4b. The sugars and phosphates are linked by the phosphodiester bonds to form a backbone from which the bases stick out sideways at right angles to the backbone.

> **KEY WORDS**
>
> **dinucleotide:** two nucleotides joined together by a phosphodiester bond
>
> **phosphodiester bond:** a bond joining two nucleotides together; there are two ester bonds, one from the shared phosphate group to each of the sugars either side of it

The structure of DNA

By the 1950s the strucure of polynucleotides as shown in Figure 6.4b was known, but this structure did not explain how DNA could store information or copy itself. A race was under way to solve this problem by learning more about the structure of DNA. The race was won in 1953 when James Watson and Francis Crick, working in Cambridge, England, published a model structure for DNA that turned out to be correct. According to James Watson, it was too pretty not to be true.

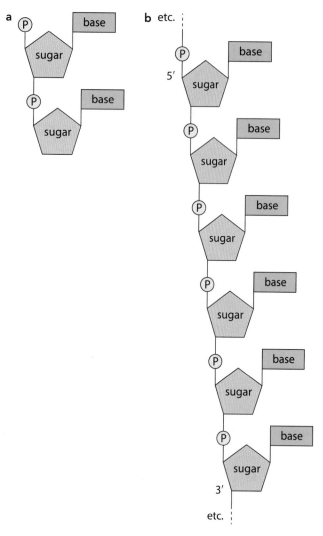

Figure 6.4: a Structure of a dinucleotide; **b** structure of a polynucleotide.

Question

3 The evidence used by Watson and Crick in building a model of DNA included data from an American chemist, Erwin Chargaff. Some of the relevant data are shown in Table 6.1. Can you spot a simple pattern in the base ratios?

The key to Watson and Crick's success was trying to make models of DNA using all the available evidence. Apart from Chargaff's data (see Question 3, Table 6.1), another vital piece of evidence came from X-ray diffraction photographs of DNA produced by Rosalind Franklin. Franklin worked at King's College in London (Figure 6.5) and her photographs suggested that DNA had a helical structure.

By playing with models, Watson and Crick eventually came up with the idea of the molecule having two polynucleotide chains, not one. The two chains could be held together by hydrogen bonding between the bases of the two chains. The model showed that the only way this could be done would be to twist each of the two strands into a helical shape – a double helix – and to run the strands in opposite directions. A sketch of this is shown in Figure 6.6.

Features of the DNA molecule

A model of DNA is shown in Figure 6.7a. A diagram of part of the molecule is shown in Figure 6.7b and Figure 6.8. The 5′ (say: five-prime) and 3′ (say: three-prime) on Figure 6.8 refer to carbon atoms 5 and 3 of the sugar. (See Chapter 2 for the numbering of carbon atoms in a sugar.) The two ends of a DNA strand are called the 5′ end and the 3′ end. At the 5′ end is phosphate and at the 3′ end is sugar.

Source of DNA	% Adenine	% Guanine	% Thymine	% Cytosine
human (mammal)	30.9	19.9	29.4	19.8
chicken (bird)	28.8	20.5	29.2	21.5
salmon (fish)	29.7	20.8	29.1	20.4
locust (insect)	29.3	20.5	29.3	20.7
wheat (plant)	27.3	22.7	27.1	22.8
E. coli (bacterium)	24.7	26.0	23.6	25.7
phage X174 (virus)	24.6	24.1	32.7	18.5

Table 6.1: Relative amounts of the four bases in different organisms. The numbers in each row add up to 100; each number is the percentage of that base in the DNA of the stated organism.

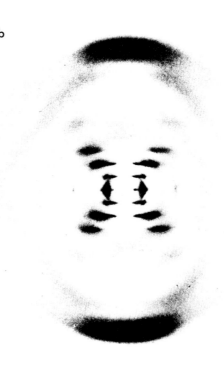

Figure 6.5: a Rosalind Franklin, whose X-ray diffraction images of DNA gave important clues to its structure; **b** X-ray diffraction photograph of a fibre of DNA.

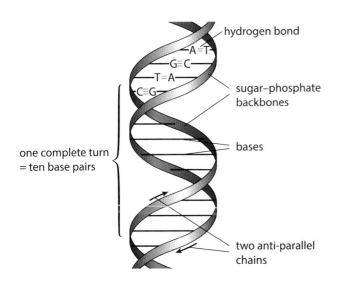

Figure 6.6: A sketch of the DNA double helix. The bases A, G, T and C are only shown in part of the molecule.

The DNA molecule has the following features:

- It is made of two polynucleotide chains.
- Each chain is a right-handed helix.

- The two chains coil around each other to form a double helix.

- The chains run in opposite directions – they are said to be antiparallel.

- Each chain has a sugar-phosphate backbone with bases projecting at right angles.

- The bases in one chain are attracted to the bases of the other chain by hydrogen bonding between the bases. This holds the chains together.

- Because of the way they fit together, like jigsaw pieces, adenine (A) always pairs with thymine (T) and guanine (G) always pairs with cytosine (C) (**complementary base pairing**). (This explains Chargaff's data – see Question 3.)

> **KEY WORD**
>
> **complementary base pairing:** the hydrogen bonding of A with T or U and of C with G in nucleic acids

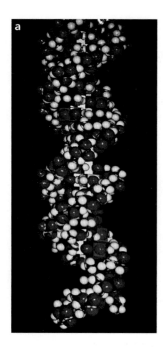

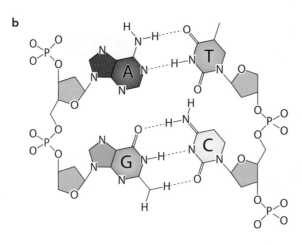

Figure 6.7: a A space-filling model of DNA. **b** A–T, G–C base pairs showing how neatly the bases fit together with hydrogen bonding. Note two hydrogen bonds between A and T, and three hydrogen bonds between G and C.

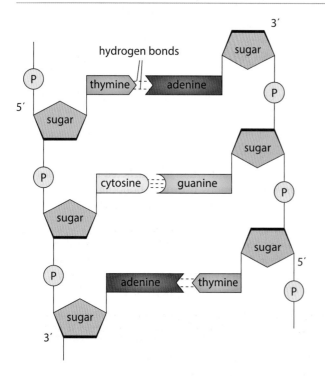

Figure 6.8: Part of a DNA molecule. Two polynucleotides, running in opposite directions, are held together by hydrogen bonds between the bases. A links with T by two hydrogen bonds; C links with G by three hydrogen bonds. This is complementary base pairing.

- A links with T by two hydrogen bonds; G links with C by three hydrogen bonds.

- Adenine and guanine are purines; thymine and cytosine are pyrimidines. A purine always pairs with a pyrimidine.

- Purines are two rings wide and pyrimidines are one ring wide; the distance between the two backbones is therefore constant and always three rings wide.

- A complete turn of the double helix takes place every 10 base pairs.

Because A must pair with T and G with C, the sequence of bases in one strand determines the sequence of bases in the other strand. The two strands are said to be complementary.

Watson and Crick realised immediately how this structure explained how DNA stores information and how it copies itself.

The information is the sequence of bases – represented by the four letters, A, G, T and C, in any order along the whole molecule. Any sequence is possible within one strand, but the other strand must be complementary. The *sequence* acts as a coded message.

The molecule can copy itself (replicate) accurately by 'unzipping' down the middle. This is relatively easy because the two strands are only held together by weak hydrogen bonds. Each half can then make a complementary copy of itself. Thus, two identical molecules of DNA are produced.

The structure of RNA

Unlike DNA, an RNA molecule is a single polynucleotide strand. Later in the chapter you will consider protein synthesis (Section 6.5). This involves three types of RNA, namely messenger RNA (mRNA), transfer RNA (tRNA) and ribosomal RNA (rRNA). Transfer RNA and rRNA fold up into complex structures, but mRNA remains as an unfolded strand.

6.3 DNA replication

Watson and Crick were quick to realise how DNA could replicate – copy itself. Scientists now know in detail how this process occurs and that it takes place during the S phase of the cell cycle (Chapter 5, Section 5.3, The cell cycle).

Replication is controlled by enzymes. It starts by the unwinding (separation) of the two strands of DNA by the breaking of the hydrogen bonds that normally hold the two strands together. This is the 'unzipping' mentioned earlier. The enzyme **DNA polymerase** is then used for the copying process. A molecule of DNA polymerase attaches to each of the single strands. It adds one new nucleotide at a time, which is held by hydrogen bonding to the strand being copied.

DNA polymerase can only copy in the 5' to 3' direction along each strand. This creates a problem. If you look at Figure 6.9, you can see that the top parent strand is being copied in the same direction as the unwinding process. The DNA polymerase simply follows the unwinding process, copying the DNA as it is unwound. The new strand being formed is called the **leading strand**. In contrast to the top parent strand, for the bottom parent strand the 5' to 3' direction of copying is in the opposite direction to the unwinding. This means that the DNA polymerase has to copy an unwound piece of DNA and then go back and copy the next piece of unwound DNA. It has to keep repeating this process. The result is a series of short fragments of copied DNA

(Figure 6.9). These are called Okazaki fragments after the biochemist who discovered them. In this case, the new strand being formed is called the **lagging strand**.

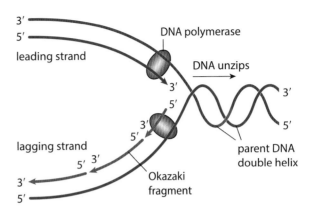

Figure 6.9: Diagram of DNA replication. The lagging strand can only be made in short fragments as the DNA unwinds.

Another enzyme called **DNA ligase** finishes the process. Its job is to connect all the new nucleotides with covalent bonds. Before this they are only holding on to the parent strand with hydrogen bonds between complementary bases. DNA ligase connects neighbouring nucleotides with phosphodiester bonds to form the sugar-phosphate backbone of the new DNA molecule. The Okazaki fragments are connected in the same way at the same time. Figure 6.10 shows you some more details of replication, including base pairing.

> ## KEY WORDS
>
> **DNA polymerase:** an enzyme that copies DNA; it runs along the separated DNA strands lining up one complementary nucleotide at a time ready for joining by DNA ligase
>
> **leading strand:** during DNA replication, the parent strand that runs in the 3' to 5' direction is copied to produce the leading strand
>
> **lagging strand:** during DNA replication, the parent strand that runs in the 5' to 3' direction is copied to produce the lagging strand
>
> **DNA ligase:** an enzyme that catalyses the joining together of two nucleotides with covalent phosphodiester bonds during DNA replication

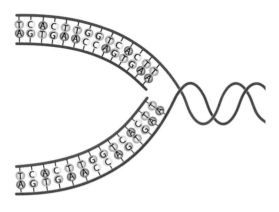

Figure 6.10: DNA replication showing base pairing.

Semi-conservative replication

The method of copying DNA described is called **semi-conservative replication**. This is because each time a DNA molecule is replicated, half the original molecule is kept (conserved) in each of the new molecules. If replication was conservative, the parent DNA molecule would remain at the end of the process and the new DNA molecule would have two newly made strands.

KEY WORDS

semi-conservative replication: the method by which a DNA molecule is copied to form two identical molecules, each containing one strand from the original molecule and one newly synthesised strand

gene: a length of DNA that codes for a particular polypeptide or protein

---

Questions

4 a Make a list of the different molecules needed for DNA replication to take place.

b State what each of these molecules does.

c In what part of a eukaryotic cell does DNA replication take place?

5 Figure 6.11 is a diagram of a DNA molecule. One strand is red and one is blue.

Using the colours red and blue as appropriate, draw the two daughter molecules resulting from replication of this parent molecule:

a if replication is semi-conservative

b if replication is conservative.

Figure 6.11: DNA – what happens in replication?

6.4 The genetic code

As soon as the race to find the structure of DNA had been won, a new race started – a race to break the genetic code. Watson and Crick had realised that the DNA code was the sequence of bases in the DNA. Scientists also realised that the sequence of bases must be the code for the sequences of amino acids in proteins.

Here is the logic that led to this realisation. The activities of a cell are controlled by enzymes. Enzymes are proteins. Each type of protein has a unique sequence of amino acids which determines its structure and, hence, its function. Therefore, if you control the sequences of amino acids in the cell's proteins, you control the enzymes that are made and thus you control the cell. The sequence of bases in the DNA of a cell is the code for all the proteins of that cell and organism. The code for one polypeptide is called a gene.

There are 20 common amino acids found in proteins, but only four different bases in DNA to code for them. It cannot be the case that each base codes for one amino acid. Even if two bases were the code for one amino acid, there would be only 16 possible codes: AA, AG, AT, AC, GA, GG, GT, GC, TA, TG, TT, TC, CA, CG, CT, CC. This is still not enough codes for 20 amino acids.

If the code were a triplet code, there would be 64 possible combinations of three bases. Although this seemed too many to code for only 20 amino acids, it *is* the case because most of the amino acids have more than one code. The nature of the code was gradually broken and, by 1964, it was possible to look up any code in a table like Appendix 2.

Question

6 Can you work out the general formula for predicting how many amino acids can be coded for by four bases?

Features of the genetic code

The DNA genetic code has the following features.

- It is a three-letter code, otherwise known as a triplet code. This means that three bases make the code for one amino acid. For example, TAC is the DNA code for the amino acid methionine (abbreviated to 'Met' in the DNA table in Appendix 2)

- The code is universal. This means that each triplet codes for the same amino acid in all living things.

- The code has punctuations. Three of the DNA triplets act as 'full stops' in the message (see Appendix 2). During protein synthesis, these stop triplets mark the end of a gene. Some triplets can act as 'start signals', where the process of copying a gene starts. An example is TAC, the DNA code for methionine.

- The code is described as redundant or degenerate. This means that some amino acids are coded for by more than one triplet. The DNA table in Appendix 2, for example, shows that the amino acid cysteine is coded for by ACA and ACG. The third letter can be A or G – note that A and G are both purines, so the code is ACpurine.

Question

7   What does the fact that the code is universal suggest?

6.5 Protein synthesis

'DNA makes RNA and RNA makes protein'

As you have seen, DNA is a code for proteins. However, DNA is found in the nucleus and proteins are made at ribosomes, which are found in the cytoplasm outside the nucleus. There must therefore be some way of getting information from the DNA to the ribosomes. The solution to this problem is to use an intermediate molecule that carries the information. In 1961, two French scientists, Jacob and Monod, suggested this molecule would be RNA and they described it as 'messenger RNA', or mRNA for short. They were correct and they neatly summarised the process of protein synthesis in the phrase 'DNA makes RNA and RNA makes protein.' This shows that protein synthesis is a two-stage process. The process by which DNA makes mRNA is called **transcription**. The process by which the message carried by mRNA is decoded to make protein is called **translation**.

KEY WORDS

transcription: copying the genetic information in a molecule of DNA into a complementary strand of mRNA; a single strand of the DNA is used as a template (this is called the template or transcribed strand) – the enzyme responsible is RNA polymerase

translation: a stage in protein synthesis during which a sequence of nucleotides in a molecule of messenger RNA (mRNA) is converted (translated) into a corresponding sequence of amino acids in a polypeptide chain; it takes place at ribosomes

Transcription

Transcription takes place in the nucleus (where the DNA is). The enzyme responsible for transcription is called RNA polymerase. RNA polymerase attaches to the beginning of the gene to be copied. It starts to unwind the DNA of the gene and another enzyme breaks the hydrogen bonds between the two strands ('unzips' the DNA). This creates two single-stranded sections of DNA with the normal double helical structure either side of the unzipped section (Figure 6.12). Only one of the exposed strands is copied. This is called the template strand or transcribed strand. The triplets in template strands are those shown in the DNA table in Appendix 2. The other strand is called the non-transcribed strand. A complementary RNA copy of the template strand is made. Remember that RNA contains the base uracil instead of thymine. This means that the bases A, G, T and C in DNA are copied in the RNA as U, C, A and G respectively.

Figure 6.12 shows a short length of a DNA molecule coding for four amino acids.

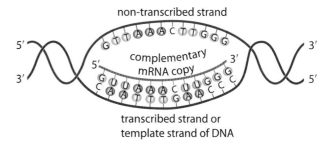

Figure 6.12: Transcription. A length of DNA coding for four amino acids with a complementary mRNA copy.

Since the code is a three-letter code (triplet code), each set of three bases codes for one amino acid. The lower strand is the template (transcribed) strand. Reading from the left-hand end of the template strand, the first triplet shown is CAA. This is the DNA code for the amino acid valine (Val in the DNA table in Appendix 2).

Question

8 Using the DNA table in Appendix 2, what are the next three amino acids coded for by the DNA (after the CAA triplet) in Figure 6.12? The full names of the amino acids are given in Appendix 1.

mRNA is made from nucleotides found free in solution in the nucleus. As the RNA polymerase moves along the gene, the nucleotides approach and hydrogen bond with their complementary nucleotides in the DNA. As each nucleotide arrives RNA polymerase joins it to the growing mRNA molecule with a phosphodiester bond. Once phosphodiester bonds are formed, hydrogen bonding of that part of the mRNA to the DNA is no longer necessary and the hydrogen bonds are broken – see the 'growing mRNA molecule' label on Figure 6.13). Eventually a stop message will be reached. At this point the RNA polymerase releases the completed mRNA. The RNA polymerase leaves the DNA. Figure 6.13 shows the process of transcription.

The mRNA leaves the nucleus through a nuclear pore in the nuclear envelope. It is a single polynucleotide chain which, unlike the two RNAs involved in translation (tRNA and rRNA – see Figure 6.13) does not fold up into a more complex structure after it has been made.

Modifying the mRNA

In eukaryotes, the mRNA is modified (partly changed) before it leaves the nucleus. The original molecule, before it is modified, is called the primary transcript. The process of modification is called RNA processing. One step in this processing is RNA splicing. Splicing is the removal of sections of the primary transcript. The sections removed are called introns (as are the sections of DNA that code for them). The nucleotide sequences that remain after the introns are removed are called exons. They have to be joined together after removal of the introns.

There is still debate about the functions of introns. Scientists know that introns in the DNA can help to regulate the activity of genes. They also know that in some cases a given primary transcript molecule can be spliced in different ways ('alternative splicing'). This results in different mRNAs being made from the original primary transcript. These different mRNAs will produce different proteins when translated. It means that one gene can code for several different proteins or different forms of the same protein.

Translation

Translation is the process by which a sequence of bases in mRNA is converted into a sequence of amino acids in a polypeptide. As you have seen, the sequence of bases in an mRNA molecule is a complementary copy of a gene coding for a particular polypeptide. The DNA code is read three bases at a time. In DNA, a set of three bases coding for an amino acid is called a triplet. In mRNA a complementary set of three bases coding for

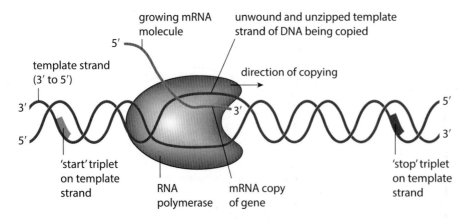

Figure 6.13: Transcription.

an amino acid is called a **codon**. Appendix 2 shows the DNA triplets and the corresponding complementary mRNA codons.

Translation is such a complex process that a special organelle, the ribosome, is used to bring all the molecules involved together. In Chapter 1 you saw that ribosomes have a small and a large subunit and that they are made of rRNA and protein.

Translation involves a third type of RNA called transfer RNA (tRNA). The job of tRNA is to transfer amino acids to the ribosome. Figure 6.14 shows the structure of a tRNA molecule.

Animations of translation are available on the internet and help to develop understanding of the dynamic nature of the process.

Transfer RNA is where the actual translation from a base sequence to an amino acid takes place. Each amino acid has a different tRNA molecule to carry it. The amino acid is attached at one end of the molecule (Figure 6.14). At the other end of the molecule three projecting bases form an **anticodon**. This is complementary to the codon for the amino acid carried by that tRNA. Enzymes are responsible for making sure that each tRNA carries the correct amino acid.

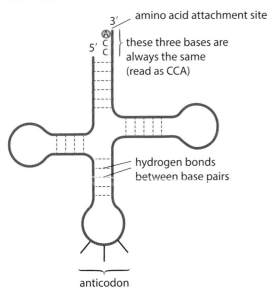

Figure 6.14: A tRNA molecule. The molecule is single-stranded, but folded back on itself, forming a clover-leaf shape. An amino acid attaches at one end of the molecule. At the other end is the anticodon that will recognise the codon for the amino acid carried by the tRNA.

When an mRNA molecule arrives at a ribosome, it enters a groove between the two subunits of the ribosome where it is held ready to receive the first tRNA molecule. The sequence of events that follows is described in Figure 6.15.

The tRNA with the anticodon complementary to the first codon on the mRNA enters the ribosome and attaches to the codon by hydrogen bonding. Two tRNA molecules can fit into the ribosome at any one time, so the second tRNA enters the ribosome. This has the anticodon which matches the second codon in the mRNA. The amino acids carried by the two tRNAs are now side by side and a peptide bond is formed between them. The first tRNA now leaves, the ribosome 'clicks' forward one codon and the third tRNA enters, carrying the next amino acid. This process is repeated until a stop codon is reached.

The completed polypeptide leaves the ribosome and folds up into its secondary and tertiary structures. The folding may be assisted and controlled by special proteins. The polypeptide may enter the endoplasmic reticulum (ER) for transport to another part of the cell.

6.6 Gene mutations

A mutation is a random change in the structure of DNA (a **gene mutation**) or in the structure and/or number of chromosomes (a **chromosome mutation**).

A gene mutation is a change in the nucleotide sequence and therefore in the base sequence of DNA. Mutation occurs when a wrong nucleotide is inserted. This may be because of errors during DNA replication (copying errors) or because damage is done to the DNA by factors such as radiation or carcinogens.

KEY WORDS

codon: sequence of three bases on an mRNA molecule that codes for a specific amino acid or for a stop signal

anticodon: sequence of three unpaired bases on a tRNA molecule that binds with a codon on mRNA

gene mutation: a change in the base sequence in part of a DNA molecule

chromosome mutation: a random and unpredictable change in the structure or number of chromosomes in a cell

---

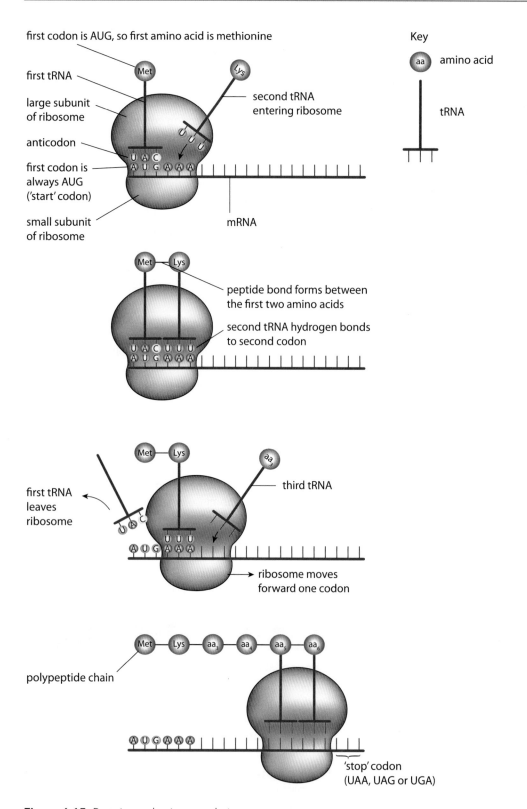

Figure 6.15: Protein synthesis – translation.

A change in the base sequence of the DNA may cause a change in the amino acid sequence of the polypeptide coded for by the mutated DNA. Something that can cause mutations is called a mutagen. X-ray radiation is an example of a mutagen.

Gene mutations are random events and are likely to be harmful. This is because making a random change in the amino acid sequence (primary structure) of a polypeptide is likely to be harmful. Such a change may affect the way the polypeptide folds up and in turn change the tertiary structure of the protein. This could affect the functioning of the polypeptide. You saw in Chapter 5 (Section 5.7, Cancers) how mutations in certain genes can cause cancers.

Types of mutation

There are different types of gene mutation. Three of the most common are:

- substitution – a base is replaced by a different base
- deletion – a base is lost and not replaced
- insertion – a base is added.

Substitution

The template sequence of bases in Figure 6.12 can be used as an example to show the effect of a substitution. The sequence is shown in the first line of bases below. Vertical lines indicate how the code is read, three bases at a time. The amino acid sequence coded for is also shown. The second line of bases shows a substitution. In the second triplet, the middle T has been substituted by A (shown in bold). The resulting change in the amino acid sequence coded for is shown.

CAA|TTT|GAA|CCC| valine | lysine | leucine | glycine

CAA|**TAT**|GAA|CCC| valine | isoleucine | leucine | glycine

The next base sequence shows how a substitution does not necessarily affect the sequence of amino acids coded for. In the second triplet, the third base, T, has been substituted by a C (shown in bold).

CAA|**TTC**|GAA|CCC| valine | lysine | leucine | glycine

You can see that this has had no effect on the amino acid sequence because lysine is coded for by both TTT and TTC. An amino acid being coded for by more than one triplet is an example of the fact that the genetic code is degenerate.

An example of substitution: sickle cell anaemia

An example of how significant a substitution can be is the genetic disorder sickle cell anaemia. It affects the protein haemoglobin.

Haemoglobin is the red pigment in red blood cells. It carries oxygen around the body. As you saw in Chapter 2 (Section 2.6, Proteins), a haemoglobin molecule is made up of four polypeptide chains. Each chain has one iron-containing haem group in the centre. Two of the polypeptide chains are called α (alpha) chains, and the other two β (beta) chains.

The gene which codes for the amino acid sequence in the β chains is not the same in everyone. In most people, the β chains begin with the amino acid sequence:

Val–His–Leu–Thr–Pro–Glu–Glu–Lys–

But in people with sickle cell anaemia, the base sequence CTT is replaced by CAT, and the amino acid sequence becomes:

Val–His–Leu–Thr–Pro–Val–Glu–Lys–

The mutation responsible is a substitution: the first T in the triplet has been substituted by A. In this case, the small difference in the amino acid sequence results in sickle cell anaemia. You can read more about sickle cell anaemia in Chapters 2 and 16.

Deletion and insertion

Deletions and insertions are much more likely to be serious than substitutions because they cause 'frame-shift mutations'.

KEY WORDS

frame-shift mutation: a type of gene mutation caused by insertion or deletion of one or more nucleotides, resulting in incorrect reading of the sequence of triplets in the genetic code due to a shift in the reading frame

The following base sequences show the effect of adding or deleting a base on how the code is read. A repeat sequence of TAG is chosen as an example because it makes the changes easier to see.

Normal code:

TAG|TAG|TAG|TAG|TAG|TAG|TAG|TAG|TAG| TAG|TAG|TAG|

Insert a base (shown in bold):

TAG|TAG|TAG|TAG|**C**TA|GTA|GTA|GTA|GTA| GTA|GTA|GTA|

Delete a base:

TAG|TAG|TAG|TAG|AGT|AGT|AGT|AGT|
AGT|AGT|AGT|

Note that for both insertion and deletion the whole of the rest of the code is altered. If you imagine a reading frame covering each triplet, the frame has been shifted by one base – hence the term *frame-shift mutation*. All the triplets from the mutation onwards are affected. Therefore, all the amino acids coded for will probably be incorrect, so the polypeptide or protein made as a result is likely to be non-functioning.

Questions

9 Copy Table 6.2. Use the table to summarise the differences between DNA and mRNA.

10 Draw a *simple* diagram, or use a flow diagram, to summarise the important stages in protein synthesis. Include the words:

> nucleus, nuclear pore, DNA, mRNA, transcription, translation, ribosome, amino acid, tRNA, amino acid-tRNA, polypeptide

Feature	DNA	messenger RNA
sugar present in structure		
bases used in structure		
number of strands		
overall structure		
location in cell		
function		

Table 6.2: Differences between DNA and mRNA.

REFLECTION

Scientists attending scientific conferences often make posters to illustrate and summarise their work. Posters need to have an attractive design and should attempt to make important points without overwhelming the viewer with too much information.

Design a poster to illustrate the process of protein synthesis. As part of the poster, you could choose a particular protein from Chapter 2 and explain its structure and why it is important.

Personal reflection question

How well do you think you communicated the science in your poster to your chosen audience? What improvements could you make to the poster given more time?

Final reflection

Discuss with a friend which, if any, parts of Chapter 6 you need to:

* read through again to make sure you really understand

* seek more guidance on, even after going over it again.

SUMMARY

DNA and RNA are polynucleotides, made up of long chains of nucleotides. A nucleotide contains a pentose sugar, a phosphate group and a nitrogen-containing base. In RNA, the sugar is ribose; in DNA, it is deoxyribose.
A DNA molecule consists of two polynucleotide chains, linked by hydrogen bonds between the bases. The overall structure is a double helix. In DNA there are four bases – adenine (A) always pairs with thymine (T), and guanine (G) always pairs with cytosine (C).
RNA has only one polynucleotide chain, although this may be twisted back on itself, as in tRNA. In RNA the base thymine is replaced by uracil.
Adenine and guanine are purines with a double ring structure and thymine, cytosine and uracil are pyrimidines with a single ring structure.
DNA molecules replicate during the S phase of interphase by semi-conservative replication. Each of the two new molecules formed contains one parent strand and one new strand.
The sequence of nucleotide bases in a DNA molecule codes for the sequence of amino acids in a polypeptide. Each amino acid is coded for by three bases. A length of DNA coding for one polypeptide is a gene.
Protein synthesis takes place in two stages, transcription and translation. During transcription, a complementary RNA copy of the base sequence of a gene is made. The RNA copy is called messenger RNA (mRNA). In mRNA each set of three bases coding for an amino acid is called a codon.
In eukaryotes, the mRNA molecule made during transcription, the primary transcript, is modified by the removal of non-coding sequences (introns) and the joining together of remaining coding sequences (exons) to form the final mRNA molecule used in translation.
During translation the mRNA moves to a ribosome in the cytoplasm. Transfer RNA (tRNA) molecules bring the appropriate amino acids to the ribosome. The ribosome moves along the mRNA molecule one codon at a time. The sequence of codons determines the sequence of amino acids joined together to form a polypeptide.
A change in the nucleotide sequence of DNA is a gene mutation. Various types of gene mutation can occur, including base substitution, insertion and deletion.

EXAM-STYLE QUESTIONS

1 What can be found in both DNA and messenger RNA (mRNA)?

  A double helix structure

  B sugar-phosphate chain

  C ribose

  D thymine   [1]

2 Which statement about base pairing in nucleic acids is not correct?

  A Adenine can pair with either thymine or uracil.

  B Guanine only pairs with cytosine.

  C Thymine can pair with either adenine or uracil.

  D Uracil only pairs with adenine.   [1]

3 How many different triplets can be coded for using four different bases?

  A $3 + 4$

  B 3×4

  C 3^4

  D 4^3 [1]

CONTINUED

4 Nucleic acids are made of chains of:

   A amino acids

   B bases

   C histones

   D nucleotides   [1]

5 Copy the drawing.

   Annotate the drawing to explain the replication of DNA.   [4]

6 Copy the table.

   The table shows all the mRNA codons for the amino acid leucine. Complete the
   table by entering, for each codon, the tRNA anticodon that would bind with it
   and the DNA triplet from which it was transcribed.

mRNA codon	tRNA anticodon	DNA triplet from which mRNA was transcribed
UUA		
UUG		
CUU		
CUC		
CUA		
CUG		

[12]

7 A gene mutation occurred in a person. The mutation occurred in a cell that
   produces gametes. The mutation resulted in a change in a DNA triplet from
   CTA to GTA. CTA codes for the amino acid aspartic acid. GTA codes for the
   amino acid histidine.

   a Name the type of mutation which resulted in the change from CTA to GTA. [1]

   b This type of mutation does not always result in a change in the amino acid
      coded for by the affected triplet. Explain why.   [2]

   c The mutation could be harmful. Explain why.   [3]

   d The mutation was more likely to be harmful because it took place in a
      gamete-producing cell. Suggest why.   [2]

   e Two other types of mutation are addition and deletion of bases.
      Suggest why the addition or deletion of three nucleotides in the DNA
      sequence of a gene often has less effect on the polypeptide coded for
      than the addition or deletion of a single nucleotide.   [4]

                                                          [Total: 12]

8 Copy the table.

Complete the table to distinguish between the processes of transcription and translation.

	Transcription	Translation
site in cell where it occurs		
molecule used as a template		
molecule produced		
component molecules (monomers) of molecule produced		
one other molecule that is essential for the process to occur		

[10]

9 The drawing shows two stages in the synthesis of a polypeptide. The polypeptide is one of the structures labelled.

a Identify **U**, **V**, **W**, **X** and **Y**. [5]

b The label **Z** shows where a chemical bond will be formed. Name the type of bond that will be formed. [1]

c Explain why the position of **V** has moved between the two stages shown. [3]

[Total: 9]

10 In the 1940s, Chargaff and his co-workers analysed the base composition of the DNA of various organisms. The relative numbers of the bases adenine (A), cytosine (C), guanine (G) and thymine (T) of three of these organisms are shown in the table.

Organism (tissue)	Relative numbers of bases			
	A	C	G	T
ox (spleen)	27.9	20.8	22.7	27.3
ox (thymus)	28.2	21.2	21.5	27.8
yeast	31.3	17.1	18.7	32.9
virus with single-stranded DNA	24.3	18.2	24.5	32.3

CONTINUED

Explain why:

a the relative numbers of each base in ox spleen and thymus are the same, within experimental error [1]

b the relative numbers of each base in yeast are different from those in ox spleen or thymus [1]

c the ratio of A to T, and of C to G, is equal to 1 in ox and yeast (within experimental error) [1]

d in the virus, the ratio of A to T, and of C to G, is not equal to 1. [1]

[Total: 4]

SELF-EVALUATION CHECKLIST

After studying this chapter, complete a table like this:

I can	See section...	Needs more work	Almost there	Ready to move on
describe the structure of nucleotides, including ATP	6.2			
describe briefly the structures of the bases found in DNA and RNA (adenine, guanine, thymine, cytosine and uracil)	6.2			
describe the structure of DNA	6.2			
describe the structure of RNA, using mRNA as an example	6.2			
describe the semi-conservative replication of DNA	6.3			
explain how the sequence of amino acids in a polypeptide is coded for by a sequence of nucleotides in DNA (a gene)	6.4			
describe the principle of the universal genetic code in which DNA bases code for amino acids and start and stop signals	6.4			
explain the roles of DNA and RNA in the transcription and translation stages of protein synthesis	6.5			
explain the modification of RNA after transcription and the nature of introns and exons	6.5			
explain the nature, types and effects of gene mutations	6.6			

> Chapter 7
Transport in plants

LEARNING INTENTIONS

In this chapter you will learn how to:

- outline the transport needs of plants and the fact that some mineral ions and organic compounds can be transported within plants dissolved in water
- draw, label and describe the overall structure of herbaceous dicotyledonous stems, roots and leaves using a light microscope
- draw the structure of the transport tissues xylem and phloem using the high-power lens of a light microscope
- explain the process of transpiration
- describe the adaptations of the leaves of xerophytic plants with the aid of annotated drawings
- explain how water moves across a leaf through the apoplast and symplast pathways
- relate the structure of xylem to its functions
- explain the movement of water up the xylem from root to leaf, including the roles of cohesion–tension and adhesion

CONTINUED

- describe the transport of water from the soil to the root xylem through the apoplast and symplast pathways
- relate the structure of phloem to its functions
- explain that assimilates dissolved in water, such as sucrose and amino acids, move through phloem sieve tubes from sources to sinks
- explain mass flow in phloem sieve tubes down a hydrostatic pressure gradient from source to sink
- explain how companion cells transfer assimilates to phloem sieve tubes.

BEFORE YOU START

In Chapter 4 you considered the effect of an increase in size on the surface area : volume ratio of a structure such as a cell.

- How does the surface area : volume ratio change with increasing size?

- How can the shape of a structure such as a leaf or a cell with microvilli affect the ratio?

- Bearing in mind your answers to these questions, try to explain why large multicellular organisms like plants and animals need transport systems.

- What features would you expect such transport systems to have (e.g. their structure and how they work)?

DOES GOLD GROW ON TREES?

Scientists studying how plants transport materials over large distances have found eucalyptus trees interesting for two reasons. First, eucalyptus trees can grow to great heights (only redwoods are taller). They are commonly over 60 metres in height, the tallest living example being 100.5 metres tall. Second, the leaves are concentrated at the top of the tree (Figure 7.1). The leaves have to supply food to the rest of the tree, including the extensive underground root system, and the roots have to supply water to the leaves. This means that any theory of how plants transport food and water has to explain how transport can occur over these very long distances through the tiny tubes of the transport system. Sugar, for example, has to move through tubes no wider than a fine human hair. Not easy!

Studying transport in eucalyptus trees recently provided an unexpected bonus. Scientists from Australia's national scientific agency, the CSIRO, discovered that the roots of eucalyptus trees growing over rocks that contain gold take up tiny quantities of gold and transport them throughout the plant. Gold is toxic to plant cells, but the trees get round this problem by depositing the gold in insoluble calcium oxalate crystals in the leaves and bark (Figure 7.2).

Figure 7.1: Leaves are concentrated at the top of a eucalyptus tree.

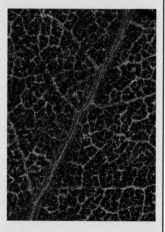

Figure 7.2: Particles of gold in a eucalyptus leaf show up as green spots in this image.

CONTINUED

The systematic sampling of eucalyptus leaves for gold opens up a new way of finding deposits of gold in the remote Australian outback. The fact that eucalyptus roots can penetrate as far as 40 metres underground in their search for water makes them very useful gold prospectors. It could save mining companies the expense of drilling in rugged terrain where exploration is difficult. It is likely that the method could also be applied to the search for other minerals such as copper and zinc.

Questions for discussion

There were once extensive forests of huge eucalyptus trees in Australia. Most of these have been logged (cut down) for timber. New trees have been planted for timber in plantations in some areas. Forests worldwide are declining.

- What factors, apart from logging for timber, are responsible?

- How should the remaining forested areas of the planet be managed?

7.1 The transport needs of plants

Animals generally get their food by eating it, but plants have to make their own organic food using photosynthesis; they can get minerals and water from the soil.

The main photosynthetic organs are the leaves. Leaves require light, so they tend to be found towards the top of the plant, especially in trees.

In order to obtain minerals and water, plants have extensive root systems below ground. The plant body therefore tends to spread out above ground to get light and to spread out below ground to get inorganic mineral ions and water.

Since the materials made by the leaves and the materials absorbed by the roots are needed by all the cells of the plant body, there must be a way of achieving long-distance transport. For example, sugars are produced in leaves, but glucose is needed by all parts of the plant, including the roots, for respiration and for making cellulose. An example of a mineral ion absorbed by roots that is needed by leaves is magnesium, which is needed to make chlorophyll (Chapter 13).

Question

1   The transport sugar made in leaves is the disaccharide, sucrose.

   a   Define a disaccharide (Chapter 2).

   b   What monosaccharides are used to make sucrose (Chapter 2)?

   c   Which isomer of glucose is used to make cellulose (Chapter 2)?

   d   Which isomer of glucose is used to make starch (Chapter 2)?

   e   Where in the plant would the process of making cellulose most be needed and why (Chapter 5)?

7.2 Vascular system: xylem and phloem

The fact that substances have to be moved around the plant body is why special long-distance transport systems have evolved in plants. The substances transported, such as mineral ions and organic compounds, dissolve in water to form solutions and these solutions are moved through specialised tubes. The tubes form a system called the **vascular system**. The term **vascular** refers to tubes or vessels. Plants contain a vascular system, but there are also vascular systems in many animals, such as the blood vascular system which carries the fluid blood, and the lymphatic system which carries the fluid lymph. In plants, the

KEY WORDS

vascular system: a system of fluid-filled tubes, vessels or spaces, most commonly used for long-distance transport in living organisms; examples are the blood vascular system in animals and the vascular system of xylem and phloem in plants

vascular: a term referring to tubes or vessels (from the Latin 'vascul', meaning vessel)

vascular system contains two tissues, **xylem** and **phloem**. Both contain specialised tubes for transporting fluids. The fluid is called sap (xylem sap or phloem sap). Xylem sap moves in tubes called xylem vessels. Phloem sap moves in tubes called sieve tubes. Xylem and phloem are together known as **vascular tissue**.

Xylem carries mainly water and inorganic ions (mineral salts) from roots to the parts above ground. Xylem sap can move in only one direction, from roots to the rest of the plant. Phloem sap carries substances made by photosynthesis from the leaves to other areas of the plant. It can also carry substances from storage organs to other parts of the plant. These might be underground. So, at any one time, the fluid in the phloem can be moving in different directions in different tubes of the phloem, up or down the plant.

In neither xylem nor phloem do fluids move as rapidly as blood does in a mammal, nor is there an obvious pump such as the heart.

7.3 Structure of stems, roots and leaves and the distribution of xylem and phloem

Stems, roots and leaves are the main organs involved in transport in plants.

The structure of stems, roots and leaves is most easily studied using prepared slides or photomicrographs of transverse sections (TS) of these organs. Drawing low-power plans and high-power detail of representative groups of cells as seen with a microscope is a useful way of understanding the structure of the organs and the distribution of xylem and phloem.

When making drawings from specimens under a microscope, you will need to follow the advice given in Practical Activity 7.1.

Dicotyledons

Flowering plants may be monocotyledons or **dicotyledons**. Each type has its own characteristics. For example, monocotyledonous plants, such as grasses, typically have long, narrow leaves. Dicotyledonous plants typically have leaves with wide blades and narrow stalks (petioles). The mechanisms of transport through both types of plant are the same, but there are differences in the distribution of xylem and phloem in their roots, stems and leaves.

> **Note:** Monocotyledons are extension content, and are not part of the syllabus.

KEY WORDS

xylem: a tissue containing tubes called vessels and other types of cell, responsible for the transport of water and mineral salts through a plant and for support

phloem: a tissue containing tubes called sieve tubes and other types of cell, responsible for the transport through the plant of organic solutes (assimilates) such as sucrose

vascular tissue: a tissue in plants consisting mainly of xylem and phloem but also containing sclerenchyma and parenchyma cells

dicotyledon: flowering plants can be classified as monocotyledons or dicotyledons; the seeds of dicotyledonous plants contain an embryo with two cotyledons (seed leaves) in their seeds and the adult plant typically has leaves with a blade (lamina) and a stalk (petiole)

PRACTICAL ACTIVITY 7.1

Biological drawing based on light microscopy

Help with biological drawing is also given in Chapter P1, Section P1.10, Drawings.

Equipment

You need the following equipment:

- Sharp pencil (HB or H) (do not use a pen or coloured pencils)

- Pencil sharpener
- Eraser
- Ruler (for label lines)
- Plain paper
- A hand lens may be useful

CONTINUED

Quality of your drawing

- Always use a sharp pencil.
- Use clear, continuous lines without any overlapping.
- *Do not* use shading.
- Use accurate proportions and observation – not a textbook version.
- Make the drawing large enough – if it is a whole organism, organ or a tissue, it should normally occupy more than half the available space on the page. Individual cells drawn at high power should be one to several centimetres in diameter.
- If you make a mistake, use a good eraser to rub out the lines completely.

Low-power drawing (see Figure 7.3)

- *Do not* draw individual cells.
- Draw all tissues completely enclosed by lines.
- Draw a correct interpretation of the distribution of tissues.
- A representative portion may be drawn (e.g. half a TS).

An example of a low-power plan drawing of a section through the stem of *Helianthus* is shown in Figure 7.3.

High-power drawing

- Draw only a few representative cells.
- Draw the cell wall of all plant cells.
- *Do not* draw the nucleus as a solid blob.

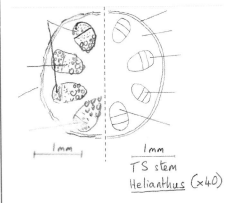

Figure 7.3: The right side of this low-power drawing shows examples of good technique, while the left side shows many of the errors you should avoid.

Quality of your labelling

- Always use a sharp pencil.
- Label all relevant structures. Also include a title, stating what the specimen is. If relevant, include a scale.
- Identify parts correctly.
- Use a ruler for label lines and scale line.
- Label lines should stop exactly at the structure being labelled; *do not* use arrowheads.
- Arrange label lines neatly and make sure they *do not* cross over each other.
- Labels should be written horizontally, as in this book. *Do not* write them at the same angle as the label lines.
- Annotate your drawing if necessary. 'Annotate' means provide short notes next to the labels in order to describe or explain features of biological interest.

Magnification

Magnification is how much bigger (or smaller) the drawing is compared with the specimen. You can calculate it as follows:

1 Measure between two suitable points of the drawing.

2 Measure between the same two points of the specimen. You may have to use an **eyepiece graticule** to do this (see Chapter 1, Section 1.4, Measuring size and calculating magnification).

3 Divide measurement 1 by measurement 2.

Scale line

A scale line is a line drawn below the drawing of the specimen which represents a certain length of the specimen. For example, if a specimen has been magnified 400 times, a scale line 40 mm long at the bottom of your drawing would represent a distance 400 times smaller than this on the specimen. 400 times smaller than 40 mm is 40/400, which is 0.4 mm or 400 μm. The scale line would therefore be labelled 400 μm.

CONTINUED

Measuring cells, tissues and organs

Using an eyepiece graticule and a **stage micrometer** will allow you to make measurements of cells, tissues and organs. It will help you to show tissues in their correct proportions. See Worked Example 1 for guidance on making measurements.

Question

2   Look at Figure 7.3. List the errors in drawing technique that you can spot in the left-hand half of the drawing.

(See Practical Investigation 6.1 in the Practical Workbook for additional information.)

Low-power plan diagrams

TSs of a typical dicotyledonous stem, root and leaf are shown in Figures 7.4–7.9. In each case, a photomicrograph from a prepared slide is shown, followed by a low-power labelled drawing of the same organ. Figure 7.10 is a diagram of a TS of a typical dicotyledonous stem. *The main tissues to concentrate on are the xylem and phloem (vascular tissue).* However, it is useful to know a little about other tissues as well because it will help you with drawing low-power plans and it becomes relevant later when you study the movement of substances through the plant.

- Phloem is usually stained green and has small cells. Xylem is usually stained red and usually contains a few large vessels.

- In stems and leaves, the xylem and phloem are found in structures called **vascular bundles** which also contain other types of cell. In roots, the xylem and phloem are found at the centre of the root.

- The epidermis is one cell thick and covers the outside of the plant.

- Most of the cells outside the vascular tissue are **parenchyma** cells. These have thin cell walls and vary in size. You may see nuclei in some of them. The outer region of stems and roots is known as the cortex and it is mainly made of parenchyma.

- Sometimes there are zones of cells like parenchyma with thicker walls (**collenchyma**) for more support. These tend to be found around the outside of stems just below the **epidermis** and in the midrib of leaves.

- The **endodermis** is relevant later when you study transport. It is one cell thick like the epidermis ('endo' means inside, so it is like an inside epidermis).

- Vascular bundles in stems have a cap of fibres (**sclerenchyma**) for extra strength in the stem. These are usually stained red like xylem because, like xylem, their walls contain the strengthening material **lignin**.

KEY WORDS

eyepiece graticule: small scale that is placed in a microscope eyepiece

stage micrometer: very small, accurately drawn scale of known dimensions, engraved on a microscope slide

vascular bundle: a strand of vascular tissue running longitudinally in a plant; within the bundle, the arrangement of tissues like xylem, phloem and sclerenchyma varies in different plants and organs

parenchyma: a basic plant tissue typically used as packing tissue between more specialised structures; it is metabolically active and may have a variety of functions such as food storage and support; parenchyma cells also play an important role in the movement of water and food products in the xylem and phloem

collenchyma: a modified form of parenchyma in which the corners of the cells have extra cellulose thickening, providing extra support, as in the midrib of leaves and at the corners of square stems; in three dimensions the tissue occurs in strands (as in celery petioles)

epidermis: the outer layer of cells covering the body of a plant or animal; in plants it is usually one cell thick and may be covered with a cuticle which provides additional protection against loss of water and disease

endodermis: the layer of cells surrounding the vascular tissue of plants; it is most clearly visible in roots

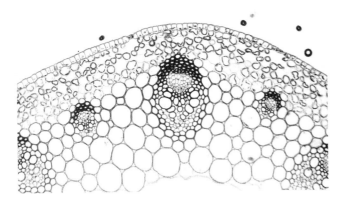

Figure 7.4: Light micrograph of part of a TS of a young *Ranunculus* (buttercup) stem (×60).

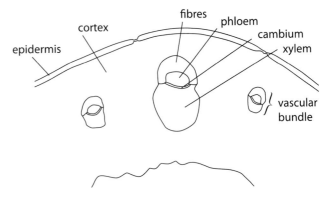

Figure 7.5: Low-power plan of the *Ranunculus* stem shown in Figure 7.4.

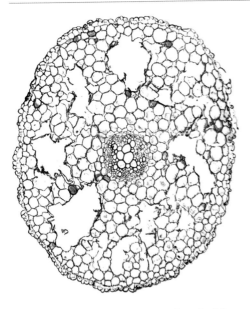

Figure 7.6: Light micrograph of a TS of *Ranunculus* (buttercup) root (×35).

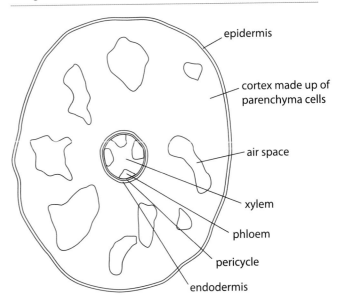

Figure 7.7: Low-power plan of the *Ranunculus* root shown in Figure 7.6.

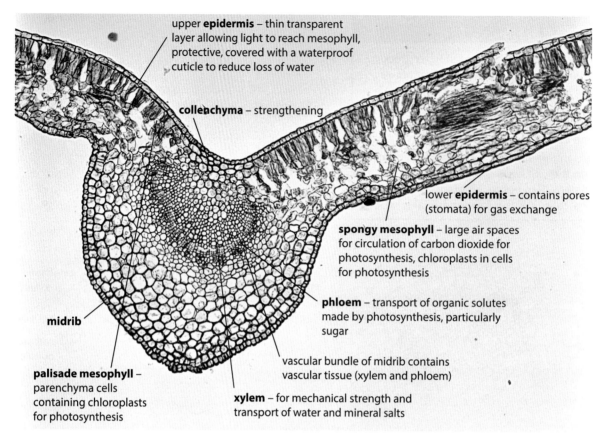

upper **epidermis** – thin transparent layer allowing light to reach mesophyll, protective, covered with a waterproof cuticle to reduce loss of water

collenchyma – strengthening

lower **epidermis** – contains pores (stomata) for gas exchange

spongy mesophyll – large air spaces for circulation of carbon dioxide for photosynthesis, chloroplasts in cells for photosynthesis

phloem – transport of organic solutes made by photosynthesis, particularly sugar

midrib

vascular bundle of midrib contains vascular tissue (xylem and phloem)

palisade mesophyll – parenchyma cells containing chloroplasts for photosynthesis

xylem – for mechanical strength and transport of water and mineral salts

Figure 7.8: TS through the midrib of a dicotyledonous leaf, *Ligustrum* (privet) (×50). Tissues are labelled in bold type with annotations.

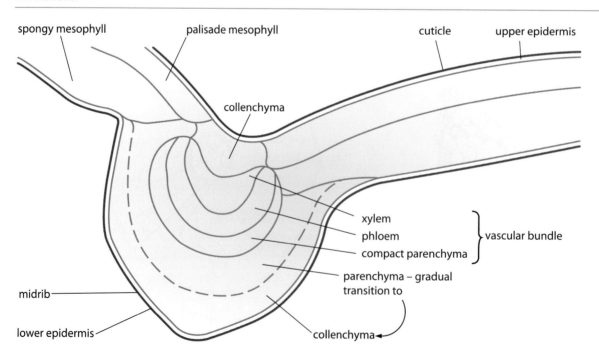

spongy mesophyll

palisade mesophyll

cuticle

upper epidermis

collenchyma

xylem

phloem

compact parenchyma

vascular bundle

parenchyma – gradual transition to

midrib

lower epidermis

collenchyma

Figure 7.9: A plan diagram of the TS through a privet leaf shown in Figure 7.8.

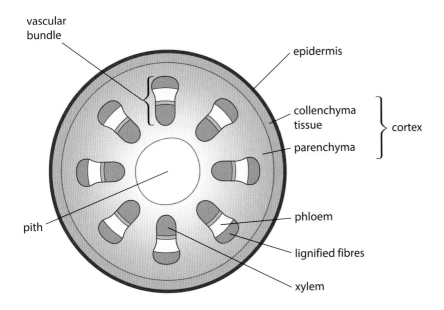

Figure 7.10: TS of a young sunflower (*Helianthus*) stem to show the distribution of tissues. The sunflower is a dicotyledonous plant.

High-power detail diagrams

When drawing cells at high power, remember the rules given in Practical Activity 7.1. The emphasis should be on drawing two or three representative cells of the selected tissue accurately, rather than trying to draw a lot of cells to make it look like the specimen on the slide or photomicrograph. High-power drawings of xylem and phloem seen in TS are shown in Figures 7.11 and 7.12.

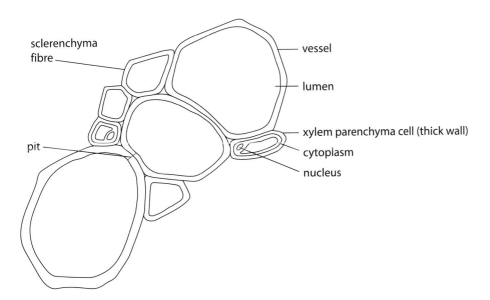

Figure 7.11: High-power drawing of xylem as seen in TS. Three large vessels are shown.

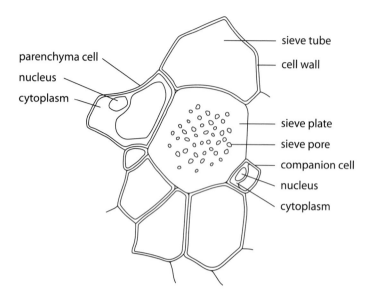

parenchyma cell
nucleus
cytoplasm
sieve tube
cell wall
sieve plate
sieve pore
companion cell
nucleus
cytoplasm

Figure 7.12: High-power drawing of phloem as seen in TS.

7.4 The transport of water

Figure 7.13 outlines the pathway taken by water as it is transported through a plant. In order to understand the transport mechanism, you need to understand that water always moves from a region of higher water potential to a region of lower water potential, as explained in Chapter 4 (Section 4.5, Movement of substances across membranes). The movement of water through the plant is driven by evaporation from the leaves.

The energy of the Sun causes water to evaporate from the leaves, a process called transpiration. This reduces the water potential in the leaves and sets up a water potential gradient throughout the plant. Water moves down this gradient from the soil into the plant. Water then moves across the root into the xylem tissue in the centre of the root. Once inside the xylem, the water moves upwards through the root to the stem and from there into the leaves.

Movement of water from leaf to atmosphere – transpiration

Figures 7.8, 7.9 and 7.14 show the structure of a dicotyledonous leaf. The cells inside the leaf (mesophyll cells) have many air spaces around them. The walls of the mesophyll cells are wet, and some of this water

evaporates into the air spaces (Figure 7.15), so the air inside the leaf is usually saturated with water vapour.

The air inside the leaf has direct contact with the air outside the leaf through small pores called stomata (singular: stoma). There is usually a water potential gradient between the air inside the leaf (higher water potential) and the air outside (lower water potential). Water vapour will diffuse out of the leaf down this gradient. This is transpiration. Stomata open during the day and close at night, so most transpiration takes place during the day.

KEY WORDS

transpiration: the loss of water vapour from a plant to its environment; it mostly takes place through the stomata in the leaves

mesophyll: the region of a leaf between the upper and lower epidermis; in dicotyledonous plants the mesophyll has an upper palisade layer and a lower mesophyll layer; the palisade mesophyll cells are column-shaped and form the main photosynthetic layer, whereas the spongy mesophyll has large air spaces between the cells for gas exchange

stoma (plural: stomata): a pore in the epidermis of a leaf, bounded by two guard cells and needed for efficient gas exchange

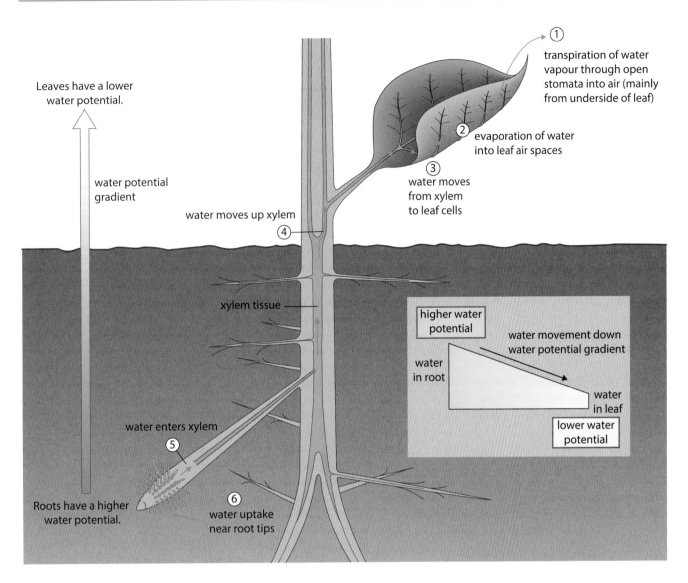

Figure 7.13: An overview of the movement of water through a plant. Water moves down a water potential gradient from the soil to the air. The process starts with loss of water vapour from the leaves and follows the sequence from **1** to **6** in the diagram.

Questions

3   Most stomata are usually found in the lower epidermis of leaves. Suggest why this is the case.

4   Suggest how the following factors may cause the rate of transpiration to increase:

   a   an increase in wind speed

   b   a rise in temperature.

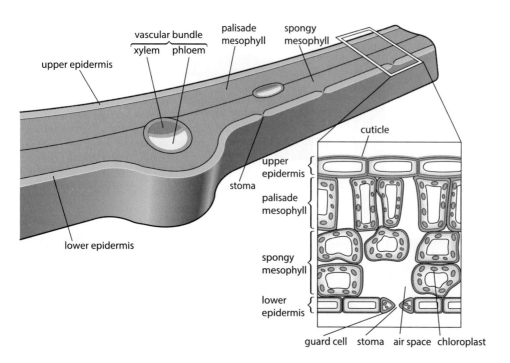

Figure 7.14: The structure of a dicotyledonous leaf. Water enters the leaf as liquid water in the xylem vessels and diffuses out as water vapour through the stomata.

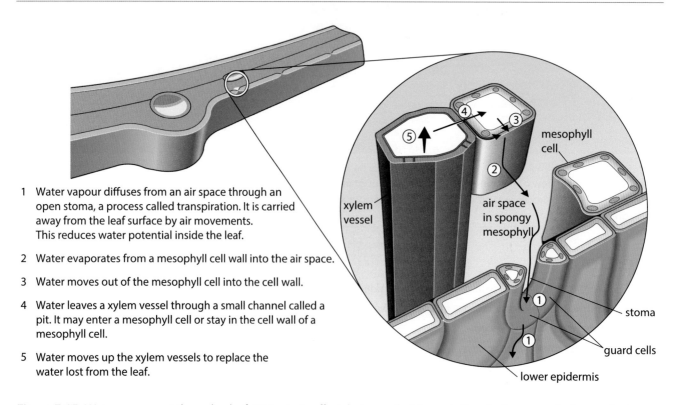

1 Water vapour diffuses from an air space through an open stoma, a process called transpiration. It is carried away from the leaf surface by air movements. This reduces water potential inside the leaf.

2 Water evaporates from a mesophyll cell wall into the air space.

3 Water moves out of the mesophyll cell into the cell wall.

4 Water leaves a xylem vessel through a small channel called a pit. It may enter a mesophyll cell or stay in the cell wall of a mesophyll cell.

5 Water moves up the xylem vessels to replace the water lost from the leaf.

Figure 7.15: Water movement through a leaf. Water is, in effect, being pulled through the plant as a result of transpiration.

Xerophytes

Xerophytes (xerophytic plants) are plants that live in places where water is in short supply. Many xerophytes have evolved special adaptations of their leaves that keep water loss down to a minimum. Some examples are shown in Figure 7.16.

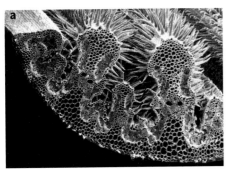

a A scanning electron micrograph of a TS through part of a rolled leaf of marram grass, *Ammophila arenaria*. This grass grows on sand dunes, where conditions are very dry. The leaves can roll up due to shrinkage of special 'hinge cells', exposing a thick, waterproof **cuticle** to the air outside the leaf. The cuticle contains a fatty, relatively waterproof substance called cutin. The stomata are found only in the upper epidermis and therefore open into the enclosed, humid space in the middle of the 'roll'. Hairs help to trap a layer of moist air close to the leaf surface, reducing the steepness of the diffusion gradient for water vapour.

b *Opuntia* is a cactus with flattened, photosynthetic stems that store water. The leaves are reduced to spines, which lessens the surface area from which transpiration can take place and protects the plant from being eaten by animals.

Figure 7.16: Some adaptations shown by xerophytes.

c False-colour scanning electron micrograph of a needle from a Sitka spruce (×1265), a large tree native to Canada and Alaska. Its leaves are in the form of needles, greatly reducing the surface area available for water loss. In addition, they are covered in a layer of waterproof wax and have sunken stomata, as shown here.

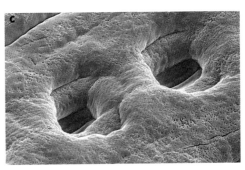

d Scanning electron micrograph of a TS through a *Phlomis italica* leaf showing its trichomes (×20). Trichomes are tiny hair-like structures that act as a barrier to the loss of water, like the marram grass hairs. *Phlomis* is a small shrub that lives in dry habitats in the Mediterranean regions of Europe and North Africa.

e The cardon *Euphorbia canariensis* grows in dry areas of Tenerife. It has swollen, succulent stems that store water and photosynthesise. The stems are coated with wax, which cuts down water loss. The leaves are extremely small.

KEY WORDS

xerophyte: a plant adapted to survive in conditions where water is in short supply

cuticle: a layer covering, and secreted by, the epidermis; in plants it is made of a fatty substance called cutin, which helps to provide protection against water loss and infection

PRACTICAL ACTIVITY 7.2

Drawing a TS of marram grass based on light microscopy

You can study the structure of a xerophytic leaf for yourself by observing a TS of a marram grass leaf (Figure 7.17). Use a light microscope and make an annotated low-power plan drawing of a representative part of the leaf. You could also draw high-power detail of chosen xerophytic features. Note the sunken stomata and hinge cells on the inner surface (upper epidermis) – they are at the bottoms of grooves in the leaf. The upper epidermis also has hairs. Note also that the outer surface (lower epidermis) has no stomata and has a thick cuticle.

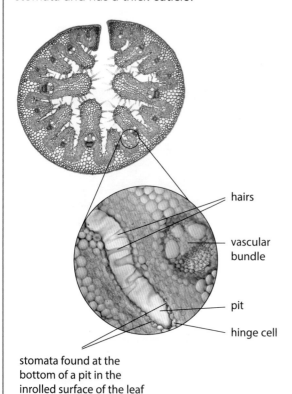

hairs

vascular bundle

pit

hinge cell

stomata found at the bottom of a pit in the inrolled surface of the leaf ('sunken stomata')

Figure 7.17: Low-power light micrograph of a TS of a rolled marram grass leaf. High-power detail of part of the leaf is also shown.

(See Practical Investigation 6.6 in the Practical Workbook for additional information).

Question

5   Identify six xerophytic features of leaves visible in Figures 7.16 and 7.17 and explain how each feature helps the plant to conserve water. Summarise your answer in a table using the following headings.

Xerophytic feature of leaves	How it helps to conserve water	Example (name of plant)

Movement of water from xylem across the leaf

As water evaporates from the cell walls of mesophyll cells, more water is drawn into the walls to replace it. This water can be traced back to the xylem vessels in the leaf. Water constantly moves out of these vessels through the unlignified parts of the xylem vessel walls (the structure of xylem is described in the next section). The water then moves down a water potential gradient from cell to cell in the leaf along two possible pathways. In one pathway, known as the **symplast pathway**, water moves from cell to cell via the plasmodesmata. In the other pathway, known as the **apoplast pathway**, water moves through the cell walls. Symplast and apoplast pathways are both described in more detail later in this chapter.

Structure of xylem

In order to understand how water moves into the xylem from the root, up the stem and into the leaves, you need to understand the structure of xylem tissue.

KEY WORDS

symplast pathway: the living system of interconnected protoplasts extending through a plant, used as a transport pathway for the movement of water and solutes; individual protoplasts are connected via plasmodesmata

apoplast pathway: the non-living system of interconnected cell walls extending throughout a plant, used as a transport pathway for the movement of water and mineral ions

Xylem contains more than one type of cell, but the ones of particular importance in transport are the xylem vessel elements. Each vessel element begins life as a normal plant cell, but later a substance called lignin is laid down in the walls. Lignin is a very hard, strong substance, which is waterproof. (Wood is made of xylem and gets its strength from lignin.) As lignin builds up around the cell, the contents of the cell die, leaving a completely empty space, or lumen, inside.

The xylem vessel elements are quite elongated and they line up end to end. The end walls of the vessel elements then break down completely, to form a continuous tube rather like a drainpipe running through the plant. This long non-living tube is a xylem vessel. It may be up to several metres long. Many of these tubes are found in the xylem.

> **KEY WORDS**
>
> xylem vessel element: a dead, lignified cell found in xylem specialised for transporting water and for support; the ends of the cells break down and join with neighbouring elements to form long tubes called xylem vessels
>
> xylem vessel: a dead, empty tube with lignified walls, through which water is transported in plants; it is formed by xylem vessel elements lined up end to end

There is one further complication. In those parts of the original cell walls where groups of plasmodesmata are found, no lignin is laid down. These non-lignified areas appear as 'gaps' in the thick walls of the xylem vessel, and are called pits. Pits are not open pores; they still have the original unthickened cell wall containing cellulose. The pits in one cell link with those in the neighbouring cells, just like the plasmodesmata did, so water can pass freely from one cell to the next (Figure 7.18d). This is necessary because it means that water can move into and out of the vessels, despite the waterproof lignin.

Because of the strength of lignin, which is hard to compress or stretch, xylem has the important function of support as well as being a transport tissue. The structural features of xylem vessels are closely related to their function, as you will see in the next section. To summarise:

- Xylem vessels are made from cells joined end to end to form tubes.
- The cells are dead.

- The walls of the cells are thickened with lignin, a hard, strong material.
- Pits in the walls allow water in and out of the tubes.

Figure 7.18 shows the structure of typical xylem vessels.

Movement of water through xylem from root to leaf

The removal of water from xylem vessels in the leaf creates a tension in the water left in the xylem vessels (the water potential at the top of the xylem vessel becomes lower than the water potential at the bottom). The tension causes water to move up the xylem vessels. The vessels are full of water, so it is just like sucking water up a straw.

If you suck hard on a straw, its walls may collapse inwards as a result of the high tension you are creating. Xylem vessels would do the same if they did not have strong, lignified walls to stop them from collapsing. Tension, or sucking, is actually a negative pressure. It is like pulling on the water.

The movement of water and mineral ions up through xylem vessels is by mass flow. This means that all the water molecules, plus any dissolved solutes, move together at the same speed, like water in a river. This is different from diffusion where the different types of molecule or ion move at different speeds and directions according to their own diffusion gradients. Mass flow through xylem is helped by the fact that water molecules are attracted to each other by hydrogen bonding (Chapter 2); this attraction is called cohesion. The water molecules are also attracted to the cellulose and lignin in the walls of the xylem vessels, which are hydrophilic. This attraction is called adhesion. Cohesion and adhesion help to keep the water in a xylem vessel moving as a continuous column. The fact that the cells are dead and empty is an advantage, because it means there is no protoplasm to get in the way of transport.

If an air bubble forms in the column of water in a vessel, the water stops moving upwards. This is called an air lock. The small diameter of xylem vessels helps to prevent such breaks from occurring. Also the pits in the vessel walls allow water to move out from one vessel to a neighbouring vessel and so bypass such an air lock. Air bubbles cannot pass through pits – remember there is a cellulose cell wall in the pit. Pits are also important because they allow water to move in and out of xylem vessels from and to surrounding living cells.

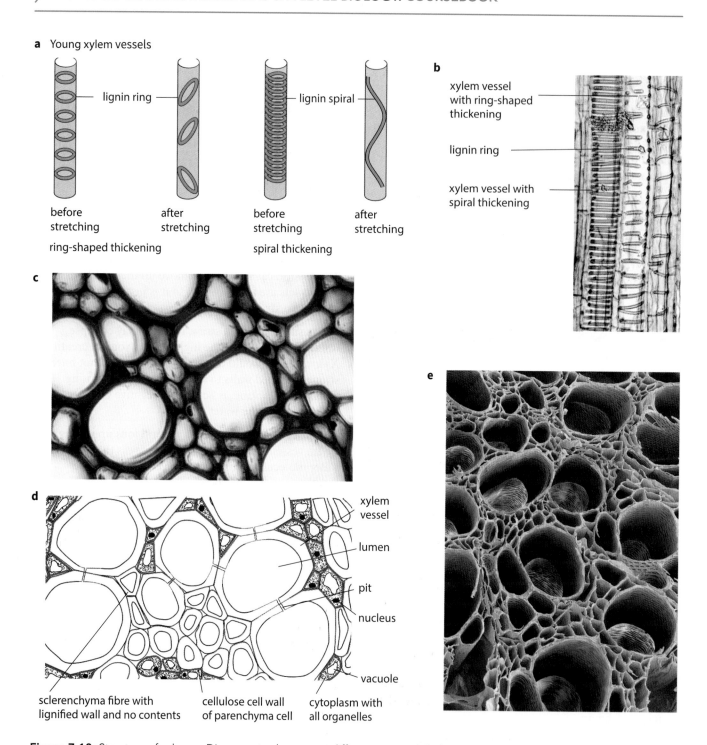

a Young xylem vessels

lignin ring

before stretching · after stretching

ring-shaped thickening

lignin spiral

before stretching · after stretching

spiral thickening

b

xylem vessel with ring-shaped thickening

lignin ring

xylem vessel with spiral thickening

c

d

xylem vessel

lumen

pit

nucleus

vacuole

sclerenchyma fibre with lignified wall and no contents

cellulose cell wall of parenchyma cell

cytoplasm with all organelles

e

Figure 7.18: Structure of xylem. **a** Diagrams to show some different types of thickening in young xylem vessels. Young vessels (protoxylem) can still stretch longitudinally. **b** Photomicrograph of xylem as seen in LS (×100). Lignin is stained red. LSs show the tube-like nature of the vessels. **c** and **d** Photomicrograph and diagram of xylem as seen in TS; lignin is stained red in **c**. Small parenchyma cells are visible between the xylem vessels in **c** and **d** (×120). **e** Scanning electron micrograph of mature xylem vessels, showing reticulate (net-like) pattern of lignification (×130).

Questions

6 Explain how each of the following features adapts xylem vessels for their function of transporting water from roots to leaves.

   a   total lack of cell contents

   b   no end walls in individual xylem elements

   c   a narrow diameter (between 0.01 mm and 0.2 mm)

   d   lignified walls

   e   pits

7 The accepted theory for how water moves through xylem is called the cohesion–tension theory. It relies largely on what is called transpirational pull. Briefly explain the use of the terms *cohesion–tension* and *transpirational pull*.

Movement of water across the root from root hairs to xylem

Figures 7.19 and 7.20 show TSs of a young root. The xylem vessels are in the centre of the root, unlike the arrangement in stems, where they are arranged in a ring and are nearer to the outside. Water is taken up by root hairs, which are on the outside of the root, growing from the epidermis. The hairs increase the surface area for absorption of water (and mineral ions). After entering the root hair, water crosses the cortex of the root and enters the xylem in the centre of the root. It does this because the water potential inside the xylem vessels is lower than the water potential in the root hairs. Therefore, the water moves down a water potential gradient across the root.

As mentioned earlier, the water takes two routes through the cortex: the apoplast pathway and the symplast pathway. Individual molecules can switch randomly from one route to the other at any time.

The cells of the cortex, like all plant cells, are surrounded by cell walls containing several layers of cellulose fibres criss-crossing one another. Water can soak into these walls, rather like soaking into blotting paper, and can move across the root from cell wall to cell wall without ever entering the cytoplasm of the cortex cells. This is the apoplast pathway (Figure 7.21a).

Another possibility is for the water to move into the cytoplasm or vacuole of a cortex cell by osmosis, and then into neighbouring cells through the interconnecting plasmodesmata. This is the symplast pathway (Figure 7.21b).

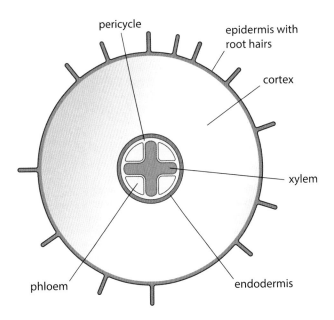

Figure 7.19: TS of a young dicotyledonous root to show the distribution of tissues.

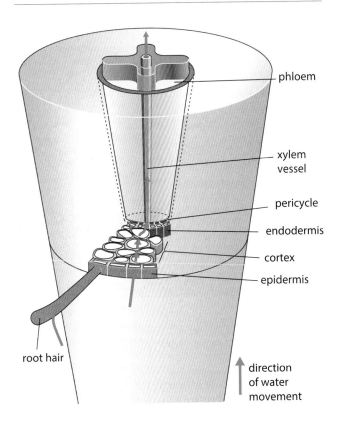

Figure 7.20: The pathway of water movement from root hair to xylem.

a

Apoplast pathway

1 Water enters the cell wall.

2 Water moves through the cell wall.

3 Water may move from cell wall to cell wall through the intercellular spaces.

4 Water may move directly from cell wall to cell wall.

b

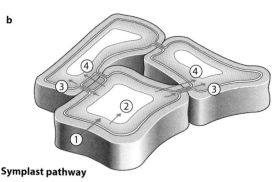

Symplast pathway

1 Water enters the cytoplasm by osmosis through the partially permeable cell surface membrane.

2 Water moves into the sap in the vacuole, through the tonoplast by osmosis.

3 Water may move from cell to cell through the plasmodesmata.

4 Water may move from cell to cell through adjacent cell surface membranes and cell walls.

Figure 7.21: a Apoplast and **b** symplast pathways for movement of water from root hairs to xylem.

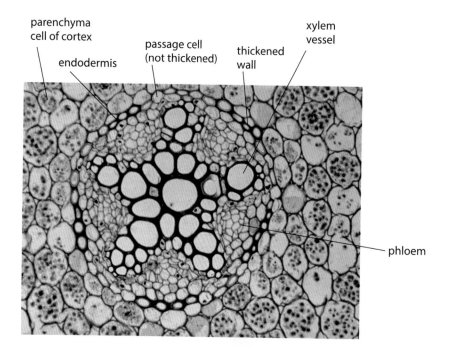

Figure 7.22: Light micrograph of part of a TS of a dicotyledonous root. The endodermis with its thickened walls is shown. Note also the passage cells which allow the passage of water (×250).

When the water reaches the endodermis (Figures 7.19 and 7.20), the apoplast pathway is blocked. The endodermis, like the epidermis, is one cell thick (Figure 7.22). It surrounds the vascular tissue in stems and roots.

The cells in the endodermis have a thick, waterproof, waxy band of suberin in their cell walls (Figure 7.23).

This band is called the Casparian strip and it goes right round the cell. It stops water moving through the apoplast. The only way for water coming across the cortex to cross the endodermis is through the unthickened parts of the wall into the cytoplasm of the endodermis cells. As the endodermis cells get older, the suberin deposits become more extensive until, except

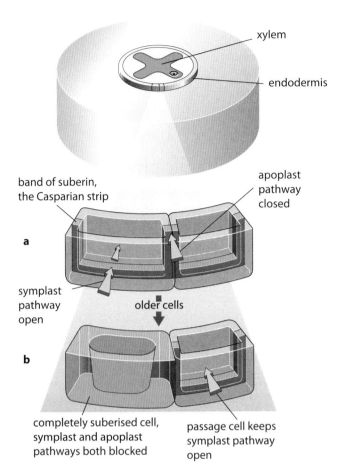

Figure 7.23: Suberin deposits in the endodermis stop water moving through the apoplast pathway. **a** In a young root, the suberin forms bands in the cell walls called Casparian strips. The symplast pathway remains open. **b** In an older root, entire cells become suberised, closing the symplast pathway too. Only passage cells are then permeable to water.

in certain cells called passage cells, no water can enter the cells. Passage cells still have a Casparian strip but water can continue to pass using the symplast pathway. It is thought that this arrangement gives a plant control over what mineral ions pass into its xylem vessels, as everything has to cross cell surface membranes.

Once across the endodermis, water continues to move down the water potential gradient towards the xylem vessels through either the symplast or apoplast pathways. Water moves into the xylem vessels through the pits or non-lignified regions of their walls. It then moves up the vessels towards the leaves as previously described.

Movement of water from the soil into root hairs

Figure 7.24a shows a young root growing through soil. The tip of the root is covered by a tough, protective root cap and is not permeable to water. However, just behind the tip you can see many fine hair-like structures. These are the root hairs. They are extensions of some of the epidermal cells of the root. They reach into spaces between the soil particles, from where they absorb water and mineral ions.

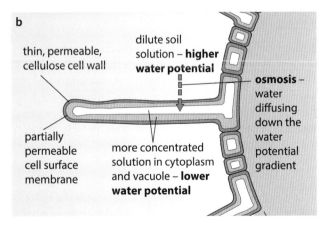

Figure 7.24: a A root of a young radish (*Raphanus*) plant showing the root cap and the root hairs. **b** Water uptake by a root hair cell. Mineral ions are also taken up.

Water moves into the root hairs by osmosis down a water potential gradient (Figure 7.24b). Although soil water contains some inorganic ions in solution, it is a relatively dilute solution and so has a relatively high water potential. However, the cytoplasm and cell sap inside the root hairs have considerable quantities of inorganic ions and organic substances such as proteins and sugars dissolved in them, and so have a relatively low water potential. Water, therefore, diffuses down this water potential gradient, through the partially permeable cell surface membrane and into the cytoplasm and vacuole of the root hair cell.

The large number of very fine root hairs provides a large surface area in contact with the soil surrounding the root, thus increasing the rate at which water can be absorbed. Root hairs are also important for the absorption of mineral ions such as nitrate and magnesium.

7.5 Transport of assimilates

Assimilates are the chemical compounds made by the plant itself as a result of assimilation. Assimilation in plants is the range of processes by which the plant converts its inorganic nutrients into organic compounds. An example of assimilation is photosynthesis. During photosynthesis, inorganic carbon dioxide and water are converted, using energy, to organic solutes like sugars. Another example of assimilation is the use of nitrates obtained from the soil to help make amino acids. Sucrose and amino acids are two of the common assimilates that are transported over long distances in the phloem.

Assimilates are transported from sources to sinks in phloem. A source is the place where the assimilate is located. A sink is the place it has to be moved to and where it is needed for growth and development or for storage. Common sources are leaves and storage organs, such as tubers. Common sinks are buds, flowers, fruits, roots and storage organs.

Question

8 Give an example of an organic molecule containing:
 a nitrogen
 b phosphorus
 c sulfur.

Structure of phloem

As a reminder, assimilates are transported in phloem and the location of phloem in the plant is shown in Figures 7.4–7.10, 7.14, 7.19 and 7.22.

Phloem tissue is made up of several types of cell. The two most important types for transport are sieve tube elements and companion cells (Figures 7.25 and 7.26).

Sieve tube elements and sieve tubes

Phloem contains tubes called sieve tubes that are made from cells called sieve tube elements. Unlike xylem vessels, sieve tubes are made of living cells. Figure 7.25

KEY WORDS

source: a site in a plant which provides food for another part of the plant, the sink

sink: a site in a plant which receives food from another part of the plant, the source

sieve tube element: a cell found in phloem tissue, with non-thickened cellulose walls, very little cytoplasm, no nucleus and end walls perforated to form sieve plates, through which sap containing sucrose is transported

companion cell: a cell with an unthickened cellulose wall and dense cytoplasm that is found in close association with a phloem sieve tube element to which it is directly linked via many plasmodesmata; the companion cell and the sieve tube element form a functional unit

sieve tube: tube formed from sieve tube elements lined up end to end

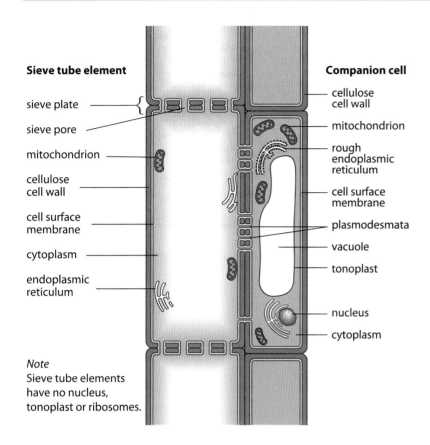

Sieve tube element

- sieve plate
- sieve pore
- mitochondrion
- cellulose cell wall
- cell surface membrane
- cytoplasm
- endoplasmic reticulum

Companion cell

- cellulose cell wall
- mitochondrion
- rough endoplasmic reticulum
- cell surface membrane
- plasmodesmata
- vacuole
- tonoplast
- nucleus
- cytoplasm

Note
Sieve tube elements have no nucleus, tonoplast or ribosomes.

Figure 7.25: A phloem sieve tube element and its companion cell.

is a diagram showing the structure of a sieve tube and its accompanying companion cells. Figure 7.26 shows diagrams based on photomicrographs and photomicrographs of TSs and LSs of phloem tissue. The LSs show the tube-like nature of sieve tubes.

Sieve tube elements are elongated in shape. The cells are joined end to end vertically to form a continuous tube. Like a typical plant cell, a sieve tube element has a cell wall containing cellulose, a cell surface membrane and cytoplasm containing endoplasmic reticulum and mitochondria. However, the amount of cytoplasm is very reduced and only forms a thin layer lining the inside of the cell wall. There is no nucleus and there are no ribosomes.

The most striking feature of sieve tube elements is their end walls. Where the end walls of two sieve tube elements meet, a sieve plate is formed. This is made up of the walls of both cells, perforated by large pores. These pores are easily visible with a good light

microscope. The pores are open, presenting little barrier to the flow of liquids through them.

Each sieve tube element has at least one companion cell lying close beside it. Companion cells have the structure of a typical plant cell, with a cell wall containing cellulose, a cell surface membrane, cytoplasm, a small vacuole and a nucleus. However, the number of mitochondria and ribosomes is greater than normal, and the cells are metabolically very active.

Companion cells are very closely linked with their neighbouring sieve tube elements in terms of their function. In fact, they are regarded as a single functional unit. Numerous plasmodesmata pass through their cell walls, making direct contact between the cytoplasm of the companion cell and that of the sieve tube element.

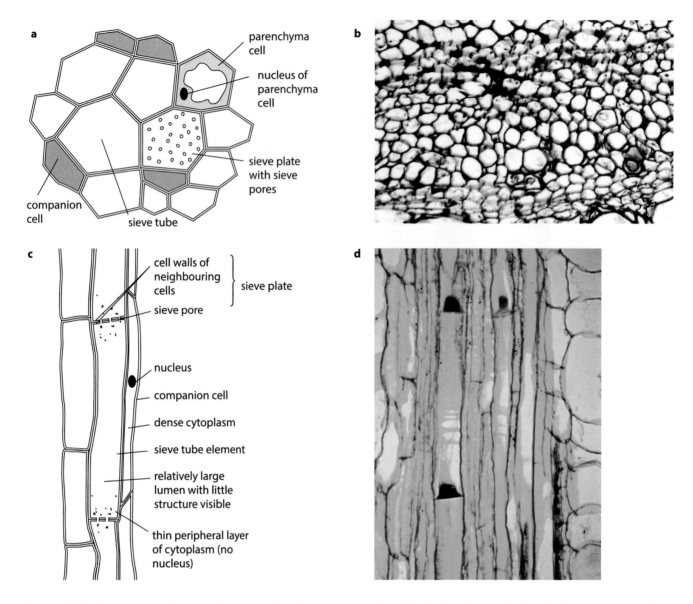

Figure 7.26: Structure of phloem: **a** diagram in TS; **b** light micrograph in TS (×300); **c** diagram in LS; **d** light micrograph in LS (×200). The red triangles are patches of callose that formed at the sieve plates between the sieve tube elements in response to the damage done as the section was being cut. You can see companion cells, with their denser cytoplasm, lying alongside the sieve tube elements. On the far right are some parenchyma cells.

The contents of phloem sieve tubes

The liquid inside phloem sieve tubes is called phloem sap, or just sap. Table 7.1 shows the composition of the sap of the castor oil plant, *Ricinus communis*.

Solute	Concentration / mol dm^{-3}
sucrose	250
potassium ions	80
amino acids	40
chloride ions	15
phosphate ions	10
magnesium ions	5
sodium ions	2
ATP	0.5
nitrate ions	0
plant growth substances (e.g. auxin, cytokinin)	small traces

Table 7.1: Composition of phloem sap.

Question

9   Which substances listed in Table 7.1 are assimilates (made by the plant)?

How transport occurs in sieve tubes

Phloem sap, like xylem sap, moves by mass flow. Mass flow moves organic solutes about 1 metre per hour on average, about 10 000 times faster than diffusion. In xylem vessels, the movement is passive, meaning it requires no energy input from the plant (only the Sun). This is not the case in phloem. To create the pressure differences needed for mass flow in phloem, the plant has to use energy. Phloem transport is therefore an active process, in contrast to the passive transport in xylem.

The pressure difference in phloem is produced by active loading (moving) of sucrose into the sieve tube elements at the source (the place where sucrose starts its journey). The source is usually a photosynthesising leaf or a storage organ. As you have seen, an area where sucrose is taken out of the phloem is called a sink – for example, the roots.

Loading a high concentration of sucrose into a sieve tube element greatly decreases the water potential of

the sap inside it. Therefore, water enters the sieve tube element, moving down a water potential gradient by osmosis. This causes a build-up of pressure inside the sieve tube element. The pressure is referred to as hydrostatic pressure. You can think of it as a pumping pressure. A pressure difference is therefore created between the source and the sink. This pressure difference causes a mass flow of water and dissolved solutes through the sieve tubes, from the high pressure area to the low pressure area (Figure 7.27). At the sink, sucrose is removed, causing the water to follow by osmosis. The loss of water from the tube reduces pressure inside the tube, thus maintaining the hydrostatic pressure gradient. Mass flow from source to sink is summarised in Figure 7.28.

Figure 7.27: The phloem sap of the sugar maple (*Acer saccharum*) contains a high concentration of sugar and can be harvested to make maple syrup. Taps are inserted into each tree and the sap runs out under its own pressure through the plastic pipelines.

Sinks can be anywhere in the plant, both above and below the photosynthesising leaves. Thus, sap flows both upwards and downwards in phloem (in contrast to xylem, in which flow is always upwards). Within any vascular bundle, phloem sap may be flowing upwards in some sieve tubes and downwards in others, but it can only flow one way in any particular sieve tube at any one time.

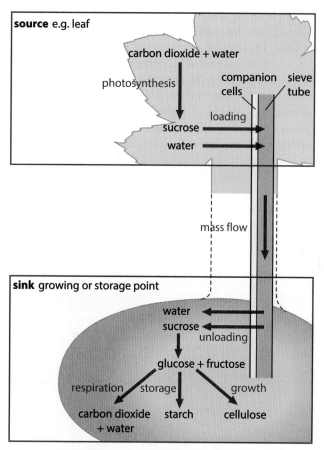

The sink is a growing point, e.g. young leaf, bud, flower or root, or a storage point, e.g. seed, fruit or tuber.

Figure 7.28: Sources, sinks and mass flow in phloem.

Question

10 Which of the following are sources, and which are sinks?

a   a nectary in a flower

b   a developing fruit

c   the storage tissue of a potato tuber (a storage organ) when the buds are beginning to sprout

d   a potato tuber being formed

Loading sucrose into phloem

In leaf mesophyll cells, photosynthesis in chloroplasts produces sugars. Some of the sugars are used to make sucrose.

The sucrose, in solution, moves from the mesophyll cells, across the leaf to the phloem tissue. It may move by the symplast pathway, moving from cell to cell

via plasmodesmata. Alternatively, it may move by the apoplast pathway, travelling along cell walls.

It is now known that companion cells and sieve tube elements work together. Sucrose is loaded into a companion cell by active transport. Figure 7.29 shows how this may be done. Hydrogen ions (protons, H^+) are pumped out of the companion cell into its cell wall by a proton pump using ATP as an energy source. Proton pumps are proteins found in the cell surface membrane. The proton pump creates a large excess of hydrogen ions in the apoplast pathway outside the companion cell. The hydrogen ions can move back into the cell by passive diffusion down their concentration gradient, through a protein which acts as a carrier for both a hydrogen ion and a sucrose molecule at the same time. Because it carries two substances at the same time, the protein is called a co-transporter. The sucrose molecules are carried through this co-transporter molecule into the companion cell, against the concentration gradient for sucrose, but down the concentration gradient for hydrogen ions. The co-transporter will only work if both a hydrogen ion and a sucrose molecule move through it together. Once inside the companion cell, the sucrose molecules can move by diffusion into the sieve tube. They do this by moving through the plasmodesmata which connect the companion cell to the sieve tube (the symplast pathway).

Questions

11 Sucrose is highly soluble in water. It is also relatively inactive metabolically. Suggest how these two properties make it suitable as a long-distance transport sugar.

12 Figure 7.26d shows a sieve tube element with red-stained 'triangles' of callose at each end. These triangles indicate the positions of the sieve plates. (The callose is only deposited when the phloem is cut during preparation of the specimen. It is not normally present in living phloem.)

a   Assuming the magnification of the micrograph is ×200, calculate the length of the sieve tube element. Show your working. (You may find it useful to refer to Chapter 1, Worked Example 4, for the method of calculation.)

b   i   Calculate how many sieve plates per metre a sucrose molecule would have to cross if it were travelling in the sieve tube identified in **a**. Show your working. (Assume all the sieve tube elements are the same size as the one measured in Figure 7.26d.)

ii What feature of the sieve plates allows materials to cross them?

c Flow rates in sieve tubes range from 0.3 m h⁻¹ to 1.5 m h⁻¹ and average about 1 m h⁻¹. If the flow rate in the sieve element shown in Figure 7.26d is 1 m h⁻¹, how long does it take a sucrose molecule to travel through it? Show your working.

Key

- sucrose
- storage product e.g. starch

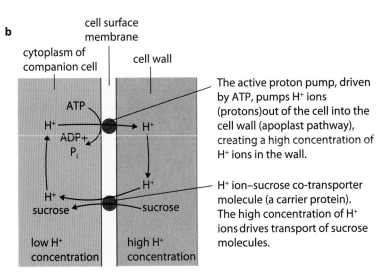

Figure 7.29: Loading phloem: **a** one of the possible methods by which sucrose is loaded and a hydrostatic pressure gradient is generated; **b** detail of the H⁺ ion–sucrose co-transporter system.

REFLECTION

This chapter has shown that there are some similarities between xylem and phloem, both in terms of their structure and in the way they function. Yet there are many important differences.

It is a useful exercise at this stage to try to compare xylem and phloem. It will help you to think of the important features of both. (Remember when you compare two things you need to think of similarities as well as differences.)

Using tables like Tables 7.2 and 7.3 will help you with the comparison.

Similarities	
structure	1
function	1
	2
	3
	4

Table 7.2: Comparing xylem and phloem – similarities.

Differences		
Feature	Xylem	Phloem
tubes are called		
cells/tubes living or dead		
cell/tube contents	empty	
walls		
end walls of tubes		
substances transported		
functional unit		
mechanism of movement – passive or active		
direction of movement		
pressure gradient		
other function		

Table 7.3: Comparing xylem and phloem – similarities.

Personal reflection question

Do you think comparing things increases your understanding, or is it a pointless exercise? If you find it helpful, think about why this is the case.

Final reflection

Discuss with a friend which, if any, parts of Chapter 7 you need to:

- read through again to make sure you really understand

- seek more guidance on, even after going over it again.

SUMMARY

Plants need long-distance transport systems.
Water and mineral salts are transported through a plant in xylem vessels. Movement of water through a plant is a passive process in which the water moves down a water potential gradient from soil to air.
The energy for this process comes from the Sun. It causes water to evaporate from the wet walls of mesophyll cells in leaves into air spaces in the leaf. From here water vapour diffuses out of the leaf through stomata in a process called transpiration. This loss of water sets up a water potential gradient throughout the plant (from high water potential in the soil and roots to low in the leaves).
Plants that are adapted to live in places where water is in short supply are called xerophytes. Xerophytes have evolved adaptations that help to reduce the rate of loss of water vapour from their leaves.
Water moves across the leaf either via the cell walls (the apoplast pathway) or through the cytoplasm of cells (the symplast pathway).
Water and mineral ions (xylem sap) move up xylem vessels by mass flow. Movement depends on cohesion of water molecules to each other and adhesion of water molecules to the walls of the vessels. Water in the xylem vessels is under tension as a result of loss of water from the leaves by transpiration. Water is therefore pulled up the vessels, a process known as transpirational pull.
Water enters the plant through root hairs by osmosis. Water crosses the root either through the apoplast pathway or the symplast pathway. It enters the xylem vessels at the centre of the root.
Transport of organic solutes, such as sucrose and amino acids, occurs through living phloem sieve tubes. Phloem sap moves by mass flow from a region known as the source to a region known as the sink.
Sucrose is produced at the source (e.g. photosynthesising leaves) and used at the sink (e.g. a flower or a storage organ). Mass flow occurs as a result of hydrostatic pressure differences between the source and the sink. Active loading of sucrose into the sieve tubes at the source results in the entry of water by osmosis, creating a high hydrostatic pressure in the sieve tubes. Phloem sap can move in different directions in different sieve tubes.
Both xylem vessels and phloem sieve tubes show unique structural features which are adaptations to their roles in transport.

EXAM-STYLE QUESTIONS

1 If sucrose is actively loaded into a companion cell, which combination of changes takes place in the cytoplasm of the companion cell?

	Water potential	Hydrogen ion concentration
A	decreases	decreases
B	decreases	increases
C	increases	decreases
D	increases	increases

[1]

CONTINUED

2 Which of the following rows correctly describes the pressure of the two types of elements?

	Pressure	
	Xylem vessel element	Phloem sieve tube element
A	negative	negative
B	negative	positive
C	positive	negative
D	positive	positive

[1]

3 The figure shows diagrams of TSs of two plant organs, X and Y, containing vascular tissue. Which of the following rows correctly identifies the tissues?

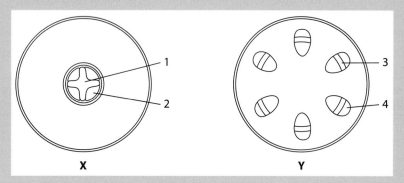

	X	Y
A	1 phloem	4 phloem
B	2 phloem	3 phloem
C	1 xylem	4 xylem
D	2 xylem	3 xylem

[1]

4 Movement of water from a root hair to xylem cannot take place entirely through the apoplast pathway due to cells in the:

A cortex   C epidermis

B endodermis   D pericycle. [1]

5 Explain how water moves from:

a the soil into a root hair cell [3]

b one root cortex cell to another [4]

c a xylem vessel into a leaf mesophyll cell. [3]

[Total: 10]

6 Arrange the following in order of water potential. Use the symbol > to mean 'greater than'.

dry atmospheric air   mesophyll cell   root hair cell   soil solution
xylem vessel contents [1]

CONTINUED

7   Figure **a** shows changes in the relative humidity of the atmosphere during the daylight hours of one 24-hour day.

Figure **b** shows changes in the tension in the xylem of a tree during the same period. Tension is measured in pressure units called kilopascals (kPa). As tension increases in the xylem, the pressure in kPa becomes increasingly negative.

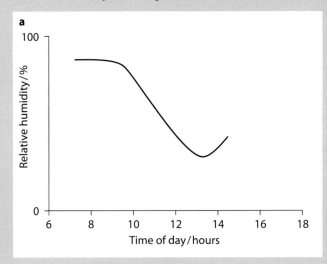

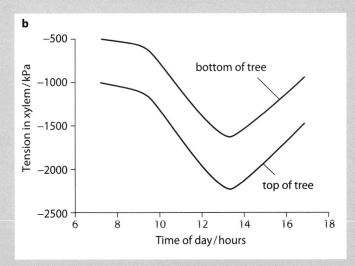

a   Describe and explain the relationship between relative humidity and xylem tension. **[4]**

b   Describe and explain the differences observed in xylem tension between the top of the tree and the bottom of the tree. **[3]**

[Total: 7]

8   An instrument called a dendrogram can be used to measure small changes in the diameter of a tree trunk. The instrument usually shows that the diameter of the tree trunk is at its lowest during daylight hours and at its greatest at night.

Suggest an explanation for these observations. **[4]**

CONTINUED

9 The graph shows the relationship between rate of transpiration and rate of water uptake for a particular plant.

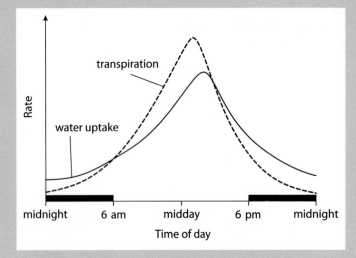

a Define the term *transpiration*. [2]

b Suggest the two environmental factors which are most likely to be responsible for the changes in transpiration rate shown in the graph. [2]

c Describe the relationship between rate of transpiration and rate of water uptake shown in the graph. [2]

d Explain the relationship. [4]

[Total: 10]

10 Explain how active loading of sucrose into companion cells leads to the following observations:

a The cytoplasm of companion cells has a relatively high pH of about pH 8. [1]

b The inside of companion cells is negatively charged relative to the outside. (There is a difference in electrical potential across the cell surface membrane, with a potential of about $-150\ mV$ on the inside.) [2]

c ATP is present in relatively large amounts inside companion cells. [1]

[Total: 4]

11 Translocation of organic solutes takes place between sources and sinks.

a Briefly explain under what circumstances:

i a seed could be a sink [1]

ii a seed could be a source [1]

iii a leaf could be a sink [1]

iv a leaf could be a source [1]

v a storage organ could be a sink [1]

vi a storage organ could be a source. [1]

b Suggest two possible roles for glucose in each of the following sinks:

i a storage organ [2]

ii a growing bud. [2]

[Total: 10]

SELF-EVALUATION CHECKLIST

After studying this chapter, complete a table like this:

I can	See section...	Needs more work	Almost there	Ready to move on
outline the transport needs of plants and the fact that some mineral ions and organic compounds can be transported within plants dissolved in water	7.1, 7.2			
draw, label and describe the overall structure of herbaceous dicotyledonous stems, roots and leaves using a light microscope	7.3			
draw the structure of the transport tissues xylem and phloem using the high-power lens of a light microscope	7.3			
explain the process of transpiration	7.4			
describe the adaptations of the leaves of xerophytic plants with the aid of annotated drawings	7.4			
explain how water moves across a leaf through the apoplast and symplast pathways	7.4			
relate the structure of xylem to its functions	7.4			
explain the movement of water up the xylem from root to leaf, including the roles of cohesion–tension and adhesion	7.4			
describe the transport of water from the soil to the root xylem through the apoplast and symplast pathways	7.4			
relate the structure of phloem to its functions	7.5			
explain that assimilates dissolved in water, such as sucrose and amino acids, move through phloem sieve tubes from sources to sinks	7.5			
explain mass flow in phloem sieve tubes down a hydrostatic pressure gradient from source to sink	7.5			
explain how companion cells transfer assimilates to phloem sieve tubes	7.5			

> Chapter 8
Transport in mammals

LEARNING INTENTIONS

In this chapter you will learn how to:

- describe the structure of the mammalian circulatory system
- explain how the structures of arteries, arterioles, veins, venules and capillaries are related to their functions
- describe and explain the structure and functions of blood, including the transport of oxygen and carbon dioxide
- make diagrams of blood vessels and blood cells from slides, photomicrographs or electron micrographs
- describe the formation and functions of tissue fluid
- explain the structure and function of the heart
- describe the cardiac cycle and its control.

BEFORE YOU START

- In your group, make lists of:

    - the different kinds of blood vessel in the mammalian circulatory system

    - the different components of blood.

- Write **two** facts about each of the items in your lists – for example, what their function is, and how they are adapted to carry it out.

Be ready to share your ideas with others in the class.

ARTIFICIAL HEARTS

Each year, about 18 million people worldwide die from cardiovascular disease, more than from any other disease. 'Cardiovascular' means to do with the heart and the circulatory system, and many of these deaths are due to the heart failing to work normally. In many countries, medical help is available for people with a failing heart, ranging from treatment with drugs to major heart surgery. But, until recently, the only hope for some heart patients was a heart transplant. However, the number of people needing a new heart is much greater than the number of hearts available. Many people wait years for a heart transplant, and many die from their heart disease before they get a new heart.

Petar Bilic (not his real name) thought that he was going to add to that statistic. The muscle in both of his ventricles had deteriorated so much that his heart was only just keeping him alive. No suitable heart could be found for a transplant.

Petar was very lucky. In recent years, biomedical engineers have developed a pumping device called a 'total artificial heart' (Figure 8.1). Petar's heart was completely removed, and an artificial heart put in its place. Petar was able to go home within a few weeks of his operation. The plan is that the artificial heart will keep him alive until a real heart is available for transplant. Some patients have lived for almost 5 years with their artificial heart in place. However, living with an artificial heart is not easy. An artificial heart needs an energy supply, and this is often provided with a battery that the patient carries in a backpack.

Figure 8.1: An artificial heart.

Biomedical engineers continue to make progress in developing new types of heart that should work for much longer – perhaps long enough for its owner to live out a long life without any need for a heart transplant. And, while the first artificial hearts were designed to fit into the body of an adult man, smaller ones are now available, which can be used for women and children.

Question for discussion

What do you think might be the advantages and disadvantages of using an artificial heart rather than a heart transplant, to treat a person whose own heart is failing?

8.1 Transport systems in animals

Most animals are far more active than plants. They must move to find their food, because they cannot make their own. Movement requires energy, for example for muscle contraction and the transmission of nerve impulses. This energy comes from glucose and other substances, which are broken down in respiration inside each individual cell.

The most efficient form of respiration – which releases the most energy from a given amount of glucose – is aerobic respiration, and this requires good supplies of oxygen. Supplying oxygen to respiring tissues is one of the most important functions of an animal's transport system. At the same time, waste products such as carbon dioxide can be removed.

Very small animals may be able to get enough oxygen to their cells by diffusion, especially if they are not particularly active. In a jellyfish, for example, oxygen simply diffuses into its body from the seawater around it, and then to the respiring cells. Carbon dioxide diffuses in the opposite direction. Because no cell is very far from the surface, each cell gets an adequate amount of oxygen quickly enough for its needs.

But in larger animals, such as mammals, diffusion is not sufficient. A transport system is needed to distribute oxygen quickly to all the body cells, and to remove their waste products. Mammals have greater requirements for oxygen than most other animals because they use respiration to generate heat inside their bodies, to help to keep their body temperature constant.

8.2 The mammalian circulatory system

Figure 8.2 shows the general layout of the main transport system of mammals – the blood system or **circulatory system**. It is made up of a pump – the heart – and a system of interconnecting tubes – the blood vessels. The blood always remains within these vessels, and so the system is known as a **closed blood system**.

Put your finger onto the left ventricle in Figure 8.2. Use your finger to follow the journey of the blood around the body. You will find that the blood travels twice through the heart on one complete 'circuit'. This is called a **double circulation**.

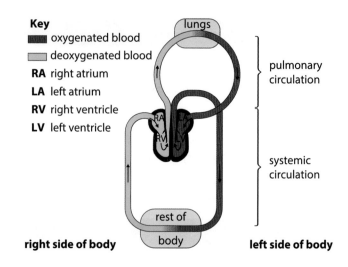

Key
- oxygenated blood
- deoxygenated blood
- **RA** right atrium
- **LA** left atrium
- **RV** right ventricle
- **LV** left ventricle

Figure 8.2: The general plan of the mammalian transport system, viewed as though looking at someone facing you. It is a closed double circulatory system.

Blood is pumped out of the left ventricle into the aorta (Figure 8.3), and travels from there to all parts of the body except the lungs. It returns to the right side of the heart in the vena cava. This is called the systemic circulation.

The blood is then pumped out of the right ventricle into the pulmonary arteries, which carry it to the lungs. The final part of the journey is along the pulmonary veins, which return it to the left side of the heart. This is called the **pulmonary circulation**.

KEY WORDS

circulatory system: a system that carries fluids around an organism's body

closed blood system: a circulatory system made up of vessels containing blood

double circulation: a circulatory system in which the blood passes through the heart twice on one complete circuit of the body

systemic circulation: the part of the circulatory system that carries blood from the heart to all of the body except the gas exchange surface, and then back to the heart

pulmonary circulation: the part of the circulatory system that carries blood from the heart to the gas exchange surface and then back to the heart

The pressure in the systemic circulation is considerably higher than in the pulmonary circulation. You can read about blood pressure in the circulatory system later in this chapter.

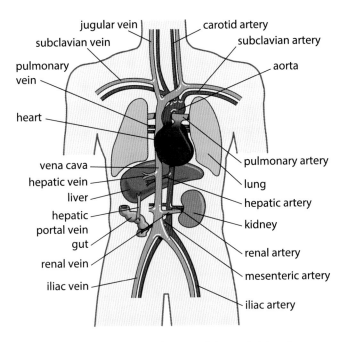

Figure 8.3: The positions of some of the main blood vessels in the human body.

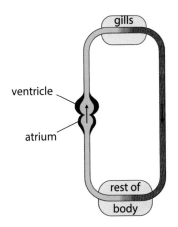

Figure 8.4: The general plan of the transport system of a fish.

Question

1 Figure 8.4 shows the general layout of the circulatory system of a fish.

   With a partner, discuss:

   a how this system differs from the circulatory system of a mammal

   b why the mammalian transport system may be able to deliver more oxygen more quickly to the tissues than the fish's transport system

   c how these differences could relate to the different requirements of a fish and a mammal.

   Be ready to share your ideas with the rest of the class.

8.3 Blood vessels

There are three main types of vessel making up the circulatory system. Figure 8.5 shows these vessels in transverse section. Vessels carrying blood away from the heart are known as **arteries**, while those carrying blood towards the heart are **veins**. Small arteries are called **arterioles**, and small veins are **venules**. Linking arterioles and venules, taking blood close to almost every cell in the body, are tiny vessels called **capillaries**.

KEY WORDS

artery: vessel with thick, strong walls that carries high-pressure blood away from the heart

vein: vessel with relatively thin walls that carries low-pressure blood back to the heart

arteriole: small artery

venule: small vein

capillary: the smallest blood vessel, whose role is to deliver oxygen and nutrients to body tissues, and to remove their waste products

Transverse section (TS) through small artery

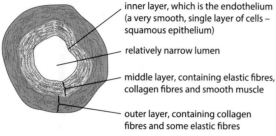

inner layer, which is the endothelium (a very smooth, single layer of cells – squamous epithelium)

relatively narrow lumen

middle layer, containing elastic fibres, collagen fibres and smooth muscle

outer layer, containing collagen fibres and some elastic fibres

Arteries in different parts of the body vary in their structure. Arteries near the heart have especially large numbers of elastic fibres in the middle layer, as shown here. In other parts of the body, the middle layer contains less elastic tissue and more smooth muscle.

TS through capillary

7 μm

wall made of endothelium, one cell thick

lumen, just big enough for a red cell to squeeze along

TS through small vein

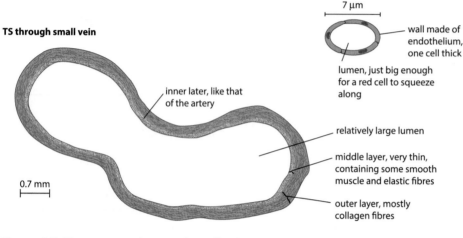

inner later, like that of the artery

relatively large lumen

middle layer, very thin, containing some smooth muscle and elastic fibres

outer layer, mostly collagen fibres

0.7 mm

Figure 8.5: The tissues making up the walls of arteries, capillaries and veins.

Arteries and arterioles

The function of arteries is to transport blood, swiftly and at high pressure, to the tissues.

Artery walls are very strong and elastic. Blood leaving the heart is at a very high pressure. Blood pressure in the human aorta may be around 120 mmHg, which can also be stated as 16 kPa. The thickness and composition of the artery wall enables it to withstand this pressure.

Both arteries and veins have walls made up of three layers (Figures 8.5 and 8.6):

- an inner layer, which is made up of a layer of **endothelium** (lining tissue) consisting of a layer of flat cells (**squamous epithelium**) fitting together like jigsaw pieces, plus a layer of elastic fibres; the endothelium is very smooth, minimising friction with the moving blood

- a middle layer containing **smooth muscle**, collagen and elastic fibres

- an outer layer containing elastic fibres and collagen fibres.

KEY WORDS

endothelium: a tissue that lines the inner surface of a structure such as a blood vessel

squamous epithelium: one or more layers of thin, flat cells forming the lining of some hollow structures, e.g. blood vessels and alveoli

smooth muscle: a type of muscle that can contract steadily over long periods of time

IMPORTANT

Blood pressure is still measured in the old units of mmHg, even though kPa is the SI unit. The abbreviation mmHg stands for 'millimetres of mercury', and refers to the distance which a column of mercury is pushed up the arm of a U-tube. 1 mmHg is equivalent to about 0.13 kPa.

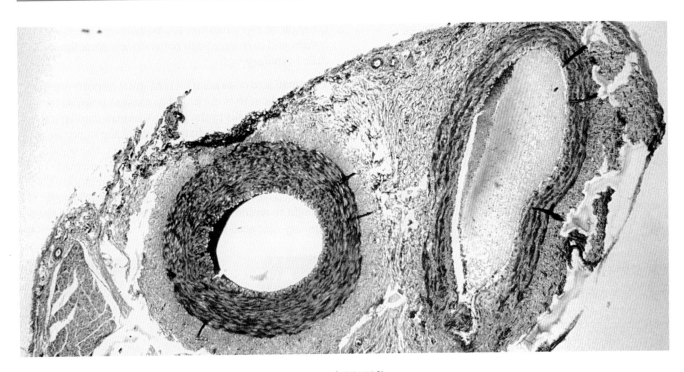

Figure 8.6: Photomicrograph of an artery (left) and a vein (right) (×110).

Arteries have the thickest walls of any blood vessel. The aorta, the largest artery, has an overall diameter of 2.5 cm close to the heart, and a wall thickness of about 2 mm. The composition of the wall provides great strength and resilience. The middle layer, which is by far the thickest part of the wall, contains a large amount of elastic fibres. These allow the wall to stretch as pulses of blood surge through at high pressure. Arteries further away from the heart have fewer elastic fibres in the middle layer but have more muscle fibres.

Arteries that have a lot of elastic tissue in their middle layer – such as the aorta – are called **elastic arteries**. The function of an elastic artery is to carry blood from the heart on the first part of its journey towards its final destination. The elasticity of these artery walls is important in allowing them to stretch, which reduces the likelihood that they will burst. This elasticity also has another very important function. Blood is pumped out of the heart in pulses, rushing out at high pressure as the ventricles contract, and slowing as the ventricles relax. The artery walls stretch as the high-pressure blood surges into them, and then recoil inwards as the pressure drops. Therefore, as blood at high pressure enters an artery, the artery becomes wider, reducing the pressure a little. As blood at lower pressure enters an artery, the artery wall recoils inwards, giving the blood a small 'push' and raising the pressure a little. The overall effect is to 'even out' the flow of blood. However, the arteries

are not entirely effective in achieving this: if you feel your pulse in your wrist, you can feel the artery, even at this distance from your heart, being stretched outwards with each surge of blood from the heart.

As arteries divide into smaller vessels, the proportion of muscle in their walls increases and the proportion of elastic tissue decreases. They are now **muscular arteries**. Muscular arteries take blood from an elastic artery and deliver it close to its final destination. The type of muscle in their walls is smooth muscle, which is able to contract slowly and steadily to alter the internal diameter of the artery and therefore control the volume of blood that can flow through it.

Muscular arteries divide to form even smaller vessels called arterioles. These also contain a lot of smooth muscle in their walls. Their narrowness provides

---

KEY WORDS

elastic arteries: relatively large arteries, which have a lot of elastic tissue and little muscle tissue in their walls

muscular arteries: arteries that are closer to the final destination of the blood inside them than elastic arteries, with more smooth muscle in their walls which allows them to constrict and dilate

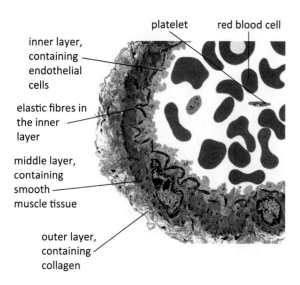

inner layer, containing endothelial cells

platelet

red blood cell

elastic fibres in the inner layer

middle layer, containing smooth muscle tissue

outer layer, containing collagen

Figure 8.7: Transmission electron micrograph (TEM) of a small artery.

resistance to blood flow, causing it to slow down, which provides extra time for exchange of gases and nutrients as the blood flows through the capillaries in the tissues.

The walls of arterioles have a nerve supply. Nerve impulses from the brain can cause their smooth muscle to contract, narrowing the arteriole. This is called **vasoconstriction**. This can be used to reduce blood flow to a particular area and divert it to other tissues. When the muscle relaxes, the diameter of the arteriole widens. This is called **vasodilation**. The smooth muscle can also respond to hormones in the blood.

KEY WORDS

vasoconstriction: the narrowing of a muscular artery or arteriole, caused by the contraction of the smooth muscle in its walls

vasodilation: the widening of a muscular artery or arteriole, caused by the relaxation of the smooth muscle in its walls

Capillaries

The arterioles themselves continue to branch, eventually forming the tiniest of all blood vessels, capillaries. The function of capillaries is to take blood as close as possible to all cells, allowing rapid transfer of substances between cells and blood. Capillaries form a network

throughout every tissue in the body except the brain, cornea and cartilage. Such networks are sometimes called capillary beds.

The small size of capillaries is of great importance in allowing them to bring blood as close as possible to each group of cells in the body. A human capillary is approximately 7 μm in diameter, about the same size as a red blood cell (Figures 8.5, 8.8 and 8.9). The walls of capillaries are extremely thin because they are made up of a single layer of endothelial cells. As red blood cells carrying oxygen squeeze through a capillary, they are brought to within as little as 1 μm of the cells outside the capillary that need the oxygen.

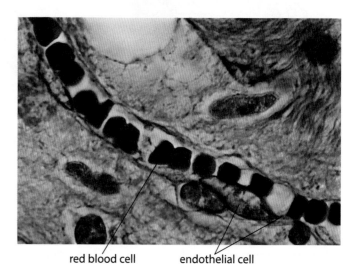

red blood cell   endothelial cell

Figure 8.8: Photomicrograph of a blood capillary containing red blood cells (dark red) (×900). The cells of the endothelium are very thin, except where there is a nucleus (red).

In most capillaries, there are tiny gaps between the individual cells that form the endothelium. As you will see later in this chapter, these gaps are important in allowing some components of the blood to seep through into the spaces between the cells in all the tissues of the body.

By the time blood reaches the capillaries, it has already lost much of the pressure originally supplied to it by the contraction of the ventricles. Blood pressure continues to drop as it passes through the capillaries. As blood enters a capillary from an arteriole, it may have a pressure of around 35 mmHg or 4.7 kPa; by the time it reaches the far end of the capillary, the pressure will have dropped to around 10 mmHg or 1.3 kPa.

Question

2   Suggest why there are no blood capillaries in the cornea of the eye. How might the cornea be supplied with oxygen and nutrients?

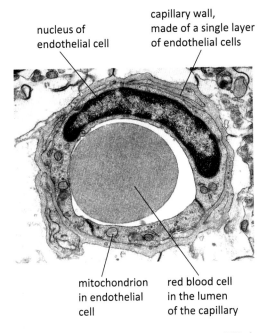

Figure 8.9: TEM of a transverse section (TS) through a small capillary (approximately ×4500).

Veins and venules

As blood leaves a capillary bed, the capillaries gradually join with one another, forming larger vessels called venules. These join to form veins. The function of veins is to return blood to the heart.

By the time blood enters a vein, its pressure has dropped to a very low value. In humans, a typical value for venous blood pressure is about 5 mmHg or less. This very low pressure means that there is no need for veins to have thick walls. They have the same three layers as arteries, but the middle layer is much thinner and has far fewer elastic fibres and muscle fibres.

The low blood pressure in veins creates a problem: how can this blood be returned to the heart? Think about how blood can return to your heart from your feet when you are standing up. Unaided, the blood in your leg veins would sink and accumulate in your feet. However, many of the veins run within, or very close to,

several leg muscles. Whenever you tense (contract) these muscles, they squeeze inwards on the veins in your legs, temporarily raising the pressure within them.

This squeezing, in itself, would not help to push the blood back towards the heart; blood would just squidge up and down as you walked. To keep the blood flowing in the right direction, veins contain half-moon valves, or **semilunar valves**, formed from their endothelium (Figure 8.10). These valves allow blood to move towards the heart, but not away from it. So, when you contract your leg muscles, the blood in the veins is squeezed up through these valves, but cannot pass down through them.

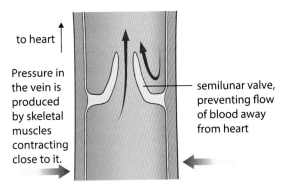

Figure 8.10: Longitudinal section (LS) through part of a small vein.

Blood pressure in the circulatory system

You have seen how blood leaves the heart at high pressure, and then gradually loses this pressure as it passes through muscular arteries, arterioles, capillaries, venules and veins. This happens in both systems – the systemic system and the pulmonary system. The pressure of blood leaving the heart is much greater in

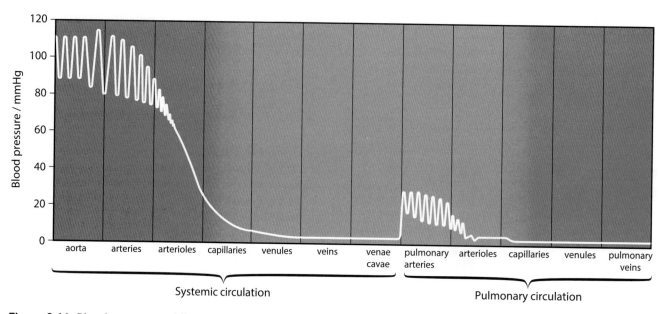

Figure 8.11: Blood pressure in different regions of the human circulatory system.

the systemic system than in the pulmonary system. These blood pressure changes are shown in Figure 8.11.

Questions

3   Suggest reasons for each of the following.

   a   Normal venous pressure in the feet is about 25 mmHg. When a soldier stands motionless at attention, the blood pressure in his feet rises very quickly to about 90 mmHg.

   b   When you breathe in – that is, when the volume of the thorax increases – blood moves through the veins towards the heart.

4   Using the graph in Figure 8.11, describe and explain in your own words how blood pressure varies in different parts of the circulatory system.

5   a   Construct a table comparing the structure of arteries, veins and capillaries. Include both similarities and differences, and give reasons for the differences you describe.

   b   Compare your table with others.

   • Are the headings of the rows and columns the same? If not, whose do you think are best, and why?

   • Has anyone else thought of a similarity or difference that you did not?

   • Who has written the best reasons? What makes these the best?

   If you think your table can be improved, make changes to it.

8.4 Tissue fluid

Blood is composed of cells floating in a pale yellow liquid called **plasma**. Blood plasma is mostly water, with a variety of substances dissolved in it. These solutes include nutrients such as glucose and waste products such as urea that are being transported from one place to another in the body. Solutes also include protein molecules, called **plasma proteins**, which remain in the blood all the time.

KEY WORDS

plasma: the liquid component of blood, in which the blood cells float; it carries a very large range of different substances in solution

plasma proteins: a range of several different proteins dissolved in the blood plasma, each with their own function; many of them are made in the liver

---

As blood flows through capillaries within tissues, some of the plasma leaks out through the gaps between the cells in the walls of the capillary, and flows gently into the spaces between the cells of the tissues. Almost one-sixth of your body consists of spaces between your cells. These spaces are filled with this leaked plasma, which is known as tissue fluid.

> **KEY WORD**
>
> **tissue fluid:** the almost colourless fluid that fills the spaces between body cells; it forms from the fluid that leaks from blood capillaries

Tissue fluid is almost identical in composition to blood plasma. However, it contains far fewer protein molecules than blood plasma, because these are too large to escape easily through the capillary endothelium. Red blood cells are much too large to pass through, so tissue fluid does not contain these, but some white blood cells can squeeze through and move around freely in tissue fluid.

The volume of fluid that leaves the capillary to form tissue fluid is the result of two opposing forces. At the arterial end of a capillary bed, the blood pressure inside the capillary is enough to push fluid out into the tissue. However, there is a greater concentration of dissolved proteins in the blood plasma than in the tissue fluid. This produces a water potential gradient from the tissue fluid into the blood plasma (see Chapter 4, Section 4.5, Movement of substances across membranes). Overall,

water moves from the capillaries into the tissue fluid (Figure 8.12).

At the venule end of a capillary bed, the blood pressure inside the capillaries is lower, so there is less tendency for water to be pushed out of the capillaries into the tissue. The water potential gradient caused by the difference in the concentration of dissolved proteins is still similar to that at the arteriole end. Now, the net movement of water is from the tissue fluid, back into the capillaries.

Overall, more fluid flows out of capillaries than into them, so there is a net loss of fluid from the blood as it flows through a capillary bed.

If blood pressure is too high, too much fluid is forced out of the capillaries and may accumulate in the tissues. This build-up of fluid is called oedema. One of the roles of arterioles is to reduce the pressure of the blood that enters the capillaries, in order to avoid this.

Tissue fluid forms the environment of each individual body cell. Exchanges of materials between cells and the blood occur through the tissue fluid. Within your body, many processes take place to maintain the composition of tissue fluid at a constant level, to provide an optimum environment in which cells can work. These processes contribute to the overall process of homeostasis – that is, the maintenance of a constant internal environment – and include the regulation of glucose concentration, water, pH, metabolic wastes and temperature.

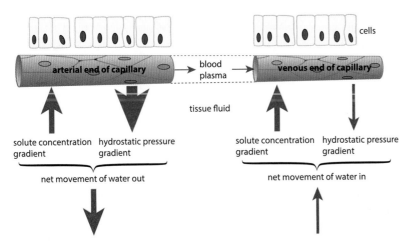

Figure 8.12: Movement of fluid into and out of capillaries.

Questions

6 Table 8.1 shows the relative permeability of capillary walls in a muscle to different substances. In the table, the permeability of water is given a value of 1, and the other values are given in proportion to this.

Use the information in the table, and your own knowledge, to discuss whether there is a relationship between the RMM of a substance and the permeability of the capillary walls to that substance. If so, how can you explain this relationship?

Substance	Relative molecular mass (RMM)	Permeability of capillary walls
water	18	1.00
sodium ions	23	0.96
urea	60	0.8
glucose	180	0.6
haemoglobin	68 000	0.01
albumin	69 000	0.00001

Table 8.1: Relative permeability of capillary walls in muscle.

7 The most abundant plasma protein is albumin. Suggest why it is important that capillary walls are not permeable to albumin.

8 The disease kwashiorkor is caused by a diet which is very low in protein. The concentration of proteins in blood plasma is much lower than usual. One of the symptoms of kwashiorkor is swelling caused by build-up of tissue fluid. Suggest why this is so.

8.5 Blood

You have about 5 dm³ of blood in your body, with a mass of about 5 kg. Suspended in the blood plasma, you have around 2.5×10^{13} red blood cells, 5×10^{11} white blood cells and 6×10^{12} platelets (small cell fragments with no nucleus) (Figures 8.13 and 8.14).

Blood plasma is a pale yellow liquid. It is about 95% water, with various substances dissolved in it. These substances are transported in the blood from one part of the body to another. For example, glucose is transported, in solution in blood plasma, from the small intestine to the liver, and from the liver to all other body cells. Urea is transported from the liver to the kidneys. Water's properties as a solvent (Chapter 2, Section 2.7, Water) make it ideal for this role.

As well as substances in solution, blood plasma transports heat around the body. You will remember that water has a high heat capacity, which allows it to absorb a lot of heat energy without altering its temperature very much.

As tissue fluid is formed from blood plasma, it also contains a high percentage of water. The high heat capacity of the water in tissue fluid helps the whole body to maintain a relatively constant temperature.

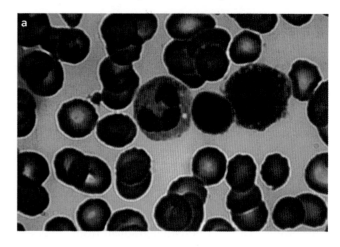

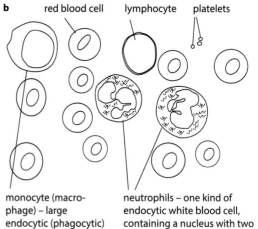

Figure 8.13: **a** Photomicrograph of human blood. It has been stained so that the nuclei of the cells are dark purple (×1600). **b** Diagram of the types of cells seen in a stained blood film.

Red blood cells

The red colour of red blood cells (Figures 8.14 and 8.15) is caused by the pigment haemoglobin, a globular protein (Chapter 2, Section 2.6, Proteins). The main function of haemoglobin is to transport oxygen from lungs to respiring tissues. This function is described in detail later in this chapter.

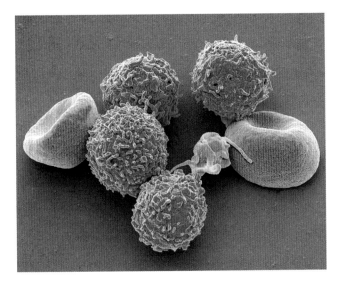

Figure 8.14: False-colour scanning electron micrograph of human blood. Red blood cells have been coloured red. The blue spheres are white blood cells. The platelet has been coloured yellow.

cell surface membrane

haemoglobin solution in cytoplasm (no nucleus, mitochondria or ER)

TS through a red blood cell

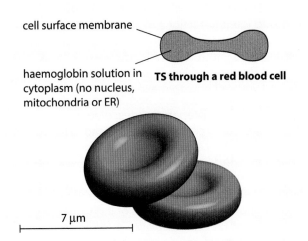

7 μm

Figure 8.15: Red blood cells.

The structure of a red blood cell is unusual in several ways.

- Red blood cells are shaped like a biconcave disc. The dent in each side of the cell increases the surface area to volume ratio (surface area : volume) of the cell. This large surface area means that oxygen can diffuse quickly into or out of the cell.

- Red blood cells are very small. The diameter of a human red blood cell is about 7 μm, compared with the diameter of an average liver cell of 40 μm. This small size means that no haemoglobin molecule within the cell is very far from the cell surface membrane, and the haemoglobin molecules can therefore quickly exchange oxygen with the fluid outside the cell. It also means that capillaries can be only 7 μm wide and still allow red blood cells to squeeze through them, so bringing oxygen as close as possible to cells which require it.

- Red blood cells are very flexible. Some capillaries are even narrower than the diameter of a red blood cell. The cells are able to be squashed so that they can pass through these vessels. This is possible because the cells have a specialised cytoskeleton (Chapter 1, Section 1.6, Plant and animal cells as seen with an electron microscope), made up of a mesh-like network of protein fibres. This allows them to be squashed into different shapes but then spring back to produce the normal biconcave shape.

- Red blood cells have no nucleus, no mitochondria and no endoplasmic reticulum. The lack of these organelles means that there is more room for haemoglobin, so maximising the amount of oxygen which can be carried by each red blood cell.

Red blood cells do not live very long. Old ones are broken down in the liver, and new ones are constantly made in the bone marrow.

Questions

9   Assuming that you have 2.5×10^{13} red blood cells in your body, that the average life of a red blood cell is 120 days, and that the total number of red blood cells remains constant, calculate how many new red blood cells must be made, on average, in your bone marrow each day.

10 Which of these functions could, or could not, be carried out by a red blood cell? In each case, briefly justify your answer.

    a   protein synthesis   c   lipid synthesis
    b   cell division   d   active transport

White blood cells

White blood cells, like red blood cells, are made in the bone marrow. They are easy to distinguish from red blood cells in a micrograph because:

- white blood cells all have a nucleus, although the shape of this varies in different types of white cell

- most white blood cells are larger than red blood cells, although one type, lymphocytes, may be slightly smaller

- white blood cells are either spherical or irregular in shape, not a biconcave disc (compare Figures 8.14 and 8.16).

There are many different kinds of white blood cell, with a wide variety of functions, although all are concerned with fighting disease. They can be divided into two main groups: phagocytes and lymphocytes.

Phagocytes are cells that destroy invading microorganisms by phagocytosis. The commonest type of phagocyte is called a **neutrophil**, and can be recognised by its lobed nucleus and granular cytoplasm. **Monocytes** (Figure 8.13) are cells that can develop into a different type of phagocyte called a **macrophage**.

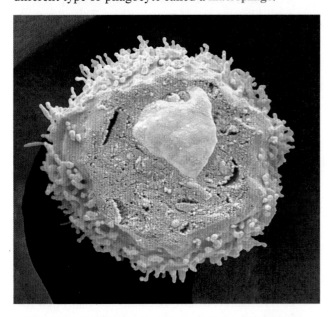

Figure 8.16: False-colour scanning electron micrograph of a section through a white blood cell (×6000). This is a lymphocyte.

Lymphocytes also destroy microorganisms, but not by phagocytosis. Some of them secrete chemicals called

antibodies, which attach to and destroy the invading cells. There are different types of lymphocyte, which act in different ways, although they all look the same. Their activities are described in Chapter 11 (Section 11.2, Cells of the immune system). Lymphocytes are smaller than most phagocytes, and they have a large round nucleus and only a small amount of cytoplasm.

PRACTICAL ACTIVITY 8.1

Observing and drawing blood vessels and blood cells

You should practise using prepared microscope slides to identify sections of arteries and veins. Plan diagrams can be used to show the different tissue layers in the walls of blood vessels. Look back at Practical Activity 7.1 in Chapter 7 to remind yourself how to make plan diagrams.

You can also use prepared slides, electron micrographs and photomicrographs to observe and draw blood cells – red cells, monocytes, neutrophils and lymphocytes. If you are viewing a prepared microscope slide, you will need to use high power, and your drawings will be high-power details, showing the structures of individual cells. Look back at Practical Activity 7.1 for advice on high-power detail drawings, and some examples.

(See Practical Investigations 7.1 and 7.3 in the Practical Workbook for additional information.)

Haemoglobin

A major role of the circulatory system is to transport oxygen from the gas exchange surfaces of the alveoli in the lungs to tissues all over the body. Body cells need a constant supply of oxygen in order to be able to carry out aerobic respiration. Oxygen is transported around the body inside red blood cells in combination with the protein haemoglobin (Figure 2.23).

As you saw in Chapter 2 (Section 2.6, Proteins), each haemoglobin molecule is made up of four polypeptides, each containing one haem group. Each haem group can combine with one oxygen molecule, O_2. Overall, then, each haemoglobin molecule can combine with four oxygen molecules (eight oxygen atoms).

$$Hb \quad + \quad 4O_2 \quad \rightarrow \quad HbO_8$$

haemoglobin   oxygen   oxyhaemoglobin

Question

11 In a healthy adult human, there is about 150 g of haemoglobin in 1 dm³ of blood.

  a 1 g of pure haemoglobin can combine with 1.3 cm³ of oxygen at body temperature. Calculate how much oxygen can be carried in 1 dm³ of blood.

  b At body temperature, the solubility of oxygen in water is approximately 0.025 cm³ of oxygen per cm³ of water. Assuming that blood plasma is mostly water, how much oxygen could be carried in 1 dm³ of blood if there was no haemoglobin?

The haemoglobin dissociation curve

A molecule whose function is to transport oxygen from one part of the body to another must be able to pick up oxygen efficiently at the lungs. It is equally important that it can release oxygen within respiring tissues. Haemoglobin performs these tasks superbly.

To investigate how haemoglobin behaves, samples are extracted from blood and exposed to different concentrations, or **partial pressures**, of oxygen. The quantity of oxygen which combines with each sample of haemoglobin is then measured. The maximum amount of oxygen with which a sample can possibly combine is given a value of 100%. A sample of haemoglobin which has combined with this maximum amount of oxygen is said to be saturated. The amounts of oxygen with which identical samples of haemoglobin combine at lower oxygen partial pressures are then expressed as a percentage of this maximum value known as the **percentage saturation**. Table 8.2 shows a series of results from such an investigation.

The percentage saturation of each sample can be plotted against the partial pressure of oxygen to obtain the curve shown in Figure 8.17. This is known as a **dissociation curve**.

The curve shows that at low partial pressures of oxygen, the percentage saturation of haemoglobin is very low – that is, the haemoglobin is combined with only a very little oxygen. At high partial pressures of oxygen, the percentage saturation of haemoglobin is very high; it is combined with large amounts of oxygen.

KEY WORDS

partial pressure: a measure of the concentration of a gas

percentage saturation: the degree to which the haemoglobin in the blood is combined with oxygen, calculated as a percentage of the maximum amount with which it can combine

dissociation curve: a graph showing the percentage saturation of a pigment (such as haemoglobin) with oxygen, plotted against the partial pressure of oxygen

---

Partial pressure of oxygen / kPa	1	2	3	4	5	6	7	8	9	10	11	12	13	14
Percentage saturation of haemoglobin	8.5	24.0	43.0	57.5	71.5	80.0	85.5	88.0	92.0	94.0	95.5	96.5	97.5	98.0

Table 8.2: Effect of oxygen partial pressure on the percentage saturation of haemoglobin with oxygen.

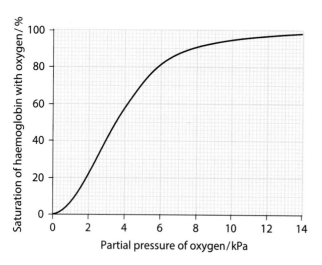

Figure 8.17: The haemoglobin dissociation curve.

Think about the haemoglobin inside a red blood cell in a capillary in the lungs. Here, the partial pressure of oxygen is high, so this haemoglobin is 95–97% saturated with oxygen. This means that almost every haemoglobin molecule is combined with its full complement of eight oxygen atoms.

In an actively respiring muscle, however, where the partial pressure of oxygen is low, the haemoglobin will be about 20–25% saturated with oxygen. In other words, the haemoglobin is carrying only a quarter of the oxygen it is capable of carrying.

This means that haemoglobin coming from the lungs carries a lot of oxygen but, when it reaches a muscle, it releases around three-quarters of it. This released oxygen diffuses out of the red blood cell and into the muscle where it can be used in respiration.

The S-shaped curve

The shape of the haemoglobin dissociation curve can be explained by the behaviour of a haemoglobin molecule as it combines with or loses oxygen molecules.

Oxygen molecules combine with the iron atoms in the haem groups of a haemoglobin molecule. You will remember that each haemoglobin molecule has four haem groups. When an oxygen molecule combines with one haem group, the whole haemoglobin molecule is slightly distorted (its 3D shape changes). The shape change makes it easier for a second oxygen molecule to combine with a second haem group. This in turn makes it easier for a third oxygen molecule to combine with a third haem group. It is then even easier for the fourth and final oxygen molecule to combine.

The shape of the haemoglobin dissociation curve reflects the way that oxygen atoms combine with haemoglobin molecules. Up to an oxygen partial pressure of around 2 kPa, on average only one oxygen molecule is combined with each haemoglobin molecule. Once this oxygen molecule is combined, however, it becomes successively easier for the second and third oxygen molecules to combine, so the curve rises very steeply. Over this part of the curve, a small change in the partial pressure of oxygen causes a very large change in the amount of oxygen which is carried by the haemoglobin.

Questions

12 Use the dissociation curve in Figure 8.17 to answer these questions.

    a i The partial pressure of oxygen in the alveoli of the lungs is about 12 kPa. What is the percentage saturation of haemoglobin in the capillaries in the lungs?

        ii If 1 g of fully saturated haemoglobin is combined with 1.3 cm³ of oxygen, how much oxygen will 1 g of haemoglobin in the capillaries in the lungs be combined with?

    b i The partial pressure of oxygen in an actively respiring muscle is about 2 kPa. What is the percentage saturation of haemoglobin in the capillaries of such a muscle?

        ii How much oxygen will 1 g of haemoglobin in the capillaries of this muscle be combined with?

13 With a partner, build up a list of the ways in which the structure of haemoglobin is related to its function as an oxygen transport molecule in the blood. (You may wish to look back at Chapter 2 to remind you about the various levels of structure of a protein molecule such as haemoglobin, but try to do this without looking if you can.)

Then use your list to write a brief but full explanation of how the structure of haemoglobin helps it to carry out its functions.

The Bohr shift

The behaviour of haemoglobin in picking up oxygen at the lungs, and readily releasing it when in conditions of low oxygen partial pressure, is exactly what is needed. But, in fact, haemoglobin is even better at this than is shown by the dissociation curve in Figure 8.17. This is because the amount of oxygen the haemoglobin carries is affected not only by the partial pressure of oxygen but also by the partial pressure of carbon dioxide.

Carbon dioxide is continually produced by respiring cells. It diffuses from the cells and into blood plasma, from where some of it diffuses into the red blood cells.

In the cytoplasm of red blood cells there is an enzyme, carbonic anhydrase, that catalyses the following reaction:

$$CO_2 + H_2O \underset{\text{carbonic anhydrase}}{\rightleftharpoons} H_2CO_3$$

carbon dioxide   water   carbonic acid

The carbonic acid dissociates:

$$H_2CO_3 \rightleftharpoons H^+ + HCO_3^-$$

carbonic acid   hydrogen ion   hydrogencarbonate ion

Haemoglobin readily combines with the hydrogen ions, forming haemoglobinic acid, HHb. When haemoglobin does this, it releases the oxygen which it is carrying.

The net result of this reaction is twofold.

- Haemoglobin removes excess hydrogen ions from solution. When carbon dioxide dissolves and dissociates, a high concentration of hydrogen ions is formed. This produces a low pH. If the hydrogen ions were left in solution, the blood would be very acidic. By removing the hydrogen ions from solution, haemoglobin helps to maintain the pH of the blood close to neutral. It is acting as a buffer.

- The presence of a high partial pressure of carbon dioxide causes haemoglobin to release oxygen. This is called the Bohr shift, after Christian Bohr who discovered it in 1904. It is exactly what is needed. High concentrations of carbon dioxide are found in actively respiring tissues, which need oxygen; these high carbon dioxide concentrations cause haemoglobin to release its oxygen even more readily than it would otherwise do.

KEY WORDS

carbonic anhydrase: an enzyme found in the cytoplasm of red blood cells that catalyses the reaction between carbon dioxide and water to form carbonic acid

Bohr shift: the decrease in affinity of haemoglobin for oxygen that occurs when carbon dioxide is present

If a dissociation curve is drawn for haemoglobin at a high partial pressure of carbon dioxide, it looks like the lower curve shown on both graphs in Figure 8.18. At each partial pressure of oxygen, the haemoglobin is less saturated than it would be at a low partial pressure of carbon dioxide. The curve therefore lies below, and to the right of, the 'normal' curve.

The effect of changes in carbon dioxide concentration on haemoglobin saturation

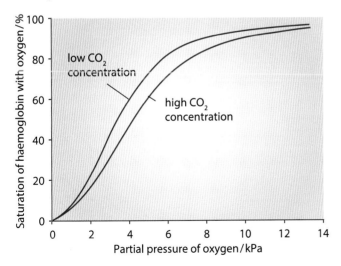

The effect of changes in carbon dioxide concentration on oxygen transport

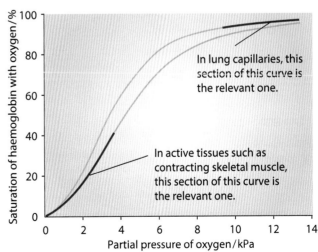

Figure 8.18: Dissociation curves for haemoglobin at two different partial pressures of carbon dioxide. The shift of the curve to the right when the haemoglobin is exposed to higher carbon dioxide concentration is called the Bohr shift.

The chloride shift

The hydrogencarbonate ions that are produced inside red blood cells, as a result of the action of carbonic anhydrase on carbon dioxide, diffuse out of the cells and into the blood plasma. These ions have a negative charge and, to balance their movement, chloride ions (which also have a negative charge) move from the blood plasma into the red blood cells. This is called the **chloride shift**.

If the chloride shift did not happen, the inside of the red blood cell would develop an overall positive charge, because hydrogen ions (from the dissociation of carbonic acid) would accumulate. Hydrogen ions cannot leave the cell, because its cell membrane is not permeable to them. The influx of chloride ions therefore helps to prevent the overall charge inside the cell from becoming too positive.

> ### KEY WORDS
>
> **chloride shift:** the movement of chloride ions into red blood cells from blood plasma, to balance the movement of hydrogencarbonate ions into the plasma from the red blood cells
>
> **carbaminohaemoglobin:** a compound formed when carbon dioxide binds with haemoglobin

Carbon dioxide transport

Carbon dioxide is produced all over the body by respiring cells. Blood transports this waste product from the cells to the lungs, where it is lost by diffusion into the alveoli (Chapter 9, Section 9.5, Alveoli). The blood transports carbon dioxide in three different ways.

As hydrogencarbonate ions in the blood plasma

The description of the Bohr shift above explains one way in which carbon dioxide is carried in the blood. One product of the dissociation of dissolved carbon dioxide is hydrogencarbonate ions, HCO_3^-. These are formed in the cytoplasm of the red blood cell, because this is where the enzyme carbonic anhydrase is found. Most of the hydrogencarbonate ions then diffuse out of the red blood cell into the blood plasma, where they are carried in solution. About 85% of the carbon dioxide transported by the blood is carried in this way.

As dissolved carbon dioxide molecules in the blood plasma

Some carbon dioxide remains as carbon dioxide molecules and some of these simply dissolve in the blood plasma. About 5% of the total is carried in this form.

As carbaminohaemoglobin

Other carbon dioxide molecules diffuse into the red blood cells but do not undergo the reaction catalysed by carbonic anhydrase. Instead, they combine directly with the terminal amine groups ($-NH_2$) of some of the haemoglobin molecules. The compound formed is called **carbaminohaemoglobin**. About 10% of the carbon dioxide is carried in this way (Figure 8.19).

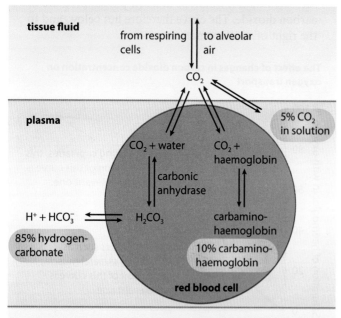

Figure 8.19: Carbon dioxide transport in the blood. The blood carries carbon dioxide partly as undissociated carbon dioxide in solution in the plasma, partly as hydrogencarbonate ions in solution in the plasma, and partly combined with haemoglobin in the red blood cells.

When blood reaches the lungs, the reactions described above go into reverse. As there is a relatively low concentration of carbon dioxide in the alveoli compared with that in the blood, carbon dioxide diffuses from the blood into the air in the alveoli. In turn, this stimulates the carbon dioxide of carbaminohaemoglobin to leave the red blood cell, and hydrogencarbonate and hydrogen ions to recombine to form carbon dioxide molecules once more. This leaves the haemoglobin molecules free to combine with oxygen, ready to begin another circuit of the body.

Question

14 The following statements were all made by candidates in examination answers. Explain what is wrong with each of the following statements.

   a Oxyhaemoglobin gradually releases its oxygen as it passes from the lungs to a muscle.

   b The strong walls of arteries enable them to pump blood around the body.

   c Each red blood cell can combine with eight oxygen atoms.

   d Red blood cells have a large surface area so that many oxygen molecules can be attached.

   e Most carbon dioxide is transported in solution in blood plasma.

8.6 The heart

The heart of an adult human has a mass of around 300 g and is about the size of your fist (Figure 8.20). It is a bag made of muscle and filled with blood. Figure 8.21 shows the appearance of a human heart, looking at it from the front of the body.

The muscle of which the heart is made is called cardiac muscle. Although you do not need to know the structure of cardiac muscle, you may find it interesting, and it is shown in Figure 8.22. It is made of interconnecting cells with cell surface membranes very tightly joined together. This close contact between the muscle cells allows waves of electrical excitation to pass easily between them. This is a very important feature of cardiac muscle, as you will see later.

> ### KEY WORD
>
> cardiac muscle: the type of muscle that makes up the walls of the heart

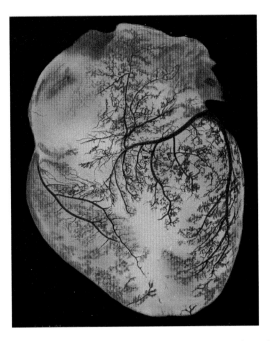

Figure 8.20: A human heart. The blood vessels in the photograph lie immediately below the surface of the heart and have been injected with gelatine containing a dye. The cardiac muscle was treated to make it transparent to a depth of 2 mm to allow the blood vessels to be seen.

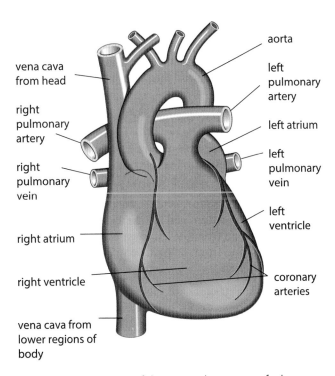

Figure 8.21: Diagram of the external structure of a human heart, seen from the front.

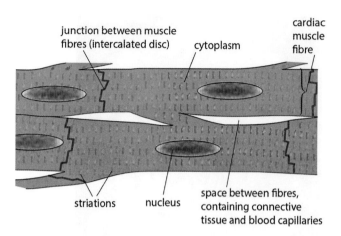

junction between muscle fibres (intercalated disc)

cytoplasm

cardiac muscle fibre

striations

nucleus

space between fibres, containing connective tissue and blood capillaries

Figure 8.22: Diagram of the structure of cardiac muscle. You do not need to know this structure, but you may like to compare it with striated muscle, shown in Chapter 15 (Figure 15.26).

On the surface of the heart, the **coronary arteries** can be seen (Figure 8.20). These branch from the aorta, and deliver oxygenated blood to the walls of the heart itself.

If the heart is cut open vertically (Figures 8.23 and 8.24), it can be seen to contain four chambers. The two chambers on the left of the heart are completely separated from those on the right by a wall of muscle called the **septum**.

Blood cannot pass through the septum; the only way for blood to get from one side of the heart to the other is for it to leave the heart, circulate around either the lungs or the rest of the body, and then return to the other side of the heart.

The upper chamber on each side of the heart is called an **atrium** (plural: **atria**). The two atria receive blood from the veins. You can see from Figure 8.24 that blood from the venae cavae flows into the right atrium, while blood from the pulmonary veins flows into the left atrium.

The lower chambers are **ventricles**. Blood flows into the ventricles from the atria, and is then squeezed out into the arteries. Blood from the left ventricle flows into the aorta, while blood from the right ventricle flows into the pulmonary arteries.

The atria and ventricles have valves between them, which are known as the **atrioventricular valves**. The one on the left is the mitral or **bicuspid valve**, and the one on the right is the **tricuspid valve**.

KEY WORDS

coronary arteries: arteries that branch from the aorta and spread over the walls of the heart, supplying the cardiac muscle with nutrients and oxygen

septum: the layer of tissue that separates the left and right sides of the heart

atrium (plural: **atria**): one of the chambers of the heart that receives low-pressure blood from the veins

ventricle: one of the chambers of the heart that receives blood from the atria and then pushes it into the arteries

atrioventricular valve: a valve between the atria and ventricles that closes when the ventricles contract and stops backflow of blood into the atria

bicuspid valve: the atrioventricular valve on the left side of the heart

tricuspid valve: the atrioventricular valve on the right side of the heart

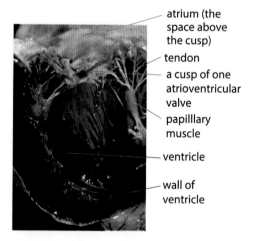

atrium (the space above the cusp)

tendon

a cusp of one atrioventricular valve

papilllary muscle

ventricle

wall of ventricle

Figure 8.23: Section through part of the left side of the heart.

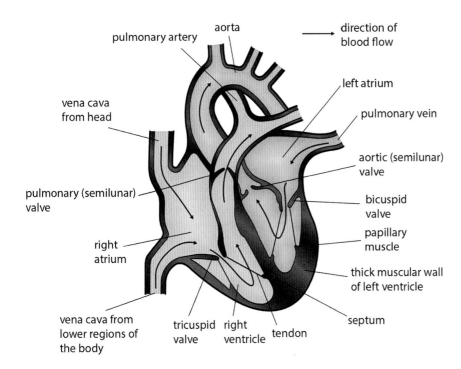

aorta

pulmonary artery

→ direction of blood flow

left atrium

pulmonary vein

aortic (semilunar) valve

bicuspid valve

papillary muscle

thick muscular wall of left ventricle

septum

vena cava from head

pulmonary (semilunar) valve

right atrium

vena cava from lower regions of the body

tricuspid valve

right ventricle

tendon

Figure 8.24: Diagrammatic section through a heart.

KEY WORD

cardiac cycle: the sequence of events that takes place during one heartbeat

The cardiac cycle

Your heart beats around 70 times a minute. The **cardiac cycle** is the sequence of events which makes up one heartbeat. Figure 8.25 shows three stages in this cycle.

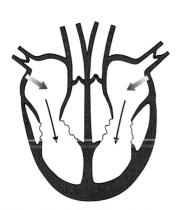
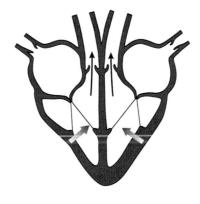

1 **Atrial systole.** Both atria contract. Blood flows from the atria into the ventricles. Backflow of blood into the veins is prevented by closure of the valves in the veins.

2 **Ventricular systole.** Both ventricles contract. The atrioventricular valves are pushed shut by the pressurised blood in the ventricles. The semilunar valves in the aorta and pulmonary artery are pushed open. Blood flows from the ventricles into the arteries.

3 **Ventricular diastole.** Atria and ventricles relax. The semilunar valves in the aorta and pulmonary artery are pushed shut. Blood flows from the veins through the atria and into the ventricles.

→ pressure exerted by contraction of muscle

→ movement of blood

Figure 8.25: The cardiac cycle. Only three stages in this continuous process are shown.

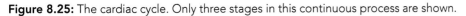

As the cycle is continuous, a description of it could begin anywhere. Let's begin with the time when the heart is filled with blood and the muscle in the atrial walls contracts. This stage is called **atrial systole** (pronounced sis-tole-ee). The pressure developed by this contraction is not very great because the muscular walls of the atria are only thin, but it is enough to force the blood in the atria down through the atrioventricular valves into the ventricles. The blood from the atria does not go back into the pulmonary veins or the venae cavae because these veins have semilunar valves to prevent backflow.

About 0.1 seconds after the atria contract, the ventricles contract. This is called **ventricular systole**. The thick, muscular walls of the ventricles squeeze inwards on the blood, increasing its pressure and pushing it out of the heart. As soon as the pressure in the ventricles becomes greater than the pressure in the atria, the pressure difference pushes the atrioventricular valves shut, preventing blood from going back into the atria. Instead, the blood rushes upwards into the aorta and the pulmonary artery, pushing open the semilunar valves in these vessels as it does so.

Ventricular systole lasts for about 0.3 seconds. The muscle then relaxes, and the stage called ventricular **diastole** begins. As the muscle relaxes, the pressure in the ventricles drops. The high-pressure blood which has just been pushed into the arteries would flow back into the ventricles, but the semilunar valves snap shut as the blood fills their cusps and so prevent this from happening.

> ### KEY WORDS
>
> **atrial systole:** the stage of the cardiac cycle when the muscle in the walls of the atria contracts
>
> **ventricular systole:** the stage of the cardiac cycle when the muscle in the walls of the ventricles contracts
>
> **diastole:** the stage of the cardiac cycle when the muscle in the walls of the heart relaxes

During **atrial systole**, the pressure of the blood is higher in the atrium than in the ventricle, and so forces the atrioventricular valve open. During **ventricular systole**, the pressure of the blood is higher in the ventricle than in the atrium. The pressure of the blood pushes up against the cusps of the atrioventricular valve, pushing it shut. Contraction of the papillary muscles, attached to the valve by tendons, prevents the atrioventricular valve from being forced inside-out.

During **ventricular systole**, the pressure of the blood forces the semilunar valves open. During **ventricular diastole**, the pressure of the blood in the arteries is higher than in the ventricles. The pressure of the blood pushes into the cusps of the semilunar valves, squeezing them shut.

Atrioventricular valve

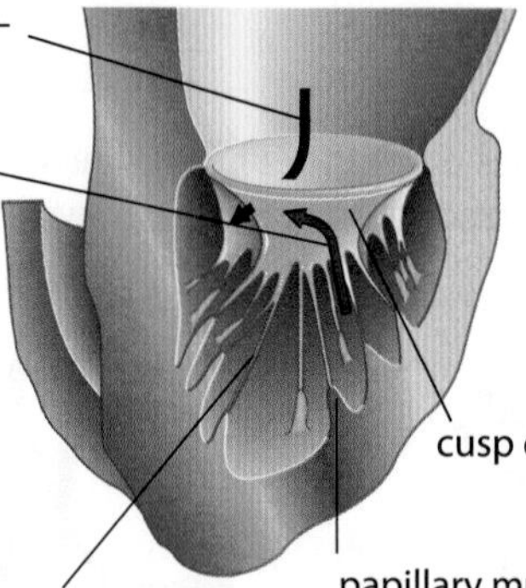

atrial systole – valve open

ventricular systole – valve shut

cusp of valve

papillary muscle

tendon

Semilunar valve

ventricular diastole – valve shut

ventricular systole – valve open

cusp of valve

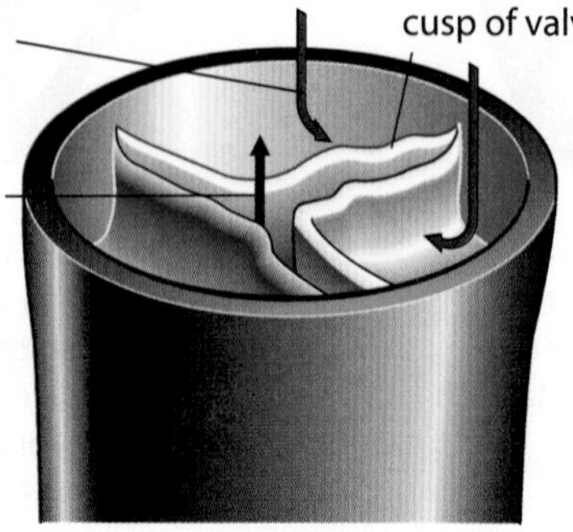

Figure 8.26: How the heart valves function.

During diastole, as all the heart muscle relaxes, blood from the veins flows into the two atria. The blood is at a very low pressure, but the thin walls of the atria are easily distended, providing very little resistance to the blood flow. Some of the blood trickles downwards into the ventricles, through the atrioventricular valves. The atrial muscle then contracts, to push blood forcefully down into the ventricles, and the whole cycle begins again.

Figure 8.26 shows how the atrioventricular and semilunar valves work. Figure 8.27 shows the pressure changes in the left side of the heart during one cardiac cycle.

The walls of the ventricles are much thicker than the walls of the atria because the ventricles need to develop much more force when they contract. Their contraction has to push the blood out of the heart and around the body. For the right ventricle, the force produced must be relatively small, because the blood goes only to the lungs, which are very close to the heart. If the pressure developed was too high, lung capillaries could be damaged and tissue fluid would accumulate in the lungs, hampering gas exchange.

The left ventricle, however, has to develop sufficient force to supply blood to all the rest of the body organs. For most organs, most of the time, the high pressures

that the left ventricle is capable of producing would be too great. So, as you have seen, arterioles play an important role in reducing this pressure before blood flows into the capillaries. However, during vigorous exercise, when muscles are working hard, the arterioles supplying blood to them dilate, increasing blood flow to them. The left ventricle must be able to develop enough force to ensure that there is still sufficient blood reaching other organs. For this reason, the thickness of the muscular wall of the left ventricle is much greater than that of the right.

Figure 8.27 shows the pressure changes in the left side of the heart and the aorta during two consecutive cardiac cycles. You can see that the pressure developed in the left ventricle is much greater than that in the left atrium.

Questions

15 From Figure 8.27, identify the time at which each stage shown in Figure 8.25 is occurring.

16 Heart valves can become weakened and fail to close effectively. Suggest how this would affect the function of the heart and the health of a person.

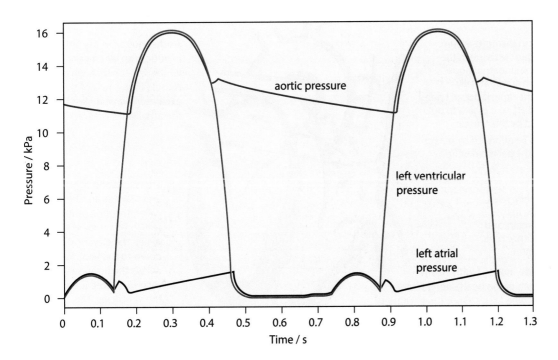

Figure 8.27: Pressure changes in the left side of the heart during the cardiac cycle.

Control of heartbeat

Cardiac muscle differs from the muscle in all other areas of the body in that it is myogenic. This means that it naturally contracts and relaxes; it does not need to receive impulses from a nerve to make it contract. If cardiac muscle cells are cultured in a warm, oxygenated solution containing nutrients, they contract and relax rhythmically, all by themselves.

However, the individual heart muscle cells cannot be allowed to contract at their own natural rhythms. If they did, parts of the heart would contract out of sequence with other parts. The cardiac cycle would become disordered, and the heart would stop working as a pump. The heart has its own built-in controlling and coordinating system which prevents this happening.

The cardiac cycle is initiated in a specialised patch of muscle in the wall of the right atrium called the sinoatrial node. It is often called the SAN for short, or pacemaker. The muscle cells of the SAN set the rhythm for all the other cardiac muscle cells. Their natural rhythm of contraction is slightly faster than that of the rest of the heart muscle. Each time the muscles of the SAN contract, they set up a wave of electrical activity which spreads out rapidly over the whole of the atrial

walls. The cardiac muscle in the atrial walls responds to this excitation wave by contracting, at the same rhythm as the SAN. Therefore, all the muscle in both atria contracts almost simultaneously.

As you have seen, the muscles of the ventricles do not contract until after the muscles of the atria. (You can imagine what would happen if they all contracted at once.) This delay is caused by a feature of the heart that briefly delays the excitation wave in its passage from the atria to the ventricles. There is a band of fibres between the atria and ventricles which does not conduct the excitation wave. This means that, as the wave spreads out from the SAN over the atrial walls, it cannot pass directly into the ventricle walls. The only route through is via a patch of conducting fibres, situated in the

> ## KEY WORDS
>
> myogenic: a word used to describe muscle tissue that contracts and relaxes even when there is no stimulation from a nerve
>
> sinoatrial node (SAN): a patch of cardiac muscle in the right atrium of the heart which contracts and relaxes in a rhythm that sets the pattern for the rest of the heart muscle

1 Each cardiac cycle begins in the right atrium. There is a small patch of muscle tissue in the right atrium wall, called the sinoatrial node (SAN) or pacemaker, which automatically contracts and relaxes all the time. It doesn't need a nerve impulse to start it off, so it is said to be myogenic - that is, "started by the muscle".

The pacemaker's rate can be adjusted by nerves transmitting impulses to the pacemaker from the brain.

5 The ventricles then relax. Then the muscle in the SAN contracts again, and the whole sequence runs through once more.

4 The excitation wave moves swiftly down through the septum of the heart, along fibres known as the Purkyne tissue. Once the excitation wave arrives at the base of the ventricles it sweeps upwards, through the ventricle walls. The ventricles contract.

2 As the muscle in the SAN contracts, it produces an electrical excitation wave which sweeps through all of the muscle in the atria of the heart. This excitation wave makes the muscle in the atrial walls contract.

3 The excitation wave sweeps onward and reaches another patch of cells, called the atrioventricular node (AVN). This node is the only way in which the electrical impulse can get down to the ventricles. The AVN delays the impulse for a fraction of second, before it travels down into the ventricles. This delay means that the ventricles receive the signal to contract after the atria receive the signal.

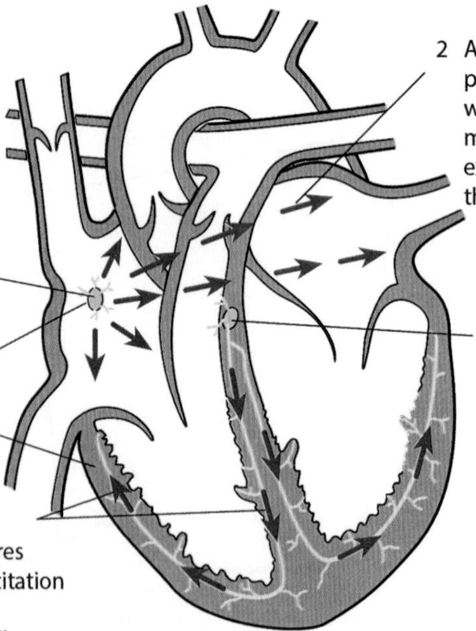

Figure 8.28: How electrical excitation waves move through the heart.

septum, known as the **atrioventricular node**, or **AVN** (Figure 8.28). The AVN picks up the excitation wave as it spreads across the atria and, after a delay of about 0.1 seconds, passes it on to a bunch of conducting fibres called the **Purkyne tissue**, which runs down the septum between the ventricles. This transmits the excitation wave very rapidly down to the base of the septum, from where it spreads outwards and upwards through the ventricle walls. As it does so, it causes the cardiac muscle in these walls to contract, from the bottom up, so squeezing blood upwards and into the arteries.

KEY WORDS

atrioventricular node (AVN): a patch of tissue in the septum of the heart which transmits the wave of excitation from the walls of the atria and transmits it to the Purkyne tissue

Purkyne tissue: a bundle of fibres that conduct the wave of excitation down through the septum of the heart to the base (apex) of the ventricles

---

REFLECTION

In your group, discuss the transport systems of flowering plants and mammals.

- What functions do they have in common, and how do the structures of each of them help to fulfil these functions?

- How do the differences between them reflect the differences in the requirements of plants and animals?

What process did you go through to produce your responses?

Final reflection

Discuss with a friend which, if any, part of Chapter 8 you need to:

- read through again to make sure you really understand

- seek more guidance on, even after going over it again.

SUMMARY

Blood is carried away from the heart in arteries, passes through tissues in capillaries, and is returned to the heart in veins. Blood pressure drops gradually as it passes along this system.

Arteries have thick, elastic walls, to allow them to withstand high blood pressures and to smooth out the pulsed blood flow. Arterioles are small arteries that help to reduce blood pressure and control the amount of blood flow to different tissues. Capillaries are only just wide enough to allow the passage of red blood cells, and they have very thin walls to allow efficient and rapid transfer of materials between blood and cells. Veins have thinner walls than arteries and possess valves to help blood at low pressure flow back to the heart.

Blood plasma leaks from capillaries to form tissue fluid.

Red blood cells are relatively small cells. They have a biconcave shape and no nucleus. Their cytoplasm is full of haemoglobin.

White blood cells include phagocytes and lymphocytes. They all have nuclei, and are either spherical or irregular in shape.

Red blood cells carry oxygen in combination with haemoglobin.

CONTINUED

Haemoglobin picks up oxygen at high partial pressures (concentrations) of oxygen in the lungs and releases it at low partial pressures of oxygen in respiring tissues. A graph showing the percentage saturation of haemoglobin at different partial pressures of oxygen is known as a dissociation curve.

At high carbon dioxide concentrations, the dissociation curve shifts downwards and to the right, showing that haemoglobin releases oxygen more easily when carbon dioxide concentration is high. This is known as the Bohr shift.

The mammalian heart has four chambers: right and left atria and right and left ventricles. The right side of the heart is divided from the left by a wall of tissue called the septum. The atrial muscular walls are thin and do not exert much pressure when they contract. The ventricular walls are much more muscular and exert a sufficient pressure to drive blood to the lungs from the right ventricle and around the rest of the body from the left ventricle. The left ventricular wall is therefore much thicker and more muscular than the right ventricular wall.

The cardiac cycle is a continuous process but can be considered in three stages. **1** Atrial systole (contraction of the atria) allows blood to flow into the ventricles from the atria. Closure of valves in the veins prevents backflow of blood into the veins. **2** Ventricular systole (contraction of the ventricles) pushes blood into the arteries by forcing open the semilunar valves. Blood is prevented from flowing back into the atria by pressure closing the atrioventricular valves. **3** In diastole (relaxation of heart muscle), the semilunar valves are pushed shut, preventing backflow of blood from the arteries into the ventricles. Blood flows into the atria and ventricles from the veins.

Beating of the heart is initiated by the sinoatrial node (SAN) or pacemaker, which has its own myogenic rhythm. A wave of excitation spreads across the atria so all the heart muscle cells in the atria contract together. The wave of excitation cannot spread to the ventricles directly because of a band of non-conducting tissue. However, the atrioventricular node (AVN) in the septum passes the wave to the Purkyne tissue, which then causes the ventricles to contract from the bottom up shortly after the atria. This is important because it pushes the blood upwards out of the ventricles into the arteries.

EXAM-STYLE QUESTIONS

1 Where is the mammalian heartbeat initiated?

   A atrioventricular node (AVN)

   B left atrium

   C Purkyne tissue

   D sinoatrial node (SAN)   [1]

2 What causes the bicuspid valve to close during ventricular systole?

   A a greater blood pressure in the left atrium than in the left ventricle

   B a greater blood pressure in the left ventricle than in the left atrium

   C contraction of muscles in the septum

   D contraction of muscles in the valve   [1]

CONTINUED

3 The diagram shows the changes in blood pressure as blood flows through the blood vessels in the human systemic circulatory system.

Which correctly identifies the vessels labelled **P** to **S**?

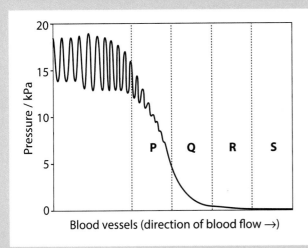

	P	Q	R	S
A	artery	capillary	arteriole	venule
B	arteriole	artery	venule	capillary
C	artery	arteriole	capillary	venule
D	venule	capillary	arteriole	artery

[1]

4 The micrograph shows an artery and a vein.

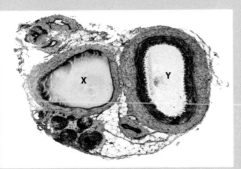

Which row correctly identifies and describes the artery and the vein?

	X	Y	Description
A	artery	vein	The artery has thick walls and the vein has thin walls.
B	artery	vein	The artery has a thin middle layer while the vein has a thick middle layer.
C	vein	artery	The artery has a thick middle layer while the vein has a thin middle layer.
D	vein	artery	The artery has thin walls and the vein has thick walls.

[1]

CONTINUED

5   Carbon dioxide is transported in the blood in various forms.

   a   Describe how carbon dioxide molecules reach red blood cells from
       respiring cells.   [2]

   b   The diagram below shows part of a capillary network and some cells of
       the surrounding tissue.

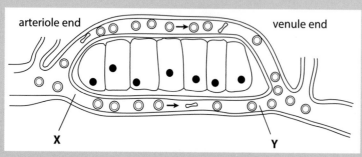

       State **three** ways in which the blood at Y differs from the blood
       at **X other than** in the concentration of carbon dioxide.   [3]

   c   An enzyme in red blood cells catalyses the reaction between carbon dioxide
       and water as blood flows through respiring tissues.

$$CO_2 + H_2O \xrightarrow{\text{enzyme}} H_2CO_3 \longrightarrow H^+ + HCO_3^-$$

   i   Name the enzyme that catalyses this reaction.   [1]

   ii Explain the significance of this reaction in the transport of
       carbon dioxide.   [3]

   d   The graph below shows the effect of increasing the carbon dioxide
       concentration on the oxygen dissociation curve for haemoglobin.

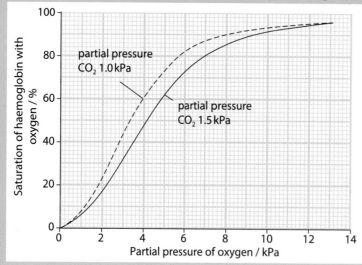

CONTINUED

   i   State the percentage saturation of haemoglobin with oxygen at a
       partial pressure of 5 kPa of oxygen when the partial pressure of
       carbon dioxide is:

       1.0 kPa

       1.5 kPa   **[1]**

   ii The percentage saturation of haemoglobin with oxygen decreases as the
       partial pressure of carbon dioxide increases. Explain how this happens.

                                                      [2]

  iii Name the effect of increasing carbon dioxide concentration on the
       oxygen dissociation curve.   **[1]**

  iv Explain the importance of the effect of carbon dioxide on haemoglobin
       as shown in the graph.   **[3]**

                                                [Total: 16]

*Cambridge International AS & A Level Biology (9700) Paper 21, Question 2,
June 2011*

6 Mammals have a closed, double circulation.

  a State what is meant by the term *double circulation*.   **[1]**

  b The figure below shows part of the circulation in a mammalian tissue.
     The central part is enlarged to show a capillary and a cell supplied by
     the capillary.

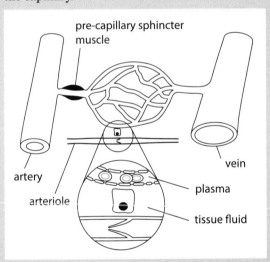

     Explain why the wall of the artery is thicker than the wall of the vein.   **[2]**

  c Suggest **one** role for the pre-capillary sphincter muscle shown in
     the figure.   **[1]**

  d With reference to the figure, describe the role of capillaries in forming
     tissue fluid.   **[3]**

  e Describe **three** ways in which plasma differs from tissue fluid.   **[3]**

                                                    [Total: 10]

*Cambridge International AS & A Level Biology (9700) Paper 2, Question
4a–ei, November 2008*

7 Figure 8.27 shows the pressure changes in the left atrium, left ventricle and aorta throughout two cardiac cycles. Make a copy of this diagram.

  a   **i**   How long does one heartbeat (one cardiac cycle) last?   **[1]**

      ii   What is the heart rate represented on this graph, in beats per minute?   **[1]**

  b   The contraction of muscles in the ventricle wall causes the pressure inside the ventricle to rise. When the muscles relax, the pressure drops again. On your copy of the diagram, mark the following periods:

      i   the time when the ventricle is contracting (ventricular systole)   **[1]**

      ii   the time when the ventricle is relaxing (ventricular diastole).   **[1]**

  c   The contraction of muscles in the wall of the atrium raises the pressure inside it. This pressure is also raised when blood flows into the atrium from the veins, while the atrial walls are relaxed. On your copy of the diagram, mark the following periods:

      i   the time when the atrium is contracting (atrial systole)   **[1]**

      ii   the time when the atrium is relaxing (atrial diastole).   **[1]**

  d   The atrioventricular valves open when the pressure of the blood in the atria is greater than that in the ventricles. They snap shut when the pressure of the blood in the ventricles is greater than that in the atria.

      On your diagram, mark the points at which these valves will open and close.   **[1]**

  e   The opening and closing of the semilunar valves in the aorta depends in a similar way on the relative pressures in the aorta and ventricles. On your diagram, mark the points at which these valves will open and close.   **[1]**

  f   The right ventricle has much less muscle in its walls than the left ventricle, and only develops about one-quarter of the pressure developed on the left side of the heart. On your diagram, draw a line to represent the probable pressure inside the right ventricle over the 1.3 seconds shown.   **[1]**

                                      [Total: 9]

8 The diagram below shows a cross section of the heart at the level of the valves.

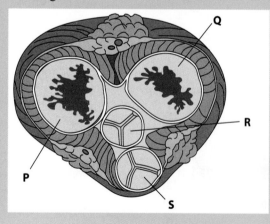

CONTINUED

a i Copy and complete the following flow chart to show the pathway of blood through the heart.

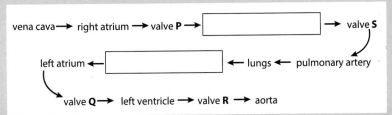

ii Explain how the valves P and Q ensure one-way flow of blood through the heart. **[2]**

b The cardiac cycle describes the events that occur during one heartbeat. The following figure shows the changes in blood pressure that occur within the left atrium, left ventricle and aorta during one heartbeat. **[2]**

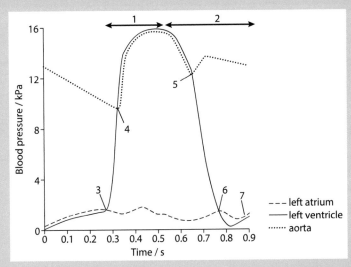

Copy and complete the table below. Match up each event during the cardiac cycle with an appropriate number from 1 to 7 on the diagram. **You should put only one number in each box. You may use each number once, more than once or not at all.**

The first answer has been completed for you.

Event during the cardiac cycle	Number
atrioventricular (bicuspid) valve opens	6
ventricular systole	
semilunar (aortic) valve closes	
left ventricle and left atrium both relaxing	
semilunar (aortic) valve opens	

[4]

CONTINUED

c   Explain the roles of the SAN, AVN and the Purkyne tissue during one
heartbeat.   [5]

[Total: 13]

*Cambridge International AS & A Level Biology (9700) Paper 21,
Question 3, May/June 2010*

SELF-EVALUATION CHECKLIST

After studying this chapter, complete a table like this:

I can	See section...	Needs more work	Almost there	Ready to move on
describe the structure of the mammalian circulatory system as a closed, double circulation, and describe its main components	8.2			
explain how the structures of arteries, arterioles, veins, venules and capillaries are related to their functions	8.3			
describe the formation and functions of tissue fluid	8.4			
describe the structure of blood, including blood plasma, red cells, monocytes, neutrophils and lymphocytes	8.5			
make diagrams of blood vessels and blood cells from slides, photomicrographs or electron micrographs	8.4, 8.5			
explain, in detail, how oxygen and carbon dioxide are transported in the blood, and interpret oxygen dissociation curves	8.5			
describe and explain the Bohr shift	8.5			
explain how the solvent properties of water, and its high heat capacity, enable blood plasma and tissue fluid to carry out their functions	8.5			
explain the structure and function of the heart	8.6			
describe the cardiac cycle and its control	8.6			

Gas exchange

BEFORE YOU START

This chapter is about the gas exchange system of mammals. This system is a collection of organs, tissues and cells that function together for the movement of air in and out of the lungs where gases are exchanged with the blood. Many organisms do not have structures specialised for gas exchange.

Discuss with your group why mammals need a complex gas exchange system.

EXAMINING THE AIRWAYS

The surgeon in Figure 9.1a is using an endoscope to examine the airways looking for any blockages or for a tumour. Endoscopes are flexible tubes with a light and camera at one end. They are used for many routine examinations of body cavities. The type of endoscope used to examine the airways and lungs is a bronchoscope.

The surgeon inserts the bronchoscope through the nose or mouth. It passes through the vocal cords in the larynx and then goes down the trachea (windpipe) and into one of the bronchi. If the bronchoscope has a video camera, it is possible for others, including the patient, to view any blockages or damage to the airways on a monitor screen.

In this case, the white area at the base of the trachea is inflamed (Figure 9.1b). If the patient is a smoker, the surgeon may suspect lung cancer. He can use the bronchoscope to carry out a biopsy by removing a small amount of tissue from this area and sending it to the lab for analysis to see if the cells are cancerous.

Question for discussion

The surgeon who is using the bronchoscope works in a Department of Respiratory Medicine of a hospital. Many health services offer screening tests for different diseases, including lung cancer.

Discuss whether screening tests should be made compulsory for those at risk of certain diseases.

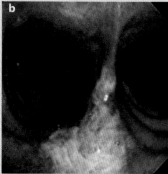

Figure 9.1: a A surgeon using a bronchoscope to view the interior of the airways. **b** A view through a bronchoscope of the base of the trachea where it branches into the two bronchi. The white area is inflammation of the tissues that line the trachea.

9.1 Gas exchange

The human gas exchange system links the circulatory system (Chapter 8, Section 8.2, The mammalian circulatory system) with the atmosphere and is adapted to:

- clean and warm the air that enters during breathing
- maximise the surface area for diffusion of oxygen and carbon dioxide between the blood and atmosphere
- minimise the distance for this diffusion
- maintain adequate gradients for this diffusion.

Most organisms need a supply of oxygen for respiration. In single-celled organisms, the oxygen simply diffuses from the fluid outside the cell, through the cell surface membrane and into the cytoplasm. In a multicellular organism such as a human, most of the cells are a considerable distance away from the external environment from which the oxygen is obtained.

Multicellular organisms, therefore, usually have a specialised **gas exchange surface** where oxygen from the external environment can diffuse into the body, and carbon dioxide can diffuse out.

In humans, the gas exchange surface is the **alveoli** (singular: **alveolus**) in the lungs. Figure 9.2 shows the distribution of alveoli in the lungs and their structure. Although each individual alveolus is tiny, the alveoli collectively have a huge surface area, probably totalling about 70–75 m^2 in an adult human. This means that a large number of oxygen and carbon dioxide molecules can diffuse through the surface at any one moment giving a high rate of gas exchange. The large surface area is also required because oxygen is not very soluble in water.

9.2 Lungs

The lungs are in the thoracic (chest) cavity surrounded by the pleural membranes, which enclose an airtight space. This space contains a small quantity of fluid to allow friction-free movement as the lungs are ventilated by the movement of the diaphragm and ribs. For this chapter, you do not need detailed knowledge of the breathing movements of diaphragm and rib cage.

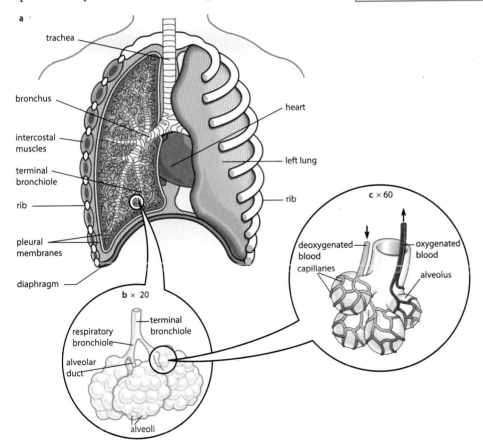

Figure 9.2: The human trachea and lungs. Air passes through **a** the trachea and bronchi to supply many branching bronchioles **b** which terminate in alveoli **c** where gas exchange occurs between alveolar air and blood in pulmonary capillaries. The gas exchange surface of around 70–75 m^2 fits into the thoracic cavity, which has a capacity of about 5 dm^3.

Airway	Number	Approximate diameter	Cartilage	Goblet cells	Smooth muscle	Cilia	Site of gas exchange
trachea	1	1.8 cm	yes	yes	yes	yes	no
bronchus	2	1.2 cm	yes	yes	yes	yes	no
terminal bronchiole	48 000	1.0 mm	no	no	yes	yes	no
respiratory bronchiole	300 000	0.5 mm	no	no	no	a few	no
alveolar duct	9×10^6	400 µm	no	no	no	no	yes
alveoli	3×10^9	250 µm	no	no	no	no	yes

Table 9.1: The structure of the airways from the trachea to the alveoli. The various airways are shown in Figure 9.2.

9.3 Trachea, bronchi and bronchioles

The lungs are ventilated with air that passes through a branching system of airways (Table 9.1). Leading from the throat to the lungs is the trachea. At the base of the trachea are two bronchi (singular: bronchus), which subdivide and branch extensively forming a bronchial 'tree' in each lung. Each bronchus divides many times to form smaller and smaller bronchioles. Terminal bronchioles divide to form even narrower respiratory bronchioles that supply the alveolar ducts with air.

Cartilage in the trachea and bronchi keeps these airways open and air resistance low; it prevents them from collapsing or bursting as the air pressure changes during breathing. In the trachea, there is a regular arrangement of C-shaped rings of cartilage; in the bronchi, there are irregular blocks of cartilage. Compare the photographs of the trachea (Figures 9.3a and 9.9) with those of bronchi (Figures 9.3b and 9.10).

Questions

1 Calculate the actual width of the regions of cartilage in the trachea and in the bronchus (Figures 9.3a and 9.3b). Give the formula you use, show all your working and express your answer to the nearest micrometre.

2 a Use Figure 9.3c to help you describe the appearance of smooth muscle in the bronchiole.

   b Explain the role of smooth muscle in the gas exchange system.

3 Explain why there are so many alveoli in the lungs.

KEY WORDS

trachea (windpipe): the tube-like structure that extends from the larynx to the bronchi; it allows movement of air into and out of the lungs

bronchus (plural: bronchi): a major branch of the trachea that extends into the lungs

bronchiole: a microscopic branch of a bronchus that leads to the alveoli

cartilage: a type of skeletal tissue that is strong and flexible and supports the larynx, trachea and bronchi in the gas exchange system; cartilage is also found at joints between bones and in the external ear

9.4 Warming and cleaning the air

As air flows through the nose and the trachea, it is warmed to body temperature and moistened by evaporation from the lining, so protecting the delicate surfaces inside the lungs from desiccation (drying out). Protection is also needed against material carried in the air, which may include dust, sand, pollen, fungal spores, bacteria and viruses. All are potential threats to the proper functioning of the lungs. Particles larger than about 5–10 µm are caught on the hairs inside the nose and the mucus lining the nasal passages and other airways.

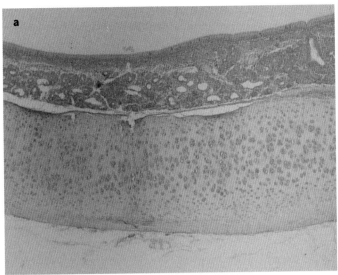

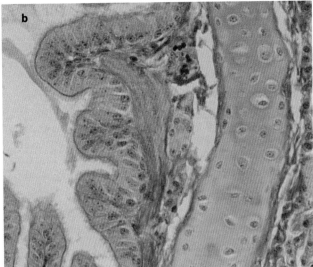

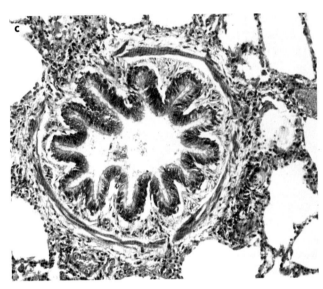

Figure 9.3:

a A photomicrograph of part of the trachea in transverse section (TS) (×65). The lining is comprised of ciliated epithelium which rests on a basement membrane made of protein fibres. In between the ciliated cells are goblet cells (stained blue). Beneath the epithelium is an area of loose tissue with blood vessels and mucous glands. The trachea as a whole is supported by C-shaped rings of cartilage. A portion of a cartilage ring appears as a thick layer running across the bottom of the picture.

b A light micrograph of part of a bronchus in TS (×300). Between the ciliated epithelial cells, the goblet cells are stained pink. There are fewer goblet cells per cm² than in the trachea, and the epithelial cells are not as tall. Beneath the epithelium there are elastic fibres. Blocks of cartilage, not rings, support the bronchus, and part of one can be seen, also stained pink, stretching from the top to the bottom of the picture.

c A light micrograph of a small bronchiole in TS (×135). Surrounding the epithelium is smooth muscle. There is no cartilage. Around the bronchiole are some alveoli. In living lung tissue there is no folding of the wall of the airways. Smooth muscle contracts at death to cause the folding you can see.

In the trachea and bronchi, the mucus is produced by goblet cells of the ciliated epithelium (Figures 9.3–9.6). The upper part of each goblet cell is swollen with mucin droplets which have been secreted by the cell. Mucus is a slimy solution of mucin, which is composed of glycoproteins with many carbohydrate chains that make them sticky and able to trap inhaled particles. The rest of the cell contains a Golgi body (Golgi apparatus), some rough endoplasmic reticulum, mitochondria and a nucleus. The lower part of the cell is thin so that the cell resembles a drinking vessel, known as a goblet. Mucus

KEY WORDS

goblet cell: a cell shaped like a drinking goblet that secretes mucus; goblet cells are found in epithelia lining parts of the gas exchange system and other organ systems, e.g. reproductive and digestive

ciliated epithelium: an epithelium that consists mainly of ciliated cells; may also contain goblet cells

mucin: any glycoprotein that forms part of the mucus secreted by goblet cells and mucous cells

is also made by mucous glands beneath the epithelium. Some chemical pollutants, such as sulfur dioxide and nitrogen dioxide, can dissolve in mucus to form an acidic solution that irritates the lining of the airways.

Between the goblet cells are ciliated epithelial cells. The continual beating of their cilia carries the layer of mucus upwards towards the larynx at a speed of about 1 cm min⁻¹ (Figure 9.5). When mucus reaches the top of the trachea it is usually swallowed so that pathogens are destroyed by acid in the stomach. The way cilia function is described in Chapter 1 (Section 1.6, Plant and animal cells as seen with an electron microscope).

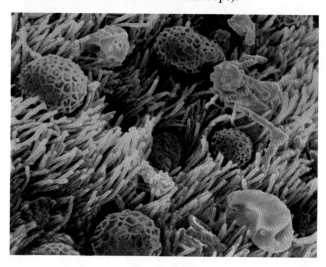

Figure 9.4: False-colour scanning electron micrograph of the surface of the trachea, showing large numbers of cilia (yellow) covered with pollen grains (pink) and dust (blue) breathed in with the air (×2000).

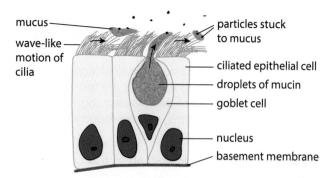

Figure 9.5: The wave-like beating of the cilia moves mucus secreted by goblet cells to the back of the throat.

Bronchioles are surrounded by smooth muscle, which can contract or relax to adjust the diameter of these tiny airways. During exercise, the muscles relax to allow a greater flow of air to the alveoli. The absence of cartilage makes these adjustments possible.

Phagocytic white blood cells known as macrophages patrol the surfaces of the airways scavenging small particles such as bacteria and fine dust particles. During an infection, the macrophages are joined by other phagocytic cells which leave the capillaries to help remove pathogens (Chapter 11, Section 11.2, Cells of the immune system).

9.5 Alveoli

At the end of the pathway between the atmosphere and the bloodstream are the alveoli (Figures 9.3c, 9.7 and 9.10). Alveolar walls contain **elastic fibres** which stretch during inspiration and recoil during expiration to help force out air. This elasticity allows alveoli to expand according to the volume of air breathed in. When the alveoli are fully expanded during exercise, the surface area available for diffusion increases, and the air is expelled efficiently when the elastic fibres recoil during exhalation. The walls also contain some collagen fibres to provide support and help prevent alveoli from bursting.

The alveoli have extremely thin walls, each consisting of a single layer of squamous epithelial cells. These cells are like fried eggs. The nucleus is like the yolk surrounded by a thin layer of cytoplasm, which is only 25 nm thick. No part of the cell is more than 0.5 μm thick. Pressed closely against the alveoli walls are blood capillaries, lined by endothelial cells that are also very thin. Oxygen and carbon dioxide molecules diffuse quickly between the air and the blood because the distance is very small.

You will remember that diffusion is the net movement of molecules or ions down a concentration gradient. So, for gas exchange to take place rapidly, a steep concentration gradient must be maintained. This is done by breathing and by the movement of the blood. Breathing brings supplies of fresh air into the lungs, with a relatively

> ## KEY WORD
>
> **elastic fibres:** bundles of the fibrous protein elastin which can stretch and recoil like elastic bands; they can stretch up to twice their length before breaking

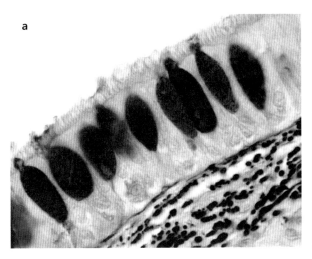
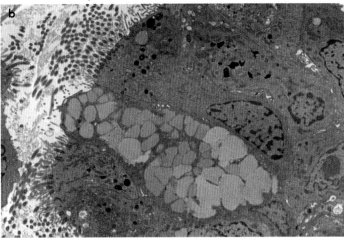

Figure 9.6: a Epithelium of the trachea with many goblet cells (purple) secreting mucus onto the surface to be moved by cilia. The tissue below the epithelium (lower right) has many elastic fibres (×550). **b** Transmission electron micrograph (TEM) of the epithelium of the bronchus. In the centre is a section of a goblet cell. The upper part of the goblet cell is filled with mucus with exocytosis occurring into the lumen on the left. At the opposite end of the goblet cell is its triangular shaped nucleus. On either side of the goblet cells are ciliated epithelial cells (×1300).

high oxygen concentration and a relatively low carbon dioxide concentration. Blood is brought to the lungs with a lower concentration of oxygen and a higher concentration of carbon dioxide than the air in the alveoli. Oxygen therefore diffuses down its concentration gradient from the air in the alveoli to the blood, and carbon dioxide diffuses down its concentration gradient in the opposite direction. The blood is constantly flowing through and out of the lungs, so, as the oxygenated blood leaves, more deoxygenated blood enters to maintain the concentration gradient with each new breath (Figure 9.8).

Questions

4   Use Figure 9.6a to make a labelled drawing of the epithelium of the trachea. Indicate on your drawing the actual depth of the epithelium, and show your calculation.

5   Goblet cells are surrounded by ciliated epithelial cells in the gas exchange system. They are also found in the small intestine where they are surrounded by cells with microvilli. What are the similarities and differences between cilia and microvilli? (You may want to refer back to Chapter 1.)

6   Describe the detail that can be seen in a TEM of a ciliated epithelial cell that cannot be seen under high power with a light microscope.

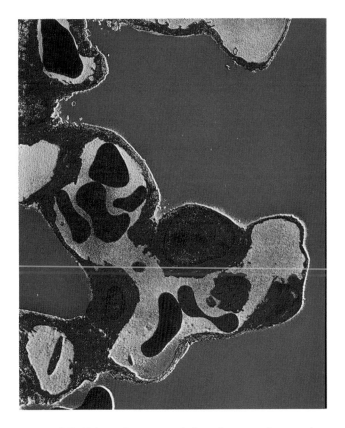

Figure 9.7: False-colour transmission electron micrograph (TEM) of the lining of an alveolus. Red blood cells fill the blood capillaries (yellow), which are separated from the air (blue) by a thin layer of cells (pink) (×2500).

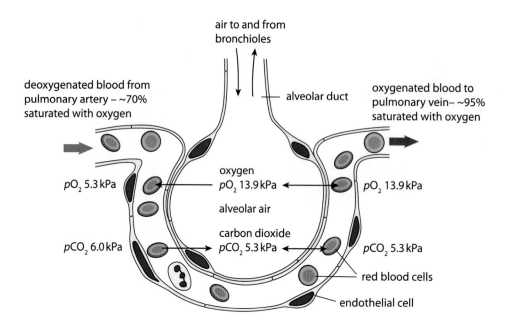

air to and from bronchioles

deoxygenated blood from pulmonary artery – ~70% saturated with oxygen

alveolar duct

oxygenated blood to pulmonary vein– ~95% saturated with oxygen

oxygen
pO_2 5.3 kPa
pO_2 13.9 kPa
pO_2 13.9 kPa

alveolar air

carbon dioxide
pCO_2 6.0 kPa
pCO_2 5.3 kPa
pCO_2 5.3 kPa

red blood cells

endothelial cell

Figure 9.8: Gas exchange between the air in the alveolus and blood in the pulmonary capillaries. Note that there is a much steeper concentration gradient for oxygen than for carbon dioxide. See the section on transport of carbon dioxide in Chapter 8 to find the reason for the shallow concentration gradient for carbon dioxide.

Questions

7 **a** Describe the pathway taken by a molecule of oxygen as it passes from the atmosphere to the blood in the lungs.

   b Explain how alveoli are adapted for gas exchange.

8 **a** Explain the advantage of being able to adjust the diameter of bronchioles.

   b How many times does an oxygen molecule cross a cell surface membrane as it moves from the air into a red blood cell? Explain your answer.

9 The electron microscope was needed to confirm that each alveolus is completely surrounded by epithelial cells. Explain why.

PRACTICAL ACTIVITY 9.1

Making drawings of prepared slides

Practical Activity 7.1 in Chapter 7 provides general guidance on biological drawing. Read the relevant sections of that activity before answering Question 10 here.

Figure 9.9: A section through the trachea. The front of the neck is at the top. At the back of the trachea between the ends of the ring of cartilage is a band of smooth muscle (×4).

(See Practical Investigations 7.1 and 7.3 in the Practical Workbook for additional information.)

CONTINUED

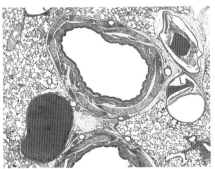

Figure 9.10: A section through lung tissue showing a cross section of a bronchus, cross sections of three blood vessels and many alveoli (×8).

(See Practical Investigation 7.4 in the Practical Workbook for additional information.)

Question

10 Before you start, remind yourself how to draw plan diagrams.

Use Figures 9.9 and 9.10 to draw low-power plan diagrams of the walls of:

a   the trachea

b   a bronchus.

Label your plan diagrams to identify the tissues. Annotate your plan diagrams to show the appearance of the tissues.

REFLECTION

Exercise physiology labs use apparatus to measure changes in the way the cardiovascular and gas exchange systems respond to different intensities of exercise. Researchers can change the resistance of the bicycle to make athletes exercise at different intensities (Figure 9.11).

Discuss how you would use the apparatus shown in Figure 9.11 to investigate how athletes respond to exercise of increasing intensity. Some decisions that you will have to make are:

•   how you will choose the athletes to use as subjects for your investigation

•   what you will measure

•   how you will process the results to make valid comparisons between the effects of different intensities of exercise

•   the variables you will standardise so you can collect valid results.

Figure 9.11: An athlete on an exercise bicycle. The face mask is attached to sensors that detect how fast she is breathing, how much air she breathes in and how much oxygen she absorbs. The clip on her finger is an oximeter that detects her pulse rate and the percentage saturation of the haemoglobin in blood entering the capillaries in her skin (SpO_2).

Final reflection

Discuss with a friend which, if any, parts of Chapter 9 you need to:

•   read through again to make sure you really understand

•   seek more guidance on, even after going over it again.

SUMMARY

Multicellular organisms often have surfaces that are specialised to allow exchange of gases to take place between their bodies and the environment. Alveoli in the lungs form the gas exchange surface in mammals.

In human lungs, air passes down the trachea and through a branching system of airways to reach the alveoli. The airways are lined by a ciliated epithelium with mucus-secreting goblet cells. The epithelium protects the alveoli by moving a carpet of mucus towards the throat, where it can be swallowed. There are C-shaped rings of cartilage in the trachea and irregularly shaped blocks of cartilage in the bronchi to keep the large airways open and so reduce resistance to the flow of air. Smooth muscle in the airways contracts and relaxes to adjust the diameter of the airways.

The alveoli are lined by a squamous epithelium that gives a short diffusion distance for the exchange of oxygen and carbon dioxide. The alveoli are well supplied with blood by the many capillaries surrounding the gas exchange surface. The constant flow of blood and the continuous ventilation of the lungs maintain concentration gradients between blood and air for oxygen and carbon dioxide. Recoil of the elastic fibres in the wall of the alveoli helps to move air out during expiration.

EXAM-STYLE QUESTIONS

1 The following structures are found in the walls of the gas exchange system.

1 cilia   4 smooth muscle cells

2 elastic fibres   5 squamous epithelial cells

3 goblet cells

Which would be found in the lining of an alveolus?

A 1 and 3   C 2 and 5

B 1, 2 and 3   D 4 and 5   [1]

2 Cartilage is found in which structure?

A alveolus   C capillary

B bronchiole   D trachea   [1]

3 Which of the following is **not** a role of elastic fibres in the gas exchange system?

A contract to decrease the volume of the alveoli during exhalation

B recoil to force air out of the alveoli during exhalation

C stretch to accommodate more air in the alveoli during deep breathing

D stretch to increase the surface area of the alveoli for gas exchange   [1]

4 Which of the following best describes the process of gas exchange in the lungs?

A Air moves in and out of the alveoli during breathing.

B Carbon dioxide diffuses from deoxygenated blood in capillaries into the alveolar air.

C Oxygen and carbon dioxide diffuse down their concentration gradients between blood and alveolar air.

D Oxygen diffuses from alveolar air into deoxygenated blood.   [1]

5 The diagram shows an alveolus.

a Name:

i cells A, B and C   [3]

ii the fluid at D.   [1]

CONTINUED

b The length of the scale bar is 13 mm.

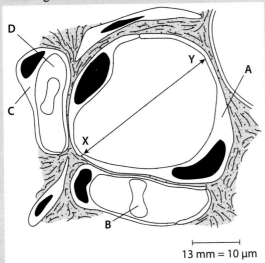

13 mm = 10 µm

Calculate the actual distance indicated by X–Y:
- write out the formula that you will use
- use the formula to calculate the actual distance
- give your answer to the nearest micrometre. **[3]**

c Explain how alveoli are adapted for the exchange of gases. **[4]**

[Total: 11]

6 The diagram shows two cells from the lining of the trachea.

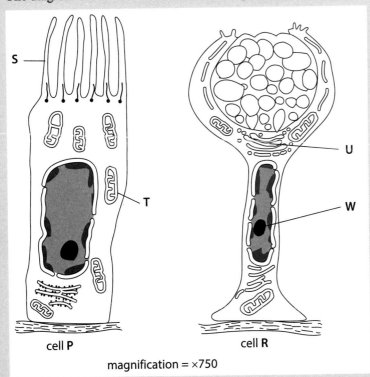

cell P   cell R

magnification = ×750

CONTINUED

a Name:

  i cells P and R [2]

  ii structures S, T, U and W. [4]

b Explain:

  i why cell P contains many of the structures labelled T [2]

  ii the role of structure U in cell R. [2]

c The magnification of the diagram is ×750.

  Calculate the actual length of cell P:

  - write out the formula that you will use

  - use the formula to calculate the actual distance

  - give your answer to the nearest micrometre. [3]

d Describe the roles of cell P and cell R in the gas exchange system. [4]

[Total: 17]

7 a Copy and complete the table to compare the trachea with a respiratory bronchiole. Use a tick (✓) to indicate that the structure is present and a cross (✗) to indicate that it is not.

Structure	Trachea	Respiratory bronchiole
smooth muscle		
ciliated epithelium		
mucous glands		
cartilage		
elastic fibres		

[5]

b Describe how the alveoli are protected against infection. [5]

c Explain the roles of elastic fibres and smooth muscle in the gas exchange system. [5]

[Total: 15]

8 The composition of alveolar air remains fairly constant even though gases are exchanged with the blood in the capillaries that surround the alveoli. The table shows the partial pressures of oxygen and carbon dioxide in four places in the human body.

Place in the human body	Partial pressure of oxygen / kPa	Partial pressure of carbon dioxide / kPa
deoxygenated blood entering capillaries around alveoli	5.3	6.0
alveolar air	13.9	5.3
oxygenated blood entering capillaries in respiring tissues	13.3	≤5.3
tissue fluid around respiring cells	5.3	≥6.0

CONTINUED

a Use the information in the table to describe the process of gas exchange between:

    i alveolar air and deoxygenated blood   **[4]**

    ii oxygenated blood and respiring tissues.   **[4]**

b Explain why the composition of alveolar air remains fairly constant.   **[3]**

c Suggest **three** ways in which the gas exchange system responds to the demands of exercise.   **[3]**

            [Total: 14]

SELF-EVALUATION CHECKLIST

After studying this chapter, complete a table like this:

I can	See section...	Needs more work	Almost there	Ready to move on
describe the structure of the human gas exchange system	9.2			
recognise the trachea, bronchi, bronchioles and alveoli in microscope slides, photomicrographs and electron micrographs and make plan diagrams of transverse sections (TSs) of the walls of the trachea and bronchus	9.3			
describe and explain the distribution of tissues and cells within the gas exchange system and recognise them in microscope slides, photomicrographs and electron micrographs	9.3			
describe the functions in the gas exchange system of cartilage, smooth muscle, elastic fibres and squamous epithelium	9.3			
describe the functions of ciliated epithelial cells, goblet cells and mucous glands in maintaining the health of the gas exchange system	9.4			
describe gas exchange between air in the alveoli and blood in the capillaries	9.5			

› Chapter 10
Infectious disease

LEARNING INTENTIONS

In this chapter you will learn how to:

- explain that infectious diseases are caused by pathogens that are transmitted from person to person
- give the names of the pathogens that cause cholera, malaria, tuberculosis (TB) and HIV/AIDS and explain how they are transmitted
- state that human pathogens can be viruses, bacteria and protoctists
- discuss the biological, social and economic factors that influence the effectiveness of control measures for cholera, malaria, TB and HIV
- outline the way in which the antibiotic penicillin acts on bacteria
- explain why antibiotics have no affect on viruses
- discuss the consequences of the resistance of pathogens to antibiotics
- outline the measures that can be taken to reduce the impact of antibiotic resistance.

- Life on humans. There are microorganisms growing all over the surfaces of our bodies and many more inside us. Most of these are either harmless or do us some good. Parasites, however, do us harm. Discuss how you think these human parasites survive and how they transfer from one person to another.

- Make a list of the ways people can protect themselves from infection by harmful parasites.

ROLL BACK MALARIA

Malaria is one of the most serious of all human diseases. It is endemic in about 100 countries in Latin America, Africa and South East Asia. An infectious disease is endemic in a country if it is maintained there by transmission between people and does not occur by being brought into the country by travellers. The burden of malaria is felt most in countries in Africa: it is estimated that 37% of all cases of malaria occur in Nigeria and the Democratic Republic of the Congo.

The word malaria derives from the Italian mala aria, which means bad air. The cause of malaria was thought to be something in the air. The French doctor Charles Laveran was the first person to see the malarial parasite in blood in 1893. Ronald Ross, a British army surgeon, discovered that mosquitoes are responsible for carrying the parasite from one person to another.

If we are to lift the burden of malaria, then we have to outsmart this disease. Many international organisations are cooperating with African governments to reduce the number of cases of malaria. For example, Roll Back Malaria is a global partnership working to implement coordinated action against malaria. Laboratory research using modern genetic methods plays an important part, but the success of new initiatives in the Roll Back Malaria campaign can only be evaluated by tracking cases of the disease and collecting accurate data. Technology is helping here too in pinpointing accurately where cases occur (Figure 10.1). Find out more by searching online for 'roll back malaria'.

Knowing when and where outbreaks occur provides key data in the fight against infectious diseases. When an outbreak of malaria occurs, the local population can be warned to take appropriate precautions to avoid getting bitten by mosquitoes. These include sleeping under bed nets and draining any bodies of water that

Figure 10.1: Modern technology in the fight against malaria: these health workers in Kenya are using GPS to record accurate locations where there are outbreaks of malaria.

female mosquitoes might use to lay their eggs. The local area can be sprayed to kill any mosquitoes. By tracking when and where malaria outbreaks occur, health agencies can direct their resources to control the spread of the disease and limit its effects on local populations. Satellite imagery is also being used in the fight against malaria. By studying weather data collected from satellites, scientists are able to predict where malaria outbreaks are likely to occur. This helps health workers concentrate resources where they will be needed and reduce the severity of any outbreaks. Using modern technology is helping to bring about a significant reduction in the effect of this dreadful disease.

Question for discussion

There are several new and emerging infectious diseases that threaten human health. Discuss how scientists can use modern technology to help them find the cause of a new infectious disease and discover how it is transmitted.

10.1 Infectious diseases

Infectious diseases are diseases that are caused by organisms known as **pathogens**. They are sometimes called communicable diseases as they are passed from infected to uninfected people – a process known as **disease transmission**. Some diseases also affect animals and are passed from animals to humans.

The word 'disease' implies something very serious, yet many conditions that make us feel ill, such as the common cold, are not as harmful to health as the diseases discussed in this chapter. 'Disease' is a difficult word to define satisfactorily as it covers a wide range of human conditions, but it is often defined as an illness or disorder of the body or mind that leads to poor health. Each disease is associated with a set of signs and symptoms.

Many infectious diseases, such as the common cold, measles and influenza, affect us for only a short period of time. Others, such as tuberculosis (TB), may last a much longer time. Indeed, in the case of HIV/AIDS, there is as yet no cure, and treatments must be taken for the whole of a person's life. Some infectious diseases can only spread from one person to another by direct contact, because the pathogen cannot survive outside the human body. Other pathogens can survive in water, human food, faeces or animals (including insects), and so are transmitted indirectly from person to person. Some people may spread a pathogen even though they do not have the disease themselves. People like this who are symptomless, as they lack any symptoms, are called **disease carriers** (or simply **carriers**), and it can be very difficult to trace them as the source of an infection.

The way in which a pathogen passes from one host to another is called the **transmission cycle**. Control methods attempt to break transmission cycles by removing the conditions that favour the spread of the pathogen. Control is only possible once the cause of the disease and its method of transmission are known and understood. Vaccination is a major control measure for many infectious diseases. Vaccination works by making us immune to specific pathogens so that they do not live and reproduce within us and do not spread to others, so breaking the transmission cycle.

Action by governments and non-governmental organisations, coordinated by the World Health Organization (WHO), are reducing the impact of these diseases. The WHO has campaigns designed to stop

all transmission of some diseases so leading to their **eradication**. Two diseases have so far been eradicated. In 1980, the WHO declared that smallpox had been eradicated. In 2011, rinderpest, a severe disease of livestock, was eradicated.

Table 10.1 lists the scientific names of the causative agents of four diseases.

Questions

1   a   State **one** structural feature of the cells of *Plasmodium* that indicates that it is eukaryotic.

    b   Explain why viruses are not classified as prokaryotes.

2   All viruses are parasites, but most bacteria are not. Explain why all viruses are parasites, but not all bacteria are parasitic.

Diseases that are always in populations are described as **endemic**. TB is an example of a disease endemic in the whole human population. Malaria is endemic in tropical and sub-tropical regions.

KEY WORDS

infectious disease: a disease caused by an organism such as a protoctist, bacterium or virus

pathogen: an organism that causes disease

disease transmission: the transfer of a pathogen from a person infected with that pathogen to an uninfected person; transmission may occur by direct contact, through the air or water or by animal vectors, such as insects

disease carrier (or simply **carrier**): person infected with a pathogen who shows no symptoms, but can be the source of infection in other people (not carrier of an inherited disease)

transmission cycle: the passage of a pathogen from one host to another is continually repeated as the pathogen infects new hosts

disease eradication: the complete breakage of the transmission cycle of a pathogen so that there are no more cases of the disease caused by the pathogen anywhere in the world

endemic disease: a disease that is always in a population

Disease	Causative agent (pathogen)	Type of pathogen
cholera	*Vibrio cholerae*	bacterium (prokaryote)
malaria	four species of *Plasmodium:* • *Plasmodium falciparum* • *Plasmodium malariae* • *Plasmodium ovale* • *Plasmodium vivax*	protoctist (eukaryote)
HIV/AIDS	human immunodeficiency virus (HIV)	virus
TB	*Mycobacterium tuberculosis* and *Mycobacterium bovis*	bacterium (prokaryote)

Table 10.1: The names and types of pathogens that cause four infectious diseases. Make sure that you can spell the names correctly. There is more about these types of organisms in Chapter 18.

You will see a number of other terms that are also used to describe the occurrence of disease.

- The *incidence* of a disease is the number of people who are diagnosed over a certain period of time, usually a week, month or year.

- The *prevalence* of a disease is the number of people who have that disease at any one time.

- An *epidemic* occurs when there is a sudden increase in the number of people with a disease.

- A *pandemic* occurs when there is an increase in the number of cases throughout a continent or across the world.

- The number of deaths over a particular length of time (usually a year) is the *mortality rate*.

Data collected for incidence, prevalence and mortality is usually standardised and expressed as a proportion of the population, for example 'per 100 000 people'. This makes it possible to make valid comparisons over time and between different populations and between different countries. (Some examples are given in Exam-style questions 5, 7 and 8 at the end of the chapter.)

Cholera

Transmission of cholera

The features of cholera are given in Table 10.2. Cholera is caused by the bacterium *Vibrio cholerae* (Figure 10.2).

As the disease is water-borne, cholera occurs where people do not have access to proper sanitation (clean water supply) and/or uncontaminated food. Infected people, three-quarters of whom may be symptomless carriers, pass out large numbers of bacteria in their faeces. If these contaminate the water supply, or if infected people handle food or cooking utensils without washing their hands, then bacteria are transmitted to uninfected people.

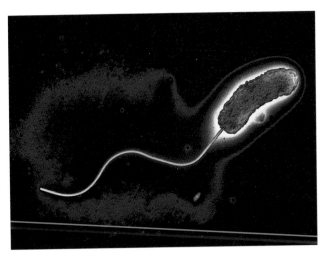

Figure 10.2: An electron micrograph of *Vibrio cholerae*. The faeces of an infected person are full of these bacteria, each with its distinctive flagellum (×13 400).

To reach their site of action in the small intestine, the bacteria have to pass through the stomach. If the contents are sufficiently acidic (pH less than 4.5), the bacteria are unlikely to survive. However, if the bacteria do reach the small intestine, they multiply and secrete the toxin choleragen. This toxin disrupts the functions of the epithelium lining the intestine, so that salts and

Pathogen	*Vibrio cholerae*
Methods of transmission	food-borne, water-borne
Global distribution	Asia, Africa, Latin America
Incubation period	two hours to five days
Site of action of pathogen	wall of small intestine
Clinical features	severe diarrhoea ('rice water'), loss of water and salts, dehydration, weakness
Methods of diagnosis	dipstick test of rectal swabs; identification of *V. cholerae* in faecal samples using microscopy
Annual incidence worldwide in 2017	1.3 million to 4.0 million (WHO estimate)
Annual mortality worldwide in 2017	21 000 to 143 000 (WHO estimate)

Table 10.2: The features of cholera.

water leave the blood. The loss of salts and water causes severe diarrhoea. The loss of fluid can be fatal if not treated within 24 hours.

Treating cholera

Almost all people with cholera who are treated make a quick recovery. A death from cholera is an avoidable death. The disease can be treated quite cheaply by a solution of salts and glucose. If people can drink, they are given oral rehydration therapy. If not, then the solution is given intravenously to rehydrate the body (Figure 10.3). Glucose is effective, because it is absorbed into the blood and this is linked to the uptake of sodium and potassium ions. It is important to make sure that a patient's fluid intake equals fluid losses in urine and faeces, and to maintain the osmotic balance of the blood and tissue fluids (Chapter 4, Section 4.5, Movement of substances across membranes).

Preventing cholera

In developing countries, large cities that have grown considerably in recent years, but as yet have no sewage treatment or clean water, create perfect conditions for the spread of the disease. Increasing quantities of untreated faeces from a growing population favour cholera's survival. These countries often do not have the financial resources to provide clean water supplies and proper drainage to many of their people. The use of raw human sewage to irrigate vegetables is a common cause of the disease, as are inadequate cooking, or washing in contaminated water.

Cholera is now almost unknown in the developed world, as a result of sewage treatment and the provision of clean piped water, which is chlorinated to kill bacteria. The transmission cycle has been broken.

Health authorities always fear outbreaks of cholera and other diarrhoeal diseases following natural disasters. In Haiti in 2010, an epidemic began several months after the earthquake that destroyed large parts of the country. In Yemen in October 2016, a cholera epidemic broke out as a consequence of civil war in that country.

An oral vaccine that gives short-term protection against cholera was approved for use in the USA in 2016. It is available for people travelling to places where there is transmission of *V. cholerae* (Figure 10.3). The same vaccine has been used in mass vaccination programmes in Africa during epidemics to prevent the spread of the disease.

Questions

3   Describe how cholera is transmitted from person to person.

4   One person can excrete 10^{13} cholera bacteria a day. An infective dose is 10^6. How many people could one person infect in one day?

5   Explain why there is such a high risk of cholera following natural disasters such as earthquakes, hurricanes, typhoons and floods.

6   Describe the precautions that a visitor to a country where cholera is endemic can take to avoid catching the disease.

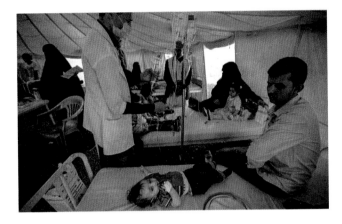

Figure 10.3: Children are most at risk of cholera. These children are being treated in a tent outside a hospital in Sana'a, the capital of Yemen, during the cholera epidemic that began in 2016. The drips contain a solution of salts to replace those lost through severe diarrhoea. Cholera can cause many deaths when normal life is disrupted by war and by natural catastrophes such as earthquakes.

Malaria

Transmission of malaria

The features of this disease are summarised in Table 10.3. Most cases of malaria are caused by one of four species of the protoctist *Plasmodium*. Genetic analysis of infections shows that some species of *Plasmodium* that cause malaria in monkeys also affect humans.

The female *Anopheles* mosquito is the **disease vector** of malaria and she transmits the disease when she passes the infective stages into an uninfected person. Malaria may also be transmitted during blood

> **KEY WORD**
>
> **disease vector:** an organism which carries a pathogen from one person to another or from an animal to a human

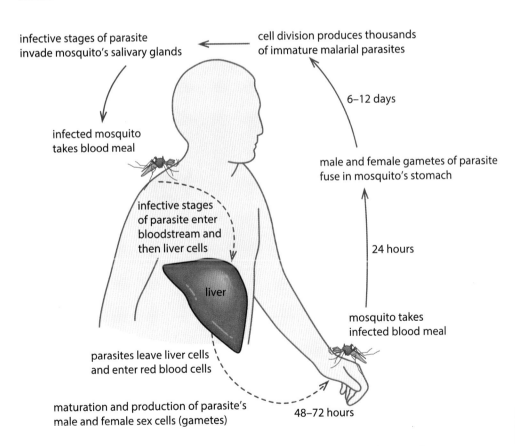

Figure 10.4: The life cycle of *Plasmodium*. The parasite has two hosts: the sexual stage occurs in mosquitoes, the asexual stage in humans. The time between infection and appearance of parasites inside red blood cells is 7–30 days in *P. falciparum*; longer in other *Plasmodium* species.

> **Note:** the malaria life-cycle is extension content, and is not part of the syllabus.

Pathogen	*Plasmodium falciparum, P. vivax, P. ovale, P. malariae*
Main method of transmission	insect vector: female *Anopheles* mosquito (about 30 different species)
Global distribution	throughout the tropics and sub-tropics (endemic in 106 countries)
Incubation period	from a week to a year
Site of action of pathogen	liver, red blood cells, brain
Clinical features	fever, anaemia, nausea, headaches, muscle pain, shivering, sweating, enlarged spleen
Method of diagnosis	dipstick test for malaria antigens in blood microscopical examination of blood (Figure 10.6)
Annual incidence worldwide in 2017	219 million cases of malaria – in 90 countries (WHO estimate) 92% of cases are in Africa
Annual mortality worldwide in 2017	435 000 deaths (WHO estimate) 93% of deaths are in Africa

Table 10.3: The features of malaria.

transfusion and when unsterile needles are re-used. *Plasmodium* can also pass across the placenta from mother to fetus.

Female *Anopheles* mosquitoes feed on human blood to obtain the protein they need to develop their eggs. If the person they bite is infected with *Plasmodium*, they will take up some of the pathogen's gametes with the blood meal. Male and female gametes fuse in the mosquito's gut and develop to form infective stages, which move to the mosquito's salivary glands. When the mosquito feeds again, she injects an anticoagulant from her salivary glands that prevents the blood meal from clotting, so that it flows out of the host into her body. The infective stages pass from the mosquito's salivary glands into the human's blood together with the anticoagulant in the saliva. The parasites enter the red blood cells, where they multiply (Figures 10.5 and 10.6).

Plasmodium multiplies in both hosts, the human and the mosquito; at each stage there is a huge increase in the number of parasites, and this improves the chances of infecting another mosquito or human host (Figure 10.6).

Transmission is more intense in places where the mosquito lifespan is longer (so that the parasite has time to complete its development inside the mosquito) and where it prefers to bite humans rather than other animals. The long lifespan and strong human-biting habit of the species of *Anopheles* found in Africa are the main reasons why about 90% of the world's malaria

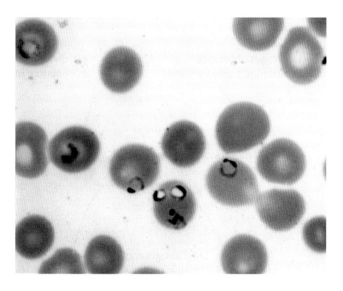

Figure 10.5: Red blood cells infected with *Plasmodium falciparum*. Notice the characteristic 'signet ring' appearance of the parasites inside the red blood cells (×1400).

cases are in Africa. Most of these cases are caused by *P. falciparum*, the species that causes severe, often fatal malaria.

Transmission also depends on climatic conditions that may affect the number and survival of mosquitoes, such as rainfall patterns, temperature and humidity. In many places, transmission is seasonal, with the peak occurring during and just after the rainy season. Malaria epidemics can occur when climate and other conditions

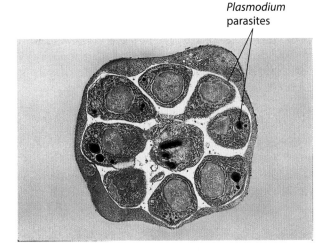
Plasmodium parasites

Figure 10.6: A transmission electron micrograph (TEM) of a section through a red blood cell packed tightly with malarial parasites. *Plasmodium* multiplies inside red blood cells; this cell will soon burst, releasing parasites which will infect other red blood cells.

suddenly favour transmission in areas where people have little or no immunity to malaria. They can also occur when people with low immunity move into areas with intense malaria transmission. This happens, for example, when people migrate to find work or to escape poverty, war or natural disasters.

If people are continually re-infected by different strains of malaria, they become immune (Chapter 11, Section 11.3, Active and passive immunity). However, this happens only if they survive the first five years of life, when mortality from malaria is very high. The immunity lasts only as long as people are in contact with the disease. This explains why epidemics in places where malaria is not endemic can be very serious, and why malaria is more dangerous in those areas where it occurs only during and after the rainy season. This often coincides with the time of maximum agricultural activity, so the disease has a disastrous effect on the economy: people cannot cultivate the land when they are sick.

Questions

7   Describe how malaria is transmitted.

8   Looking at Figures 10.5 and 10.6, explain how the cells of *Plasmodium* differ from the red blood cells of the host.

Treating malaria

WHO recommends that all cases of suspected malaria are confirmed by using a test that shows the presence of *Plasmodium* (Table 10.3) before treatment is started. The results of these tests can be available within 30 minutes or less.

Anti-malarial drugs such as quinine and chloroquine are used to treat infected people. Chloroquine is also used as a prophylactic (preventative) drug, stopping an infection occurring if a person is bitten by an infected mosquito. Prophylactic drugs are taken before, during and after visiting an area where malaria is endemic. Chloroquine inhibits protein synthesis and prevents the parasite spreading within the body. Another prophylactic, proguanil, has the added advantage of inhibiting the sexual reproduction of *Plasmodium* inside the biting mosquito.

Where anti-malarial drugs have been used widely, there are strains of drug-resistant *Plasmodium* – the drug is no longer effective against the pathogen. Chloroquine resistance is widespread in parts of South America, Africa and South East Asia. Newer drugs such as mefloquine are used in some of these areas. However, mefloquine sometimes causes unpleasant side-effects such as restlessness, dizziness, vomiting and disturbed sleep. Resistance to mefloquine has developed in South East Asia.

Currently, the best available treatment, particularly for malaria caused by *P. falciparum*, is artemisinin-based combination therapy (ACT). Drugs derived from the plant *Artimisia annua* are used in combination with another drug, such as mefloquine, to treat infections of *P. falciparum*.

People from non-malarial countries visiting many parts of the tropics are at great risk of contracting malaria. Doctors in developed countries, who see very few cases of malaria, often misdiagnose it as influenza, since the initial symptoms are similar. Many of these cases are among settled immigrants who have been visiting relatives in Africa or India. These people do not take prophylactic drugs because they do not realise that they have lost their immunity.

Preventing malaria

Malaria is one of the world's biggest threats to health: 40% of the world's population lives in areas where there is a risk of malaria.

There are three main ways to control malaria:

- reduce the number of mosquitoes

- avoid being bitten by mosquitoes

- use prophylactic drugs to prevent *Plasmodium* infecting people.

The most effective method is to kill the insect vector and break the transmission cycle. Mosquitoes lay their eggs in water. Larvae hatch and develop in water but breathe air by coming to the surface. Oil can be spread over the surfaces of water to make it impossible for mosquito larvae and pupae to breathe. Marshes can be drained and vegetation cleared to reduce the breeding sites for mosquitoes.

Two biological control measures that can be used are:

- stocking ponds, irrigation and drainage ditches and other permanent bodies of water with fish which feed on mosquito larvae

- spraying a preparation containing the bacterium *Bacillus thuringiensis*, which kills mosquito larvae but is not toxic to other forms of life.

However, mosquitoes will lay their eggs in any small puddle or pool, which makes it impossible to completely eradicate breeding sites, especially in rainy seasons.

The best protection against malaria is to avoid being bitten. People should not expose their skin when mosquitoes are most active, which is usually at dusk. People are advised to sleep beneath mosquito nets and use insect repellents (Figure 10.7). Using mosquito nets treated with long-lasting insecticide has been shown to

Figure 10.7: These children in Vanuatu in the Pacific are sleeping under mosquito nets that have been soaked in a long-lasting insecticide.

reduce mortality from malaria significantly. These nets prevent mosquitoes biting and kill any mosquitoes that land on the nets. Replacing the nets every 2–3 years is recommended. Between 2010 and 2015 there was an 80% increase in insecticide-treated nets (ITNs) in sub-Saharan Africa.

Insecticides are also sprayed inside houses. This control method is effective for between three and six months, depending on the insecticides used and the type of surface on which they are sprayed. The use of nets and insecticides protects the whole population, even those people who do not have nets and have not had their houses sprayed.

Young children are the most at risk of dying from malaria. Pregnant women and young children can be treated with drugs that prevent infections of *Plasmodium*. The WHO recommends that pregnant women are treated with a prophylactic drug each time they visit an antenatal clinic in the latter two-thirds of their pregnancy. Similarly, WHO recommends that infants living in high-transmission areas in Africa are given three doses of the same drugs when they attend clinics for routine vaccinations.

Several recent advances give hope that malaria may one day be controlled so that death rates are very low. The introduction of simple dip stick tests for diagnosing malaria means that diagnosis can be done quickly without the need for laboratories. The whole genome of *Plasmodium* has been sequenced and this is leading to developments of new treatments and vaccines.

RTS,S/AS01 (RTS,S) – also known as Mosquirix – is an injectable vaccine that provides partial protection against malaria in young children. In November 2016, WHO announced that this vaccine would be used in pilot projects in selected areas in three countries in sub-Saharan Africa: Ghana, Kenya and Malawi. Funding was secured for the initial phase of the programme and vaccinations began in Malawi in early 2019. Other vaccines are under development or being trialled. You can find out the progress in developing vaccines to protect people against malaria by searching online.

Three factors may lead to improvements in the control of malaria:

- use of modern techniques in gene sequencing and drug design

- development of vaccines targeted against different stages of the parasite's life cycle

- a renewed international will to remove the burden of malaria from the poorest parts of the world, allied to generous donations from wealthy individuals and foundations.

Questions

9 Figure 10.8 shows the number of cases of malaria and number of deaths from malaria recorded in hospitals in Zanzibar, United Republic of Tanzania, between 1999 and 2008. (Adapted from: *WHO World Malaria Report* 2009)

 a i Looking at the graph, describe the data collected from hospitals in Zanzibar.

 ii Suggest possible reasons for the pattern you describe.

 iii Suggest other data that could have been collected in Zanzibar to assess the effectiveness of methods to control malaria.

 b Suggest why WHO recommends that cases of suspected malaria are confirmed using the parasite diagnostic tests before treatment is given.

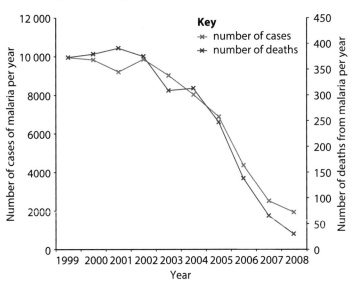

Figure 10.8: Malaria in Zanzibar hospitals between 1999 and 2008.

10 List the factors that make malaria a difficult disease to control.

11 Describe the precautions that people can take to avoid developing malaria.

HIV/AIDS

Infection with the human immunodeficiency virus (**HIV**) may lead to acquired immunodeficiency syndrome (**AIDS**) (Figure 10.9). The features of AIDS and HIV are listed in Table 10.4. The features of viruses are described in Chapter 1 (Section 1.9, Viruses).

HIV is a retrovirus, which means that its genetic material is RNA, not DNA. Once inside a host cell, the viral RNA is converted 'back' to DNA (hence 'retro') to be incorporated into human chromosomes. The virus infects

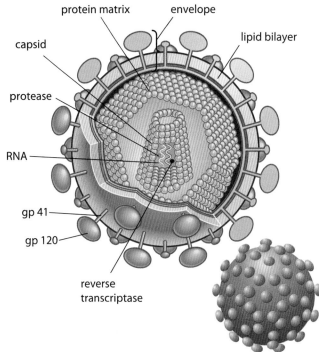

Figure 10.9: Human immunodeficiency virus (HIV). The outer lipid membrane forms the envelope, which also has two glycoproteins: gp120 and gp41. The protein core contains genetic material (RNA) and two enzymes: a protease and reverse transcriptase. Reverse transcriptase uses the RNA as a template to produce DNA once the virus is inside a host cell.

KEY WORDS

HIV: human immunodeficiency virus

AIDS: acquired immunodeficiency syndrome

Pathogen	human immunodeficiency virus (HIV)
Methods of transmission	in semen and vaginal fluids during sexual intercourse
	infected blood or blood products
	contaminated hypodermic syringes
	mother to fetus across placenta and at birth
	mother to infant in breast milk
Global distribution	worldwide, especially in sub-Saharan Africa and South East Asia
Incubation period	initial incubation a few weeks, but up to ten years or more before symptoms of AIDS may develop
Site of action of pathogen	T-helper lymphocytes, macrophages, brain cells
Clinical features	HIV infection – flu-like symptoms and then symptomless
	AIDS – opportunistic infections including pneumonia, TB and cancers; weight loss, diarrhoea, fever, sweating, dementia
Method of diagnosis	testing blood, saliva or urine for the presence of antibodies produced against HIV
Estimated total number of people living with HIV worldwide in 2017	36.9 million (approximately 67% of these in sub-Saharan Africa) (UNAIDS estimate)
Estimated number of new cases of HIV infection worldwide in 2017	1.8 million (UNAIDS estimate)
Estimated number of deaths from AIDS-related diseases worldwide in 2017	940 000 (UNAIDS estimate)

Table 10.4: The features of HIV/AIDS.

and destroys cells of the body's immune system so that their numbers gradually decrease (Figure 10.10). These cells, known as T-helper lymphocytes, control the immune system's response to infection (Chapter 11, Section 11.2, Cells of the immune system). When the numbers of these cells are low, the body is unable to defend itself against infection, so allowing a range of pathogens to cause a variety of **opportunistic infections**. AIDS is not a disease; it is a collection of these opportunistic diseases associated with immunodeficiency caused by HIV infection.

Since HIV is an infective agent, AIDS is called an acquired immunodeficiency to distinguish it from other types – for example, an inherited form.

> **KEY WORD**
>
> **opportunistic infection:** an infection caused by pathogens that take advantage of a host with a weakened immune system, as may happen in someone with an HIV infection

Transmission of HIV

After initial uncertainties in the early 1980s surrounding the emergence of an apparently new disease, it soon became clear that an epidemic and then a pandemic was underway. The WHO estimated that, by 2017, 70 million people had been infected with HIV and 35 million people had died of HIV/AIDS.

HIV is a virus that is spread by intimate human contact; there is no vector (unlike in malaria) and the virus is unable to survive outside the human body (unlike cholera or malarial pathogens). Transmission is only possible by direct exchange of body fluids. In practice, this means that HIV is spread most easily through sexual intercourse, blood donation and the sharing of needles by intravenous drug users. HIV is also transmitted from mother to child across the placenta and, more often, through the mixing of blood during birth.

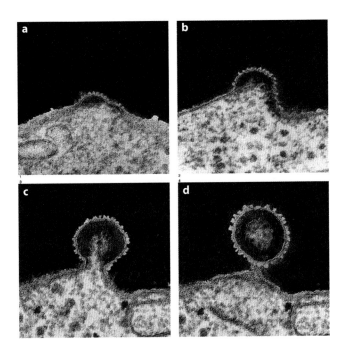

Figure 10.10: A series of transmission electron micrographs (TEMs) showing HIV budding from the surface of an infected T-lymphocyte and becoming surrounded by an envelope derived from the cell surface membrane of the host cell (×176 000). **a** The viral particle first appears as a bump, **b** which then buds out and **c** is eventually cut off. **d** The outer region of dense material and the less dense core are visible in the released virus.

The initial epidemic in North America and Europe was among male homosexuals who practised anal intercourse and had many sex partners, two forms of behaviour that put them at risk. The mucous lining of the rectum is not as thick as that of the vagina, and there is less natural lubrication. As a result, the rectal lining is easily damaged during intercourse and the virus can pass from semen to blood. Having multiple partners, both homosexual and heterosexual, allows the virus to spread more widely.

Also at high risk of infection were haemophiliacs who were treated with a clotting substance (factor VIII) isolated from blood pooled from many donors. Such blood products are now largely synthetic (Chapter 19, Section 19.6, Genetic technology and medicine). Much of the transmission of HIV has been by heterosexual intercourse. This is particularly rapid in some African states, where equal numbers of males and females are now HIV-positive (HIV+).

HIV is a slow virus and, after infection, there may not be any symptoms until years later. Some people who

have the virus even appear not to develop any initial symptoms, although there are often flu-like symptoms for several weeks after becoming infected. At this stage, a person is HIV+ but does not have AIDS.

The infections that can opportunistically develop to create AIDS tend to be characteristic of the condition. Two of these are caused by fungi: oral thrush caused by *Candida albicans*, and a rare form of pneumonia caused by *Pneumocystis jiroveci*. During the early years of the AIDS epidemic, people in developed countries died within 12 hours of contracting this unusual pneumonia. Now this condition is managed much better and drugs are prescribed to prevent the disease developing.

As the immune system collapses further, it becomes less effective in finding and destroying cancers. A rare form of skin cancer, Kaposi's sarcoma, caused by a herpes-like virus, is associated with AIDS. Kaposi's sarcoma and cancers of internal organs are now the most likely causes of death of people with AIDS in developed countries, along with degenerative diseases of the brain, such as dementias.

At about the same time that AIDS was first reported on the west coast of the USA and in Europe, doctors in Central Africa reported seeing people with similar opportunistic infections. HIV/AIDS is now widespread throughout sub-Saharan Africa from Uganda to South Africa. It is a serious public health problem there because HIV infection makes people more vulnerable to existing diseases such as malnutrition, TB and malaria. AIDS is having an adverse effect on the economic development of countries in the region, as it affects sexually active people in their twenties and thirties who are also potentially the most economically productive, and the purchase of expensive drugs drains government funds. The World Bank estimated that AIDS had reversed 10–15 years of economic growth for some African states by the end of the 20th century.

Treating HIV/AIDS

There is as yet no cure for AIDS and no vaccine for HIV. However, there has been much success in recent years in treating people with drugs so that they can live with HIV. Drug therapy can slow down the onset of AIDS quite dramatically so that many HIV+ people may now have a normal life expectancy.

However, the drugs are expensive and have a variety of side-effects ranging from the mild and temporary (rashes, headaches, diarrhoea) to the severe and permanent (nerve damage, abnormal fat distribution). If used in combination, two or more drugs which prevent the replication of the virus inside host cells can prolong life, but they are not a cure. The drugs are similar to DNA nucleotides (e.g., zidovudine is similar to the nucleotide that contains the base thymine). Zidovudine binds to the viral enzyme reverse transcriptase and blocks its action. This stops the replication of the viral genetic material and leads to an increase in some of the body's lymphocytes. A course of combination therapy (taking several drugs) can be very complicated to follow. The pattern and timing of medication through the day must be strictly followed. People who are unable to keep to this pattern can become susceptible to strains of HIV that have developed resistance to the drugs.

Global scale-up of antiretroviral therapy has been the primary contributor to a 48% decline in deaths from AIDS-related causes, from a peak of 1.9 million in 2005 to 1.0 million in 2016. The number of children (aged 0–14 years) dying of AIDS-related illnesses has been nearly cut in half in just six years, from 210 000 in 2010 to 120 000 in 2016. Much of the decline is due to steep reductions in new HIV infections among children, with increased access to treatment with antiretroviral drugs for pregnant women.

Preventing HIV/AIDS

The spread of HIV/AIDS is difficult to control. The virus's long latent stage means it can be transmitted by people who are HIV+ but who show no symptoms of AIDS and do not know they are infected. The virus changes its surface proteins, which makes it hard for the body's immune system to recognise it (Chapter 11, Section 11.1, Defence against disease). This also makes the development of a vaccine very difficult.

There has been much success in treating pregnant women so that HIV does not infect their fetuses. This has led to a considerable decrease in the number of children born with HIV.

Public health measures are used to prevent the spread of HIV. People can be educated about the spread of the infection and encouraged to change their behaviour so as to protect themselves and others. Condoms, femidoms and dental dams are the only effective methods of reducing the risk of infection during intercourse, as they form a barrier between body fluids, reducing the chances of transmission of the virus. Some countries have promoted the use of condoms as well as other measures. As a result, infection rates in these countries have slowed and the number of new cases reported each year has either decreased or remained the same year on year. It is estimated that the rate of HIV

infection across the world decreased by 25% between 2001 and 2009, but only by 18% between 2010 and 2017.

Contact tracing is an important part of controlling the spread of HIV. If a person who is diagnosed as HIV+ is willing and able to identify the people he or she has put at risk of infection by sexual intercourse or needle sharing, then these people will be offered an HIV test. This test identifies the presence of antibodies to HIV, although these only appear several weeks after the initial infection. Home testing kits for HIV are now available (Figure 10.11).

Injecting drug users are advised to give up their habit, stop sharing needles or take their drug in some other way. Needle-exchange schemes operate in some places to exchange used needles for sterile ones to reduce the chances of infection with HIV and other blood-borne diseases.

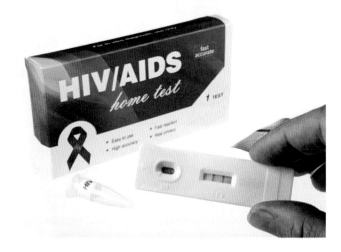

Figure 10.11: A home testing kit for HIV.

Blood collected from blood donors is screened for HIV and heat-treated to kill any viruses. People who think they may have been exposed to the virus are strongly discouraged from donating blood. In some low-income countries, not all donated blood is tested. Anyone concerned about becoming infected by blood transfusion during an operation may donate their own blood before the operation to be used instead of blood from a blood bank.

Widespread testing of a population to find people who are HIV+ is not expensive, but governments are reluctant to introduce such testing because of the infringement of personal freedom. In the developed world, HIV testing is promoted most strongly to people in high-risk groups, such as male homosexuals, prostitutes, injecting drug users and their sexual partners. If tested positive, they can be given the medical and psychological support they need. In Africa and South East Asia, the epidemic is not restricted to such easily identifiable groups and widespread testing is not feasible due to the difficulty of reaching the majority of the population and organising testing. People in these regions find out that they are HIV+ when they develop the symptoms of AIDS.

Both viral particles and infected lymphocytes are found in breast milk. Mother-to-child transmission is reduced by treating HIV+ women and their babies with drugs. However, HIV+ women in high-income countries are advised not to breastfeed their babies, because of the risk of transmission even if they have a secure supply of drugs during this period. In contrast, HIV+ women in low- and middle-income countries are advised to breastfeed, especially if they have a secure supply of drugs during this period, as the protection this gives the babies against other diseases and the lack of clean water to make up formula milk may outweigh the risks of transmitting HIV.

Questions

12 Table 10.5 shows the number of people across the world who are estimated to be infected with HIV, and the number of those estimated to be receiving treatment for HIV between 2000 and 2017.

   a   i   Calculate the percentage change in the number of people living with HIV between 2000 and 2017.

      ii   Looking at Table 10.5, explain what is meant by the phrase 'living with HIV'.

   b   i   Summarise the data in Table 10.5.

      ii   Suggest why the numbers given in the table are estimates.

13 Suggest the types of advice which might be offered as part of an HIV/AIDS education programme.

14 Children in Africa with sickle cell anaemia or malaria often receive blood transfusions. Explain how this puts them at risk of HIV infection.

15 Explain why the early knowledge of HIV infection is important in transmission control.

Year	Numbers estimated to be living with HIV in millions	Numbers estimated to be receiving treatment in millions	Proportion of people living with HIV who are receiving treatment
2000	28.9	0.8	0.03
2005	31.8	2.2	0.07
2010	33.3	7.5	0.23
2013	35.3	13.0	0.37
2014	35.9	15.0	0.42
2015	36.7	17.0	0.46
2016	36.7	19.5	0.53
2017	36.9	21.7	0.59

Table 10.5: Estimates of the numbers of people living with HIV and those receiving treatment 2000–2017.

Tuberculosis (TB)

Table 10.6 gives the main features of this disease. TB is caused by either of two bacteria, *Mycobacterium tuberculosis* (Figure 10.12) and *Mycobacterium bovis*. These are pathogens that live inside human cells, particularly in the lungs. This is the first site of infection, but the bacteria can spread throughout the whole body and even infect bone tissue.

Some people become infected and develop TB quite quickly, while in others the bacteria remain inactive for many years. It is estimated that about 30% of the world's population is infected with TB without showing any symptoms of the infection; people with this inactive, or latent, infection do not spread the disease to others. However, the bacteria can later become active, and this is most likely to happen when people are weakened by other diseases, suffer from malnutrition, smoke, have diabetes, consume large quantities of alcohol or become infected

Pathogen	*Mycobacterium tuberculosis*; *Mycobacterium bovis*
Methods of transmission	airborne droplets (*M. tuberculosis*); via undercooked meat and unpasteurised milk (*M. bovis*)
Global distribution	worldwide
Incubation period	a few weeks or up to several years
Site of action of pathogen	primary infection in lungs; secondary infections in lymph nodes, bones and gut
Clinical features	racking cough, coughing blood, chest pain, shortness of breath, fever, sweating, weight loss
Methods of diagnosis	rapid molecular test detecting presence of DNA from *M. tuberculosis* microscopical examination of sputum for bacteria chest X-ray long-term culture of bacteria (up to 12 weeks)
Annual incidence worldwide in 2017	10 million (WHO estimate) Over 90% of cases among adults; more men than women
Annual mortality worldwide in 2017	1.6 million, including about 300 000 deaths of people who were HIV+ (WHO estimate)

Table 10.6: The features of TB.

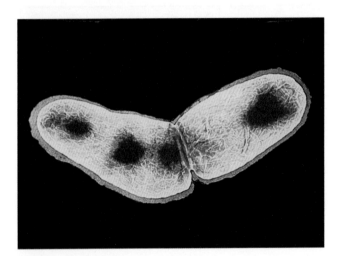

Figure 10.12: False-colour TEM of *Mycobacterium tuberculosis* dividing into two. The bacterium may multiply like this inside the lungs and then spread throughout the body or lie dormant, becoming active many years later (×67 000).

Figure 10.13: A TB patient undergoes treatment in a hospital in Russia.

with HIV. Those who have the active form of TB often suffer from debilitating illness for a long time. They have a persistent cough and, as part of their defence, cells release hormone-like compounds, which cause fever and suppress the appetite. As a result, people with TB lose weight and often look emaciated (Figure 10.13).

TB is often the first opportunistic infection to strike HIV+ people. HIV infection may reactivate dormant infections of *M. tuberculosis* which may have been present from childhood or, if people are uninfected, make them susceptible to infection. TB is the leading causes of death among people living with HIV. The HIV pandemic has been followed very closely by a TB pandemic.

Transmission of TB

TB is spread when infected people with the active form of the illness cough or sneeze and the bacteria are carried in the air in tiny droplets of liquid. The transmission cycle is complete when people who are uninfected inhale the droplets. TB spreads most rapidly among people living in overcrowded conditions. People who sleep close together in large numbers are particularly at risk. The disease primarily attacks the homeless and people who live in poor, substandard housing; those with low immunity, because of malnutrition or being HIV-positive, are also particularly vulnerable.

The form of TB caused by *M. bovis* also occurs in cattle and is spread to humans in meat and milk. It is estimated that there were about 800 000 deaths in the UK between 1850 and 1950 as a result of TB transmitted from cattle. Very few now acquire TB in this way in developed countries for reasons explained later, although meat and milk still remain a source of infection in some developing countries.

The incidence of TB in the UK decreased steeply well before the introduction of a vaccine in the 1950s, because of improvements in housing conditions and diet. The antibiotic streptomycin was introduced in the 1940s, and this hastened the decrease in the incidence of TB. This pattern was repeated throughout the developed world.

Once thought to be practically eradicated, TB is increasing. There are high rates of incidence all across the developing world and in Russia and surrounding countries. High rates are also found in cities with populations of migrants from countries where TB is more common. Parts of London, for example, have rates of TB much higher than the rest of the UK. The incidence in such areas is as high as in less economically developed countries. This increase is due in part to the following factors:

- some strains of TB bacteria are resistant to drugs
- the HIV/AIDS pandemic
- poor housing in inner cities and homelessness
- the breakdown of TB control programmes; partial treatment for TB increases the chance of drug resistance in *Mycobacterium*.

Treating TB

When a doctor first sees a person with the likely symptoms of TB, samples of the sputum (mucus and pus) from their lungs are collected for analysis. The identification of the TB bacteria can be done very quickly by microscopy. If TB is confirmed, then patients should be isolated while they are in the most infectious stage (which is at two to four weeks). This is particularly if they are infected with a drug-resistant strain of the bacterium. The treatment involves using several drugs to ensure that all the bacteria are killed. If not killed, drug-resistant forms remain to continue the infection. The treatment is a long one (six to nine months, or longer), because it takes a long time to kill the bacteria, which are slow growing and are not very sensitive to the drugs used. Unfortunately, many people do not complete their course of drugs, because they think that they are cured when they feel better. People who do not complete their treatment may be harbouring drug-resistant bacteria and may spread these to others if the bacteria become active.

The WHO promotes a scheme to ensure that patients complete their course of drugs. DOTS (direct observation treatment, short course) involves health workers or responsible family members making sure that patients take their medicine regularly for six to eight months (Figure 10.14). The drugs widely used are isoniazid and rifampicin, often in combination with others. This drug therapy cures 95% of all patients, and is twice as effective as other strategies.

Figure 10.14: The WHO DOTS scheme in action: TB patients take their drugs under supervision in a hospital clinic in Tomsk, Russia. DOTS is helping to reduce the spread of MDR strains of TB.

Drug-resistant TB

Strains of drug-resistant *M. tuberculosis* were identified when treatment with antibiotics began in the 1950s. Antibiotics act as selective agents, killing drug-sensitive strains and leaving resistant ones behind (Chapter 17, Section 17.2, Natural selection). Drug resistance occurs as a result of mutation in the bacterial DNA. Mutation is a random event and occurs with a frequency of about one in every thousand bacteria. If three drugs are used in treatment, then the chance of resistance arising to all three of them by mutation is reduced to one in a thousand million. If four drugs are used, the chance is reduced to one in a billion.

If TB is not treated, or the person stops the treatment before the bacteria are completely eliminated, the bacteria spread throughout the body, increasing the likelihood that mutations will arise, as the bacteria survive for a long time and multiply. Stopping treatment early can mean that *M. tuberculosis* develops resistance to all the drugs being used. People who do not complete a course of treatment are highly likely to infect others with drug-resistant forms of TB. It is estimated that one person may transmit the disease to 10 to 15 other people, especially if the person lives in overcrowded conditions.

Multiple-drug-resistant forms of TB (MDR-TB) now exist. MDR-TB strains of TB are resistant to at least the two main drugs used to treat TB – isoniazid and rifampicin – which are known as first-line drugs. Extensively (or extremely) drug-resistant TB (XDR-TB) has also emerged as a very serious threat to health, especially for those people who are HIV+. XDR-TB strains are resistant to first-line drugs and to the drugs used to treat MDR-TB. These resistant strains of TB do not respond to the standard six-month treatment with first-line anti-TB drugs and can take two years or more to treat with drugs that are less potent and much more expensive. Treatment for MDR-TB takes longer, uses more toxic drugs and is more expensive. A new drug called bedaquiline is now available to treat MDR-TB.

Drug-resistant TB continues to be a public health crisis. The best estimate is that, worldwide in 2017, 558 000 people developed TB that was resistant to rifampicin, the most effective drug, and of these, 82% had MDR-TB. Among cases of MDR-TB in 2017, 8.5% were estimated to have XDR-TB.

Preventing TB

TB is a global problem. Worldwide, TB is one of the top ten causes of death, yet the majority of people who fall ill with TB live in one of eight countries. Of those that fell ill with MDR-TB, almost half lived in just three countries. Contact tracing and the subsequent testing of contacts for the bacterium are essential parts of controlling TB. Contacts are screened for symptoms of TB infection, but the diagnosis can take up to two weeks.

The only vaccine currently available for TB is the BCG vaccine, which is derived from *M. bovis* and protects up to 70–80% of people who receive it. The effectiveness of the vaccine decreases with age unless there is exposure to TB. Many countries with high numbers of people with TB use the BCG vaccine to protect children from getting the disease. Countries such as the UK and USA do not include BCG vaccination in their immunisation programmes. Instead, it may be given only to people who are at high risk of becoming infected because, for example, they live with an adult who is being treated for the disease. There are no vaccines that can be administered to protect adults. In 2019, there were 12 vaccines for TB being trialled.

TB can be transmitted between cattle and humans. To prevent people catching TB in this way, cattle are routinely tested for TB and any found to be infected are destroyed. TB bacteria are killed when milk is pasteurised. These control methods are very effective and have reduced the incidence of human TB caused by *M. bovis* considerably, so that it is virtually eliminated in countries where these controls operate.

Questions

16 The WHO collects data on the impact of TB from countries across the world. It published the following estimates for one country in South East Asia:

   In 2018, the population was 69 million. The country had about 106 000 new cases of TB that year with 10% of these found to be living with HIV. The total mortality in 2018 from TB was 11 500.

   a Suggest how the data about this country should be processed to allow valid comparisons to be made with similar data for other countries in the world.

   b Suggest the data that should be collected to evaluate the success of programmes for treating TB in this country.

17 Explain why there is a high death rate from TB in countries with a high proportion of the population who are HIV+.

18 Describe the precautions that a visitor should take when travelling to a country with a high prevalence of TB.

10.2 Antibiotics

An **antibiotic** is a drug that kills or stops the growth of bacteria, without harming the cells of the infected organism. Antibiotics are derived from living organisms, although they are often made more effective by various chemical processes. There are a wide range of antibiotics to treat bacterial infections. Other antimicrobial drugs such as isoniazid, used for the treatment of TB, are synthetic (made in laboratories).

> **KEY WORD**
>
> **antibiotic:** a substance derived from a living organism that is capable of killing or inhibiting the growth of a microorganism

How antibiotics work

Antibiotics interfere with some aspect of growth or metabolism of the target bacterium (Figure 10.15). These include:

- synthesis of bacterial cell walls

- activity of proteins in the cell surface membrane (Chapter 4, Section 4.2, Structure of membranes)

- enzyme action (Chapter 3, Section 3.2, Mode of action of enzymes)

- DNA synthesis (Chapter 6, Section 6.3, DNA replication)

- protein synthesis (Chapter 6, Section 6.5, Protein synthesis).

Bacterial cells have walls made of peptidoglycans (Chapter 1, Section 1.7, Bacteria). These are long molecules containing peptides (chains of amino acids) and sugars. In the bacterial cell wall, peptidoglycans are held together by cross-links that form between them. Penicillin prevents the synthesis of the cross-links between the peptidoglycan polymers in the cell walls of bacteria by inhibiting the enzymes that build these cross-links. This means that penicillin is only active against bacteria while they are growing.

When a newly formed bacterial cell is growing, it secretes enzymes called autolysins, which make little holes in its cell wall. These little holes allow the wall to stretch so that new peptidoglycan chains can link together. Penicillin prevents the peptidoglycan chains from linking up, but the autolysins keep making new holes. The cell wall therefore becomes progressively weaker. Bacteria live in watery environments and take up water by osmosis. When they are weakened, the cell walls cannot withstand the turgor pressure exerted on them by the cell contents and the cells burst (Figure 10.16).

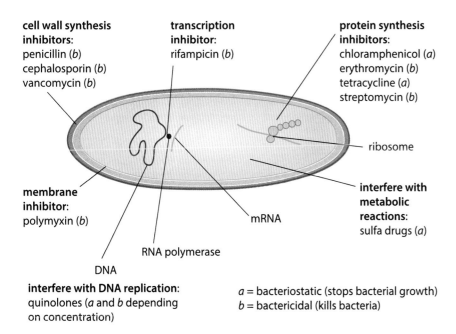

cell wall synthesis inhibitors:
penicillin (*b*)
cephalosporin (*b*)
vancomycin (*b*)

transcription inhibitor:
rifampicin (*b*)

protein synthesis inhibitors:
chloramphenicol (*a*)
erythromycin (*b*)
tetracycline (*a*)
streptomycin (*b*)

ribosome

membrane inhibitor:
polymyxin (*b*)

mRNA

interfere with metabolic reactions:
sulfa drugs (*a*)

RNA polymerase

DNA

interfere with DNA replication:
quinolones (*a* and *b* depending on concentration)

a = bacteriostatic (stops bacterial growth)
b = bactericidal (kills bacteria)

Figure 10.15: The sites of action of antibiotics in bacteria.

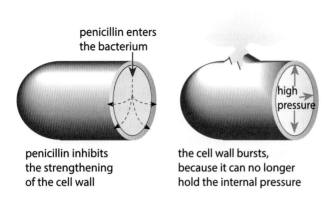

Figure 10.16: How penicillin works.

This explains why penicillin does not affect human cells. Our cells do not have cell walls. This also explains why penicillin and other antibiotics do not affect viruses, which do not even have cells, let alone cell walls. Viruses do not have the targets shown in Figure 10.15. For example, when a virus replicates, it uses the host cell's mechanisms for transcription and translation, and antibiotics do not bind to the proteins that host cells use in these processes. Eukaryotic cells have proteins that are different from those in bacteria so they are unaffected by such antibiotics. Other drugs, called antivirals, are used to control viral infections. There are fewer antivirals than there are antibiotics.

Question

19 Explain why antibiotics are not effective against viruses.

Antibiotic resistance

Penicillin first became available for treating disease in the 1940s. It was hailed as a wonder drug that could be used to wipe out all the diseases caused by bacteria. To begin with, this seemed to be true, but very quickly it became clear that this was not going to happen even though other antibiotics, such as streptomycin, soon became available.

Some types of bacteria are not sensitive to particular antibiotics: for example, penicillin is not effective against *M. tuberculosis*. Even among the types of bacteria that were killed by penicillin, there were certain strains that were not affected. These strains had become resistant to penicillin. During the 70 years since the introduction of antibiotics, most pathogenic bacteria have become resistant to one or more types of antibiotic; they have developed **antibiotic resistance**.

Penicillin has no effect on *M. tuberculosis* because the thick cell wall of this bacterium is not very permeable and because the bacterium has a gene that codes for an enzyme that catalyses the breakdown of penicillin. Proteins in the membranes of other species of bacteria can inactivate antibiotics so they have no effect; bacterial membranes also have proteins that pump out antibiotics if they enter the cytoplasm. In some cases, the antibiotic simply cannot bind to the intended site of action.

Bacteria that are sensitive to an antibiotic are described as being susceptible to that antibiotic. They may become resistant if they gain a gene coding for a protein that protects them from the antibiotic.

Soil bacteria have many resistance mechanisms as they grow in an environment where there are many molecules that interfere with their metabolism. These resistance mechanisms are very similar to those found in some pathogenic bacteria. Before the introduction of antibiotics, enzymes known as beta-lactamases were not common among pathogenic bacteria. The genes for these enzymes have spread into many different forms of bacteria and it is believed that they have come from soil bacteria.

Penicillin has a structure that can be broken down by β-lactamase (penicillinase) enzymes. Pathogenic bacteria that have become resistant to penicillin have often done so because they have acquired the genes that code for these enzymes. How bacteria become resistant to antibiotics is described in Chapter 17 (Section 17.2, Natural selection).

Genes for antibiotic resistance often occur on plasmids, which are small loops of double-stranded DNA. Plasmids are quite frequently transferred from one bacterium to another, even between different species. This happens during conjugation when a tube forms between two bacteria to allow the movement of DNA. During conjugation, plasmids are transferred from a donor bacterium to a recipient. Transfer of part of the DNA from the circular DNA also occurs in the same way. Thus it is possible for resistance to a particular antibiotic to arise in one species of bacterium and be passed on to another.

KEY WORD

antibiotic resistance: the ability of bacteria or fungi to grow in the presence of an antibiotic that would normally slow their growth or kill them; antibiotic resistance arises by mutation and becomes widespread when antibiotics are overused

Consequences of antibiotic resistance

The more we misuse antibiotics, the greater the selection pressure we exert on bacteria to evolve resistance to them. Antibiotic-resistant strains of bacteria are continually appearing (Figure 10.17). Antibiotic-resistant infections increase the risk of death, and they are often associated with long stays in hospital, and sometimes serious complications.

There is a constant race to find new antibiotics as resistant strains keep arising.

Where there is widespread use of antibiotics, such as in hospitals or on farms, resistance quickly spreads among different species of bacteria. Resistance may first appear in a non-pathogenic bacterium, but then be passed to a pathogenic species. Bacteria living where there is widespread use of antibiotics may have plasmids carrying resistance genes for several different antibiotics, giving multiple resistance. This presents major problems for doctors. For example, methicillin-resistant *Staphylococcus aureus* (MRSA) has become a problem in hospitals around the world and in prisons in the USA. It is now also infecting people in the general population. MRSA caused dangerous infections after surgery, which were mostly controlled by vancomycin,

an antibiotic often used as a last resort for treating infections when everything else has failed, so as to lessen the chances of the development of more such resistant organisms. Then, another bacterium common in hospitals, *Enterococcus faecalis*, developed resistance to vancomycin and this resistance passed to *S. aureus*.

Questions

20 Describe the ways in which bacteria can resist the effects of antibiotics.

21 Suggest why an organism resistant to many antibiotics has evolved in hospitals and is common in prisons.

Reducing the impact of antibiotic resistance

Antibiotics should be chosen carefully. Testing antibiotics against the strain of the bacterium isolated from people ensures that the most effective antibiotic can be used in treatment.

As fast as we develop new antibiotics, bacteria seem to develop resistance to them. It follows from this that there is a constant search for new antibiotics, especially ones that work in a completely different way from those currently in use.

Fortunately, a bacterium resistant to a particular antibiotic may not be resistant to that antibiotic with a slightly altered chemical structure. Chemists can make such semi-synthetic antibiotics to extend the range available. However, many experts believe that we will not be able to keep up and that soon there will be no antibiotics left to treat diseases. This is fast becoming the case with pneumonia, blood poisoning, gonorrhoea and some forms of TB.

Clearly, we should try to reduce the number of circumstances in which bacteria develop resistance to antibiotics. Some of the ways in which we can do this include:

- using antibiotics only when appropriate and necessary; not prescribing them for viral infections

- reducing the number of countries in which antibiotics are sold without a doctor's prescription

- avoiding the use of so-called wide-spectrum antibiotics and using instead an antibiotic specific to the infection (known as narrow spectrum)

- making sure that patients complete their course of medication, which is essential in the treatment of TB

- making sure that patients do not keep unused antibiotics for self-medication in the future or give them to someone else

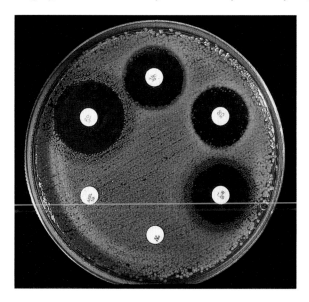

Figure 10.17: The grey areas on the agar jelly in this Petri dish are colonies of the bacterium *Escherichia coli*. The white discs are pieces of card impregnated with different antibiotics. Where there are clear areas around the discs the antibiotic has prevented the bacteria from growing. However, you can see that this strain of *E. coli* is resistant to the two antibiotics on the discs at the bottom and has been able to grow right up to the discs.

- changing the type of antibiotics prescribed for certain diseases so that the same antibiotic is not always prescribed for the same disease

- avoiding using antibiotics in farming to prevent, rather than cure, infections.

Questions

22 Suggest how each of the following might decrease the chances of an antibiotic-resistant strain of bacteria developing:

a limiting the use of antibiotics to cases where there is a real need

b regularly changing the type of antibiotic that is prescribed for a particular disease

c using two or more antibiotics together to treat a bacterial infection.

23 Figure 10.18 shows the results of an antibiotic sensitivity test carried out on a pathogenic strain of the human gut bacterium *Escherichia coli* O157.

Bacteria are collected from faeces, food or water, and grown on an agar medium. Various antibiotics are absorbed onto discs of filter paper and placed on the agar plate. The plate is incubated, and the diameters of the inhibition zones where no bacteria are growing are measured.

Table 10.7 shows the inhibition zone diameters for the antibiotics included in Figure 10.18.

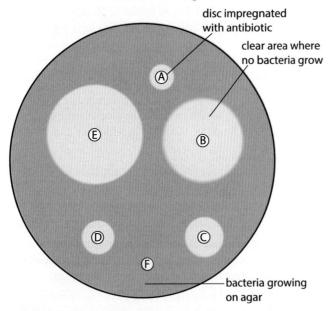

Figure 10.18: An antibiotic sensitivity test for a pathogenic strain of *E. coli*. Table 10.7 shows the inhibition zone diameters for the six antibiotics.

If the diameter of the inhibition zone for an antibiotic is equal to or less than ($\leq$) the figure given in the first column of Table 10.7, the bacteria are resistant to it. If the diameter is equal to or greater than ($\geq$) the figure in the right-hand column, the bacteria are sensitive, and the antibiotic may be chosen for treatment.

Which of the antibiotics in Figure 10.18 and Table 10.7 would be chosen to treat the patient with the pathogenic strain of *E. coli* O157? Explain your answer.

Antibiotic	Inhibition zone diameter / mm	
	Resistant	Sensitive
A	≤ 11	≥ 14
B	≤ 12	≥ 18
C	≤ 9	≥ 14
D	≤ 11	≥ 22
E	≤ 12	≥ 15
F	≤ 14	≥ 19

Table 10.7: Inhibition zone diameters for the antibiotics tested in Figure 10.18.

REFLECTION

Some scientists think that we are reaching the end of the 'age of antibiotics'.

Research the reasons for this statement and the likely consequences for the future of human populations. Summarise the results of your discussion as a presentation.

How did you research your answers to this activity? Did you find information in support of this statement and any that supports alternative views?

Final reflection

Discuss with a friend which, if any, parts of Chapter 10 you need to:

- read through again to make sure you really understand

- seek more guidance on, even after going over it again.

SUMMARY

Infectious diseases are caused by organisms known as pathogens that invade the body.

Cholera, malaria, HIV/AIDS and tuberculosis (TB) are all examples of infectious diseases.

Cholera is caused by the bacterium *Vibrio cholerae* and is transmitted in water or food contaminated by the faeces of infected people. Cholera can be controlled by treating patients with intravenous or oral rehydration therapy and making sure that human faeces do not reach the water supply. The disease is prevented by providing clean, chlorinated water and good sanitation.

Malaria is caused by four species of *Plasmodium*. The most dangerous is *P. falciparum*. Malaria is transmitted by an insect vector: female *Anopheles* mosquitoes transfer *Plasmodium* from infected to uninfected people. Malaria is controlled in three main ways: by reducing the number of mosquitoes through insecticide spraying or draining breeding sites; by using mosquito nets (more effective if soaked in long-lasting insecticide); by using drugs to prevent *Plasmodium* infecting people.

AIDS is a set of diseases caused by the destruction of the immune system by infection with human immunodeficiency virus (HIV). HIV is transmitted in certain body fluids: blood, semen, vaginal secretions and breast milk. HIV primarily infects economically active members of populations in developing countries and has an extremely adverse effect on social and economic development.

The transmission of HIV can be controlled by using barrier methods (e.g. condoms and femidoms) during sexual intercourse. Educating people to practise safer sex is the only control method currently available to health authorities. Contact tracing is used to find people who may have contracted HIV, so that they can be tested and counselled.

Life expectancy can be greatly extended by using combinations of drugs which interfere with the replication of HIV. However, such treatment is expensive, is difficult to maintain and some side effects are unpleasant. There is no vaccine for HIV and no cure for AIDS.

TB is caused by the bacteria *Mycobacterium tuberculosis* and *M. bovis*. *M. tuberculosis* is spread when people infected with the active form of the disease release bacteria in droplets of liquid when they cough or sneeze. Transmission occurs when uninfected people inhale the bacteria. This is most likely to happen where people live in overcrowded housing conditions, and especially where many sleep close together. *M. bovis* causes TB in cattle, but can be passed to humans.

Many people have the inactive form of TB in their lungs, but they do not have the disease and do not spread it. The inactive bacteria may become active in people who are malnourished or who become infected with HIV. Drugs are used to treat people with the active form of TB. The treatment may take nine months or more as it is difficult to kill the bacteria. Contact tracing is used to find people who may have caught the disease. These people are tested for TB and treated if found to be infected. The BCG vaccine provides some protection against TB, but its effectiveness varies in different parts of the world and decreases with age.

Public health measures are taken to reduce the transmission of all of these infectious diseases, but to be effective they must be informed by a knowledge of the life cycle of each pathogen.

Antibiotics are drugs that are used to treat infections caused by pathogenic bacteria. They are compounds that are made by microorganisms and modified chemically to increase their effectiveness. Penicillin prevents the production of new cell walls in bacteria and so does not affect viruses or human cells, neither of which have cell walls. Not all antibiotics are effective against all bacteria.

Resistance to antibiotics can arise because some bacteria may, by chance, contain a resistance gene. The bacteria survive when exposed to the antibiotic and can then reproduce to form a large population of bacteria all containing this gene. Resistance can also be spread between bacteria when plasmids are transferred during conjugation.

CONTINUED

The widespread and indiscriminate use of antibiotics has led to the growth of resistant strains of bacteria. This poses a serious challenge to the maintenance of health services in the 21st century.

Various measures can be taken to reduce the impact of antibiotic resistance. Examples are restricting the use of antibiotics, making sure that they are only available on prescription from a doctor and using antibiotics in combination.

EXAM-STYLE QUESTIONS

1 Cholera, malaria, HIV/AIDS and TB are infectious diseases. Which row shows the type of organism that causes each of these diseases?

	Cholera	Malaria	HIV/AIDS	TB
A	bacterium	protoctist	virus	bacterium
B	bacterium	virus	bacterium	protoctist
C	protoctist	insect	bacterium	virus
D	virus	protoctist	virus	bacterium

[1]

2 Infectious diseases are best defined as:

A all diseases that are transmitted through the air

B all diseases that are caused by bacteria and viruses

C all diseases that are caused by a pathogen

D all diseases that are transmitted from mother to child. [1]

3 An antibiotic sensitivity test was carried out on bacteria isolated from a patient with a blood disease.

Four antibiotics were tested, **A**, **B**, **C** and **D**. The results are shown in the diagram. Which antibiotic is likely to be the most effective in treating the blood disease? [1]

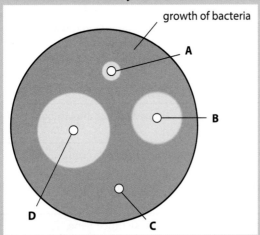

4 Which of the following diseases is transmitted by an insect vector?

A cholera   C malaria

B HIV/AIDS   D TB [1]

5 a State **three** ways in which HIV is transmitted. **[3]**

The table shows statistics published in 2017 for four regions of the world and the global totals for HIV/AIDS in 2016 (data from UNAIDS).

Region	Estimated number of people newly infected with HIV	Estimated number of people living with HIV	Estimated number of people who died from AIDS
1 Eastern Europe and Central Asia	190 000	1.6 million	40 000
2 Sub-Saharan Africa	1.16 million	25.5 million	730 000
3 Asia and the Pacific	270 000	5.1 million	170 000
4 North America, Western and Central Europe	73 000	2.1 million	18 000
Global total	1.8 million	36.7 million	1.0 million

b Suggest **three** sources of data that UNAIDS may have used to compile the data in the table. **[3]**

c Explain why it is important to collect the data on the HIV/AIDS pandemic shown in the table. **[3]**

d i For region 4, the ratio of the number of people dying from AIDS to the number of people living with HIV in 2016 was 18 000 : 2.1 million or 0.009 : 1.

Calculate the ratio for region 2. **[1]**

ii Suggest reasons for the difference between the ratios for regions 4 and 2. **[3]**

[Total: 13]

6 The photograph is a transmission electron micrograph (TEM) of *Plasmodium falciparum* in a host red blood cell just after it has divided and split into separate cells.

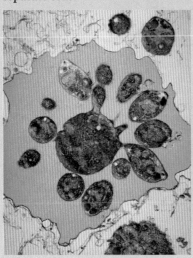

CONTINUED

a Describe how *P. falciparum* is transmitted from one host to another. [3]

b Suggest the likely effect on the host of the destruction of red blood cells shown in the photograph. [3]

c The WHO recommends the following steps for controlling malaria:

- the use of long-lasting insecticidal nets (LLINs) for all people at risk of malaria

- indoor spraying with long-lasting insecticides every three to six months

- providing preventative drugs to children under five years of age during rainy seasons.

   i Explain the reasons for these steps. [4]

   ii Suggest potential problems with these steps. [3]

[Total: 13]

7 a Describe how cholera is transmitted. [2]

  b List **three** risk factors for cholera. [3]

  c The table shows the number of cases of cholera and deaths from the disease for the five countries with the greatest outbreaks as reported to the WHO in 2016.

Country	Region	Total number of reported cases	Number of reported deaths	Case fatality rate / %
Democratic Republic of Congo	Central Africa	28 093	759	2.70
Haiti	Caribbean	41 421	447	
Kenya	East Africa	5 866	80	1.36
Nigeria	West Africa	768	32	4.17
Somalia	East Africa	15 619	548	3.51
South Sudan	Central Africa	4 295	82	1.91
United Republic of Tanzania	East Africa	11 360	172	1.51
Yemen	Arabia	15 751	164	1.04
Total	All regions of the world	132 118	2420	1.83

With reference to the table:

   i calculate the case fatality rate for Haiti in 2016 [1]

   ii suggest why the case fatality rate varies between countries [3]

   iii explain why it is important that the WHO collects data on outbreaks of cholera. [3]

CONTINUED

d The WHO also collects data on 'imported' cases of cholera. Among countries reporting these cases in 2016 were Australia, Singapore and the USA.

   i   Suggest what is meant by the term *imported case*.   **[1]**

   ii   Explain why there are no epidemics of cholera in highly economically developed countries such as Australia and the USA.   **[2]**

e 'Every death from cholera is avoidable.' Explain why there are deaths from cholera.   **[2]**

[Total: 17]

8 a i   Name the causative organism of TB.   **[1]**

   ii   Explain how TB is transmitted.   **[2]**

b The graph shows the number of new cases of TB between 1990 and 2012 in five countries in the Commonwealth of Independent States (CIS).

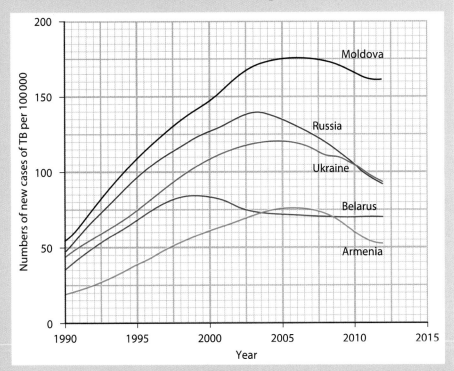

   i   Explain why the number of new cases is shown as 'per 100 000'.   **[2]**

   ii   Describe the trends shown in the graph.   **[3]**

   iii Countries in the CIS have found it difficult to control the spread of TB. Explain why TB is a difficult disease to control.   **[5]**

[Total: 13]

CONTINUED

9 In 2004, scientists in Switzerland published the results of a study to see if there was a correlation between the use of antibiotics and the number of cases of antibiotic resistance. They recorded the use of penicillin in outpatient departments of hospitals and penicillin resistance in bacteria recorded in the patients attending those departments. The scientists collected data from hospitals in the USA, Canada and 18 European countries.

The results of the study are shown in the scatter graph.

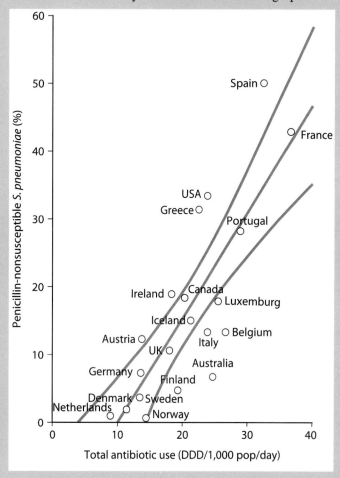

a The scientists concluded that bacterial resistance is directly associated with antibiotic use.

   i State the evidence in the scatter graph that supports the scientists' conclusion. **[2]**

   ii State **one** piece of evidence from the scatter graph that does **not** support their conclusion. **[2]**

b Antibiotic resistance is a serious threat to the health of the global population.

Discuss the steps that health authorities across the world could take to reduce the spread of antibiotic resistance. **[5]**

[Total: 9]

COMMAND WORD

Discuss: write about issue(s) or topic(s) in a structured way.

CONTINUED

10 The minimum inhibitory concentration (MIC) is defined as the lowest concentration of an antibiotic required to prevent the growth of bacteria. It is used to determine if a pathogen is susceptible or resistant to an antibiotic. E-test strips are used to determine the MIC for specific antibiotics.

- Each E-test strip is a plastic strip which is placed on an agar plate that has been inoculated with the bacteria to be tested.

- As soon as an E-test strip is put on an inoculated agar plate, the antibiotic is released immediately to establish a concentration gradient in the agar along either side of the strip.

- The agar plates are left overnight to allow time for the bacteria to grow.

- After incubation, a symmetrical inhibition ellipse is produced as shown in the drawing.

- The MIC is determined by reading the scale on the E-test strip at the lowest point where bacterial growth is prevented.

Bacteria of a strain of *Staphylococcus aureus* were tested with E-test strips for three antibiotics, **A**, **B** and **C**. The results are shown in the diagram.

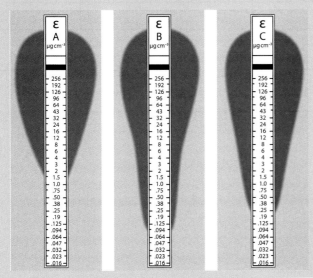

a State the MIC for each of the antibiotics.   **[3]**

b With reference to the results in the diagram, suggest the advantages of using E-test strips.   **[4]**

c Make a drawing to show the result you would expect if the MIC for an antibiotic was $8\,\mu g\,cm^{-3}$.   **[3]**

d In 1993, bacteria were isolated from hospital patients that only grow in the presence of vancomycin at concentrations greater than $6\,\mu g\,cm^{-3}$.

Describe the results that would be obtained if these vancomycin-dependent bacteria are tested with an E-test strip containing vancomycin at different concentrations.   **[2]**

[Total: 12]

SELF-EVALUATION CHECKLIST

After studying this chapter, complete a table like this:

I can	See section...	Needs more work	Almost there	Ready to move on
explain that infectious diseases are caused by pathogens that are transmitted from person to person	10.1			
give the names of the pathogens that cause cholera, malaria, TB and HIV/AIDS and explain how they are transmitted	10.1			
state that human pathogens can be viruses, bacteria and protoctists	10.1			
discuss the biological, social and economic factors that influence the effectiveness of control measures for cholera, malaria, TB and HIV	10.1			
outline the way in which the antibiotic penicillin acts on bacteria	10.2			
explain why antibiotics have no affect on viruses	10.2			
discuss the consequences of the resistance of pathogens to antibiotics	10.2			
outline the measures that can be taken to reduce the impact of antibiotic resistance	10.2			

> Chapter 11

Immunity

LEARNING INTENTIONS

In this chapter you will learn how to:

- describe the mode of action of macrophages and neutrophils
- explain what is meant by the term *antigen* and state the difference between self antigens and non-self antigens
- describe what happens during a primary immune response and explain the role of memory cells in long-term immunity
- explain how the molecular structure of antibodies is related to their functions
- outline the hybridoma method for the production of monoclonal antibodies and the principles of using monoclonal antibodies in the diagnosis and treatment of diseases
- describe the differences between the different types of immunity: active and passive and natural and artificial
- explain that vaccines contain antigens that stimulate immune responses to provide long-term immunity and how vaccination programmes are used to control the spread of infectious diseases.

BEFORE YOU START

Immunity is a topic that relies on a good understanding of many topics from the whole of your course so far. In your group, prepare presentations on some topics that you can deliver *without notes*. You should have no more than five slides (if you need them) and each slide should have fewer than ten words. Your presentation should take no longer than 60 seconds. Here is a list of some suggested topics.

- Structure and roles of proteins

- Structure of animal cells

- Protein synthesis

- Structure and functions of mammalian blood cells

- Cell cycle of animal cells

- Specialisation of mammalian cells

- Roles of stem cells in mammals

- Cell signalling

- Movement into and out of animal cells

SMALLPOX WAS FIRST – WILL POLIO BE SECOND?

You have probably been vaccinated against polio. You may wonder why people make such a fuss about having a vaccination against a disease that you are unlikely ever to come across. There may be very few cases of polio now but, in the past, large numbers of people contracted the disease. In many cases, the disease was mild but the virus that causes polio can infect the base of the nerves and cause paralysis. This happened in about 1% of all cases.

Vaccines against polio became available in the 1950s and mass vaccination programmes began immediately. These have proved very successful: the last case of polio in the Americas was in 1991. In 1994 it was declared that transmission of polio had been broken so that the disease was no longer endemic in the Western Hemisphere. Success has been slower coming in the rest of the world. In 2018 there were only 29 reported cases of polio throughout the world. These cases occurred in three countries: Nigeria, Pakistan and Afghanistan (Figure 11.1).

India has mobilised huge numbers of medical staff and around 230 000 volunteers to vaccinate children throughout the country. This didn't just happen once, but on many occasions in the government's drive to eradicate polio. In 2014 the World Health Organization (WHO) declared that India was a polio-free country although vaccination programmes continue with two throughout the country in 2018. Other countries where polio

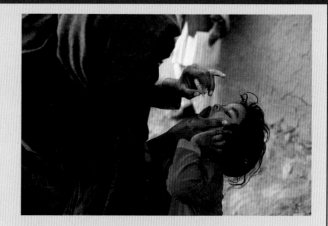

Figure 11.1: A child receiving polio vaccine during an anti-polio campaign in Kandahar province in Afghanistan in 2016.

remains endemic have not been as successful as India. One reason is that some people have resisted attempts by medical staff to vaccinate the local population. Some medical staff have been attacked, even killed, while working on polio eradication campaigns in Pakistan and Afghanistan.

In 1980 the WHO announced that the viral disease smallpox had been eradicated as there had not been a new case anywhere in the world for the previous three years. Polio is the most likely candidate for the second infectious disease of humans to be eradicated. This may happen in the near future although global eradication is proving more difficult than it was with smallpox. You can

CONTINUED

follow the progress of the campaign by searching online for 'polio eradication'.

Question for discussion

What are the long-term advantages of mass vaccination programmes for individuals and for society?

You are now going to consider in detail something that was mentioned in Chapter 10: humans can defend themselves against infection by pathogens (disease-causing organisms). You have seen that some people experience few or no symptoms when exposed to certain infectious diseases. Even though a person may be a carrier of disease to other people, he or she has immunity. How is this possible? The disease measles is used as an example here.

Measles is caused by a virus that enters the body and multiplies inside cells in the upper respiratory tract (nasal cavity and trachea). Most people have measles only once. It is very unlikely that anyone surviving the disease will have it again. They are immune. Their body's internal defence system has developed a way of recognising the measles virus and preventing it from doing any harm again. Immunity is the protection against disease provided by the body's internal defence or immune system.

11.1 Defence against disease

External defence system

Humans have a variety of mechanisms to protect them against infectious diseases such as measles and those described in Chapter 10. Many pathogens do not harm us, because, if we are healthy, we have physical, chemical and cellular defences that prevent them entering. For example, the epithelia that cover the airways are an effective barrier to the entry of pathogens; hydrochloric acid in the stomach kills many bacteria that we ingest with food and drink; blood clotting is a defence mechanism that stops the loss of blood and prevents the entry of pathogens through wounds in the skin.

Internal defence system

If pathogens do successfully enter the body, white blood cells can recognise them as something foreign and destroy them. The structure of white blood cells is described in Chapter 8 (Section 8.5, Blood).

White blood cells are part of the immune system and they recognise pathogens by the distinctive, large molecules that cover the pathogen surfaces. These molecules include proteins, glycoproteins, glycolipids and polysaccharides, and the toxins and waste materials which some pathogens produce. Any molecule which the body recognises as foreign is an antigen.

There are two types of white blood cell: phagocytes and lymphocytes. Before looking at their function in detail, it will be useful to look at an example of the immune response in humans. This example introduces further important features of the immune system: the ability to distinguish between self and non-self, and the

KEY WORDS

immune system: the body's internal defence system

antigen: a substance that is foreign to the body and stimulates an immune response (e.g. any large molecule such as a protein)

self: refers to substances produced by the body that the immune system does not recognise as foreign, so they do not stimulate an immune response

non-self: refers to any substance or cell that is recognised by the immune system as being foreign and will stimulate an immune response production of **antibodies**. Antibodies are glycoprotein molecules that act against specific antigens.

Everyone has molecules on the surfaces of their cells that are not found in other organisms, or even in other humans. These are often called cell surface antigens. Although cell surface antigens do not stimulate production of antibodies in their own body, they may do if they enter someone else. The cell surface antigens of the human ABO blood group system are a good example. If you are blood group A, then you have a specific carbohydrate chain on the glycolipids and glycoproteins on your red blood cells that is not on the red cells of people who are blood group B. If blood of type A is given to someone who has blood of type B during a transfusion, the recipient's immune systems will recognise the blood cells as foreign and start to produce antibodies. This happens because the recipient's immune system has recognised the antigens on blood cells of type A as non-self. If blood of type B is used during the transfusion, as it should be, the recipient's immune system recognises the antigens on the red blood cells as self and no antibodies are produced.

The response of lymphocytes to the presence of a foreign antigen is known as the **immune response**. In some cases, lymphocytes respond by producing antibodies; in others, they respond by killing cells that have become infected by pathogens.

KEY WORDS

antibody: a glycoprotein (immunoglobulin) made by specialised lymphocytes in response to the presence of a specific antigen; each type of antibody molecule has a shape that is complementary to its specific antigen

immune response: the complex series of responses of the body to the entry of a foreign antigen; it involves the activity of lymphocytes and phagocytes

---

Question

1 a Antibodies and antibiotics are often confused. State the differences between them.

   b Using the ABO blood group system as an example, explain why red blood cells can be recognised as self or as non-self.

   c Explain why blood of type B is not given to someone with blood type A during a blood transfusion.

11.2 Cells of the immune system

The cells of the immune system are produced from stem cells in bone marrow. There are two groups of these cells involved in defence:

- phagocytes (neutrophils and macrophages)
- lymphocytes.

All of these cells are visible among red blood cells when a blood smear is stained to show nuclei (Figure 11.2).

Phagocytes

Phagocytes are produced throughout life in the bone marrow. They are stored there before being distributed around the body in the blood. They are scavengers, removing any dead cells as well as invasive microorganisms.

Neutrophils are a kind of phagocyte and form about 60% of the white cells in the blood (Figures 11.2 and 11.3).

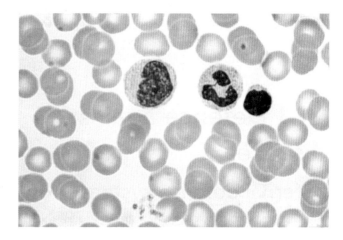

Figure 11.2: A monocyte (left), which will develop into a macrophage, a neutrophil (centre) and a lymphocyte (right), together with red blood cells in a blood smear which has been photographed through a light microscope. The cytoplasm of the neutrophil contains vacuoles full of hydrolytic enzymes (×1000).

They travel throughout the body, often leaving the blood by squeezing through the walls of capillaries to move through the tissues engulfing any pathogens that they find. During an infection, neutrophils are released in large numbers from their stores, but they are short-lived cells.

Macrophages are also phagocytes but are larger than neutrophils and tend to be found in organs such as the lungs, liver, spleen, kidney and lymph nodes, rather than remaining in the blood. After they are made in the bone marrow, macrophages travel in the blood as monocytes (Figure 11.2), which develop into macrophages once they leave the blood and settle in the organs, removing any foreign matter found there.

Macrophages are long-lived cells and play a crucial role in initiating immune responses, since they do not destroy pathogens completely, but cut them up to display antigens that can be recognised by lymphocytes.

Phagocytosis

If pathogens invade the body and cause an infection, some of the cells under attack respond by releasing chemicals such as histamine. These, together with any chemicals released by the pathogens themselves, attract passing neutrophils to the site. (This movement towards a chemical stimulus is called chemotaxis.) The neutrophils destroy the pathogens by phagocytosis (see Figures 4.19 and 11.4).

The neutrophils move towards the pathogens, which may be clustered together and covered in antibodies.

The antibodies further stimulate the neutrophils to attack the pathogens. This is because neutrophils have receptor proteins on their surfaces that recognise antibody molecules and attach to them. When the neutrophil attaches to the pathogens, the neutrophil's cell surface membrane engulfs the pathogens, and traps them within a phagocytic vacuole in a process called endocytosis. Lysosomes fuse with the phagocytic vacuoles releasing enzymes that breakdown the pathogens.

Neutrophils have a short life: after killing and digesting some pathogens, they die. Dead neutrophils often collect at a site of infection to form pus.

Questions

2 Looking at Figure 11.2, describe the differences between the neutrophil and the lymphocyte.

3 Looking at Figure 11.3, calculate the actual width of:

a one of the bacteria

b the neutrophil on the right of the TEM.

4 State how the cells in Figure 11.3 can be identified as neutrophils.

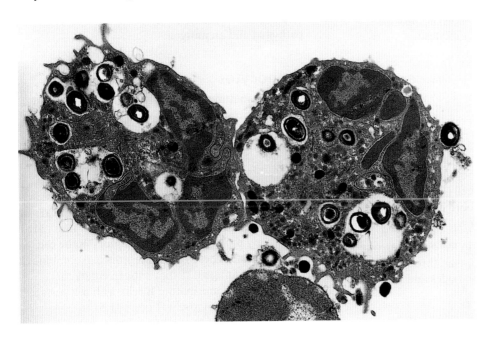

Figure 11.3: A transmission electron micrograph (TEM) of two neutrophils that have ingested several *Staphylococcus* bacteria (×6000). Notice at the extreme right, one bacterium is just about to be engulfed. Compare this photograph with Figure 11.4.

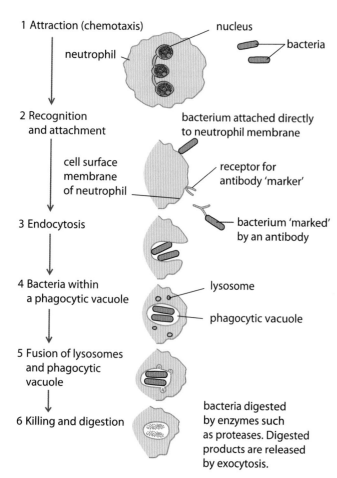

1 Attraction (chemotaxis)

neutrophil — nucleus — bacteria

2 Recognition and attachment

bacterium attached directly to neutrophil membrane

cell surface membrane of neutrophil

receptor for antibody 'marker'

3 Endocytosis

bacterium 'marked' by an antibody

4 Bacteria within a phagocytic vacuole

lysosome

phagocytic vacuole

5 Fusion of lysosomes and phagocytic vacuole

6 Killing and digestion

bacteria digested by enzymes such as proteases. Digested products are released by exocytosis.

Figure 11.4: The stages of phagocytosis. The antibody and antibody receptor are not drawn to the same scale as the rest of the diagram.

Lymphocytes

Lymphocytes are smaller than phagocytes. They have a large nucleus that fills most of the cell (Figure 11.2). There are two types of lymphocyte, both of which are produced before birth in bone marrow.

- B-lymphocytes (B cells) remain in the bone marrow until they are mature and then spread throughout the body, concentrating in lymph nodes and the spleen.

- T-lymphocytes (T cells) leave the bone marrow and collect in the thymus where they mature. The thymus is a gland that lies in the chest just beneath the sternum. It doubles in size between birth and puberty, but after puberty it shrinks.

Only mature lymphocytes can carry out immune responses. During the maturation process, many different types of B- and T-lymphocyte develop, perhaps many millions. Each type is specialised to respond to one antigen, giving the immune system as a whole the ability to respond to almost any type of pathogen that enters the body. When mature, all these B and T cells circulate between the blood and the lymph (Chapter 8). This ensures that they are distributed throughout the body so that they come into contact with any pathogens *and* with each other.

Immune responses depend on B and T cells interacting with each other to give an effective defence. You will look in detail at the roles of B and T cells and how they interact in the following sections. Put briefly, some T cells coordinate the immune response stimulating B cells to divide and then secrete antibodies into the blood. The antibodies recognise the antigens on the pathogens and help to destroy the pathogens. Other T cells seek out and kill any of the body's own cells that are infected with pathogens. To do this they must make direct contact with infected cells.

Question

5 Explain to someone else the difference between a pathogen and an antigen.

B-lymphocytes

As each B cell matures, it gains the ability to make just one type of antibody molecule. Many different types of B cell develop in each of us, perhaps as many as 10 million. While B cells are maturing, the genes that code for antibodies are changed in a variety of ways to code for different antibodies. Each cell then divides to give a small number of cells that are able to make the same type of antibody. Each small group of identical cells is called a clone. At this stage, each B cell uses part of the antibody molecule to make receptors in the cell surface membrane. These B cell receptors can combine with one specific antigen. If that antigen enters the body, there will be some mature B cells with cell surface receptors that will recognise it (Figure 11.5).

Figure 11.6 shows what happens to B cells during the immune response when an antigen enters the body on two separate occasions. When the antigen enters the body for the first time, the small numbers of B cells with cell membrane receptors complementary to the

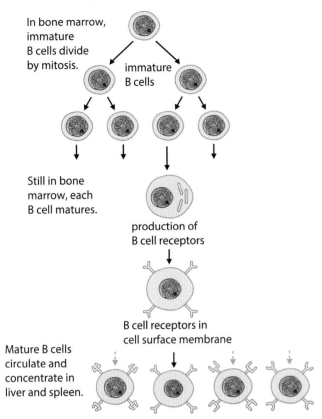

In bone marrow, immature B cells divide by mitosis.

immature B cells

Still in bone marrow, each B cell matures.

production of B cell receptors

B cell receptors in cell surface membrane

Mature B cells circulate and concentrate in liver and spleen.

mature B cells each with different B cell receptors

Figure 11.5: Origin and maturation of B-lymphocytes. As they mature in bone marrow, the cells become capable of secreting one type of antibody molecule with a specific shape. Some of these molecules become receptor proteins in the cell surface membrane and act like markers. By the time of a child's birth, there are millions of different B cells, each with specific B cell receptors. The diagram shows just four of these.

antigen are stimulated to divide by mitosis. This stage is known as **clonal selection**. The small clone of cells with receptors specific to antigens on the surface of the invading pathogen divides repeatedly by mitosis in the **clonal expansion** stage so that huge numbers of identical B cells are produced over a few weeks.

Questions

6   Some people say that in an immune response a pathogen chooses the lymphocytes that will destroy them. Do you agree?

7   The receptors on the surface of the mature B cells illustrated in Figure 11.5 are not drawn to scale. Receptors on cell surfaces are not visible at this magnification, but can be shown in diagrams like this. Discuss with others why each clone only has one type of B cell receptor.

8   Analogies are often useful in science. An analogy is used to try to explain an unfamiliar topic by comparing it to something that is more familiar, for example the action of the heart is often compared with a pump. Try to think of an analogy to explain clonal selection.

9   Looking at Figure 11.6, explain why only cells in clone **Y** have responded to the antigen.

Some of the activated B cells become **plasma cells** that produce antibody molecules very quickly – up to several thousand a second. Plasma cells secrete antibodies into the blood, lymph or onto the linings of the lungs and the gut (Figure 11.7). These plasma cells do not live long: after several weeks their numbers decrease. The antibody molecules they have secreted stay in the blood for longer, however, until they too eventually decrease in concentration.

Other B cells become **memory cells**. These cells remain circulating in the body for a long time. If the same

KEY WORDS

clonal selection: individual lymphocytes have cell surface receptors specific to one antigen; this specificity is determined as lymphocytes mature and before any antigens enter the body (during an immune response the only lymphocytes to respond are those with receptors specific to antigens on the surface of the invading pathogen)

clonal expansion: the increase in number of specific clones of lymphocytes by mitosis during an immune response

plasma cell: short-lived, activated B-lymphocyte produced during clonal expansion; plasma cells produce and release antibody molecules

memory B cell: long-lived, activated B-lymphocyte that is specific to one antigen; memory cells are activated to differentiate (develop) into plasma cells during secondary immune responses to the specific antigen

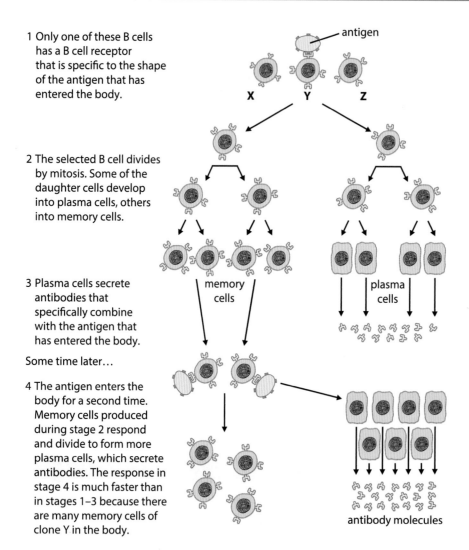

1 Only one of these B cells has a B cell receptor that is specific to the shape of the antigen that has entered the body.

2 The selected B cell divides by mitosis. Some of the daughter cells develop into plasma cells, others into memory cells.

3 Plasma cells secrete antibodies that specifically combine with the antigen that has entered the body.

Some time later…

4 The antigen enters the body for a second time. Memory cells produced during stage 2 respond and divide to form more plasma cells, which secrete antibodies. The response in stage 4 is much faster than in stages 1–3 because there are many memory cells of clone Y in the body.

antigen

X   Y   Z

memory cells

plasma cells

antibody molecules

Figure 11.6: The role of B-lymphocytes during an immune response. **X**, **Y** and **Z** are cells from three clones of B-lymphocytes. The resulting changes in antibody concentration are shown in Figure 11.8.

antigen is reintroduced a few weeks or months after the first infection, memory cells divide rapidly and develop into plasma cells and more memory cells. This is repeated on every subsequent invasion by the pathogen with the same antigen, meaning that the invading pathogens can be destroyed and removed before the development of any symptoms of the disease.

Figure 11.8 shows the changes in the concentration of antibody molecules in the blood when the body encounters an antigen. The first or primary immune response is slow because, at this stage, there are very few B cells that are specific to the antigen. The secondary immune response is faster because there are now many memory cells, which quickly divide and differentiate into plasma cells. During the primary response, the number of cells in each clone of

B cells that is selected has increased in size. There are many more B cells specific to the pathogen that has invaded the body. As you can see in Figure 11.8, many more antibodies are produced in the secondary response and they are produced almost immediately when the antigen is detected.

> ### KEY WORDS
>
> **primary immune response:** the first immune response to a specific antigen
>
> **secondary immune response:** the second and any subsequent immune responses to a specific antigen

Memory cells are the basis of immunological memory. Memory cells last for many years, often a lifetime. This explains why someone is very unlikely to catch measles twice. There is only one strain of the virus that causes measles, and each time it infects the body there is a fast secondary response. However, people do suffer from repeated infections of the common cold and influenza, because there are many different and new strains of the viruses that cause these diseases, and each has different antigens. When a pathogen with different antigens infects you, the primary response must occur before you become immune, and during that time you can become ill.

Questions

10 Calculate the diameter of the plasma cell in Figure 11.7 at its widest point.

11 Explain why B cells divide by mitosis during an immune response.

12 Explain how plasma cells, such as the one shown in Figure 11.7, are adapted to secrete large quantities of antibody molecules.

B cells and antibodies

Antibodies are all globular glycoproteins with quaternary structure (Chapter 2, Section 2.6, Proteins). They form the group of plasma proteins called immunoglobulins. Each antibody molecule consists of four polypeptide chains: two 'long' or 'heavy' chains and two 'short' or 'light' chains (Figures 11.9 and 11.10). Disulfide bonds hold the chains together. Each molecule has two identical variable regions formed from parts of both light and heavy chains. The sequences of amino acids in these variable regions make specific 3D shapes which bind to one antigen. Each clone of B cells makes antibody molecules all with the same variable regions which are complementary in shape to one antigen. The 'hinge' region gives the flexibility for the antibody molecule to bind to antigens on the surface of a pathogen.

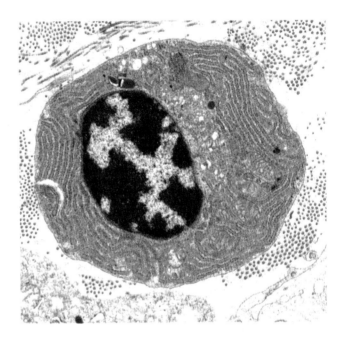

Figure 11.7: False-colour TEM of the contents of a plasma cell (×6000). There is an extensive network of rough endoplasmic reticulum in the cytoplasm (green) for the production of antibody molecules, which plasma cells secrete into blood or lymph by exocytosis (Chapter 4). The mitochondria (blue) provide adenosine triphosphate (ATP) for protein synthesis and the movement of secretory vesicles.

KEY WORDS

immunological memory: the ability of the immune system to mount a larger and more rapid response to an antigen that has already been encountered before

variable region: region of an antibody molecule composed of parts of the light and heavy polypeptide chains that form the antigen-binding site; the amino acid sequences of the variable site form a specific shape that is complementary to a particular antigen

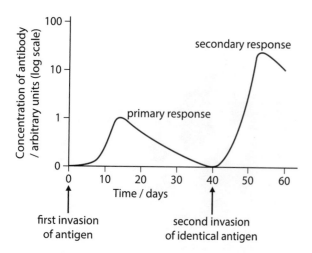

Figure 11.8: The changes in antibody concentration in the blood during a primary and secondary response to the same antigen.

Questions

13 Looking at Figure 11.8, state how the secondary immune response differs from the primary immune response.

14 Explain why people are often ill for several weeks after they catch a disease, even though they can make antibodies against the disease.

15 Look again at Figure 11.4. Explain why it is important that the constant region of all antibodies is the same.

16 Explain why the antibody molecule shown in Figure 11.10:

   a   shows all four levels of protein structure

   b   is a glycoprotein.

17 Explain why polysaccharides would not be suitable for making antibody molecules.

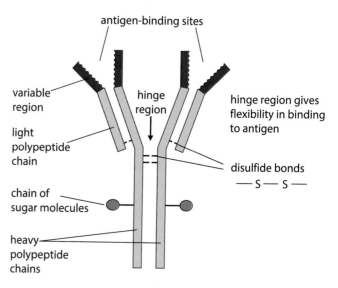

Figure 11.10: A diagram of an antibody molecule. Antigen–antibody binding occurs at the variable regions. An antigen fits into the binding site like a substrate fitting into the active site of an enzyme. The part of the molecule shown in green is identical in all antibodies known as IgG that have four polypeptides.

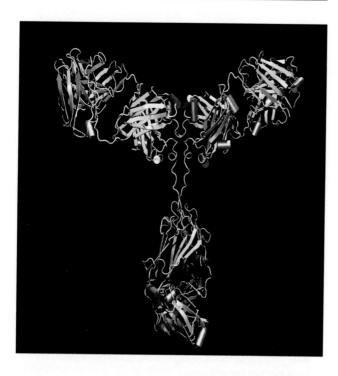

Figure 11.9: A model of an antibody made using computer graphics. The molecule is Y-shaped with the constant region forming the lower part and the two variable regions at the ends of the branches of the Y. α-helices are shown in purple and β-pleated sheets in yellow. Compare this with Figure 11.10. This type of antibody molecule with four polypeptides is known as immunoglobulin G, IgG for short. Larger types of antibody molecules are IgA (four antigen-binding sites) and IgM (ten antigen-binding sites).

Figure 11.11 shows the different ways in which antibodies work to protect the body from pathogens. As you saw earlier, some antibodies act as labels to identify antigens as appropriate targets for phagocytes to destroy (diagram 5, Figure 11.11). A special group of antibodies are antitoxins. These bind to and block the toxins released by bacteria, such as those that cause cholera,

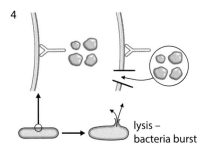

Antibodies combine with viruses preventing them entering or damaging cells.

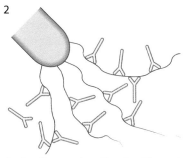

Antibodies attach to flagella of bacteria making them less active and easier for phagocytes to engulf.

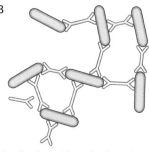

Antibodies with multiple antigen binding sites cause agglutination (clumping together) of bacteria reducing the chances of spread throughout the body.

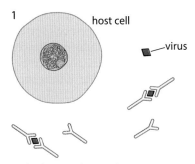

Together with other molecules, some antibodies 'punch' holes in the cell walls of bacteria, causing them to burst when they absorb water by osmosis.

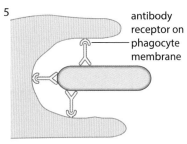

Antibodies coat bacteria, making it easier for phagocytes to ingest them; phagocytes have receptor proteins for the constant regions of antibodies.

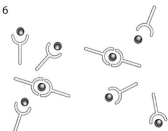

Antibodies combine with toxins, neutralising them and making them harmless; these antibodies are called antitoxins.

Figure 11.11: The functions of antibodies. Antibodies have different functions according to the type of antigen to which they bind.

diphtheria and tetanus, to prevent them damaging the host cells (diagram 6, Figure 11.11).

T-lymphocytes

Mature T cells have specific cell surface receptors called T-cell receptors (Figure 11.12). T-cell receptors have a structure similar to that of antibodies, and they are each specific to one antigen. T cells are activated when they recognise this antigen on another cell of the host (that is, on the person's own cells). Sometimes this cell is a macrophage that has engulfed a pathogen and cut it up to expose the pathogen's surface molecules, or it may be a body cell that has been invaded by a pathogen and is similarly displaying the antigen on its cell surface membrane as a kind of 'help' signal. The display of antigens on the surface of cells in this way is known as **antigen presentation**. The T cells that have receptors complementary to the antigen respond by dividing by mitosis to increase the number of cells. T cells go through the same stages of clonal selection and clonal expansion as clones of B cells (Figure 11.13).

There are two main types of T cell:

- **T-helper cells**
- **T-killer cells** (also known as T-cytotoxic cells).

When T-helper cells are activated, they release **cytokines** – cell-signalling molecules that stimulate appropriate B cells to divide, develop into plasma cells and secrete antibodies. Some T-helper cells secrete cytokines that stimulate macrophages to carry out phagocytosis more vigorously. T-killer cells search the body for cells that have become invaded by pathogens and are displaying foreign antigens from the pathogens on their cell surface membranes. T-killer cells recognise the antigens, attach themselves to the surface of infected cells, and secrete toxic substances such as hydrogen peroxide, killing the body cells and the pathogens inside (Figure 11.13). Some T-helper cells secrete cytokines that stimulate T-killer cells to divide by mitosis and to differentiate by producing vacuoles full of toxins.

Memory T-helper cells and memory T-killer cells are produced, which remain in the body and become active very quickly during the secondary response to antigens.

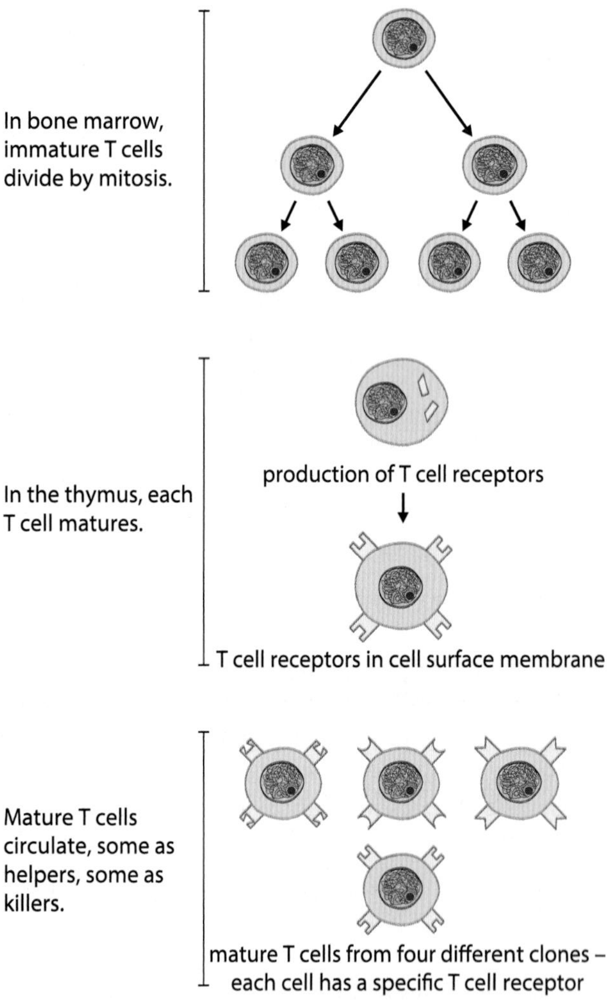

> ### KEY WORD
>
> **cytokine:** any signalling molecule released by cells to influence the growth and/or differentiation of the same or another cell

In bone marrow, immature T cells divide by mitosis.

In the thymus, each T cell matures.

production of T cell receptors

T cell receptors in cell surface membrane

Mature T cells circulate, some as helpers, some as killers.

mature T cells from four different clones – each cell has a specific T cell receptor

Figure 11.12: Origin and maturation of T-lymphocytes. As T cells mature in the thymus gland they produce T cell receptor proteins. Each cell has a specific receptor. Some cells become T-helper cells, others become T-killer cells.

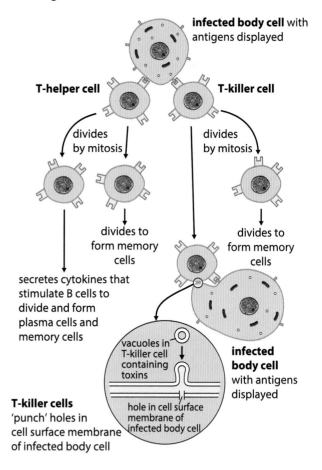

infected body cell with antigens displayed

T-helper cell   **T-killer cell**

divides by mitosis   divides by mitosis

divides to form memory cells   divides to form memory cells

secretes cytokines that stimulate B cells to divide and form plasma cells and memory cells

vacuoles in T-killer cell containing toxins

infected body cell with antigens displayed

hole in cell surface membrane of infected body cell

T-killer cells 'punch' holes in cell surface membrane of infected body cell

Figure 11.13: The functions of T-lymphocytes during an immune response. T-helper cells and T-killer cells with T-cell receptor proteins specific to the antigen respond and divide by mitosis. Activated T-helper cells stimulate B cells to divide and develop into plasma cells (Figure 11.6). T-killer cells attach themselves to infected cells and kill them.

Questions

18 Use what you learnt from Chapter 4 about cell signalling to make a diagram showing how T-helper cells coordinate the activity of other lymphocytes during an immune response. Share your diagram with others.

19 Outline the sequence of events that follows:

a the release of a toxin by *Corynebacterium diphtheriae*, the causative organism of diphtheria

b the invasion of cells in the gas exchange system by the virus that causes measles.

20 There are many different strains of the rhinovirus, which causes the common cold. Explain why people can catch several different colds in the space of a few months.

11.3 Active and passive immunity

The type of immunity just described occurs during the course of an infection. It is called **active immunity** because the person makes their own antibodies. This happens when the lymphocytes are activated by antigens on the surface of pathogens that have invaded the body. As this activation occurs naturally during an infection, it is called **natural active immunity**.

The immune response can also be activated artificially. There are two ways to do this: by injecting **vaccines** into the body or (for certain diseases such as polio and cholera) taking them by mouth. This is the basis of **artificial active immunity**, more commonly known as **vaccination**. The immune response is similar to that following an infection, and the effect is the same – long-term immunity. In both natural and artificial active immunity, antibody concentrations in the blood change in the way shown in Figure 11.8.

In both forms of active immunity, it takes time for enough B and T cells to be produced to give an effective defence. If a person becomes infected with a potentially fatal disease such as tetanus, a more immediate defence than that provided by active immunity is needed for survival. Tetanus can kill quickly, before the body's natural primary response can take place. So people who have a wound that may be infected with the bacterium that causes tetanus are given an injection of antitoxin. This is a preparation of human antibodies against the tetanus toxin. The antibodies are collected from blood donors who have recently been vaccinated against tetanus. Antitoxin provides immediate protection, but this is only temporary as the antibodies are not produced by the body's own B cells and are therefore non-self. They are removed from the circulation by phagocytes in the liver and spleen.

This type of immunity is called **passive immunity** because the person has not produced the antibodies themselves. B and T cells have not been activated and plasma cells have not produced any antibodies. More specifically, antitoxins provide **artificial passive immunity**, because the antibodies have not entered the body by a natural process: they have come from another person who has encountered the antigen.

The immune system of a newborn infant is not as effective as that of a child or an adult. However, infants are not entirely unprotected against pathogens, because antibodies from their mothers cross the placenta during pregnancy and remain in the infant for several months (Figure 11.14). For example, antibodies against measles may last for four months or more in the infant's blood. This is **natural passive immunity**.

KEY WORDS

active immunity: immunity gained when an antigen enters the body, an immune response occurs and antibodies are produced by plasma cells

natural active immunity: immunity gained by being infected by a pathogen

vaccine: a preparation containing antigens to stimulate active immunity against one or several diseases

artificial active immunity: immunity gained by putting antigens into the body, either by injection or by mouth

vaccination: giving a vaccine containing antigens for a disease, either by injection or by mouth; vaccination confers artificial active immunity without the development of symptoms of the disease

passive immunity: the temporary immunity gained without there being an immune response

artificial passive immunity: the immunity gained by injecting antibodies

natural passive immunity: the immunity gained by a fetus when maternal antibodies cross the placenta or the immunity gained by an infant from breast milk

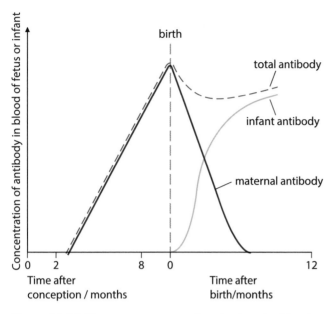

Figure 11.14: The concentrations of antibody in the blood of a fetus and an infant.

Colostrum, the thick yellowish fluid produced by a mother's breasts for the first four or five days after birth, contains a type of antibody known as IgA. Some of these antibodies remain on the surface of the infant's gut wall, while others pass into the blood undigested. IgA acts in the gut to prevent the growth of bacteria and viruses and also circulates in the blood. This is also natural passive immunity.

The features of active and passive immunity are compared in Table 11.1 and Figure 11.15.

Immunity	Features				
	Antigen encountered	Immune response	Time before antibodies appear in blood	Production of memory cells	Protection
active	yes	yes	1–2 weeks during an immune response	yes	permanent
passive	no	no	immediate	no	temporary

Table 11.1: Features of active and passive immunity.

Active immunity
Immunity developed after contacting pathogens inside the body.

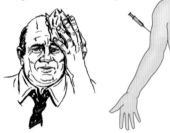

Natural
infection

Artificial
injection of live or attenuated pathogen

Passive immunity
Immunity provided by antibodies or antitoxins provided from outside the body.

Natural
antibodies from a mother in breast milk or across the placenta

Artificial
injection of antibodies (e.g. antitoxins)

Figure 11.15: Active and passive immunity

Vaccines

A vaccine is a preparation containing antigens which is used to stimulate an immune response artificially. It may contain a whole live microorganism, a dead one, a harmless version (known as an attenuated organism), a harmless form of a toxin (known as a toxoid) or a preparation of surface antigens. Vaccines are either given by injection into a vein or muscle, or taken orally (by mouth). Some are produced using techniques of genetic engineering (Chapter 19, Section 19.1, Genetic engineering).

Questions

21 Write definitions of *natural immunity* and *artificial immunity*.

22 Explain the difference between artificial active immunisation (vaccination) and artificial passive immunisation.

23 a Explain the pattern of maternal and infant antibody shown in Figure 11.14.

  b Explain the advantages of natural passive immunity for newborn infants.

24 Explain the difference between immunity to a disease and resistance to an antibiotic.

Immunity derived from a natural infection is often extremely good at providing protection, because the immune system has met living organisms which persist inside the body for some time, so the immune system has time to develop an effective response. When possible, vaccination tries to mimic this. Sometimes this works very well, when vaccines contain live microorganisms. The microorganisms reproduce, often rather slowly, so that the immune system is continually presented with a large dose of antigens. Less effective are those vaccines that do not mimic an infection because they are made from dead bacteria or from viruses that do not reproduce inside cells of the body. Some vaccines contain only antigens derived from a pathogen, not the pathogen (dead or alive) itself.

Some vaccines are highly effective, and one injection may give a lifetime's protection. Less effective vaccines need booster injections to stimulate secondary responses that give enhanced protection (Figure 11.8). It is often a good idea to receive booster injections if you are likely to be exposed to a disease, even though you may have been vaccinated as a child.

Herd immunity is gained by vaccinating nearly everyone in a population. If most of the population are immune to a specific disease, it is unlikely that the pathogen will be transmitted to those who do not have immunity for whatever reason. Herd immunity interrupts the transmission cycle in a population, so that those who are susceptible are very unlikely to be infected by the pathogens concerned. For example, some people do not respond to a vaccine by making antibodies. Young children may have lost their passive immunity to measles but not yet been vaccinated. Some people may have a medical condition that prevents them being vaccinated; for example, children receiving cancer treatment or who are on drugs that suppress the immune system.

Question

25 Discuss why the primary immune response to a pathogen cannot occur immediately, whereas it does in the secondary immune response.

Vaccination programmes

Vaccination is one of the most effective ways in which governments can protect the health of their peoples. The WHO recommends a schedule of vaccinations that is adapted by health authorities across the world to their own circumstances. For example, the schedule recommends that children receive the first dose of the MMR vaccine for measles, mumps and rubella at about nine months of age and a second dose at any time after a minimum interval of four weeks. The second dose is usually given between 15 months and 4 years of age. If a large proportion of the children in the target age group receives the vaccine, herd immunity is achieved. Vaccination programmes for the diseases on the WHO schedule should always attempt to achieve nearly 100% coverage to achieve good herd immunity. Even though many people have no experience of the diseases listed in the schedule and the incidence of the diseases is very low in many countries, it is still possible for visitors, migrants or returning travellers to introduce these diseases.

WHO also makes recommendations for vaccines that protect against diseases not listed in the schedule. There is little point in routinely vaccinating children against cholera when outbreaks occur rarely and only under certain circumstances. Also the protection provided by the vaccine is short-lived and boosters should be given to children every six months.

> **KEY WORD**
>
> **herd immunity:** vaccinating a large proportion of the population; provides protection for those not immunised as transmission of a pathogen is reduced

Vaccines are also used to contain outbreaks of disease. In the UK the BCG vaccine is not given routinely to all children to protect against TB. However, if there is an outbreak of TB, then everyone who has been in contact with the infected people and others living in the area concerned are vaccinated to stop the spread of TB. This is an example of **ring immunity** ensuring that people living in the area where an outbreak has occurred provide a 'zone of immunity' to prevent spread into the wider population. This was the strategy used in the latter stages of the smallpox eradication programme in Ethiopia and Somalia.

Immunisation schedules will change in the future as some diseases are eradicated and new diseases emerge. In 2019 the new vaccine for Ebola was offered to health workers in Central Africa to give them protection against a strain of the virus for this emergent disease that the WHO hopes to contain. It is possible that the vaccine will become more widely available to the general population whenever there is an outbreak.

As of 2019, no vaccination programme has repeated the success of the smallpox eradication programme. A vaccine for measles was introduced in the 1960s. However, a programme of one-dose vaccination has not eliminated the disease in any country, despite high coverage of the population. This is explained by the poor response to the vaccine shown by some children who need at least one booster to develop full immunity. In large cities with high birth rates and shifting populations, it can be difficult to give boosters, follow up cases of measles and trace

contacts (Figure 11.16). Measles is highly infectious and migrants and refugees can form reservoirs of infection, experiencing epidemics within their communities and then spreading the disease to surrounding populations.

It is estimated that herd immunity of 93–95% is required to prevent transmission in a population. As the currently available measles vaccine has a success rate of 95%, this means that the whole population needs to be vaccinated. Many countries struggle to achieve 80% coverage with measles vaccination and therefore it is likely that the disease will persist for many years to come (Figures 11.17).

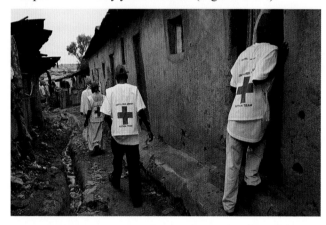

Figure 11.16: The success of immunisation programmes relies on people, such as these Red Cross workers in Nairobi, Kenya, ensuring that all families know when and where vaccinations are available.

KEY WORD

ring immunity: vaccinating all those people in contact with a person infected with a specific disease to prevent transmission in the immediate area

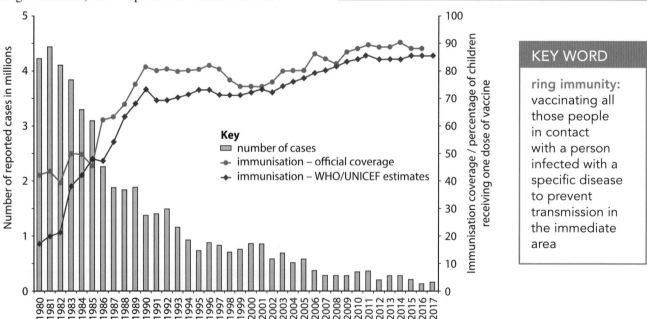

Figure 11.17: The progress of the global measles immunisation programme coordinated by the WHO. The chart shows the number of cases of measles between 1980 and 2017 and the global coverage with one-dose vaccination.

Questions

26 **a**   Search online for the WHO immunisation schedule and for the immunisation schedule currently used in your country and find out which diseases you should be protected against.

b   Use Figure 11.17 to describe the effectiveness of the one-dose immunisation programme for measles.

27 Explain:

a   why the WHO recommends that children receive a second (booster) dose of measles vaccine

b   the advantages of achieving very high immunisation rates for vaccine-preventable diseases, such as measles.

28 Look at the summary you made in response to the question in the feature about smallpox and polio at the start of this chapter. Discuss with others how your knowledge of immunity has changed as you have studied this chapter.

Monoclonal antibodies

Figure 11.6 shows that, during an immune response, B cells become plasma cells that secrete antibodies in response to the presence of a non-self antigen. As you have seen, antibodies bind to pathogens and kill them or mark them for destruction by phagocytes. Antibodies have high degrees of specificity. This specificity of antibodies has made them very desirable for use in the diagnosis and treatment of diseases.

For some time, no one could see how to manufacture antibodies on a large scale. This requires a very large number of cells of a particular B cell clone, all secreting identical or **monoclonal antibodies** (**Mabs**). There is a major problem in achieving this: B cells that divide by mitosis do not produce antibodies, and plasma cells that secrete antibodies do not divide.

The breakthrough came in the 1970s using the technique of cell fusion. A small number of plasma cells producing a particular antibody were fused with cancer cells. Cancer cells, unlike other cells, go on dividing indefinitely. The cell produced by this fusion of a plasma cell and a cancer cell is called a **hybridoma** (Figure 11.18). The hybridoma cells divide by mitosis *and* secrete antibodies.

Mabs have many different uses in medicine and new applications for them are the subject of research.

Using monoclonal antibodies in diagnosis

Mabs are used both for diagnosis and treatment. For example, Mabs can be used to locate the position of blood clots in the body of a person thought to have a deep vein thrombosis (DVT). The antibodies are produced by injecting a mouse with human fibrin, the main protein found in blood clots. The mouse makes many plasma cells that secrete the antibody against

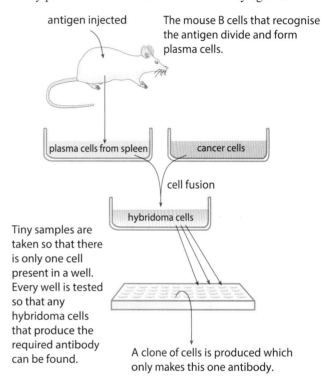

Figure 11.18: How Mabs are produced. Mabs have many different uses in research and in medicine, both in diagnosis and in treatment.

KEY WORDS

monoclonal antibody (**Mab**): an antibody made by a single clone of hybridoma cells; all the antibody molecules made by the clone have identical variable regions so are specific to one antigen

hybridoma: a cell formed by the fusion of a plasma cell and a cancer cell; it can both secrete antibodies and divide to form other cells like itself

fibrin; these plasma cells are collected from its spleen. The plasma cells are fused with cancer cells to form hybridomas that secrete the antifibrin antibody. A radioactive chemical that produces gamma radiation is attached to each antibody molecule to make a radioactively labelled Mab.

The labelled antibodies are then introduced into the patient's blood. As the Mabs are carried around the body in the bloodstream, they bind to any fibrin molecules with which they come into contact. The radioactivity emitted by these labelled antibodies is used to detect where they are in the body. A gamma-ray camera is used to detect the exact position of the antibodies in the person's body. The position of the labelled Mabs indicates the position of any blood clots.

Mabs are also used routinely in blood typing before transfusion, and tissue typing before transplants.

There are now many Mabs available to diagnose hundreds of different medical conditions. For example, they can be used to locate cancer cells which have proteins in their cell surface membranes that differ from the proteins on normal body cells and can therefore be detected by antibodies (Figure 11.19). They can also be

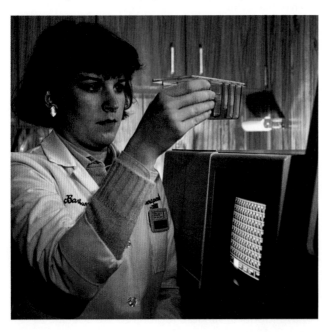

Figure 11.19: A technician examines a reagent tray containing monoclonal antibodies, before inserting it into an automated screening machine to find the most suitable Mabs. Hybridomas are screened for the required antibody. Once isolated, each hybridoma is cloned and then cultured to produce one type of useful antibody.

used to identify the exact strain of a virus or bacterium that is causing an infection; this speeds up the choice of the most appropriate treatment for the patient.

Using monoclonal antibodies in treatment

When Mabs are used in diagnosis, they are normally administered on just one occasion. Mabs used as a treatment need to be administered more than once, and that causes problems.

The antibodies are produced by mice, rabbits or other laboratory animals. When introduced into humans, they trigger an immune response because they are foreign (non-self) and act as antigens. This problem has now been largely overcome by humanising Mabs in two ways:

- altering the genes that code for the heavy and light polypeptide chains of the antibodies so that they code for human sequences of amino acids rather than mouse or rabbit sequences (Figure 11.10)

- changing the type and position of the sugar groups that are attached to the heavy chains to the arrangement found in human antibodies.

Some Mabs have had significant success in treatments that involve modifying immune responses. These monoclonals are trastuzumab, ipilimumab, infliximab and rituximab.

Trastuzumab (also known as Herceptin™) is used in the treatment of some breast cancers (Chapter 19, Section 19.6, Genetic technology and medicine). It is a humanised mouse Mab. Trastuzumab binds to a receptor protein that is produced in abnormal quantities in the cell surface membranes of some breast cancers.

The receptor protein is not unique to cancer cells, but cells with between 10 and 100 times the usual number of these receptor molecules in their cell surface membranes can only be cancer cells. Trastuzumab binds to these cells, and this marks them out for destruction by the immune system.

Ipilimumab is a therapy for melanoma, a type of skin cancer. It also works by activating the immune system, but in a different way to trastuzumab. Ipilimumab binds to a protein produced by T cells, the role of which is to suppress the immune response. By blocking the action of the protein, an immune response can be maintained against the cancer cells.

Infliximab is used to treat rheumatoid arthritis. This condition involves a protein secreted by T-lymphocytes that causes damage to the cartilage in joints. Infliximab binds to the protein and blocks its action. Most of those treated for rheumatoid arthritis receive this therapy at monthly or two-monthly intervals, so it is important that the Mab is humanised and does not itself trigger an immune response.

Rituximab is used to control B-lymphocytes. This Mab binds to a cell surface receptor protein found on the surface of B cells, but not on the surface of plasma cells. Following binding to B cells, rituximab causes a variety of changes that lead to the death of the cell. Rituximab is used to treat diseases in which there is an overproduction or inappropriate production of B-lymphocytes, such as leukaemias. Reducing the numbers of B-lymphocytes appears to reduce the severity of other diseases, such as multiple sclerosis and rheumatoid arthritis.

Questions

29 Mabs anti-A and anti-B are used in blood typing to distinguish between the A, B, AB and O blood groups. The Mab anti-D is used to detect the Rhesus blood group antigen. This antigen, known as D, is present on the red blood cells of people who have Rhesus-positive blood, but absent from those who are Rhesus negative. If the red blood cells agglutinate and clump together when tested with a Mab, then the antigen is present. If there is no agglutination, then the antigen is absent. For example, agglutination with the Mab anti-A indicates the presence of antigen A on the red blood cells; if no agglutination occurs, antigen A is absent.

   a Make a table to show the expected results when blood of the following types is tested separately with anti-A, anti-B and anti-D: A positive; B positive; AB negative; AB positive; O positive.

   b Explain why it is important to carry out blood tests on people who need blood transfusions or who are about to receive a transplanted organ, such as a kidney.

30 a What are the advantages of using Mabs in diagnosis?

   b Suggest how treating cancers using Mabs could cause fewer side effects than treating them using conventional anti-cancer drugs or radiotherapy.

SUMMARY

Phagocytes and lymphocytes are the cells of the immune system. Phagocytes originate from stem cells in the bone marrow and are produced in the bone marrow throughout life. There are two types of phagocyte: neutrophils circulate in the blood and enter infected tissues; macrophages remain inside tissues. Neutrophils and macrophages engulf bacteria and viruses by phagocytosis and destroy them by intracellular digestion using enzymes from lysosomes.

Antigens are 'foreign' (non-self) molecules that stimulate the immune system.

Lymphocytes also originate from stem cells in bone marrow. There are two types: B-lymphocytes (B cells) and T-lymphocytes (T cells). B cells and T cells gain glycoprotein receptors that are specific to each cell as they mature. B cells mature in bone marrow. T cells mature in the thymus gland. As they mature individual B cells and T cells gain specific glycoprotein receptors. During maturation, many T cells are destroyed, as they express receptors that interact with self-antigens. If left to circulate in the body, they would destroy cells and tissues. The T cells that are not destroyed recognise non-self antigens, such as those on the surfaces of pathogens. T cells differentiate into either T-helper cells or T-killer cells. Each T cell and B cell divides to form a small clone of cells that spreads throughout the body in the blood and in the lymphoid tissue (e.g. lymph nodes and spleen).

During an immune response, those B and T cells with receptors that are specific to the antigen are activated. When B cells are activated, they form plasma cells which secrete antibodies. T cells do not secrete antibodies. T-helper cells secrete cell-signalling molecules (cytokines) that control the immune system by stimulating B cells and T cells to divide and become active. Active T-killer cells can seek out and destroy any host cells that are infected by pathogens.

During an immune response, memory cells are formed which retain the ability to divide rapidly and develop into active B or T cells on a second exposure to the same antigen (immunological memory).

Antibodies are also known as immunoglobulins. They are globular glycoproteins. IgG is the class of antibodies that have a quaternary structure composed of two identical long polypeptides (heavy chains) and two identical short polypeptides (short chains). The two variable regions of the antibody molecule form antigen-binding sites. Each type of IgG antibody can bind to two antigen molecules. Antibodies agglutinate bacteria, prevent viruses infecting cells, coat bacteria and viruses to aid phagocytosis, act with plasma proteins to burst bacteria, and neutralise toxins.

Active immunity is the production of antibodies and active T cells during a primary immune response to an antigen acquired either naturally by infection or artificially by vaccination. Active immunity gives long-term immunity. Passive immunity is the introduction of antibodies either naturally across the placenta or in breast milk, or artificially by injection. Passive immunity gives temporary immunity.

Vaccination confers artificial active immunity by introducing a small quantity of an antigen by injection or by mouth. A vaccine may be a whole living organism, a dead one, a harmless version of a toxin (toxoid) or a preparation of antigens.

Monoclonal antibodies (Mabs) are antibodies that are all identical to each other. Mabs are produced by fusing a plasma cell with a cancer cell to produce a hybridoma, which divides repeatedly to form many genetically identical cells that all produce the same antibody.

Mabs are used in diagnosis, for example in locating blood clots in veins, and in the treatment of diseases, such as breast cancer.

EXAM-STYLE QUESTIONS

1 A student made drawings of four blood cells as shown in the diagrams.

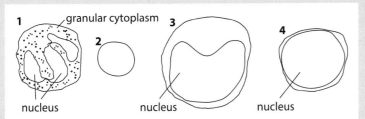

The correct identification of the cells is:

	1	2	3	4
A	lymphocyte	monocyte	red blood cell	neutrophil
B	monocyte	lymphocyte	neutrophil	red blood cell
C	neutrophil	red blood cell	monocyte	lymphocyte
D	red blood cell	neutrophil	lymphocyte	monocyte

[1]

2 The following occur during the response to infection:
1 attachment of bacteria to cell surface membrane of phagocyte
2 movement of phagocyte to site of infection by bacteria
3 formation of a phagocytic vacuole
4 fusion of lysosomes to the phagocytic vacuole
5 infolding of cell surface membrane
6 release of enzymes into the phagocytic vacuole

In which order do these events occur?

A 1, 2, 3, 4, 6, 5

B 1, 2, 3, 5, 4, 6

C 2, 1, 3, 6, 5, 4

D 2, 1, 5, 3, 4, 6 [1]

3 Which of the following explains why antibody molecules have quaternary structure?

A Antibodies have a variable region.

B Antibodies have complex three-dimensional shapes.

C Antibodies have different sequences of amino acids.

D Antibodies have more than one polypeptide. [1]

4 Which type of immunity is provided by vaccination?

A artificial active

B artificial passive

C natural active

D natural passive [1]

CONTINUED

5 Which describes the cells that produce monoclonal antibodies (Mabs)?

   A a clone of B-lymphocytes, all of which secrete different antibodies

   B a clone of hybridoma cells, all of which secrete identical proteins

   C a clone of T-lymphocytes, all of which secrete the same cytokine

   D a clone of T-lymphocytes, all of which secrete identical antibodies   [1]

6 Macrophages in the liver and spleen remove red blood cells from the circulation and break them down. The figure is a transmission electron micrograph (TEM) of a macrophage engulfing two red blood cells.

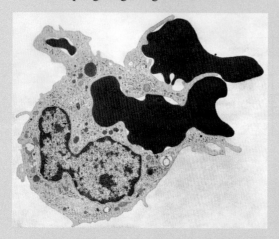

   a Explain why red blood cells are removed from the circulation by macrophages.   [3]

   b Outline how macrophages take up and break down red blood cells.   [6]

   [Total: 9]

7 *Candida albicans* is a yeast-like fungus that causes opportunistic infections.

   Researchers compared the effectiveness of macrophages and neutrophils at removing cells of *C. albicans*. They cultured macrophages and neutrophils separately and added cells of *C. albicans* to both cultures. In Experiment 1, they added the fungal cells at a ratio of 1 fungal cell : 1 phagocytic cell. In Experiment 2, they used a ratio of 3 fungal cells : 1 phagocytic cell.

   The researchers used video microscopy to record the behaviour of the phagocytes for a period of six hours. They analysed the videos recording the number of fungal cells taken up by each phagocytic cell in the cultures. The researchers processed the results by calculating the percentage of phagocytes in each culture that had taken up fungal cells. The processed results are shown in the bar charts.

CONTINUED

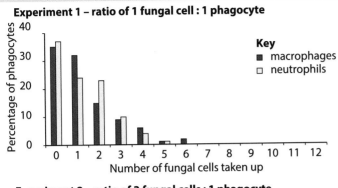

Experiment 1 – ratio of 1 fungal cell : 1 phagocyte

Key
■ macrophages
□ neutrophils

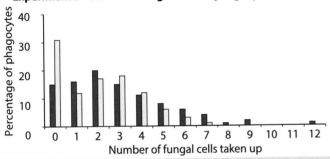

Experiment 2 – ratio of 3 fungal cells : 1 phagocyte

a State **five** conclusions that can be made from the results shown in the bar charts. [5]

b Suggest the limitations of the investigation as far as applying the results to the effectiveness of the two types of phagocyte at providing protection against infections of *C. albicans*. [3]

[Total: 8]

8 Tetanus is a bacterial disease that may be acquired during accidents in which a wound is exposed to the soil.

B-lymphocytes originate from stem cells in bone marrow, mature and circulate around the body. Following infection by tetanus bacteria, some B-lymphocytes will become activated as shown in the diagram.

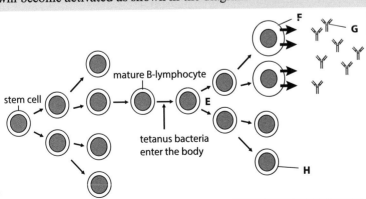

CONTINUED

   a Explain the role of stem cells in the production of lymphocytes. [2]

   b With reference to the diagram, name:

     i the type of division that occurs at **E** [1]

     ii the activated B-lymphocyte, **F** [1]

     iii the molecule **G**. [1]

   c Use the information in the figure to explain the differences between the following pairs of terms:

     i antigen and antibody [3]

     ii self and non-self. [2]

   d Explain how cell **H** is responsible for long-term immunity to tetanus. [3]

[Total: 13]

9 Phagocytes and lymphocytes are both present in samples of blood.

   a Describe how the structure of a phagocyte differs from the structure of a lymphocyte. [3]

T-lymphocytes are involved in immune responses to pathogens that invade the body. Immune responses involve the following:

- antigen presentation
- clonal selection
- clonal expansion.

Measles is a viral disease. Certain groups of T-lymphocytes are activated when the body is infected with the measles virus.

   b Using the information above, describe what happens to T-lymphocytes during an immune response to measles. [6]

   c State how the response of B-lymphocytes during an immune response is different to the response of T-lymphocytes. [2]

[Total: 11]

10 Measles is a common viral infection. Babies gain natural passive immunity to measles.

   a Explain:

     i the term *natural passive immunity* [2]

     ii how babies gain natural passive immunity. [2]

Vaccines for measles have been available since the 1960s. Global vaccination programmes include providing vaccination for measles, but it is important that the vaccine is not given to babies too early.

   b Explain why the vaccine for measles should not be given too early. [3]

   c Suggest why diseases such as polio and measles have not been eradicated, even though vaccines have existed for 60 years or more. [3]

[Total: 10]

CONTINUED

11 The diagram shows an antibody molecule.

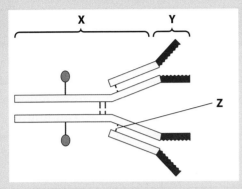

a Name:
  i the regions **X** and **Y** [2]
  ii the bond labelled **Z**. [1]

b Describe briefly how antibody molecules are produced and secreted. [4]

c Explain how the structure of an antibody is related to its function. [4]

d Explain the advantages of using Mabs in diagnosis. [4]

[Total: 15]

12 a Rearrange the following statements to produce a flow diagram to show how Mabs are produced.

  1 Hybridoma cells are cultured.

  2 Mouse is injected with antigen.

  3 Mouse plasma cells are fused with cancer cells.

  4 Hybridoma cells that make an appropriate antibody are cloned.

  5 Mouse B-lymphocytes that recognise the antigen become plasma cells. [1]

b A monoclonal antibody has been produced that binds to a glycoprotein called tumour-associated antigen (TAG). TAG is found in ovarian cancer and colon cancer cells.

The antibody is labelled with the radioactive isotope indium-111, (^{111}In). This isotope emits low-energy gamma rays that can pass through soft tissues of the body. The half-life of ^{111}In is 2.8 days.

  i Explain how this monoclonal antibody can be used in the diagnosis of cancer. [3]

  ii Suggest why ^{111}In is a suitable radioactive label for this diagnostic antibody. [3]

  iii Suggest how the antibody could be modified in order to treat a cancer. [2]

[Total: 9]

SELF-EVALUATION CHECKLIST

After studying this chapter, complete a table like this:

I can	See section...	Needs more work	Almost there	Ready to move on
describe the mode of action of macrophages and neutrophils	11.2			
explain what is meant by the term *antigen* and state the difference between self antigens and non-self antigens	11.1, 11.3			
describe what happens during a primary immune response and explain the role of memory cells in long-term immunity	11.2			
explain how the molecular structure of antibodies is related to their functions	11.2			
outline the hybridoma method for the production of Mabs and the principles of using Mabs in the diagnosis and treatment of disease of diseases	11.3			
describe the differences between the different types of immunity: active and passive and natural and artificial	11.3			
explain that vaccines contain antigens that stimulate immune responses to provide long-term immunity and how vaccination programmes are used to control the spread of infectious diseases	11.3			

> **Chapter P1**
Practical skills for AS Level

LEARNING INTENTIONS

In this chapter you will learn how to:

- collect data and observations
- make decisions about measurements and observations
- record data and observations appropriately
- display calculations and reasoning clearly
- use tables and graphs to display data
- interpret data and observations
- draw conclusions
- identify significant sources of error
- suggest improvements to a procedure, or suggest how an investigation could be extended.

The information in this section is taken from the Cambridge International syllabus (9700) for examination from 2022. You should always refer to the appropriate syllabus document for the year of your examination to confirm the details and for more information. The syllabus document is available on the Cambridge International website at www.cambridgeinternational.org.

P1.1 Practical skills

During your AS Level course, you will use a variety of skills each time you carry out an experiment. In this chapter you will look at the different components of the skills in detail, and consider what you must be able to do in order to work to the best of your abilities.

Your examination may include a 'wet practical' – an experiment that will involve you in manipulating apparatus, perhaps making up and measuring out solutions, making measurements and observations, recording them and drawing conclusions from a set of results. You should also be able to observe a biological structure, perhaps using a microscope, and recording your observations in the form of a diagram.

P1.2 Experiments

Many of the experiments that you will do during your course involve investigating how one thing affects another. For example:

- investigating how enzyme concentration affects the rate of activity of rennin
- investigating how temperature affects the rate of activity of catalase
- investigating how surface area affects the rate of diffusion
- investigating how the concentration of a solution affects the percentage of onion cells that become plasmolysed.

Let's concentrate on the first of these experiments – the effect of enzyme concentration on the rate of activity of rennin – to illustrate how you should approach an experiment, and how you should answer questions about it.

Rennin is an enzyme that clots milk. It is found in the stomachs of young mammals, which are fed on milk. Rennin (also known as chymosin) is used commercially in cheese-making. Its substrate is a protein called casein. In fresh milk, the casein molecules are dispersed in the milk as little micelles (groups of molecules organised rather like a cell membrane). These are spread evenly through the milk to form a homogeneous emulsion. Rennin splits the casein molecules into smaller molecules. This breaks up the micelles and causes the protein to clump together into small lumps, a process called clotting (Figure P1.1). These lumps separate out from the liquid milk, producing the curd that can be made into cheese.

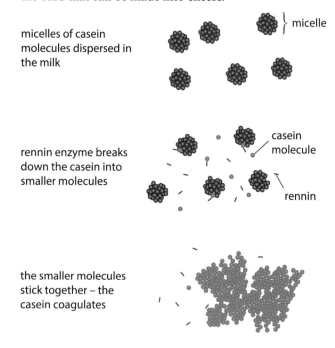

micelles of casein molecules dispersed in the milk

} micelle

rennin enzyme breaks down the casein into smaller molecules

casein molecule

rennin

the smaller molecules stick together – the casein coagulates

Figure P1.1: The effect of rennin on milk.

P1.3 Variables and making measurements

In the rennin experiment you would be investigating the effect of the concentration of rennin on the rate at which it causes milk to clot.

The concentration of rennin is the **independent variable.** This is the factor whose values you decide on, and which you change.

> KEY WORD
>
> **independent variable:** the variable (factor) that you purposefully change in an experiment

The rate at which the rennin causes the milk to clot is the **dependent variable**. This is the variable which is not under your control; you do not know what its values will be until you collect your results.

In an experiment such as this, it is important that all other variables that might affect the results are kept constant. These are called **standardised variables**. In this experiment important standardised variables include:

- temperature
- the type of milk used
- pH.

If you allow any of these to change during the experiment, then they could affect the results and would make it difficult – if not impossible – to know what effect the enzyme concentration was having on the rate of reaction.

When doing any experiment, it is important to decide which variables you should standardise. You should know which are important to keep constant and which do not really matter. In this case, anything that could affect the rate of enzyme activity – other than the independent variable, enzyme concentration – must be kept constant. Other variables (such as the amount of light, the time of day or the kind of glassware you use) are unlikely to have any significant effects, so you do not need to worry about them.

Changing the independent variable

You may be asked to decide what values of the independent variable to use in your experiment. You will need to make decisions about the **range** and the **interval**.

The range of the independent variable is the spread of values from lowest to highest. In this case, you might use concentrations of rennin ranging from 0 to 1%. If you are asked to do this, you will usually be given some clues that will help you to decide the range. For example, if you are given a solution with a concentration of 1% to work with, then that will be your highest concentration, because you cannot make a more concentrated solution from it, only more dilute ones.

The interval is the 'spacing' between the values that you choose within the range. In this case, you could use concentrations of rennin of 0, 0.2, 0.4, 0.6, 0.8 and 1%. The interval would then be 0.2%. Another possibility would be to use a series of values that are each one tenth of each other – 0.0001, 0.001, 0.01, 0.1 and 1.0. In either case, you can produce this range of concentrations by diluting the original solution. Figure P1.2 explains how to do this.

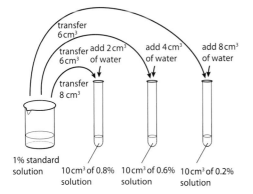
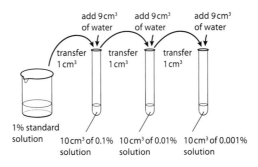

Figure P1.2: Producing a range of concentrations from a standard solution. This is serial dilution.

If you are planning to display your results as a graph, then you should have at least five values for the independent variable. This is because it is difficult to see clear trends or patterns in a line graph unless you have at least five plotted points.

Question

1 A student is investigating the effect of temperature on the activity of amylase on starch.

   a Identify the independent variable and the dependent variable in this investigation.

   b Suggest a suitable range for the independent variable. Explain why you have chosen this range.

   c Suggest a suitable interval for the independent variable. Explain why you have chosen this interval.

Measuring the dependent variable

You may be told exactly how to measure the dependent variable. But sometimes you may have to decide for yourself the best way to do this.

In an enzyme experiment such as the rennin one, there are three possible methods for taking measurements. (You can remind yourself about ways of measuring reaction rate by looking back at Chapter 3.)

- You could determine the initial rate of reaction – taking measurements very quickly to find how much product has been formed, or how much substrate has disappeared, in the first minute or so of the reaction.

- You could leave the reaction to take place until it has completely finished – that is, all the substrate has been converted to product – and record the time taken to do this.

- You could time how long it takes to reach a clearly identifiable stage of the reaction, called an end-point.

Let's say that you decide to use the last of these three methods. You will measure the time taken for the rennin to produce clots of milk that stick to the sides of the test tube in which the reaction is taking place. You add the rennin to the milk in the tube, and twist the tube gently. The end-point is the moment when you first see little clots remaining on the sides of the tube (Figure P1.3).

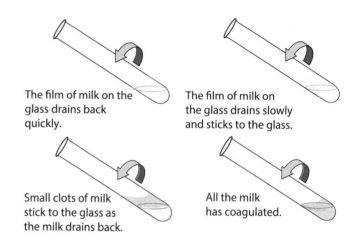

The film of milk on the glass drains back quickly.

The film of milk on the glass drains slowly and sticks to the glass.

Small clots of milk stick to the glass as the milk drains back.

All the milk has coagulated.

Figure P1.3: Determining the end-point of the clotting of milk by rennin.

In some experiments the dependent variable is colour. You may need to record this qualitatively – that is, you cannot measure anything, but can only describe it. It is important to communicate clearly when describing colour changes. Use simple words to describe colours – for example, red, purple, green. You can qualify these by using simple terms such as pale or dark. You could also use a scale such as + for the palest colour, ++ for the next darkest and so on. If you do that, include a key to say what your symbols represent.

Always state the actual colour that you observe. For example, if you are doing a Benedict's test and get a negative result, do not write 'no change'; say that the colour is blue.

It is sometimes useful to use colour standards, against which you can compare a colour you have obtained in your results. For example, if you are doing a Benedict's test, you could first carry out the test using a set volume of a series of solutions with known concentrations of glucose, using excess Benedict's solution. Stand these in a rack, and use them as colour comparison for the results you obtain with an unknown solution.

Practical Activity P1.1 describes how you can measure colour changes quantitatively, using a colorimeter. You may not have a colorimeter in your laboratory, and you will not be expected to use one in your examination. However, if you are suggesting improvements to a procedure, you could outline how a colorimeter could be used to give quantitative values for colour differences (see also Chapter 3, Section 3.3, Investigating the progress of an enzyme-catalysed reaction).

Question

2   Look back at the experiment described in Question 1. Suggest **two** ways in which you could measure the dependent variable.

PRACTICAL ACTIVITY P1.1

Observing and measuring colour changes and intensities

A colorimeter is an instrument that measures the amount of light that is absorbed by a tube containing a coloured liquid. The deeper the colour, the more light is absorbed.

It is important to choose a suitable colour of light to shine through your coloured liquid. For example, if you want to measure how much red pigment is in a sample, you should use green light. (Red things look red because they reflect red light but absorb blue and green light.) You can change the colour of the light by using different coloured filters, which are supplied with the colorimeter (Figure P1.4).

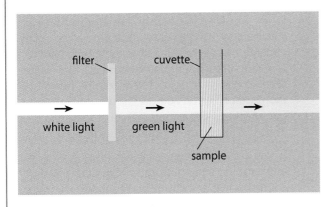

Figure P1.4: The path of light through the filter and cuvette in a colorimeter.

Special tubes called cuvettes are used to contain the liquid. To measure the concentration of an unknown solution, a colorimeter has to be calibrated using standards of known concentration.

Calibration

Step 1   Put a set volume of liquid that is identical to your samples of known concentrations, but which does not contain any red pigment, into a cuvette. This is called the blank. Put the blank into the colorimeter and set the absorbance reading on the colorimeter to 0.

Step 2   Put the same volume of one of your samples of known concentrations (standards) into an identical cuvette. Put this into the colorimeter and read the absorbance.

Step 3   Put the blank back into the colorimeter and check that the absorbance still reads 0. If it does not, start from step 1 again.

Step 4   Repeat steps 2 and 3 with each standard.

Step 5   Use your readings to draw a calibration curve (absorbance against concentration).

Measuring unknown samples

Step 5   Measure the absorbance of each of your samples containing unknown concentrations of red pigment. Use your calibration curve to determine concentrations.

Standardising or changing other variables

You have seen that it is very important to try to keep all significant variables other than the independent and dependent variable as constant as possible throughout your experiment. In a question you might be expected to identify which variables you should keep constant and describe how you would do this.

Two variables which often crop up in experiments, either as independent variables or standardised variables, are temperature and pH. You may also need to use biological material, such as seeds or plants, and may want to try to keep these individuals as similar as possible.

These three variables are discussed here.

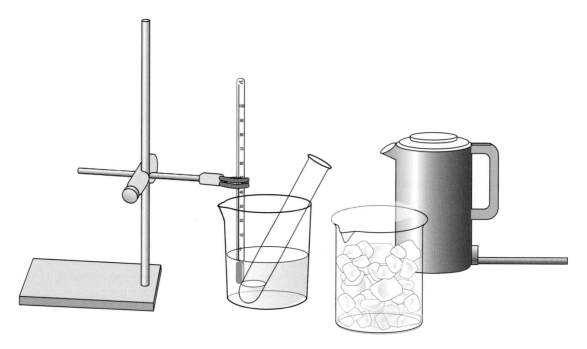

Figure P1.5: Controlling temperature using a water bath. You can use this method for producing a range of temperatures if temperature is your independent variable, or for keeping temperature constant if it is a standardised variable.

Temperature

To control temperature, you can use a water bath. You might be provided with an electronically controlled water bath. But it is more likely that you will have to make your own water bath, using a large beaker of water. Figure P1.5 shows how you can do this.

Whichever type of water bath you use, it is important to measure the temperature carefully.

- Don't assume that because an electric water bath says the temperature is 30 °C, it really is that temperature. Use a thermometer, held in the water and not touching the sides or base of the container, to measure the temperature.

- If possible, read the thermometer while its bulb is still in the water – if you take it out to read it, then you will be measuring the temperature of the air.

- If you are standing tubes of liquid in the water bath, you should allow enough time for their contents to reach the same temperature as the water. This can take a surprisingly long time. It is a good idea to measure the temperature of the liquids in the tubes, rather than to assume that they are at the same temperature as the water bath.

- If you are doing an enzyme experiment, you may need to bring both the enzyme solution and the substrate solution to the same temperature before you add one to the other. Stand them, in two separate tubes, in the same water bath and leave them to reach the desired temperature. Remember that as soon as you add the enzyme and substrate to one another, the reaction will start, so don't do that until you are ready to begin taking measurements.

- If you are using animals in your investigation, you must not use temperatures so high that it would distress or harm them. A maximum of 350 might be suitable.

pH

To control pH, you can use **buffer solutions**. These solutions have a particular pH and keep that pH even when the reaction taking place produces an acidic or alkaline substance that would otherwise cause pH to change. You simply add a measured volume of the buffer to your reacting mixture.

> **KEY WORD**
>
> **buffer solution:** a solution that has a known pH, which can be added to a reacting mixture to maintain the pH at that level

You can measure pH using an indicator. Universal indicator is especially useful, as it produces a range of colours over the whole pH range, from 0 to 14. You will not be expected to remember these colours – if you need to interpret them, you will be provided with a colour chart.

Alternatively, you may be able to measure pH using a pH meter.

Biological material

It is often very difficult to make sure that samples of biological material used in an experiment are all identical. Depending on the kind of material you are using, you should try to keep as many features as possible the same. These could include: age, storage conditions, genotype (including sex), mass, volume, position in the organism from which the sample was taken.

Question

3   Look back at the experiment described in Question 1.

   a   Describe how you would change and measure the independent variable.

   b   Suggest **two** important variables that you should try to keep constant.

   c   Describe how you would keep these variables constant.

Controls

Think back to the rennin experiment. How can you be sure that it is the rennin that is making the milk clot, and not some other factor? To check this, you need to use a control, where the factor that you are investigating is absent.

In this experiment the control is a tube that has no rennin in it. Everything else must be the same, so the same volume of water is added to match the volume of enzyme solution that is added to all the other tubes.

Another possible control could be a tube containing boiled rennin solution. Boiling denatures the rennin enzyme so it is inactive.

More about measurements – accuracy, precision and replicates

No measuring instrument is perfect. You can never be completely certain that a measurement you make gives you an absolutely 'correct' value.

The accuracy of a measurement is how 'true' it is. If you are measuring a temperature, then the accuracy of your measurement will depend on whether or not the thermometer is perfectly calibrated. If the thermometer is accurate, then when the meniscus is at 31 °C, the temperature really is exactly 31 °C.

The precision of a measurement depends on the ability of the measuring instrument or technique to give you the same reading every time it measures the same thing. This does not have to be the 'true' value. So, if your thermometer *always* reads 32 °C when the temperature is really 31 °C, it is not accurate but it *is* precise.

For example, in the rennin experiment, you have to make a decision about exactly when the end-point is reached. This is really difficult: there is no precise moment at which you can say the clots definitely form, so your measurement of the time at which this happens cannot be accurate or precise. It is very unlikely that you will measure exactly the same time in two experiments, even if everything in those experiments is exactly the same.

Using replicates can help to identify whether or not your readings are precise. For example, with the rennin experiment, you could set up three tubes of each concentration of the enzyme and measure the time to the end-point for each of them. You would then have three results for this particular enzyme concentration, which you could use to calculate a mean. If the three readings are very different from one another, this reduces your trust that they are precise.

KEY WORDS

control: a standard of comparison in an experiment; it is used to compare the results of changing the independent variable with a sample in which the independent variable is not present, or is unchanged

accuracy: how close a reading is to the 'true' value

precision: how close two or more measurements of the same value are to each other

replicates: two or more trials of the same experiment, using the same materials and apparatus

---

P1.4 Recording quantitative results

Most of the experiments that you will do, either during your course or in your practical examination, will involve the collection and display of quantitative (numerical) results. You may be given a results table to complete, but often you will have to design and draw your own results table.

Table P1.1 shows a results table that you could use for your results from the experiment investigating the effect of enzyme concentration on the rate of activity of rennin. Three replicates were done for each enzyme concentration, and a mean has been calculated.

There are several important points to note about this results table, which you should always bear in mind whenever you construct and complete one.

- The table is drawn with ruled columns, rows and a border. The purpose of a results table is to record your results clearly, so that you and others can easily see what they are, and so that you can use them easily to draw a graph or to make calculations. Drawing neat, clear lines makes it much easier to see the results at a glance.

- The columns are clearly headed with the quantity and its unit. (Use SI units.) Sometimes, you might want to arrange the table the other way round, so that it is the rows that are headed. Sometimes, both rows and columns might need to include units. The important thing to remember is that the units go in the heading, not with the numerical entries in the table.

- The results are organised in a sensible sequence. The values for the rennin concentration go up from the lowest to the highest.

- The independent variable (rennin concentration) comes first, followed by the readings of the dependent variable (time taken to reach end-point).

- Each measurement of the dependent variable is given to the same number of decimal places. You would have used a stopwatch to take these readings, and it probably gave a reading to one hundredth, or even one thousandth, of a second. So the first reading on the watch could have been 67.207. However, as you have seen, it is very difficult to judge this end-point, so to suggest that you can time it to the nearest thousandth of a second is not sensible. You can perhaps justify, however, recording the values to the nearest one tenth of a second, rounding up or down the reading on the watch.

- The values calculated for the mean are given to the same number of decimal places as the individual readings. This is very important to remember. If you have only recorded the individual readings to the nearest one tenth of a second, then it is wrong to suggest you can calculate the mean to one hundredth or one thousandth of a second.

- In the last row, the readings for the rennin at a concentration of 1% contain an anomalous result. The second reading (shown in bold italics) is clearly out of line with the other two, and looks much too close to the readings for the 0.8% rennin solution. You can't know what went wrong here, but something clearly did. If you are in a position to do so, the best thing to do about an anomalous result is to measure it again. However, if you can't do that, then you should ignore it. Do not include it in your calculation of the mean. The mean for this row is therefore calculated as (13.1 + 12.7) ÷ 2 = 12.9.

- The first row of the table records that the milk 'did not clot'. An alternative way of recording this

Rennin concentration/%	Time to reach end-point/s			
	1st reading	2nd reading	3rd reading	Mean
0.0	did not clot	did not clot	did not clot	did not clot
0.2	67.2	68.9	67.8	68.0
0.4	48.1	46.9	47.3	47.4
0.6	30.1	31.9	30.1	30.7
0.8	20.3	19.2	19.9	19.8
1.0	13.1	*18.9*	12.7	12.9

Table P1.1: Results for an experiment to investigate the effect of enzyme concentration on the rate of activity of rennin. The reading in **bold italics** is an anomalous result and has been excluded from the calculation of the mean.

would be to record the time as infinite (symbol: ∞). This can then be converted to a rate like all the other results by calculating $\dfrac{1}{time}$

Note that $\dfrac{1}{\infty} = 0$ (zero rate).

Question

4 Look back at the experiment described in Question 1 earlier in the chapter, and your answers to Questions 2 and 3. Construct a results table, with full headings, in which you could record your results.

P1.5 Displaying data

Constructing a line graph

You will generally want to display quantitative results in a table as a graph. Figure P1.6 shows a line graph constructed using the results in Table P1.1.

Once again, there are several important points to note about this graph, which you should always bear in mind whenever you construct and complete a graph.

- The independent variable goes on the x-axis (horizontal axis), and the dependent variable on the y-axis (vertical axis).

- Each axis is fully labelled, including the units. Usually, you can simply copy the headings that you have used in the results table.

- The scale on each axis goes up in equal intervals, such as 1 s, 2 s, 5 s or 10 s intervals. You would not therefore, have an axis that read 20 °C, 30 °C, 50 °C, 60 °C, 80 °C.

- The intervals chosen make it easy to read intermediate values.

- The scales cover the entire range of the values to be plotted, but don't go too far above and below them. This makes best use of the graph paper. The more spread out the scale is, the easier it is to see any trends and patterns in the relationship between the independent variable and the dependent variable. (Note that there is not always a need to begin your scale at 0.)

- The points are plotted as neat, carefully placed crosses. An acceptable alternative is a dot with a circle around it. Do not use a simple dot, as this may be hidden when the line is drawn.

- A best-fit line has been drawn. This is a smooth line which shows the trend that the points seem to fit. There is not a single perfect place to put a best-fit line, but you should ensure that approximately the same number of points, roughly the same distances

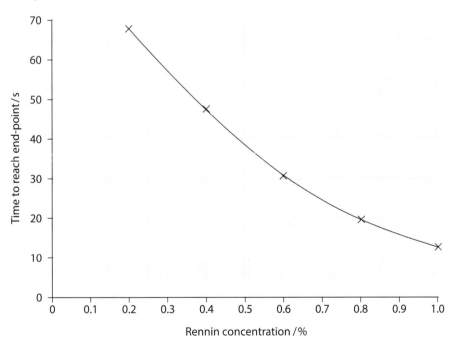

Figure P1.6: Line graph displaying the results in Table P1.1.

from the line, lie above and below it. There is no need for your line to go through either the first or last point – these points are no more 'special' than any of the others, so should not get special treatment.

- An alternative way to draw the line would be to join each point to the next one with a ruled, straight line. Generally, you should use a best-fit line when told to do so, or when you can see a clear trend in which you have confidence. If you are not sure of the trend, then draw straight lines between points.

- It is almost always incorrect to extend the line beyond the plotted points (extrapolate). However, it can sometimes be allowable to do this – for example, if you have not made a measurement when the independent variable (*x*-axis value) is 0, and when you are absolutely certain that the dependent variable (*y*-axis value) would also be 0 at that point. You could then extend your line back to meet the origin, at point 0, 0.

Constructing bar charts and histograms

Not all experiments generate results that can be displayed as a line graph. Some results are best shown in bar charts or histograms.

A **bar chart** is drawn when you have a **discontinuous variable** on the *x*-axis and a **continuous variable** on the *y*-axis. A discontinuous variable is one where there is no continuous relationship between the items listed on the scale. Each category is discrete. Figure P1.7 shows an example. The *x*-axis lists five species of tree; each

type of tree is separate from the others, and there is no continuous relationship between them. The bars are therefore drawn with gaps between them.

A continuous variable is one where there is a smooth, numerical relationship between the values. (Line graphs always have a continuous variable on both the *x*-axis and *y*-axis, as in Figure P1.6.) Sometimes, you will want to draw a graph where there is a continuous range of categories on the *x*-axis, and the frequency with which each of these categories occurs is shown on the *y*-axis. In this case, the bars are drawn so that they touch. This kind of graph is a **histogram**, sometimes called a frequency diagram. Figure P1.8 shows an example.

KEY WORDS

bar chart: a graph in which the categories on the *x*-axis are discontinuous – i.e., entirely separate from one another; the bars are drawn with spaces between them

discontinuous variable: a variable in which the different categories are separate from one another

continuous variable: a variable which can have any value within a range

histogram: a graph in which the categories on the *x*-axis are continuous; the bars are drawn with no gaps between them

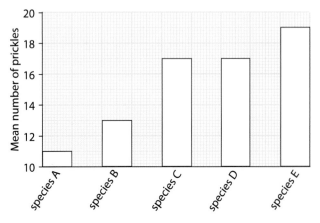

Figure P1.7: Bar chart showing the mean number of prickles on leaves from five different species of tree.

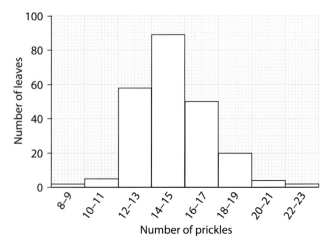

Figure P1.8: Histogram showing the numbers of leaves with different numbers of prickles on a holly tree.

P1.6 Making conclusions

A conclusion is a simple, well-focused and clear statement describing what you can deduce from the results of your experiment. The conclusion should relate to the initial question you were investigating or the hypothesis you were testing.

For example, the results shown in Table P1.1 could lead you to write a conclusion like this:

> *The greater the concentration of rennin, the shorter the time taken to reach the end-point. An increase in rennin concentration increases the rate of reaction.*

If the experiment was testing a hypothesis, then the conclusion should say whether or not the results support the hypothesis. Note you can almost never say that a hypothesis is 'proved' by a set of results. You generally need many more sets of results before you can be sure that a hypothesis really is correct.

P1.7 Describing data

You may be asked to describe your results in detail. You can do this from a table of results, but it is often best done using the graph that you have drawn. The graph is likely to show more clearly any trends and patterns in the relationship between your independent and dependent variables.

For example, you could describe the results shown in Figure P1.6 like this:

> *When no rennin was present, no end-point was reached (time taken = ∞), indicating that no reaction was taking place. At a concentration of 0.2% rennin, the end-point was reached in a mean time of 68.0 seconds. As the concentration of rennin increased, the mean time to reach the end-point decreased, with the shortest mean time (12.9 s) occurring at a concentration of 1% rennin. This indicates that the rate of reaction increases as the concentration of rennin increases.*

> *The line on the graph is a curve with decreasing gradient, not a straight line, so the relationship between concentration of rennin and the rate of reaction is not proportional (linear). The curve is steepest for the lower concentrations of rennin, gradually flattening out for the higher concentrations. This shows that a 0.2% increase in rennin concentration has a greater effect on reaction rate at low rennin concentrations than at high rennin concentrations.*

There are several points to bear in mind when you are describing results shown on a graph.

- Begin by describing the overall trend – the overall relationship between what is shown on the x-axis and what is shown on the y-axis.

- Look for any changes in gradient on the graph, and describe these. In this case, the change in gradient is a steady one (the gradient gets gradually less and less as the rennin concentration increases). Sometimes, there are sharp changes in gradient at particular key points, and you should focus on those and describe the gradient changes and precisely where they occur.

- Quote figures from the graph. You will need to pick on points of particular interest (e.g. where gradient changes occur), and quote the coordinates of those points – that is, you should state both the x-axis value and the y-axis value.

- Take great care not to use phrases that suggest something is happening over time, if time is not shown on the x-axis. For example, it would be wrong to say that the gradient of the graph in Figure P1.6 'is steep at first and gradually gets less'. 'At first' suggests time – but the x-axis shows concentration, not time. Words such as 'more quickly', 'slower' and 'rapidly' should all be avoided unless the x-axis shows time.

P1.8 Making calculations from data

You may be asked to carry out a calculation from a set of results – either the results that you have collected, or a set of results that is presented to you.

It is very important to show every step in any calculation that you make. For example, you might be given a set of five measurements and asked to **find the mean value**. You should set out your calculation clearly, like this:

measurements: 12.5 μm, 18.6 μm, 13.2 μm, 10.8 μm, 11.3 μm

$$mean = \frac{(12.5 + 18.6 + 13.2 + 10.8 + 11.3)}{5}$$
$$= \frac{66.4}{5}$$
$$= 13.3 \ \mu m$$

Remember that, even though your calculator will show an answer of 13.28, you must give your answer to only one decimal place, the same as for the original measurements.

You could also be asked to **calculate rate of change** by finding the gradient at one or more points on your graph. Figure P1.9 explains how to do this when there is a straight line, and also when the line is curved.

Question

5   a   Choose two different points on the graph in Figure P1.6, and calculate the gradient at each point. Remember to show all the steps in your calculation fully and clearly.

b   Use your calculated values to add to the description of the results given in Section P1.7, Describing data.

A third type of calculation you could be asked to do is to **find the percentage change**. To do this, you should follow these steps.

Step 1   Find the difference between the first reading and the second reading, by subtracting one from the other.

Step 2   Divide this value by the first reading, and multiply by 100; this figure gives you the percentage change – remember to state whether the change is an increase or a decrease.

For example, imagine that the mass of a plant on day 1 was 250 g. On day 5, after it had lost a lot of water by transpiration, its mass was 221 g.

$$\text{change in mass} = 250 - 221 = 29\text{g}$$

$$\text{percentage change in mass} = \frac{\text{change in mass}}{\text{original mass}} \times 100$$

$$= \frac{29}{250} \times 100$$

$$= 11.6\% \text{ decrease}$$

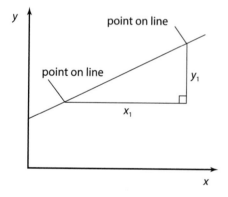

To determine the gradient of a straight line graph:
1 Select two points which are at least half as far apart as the length of the line of the graph.
2 Draw a right-angle triangle between these points.
3 Calculate the gradient using the lengths of the triangle sides x_1 and y_1:
$$\text{gradient} = \frac{y_1}{x_1}$$

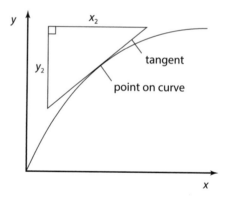

To determine the gradient at a point on a curved graph:
1 Draw a tangent to the curve at that point, making sure it is at least half as long as the line of the graph.
2 Draw a right-angle triangle on the tangent.
3 Calculate the gradient using the lengths of the triangle sides x_2 and y_2:
$$\text{gradient} = \frac{y_2}{x_2}$$

Figure P1.9: Calculating the gradients of a straight line and a curve at a point.

Explaining your results

You may be asked to explain your results. This requires you to use your scientific knowledge to explain why the relationship you have found between your independent variable and your dependent variable exists.

Question

6   Use your knowledge and understanding of enzyme activity to explain the results shown in Figure P1.6.

P1.9 Identifying sources of error and suggesting improvements

You will often be asked to identify important sources of error in your experiment. It is very important to realise that you are not being asked about mistakes that you might have made – for example, not reading the thermometer correctly or not measuring out the right volume of a solution, or taking a reading at the wrong time. These are all avoidable human mistakes and you should not be making them!

Sources of error are unavoidable limitations of your apparatus, measuring instruments, experimental technique or experimental design that reduce your confidence in your results. This, in turn, can reduce confidence in the conclusions that you make. Sources of error generally fall into three major categories.

*   **Uncertainty in measurements** resulting from lack of accuracy or precision in the measuring instruments that you were using, and from the limitations in reading the scale. These errors are likely to be the same all through your experiment. They will be about the same size, and act in the same direction, on all of your readings and results. They are **systematic errors**. Systematic errors do not affect the trend in your results, but they do affect their absolute values.

*   **Difficulties in controlling the standardised variables.** For example, if you were using a water bath to maintain a constant temperature in the rennin experiment, it may have been impossible to keep the temperature absolutely constant. Variations in temperature could have affected the rate of activity of the rennin, making it impossible to be

sure that all changes in rate of activity were due to differences in your independent variable – the concentration of the rennin. These errors are likely to be different for different stages of your investigation. They are **random errors**. Random errors may affect the trend shown by the results.

*   **Difficulties in measuring the dependent variable,** due to human limitations. For example, in the rennin experiment, you needed to judge the end-point, which is impossible to do precisely using just the human eye. You may sometimes have chosen a moment for the end-point that was relatively early and sometimes chosen a moment that was too late. So these types of errors are also random errors.

It is very important to learn to spot the really important sources of error when you are doing an experiment. Be aware of when you are having difficulties, and don't assume that this is just because you are not very good at doing practical work! If you carry out the rennin experiment, you will quickly realise how difficult it is to keep your water bath at exactly the correct temperature and to judge the end-point of the reaction precisely. These are the really important errors in this experiment, and they outweigh any others such as the error in measuring a volume or in measuring temperature.

If you are asked to suggest improvements to an experiment, your suggestions should be focused on increasing the accuracy of the procedure or the accuracy of your measurements or observations. This often means considering how to reduce the major sources of error that you have identified. Improvements here could include:

*   using measuring instruments that are likely to be more precise or accurate – for example, measuring volumes with a graduated pipette rather than a syringe

KEY WORDS

systematic error: a source of uncertainty in your results that gives incorrect values that are always the same magnitude and always err in the same direction; systematic errors do not affect trends shown by results

random error: a source of uncertainty in your results that gives incorrect values that can be of different magnitudes and err in different direction; random errors can affect trends shown by results

- using techniques for measuring the dependent variable that are likely to provide more precise or accurate readings – for example, using a colorimeter to measure colour changes rather than the naked eye

- using techniques or apparatus that are better able to keep standardised variables constant, such as using a thermostatically controlled water bath rather than a beaker of water

- standardising important variables that were not standardised in the original experiment (note that it is also important to say how you would standardise these variables)

- doing replicates so that you have several readings of your dependent variable for each value of your independent variable, and then calculating a mean value of the dependent variable.

P1.10 Drawings

You may be asked to make observations of a photograph or specimen – which will often be on a microscope slide – and to record your observations as a diagram or drawing.

You may be asked to calculate a magnification, which is described in Chapter 1. You could be asked to use an eyepiece graticule to measure an object using a microscope, and perhaps to calculate its real size by calibrating the graticule against a stage micrometer. This is also described n Chapter 1. Remember always to show every step of your working clearly and fully.

You do not have to be a good artist to be good at doing biological drawings. A good biological drawing looks simple and uncomplicated. Here are some guidelines.

- Draw with clear, single lines.

  - Do not have several 'goes' at a line so that it ends up being fuzzy.

  - Use an HB pencil and a good eraser, so that when you make a mistake (which you almost certainly will) you can rub it out completely.

- Show the overall shape, and the proportions of the different components of the structure you are drawing, accurately; you may be able to use an eyepiece graticule to measure the width of different structures in eyepiece graticule units, to help you to get the proportions correct.

- Do not include any shading or colouring.

- Drawings should be large, using most of the space available but not going outside that space (e.g. it should not go over any of the words printed on the page).

It is very important to draw what you can see, and not what you think you should see. The microscope slide that you are given might be something that is different from anything you have seen before. Remember that you are being tested on your ability to observe carefully and to record what you see, rather than any knowledge you might have about what you are looking at. During your course, you should become confident in using a microscope and learn to look carefully at what you can see through the eyepiece.

You may be asked to draw a low-power plan (a plan diagram). This is a diagram in which only the outlines of the different tissues are shown. Look back to Chapter 7. Figure 7.9 is a plan diagram of the transverse section (TS) through a privet leaf shown in Figure 7.8. Plan diagrams should never show individual cells. You will need to look carefully to determine where one tissue ends and another one begins, and it may be a good idea to move up to a high-power objective lens to help with this. You can then go back down to a lower-power lens to enable you to see the whole area that you will show in your drawing.

You may be asked to draw a more detailed drawing, using high power. This is sometimes called a high-power detail, and it generally does show individual cells. Figure P1.10 shows a drawing of some plant cells as seen using the high-power objective on a light microscope. When you are drawing plant cells, take care to use two lines to show the thickness of a cell wall. When two plant cells are in contact, there will be three lines close together, showing the thickness of each cell wall and the division between them.

You may be asked to label your drawings. The label lines should be drawn with a ruler and pencil. The end of the line should precisely touch the part of the diagram you are labelling. Do not use arrowheads. The label lines should not cross over one another. The labels themselves should be written horizontally (no matter what angle the label line is at), and they should not be written on the drawing.

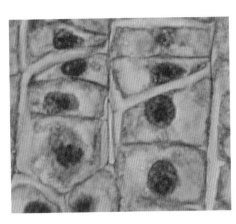

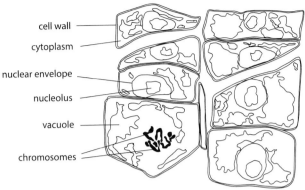

cell wall
cytoplasm
nuclear envelope
nucleolus
vacuole
chromosomes

Figure P1.10: A high-power drawing of a group of plant cells, showing the detail visible using a high-power objectives lens of a light microscope.

REFLECTION

Do you find that you have a better understanding of an investigation when you follow detailed instructions, or when you have been involved in planning the investigation yourself? How can you help yourself to gain a deeper understanding of each experiment or investigation that you do?

Final reflection

Discuss with a friend which, if any, parts of Chapter P1 you need to:

• read through again to make sure you really understand

• seek more guidance on, even after going over it again.

SUMMARY

In an experiment investigating the effect of one variable on another, the independent variable is the one that you change and the dependent variable is the one that you measure. All other variables should be standardised (kept constant). The range of the independent variable is the spread from lowest to highest value. The interval is the distance between each value in the range. Temperature can be kept constant or varied using a water bath. pH can be kept constant or varied using buffer solutions.

The accuracy of a measurement is how true it is. For example, an accurate measuring cylinder reads exactly $50\,cm^3$ when it contains $50\,cm^3$ of liquid. The precision of a measuring instrument is how consistent it is in giving exactly the same reading for the same value. You can increase confidence in your results by doing replicates and calculating a mean.

Results tables should be constructed with the independent variable in the first column and the readings for the dependent variable(s) in the next column(s). Units go in the headings, not in the body of the table. Each value should be recorded to the same number of decimal places. This is also the case for any calculated values.

In a line graph, the independent variable goes on the x-axis and the dependent variable on the y-axis. Headings must include units. Scales must go up in even and sensible steps. Points should be plotted as small crosses or as encircled dots. Lines should be best-fit or ruled between successive points. Do not extrapolate.

Bar charts are drawn when there is a discontinuous variable on the x-axis. Bars in a bar chart do not touch. Frequency diagrams or histograms are drawn when there is a continuous variable on the x-axis. Bars touch.

Conclusions should be short and to the point. They should use the results to answer the question posed by the investigation. They should not go beyond what is shown by the results. Do not confuse conclusion with discussion.

CONTINUED

When describing data displayed on a graph, begin by stating the general trend and then describe any points at which the gradient of the curve changes. Quote figures from the x-axis and y-axis coordinates for these points. Do not use language suggesting time (e.g. 'faster') if time is not shown on the x-axis or y-axis.
Show every small step whenever you are asked to do a calculation.
Do not confuse mistakes with experimental errors. Mistakes should not happen. Experimental errors are often unavoidable, unless you have the opportunity to use a better technique or better apparatus. Systematic errors are those which have the same magnitude and direction throughout the experiment, and are usually caused by limitations in the measuring instruments. Random errors are those which vary in magnitude and direction during the experiment, and may be caused by difficulty in standardising variables or in making judgements. When asked to suggest improvements in an experiment, concentrate on the main sources of error and suggest ways of reducing them.
When making drawings from a microscope, a low-power plan should show only the outlines of tissues and no individual cells. Be prepared to go up to high power to get more information about where one tissue ends and another begins. High-power drawings should show as much detail as possible, including details of individual cells.

EXAM-STYLE QUESTIONS

At AS Level, practical skills are examined in a laboratory-based practical examination. The questions that follow will give you practice in the theoretical aspects of these skills.

1 An investigation is carried out into the effect of substrate concentration on the activity of catalase. What could be the dependent variable?

A the concentration of catalase   C the rate of production of oxygen

B the pH of the enzyme solution   D the temperature of the substrate

[1]

2 An investigation is carried out into the effect of temperature on the activity of lipase. Separate tubes of substrate solution and enzyme solution are left in temperature-controlled water baths for ten minutes before mixing. Why is this done?

A to activate the enzyme

B to allow time for the enzyme and substrate to react

C to control the independent variable

D to keep a standardised variable constant   [1]

3 Copy and complete the table.

Investigation	Independent variable	Dependent variable	Two important control variables
The effect of sucrose concentration on plasmolysis of onion cells			
The effect of pH on the rate of activity of amylase			
The effect of temperature on the percentage of open stomata in a leaf			

[9]

CONTINUED

4 For this question you need two sheets of graph paper.

The light micrographs below are **a** a cross section of a young root, and **b** a representative part of a young stem of *Ranunculus* (buttercup).

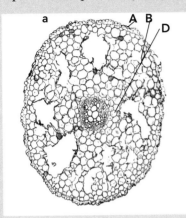

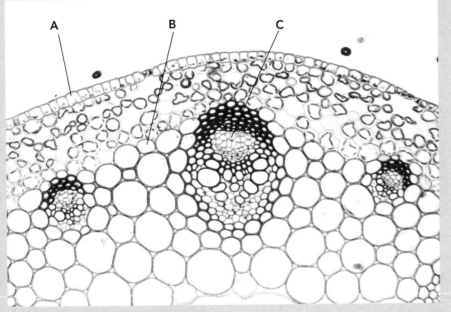

a Name the tissues **A**, **B**, **C** and **D**. [4]

b i On one of the sheets of graph paper, draw the outline of the root. Use at least half the width of the graph paper when making your drawing.

Now draw inside your outline a low-power plan of the xylem only. Be as accurate as you can in drawing the correct proportions compared with the overall size of the root – you may find it useful to make some measurements with a ruler. [4]

ii Now take the second sheet of graph paper and draw the outline of the stem. It does not have to be exactly the same size as your drawing of the root.

Carefully make a low-power plan to show the vascular bundles **only**. Draw in outline the lignified tissues sclerenchyma and xylem, and the tissue labelled **C** between them. [2]

CONTINUED

    iii Sclerenchyma and xylem are tissues which contain dead cells whose walls are thickened with a mechanically strong substance called lignin. Lignin is used for strength and support. Count the number of squares of graph paper covered by lignified tissue (xylem) in the root. Count the squares that are more than half included in the drawing as whole squares, and do not count squares that are less than half included. **[1]**

    iv Count the number of squares covered by the whole root section (including the lignified tissue). **[1]**

    v Calculate the percentage of squares occupied by lignified tissue in the root as follows:

$$\frac{\text{number of squares occupied by lignified tissue}}{\text{number of squares occupied by whole root}} \times 100$$

[1]

    vi Repeat steps **iii** to **v** for the stem (remember lignified tissue in the stem is sclerenchyma plus xylem). **[3]**

    vii Assuming the results you have obtained are typical of the whole stem, suggest an explanation for the difference in percentage of lignified tissue in the root and the stem. **[2]**

c If you try to imagine these structures in three dimensions, the lignified tissue in the root is a central rod, but in the stem it is a circle of separate rods. Suggest the reasons for the different distribution of lignified tissues in the root and the stem. **[2]**

[Total: 20]

5 A student investigated the effect of temperature on the activity of enzymes in yeast. The student measured the activity of the enzymes by counting the number of bubbles of carbon dioxide which were released in three minutes. The results of the student's investigation are shown in the table.

Temperature/°C	Enzyme activity/mean number of carbon dioxide bubbles released per minute
15	5
20	7
30	11
35	15
40	18

a i Plot a graph of the data shown in the table. **[4]**

    ii From the graph, estimate the enzyme activity at 25 °C. **[1]**

    iii Suggest how the student should make sure that the results of this investigation are as accurate and reliable as possible. **[3]**

b In carrying out this investigation, the student made the hypothesis that 'The activity of the enzymes in yeast increases as temperature increases.' State whether you think this hypothesis is supported by the student's results. Explain your answer. **[2]**

[Total: 10]

Cambridge International AS & A Level Biology (9700)
Paper 31, Question 1c and d, June 2009

CONTINUED

6   A student investigated the time taken for the complete digestion of starch by amylase found in the saliva of 25 individuals of a species of mammal.

A sample of saliva was collected from each individual and mixed with $5\,cm^3$ of starch suspension. Samples of the mixture were tested for the presence of starch.

The student recorded the time taken for the complete digestion of starch.

The investigation was repeated with the same individuals on the following day.

The results of the student's investigation are shown in the table.

Time taken for complete digestion of starch / min	Number of individuals	
	day 1	day 2
35	2	8
40	6	10
45	9	4
50	5	2
55	3	1

a   Plot a graph to display these data.   [4]

b   Describe the patterns in the results.   [3]

c   Suggest a reason for the differences between the results for day 1 and day 2.   [1]

d   Suggest how you might control the variables in this investigation to compare a different species of mammal with the mammal studied.   [3]

[Total: 11]

Cambridge International AS & A Level Biology (9700) Paper 33, Question 1b, November 2009

SELF-EVALUATION CHECKLIST

After studying this chapter, complete a table like this:

I can	See section...	Needs more work	Almost there	Ready to move on
collect data and observations	P1.3			
make decisions about measurements and observations	P1.3			
record data and observations appropriately	P1.4, P1.9			
display calculations and reasoning clearly	P1.8			
use tables and graphs to display data	P1.4, P1.5			
interpret data and observations	P1.6, P1.7			
draw conclusions	P1.6			
identify significant sources of error	P1.9			
suggest improvements to a procedure, or suggest how as investigation could be extended	P1.9			

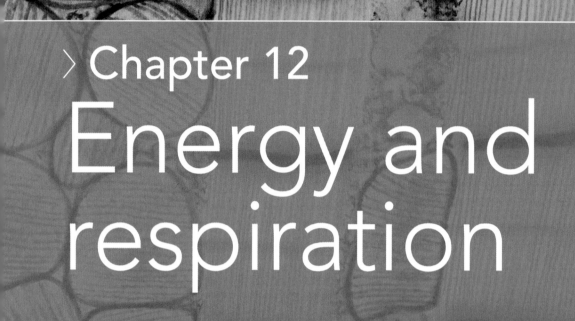

> Chapter 12
Energy and respiration

LEARNING INTENTIONS

In this chapter you will learn how to:

- outline the need for energy in living organisms
- explain how ATP is suited for the role as the universal energy currency
- describe how ATP is synthesised
- describe the stages in aerobic respiration – glycolysis, the link reaction, the Krebs cycle and oxidative phosphorylation – including the roles of NAD, FAD and coenzyme A
- describe the relationship between structure and function of mitochondria
- outline lactic acid fermentation and ethanol formation, in anaerobic conditions
- explain how rice is adapted to grow with its roots submerged in water
- compare the energy values of different respiratory substrates
- calculate respiratory quotients
- describe how to carry out investigations using respirometers
- describe how to carry out investigations using redox indicators.

Discuss these questions with a partner.

*   Why do your cells need energy?

*   How does respiration provide cells with useful energy?

*   In which cells of your body does respiration take place?

Be ready to share your ideas with the rest of the class.

A BABY WITH THREE PARENTS

In 2016 the first baby was born whose cells contain DNA from three parents. His two 'main' parents were Jordanian, and the addition of the third type of DNA to their egg and sperm was done in Mexico, by a team from the USA. So this was a truly international break-through.

The parents chose to have this treatment because the mother has a faulty gene in some of her mitochondria. During normal fertilisation, the mitochondria of the zygote all come from the mother's egg, not from the sperm. If her egg contained these faulty mitochondria, the baby could be born with a fatal condition.

Mitochondria contain small circles of DNA which contain genes that code for the ribosomal RNA and transfer RNAs that mitochondria use for making proteins. Faulty versions of these genes result in serious metabolic disorders, particularly affecting tissues that have a high energy demand, such as nerve tissue, cardiac muscle and liver cells.

In this case, the woman was helped to avoid passing on her faulty mitochondrial DNA by an in-vitro fertilisation treatment involving three biological parents: herself, the father and a female donor with healthy mitochondria.

The nucleus was removed from one of the mother's eggs (Figure 12.1). The aim was to do this without taking any mitochondria, but in practice this is difficult to do. It was then inserted into a donor egg from which the nucleus had also been removed. Then the donor egg, with its healthy mitochondria

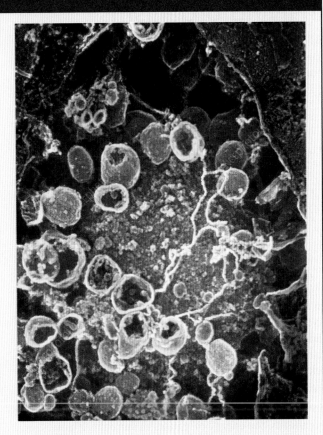

Figure 12.1: Scanning electron micrograph of a section through a human egg cell. The mitochondria have been coloured yellow (×6000).

and a nucleus from the mother, was placed in a dish. Sperm cells from the father were added. One fertilised egg developed into a healthy embryo, which was inserted into the mother's uterus.

CONTINUED

Questions for discussion

- How do you feel about the ethics of this procedure? What do others in your class feel?

- This was an experimental procedure, but the parents of the child decided not to allow scientists to test his mitochondria or health as he grows up. What are your opinions about this decision?

12.1 The need for energy in living organisms

All living organisms need a constant supply of energy to stay alive. Energy is needed for a wide variety of purposes in every living organism, and every living cell.

- Substances must be moved across membranes against their concentration gradient, by active transport (Chapter 4).

- Movement requires energy; this can be inside a cell, such as transporting a protein from where it is made on a ribosome to the Golgi apparatus; or it can involve whole cells, tissues or organs, such as contracting a muscle (Chapter 15).

- Synthesising large molecules from smaller ones, such as replicating DNA molecules or synthesising proteins (both described in Chapter 6), always requires energy; this type of reaction is said to be **anabolic**.

In all known organisms, the same substance is used to supply energy for these processes. This is ATP (adenosine triphosphate). ATP is the universal energy currency of cells. Each cell makes its own ATP and then releases energy from ATP molecules to fuel the processes outlined above.

So where does the energy in ATP come from? For most organisms, the energy originates in sunlight. Plants and other photosynthetic organisms capture energy from sunlight, and transfer it to chemical potential energy in organic molecules such as carbohydrates, fats and proteins. They do this by photosynthesis, which is described in Chapter 13. In this chapter you will learn how the energy locked into carbohydrates, fats and proteins is transferred to ATP, in the process of **respiration**.

ATP

In Chapter 6 you learnt about the structure of ATP. You may remember that ATP is a phosphorylated nucleotide. An ATP molecule is made up of the base adenine, ribose sugar and three phosphate groups (Figure 12.2).

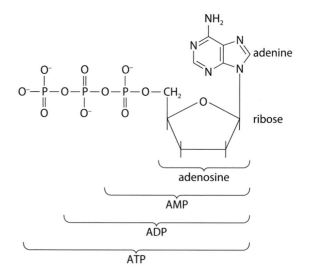

Figure 12.2: The structure of an ATP molecule.

When one phosphate group is removed from ATP, ADP (adenosine diphosphate) is formed and $30.5\,\text{kJ}\,\text{mol}^{-1}$ of energy is released. Removal of a second phosphate produces AMP (adenosine monophosphate), and

KEY WORDS

anabolic: a chemical reaction in which small molecules are built up into larger ones

respiration: the enzymatic release of energy from organic compounds in living cells

30.5 k mol^{-1} of energy is again released. Removal of the last phosphate, leaving adenosine, releases only 14.2 kJ mol^{-1} (Figure 12.3).

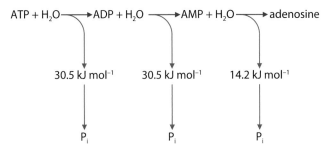

Figure 12.3: Hydrolysis of ATP to release energy. P$_i$ is inorganic phosphate, H_3PO_4.

ATP makes the perfect energy currency for a number of reasons.

- The hydrolysis of a molecule of ATP can be done quickly and easily, in whichever part of the cell the energy is required.

- The hydrolysis of one molecule of ATP releases a useful quantity of energy – enough to fuel an energy-requiring process in a cell, but not so much that it will be wasted.

- ATP is a relatively stable molecule in the range of pH that normally occurs in cells; it does not break down unless a catalyst such as the enzyme ATPase is present.

You probably have between 50 g and 200 g of ATP in your body at this moment, and you will use more than 50 kg of ATP today. (That may be similar to your entire body mass.) So, as you can see, your cells need to make ATP constantly. They cannot build up large stores of it, but tend to make it as they need it.

ATP is made when a phosphate group is combined with ADP, in a reverse of the reaction shown in Figure 12.3. This is done in two main ways:

- using energy provided directly by another chemical reaction – this is called a **substrate-linked reaction**

- by **chemiosmosis**, a process that takes place across the inner membranes of mitochondria, using energy released by the movement of hydrogen ions down their concentration gradient.

In humans, all of the ATP is made in respiration, both by substrate-linked reactions and by chemiosmosis.

These processes are described later in this chapter. In plants, ATP is again made in respiration, and also by photosynthesis, which is described in Chapter 13.

It is the need for constant supplies of ATP that requires humans to breathe continuously. Breathing supplies oxygen to the cells, which use the oxygen to oxidise glucose and release energy from it, which is used to synthesise ATP molecules. The next section describes how this is done.

Questions

1   Using Figure 12.3 to help you, write the equation for the formation of ATP from ADP.

2   'Currency' is a term that is normally used to describe money. With a partner, discuss the meaning of the term *energy currency*, and why this term is used to describe ATP. Be ready to share your ideas with the rest of the class.

12.2 Aerobic respiration

Respiration is a process in which organic molecules are broken down in a series of stages to release chemical potential energy, which is used to synthesise ATP. The main organic molecule that is used in this process in most cells is carbohydrate, usually glucose. Many cells – including brain cells – can use only glucose as their respiratory substrate. However, other cells break down fatty acids, glycerol and amino acids in respiration. Heart muscle, for example, uses fatty acids.

Glucose breakdown can be divided into four stages: glycolysis, the link reaction, the Krebs cycle and oxidative phosphorylation (Figure 12.4).

KEY WORDS

substrate-linked reaction: in the context of ATP formation, the transfer of phosphate from a substrate molecule directly to ADP to produce ATP, using energy provided directly by another chemical reaction

chemiosmosis: the synthesis of ATP using energy released by the movement of hydrogen ions down their concentration gradient, across a membrane in a mitochondrion or chloroplast

---

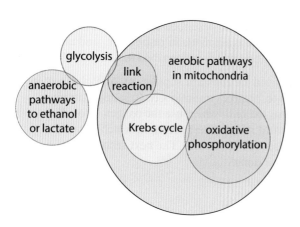

Figure 12.4: The sequence of events in respiration. In aerobic respiration, glycolysis takes place in the cytoplasm, and the link reaction, the Krebs cycle and oxidative phosphorylation take place inside mitochondria. Anaerobic respiration involves other pathways that take place in the cytoplasm.

Glycolysis

Glycolysis is the splitting, or lysis, of glucose. It takes place in the cytoplasm of a cell.

Glycolysis is a series of reactions (steps) in which a glucose molecule with six carbon atoms (6C) is eventually split into two molecules of pyruvate. Each pyruvate molecule has three carbon atoms (3C).

Perhaps surprisingly, energy from ATP is used, rather than made, at the start of glycolysis. However, energy is released in later steps, when it can be used to make ATP. More energy is released than is used, and overall there

---

KEY WORDS

glycolysis: the splitting (lysis) of glucose; the first stage in aerobic respiration

phosphorylation: the addition of a phosphate group to a molecule

NAD (nicotinamide adenine dinucleotide): a hydrogen carrier used in respiration

oxidation: the addition of oxygen, or the removal of hydrogen or electrons from a substance

reduction: the removal of oxygen, or the addition of hydrogen or electrons to a substance

---

is a net gain of two ATP molecules per molecule of glucose broken down.

A simplified flow diagram of the series of steps in glycolysis is shown in Figure 12.5.

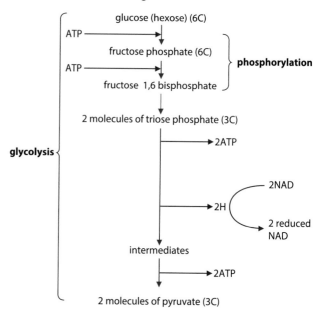

Figure 12.5: The series of steps that make up glycolysis. These steps all happen in the cytoplasm of a cell.

The first step is called **phosphorylation**. Phosphate groups are transferred from ATP molecules to glucose. This raises the energy level of the glucose molecules, making it easier for them to react in the next step.

Two ATP molecules are used for each molecule of glucose. The donation of the first phosphate group produces glucose phosphate, whose atoms are rearranged to form fructose phosphate. The second ATP molecule donates another phosphate group, forming fructose 1,6 bisphosphate. Fructose 1,6 bisphosphate (6C) then breaks down to produce two molecules of triose phosphate (3C).

Hydrogen is then removed from triose phosphate and transferred to the carrier molecule **NAD (nicotinamide adenine dinucleotide)**. The removal of hydrogen is called **oxidation**, so triose phosphate is oxidised during this process. The addition of hydrogen to a substance is called **reduction**. The NAD is now reduced NAD.

Two molecules of reduced NAD are produced for each molecule of glucose entering glycolysis. The hydrogens carried by reduced NAD can easily be transferred to other molecules. As you will see later, these hydrogens can be used in oxidative phosphorylation to generate ATP.

During the same step (the conversion of triose phosphate to pyruvate), ATP is produced. This is done by directly transferring a phosphate group from a substrate – in this case, a phosphorylated molecule that is one of the intermediates in this step – to an ADP molecule. This is an example of substrate-linked phosphorylation.

So, although two molecules of ATP were used for each glucose molecule at the beginning of glycolysis, four molecules of ATP are formed at the end. There is therefore a net gain of two ATPs per glucose.

The end product of glycolysis is pyruvate. Pyruvate still contains a great deal of chemical potential energy. If oxygen is available in the cell, the pyruvate now moves through the two membranes that make up the envelope of a mitochondrion. It is moved by active transport (so, again, a small amount of ATP is used). The pyruvate enters the mitochondrial matrix.

The link reaction

When pyruvate arrives in the matrix of a mitochondrion, enzymes remove carbon dioxide and hydrogen from it. The removal of carbon dioxide is called decarboxylation. The removal of hydrogen is dehydrogenation. The remainder of the molecule combines with coenzyme A (CoA) to produce acetyl coenzyme A. This process is known as the link reaction (Figure 12.6), because it joins or links glycolysis with the Krebs cycle.

CoA is a complex molecule composed of a nucleoside (adenine plus ribose) combined with a vitamin (pantothenic acid, vitamin B_5). A coenzyme is a molecule that is needed for an enzyme to catalyse a reaction, though it does not take part in the reaction itself. In this case, CoA carries and supplies acetyl groups, which are required for the conversion of oxaloacetate to citrate.

The hydrogen removed from pyruvate in the link reaction is transferred to NAD, producing more reduced NAD:

pyruvate + CoA + NAD ⟶ acetyl CoA + carbon dioxide + reduced NAD

The Krebs cycle

The Krebs cycle is named after Sir Hans Krebs, who earned a Nobel Prize for his discovery in 1937 of the sequence of reactions that happens next. This cycle is also known as the citric acid cycle. The Krebs cycle is shown in Figure 12.6. (Notice that the scientist's name was Krebs, so the correct name of this cycle is the Krebs cycle, not Kreb's cycle.)

The Krebs cycle is a circular pathway of enzyme-controlled reactions.

- Acetyl coenzyme A (2C) combines with oxaloacetate (4C) to form citrate (6C).

- The citrate is decarboxylated and dehydrogenated in a series of steps. This releases carbon dioxide, which is given off as a waste gas. It also releases hydrogens, which are accepted by the carriers NAD and FAD. You will see what happens to these in the next section.

- Oxaloacetate is regenerated to combine with another acetyl coenzyme A.

For each turn of the cycle, two carbon dioxide molecules are produced, one FAD and three NAD molecules are reduced, and one ATP molecule is generated. This ATP is made by the direct transfer of a phosphate group from one of the substrates in the reactions, to an ADP molecule, in the matrix of the mitochondrion. This is a substrate-linked reaction.

> ### KEY WORDS
>
> decarboxylation: the removal of carbon dioxide from a substance
>
> dehydrogenation: the removal of hydrogen from a substance
>
> coenzyme A (CoA): a molecule that supplies acetyl groups required for the link reaction
>
> acetyl coenzyme A: a molecule made up of CoA and a 2C acetyl group, important in the link reaction
>
> link reaction: decarboxylaytion and dehydrogenation of pyruvate, resulting in the formation of acetyl coenzyme A, linking glycolysis with the Krebs cycle
>
> Krebs cycle: a cycle of reactions in aerobic respiration in the matrix of a mitochondrion in which hydrogens pass to hydrogen carriers for subsequent ATP synthesis and some ATP is synthesised directly; also known as the citric acid cycle

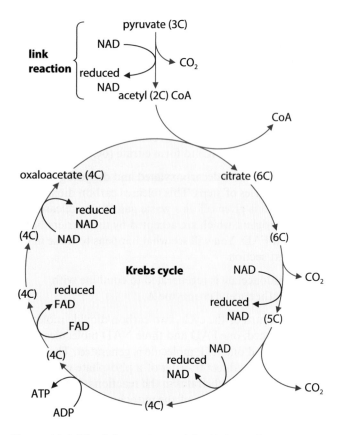

Figure 12.6: The link reaction and the Krebs cycle.

Questions

3 Look at the diagram of the link reaction and the Krebs cycle, in Figure 12.6. Outline how the carbon dioxide that is produced moves from the matrix of the mitochondrion to the air surrounding the organism.

4 Explain how the events of the Krebs cycle can be cyclical.

You have now read about three stages in aerobic respiration – glycolysis, the link reaction and the Krebs cycle. But, so far, no oxygen has been involved. This is only required for the next and final stage, which is called oxidative phosphorylation.

Oxidative phosphorylation and the electron transport chain

The final stage of aerobic respiration, **oxidative phosphorylation**, takes place in the inner mitochondrial membrane (Figure 12.7).

KEY WORD

oxidative phosphorylation: the synthesis of ATP from ADP and P_i using energy from oxidation reactions in aerobic respiration

---

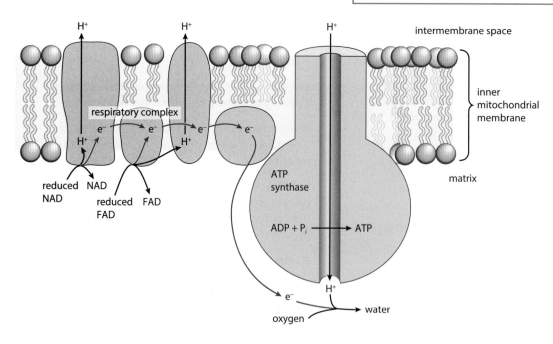

Figure 12.7: Oxidative phosphorylation: the electron transfer chain.

The **electron transport chain** is a series of membrane proteins, called electron carriers, held in position in the inner membrane (cristae) of a mitochondrion. They are arranged close to one another, and electrons can easily be passed from one to the next, along the chain. Each carrier is first reduced (as an electron is added to it) and then oxidised (as the electron is passed on). The reactions are **redox reactions**.

You have seen that reduced NAD is produced in glycolysis, and both reduced NAD and reduced FAD are produced in the Krebs cycle. The reduced NAD from glycolysis was formed in the cytoplasm, but it can pass through the mitochondrial envelope and enter the matrix. All of these reduced NAD and reduced FAD molecules move from the mitochondrial matrix to the inner membrane. Here, the hydrogens that they are carrying are removed. Each hydrogen atom is made up of a proton and an electron, and these now split apart. The proton can also be referred to as a hydrogen ion, H^+. The electron, e^-, is transferred to the first in the series of electron carriers.

This electron has energy, which started off as chemical potential energy in the glucose molecule, right back at the start of glycolysis. As the electron moves from one carrier to the next, some of its energy is released.

Some of this energy is used to actively move protons from the matrix of the mitochondrion (Figure 12.8) into the space between the inner and outer membranes of the mitochondrial envelope. This produces a higher concentration of protons in the intermembrane space than in the matrix. So now there is a concentration gradient for protons, across the inner mitochondrial membrane.

Now, protons pass back into the mitochondrial matrix by facilitated diffusion. The protons move passively down their concentration gradient through protein channels in the inner membrane. Each channel is formed

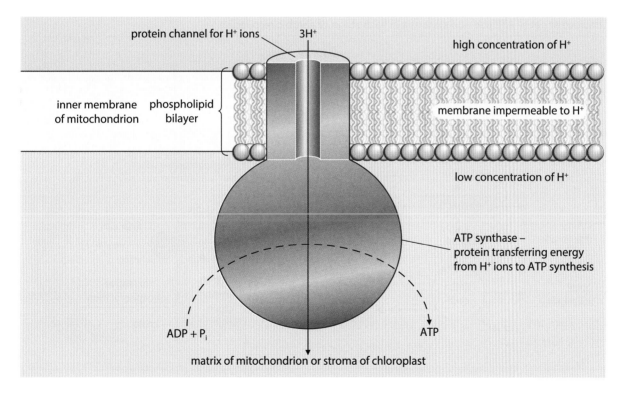

Figure 12.8: ATP synthesis by chemiosmosis in the inner mitochondrial membrane. Protons move by facilitated diffusion through ATP synthase molecules, which use the protons' energy to add phosphate groups to ADP.

by a large protein molecule, the enzyme ATP synthase. As the protons pass through the channel, their energy is used to synthesise ATP in the process called chemiosmosis (Figure 12.8).

> ### KEY WORD
>
> ATP synthase: the enzyme that catalyses the phosphorylation of ADP to produce ATP

And now, at last, oxygen comes into the process. Oxygen is required to accept the electrons as they arrive at the end of the electron transport chain. Four electrons recombine with four protons and an oxygen molecule to form water:

$$O_2 + 4H^+ + 4e^- \longrightarrow 2H_2O$$

Without oxygen available as the final electron acceptor, none of the reactions inside the mitochondrion – the link reaction, the Krebs cycle or oxidative phosphorylation – can take place. These stages, especially oxidative phosphorylation, produce much more ATP than glycolysis alone. Effectively, glycolysis releases only a small quantity of chemical potential energy from glucose, because the glucose is only partly oxidised. The reactions in the mitochondrion complete this oxidation, releasing much more energy.

You do not need to know the details of the total yield of ATP but, if you are interested, this is shown in Table 12.1.

A summary of the sequence of events in aerobic respiration, and where they take place, is shown in Figure 12.9.

Stage	ATP used	ATP made	Net gain in ATP
glycolysis	2	4	2
link reaction	0	0	0
Krebs cycle	0	2	2
oxidative phosphorylation	0	28	28
Total	2	34	32

Table 12.1: Balance sheet of ATP use and synthesis in each stage of aerobic respiration.

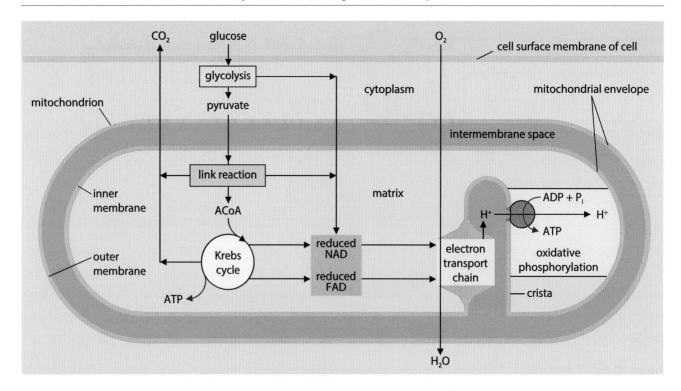

Figure 12.9: The sites of the various stages of aerobic respiration in a cell.

Questions

5   State the roles in respiration of:

   a   NAD

   b   CoA

   c   oxygen.

6   In your group, think how you could use role play to show the events that take place during oxidative phosphorylation. For example, one person could represent an NAD molecule, and two more could represent a hydrogen that it carries (made up of a proton and an electron), and so on.

   If there are enough people in your class (you will probably need at least 12 people), you can try out your plan. If you do not have enough people, write down your ideas in the form of a script for a short play.

12.3 Mitochondrial structure and function

You have seen that the link reaction, the Krebs cycle and the electron transport chain all take place inside mitochondria. Mitochondria are rod-shaped or filamentous organelles about 0.5–1.0 µm in diameter. Time-lapse photography shows that they are not rigid, but can change their shape.

The number of mitochondria in a cell depends on its activity. For example, a highly active mammalian liver cell contains between 1000 and 2000 mitochondria, occupying 20% of the cell volume.

The structure of a mitochondrion is shown in Figures 1.28 and 12.10. Like a chloroplast, each mitochondrion is surrounded by an envelope of two phospholipid membranes. The outer membrane is smooth, but the inner membrane is very folded. You may remember that these folds are called cristae (singular: crista) (Chapter 1, Section 1.6, Plant and animal cells as seen with an electron microscope). The cristae give the inner membrane a large total surface area. Cristae in mitochondria from different types of cell show considerable variation but, in general, mitochondria from active cells have longer, more densely packed cristae than mitochondria from less active cells.

The two membranes have different compositions and properties. The outer membrane is relatively permeable to small molecules. This allows the movement of substances required and produced by the link reaction, the Krebs cycle and oxidative phosphorylation, such as oxygen, carbon dioxide, ATP, ADP and P_i.

The inner membrane is less permeable. In an electron micrograph, you can see that tiny spheres, about 9 nm in diameter, are scattered all over it. These are attached to the inner membrane by stalks (Figure 12.11). The

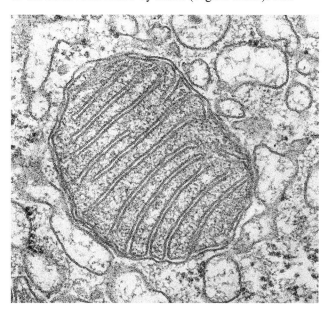

Figure 12.10: Transmission electron micrograph (TEM) of a mitochondrion (x15 000).

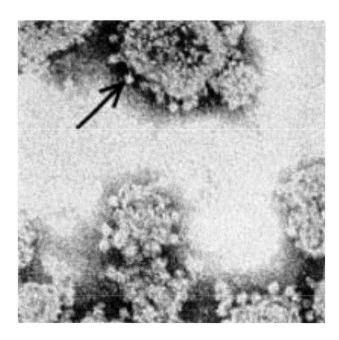

Figure 12.11: Stalked particles.

spheres are the enzyme ATP synthase. (The fact that these are visible in an electron micrograph is a reminder of how large this protein molecule is.)

The inner membrane is also the site of the electron transport chain and contains the proteins necessary for this. (These are not visible in an electron micrograph.)

The space between the two membranes of the envelope usually has a lower pH than the matrix of the mitochondrion. This is because protons are transported across the inner membrane from the matrix, to set up the concentration gradient needed for ATP formation. You will remember that a high concentration of protons – otherwise known as hydrogen ions – means high acidity (i.e. low pH).

The matrix of the mitochondrion is the site of the link reaction and the Krebs cycle. It contains the enzymes needed for these reactions. It also contains small (70S) ribosomes and several identical copies of mitochondrial DNA. These are used to synthesise some of the proteins required for the mitochondrion to function. This DNA is circular. The small ribosomes and the circular DNA should remind you that mitochondria were once bacteria, which now live symbiotically within your cells.

Question

7   Make a large diagram of a mitochondrion. Add annotations to your diagram to explain how the structure of the mitochondrion is adapted for its functions.

12.4 Respiration without oxygen

If there is no – or very little – oxygen inside a mitochondrion, there is nothing to accept the electrons at the end of the chain. So the electron transfer chain stops working and no further ATP is formed by oxidative phosphorylation. There is therefore no free carrier in the chain to accept hydrogens from reduced NAD and reduced FAD, so these remain reduced. The Krebs cycle therefore stops running, because there is no oxidised NAD or FAD to enable the dehydrogenation steps to take place.

However, all is not lost. A cell can still produce a small amount of ATP, even in **anaerobic** conditions – that is, when no oxygen is present. If the reduced NAD that

is produced in glycolysis can somehow be oxidised again, then glycolysis can continue to take place. Cells have evolved two different ways of achieving this. Both pathways take place in the cytoplasm of the cell.

In yeast and some other microorganisms, and in some plant tissues, the hydrogen from reduced NAD is passed to ethanal (CH_3CHO). The pathway is shown in Figure 12.12. First, pyruvate is decarboxylated to ethanal; then the ethanal is reduced to ethanol (C_2H_5OH) by the enzyme alcohol dehydrogenase. This process is known as **ethanol fermentation**.

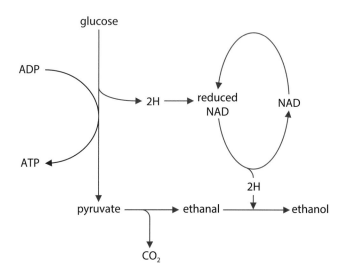

Figure 12.12: Ethanol fermentation.

In other microorganisms, and in mammalian muscles when deprived of oxygen, pyruvate acts as the hydrogen acceptor. In the process, it is converted to lactate by the enzyme lactate dehydrogenase (named after the reverse reaction, which it also catalyses). This pathway, known as **lactate fermentation**, is shown in Figure 12.13.

An important difference between ethanol fermentation and lactate fermentation is what happens to the products. Lactate can be oxidised, converting it back to pyruvate which can then be fed into the Krebs cycle

> **KEY WORDS**
>
> **anaerobic:** without oxygen
>
> **ethanol fermentation:** anaerobic respiration in which pyruvate is converted to ethanol
>
> **lactate fermentation:** anaerobic respiration in which pyruvate is converted to lactate

and generate ATP. Alternatively, the lactate can be converted to the polysaccharide glycogen, and stored. In mammals, these processes happen in the liver. The oxidation of lactate requires extra oxygen, sometimes referred to as an 'oxygen debt' or EPOC (excess post-exercise oxygen consumption), which is why we continue to breathe more deeply and heavily than usual after exercise has finished. In contrast, ethanol cannot be further metabolised. It is simply a waste product.

Both ethanol fermentation and lactate fermentation return reduced NAD to its oxidised state, ready to accept more hydrogens. This allows glycolysis to keep running, even though no oxygen is available.

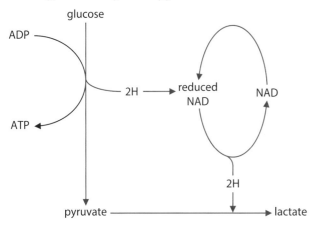

Figure 12.13: Lactate fermentation.

Question

8   Glucose can be used to produce ATP, without the use of oxygen:

$$\text{glucose} \rightarrow X \rightarrow Y \text{ in mammals}$$
$$\downarrow$$
$$Z \text{ in yeast}$$

Which compounds are represented by the letters **X**, **Y** and **Z**?

	X	Y	Z
A	ethanol	pyruvate	lactate
B	lactate	ethanol	pyruvate
C	pyruvate	ethanol	lactate
D	pyruvate	lactate	ethanol

Ethanol fermentation in rice

Rice is a very important food plant – a staple crop – in many parts of the world. Most varieties of rice can survive in dry conditions, but for maximum yield rice is often grown in 'paddies'. Paddies are fields where the ground is intentionally flooded. Rice can tolerate growing in water, whereas most of the weeds that might compete with it are not able to do so (Figure 12.14). This reduction in competition for light and mineral salts increases yields.

Figure 12.14: Rice growing in Madagascar. The blocks of rice were planted at different times and are at different stages of growth.

Most plants cannot grow in deep water because their roots do not get enough oxygen for aerobic respiration. Nor, if the leaves are submerged, can photosynthesis take place, because there is not enough carbon dioxide available. This happens because gases diffuse much more slowly in water than they do in air. Moreover, the concentrations of dissolved oxygen and dissolved carbon dioxide in water are much less than they are in air. This is especially true in rice paddies, where the rich mud in which the rice roots are planted contains large populations of microorganisms, many of which are aerobic and take oxygen from the water.

Some varieties of rice respond to flooding by quickly growing taller. As the water rises around them, they keep growing upwards so that the top parts of their leaves and flower spikes are always held above the water. This allows oxygen and carbon dioxide to be exchanged through the stomata on the leaves.

The stems and roots of the rice plants contain loosely packed cells forming a tissue known as **aerenchyma** (Figure 12.15). Gases, including oxygen, are able to diffuse through the aerenchyma to other parts of the plant, including those under the water. This ensures that the cells in the roots have at least some oxygen present, and so they are able to respire aerobically.

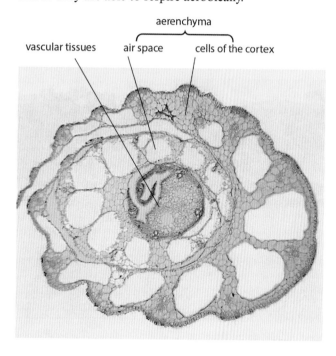

Figure 12.15: Transverse section (TS) across a rice stem, showing the large air spaces.

Nevertheless, oxygen supply is not usually enough to supply all the energy the cells need by aerobic respiration. The cells in the submerged roots therefore also use ethanol fermentation at least some of the time. Ethanol can build up in the tissues. Ethanol is toxic, but the cells in rice roots can tolerate much higher levels than most plants. They also produce more ethanol dehydrogenase, which breaks down ethanol. This allows the plants to grow actively even when oxygen is scarce, using ATP produced by ethanol fermentation.

Question

9   Construct a table to summarise the features of rice that adapt it to grow with its roots submerged in water, and how each feature contributes to this adaptation.

12.5 Respiratory substrates

In the descriptions of the stages in aerobic and anaerobic respiration in the previous sections of this chapter, the initial source of energy is assumed to be glucose. However, most cells are able to use other substrates as well. Lipids, amino acids and types of carbohydate other than glucose can all be used as respiratory substrates.

Energy values of respiratory substrates

When lipids are respired, pairs of carbon atoms are removed and fed directly into the Krebs cycle. When amino acids are respired, they are first converted into pyruvate or acetyl coenzyme A, and again move directly into the Krebs cycle. In most cells, glucose is the first substrate to be used, with lipids only respired when the immediate supply of glucose has been used up. Amino acids are generally used only as a last resort, because they normally have more important, specialised functions, rather than just being sources of energy.

These different types of substrate release different quantities of energy when they are respired. Typical energy values are shown in Table 12.2. They are given as energy densities – that is, the quantity of energy released from 1 g of the substrate.

Respiratory substrate	Energy density / kJ g^{-1}
carbohydrate	15.8
lipid	39.4
protein	17.0

Table 12.2: Energy values of different respiratory substrates.

You can see that lipids have a much greater energy density than carbohydrate or protein. This is because they contain a greater proportion of hydrogen atoms in their molecules. (You may like to look back at information about the structure of these molecules, in Chapter 2.) Most of the energy released in aerobic respiration comes from the oxidation of hydrogen to water when reduced NAD and reduced FAD have released their hydrogens to the electron transport chain. The more hydrogens the molecule contains per gram, the more energy it can provide.

Respiratory quotients

The overall equation for the aerobic respiration of glucose shows that the number of molecules of oxygen used and carbon dioxide produced are the same:

$$C_6H_{12}O_6 + 6O_2 \longrightarrow 6CO_2 + 6H_2O$$

The same number of molecules of any gas takes up the same volume, so the aerobic respiration of glucose uses the same volume of oxygen as the volume of carbon dioxide that it produces.

You can therefore say that the ratio of oxygen taken in and carbon dioxide released is 1 : 1. However, when other substrates are respired, the ratio of the volumes of oxygen used and carbon dioxide given off are not the same as each other. Measuring this ratio is necessary to work out which substrate is being used in respiration. It can also show whether or not anaerobic respiration is occurring.

The ratio of carbon dioxide produced to oxygen used is called the **respiratory quotient (RQ)**.

$$RQ = \frac{\text{volume of carbon dioxide given out in unit time}}{\text{volume of oxygen taken in unit time}}$$

Or, from an equation:

$$RQ = \frac{\text{moles or molecules of carbon dioxide given out}}{\text{moles or molecules of oxygen taken in}}$$

For the aerobic respiration of glucose:

$$RQ = \frac{CO_2}{O_2}$$
$$= \frac{6}{6}$$
$$= 1.0$$

KEY WORD

respiratory quotient (RQ): the ratio of the volume of carbon dioxide produced to the volume of oxygen used

---

What happens when lipids are respired? If you know the molecular formula of the lipid, you can construct a balanced equation. And from the equation, you can calculate the RQ.

For example, when the fatty acid oleic acid (from olive oil) is respired aerobically, the equation is:

$$C_{18}H_{34}O_2 + 25.5O_2 \longrightarrow 18CO_2 + 17H_2O$$

So, for the aerobic respiration of oleic acid:

$$RQ = \frac{CO_2}{O_2}$$
$$= \frac{18}{25.5}$$
$$= 0.7$$

Typical RQs for the aerobic respiration of different substrates are shown in Table 12.3.

Respiratory substrate	Respiratory quotient (RQ)
carbohydrate	1.0
lipid	0.7
protein	0.9

Table 12.3: RQs of different substrates.

Question

10 Calculate the RQ for the aerobic respiration of the fatty acid stearic acid, $C_{18}H_{36}O_2$.

What happens when respiration is not aerobic? The equation for the ethanol fermentation of glucose in a yeast cell is:

$$C_6H_{12}O_6 \longrightarrow 2C_2H_5OH + 2CO_2 + energy$$

$$RQ = \frac{CO_2}{O_2}$$
$$= \frac{2}{0}$$
$$= \infty$$

In reality, some respiration in the yeast cell will be aerobic. This means that at least a small volume of oxygen will be taken up and the RQ will be less than infinity. High RQ values indicate that alcoholic fermentation is occurring. Note that no RQ can be calculated for muscle cells using the lactate pathway because no carbon dioxide is produced:

glucose ($C_6H_{12}O_6$) $\longrightarrow$ 2 lactic acid ($C_3H_6O_3$)

PRACTICAL ACTIVITY 12.1

Measuring oxygen uptake and calculating RQs

Oxygen uptake during respiration can be measured using a **respirometer**. A respirometer suitable for measuring the rate of oxygen consumption of seeds or small terrestrial invertebrates at different temperatures is shown in Figure 12.16.

As the organisms respire, they absorb oxygen from the air around them. This reduces the volume of the air. Carbon dioxide produced in respiration is absorbed by a suitable chemical such as soda lime or a concentrated solution of potassium hydroxide (KOH) or sodium hydroxide (NaOH). Thus, the carbon dioxide produced does not increase the volume of the air.

Any change in the volume of air surrounding the organisms therefore results only from their oxygen consumption. Oxygen consumption can be measured by reading the level of the manometer fluid against the scale. You can measure the rate of oxygen consumption by dividing the volume of oxygen used by the time taken.

You may remember that any changes in temperature and pressure will also alter the volume of air in the apparatus. It is therefore important

that the temperature of the surroundings is kept constant while readings are taken. This could be done, for example, by using a thermostatically controlled water bath. You cannot do anything to control pressure, but if you use a second tube with no organisms inside it, then any changes in pressure will be the same in both tubes, and there will be no movement of the manometer fluid as a result. The presence of a control tube containing an equal volume of inert material to the volume of the organisms used helps to compensate for changes in atmospheric pressure.

You can investigate the effect of temperature on the rate of respiration by placing the apparatus in water baths at different temperatures, and measure the rate of oxygen consumption at each temperature.

Several repeat measurements should be made at each temperature, and mean values for oxygen

KEY WORD

respirometer: a piece of apparatus that can be used to measure the rate of oxygen uptake by respiring organisms

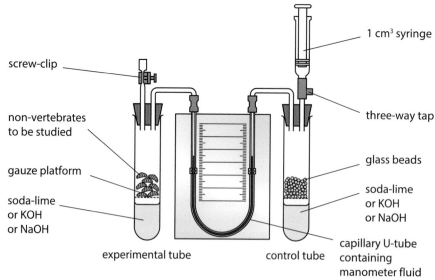

Figure 12.16: A respirometer.

CONTINUED

consumption calculated. A graph can then be plotted of mean rate of oxygen consumption against temperature.

The same apparatus can be used to measure the RQ of an organism. First, oxygen consumption at a particular temperature is found, exactly as described above. Let's say that this is $x\,cm^3\,min^{-1}$. Then the respirometer is set up with the same organism at the same temperature, but with no chemical to absorb carbon dioxide. Now, carbon dioxide given out will affect the volume and therefore the reading on the manometer. When the volumes of oxygen used and carbon dioxide released are the same, the level of the manometer fluid will not change and the RQ = 1. When more carbon dioxide is produced than

oxygen absorbed, the scale will show an increase in the volume of air in the respirometer (by $y\,cm^3\,min^{-1}$). The RQ can then be calculated:

$$RQ = \frac{CO_2}{O_2} - \frac{x + y}{x}$$

However, when less carbon dioxide is produced than oxygen absorbed, the volume of air in the respirometer will decrease (by $z\,cm^3\,min^{-1}$) and the calculation will be:

$$RQ = \frac{CO_2}{O_2} - \frac{x + y}{x}$$

(See Practical Investigations 8.1 and 8.2 in the Practical Workbook for additional information.)

PRACTICAL ACTIVITY 12.2

Measuring rate of respiration using redox indicators

One way of investigating the rate of respiration of yeast is to use a dye such as a solution of dichlorophenolindophenol, usually known as DCPIP, or a solution of methylene blue. These dyes do not damage cells and so can be added to a suspension of living yeast cells. Both of these dyes are blue, but they become colourless when they are reduced. They are examples of **redox indicators**.

You have seen that the removal of hydrogens from substrates is an important part of respiration. Usually, these hydrogens are picked up by NAD and FAD. However, if DCPIP or methylene blue is present, the dye can also pick up hydrogens and

become reduced. The faster the rate of respiration, the more hydrogens are released per unit time, and the faster the dyes are reduced. The rate of change from blue to colourless is a measure of the rate of respiration of the yeast.

This technique can be used to investigate the effect of various factors on yeast respiration, such as temperature, substrate concentration or different substrates.

(See Practical Investigation 8.3 in the Practical Workbook for additional information.)

KEY WORD

redox indicator: a substance that changes colour when it is oxidised or reduced

REFLECTION

It is thought that mitochondria were originally prokaryotic organisms (Archaea) that invaded another cell and somehow avoided being destroyed inside it.

*   What evidence is there, from the structure of mitochondria and their relationship with the rest of the cell, that supports this hypothesis?

*   If the original cell (before the mitochondrial invasion) could only produce ATP by glycolysis, how might this new symbiosis have affected the survival chances of the cell and its descendants?

What problems did you encounter while you were working on this activity? How did you solve them?

CONTINUED

Final reflection

Discuss with a friend which, if any, part of Chapter 12 you need to:

- read through again to make sure you really understand

- seek more guidance on, even after going over it again.

SUMMARY

Organisms require energy to stay alive. The energy used is normally the chemical potential energy of organic molecules, especially carbohydrates and lipids. The uses of the energy include anabolic reactions, active transport and movement.

ATP is used as the universal energy currency. ATP can be synthesised from ADP and phosphate using energy, and hydrolysed to ADP and phosphate to release energy.

Respiration is the sequence of enzyme-controlled steps by which an organic molecule, usually glucose, is broken down so that its chemical potential energy can be used to make ATP. In aerobic respiration, the sequence involves four main stages: glycolysis, the link reaction, the Krebs cycle and oxidative phosphorylation.

In glycolysis, glucose is first phosphorylated and then split into two triose phosphate molecules. These are further oxidised to pyruvate, giving a small yield of ATP and reduced NAD. Glycolysis occurs in the cell cytoplasm. When oxygen is available (aerobic respiration), the pyruvate passes to the matrix of a mitochondrion. In a mitochondrion, in the link reaction, pyruvate is decarboxylated and dehydrogenated and the remaining 2C acetyl unit combined with coenzyme A to give acetyl coenzyme A.

The acetyl coenzyme A enters the Krebs cycle in the mitochondrial matrix and donates the acetyl unit to oxaloacetate (4C) to make citrate (6C). The Krebs cycle decarboxylates and dehydrogenates citrate to oxaloacetate in a series of small steps. The oxaloacetate can then react with another acetyl coenzyme A from the link reaction.

Dehydrogenation provides hydrogen atoms, which are accepted by the carriers NAD and FAD. These pass to the inner membrane of the mitochondrial envelope, where the hydrogen atoms are split into protons and electrons.

In oxidative phosphorylation, the electrons are passed along a series of carriers. Some of the energy released as this happens is used to move protons from the mitochondrial matrix to the intermembrane space. This sets up a gradient of protons across the inner membrane of the mitochondrial envelope. Protons pass back into the matrix, moving down their concentration gradient by facilitated diffusion through protein channels in the inner membrane. An enzyme, ATP synthase, is associated with each of the proton channels. ATP synthase uses the energy of the proton gradient to phosphorylate ADP to ATP. At the end of the carrier chain, electrons and protons are recombined and reduce oxygen to water.

In the absence of oxygen as a hydrogen acceptor (in ethanol fermenation and lactate fermentation), a small yield of ATP is made through glycolysis, then removing hydrogen and producing ethanol or lactate. Rice has adaptations to allow it survive in anaerobic conditions.

The energy values of respiratory substrates depend on the number of hydrogen atoms per molecule. Lipids have a higher energy density than carbohydrates or proteins. The respiratory quotient (RQ) is the ratio of the volume of oxygen absorbed and the volume of carbon dioxide given off in respiration. The RQ reveals the nature of the substrate being respired. Carbohydrate has an RQ of 1.0, lipid 0.7 and protein 0.9. Rate of oxygen uptake, and hence RQ, can be measured using a respirometer.

Redox indicators can be used to measure the rate of respiration in yeast, and therefore to investigate the effect of factors such as temperature or substrate on concentration on the rate of respiration.

EXAM-STYLE QUESTIONS

1 a **Explain** why the energy value of lipid is more than twice that of carbohydrate. **[2]**

b Explain what is meant by *respiratory quotient (RQ)*. **[2]**

c Copy and complete the table to show the respiratory substrates with each of the given RQs.

Respiratory substrate	RQ
	1.0
	0.7
	0.9

[3]

d Measurements of oxygen uptake and carbon dioxide production by germinating seeds in a respirometer showed that $25\,cm^3$ of oxygen was used and $17.5\,cm^3$ of carbon dioxide was produced over the same time period.

  i **Calculate** the RQ for these seeds. **[2]**

  ii **Identify** the respiratory substrate used by the seeds. **[1]**

e Dahlia plants store a compound called inulin, which is a polymer of fructose. The structure of fructose is shown in the diagram.

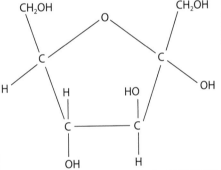

Calculate the RQ when inulin is hydrolysed and then respired aerobically. **[2]**

[Total: 12]

2 Copy and complete the following passage describing the adaptations of rice for growing with its roots submerged in water.

The stems and leaves of rice plants have very large .... in tissue called ...., which allow oxygen to pass from the air to the ....The roots are very shallow, giving them access to the higher concentration of ....in surface water. When oxygen concentrations fall, the roots can oxidise glucose through .... This produces ...., which is toxic. However, the root cells are tolerant of higher concentrations of this than are most cells and they also contain high concentrations of the enzyme ....to break it down. **[Total: 7]**

COMMAND WORDS

Explain: set out purposes or reasons / make the relationships between things evident / provide why and/or how and support with relevant evidence.

Calculate: work out from given facts, figures or information.

Identify: name / select / recognise.

CONTINUED

3 In aerobic respiration, the Krebs cycle is regarded as a series of small steps. One of these steps is the conversion of succinate to fumarate by an enzyme, succinate dehydrogenase A.

a **State** the role played by dehydrogenase enzymes in the Krebs cycle AND explain briefly the importance of this role in the production of ATP. **[3]**

b An investigation was carried out into the effect of different concentrations of aluminium ions on the activity of succinate dehydrogenase. The enzyme concentration and all other conditions were kept constant. The graph below shows the results of this investigation.

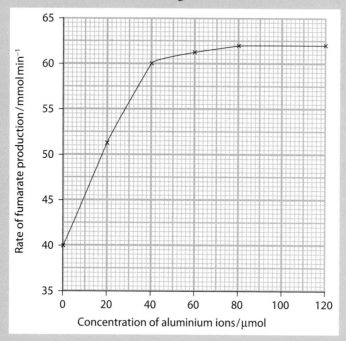

With reference to the graph:

i **describe** the effect of the concentration of aluminium ions on the rate of production of fumarate **[2]**

ii **suggest** an explanation for this effect. **[2]**

[Total: 7]

Cambridge International AS & A Level Biology (9700/04), Question 7, October/November 2007

SELF-EVALUATION CHECKLIST

After studying this chapter, complete a table like this:

I can	See section...	Needs more work	Almost there	Ready to move on
explain why living organisms need energy	12.1			
explain how ATP is suited for the role as the universal energy currency	12.1			
describe how ATP is synthesised in respiration	12.2			
describe glycolysis, the link reaction, the Krebs cycle and oxidative phosphorylation, and outline the roles of NAD, FAD and CoA	12.2			
describe how the structure of a mitochondrion is related to its function	12.3			
outline how lactate fermentation and ethanol formation provide a small quantity of ATP in anaerobic conditions	12.4			
explain how rice is adapted to grow with its roots submerged in water	12.4			
compare the energy values of different respiratory substrates	12.5			
calculate respiratory quotients	12.5			
describe how to carry out investigations using respirometers	12.5			
describe how to carry out investigations using redox indicators	12.5			

> Chapter 13
Photosynthesis

LEARNING INTENTIONS

In this chapter you will learn how to:

- explain how photosynthesis transfers energy from light to carbohydrate molecules
- describe how the structure of a chloroplast is related to its functions
- describe the roles of chloroplast pigments, and interpret absorption spectra and action spectra
- describe how to use chromatography to separate chloroplast pigments and calculate R_f values
- describe the reactions of the light-dependent stage of photosynthesis, including cyclic photophosphorylation and non-cyclic photophosphorylation
- describe the light-independent stage of photosynthesis
- explain the main limiting factors for photosynthesis, and interpret graphs showing the effects of these on the rate of photosynthesis
- describe how to investigate the effects of limiting factors on the rate of photosynthesis using aquatic plants
- describe how to investigate the effect of light intensity and light wavelengths on a chloroplast suspension, using a redox indicator.

BEFORE YOU START

Try this problem by yourself, and then discuss your ideas with a partner.

Two plants are placed in sealed containers, each with a small tube of hydrogencarbonate indicator. One container is covered with black paper. Light is shone on the other container.

What would you expect to happen to the indicator in each container over the next few hours? Why?

FUEL FROM ALGAE

Plants have evolved a chemical manufacturing system that humans still cannot equal in even the most sophisticated chemical laboratories. Despite millions of hours of research, we still have not managed to set up a chemical manufacturing system that can harvest light energy and use it to make complex chemicals, in the way that plants and other photosynthetic organisms do.

Various companies around the world have therefore been investigating the possibility of simply using photosynthetic protoctists to do this. The protoctists could use their chloroplasts and enzymes to produce fuel for use in machines, rather than fuel (in the form of carbohydrates) for the organisms themselves.

Figure 13.1 shows researchers working with flasks containing a single-celled photosynthetic protoctist called *Euglena*. They are using this organism to produce compounds that could be converted into fuel for aircraft and cars. In theory, this should be a big money-earner. Provide light, a suitable temperature and sufficient carbon dioxide, and just let the *Euglena* get on with the task. However, despite huge amounts of capital that have been invested in companies like this, so far none has been able to develop a large-scale production facility that can actually make a profit. Most of these companies have turned away from trying to produce fuel that can out-compete fossil fuels on costs. Instead, they are using the photosynthetic protoctists to produce higher-value products, such as cosmetics and animal feeds.

Figure 13.1: Researchers in San Diego, California, are investigating the conditions required for *Euglena* to produce fuels that can be processed to make diesel and gasoline.

Questions for discussion

- What could be the environmental advantages of using protoctists to produce fuels?

- What conditions would the protoctists need, in order to be able to produce large quantities of fuel?

- What might explain why it has proved to be so difficult to make this process work commercially on a large scale?

13.1 An energy transfer process

In Chapter 12 you learnt how all organisms use ATP as their energy currency. They make ATP by using the chemical potential energy contained in glucose and other organic molecules to join a phosphate group to ADP. This is done by respiration, which is a series of enzyme-controlled reactions that take place in every living cell.

In this chapter you will find out how the glucose that is used in respiration is produced. It is done by photosynthesis, in which energy in sunlight is transferred to carbohydrates such as glucose. Like three of the stages in respiration, photosynthesis happens in specialised organelles inside cells. These are chloroplasts, and they are found in all green plants and in many protoctists, such as *Euglena*.

An outline of photosynthesis

Before you look in detail at the series of reactions that happens during photosynthesis, it is useful to have an overview of the entire process.

Photosynthesis involves taking in carbon dioxide and reducing it – that is, adding hydrogen to it – to produce carbohydrate. The hydrogen for this process comes from water. The energy that drives the reactions comes from light, which is absorbed by a green pigment called **chlorophyll**.

The overall equation for photosynthesis is:

$$6CO_2 + 6H_2O \xrightarrow[\text{of chlorophyll}]{\text{light energy} \atop \text{in the presence}} C_6H_{12}O_6 + 6O_2$$

carbon dioxide   water   carbohydrate   oxygen

The two products of the reaction are carbohydrate and oxygen. Oxygen is a waste product of photosynthesis. It may be lost from the cells, or it may be used in respiration.

The reaction shown in the overall equation is actually made up of many smaller steps. These can be divided into two main stages – the **light-dependent stage** and the **light-independent stage**.

In the light-dependent stage, pigments including chlorophyll absorb energy from light. Some of this energy is used to split water molecules into hydrogen and oxygen. This is called **photolysis** (which means light splitting). The energy in the hydrogen is used make ATP, in a process called **photophosphorylation**. The hydrogen is eventually picked up by a coenzyme called **NADP**, to make reduced NADP.

Figure 13.2 summarises the inputs and outputs of the light-dependent stage.

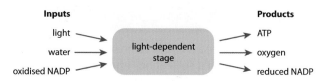

Figure 13.2: A simplified overview of the light-dependent stage of photosynthesis.

In the light-independent stage, the energy in the ATP, and the energy and hydrogens in the reduced NADP are used to reduce carbon dioxide and produce carbohydrates. This stage is also known as the **Calvin cycle**.

Both the light-dependent stage and the light-independent stage take place inside chloroplasts. Section 13.2 looks at the structure of a chloroplast, and how this is adapted for its function.

> ## KEY WORDS
>
> **chlorophyll:** a green pigment that absorbs energy from light, used in photosynthesis
>
> **light-dependent stage:** the first series of reactions that take place in photosynthesis; it requires energy absorbed from light
>
> **light-independent stage:** the final series of reactions that take place in photosynthesis; it does not require light but does need substances that are produced in the light-dependent stage
>
> **photolysis:** splitting a water molecule, using energy from light
>
> **photophosphorylation:** producing ATP using energy that originated as light
>
> **NADP:** a coenzyme that transfers hydrogen from one substance to another, in the reactions of photosynthesis
>
> **Calvin cycle:** a cycle of reactions in the light-independent stage of photosynthesis in which carbon dioxide is reduced to form carbohydrate

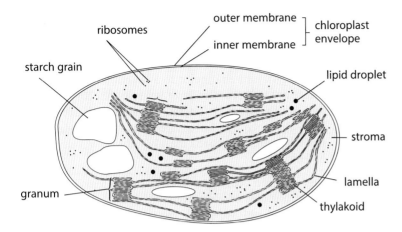

Figure 13.3: The structure of a chloroplast. Like mitochondria, chloroplasts have two membranes separating them from the cytoplasm, forming an envelope.

13.2 Structure and function of chloroplasts

Figure 13.3 and Figure 13.4 show the structure of a typical chloroplast. Chloroplasts are found in only some types of plant cell – mainly in palisade mesophyll and spongy mesophyll tissues in leaves. Each cell may contain many chloroplasts.

Each chloroplast is surrounded by an envelope of two membranes. Inside the chloroplast is a watery material that makes up the stroma. There are many enzymes and other substances in the stroma which, as you will see, are required for the reactions of the light-independent stage of photosynthesis. Like the matrix of a mitochondrion, the stroma of a chloroplast contains small ribosomes and small circles of DNA, used to synthesise proteins. The stroma also contains starch grains, which store some of the carbohydrate made, in an insoluble form.

Apart from the two membranes of the envelope, there are more membranes inside the chloroplast. These membranes are called lamellae. The membranes are arranged so that they produce fluid-filled sacs. The membranes that form these sacs are called thylakoid membranes, and the spaces inside the sacs are thylakoid spaces. In some parts of the chloroplast, the thylakoids are stacked up like a pile of coins or pancakes, and these stacks are called grana (singular: granum).

The membranes of the lamellae and thylakoids hold carrier molecules that work as an electron transport chain, in a very similar way to the membranes of the

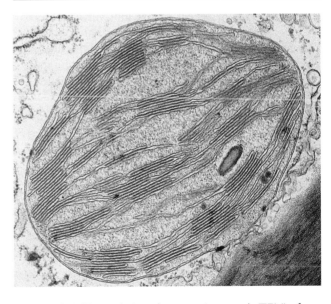

Figure 13.4: Transmission electron micrograph (TEM) of a chloroplast from a *Potamogeton* leaf (×21 000).

cristae in a mitochondrion. You will find out about the function of these carrier molecules later in this chapter.

Embedded tightly in the lamellae and thylakoid membranes are several different photosynthetic pigments. These are coloured substances that absorb energy from certain wavelengths (colours) of light. The most abundant pigment is chlorophyll, which comes in two forms – chlorophyll *a* and chloropyll *b*. Other pigments include carotene and xanthophyll.

Questions

1   Make a large, labelled diagram of the chloroplast shown in Figure 13.4. Use information in Figure 13.3 to label your diagram.

2   Compare the structures of a chloroplast and a mitochondrion.

Functions of chloroplast pigments

A pigment is a substance that absorbs some wavelengths of light and reflects others. The wavelengths it does not absorb are reflected back into our eyes. Chlorophyll looks green because it absorbs red light and reflects green light.

The majority of pigments in a chloroplast are chlorophyll *a* and chlorophyll *b*. This is why chloroplasts and the cells that contain them, and the leaves in which these cells are found, look green. Chlorophyll *a* absorbs slightly longer wavelengths of light than chlorophyll *b*. Carotene is also found in chloroplasts, and this absorbs blue light. The range of wavelengths absorbed by these three pigments is shown in Figure 13.5. This is called an absorption spectrum.

Questions

3   Use Figure 13.5 to work out what colour carotene is. Explain your answer.

4   Xanthophyll is yellow. Which wavelengths of light does xanthophyll **not** absorb?

The pigments in a thylakoid membrane are arranged in clusters called photosystems. Each photosystem is made up of large numbers of pigment molecules, plus some proteins. The pigments absorb energy from light, and channel it to a reaction centre. There are two types of photosystem, photosystem I and photosystem II. The main wavelength of light absorbed by photosystem I is 700 nm, while photosystem II absorbs mainly light of wavelength 680 nm.

The reaction centres of both photosystems contain two molecules of chlorophyll *a*. All the other pigments – chlorophyll *b*, carotene and xanthophyll – help to channel energy harvested from light to these chlorophyll *a* molecules. This increases the energy level of the electrons in the chlorophyll *a* molecules. It is these high-energy electrons that drive the steps that take place in the light-dependent stage of photosynthesis.

KEY WORDS

photosynthetic pigments: coloured substances that absorb light of particular wavelengths, supplying energy to drive the reactions in the light-dependent stage of photosynthesis

absorption spectrum: a graph showing the absorbance of different wavelengths of light by a photosynthetic pigment

photosystem: a cluster of light-harvesting pigments surrounding a reaction centre

reaction centre: the part of a photosystem towards which energy from light is funnelled; it contains a pair of chlorophyll a molecules, which absorb the energy and emit electrons

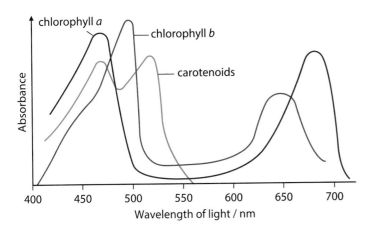

Figure 13.5: Absorption spectrum for chlorophyll *a*, chlorophyll *b* and carotene.

PRACTICAL ACTIVITY 13.1

Using chromatography to identify chloroplast pigments

Chromatography is a technique that can separate substances in a mixture according to their solubility in a solvent.

To separate and identify the pigments in a chloroplast, you first need to extract them. This can be done by crushing a leaf in a suitable solvent, such as a mixture of propanone and petroleum ether. It is important to make this extract as concentrated as you can, by using only a small amount of solvent and crushing the leaves very thoroughly. The extract must then be filtered, to obtain a dark green solution of the pigments.

Next, use a ruler and pencil to draw a line about 2 cm from the base of a rectangular piece of chromatography paper (Figure 13.6). Use a capillary tube, or a pipette with a very narrow point, to place a small drop of the green filtrate onto this line. Repeat over and over again, trying to produce an intensely green, very small spot of the filtrate. If you like, you can put more than one spot at different positions on the line, for example using extracts made from different kinds of leaves. Dry the spots, for example, using a hairdryer.

Now you can place the paper in a small amount of solvent in a glass vessel, such as gas jar or test tube, with the pencil line above the level of solvent. The

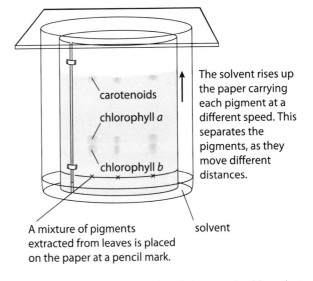

Figure 13.6: Chromatography of pigments in chloroplasts.

KEY WORD

chromatography: a technique that can separate substances in a mixture according to their solubility in a solvent

solvent will gradually move up the chromatography paper, taking the pigments in the spot with it. Some pigments will travel faster than others, and you will

CONTINUED

be able to see spots of colour in different positions up the paper.

When the solvent is close to the top of the paper, take the paper out of the solvent. Use a pencil to mark the position reached by the solvent. This is the solvent front. When the paper is dry, measure the distance of the solvent front from the original spot on the base line, and also the distances travelled by each of the pigments. You can then calculate the R_f values for each one:

$$R_f = \frac{\text{distance travelled by pigment spot}}{\text{distance travelled by solvent}}$$

The precise R_f values of the different pigments depend on the solvent you use. However, in general, carotenoids travel almost as far as the solvent front, and their R_f value is therefore close to 1. Next highest on the chromatogram is chlorophyll *a*, with chlorophyll *b* below it.

(See Practical Investigation 9.1 in the Practical Workbook for additional information.)

Action spectra

An **action spectrum** is a graph showing the rate of photosynthesis at different wavelengths of light.

You would expect the action spectrum to be related to the ability of the various pigments in the chloroplasts to absorb energy from different wavelengths of light. Look back at the absorption spectrum in Figure 13.5, which shows this ability. Compare Figure 13.5 with the action spectrum shown in Figure 13.7.

KEY WORDS

R_f **value:** a number that indicates how far a substance travels during chromatography, calculated by dividing the distance travelled by the substance by the distance travelled by the solvent; R_f values can be used to identify the substance

action spectrum: a graph showing the effect of different wavelengths of light on a process, for example the rate of photosynthesis

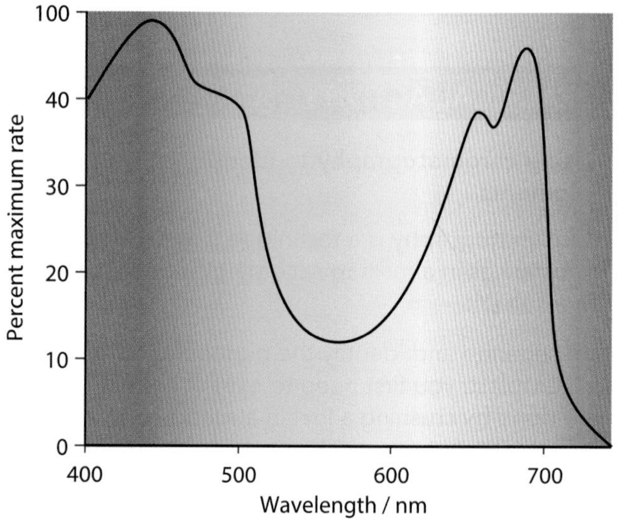

Figure 13.7: Action spectrum for photosynthesis.

Question

5   With a partner, discuss the similarities and differences between the absorption spectra for chloroplast pigments in Figure 13.5 and the action spectrum for photosynthesis in Figure 13.7. If you drew a 'composite' line for the absorption spectrum, combining all of the absorption spectra for the different pigments, how similar would this line be to the action spectrum for photosynthesis? Suggest reasons for any differences.

Be ready to share your ideas with the rest of the class.

13.3 The light-dependent stage of photosynthesis

We have seen that the light-dependent reactions include the splitting of water by photolysis to give hydrogen ions (protons) and the synthesis of ATP in photophosphorylation. The hydrogen ions combine with a carrier molecule, NADP, to make reduced NADP. ATP and reduced NADP are passed from the light-dependent to the light-independent stage.

Photophosphorylation of ADP to ATP can be cyclic or non-cyclic, depending on the pattern of electron flow in one or both types of photosystem.

Cyclic photophosphorylation

Cyclic photophosphorylation involves only photosystem I. ATP is formed, but not reduced NADP (Figure 13.8).

Light energy is absorbed by photosystem I and is passed to the reaction centre. This energy excites an electron in the chlorophyll *a* molecule to a higher energy level –

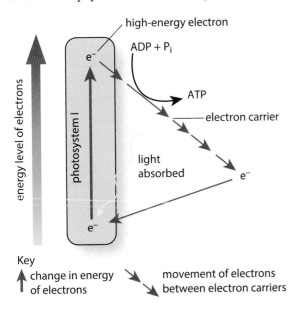

Key

↑ change in energy of electrons

↘ movement of electrons between electron carriers

Figure 13.8: Cyclic photophosphorylation.

so high that it is actually emitted from the chlorophyll molecule. This is called photoactivation.

The excited electrons are captured by an electron acceptor in a thylakoid membrane and passed along a chain of electron carriers. The carriers are alternately reduced (as they gain an electron) and oxidised (as they pass it to the next carrier). The electrons gradually lose energy as they pass along the chain. This energy is used to actively move protons from the stroma, across the thylakoid membrane, into the thylakoid space. This sets up a gradient for protons. They then move down their concentration gradient, by facilitated diffusion, through ATP synthase molecules. ATP is synthesised by adding P_i to ADP. This process is chemiosmosis, and you can see that it is almost identical to the process that takes place in mitochondria.

Question

6   In both mitochondria and chloroplasts, an energetic electron passes along a chain of carriers and the energy released is used to synthesise ATP by chemiosmosis. Suggest why the process occurring in mitochondria is known as oxidative phosphorylation, whereas in chloroplasts it is photophosphorylation.

KEY WORDS

cyclic photophosphorylation: the production of ATP using energy from light, involving only photosystem I

photoactivation: the emission of an electron from a molecule as a result of the absorption of energy from light

Non-cyclic photophosphorylation

Non-cyclic photophosphorylation involves both photosystems in the so-called 'Z scheme' of electron flow (Figure 13.9).

Energy from light is absorbed by both photosystems and excited electrons are emitted from their reaction centres. In both cases, these electrons are absorbed by electron acceptors and pass along chains of electron carriers in the thylakoid membranes. As you can see in Figure 13.9, the energy from the electron emitted from photosystem II is used to form ATP, but the energy from the electron emitted from photosystem I is passed to the coenzyme NADP. This produces reduced NADP. (NADP is very similar to the NAD that is used in respiration.)

The electrons lost from the photosystems must be replaced. Photosystem I receives the electron that was emitted from photosystem II, while photosystem II receives an electron from the splitting of water – which is described in the next section.

Photolysis of water

Photosystem II includes a water-splitting enzyme that catalyses the breakdown of water. This enzyme is sometimes known as the **oxygen-evolving complex**, or the water-splitting complex. It splits a water molecule into hydrogen ions (protons), electrons and oxygen:

$$H_2O \rightarrow 2H^+ + 2e^- + \tfrac{1}{2}O_2$$

Oxygen is a waste product of this process. It diffuses out of the chloroplast and is eventually lost from the cell or used in a mitochondrion for aerobic respiration.

The hydrogen ions combine with electrons from photosystem I and the coenzyme molecule NADP to give reduced NADP:

$$2H^+ + 2e^- + NADP \rightarrow reduced\ NADP$$

The ATP and reduced NADP that are synthesised in these light-dependent reactions can now be used in the light-independent reactions.

Question

7   It is often said that photosynthesis converts carbon dioxide to oxygen. Is this correct? Explain your answer.

KEY WORDS

non-cyclic photophosphorylation: the production of ATP using energy from light, involving both photosystem I and photosystem II; this process also produces reduced NADP

oxygen-evolving complex: an enzyme found in photosystem II that catalyses the breakdown of water, using energy from light

---

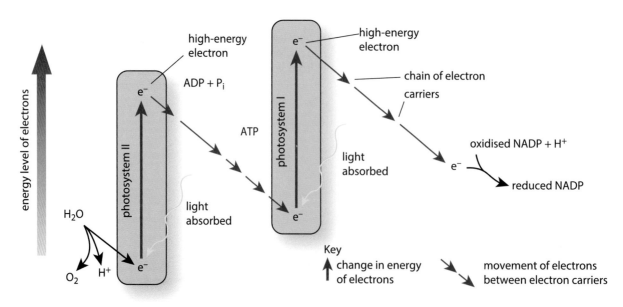

Figure 13.9: Non-cyclic photophosphorylation. This diagram is sometimes called the Z-scheme.

13.4 The light-independent stage of photosynthesis

In this stage, ATP and reduced NADP from the light-dependent stage are used to convert carbon dioxide to carbohydrates. These reactions all take place in the stroma of the chloroplast. They are known as the Calvin cycle, after Melvyn Calvin, who was one of the first scientists to work out the sequence of reactions (Figure 13.10).

This stage does not, in itself, require energy from light. It can take place either in light or in darkness. However, it does need inputs from the light-dependent stage, so it cannot go on for very long in darkness, as these supplies will run out.

The first step is the reaction of carbon dioxide with a five-carbon (5C) compound called **ribulose bisphosphate** (**RuBP**). This reaction is catalysed by an enzyme called ribulose bisphosphate carboxylase, or **rubisco**. The reaction produces two molecules of a 3C compound called **glycerate-3-phosphate** (**GP**). The carbon dioxide is now said to be 'fixed', as it has been removed from the environment and has become part of the plant cell.

GP is not a carbohydrate, but the next step converts it to one. Energy from ATP and hydrogen from reduced NADP – both made in the light-dependent stage – are used to reduce the GP to a phosphorylated three-carbon sugar, **triose phosphate** (**TP**).

Most (five-sixths) of the triose phosphates are used to regenerate RuBP. This process requires more ATP to be used. The rest of the triose phosphates (one-sixth) are used to produce other molecules needed by the plant.

Some of these triose phosphates condense to become hexose phosphates. These are used to produce starch for storage, sucrose for translocation around the plant, or cellulose for making cell walls. GP can be converted to glycerol and fatty acids to produce lipids for cellular membranes. Plants can also produce all 20 of the naturally occurring amino acids that they need for protein synthesis, using ammonium ions absorbed from the soil and carbohydrates produced in the light-independent reactions.

Questions

8   In your group, plan how you could use role-play to illustrate the events in the Calvin cycle.

   If there are enough people in your class, you can try out your plan. If not, write down your ideas in the form of a screenplay.

9   In separate experiments, an actively photosynthesising plant was supplied with one of two labelled reactants:

   - water containing the ^{18}O isotope of oxygen
   - carbon dioxide containing the ^{17}O isotope of oxygen.

   In which products of photosynthesis would these isotopes be found?

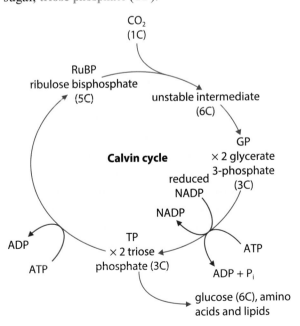

Figure 13.10: The Calvin cycle.

> **KEY WORDS**
>
> **ribulose bisphosphate (RuBP):** a five-carbon phosphorylated sugar which is the first compound to combine with carbon dioxide during the light-independent stage of photosynthesis
>
> **rubisco:** the enzyme that catalyses the combination of RuBP with carbon dioxide
>
> **glycerate-3-phosphate (GP):** a three-carbon compound which is formed when RuBP combines with carbon dioxide
>
> **triose phosphate (TP):** a three-carbon phosphorylated sugar, the first carbohydrate to be formed during the light-independent stage of photosynthesis

10 Explain why the Calvin cycle stops running when there is no light and the TP is used up.

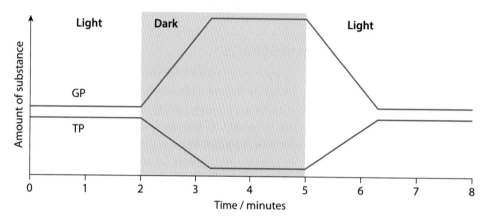

	¹⁸O	¹⁷O
A	oxygen produced by chloroplast grana	carbohydrate produced by the chloroplast stroma
B	oxygen produced by the chloroplast stroma	carbohydrate produced by chloroplast grana
C	carbohydrate produced by chloroplast grana	oxygen produced by the chloroplast stroma
D	carbohydrate produced by the chloroplast stroma	oxygen produced by chloroplast grana

11 The graph in Figure 13.11 shows the effect on the levels of GP and TP in a chloroplast when it is exposed to light, dark and then light again.

Describe **and** explain these results.

Figure 13.11: The effect of light and dark on the relative amounts of GP and TP in a chloroplast.

13.5 Limiting factors in photosynthesis

If you think back to what you have learnt about photosynthesis in this chapter, you will appreciate that plants need several different factors for photosynthesis to occur. These are:

- the presence of photosynthetic pigments
- a supply of carbon dioxide
- a supply of water
- light energy
- a suitable temperature.

A shortage of any one of these factors reduces the rate of photosynthesis below its maximum possible rate. In practice, the main external factors affecting the rate of photosynthesis are light intensity, light wavelength, temperature and carbon dioxide concentration. A shortage of water usually affects other processes in the plant before it affects photosynthesis.

Figure 13.12 shows how light intensity affects the rate of photosynthesis when temperature and carbon dioxide concentration are constant. You can see that the rate of photosynthesis increases as the light intensity increases.

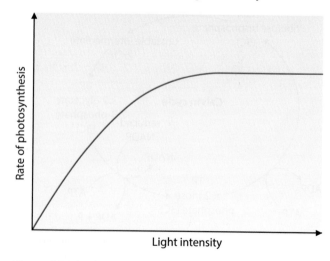

Figure 13.12: The rate of photosynthesis at different light intensities and constant temperature.

This is what you would expect – the greater the light intensity, the more energy is supplied and therefore the faster the light-dependent stage can occur. This in turn will supply more ATP and reduced NADP to the Calvin cycle, so that will also take place faster.

Over this part of the graph, light is said to be the **limiting factor** for photosynthesis. The limiting factor for any process is the factor that is in the shortest supply. If you increase the value of the limiting factor, then the rate will increase. Here, if you increase light intensity, then the rate of photosynthesis increases.

KEY WORD

limiting factor: the requirement for a process to take place that is in the shortest supply; an increase in this factor will allow the process to take place more rapidly

However, at higher light intensities, this relationship no longer holds and the rate of photosynthesis reaches a plateau. Something else must be limiting the rate of photosynthesis at these high light intensities. This could be any one of the factors in the bullet list above.

Figure 13.13 shows how temperature affects the rate of photosynthesis. For most metabolic reactions, temperature has a large effect, but it has no significant effect on light-dependent reactions. This is because these are driven by energy from light, not the kinetic energy of the reacting molecules. However, the Calvin cycle *is* affected by temperature, because these are more 'normal' enzyme-controlled reactions.

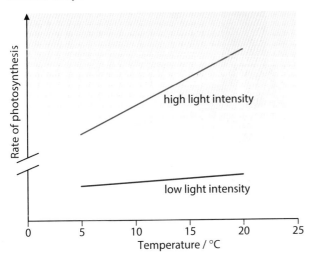

Figure 13.13: The rate of photosynthesis at two different light intensities and varying temperature.

In the graph in Figure 13.13, there are two lines – one for a plant provided with high light intensity, and one with only low light intensity. At high light intensity, the rate of photosynthesis increases as the temperature is increased. At low light intensity, increasing the temperature has little effect on the rate of photosynthesis.

What can explain this graph? At low light intensities, the limiting factor governing the rate of photosynthesis is the light intensity. It is light that is the factor in shortest supply. You can increase the rate by increasing the light intensity – which is why the 'high light intensity' line is above the 'low light intensity' line.

At high light intensity, the plant has more than enough light, so temperature is the limiting factor. You can increase the rate of photosynthesis by increasing the temperature. This is why the line slopes upwards steeply.

But at low light intensity, increasing the temperature does not have much effect on the rate. This is because, at low light intensity, it is light intensity, not temperature, that is the limiting factor. You can only increase the rate substantially by increasing the light intensity.

Now let's think about how three factors – temperature, light intensity and carbon dioxide concentration – can interact. The way in which these factors affect the rate of photosynthesis is shown in Figure 13.14.

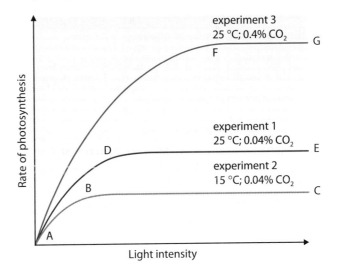

Figure 13.14: The effects of varying temperature, light intensity and carbon dioxide concentration on the rate of photosynthesis.

To interpret this graph, think about which factor is likely to be in the shortest supply at any point on the graph. Let's start with the lowest line, where both temperature and carbon dioxide concentration are low. As you increase the light intensity from its lowest level, you see a small rise in the rate because, at this left-hand side of the graph, it is light intensity that is the limiting factor. But the line levels out at a relatively low light intensity. This is because either temperature or carbon dioxide concentration is now the limiting factor – you need to increase one of these if you want to increase the rate of photosynthesis. It does not matter how much more light you give to the plant; it cannot photosynthesise any faster because it is too cold or it has too little carbon dioxide.

Now concentrate your attention on the middle line. Here, the plant is being kept at a higher temperature. You can see that this is allowing it to photosynthesise faster than at the lower temperature. Once again, increasing light intensity does increase the rate of photosynthesis at first, but, once again, the line levels off at a relatively low light intensity.

Finally, look at the top line. Now the plant has a higher temperature and a much higher concentration of carbon dioxide. The increased carbon dioxide is allowing it to photosynthesise faster. Increasing the light intensity has a much greater effect – the line rises much more steeply and over a much greater range of light intensities.

Questions

These questions are about Figure 13.14.

12 In your group, discuss the probable limiting factor at each of these areas of the graph. Be ready to share your decisions, and your reasoning, with the rest of the class.

a	A to B	**c**	A to D	**e**	A to F
b	B to C	**d**	D to E	**f**	F to G

13 Which stage of photosynthesis is limited by each of these factors? Explain your answers.

a   light intensity

b   temperature

c   carbon dioxide concentration

PRACTICAL ACTIVITY 13.2

Investigating the effect of factors on the rate of photosynthesis in aquatic plants

You can use *Elodea*, or other similar aquatic plants such as *Cabomba*, to investigate the effect on the rate of photosynthesis of altering:

- light intensity – by altering the distance, *d*, of a small light source from the plants (light intensity is proportional to $\frac{1}{d^2}$)

- wavelength of light – by using different colour filters, making sure that they each transmit the same light intensity

- concentration of carbon dioxide – by adding different quantities of sodium hydrogencarbonate ($NaHCO_3$) to the water surrounding the plant

- temperature of the water surrounding the plant – using a large container, such as a beaker, to help maintain the chosen temperatures.

It is important that the aquatic plant has been well illuminated before use and that the chosen stem is cut cleanly just before you put it into a test tube (Figure 13.15).

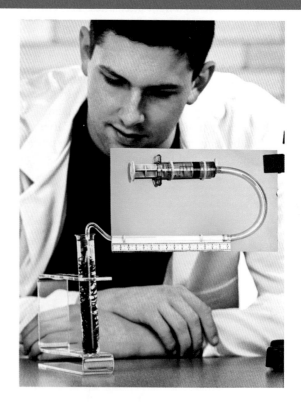

Figure 13.15: Investigating the effect of a factor on the rate of photosynthesis.

CONTINUED

The bubbles given off are mostly oxygen but they contain some nitrogen. To prevent these gases from dissolving in the water, rather than forming bubbles, the water needs to be well aerated (by bubbling air through it) before use.

The photograph shows a student collecting the gas in a special tube with a flared end, and then measuring the volume of gas produced in a certain length of time. Another method of measuring the rate is to cut discs from a leaf and push them to the bottom of a tube containing water. As the leaf discs photosynthesise, they release oxygen from the stomata on their lower surfaces. The oxygen bubbles attach to the disc and make it float. The faster the rate of photosynthesis, the faster the discs float to the water surface.

(See Practical Investigations 9.2 and 9.5 in the Practical Workbook for additional information.)

PRACTICAL ACTIVITY 13.3

Using a redox indicator to determine the effect of light intensity and light wavelength on the rate of photosynthesis

You have seen that the light-dependent reactions of photosynthesis involve the release of high-energy electrons from chlorophyll a molecules. In a chloroplast, these electrons are picked up by electron acceptors and then passed along the electron transport chain. But if you provide a redox indicator such as DCPIP or methylene blue (Chapter 12, Practical Activity 12.2), then the indicator takes up the electrons instead. This makes it change colour.

The rate at which the indicator changes colour from its oxidised state (blue) to its reduced state (colourless) is a measure of how quickly photosynthesis is taking place.

First, crush some leaves in a liquid called an isolation medium, to produce a concentrated leaf extract containing a suspension of chloroplasts. The medium must have approximately the same water potential as the leaf cells and contain a buffer, to keep the pH constant, and it should be ice cold, to avoid damage to the chloroplasts.

Then you need to set up several small tubes with different light intensities shining on them, or with different colours (wavelengths) of light of the same intensity shining on them. Add DCPIP or methylene blue indicator to each tube along with a small volume of the leaf extract. The time taken for the redox indicator to decolourise is an indication of the rate of photosynthesis.

(See Practical Investigation 9.4 in the Practical Workbook for additional information.)

REFLECTION

Aerobic respiration and photosynthesis take place inside mitochondria and chloroplasts respectively.

Thinking about these two organelles, and the reactions that take place inside them, what similarities can you identify?

Thinking about the two processes, how do their combined activities supply energy to all living cells?

Personal reflection question

If you were the teacher, what comments would you make about your performance in this activity?

Final reflection

Discuss with a friend which, in any, parts of Chapter 13 you need to:

- read through again to make sure you really understand
- seek more guidance on, even after going over it again.

SUMMARY

In photosynthesis, energy from light is absorbed by chloroplast pigments and transferred to chemical potential energy, which is used to produce complex organic molecules. In the light-dependent stage, water is split by photolysis to give hydrogen ions, electrons and oxygen. The hydrogen ions and electrons are used to reduce the coenzyme molecule NADP, and the oxygen is given off as a waste product.

Chloroplasts are adapted for the efficient absorption of light for the process of photosynthesis, and to provide a suitable environment for the reactions of the light-dependent and light-independent stages to occur efficiently.

A graph of the particular wavelengths of light that are absorbed by a photosynthetic pigment is called an absorption spectrum. A graph of the rate of photosynthesis at different wavelengths of light is called an action spectrum.

The different pigments present in a chloroplast can be separated by paper chromatography.

ATP is synthesised in the light-dependent stage by cyclic and non-cyclic photophosphorylation. During these reactions, the photosynthetic pigments of the chloroplast absorb energy from light and emit excited electrons. Energy from the electrons is used to synthesise ATP. ATP and reduced NADP are the two main products of the light-dependent stage of photosynthesis, and they then pass to the light-independent stage.

In the light-independent stage, carbon dioxide is fixed by combination with a 5C compound, RuBP. This reaction is catalysed by the enzyme ribulose bisphosphate carboxylase (rubisco). This produces two molecules of a 3C compound, GP. GP is reduced to carbohydrate, using ATP and reduced NADP from the light-dependent stage. This carbohydrate can be converted into other carbohydrates, amino acids and lipids or used to regenerate RuBP. This sequence of light-independent events is called the Calvin cycle.

When a process is affected by more than one factor, the rate of the process is limited by the factor closest to its lowest value, known as the limiting factor. Limiting factors for photosynthesis include light intensity and wavelength, carbon dioxide concentration and temperature.

The rate of production of oxygen of an aquatic plant can be used to measure the rate of photosynthesis.

The rate of decolourisation of a redox indicator such as DCPIP can be used to measure the rate of activity of a chloroplast suspension.

EXAM-STYLE QUESTIONS

1 a Explain how the inner membrane system of a chloroplast makes it well adapted for photosynthesis. [5]

   b Copy the table below and insert ticks or crosses to show which structural features are shared by a plant chloroplast and a typical prokaryotic cell.

   ✓ = structural feature shared; ✗ = structural feature not shared.

CONTINUED

Structural feature	Shared by chloroplast and typical prokaryotic cell
circular DNA	
DNA combined with structural protein to form chromosomes	
ribosomes about 18 nm in diameter	
complex arrangement of internal membranes	
peptidoglycan wall	
size ranges overlap	

[6]

[Total: 11]

2 a When isolated chloroplasts are placed in buffer solution with a blue dye such as DCPIP or methylene blue and illuminated, the blue colour disappears. Explain this observation. [4]

b Name the compound, normally present in photosynthesis, that is replaced by the blue dye in this investigation. [1]

[Total: 5]

3 Distinguish between:

a cyclic and non-cyclic photophosphorylation [2]

b photophosphorylation and oxidative phosphorylation [2]

c the roles of NAD and NADP in a plant. [2]

[Total: 6]

4 a Draw a simple flow diagram of the Calvin cycle to show the relative positions in the cycle of the following molecules:

- CO_2 (1C)
- triose phosphate (3C)
- GP (3C)
- RuBP (5C). [4]

b Show the point in the cycle at which the enzyme rubisco is active. [1]

[Total: 5]

5 a Explain what is meant by a limiting factor. [1]

b List **four** factors that may be rate-limiting in photosynthesis. [4]

c At low light intensities, increasing the temperature has little effect on the rate of photosynthesis. At high light intensities, increasing the temperature increases the rate of photosynthesis. Explain these observations. [5]

[Total: 10]

SELF-EVALUATION CHECKLIST

After studying this chapter, complete a table like this:

I can	See section...	Needs more work	Almost there	Ready to move on
explain how photosynthesis transfers energy from light to carbohydrate molecules	13.1			
explain how the structure of a chloroplast is related to its functions	13.2			
describe the roles of chloroplast pigments, and interpret absorption spectra and action spectra	13.2			
describe how to use chromatography to separate chloroplast pigments and calculate R_f values	13.2			
describe the reactions of the light-dependent stage of photosynthesis, including cyclic photophosphorylation and non-cyclic photophosphorylation	13.3			
describe the light-independent stage of photosynthesis	13.4			
explain the main limiting factors for photosynthesis, and intepret graphs showing the effects of these on the rate of photosynthesis	13.5			
describe how to investigate the effects of limiting factors on the rate of photosynthesis using aquatic plants	13.5			
describe how to investigate the effect of light intensity and light wavelengths on a chloroplast suspension, using a redox indicator	13.5			

› Chapter 14

Homeostasis

LEARNING INTENTIONS

In this chapter you will learn how to:

- explain the meaning of the term *homeostasis* and explain why homeostasis is important for mammals
- explain the principles of homeostasis in terms of: stimuli, receptors, effectors and the way in which responses are coordinated by the nervous and endocrine systems
- explain how negative feedback is involved in homeostatic mechanisms
- state that urea is produced by deamination of excess amino acids in the liver
- describe the structure of the human kidney and identify in diagrams the parts of a nephron and its associated blood vessels
- describe and explain how urine is formed in nephrons
- describe the detailed structure of the Bowman's capsule and proximal convoluted tubule and explain how they are adapted for ultrafiltration and selective reabsorption
- describe how the kidneys control the water potential of the blood and explain how osmoregulation is coordinated
- describe the principles of cell signalling as applied to the control of blood glucose concentration by glucagon
- explain how blood glucose concentration is controlled
- explain how test strips and biosensors are used for measuring the concentration of glucose in blood and urine and explain the roles of glucose oxidase and peroxidase enzymes

CONTINUED

- describe the structure and function of guard cells and explain how they regulate the width of the stomatal aperture
- explain that stomata control the entry of carbon dioxide by diffusion and regulate water loss by transpiration so balancing the needs for photosynthesis and conservation of water
- explain that stomata have daily rhythms of opening and closing and respond to changes in environmental conditions
- describe how abscisic acid is involved in the closure of stomata during times of water shortage.

BEFORE YOU START

Imagine a cell deep inside your liver and think about how it is kept alive. Think of all the substances that it needs to survive and all the waste it produces. Think also of the conditions which are kept at optimum levels for it to function efficiently and the systems of the body that work together to keep the cell alive.

Discuss your ideas with the class.

THE BLACK BEAR'S BIG SLEEP

It is metabolically expensive for a mammal such as the black bear, *Ursus americanus*, to maintain a constant, warm body temperature in long winters when it is very cold and food is hard to find. Black bears feed well during the summer to build up stores of energy-rich fat (Figure 14.1). In the autumn and early winter, the bears dig dens for themselves or find a ready-made one in somewhere like a cave. Once in their den, they curl up and sleep until the weather improves. Their metabolism adjusts for this lengthy period of inactivity when they do not eat, drink, urinate or defaecate. Their stores of fat and some muscle protein provide energy. The waste product of protein breakdown is urea, which is filtered from the blood by the kidneys. The kidneys continue to produce urine, but it is all reabsorbed by the bladder. The urea cannot be stored; instead, it is recycled by bacteria in the bear's gut. These bacteria break down urea to ammonia and carbon dioxide, which are absorbed into the blood. Carbon dioxide is breathed out and ammonia combined with glycerol from the breakdown of fat to make amino acids. The amino acids are used to synthesise the enzymes that are needed in larger quantities for the increased hydrolysis of fat to form fatty acids that are respired to provide energy during the bear's hibernation.

Figure 14.1: During the summer, black bears build up stores of fat for survival during the seven months or so when they do not eat.

Question for discussion

The weightlessness experienced by astronauts during space travel has significant effects on the normal working of their bodies.

There are plans for astronauts to travel long distances into space. For example, it takes spacecraft about seven months to reach Mars from Earth. Discuss the problems involved in maintaining the health of astronauts on a manned mission to Mars and suggest some solutions to the problems you identify.

14.1 Homeostasis

To function efficiently, organisms have control systems to keep their internal conditions near constant. This is known as homeostasis. Information about conditions inside the body and the external surroundings are detected by sensory cells. Some of the physiological factors controlled in homeostasis in mammals are:

- core body temperature

- metabolic wastes, particularly carbon dioxide and urea

- blood pH

- blood glucose concentration

- water potential of the blood

- the concentrations in the blood of the respiratory gases, oxygen and carbon dioxide.

Internal environment

The internal environment of an organism refers to all the conditions inside the body. These are the conditions in which cells function. For a cell, its immediate environment is the tissue fluid that surrounds it. Many features of the tissue fluid influence how well the cell functions. Four features of tissue fluid that influence cell activities are:

- temperature – low temperatures slow down metabolic reactions; at high temperatures proteins, including enzymes, are denatured and cannot function (Chapter 3, Section 3.4, Factors that affect enzyme action)

- water potential – if the water potential decreases, water may move out of cells by osmosis, causing metabolic reactions in the cell to slow or stop; if the water potential increases, water may enter the cell causing it to swell and maybe burst (Chapter 4, Section 4.5, Movement of substances across membranes)

- concentration of glucose in the blood – glucose is the fuel for respiration, so lack of it causes respiration to slow or stop, depriving the cell of an energy source; too much glucose may cause water to move out of the cell by osmosis, again disturbing the metabolism of the cell (Section 14.4, The control of blood glucose)

- pH – enzyme activity is influenced by pH; the pH of cytoplasm is between 6.5 and 7.0 and if it fluctuates outside this range, enzymes will function less efficiently and will be denatured at extreme values of pH (Chapter 3, Section 3.4 Factors that affect enzyme action).

In general, homeostatic mechanisms work by controlling the composition of blood, which controls the composition of tissue fluid. See Chapter 8 to remind yourself about the relationship between blood and tissue fluid. There are control mechanisms for the different aspects of the blood and tissue fluid. These include the four physiological factors listed above. In this chapter, you look at two of these – water potential (Section 14.2) and blood glucose concentration (Section 14.4).

Homeostatic control

Most control mechanisms in living organisms use a negative feedback control loop (Figure 14.2) to maintain homeostatic balance. This involves a receptor

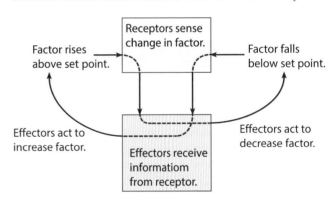

Figure 14.2: A negative feedback control loop.

(or sensor) and an **effector**. Effectors include muscles and glands. The receptor detects **stimuli** (singular: **stimulus**) that are involved with the condition (or physiological factor) being regulated. A stimulus is any change in a factor, such as a change in blood temperature or the water content of the blood. The body has receptors which detect external stimuli and other receptors that detect internal stimuli. These receptors send information about the changes they detect through the nervous system to a central control in the brain or spinal cord. This sensory information is known as the input. The central control instructs an effector to carry out an action, which is called the output. These actions are sometimes called **corrective actions** as their effect is to correct (or reverse) the changes that are detected.

Continuous monitoring of the factor by receptors produces a steady stream of information to the control centre so that continuous adjustments to the output can be made. As a result, the factor fluctuates around a particular 'ideal' value or **set point**. The mechanism that keeps changes in the factor at or near the set point is known as negative feedback. In these systems, an increase in the factor results in something happening that makes the factor decrease. Similarly, if there is a decrease in the factor, then something happens to make it increase.

Homeostatic mechanisms involve negative feedback because it minimises the difference between the actual value of the factor and the ideal value or set point. The factor never stays exactly constant, but fluctuates a little above and a little below the set point. Human body temperature as measured in the mouth often fluctuates between 36.4 °C and 37.6 °C. The actual range depends on a variety of factors such as age, sex and the time of day.

The homeostatic mechanisms in mammals require information to be transferred between different parts of the body. There are two coordination systems in mammals that do this: the nervous system and the endocrine system.

- In the nervous system, information in the form of electrical impulses is transmitted along neurones.

- The endocrine system uses chemical messengers called **hormones** that travel in the blood, in a form of long-distance cell signalling.

Question

1   a   Describe the immediate environment of a typical cell within the body of mammal.

   b   Explain why it is important that the internal environment of a mammal is carefully regulated.

   c   Explain how the following are involved in maintaining the internal environment of a mammal: stimuli, receptors, coordination systems and effectors.

   d   Distinguish between the input and the output in a homeostatic control mechanism.

Sometimes control mechanisms do not respond via negative feedback. If a person breathes air that has very high carbon dioxide content, a high concentration of carbon dioxide in the blood results. This is sensed by carbon dioxide receptors, which cause the breathing rate to increase. So the person breathes faster, taking in even more carbon dioxide, which stimulates the receptors even more, so the person breathes faster and faster. This is an example of a **positive feedback**. You can see that positive feedback cannot play any role in keeping conditions in the body constant.

KEY WORDS

effector: a tissue or organ that carries out an action in response to a stimulus; muscles and glands are effectors

stimulus (plural: **stimuli**): a change in the external or internal environment that is detected by a receptor and which may cause a response

corrective action: a response or series of responses that return a physiological factor to the set point so maintaining a constant environment for the cells within the body

set point: the ideal value of a physiological factor that the body controls in homeostasis

hormone: a substance secreted by an endocrine gland that is carried in blood plasma to another part of the body where it has an effect

positive feedback: a process in which a change in some parameter such as a physiological factor brings about processes that move its level further in the direction of the initial change

---

Excretion

Many of the metabolic reactions occurring within the body produce unwanted substances. Some of these are toxic (poisonous). The removal of these unwanted products of metabolism is known as excretion.

Many excretory products are formed in humans, but two are made in much greater quantities than others. These are carbon dioxide and urea. Carbon dioxide is produced continuously by cells that are respiring aerobically. The waste carbon dioxide is transported from the respiring cells to the lungs, in the bloodstream (Chapter 8, Section 8.5, Blood). Gas exchange occurs within the lungs, and carbon dioxide diffuses from the blood into the alveoli; it is then excreted in the air we breathe out (Chapter 9, Section 9.5, Alveoli).

Urea is produced in the liver. It is produced from excess amino acids and is transported from the liver to the kidneys, in solution in blood plasma. The kidneys remove urea from the blood and excrete it dissolved in water; the solution is called urine.

Deamination

If more protein is eaten than is needed, the excess cannot be stored in the body. It would be wasteful, however, simply to get rid of all the excess, because the amino acids provide useful energy. To make use of this energy, the liver removes the amine groups in a process known as deamination.

Figure 14.3 shows how deamination takes place. In the liver cells, the amine group ($-NH_2$) of an amino acid is removed, together with an extra hydrogen atom. These combine to produce ammonia (NH_3). The keto acid that remains may enter the Krebs cycle and be respired or it may be converted to glucose or converted to glycogen or fat for storage.

Ammonia is a very soluble and highly toxic compound. In many aquatic animals (e.g. fish that live in fresh water) ammonia diffuses from the blood and dissolves in the water around the animal. However, in terrestrial animals such as humans, ammonia increases the pH in cytoplasm; it interferes with metabolic processes such as respiration and with cell signalling in the brain. Damage is prevented by immediately converting ammonia to urea, which is less soluble and less toxic. Several reactions, known as the urea cycle, are involved in combining ammonia and carbon dioxide to form urea. An adult human produces around 25–30 g of urea per day.

Urea is the main nitrogenous excretory product of humans. We also produce small quantities of other nitrogenous excretory products, mainly creatinine and uric acid. A substance called creatine is made in the liver, from certain amino acids. Much of this creatine is used in the muscles, in the form of creatine phosphate, where it acts as an energy store. However, some is converted to creatinine and excreted. Uric acid is made from the breakdown of purines from nucleotides, not from amino acids.

> **KEY WORDS**
>
> **excretion:** the removal of toxic or waste products of metabolism from the body
>
> **urea:** a nitrogenous excretory product produced in the liver from the deamination of amino acids
>
> **deamination:** the breakdown of excess amino acids in the liver, by the removal of the amine group; ammonia and, eventually, urea are formed from the amine group

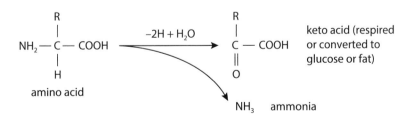

Figure 14.3: Amino acids are deaminated in the liver to form ammonia and keto acids. Ammonia is converted into urea, which is then released into the blood to be excreted by the kidneys.

Urea diffuses from liver cells into the blood plasma. All of the urea made each day must be excreted, or its concentration in the blood would build up and become dangerous. As the blood passes through the kidneys, the urea is filtered out and excreted. To explain how this happens, you must first look at the structure of a kidney.

Question

2 a   Uric acid is a nitrogenous waste product, which is produced from the breakdown of purines. What are purines and what are they used for?

   b   Explain why it is important that carbon dioxide and nitrogenous wastes are excreted and not allowed to accumulate in the body.

14.2 The structure of the kidney

Figure 14.4 shows the position of the kidneys in the body, together with their related structures. Each kidney receives blood from a renal artery, and returns blood via a renal vein. A narrow tube, called the ureter, carries urine from the kidney to the bladder. From the bladder, a single tube, called the urethra, carries urine to the outside of the body.

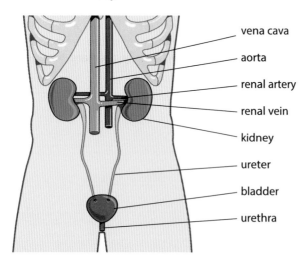

vena cava
aorta
renal artery
renal vein
kidney
ureter
bladder
urethra

Figure 14.4: Position of the kidneys and associated structures in the human body.

A longitudinal section through a kidney (Figure 14.5b) shows that it has three main areas. The whole kidney is covered by a fairly tough fibrous capsule, beneath which is the cortex. The central area is made up of the medulla. Where the ureter joins, there is an area called the renal pelvis.

A section through a kidney, seen through a microscope (Figure 14.6), shows it to be made up of thousands of tubules, called **nephrons**, and many blood vessels. Figure 14.7a shows the position of a single nephron, and Figure 14.7b shows its structure. One end of the tubule forms a cup-shaped structure called **Bowman's capsule**, which surrounds a network of capillaries called a **glomerulus**. The glomeruli and capsules of all the nephrons are in the cortex of the kidney. From the capsule, the tubule runs towards the centre of the kidney, first forming a twisted region called the **proximal convoluted tubule**, and then a long U-shaped tubule in the medulla called the **loop of Henle**. The first part of the loop is the descending limb. The ascending limb runs back into the cortex, where it forms another twisted region called the **distal convoluted tubule**, before finally joining a **collecting duct** that leads down through the medulla and into the renal pelvis.

KEY WORDS

nephron: the structural and functional unit of the kidney composed of Bowman's capsule and a tubule divided into three regions: proximal convoluted tubule, loop of Henle and distal convoluted tubule

Bowman's capsule: the cup-shaped part of a nephron that surrounds a glomerulus and collects filtrate from the blood

glomerulus: a group of capillaries within the 'cup' of a Bowman's capsule in the cortex of the kidney

proximal convoluted tubule: part of the nephron that leads from Bowman's capsule to the loop of Henle

loop of Henle: the part of the nephron between the proximal and distal convoluted tubules

distal convoluted tubule: part of the nephron that leads from the loop of Henle to the collecting duct

collecting duct: tube in the medulla of the kidney that carries urine from the distal convoluted tubules of many nephrons to the renal pelvis

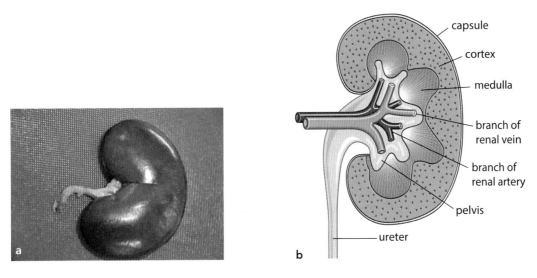

Figure 14.5: a A kidney with ureter attached; **b** a kidney cut in half longitudinally.

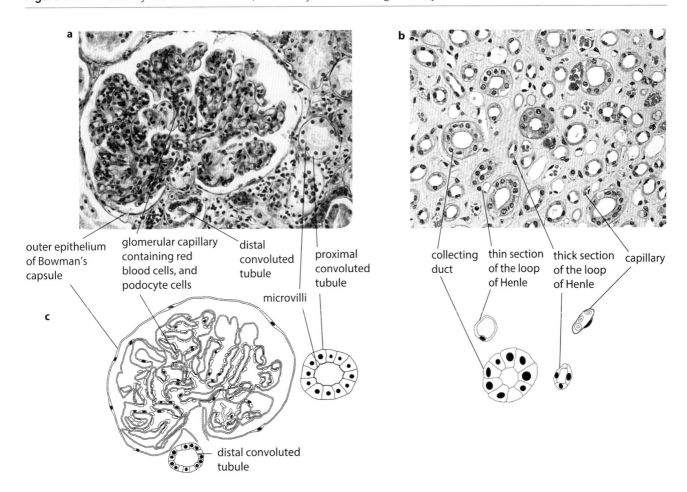

Figure 14.6: a Photomicrograph of a section through the cortex of the kidney showing a glomerulus and Bowman's capsule surrounded by proximal and distal convoluted tubules (×150); **b** photomicrograph of a section through the medulla of a kidney (×300); **c** interpretive drawings.

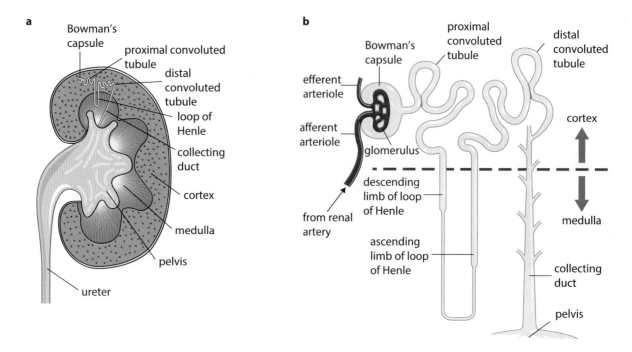

Figure 14.7: a Section through the kidney to show the position of a nephron; **b** a nephron. The fluid in the nephron is filtrate, formed from blood plasma. By the time the fluid reaches the collecting duct it is urine.

Blood vessels are closely associated with the nephrons (Figure 14.8). Each glomerulus is supplied with blood that flows from a branch of the renal artery through an **afferent arteriole**. The capillaries of the glomerulus rejoin to form an **efferent arteriole**. Blood flows through the efferent arteriole into a network of capillaries running closely alongside the rest of the nephron and the collecting duct. Blood from these capillaries flows into venules that empty into a branch of the renal vein.

The kidney makes urine in a two-stage process. The first stage, **ultrafiltration**, involves filtering small molecules,

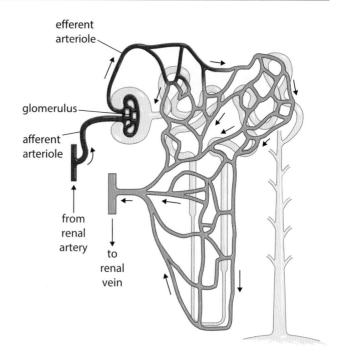

Figure 14.8: The blood supply associated with a nephron. There are also many capillaries around the collecting ducts (see Figures 14.6 and 14.18).

KEY WORDS

afferent arteriole: arteriole leading to glomerular capillaries

efferent arteriole: arteriole leading away from glomerular capillaries

ultrafiltration: filtration on a molecular scale separating small molecules from larger molecules, such as proteins (e.g. the filtration that occurs as blood flows through capillaries, especially those in glomeruli in the kidney)

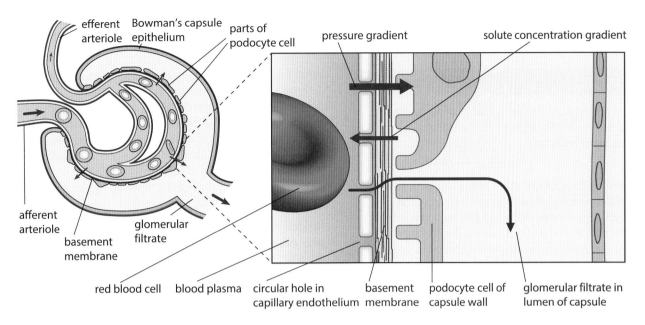

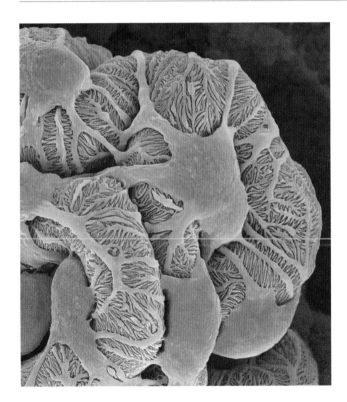

Figure 14.9: Detail of the endothelium of a glomerular capillary and Bowman's capsule. The arrows show how the net effect of higher pressure in the capillary and lower solute concentration in the Bowman's capsule forces fluid from the plasma into the lumen of the capsule to form filtrate. The basement membrane acts as a molecular filter.

Figure 14.10: A false-colour scanning electron micrograph (SEM) of podocytes (×3900). The podocytes are the blue-green cells with their extensions wrapped around the blood capillary, which is purple.

including urea, out of the blood and into the Bowman's capsule to form filtrate. From Bowman's capsule, the filtrate flows along the nephron towards the collecting duct. The second stage, **selective reabsorption**, involves taking back any useful molecules from the filtrate as it flows along the nephron.

> ### KEY WORD
>
> **selective reabsorption:** movement of certain substances from the filtrate in nephrons back into the blood

Ultrafiltration

Figure 14.9 shows a section through part of a glomerulus and Bowman's capsule. The blood in the glomerular capillaries is separated from the lumen of the Bowman's capsule by two cell layers and a basement membrane. The first cell layer is endothelium of the capillary. Each endothelial cell is perforated by many thousands of tiny membrane-lined circular holes which are about 60–80 nm in diameter. Next comes the basement membrane, which is made up of a network of collagen and glycoproteins. The second cell layer is formed from epithelial cells, which make up the inner lining of Bowman's capsule.

These cells have many tiny finger-like projections with gaps in between them, and are called **podocytes** (Figure 14.10).

KEY WORD

podocyte: one of the cells that makes up the lining of Bowman's capsule surrounding the glomerular capillaries

The holes in the capillary endothelium and the gaps between the podocytes make it relatively easy for substances dissolved in the blood plasma to pass from the blood into the capsule. However, the basement membrane stops large protein molecules from getting through. Any protein molecule with a relative molecular mass over about 69 000 cannot pass through the basement membrane and so cannot escape from the glomerular capillaries. This basement membrane, therefore, acts as a filter. Red and white blood cells and platelets are too large to pass through the perforations in the endothelium, so they remain in the blood. Table 14.1 shows the relative concentrations of substances in the blood and in the glomerular filtrate. You will see that glomerular filtrate is identical to blood plasma except that there are almost no plasma proteins in it.

Factors affecting glomerular filtration rate

The rate at which the fluid filters from the blood in the glomerular capillaries into the Bowman's capsule

Substance	Concentration in blood plasma / g dm⁻³	Concentration in glomerular filtrate / g dm³
water	900	900
plasma proteins	80.0	0.05
amino acids	0.5	0.5
glucose	1.0	1.0
urea	0.3	0.3
uric acid	0.04	0.04
creatinine	0.01	0.01
inorganic ions (mainly Na⁺, K⁺ and Cl⁻)	7.2	7.2

Table 14.1: Concentrations of substances in the blood and in the glomerular filtrate.

is called the glomerular filtration rate. In a human, for all the glomeruli in both kidneys, the rate is about 125 cm³ min⁻¹.

What makes the fluid filter through so quickly? This is determined by the differences in water potential between the plasma in glomerular capillaries and the filtrate in the Bowman's capsule. You will remember that water moves from a region of higher water potential to a region of lower water potential, down a water potential gradient (Chapter 4, Section 4.5, Movement of substances across membranes). Water potential is lowered by the presence of solutes, and raised by high pressures.

Inside the capillaries in the glomerulus, the blood pressure is relatively high, because the diameter of the afferent arteriole is wider than that of the efferent arteriole, causing pressure inside the glomerulus. This tends to raise the water potential of the blood plasma above the water potential of the contents of Bowman's capsule (Figure 14.9).

However, the concentration of solutes in the blood plasma in the capillaries is *higher* than the concentration of solutes in the filtrate in the Bowman's capsule. This is because, while most of the contents of the blood plasma can filter through the basement membrane and into the capsule, the plasma protein molecules are too big to get through, and so they stay in the blood (Table 14.1). This difference in solute concentration tends to make the water potential in the blood capillaries *lower* than that of the filtrate in the Bowman's capsule.

Overall, the effect of differences in pressure outweighs the effect of the differences in solute concentration so that the water potential of the blood plasma in the glomerulus is higher than the water potential of the filtrate in the capsule. As a result, water continues to move down the water potential gradient from the blood into the capsule as blood flows through the glomerulus.

Selective reabsorption

Many of the substances in the glomerular filtrate need to be kept in the body, so they are reabsorbed into the blood as the fluid passes along the nephron. As only certain substances are reabsorbed, the process is called selective reabsorption.

Reabsorption in the proximal convoluted tubule

Most of the reabsorption takes place in the proximal convoluted tubule. The lining of this part of the nephron is made of a single layer of cuboidal epithelial cells. These cells are adapted for their function of reabsorption by having:

- many microvilli on the surface facing the lumen (the luminal membrane) of the nephron to increase the surface area for reabsorption of substances from filtrate in the lumen (Figure 14.11)
- many co-transporter proteins in the luminal membrane

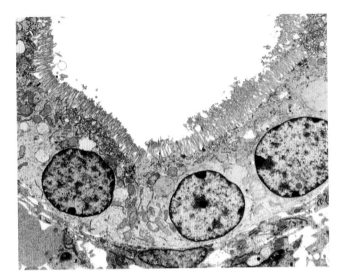

Figure 14.11: A false-colour transmission electron micrograph (TEM) of cuboidal epithelial cells that form the lining of the proximal convoluted tubule (×2200). There are many microvilli over the luminal surface of the cells to give a large surface area and many mitochondria to provide energy for selective reabsorption of ions, glucose and amino acids.

- tight junctions that hold adjacent (neighbouring) cells together firmly so that fluid cannot pass *between* the cells (all substances that are reabsorbed must go through the cells)
- many mitochondria to provide energy for sodium–potassium (Na^+–K^+) pump proteins in the basal membranes of the cells.

Blood capillaries are very close to the outer surface of the tubule. The blood in these capillaries has come directly from the glomerulus, so it has much less plasma in it than usual and has lost much of its water and many of the ions and other small solutes.

The basal membranes of the cells lining the proximal convoluted tubule are those nearest the blood capillaries. Sodium–potassium pumps in these membranes move sodium ions out of the cells (Figure 14.12). The sodium

ions are carried away in the blood. The pumping of sodium ions out of the cells lowers the concentration of sodium ions inside the cells, so that sodium ions in the filtrate diffuse down their concentration gradient through the luminal membranes. However, sodium ions do not diffuse freely through the membrane: they can only enter through special co-transporter proteins in the membrane. There are several different kinds of co-transporter protein, each of which transports a sodium ion and something else, such as glucose or a specific type of amino acid. This is the same method of membrane transport that moves sucrose into companion cells in phloem tissue (Chapter 7, Section 7.5, Transport of assimilates)

The passive movement of sodium ions *into* the cells down their concentration gradient provides the energy to move glucose molecules in this way into the cells, even against a concentration gradient. This movement of glucose and amino acids is an example of indirect or secondary active transport, since the energy (as ATP) is used in the pumping of sodium ions, not in moving these solutes. Once inside the cell, glucose diffuses down its concentration gradient, through a transport protein in the basal membrane, into the blood.

All of the glucose in the glomerular filtrate is transported out of the proximal convoluted tubule and into the blood. Normally, no glucose is left in the filtrate, so no glucose is present in urine. Similarly, amino acids, vitamins, and many sodium ions and chloride ions (Cl^-) are reabsorbed in the proximal convoluted tubule.

The removal of these solutes from the filtrate greatly *increases* its water potential. The movement of these solutes into capillaries *decreases* the water potential of the blood. There is now a steep water potential gradient between filtrate and blood. Water moves down this gradient through the cells and into the blood by osmosis. The water and reabsorbed solutes are carried away, back into the circulation.

Surprisingly, quite a lot of urea is reabsorbed too. Cell surface membranes are slightly permeable to urea. Its concentration in the filtrate is considerably higher than in the capillaries, so it diffuses passively through the cells of the proximal convoluted tubule and into the blood. About half of the urea in the filtrate is reabsorbed in this way.

The reabsorption of so much water and solutes from the filtrate in the proximal convoluted tubule greatly reduces the volume of filtrate remaining. In an adult human, around $125\,cm^3$ of filtrate enters the proximal tubules every minute, but only about 64% of this passes into the loop of Henle (Figure 14.8).

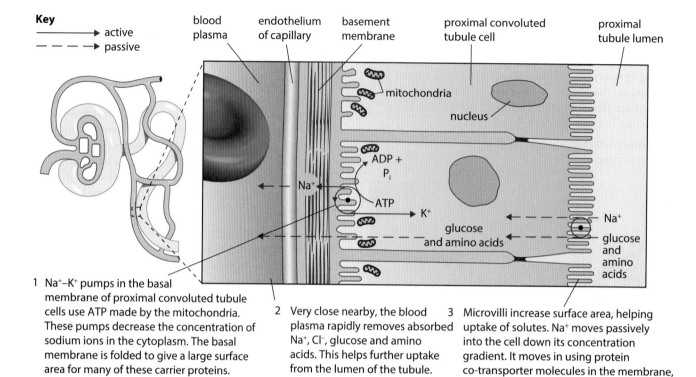

Key

→ active

– – – → passive

1 Na⁺–K⁺ pumps in the basal membrane of proximal convoluted tubule cells use ATP made by the mitochondria. These pumps decrease the concentration of sodium ions in the cytoplasm. The basal membrane is folded to give a large surface area for many of these carrier proteins.

2 Very close nearby, the blood plasma rapidly removes absorbed Na⁺, Cl⁻, glucose and amino acids. This helps further uptake from the lumen of the tubule.

3 Microvilli increase surface area, helping uptake of solutes. Na⁺ moves passively into the cell down its concentration gradient. It moves in using protein co-transporter molecules in the membrane, which bring in glucose and amino acids at the same time.

Figure 14.12: Reabsorption in the proximal convoluted tubule. As well as Na⁺–K⁺ pump proteins, the basal membrane has many transport proteins for the facilitated diffusion of solutes, such as glucose and amino acids from the cells into the blood.

Questions

3   a   Where has the blood in the capillaries surrounding the proximal convoluted tubule come from?

   b   What solutes will this blood contain that are **not** present in the glomerular filtrate?

   c   How might this help in the reabsorption of water from the proximal convoluted tubule?

   d   State the name of the process by which water is reabsorbed.

4   a   Calculate the volume of filtrate that enters the loops of Henle from the proximal convoluted tubules each minute.

   b   Although almost half of the urea in the glomerular filtrate is reabsorbed from the proximal convoluted tubule, the concentration of urea in the fluid in the nephron actually increases as it passes along the proximal convoluted tubule. Explain why this is so.

   c   Explain how each of these features of the cells in the proximal convoluted tubules adapts them for the reabsorption of solutes:

      i   microvilli

      ii   many mitochondria

      iii folded basal membranes.

Reabsorption in the loop of Henle and collecting duct

You can see from Figure 14.7 that the loops of Henle are parallel to the collecting ducts in the medulla. The function of these loops is to create a very high concentration of sodium and chloride ions in the tissue fluid in the medulla. This is partly achieved by active transport by the cells of the thick region of the ascending limb of each loop (Figure 14.6b and c). The concentration of solutes in the medulla of human kidneys can be as much as four times the concentration of blood plasma. As you will see, creating a tissue fluid in the medulla enables a lot of water to be reabsorbed from the fluid in the collecting duct as it flows through the medulla. As a result, the kidneys retain water in the body rather than excreting it in the urine, so helping to prevent dehydration.

After leaving the loop of Henle, the filtrate continues through the distal convoluted tubule into the collecting duct, which runs into the medulla again. It passes again through the regions where the solute concentration of the tissue fluid is very high and the water potential very low. Therefore, water can move out of the collecting duct by osmosis until the water potential of urine is the same as the water potential of the tissue fluid in the medulla, which may be much greater than the water potential of the blood. The degree to which this happens is controlled by antidiuretic hormone (ADH).

KEY WORD

antidiuretic hormone (ADH): hormone secreted from the posterior pituitary gland that increases water reabsorption in the kidneys and therefore reduces water loss in urine

---

Question

5   Discuss with others how human kidneys can reabsorb so much water from the filtrate that they are able to produce urine four times more concentrated than blood plasma. Look back to Chapter 4 to make sure you use the term *water potential* correctly.

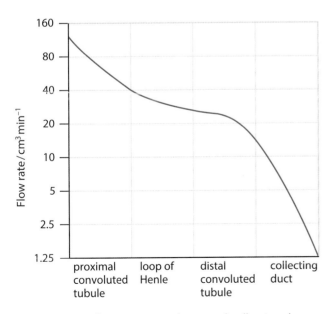

Figure 14.13: Flow rates in nephrons and collecting ducts.

The ability of some small mammals, such as rodents, to produce very concentrated urine is related to the relative thickness of the medulla in their kidneys. The maximum concentration of urine that humans can produce is four times that of the blood plasma. Desert rodents, such as gerbils and kangaroo rats, can produce urine that is about 20 times the concentration of their blood plasma. This is possible because the medulla is relatively large and the cells that line the ascending limb of their loops of Henle have deep infolds. They also have many Na^+–K^+ pumps and their cytoplasm has many mitochondria, each with many cristae. This means the cells can produce a lot of ATP to provide energy to pump sodium ions into the tissue fluid.

Reabsorption in the distal convoluted tubule and collecting duct

The first part of the distal convoluted tubule functions in the same way as the ascending limb of the loop of Henle. The second part of the distal tubule functions in the same way as the collecting duct.

In the distal convoluted tubule and collecting duct, sodium ions are actively pumped from the fluid in the tubule into the tissue fluid, from where they pass into the blood. But potassium ions are actively transported

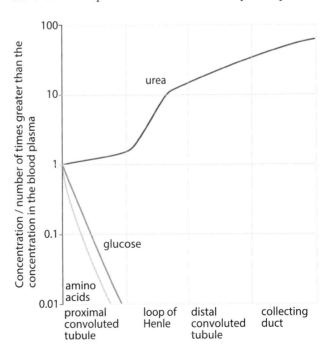

Figure 14.14: Relative concentrations of three substances in the different parts of nephrons and in collecting ducts.

into the tubule. The rate at which these two ions are moved into and out of the fluid in the nephron can be varied, and helps to regulate the concentration of these ions in the blood. Sodium ions and potassium ions are important in the conduction of nerve impulses (see Chapter 15, Section 15.2, Nervous communication).

Question

6 a Figure 14.13 shows the relative rate at which fluid flows through nephrons and collecting ducts. If water flows into an impermeable tube such as a hosepipe, it will flow out of the far end at the same rate that it flows in. However, this clearly does not happen in a nephron. Consider what happens in each region, and suggest an explanation for the shape of the graph.

b Figure 14.14 shows the relative concentrations of three substances in each part of a nephron. Explain the shapes of the curves for:

i glucose

ii amino acids

iii urea.

14.3 Control of water content

Osmoreceptors, the hypothalamus and ADH

Osmoregulation is the control of the water potential of body fluids. This regulation is an important part of homeostasis and involves the hypothalamus, posterior pituitary gland and the kidneys (Figure 14.15).

The water potential of the blood is constantly monitored by specialised sensory neurones in the hypothalamus, known as **osmoreceptors**. When these cells detect a *decrease* in the water potential of the blood below the set point, nerve impulses are sent along the neurones to where they terminate in the posterior pituitary gland (Figure 14.16). These impulses stimulate the release of antidiuretic hormone (ADH), which is a peptide hormone made of nine amino acids. Molecules of ADH enter the blood in

capillaries and are carried all over the body. The effect of ADH is to reduce the loss of water in the urine by making the kidneys reabsorb as much water as possible. The word 'diuresis' means the production of dilute urine. Antidiuretic hormone gets its name because it stops dilute urine being produced, by stimulating the reabsorption of water.

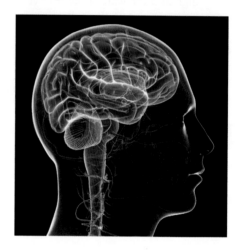

Figure 14.15: The position of the hypothalamus, shown in red, in the brain. The pituitary gland is just below the hypothalamus.

How ADH affects the kidneys

You have seen that water is reabsorbed by osmosis from the filtrate in the nephron as it passes through the collecting ducts. The cells of the collecting duct are the target cells for ADH. ADH acts on the luminal membranes of the collecting ducts cells, making them more permeable to water than usual (Figure 14.17).

This change in permeability is brought about by increasing the number of the water-permeable channels known as aquaporins in the luminal membranes of the collecting duct cells. The cells contain ready-made

---

KEY WORDS

osmoregulation: the control of the water potential of blood and tissue fluid by controlling the water content and/or the concentration of ions, particularly sodium ions

osmoreceptor: type of receptor that detects changes in the water potential of blood

---

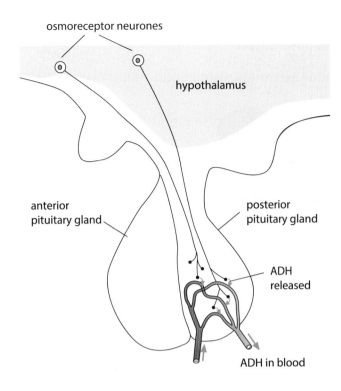

osmoreceptor neurones

hypothalamus

anterior
pituitary gland

posterior
pituitary gland

ADH
released

ADH in blood

Figure 14.16: ADH is produced by neurones in the hypothalamus and is released into the blood where the neurones terminate in the posterior pituitary gland.

vesicles that have many aquaporins in their membranes (Figure 14.18). ADH molecules bind to receptor proteins which stimulate the production of cyclic AMP (cAMP), which is a second messenger. Cyclic AMP activates a signalling cascade leading to the phosphorylation of the aquaporin molecules. The activation of the aquaporin molecules causes the vesicles to move towards the luminal membrane and fuse with it, so increasing the permeability of the membrane to water. You can read more about signalling cascades in Chapter 4 (Section 4.4, Cell signalling). The role of cAMP or c-AMP as a second messenger in the control of blood glucose is discussed in Section 14.4, The control of blood glucose.

As the fluid flows through the collecting duct, water molecules move through the aquaporins (Figure 14.19), out of the tubule and into the tissue fluid. This happens because the tissue fluid in the medulla has a very low water potential and the fluid in the collecting ducts has a very high water potential. The fluid in the collecting duct loses water and becomes more concentrated. The secretion of ADH has caused the increased reabsorption of water into the blood. A small volume of concentrated urine will flow from the kidneys through the ureters into the bladder (Figure 14.20).

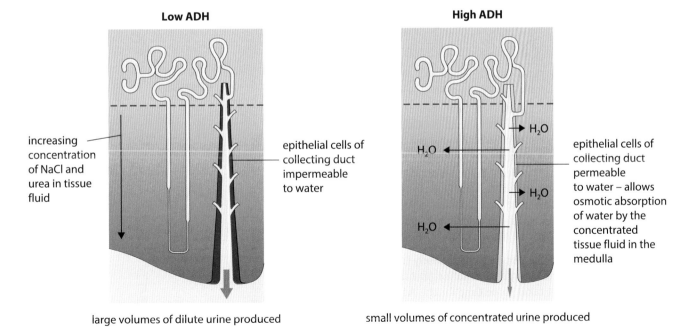

Low ADH

High ADH

increasing
concentration
of NaCl and
urea in tissue
fluid

epithelial cells of
collecting duct
impermeable
to water

H_2O

H_2O

H_2O

epithelial cells of
collecting duct
permeable
to water – allows
osmotic absorption
of water by the
concentrated
tissue fluid in the
medulla

large volumes of dilute urine produced

small volumes of concentrated urine produced

Figure 14.17: The effects of ADH on the reabsorption of water from urine in the collecting ducts.

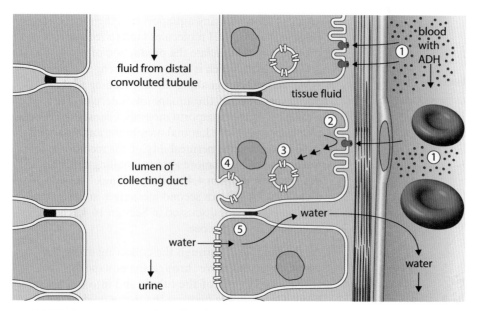

1 ADH binds to receptors in the cell surface membrane of the cells lining the collecting duct.
2 This activates a series of enzyme-controlled reactions, ending with the production of an active phosphorylase enzyme.
3 The phosphorylase causes vesicles, surrounded by membrane containing water-permeable channels (aquaporins), to move to the cell surface membrane.

4 The vesicles fuse with the cell surface membrane.
5 Water can now move freely through other aquaporins (not shown) from the cells down the water potential gradient into the concentrated tissue fluid and blood plasma in the medulla of the kidney.

Figure 14.18: How ADH increases water reabsorption in the collecting duct.

What happens when you have more than enough water in your body – for example, after enjoying a large volume of your favourite drink? When there is an *increase* in the water potential of the blood, the osmoreceptors in the hypothalamus are no longer stimulated and the neurones in the posterior pituitary gland stop secreting ADH. With no stimulus from ADH, the aquaporins are moved out of the cell surface membrane of the collecting duct cells, back into the cytoplasm as part of the vesicles. The collecting duct cells are now impermeable to water. The fluid flows down the collecting duct without losing any water, so a dilute urine collects in the renal pelvis and flows down the ureter to the bladder. Under these conditions, you tend to produce large volumes of dilute urine, losing much of the water you drank, in order to keep the water potential of the blood constant.

Collecting duct cells do not respond immediately to the reduction in ADH secretion by the posterior pituitary gland. This is because it takes some time for the ADH already in the blood to be broken down; approximately half of it is destroyed every 15–20 minutes. However, once ADH stops arriving at the collecting duct cells, it takes only 10–15 minutes for aquaporins to be removed from the cell surface membrane and taken back into the cytoplasm until they are needed again.

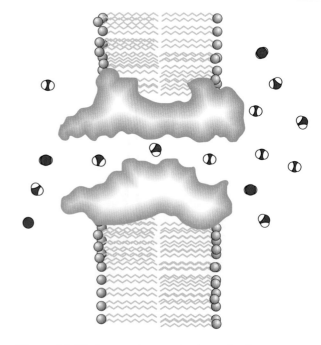

Figure 14.19: Aquaporin protein channels allow water to diffuse through membranes such as those in the cells that line collecting ducts.

Questions

7 Aquaporins are found in the cell surface membranes of many plant and animal cells. Look at Chapter 4 and then explain why they are so common.

8 **a** Use the example of water content of the blood to explain the terms *set point* and *homeostasis*.

  b Construct a diagram to show how the water potential of the blood is controlled. In your diagram, identify the following: receptors, input, effector and output. Indicate clearly how different parts of the body are coordinated and show how negative feedback is involved.

  c Describe the problems that would occur if the water potential of blood plasma was not controlled and not kept within narrow limits.

9 **a** Match the letters given in the diagram (Figure 14.21) to the following statements:

  i site of ultrafiltration

  ii site of selective reabsorption

  iii blood vessel with the highest concentration of urea

  iv region of lowest water potential

  v site of action of the hormone ADH.

  b Explain the functional advantage of the parallel arrangement of structures E, G and H in the medulla of the kidney.

  c Looking at Figure 14.20, describe and explain the concentrations of fluid in the proximal convoluted tubule and in the collecting duct.

  d **i** Describe how ADH acts as a cell-signalling compound.

  ii Explain the effect of ADH on its target organ.

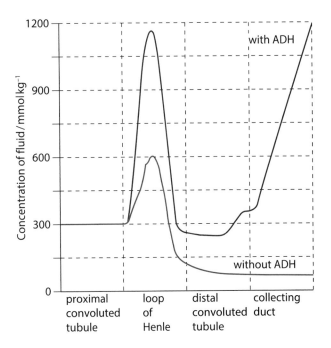

Figure 14.20: The concentration of fluid in different regions of human nephrons and collecting ducts, with and without the presence of ADH.

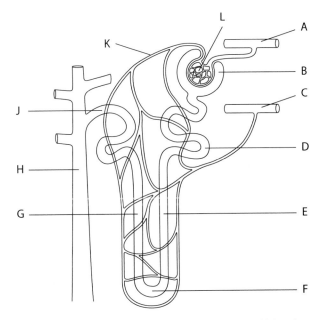

Figure 14.21: A kidney nephron and associated blood vessels.

14.4 The control of blood glucose

Carbohydrate is transported in the human bloodstream as glucose in solution in the blood plasma.

In a healthy human, each $100 cm^3$ of blood normally contains between 80 mg and 120 mg of glucose ($4.4–6.7 mmol dm^{-3}$). If the concentration decreases below this, cells may not have enough glucose for respiration, and may be unable to carry out their normal activities. This is especially important for cells that can respire only glucose, such as brain cells. Very high concentrations of glucose in the blood can also cause major problems, again upsetting the normal behaviour of cells. The homeostatic control of blood glucose concentration is carried out by two hormones secreted by endocrine tissue in the pancreas. This tissue consists of groups of cells, known as the **islets of Langerhans**, which are found throughout the pancreas (Figure 14.22). The word 'islet' means a small island, as you might find in a river. The islets contain two types of cell:

- α cells which secrete **glucagon**

- β cells which secrete **insulin**.

The α and β cells act as the receptors *and* the central control for this homeostatic mechanism. The hormones glucagon and insulin coordinate the actions of the effectors.

Figure 14.23 shows how the blood glucose concentration normally fluctuates within limits around the set point, which is indicated by the dashed line.

Increase in blood glucose concentration

After a meal containing carbohydrate, glucose from the digested food is absorbed from the small intestine and passes into the blood. As this blood flows through the pancreas, the α and β cells detect the increase in glucose concentration. The α cells respond by stopping the secretion of glucagon, whereas the β cells respond by secreting insulin into the blood plasma. The insulin is carried to all parts of the body, in the blood.

Insulin is a protein and cannot pass through cell surface membranes to stimulate the mechanisms within the cell directly. Instead, insulin binds to a receptor in the cell surface membrane and affects the cell indirectly through the action of intracellular messengers (Figure 14.24 and Chapter 4, Section 4.4, Cell signalling).

There are receptors specific for insulin on many cells (e.g. cells in the liver, muscle tissue and adipose (fat storage) tissue). Insulin stimulates cells with these receptors to increase the rate at which they absorb glucose from the blood and convert it into glycogen. Insulin also increases the use of glucose in respiration. Thus, there is a decrease in the concentration of glucose in the blood.

Glucose can only enter cells by facilitated diffusion through transporter proteins known as GLUT. There are several different types of GLUT proteins. Muscle cells have the type called GLUT4. Normally, the GLUT

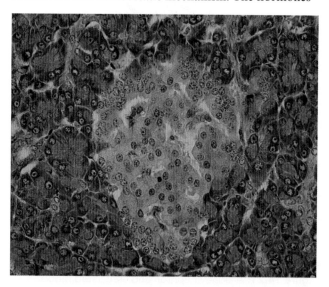

Figure 14.22: A photomicrograph of an islet of Langerhans (pink) surrounded by darker-staining tissue that secretes enzymes which act in the small intestine. Islets like this one are found throughout the pancreas and together form the endocrine pancreas (×360).

KEY WORDS

islet of Langerhans: a group of cells in the pancreas which secrete glucagon and insulin

glucagon: a small peptide hormone secreted by the α cells in the islets of Langerhans in the pancreas to bring about an increase in the concentration of glucose in the blood

insulin: a small peptide hormone secreted by the β cells in the islets of Langerhans in the pancreas to bring about a decrease in the concentration of glucose in the blood

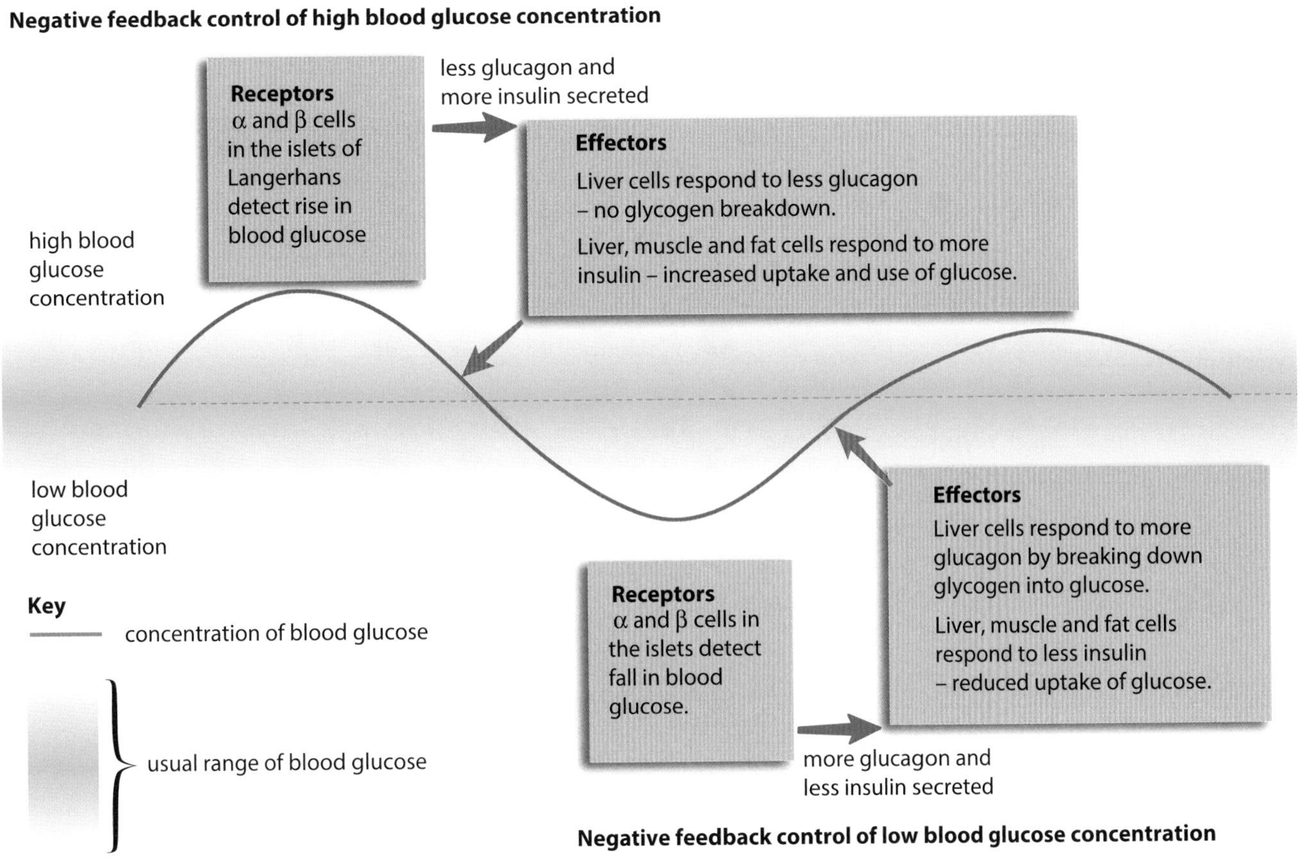

Negative feedback control of high blood glucose concentration

Figure 14.23: The control mechanism for the concentration of glucose in the blood.

proteins are kept in the cytoplasm in the same way as the aquaporins in collecting duct cells. When insulin molecules bind to receptors on muscle cells, the vesicles with GLUT4 proteins are moved to the cell surface membrane and fuse with it. GLUT4 proteins facilitate the movement of glucose into the cell (Figure 14.24). Brain cells have GLUT1 proteins and liver cells have GLUT2 proteins. Both GLUT1 and GLUT2 are always in the cell surface membrane, and their distribution is not altered by insulin.

Insulin stimulates the activation of the enzyme glucokinase, which phosphorylates glucose. This traps glucose inside cells, because phosphorylated glucose cannot pass out through glucose transporters in the cell surface membranes.

Glucose can be converted into the polysaccharide glycogen, a large, insoluble molecule made up of many glucose units linked together by 1,4 glycosidic bonds with 1,6 branching points (see Figure 2.7). Glycogen is a short-term energy store that is found in liver and

muscle cells and is easily converted back to glucose (Figure 14.25). Insulin stimulates the activation of two enzymes, phosphofructokinase and glycogen synthase, which together catalyse the addition of glucose molecules to glycogen – a process known as **glycogenesis**. When insulin is secreted, there is an increase in the size of the glycogen granules inside liver and muscle cells (Figure 14.25).

> **KEY WORD**
>
> **glycogenesis:** synthesis of glycogen by addition of glucose monomers

Question

10 Identify the structures in the liver cell visible in Figure 14.25. Suggest the roles of the structures in liver cells.

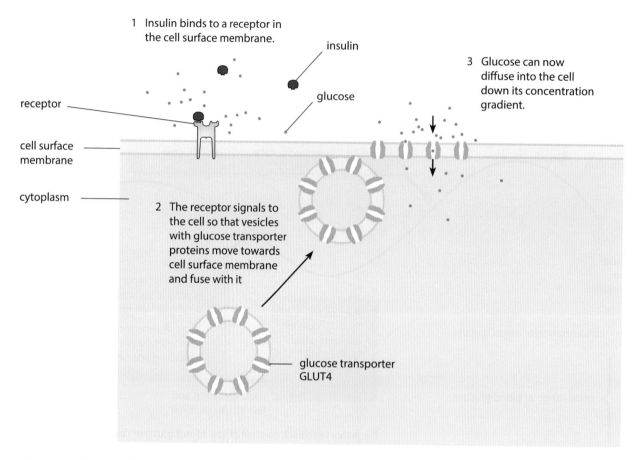

1 Insulin binds to a receptor in the cell surface membrane.

insulin

glucose

3 Glucose can now diffuse into the cell down its concentration gradient.

receptor

cell surface membrane

cytoplasm

2 The receptor signals to the cell so that vesicles with glucose transporter proteins move towards cell surface membrane and fuse with it

glucose transporter GLUT4

Figure 14.24: Insulin increases the permeability of muscle cells to glucose by stimulating the movement of vesicles with GLUT4 to the cell surface membrane.

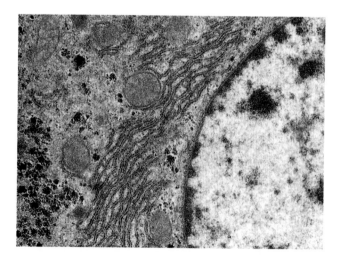

Figure 14.25: TEM of part of a liver cell (×22 000). The dark spots on the left are glycogen granules in the cytoplasm. Mitochondria can also be seen.

Decrease in blood glucose concentration

When a decrease in blood glucose concentration is detected by the α and β cells in the pancreas, the α cells respond by secreting glucagon, while the β cells respond by stopping the secretion of insulin. The stages in cell signalling following the arrival of glucagon at the surface of liver cells is shown in Figure 14.26.

The decrease in the concentration of insulin in the blood reduces the rates of uptake and use of glucose by liver and muscle cells. Uptake still continues, but at a lower rate. Glucagon binds to different specific receptor molecules in the cell surface membranes of liver cells. There are no glucagon receptors on muscle cells. The method of cell signalling in response to glucagon is the same as described earlier and in Figure 4.7. Transduction occurs following the binding of glucagon to its receptor. The binding causes a conformational change in the receptor

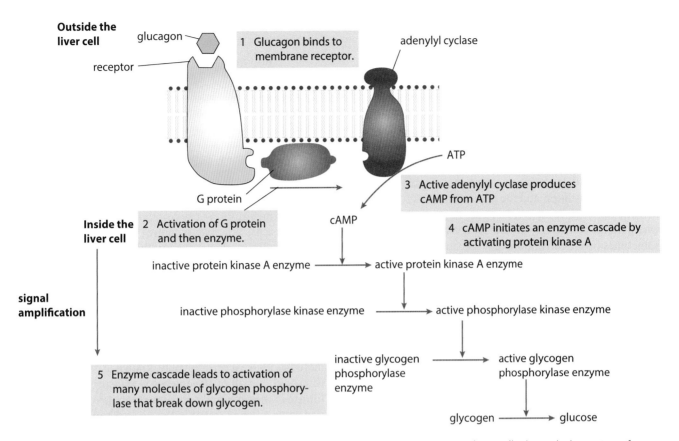

Figure 14.26: Glucagon stimulates the activation of glycogen phosphorylase enzymes in liver cells through the action of cAMP or c-AMP and an enzyme cascade that amplifies the original signal that arrives at the cell surface.

protein that activates a G protein that in turn activates the enzyme adenylyl cyclase which, like the receptor, is part of the cell surface membrane. Adenylyl cyclase catalyses the conversion of ATP to cyclic AMP, which is a second messenger (Figure 14.26). Molecules of cAMP or c-AMP bind to protein kinase A enzymes within the cytoplasm and activate them. In turn, active protein kinase enzymes activate phosphorylase kinase enzymes by adding phosphate groups to them. Phosphorylase kinase enzymes activate glycogen phosphorylase by adding phosphate groups to them. This is an enzyme cascade that amplifies the original signal from glucagon.

When activated, glycogen phosphorylase catalyses the breakdown of glycogen to glucose – a process known as glycogenolysis. It does this by removing glucose units from the numerous 'ends' of each glycogen molecule. The concentration of glucose inside the cell increases and molecules of glucose diffuse out through GLUT2 transporter proteins into the blood. Glucagon also stimulates the formation of glucose from amino acids, fatty acids, glycerol, pyruvate and lactate in a process known as gluconeogenesis, which literally means the formation of 'new' glucose.

> ## KEY WORDS
>
> **adenylyl cyclase:** enzyme that catalyses formation of the second messenger cyclic AMP
>
> **cyclic AMP (c-AMP):** a second messenger in cell-signalling pathways
>
> **protein kinase A:** enzyme that is activated by c-AMP and once activated adds phosphate groups to other proteins, including phosphorylase kinase, to activate them
>
> **phosphorylase kinase:** an enzyme that is part of the enzyme cascade that acts in response to glucagon; the enzyme activates glycogen phosphorylase by adding a phosphate group
>
> **glycogenolysis:** the breakdown of glycogen by removal of glucose monomers
>
> **gluconeogenesis:** the formation of glucose in the liver from non-carbohydrate sources such as amino acids, pyruvate, lactate, fatty acids and glycerol

As a result of glucagon secretion, the liver releases extra glucose to increase the concentration in the blood.

Glucagon and insulin work together as part of the negative feedback system in which any deviation of the blood glucose concentration from the set point stimulates actions by effectors to bring it back to normal.

Blood glucose concentrations never remain constant, even in the healthiest person. One reason for this is the inevitable time delay between a change in the blood glucose concentration and the onset of actions to correct it. Time delays in control systems result in oscillation, where things do not stay absolutely constant but sometimes rise slightly above and sometimes drop slightly below the 'required' level, as shown in Figure 14.23.

The hormone adrenaline also increases the concentration of blood glucose. It does this by binding to different receptors on the surface of liver cells that activate the same enzyme cascade as activated by glucagon (Figure 14.26). Thus, the same end result is achieved – the breakdown of glycogen by glycogen phosphorylase. Adrenaline also stimulates the breakdown of glycogen stores in muscle during exercise. The glucose produced remains in the muscle cells where it is needed for respiration.

Questions

11 The control of blood glucose concentration involves a negative feedback mechanism.

a What are the stimuli, receptors and effectors in this control mechanism?

b Explain how negative feedback is involved in this homeostatic mechanism. (You may have to look back to Section 14.1.)

12 a Name the process by which glucose enters and leaves cells.

b Explain why:

i muscle cells do not have receptors for glucagon

ii there are second messengers for insulin and glucagon

iii insulin and glucagon have different second messengers.

13 Explain why signal amplification in liver cells is necessary in the control of blood glucose.

Measuring concentration of glucose in the urine

Diabetes mellitus is a very common disease. People with the disease are not able to control their blood glucose concentration so that it stays within normal limits. Some people develop the disease early in life because the β cells in the pancreas stop producing insulin. Most people with diabetes develop the disease later in life when their cells fail to respond to insulin.

The presence of glucose in urine may indicate that a person has diabetes. If blood glucose concentration increases above a certain value, known as the renal threshold, not all of the glucose is reabsorbed from the filtrate in the proximal convoluted tubule of the kidney and some will be present in the urine. Simple tests on urine can give early indications of health problems, including diabetes, which can then be investigated more thoroughly.

You can use test strips to test urine for a range of different factors including pH, glucose, ketones and protein. The test strips for detecting glucose contain the enzymes glucose oxidase and peroxidase. These two enzymes are immobilised on a small pad at one end of the stick. Covering the pad is a cellulose membrane that only allows small molecules from the blood to reach the enzymes. The pad is immersed in urine for a brief time, and if it contains glucose, glucose oxidase catalyses a chemical reaction in which glucose is oxidised into gluconic acid. Hydrogen peroxide is also produced. Peroxidase catalyses a reaction between hydrogen peroxide and a colourless chemical in the pad to form a brown compound:

$$\text{glucose} + \text{oxygen} \xrightarrow{\text{glucose oxidase}} \text{gluconic acid} + \text{hydrogen peroxide}$$

$$\text{hydrogen peroxide} + \text{chromogen (colourless)} \xrightarrow{\text{peroxidase}} \text{oxidised chromogen (coloured)} + \text{water}$$

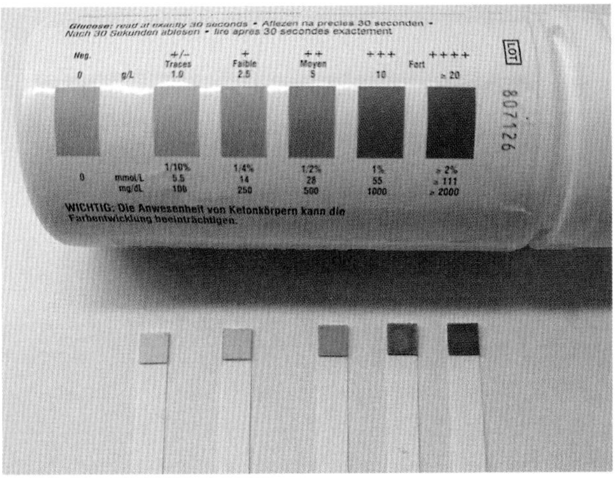

Figure 14.27: Test strips for detecting glucose in urine. After being immersed in urine the colours on the pads are compared with a colour chart provided with the test strips.

The resulting colour of the pad is matched against a colour chart which shows colours that indicate different concentrations of glucose. The more glucose is present, the darker the colour (Figure 14.27 and Figure 14.28).

negative

| mg / cm³ | 0 | 1.0 | 2.5 | 5.0 | 10.0 | 20.0 or more |

Figure 14.28: The colour chart for interpreting the colour of the pads on the test strips in Figure 14.27. The concentrations of glucose are given here in mg per cm³.

Glucose oxidase is specific for glucose, so the test gives negative results for other sugars, such as fructose, lactose and sucrose. This makes it a good example of enzyme specificity and the use of immobilised enzymes.

Measuring glucose in the blood

One problem with urine tests is that they do not indicate the current blood glucose concentration. They show whether or not the concentration was higher than the renal threshold in the period of time while urine was collecting in the bladder.

KEY WORD

biosensor: a device that uses a biological material such as an enzyme to measure the concentration of a chemical compound

A biosensor like the one shown in Figure 14.29 allows people with diabetes to check their blood to see how well they are controlling their glucose concentration. Like the test strips, the biosensor uses glucose oxidase immobilised on a recognition layer (Figure 14.30). A small sample of blood is tested. Small molecules in the plasma pass through the membrane. Glucose molecules enter the active sites of the enzyme that catalyses the reaction to produce gluconic acid and hydrogen peroxide. Hydrogen peroxide is oxidised at an electrode that detects electron transfers. The electron flow is proportional to the number of glucose molecules in the blood; the biosensor amplifies the current which is read by the meter which produces a digital reading for blood glucose concentration within seconds. Results can be stored and sent electronically to a doctor's surgery (Figure 14.29).

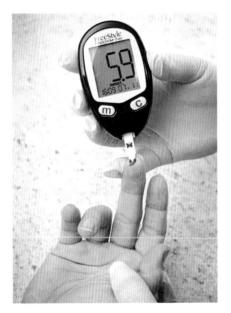

Figure 14.29: Biosensors use biological materials, such as enzymes, to measure the concentration of molecules such as glucose. This glucose biosensor is used to check the glucose concentration in a sample of blood. The meter shows a reading in the normal range.

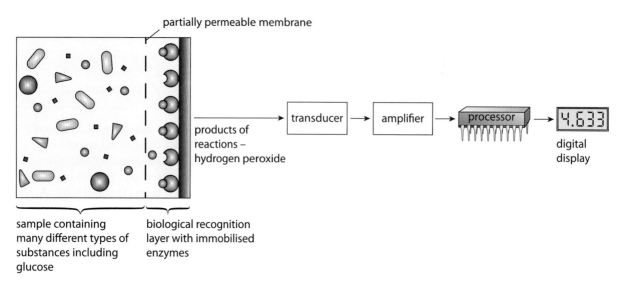

Figure 14.30: A diagram showing the parts of a glucose biosensor.

Questions

14 Test strips can be used for testing biological samples other than urine for glucose. State the advantage of using test strips rather than Benedict's solution to test for glucose.

15 a Looking at Figure 14.31:

  i describe the changes in the concentrations of glucose and insulin in the blood over the three hours of the investigation

  ii explain the differences between the responses to the ingestion of glucose in the two people.

b People with diabetes are taught how to inject themselves with insulin.

  i Explain why insulin cannot be taken by mouth.

  ii Suggest how people with diabetes can monitor the effectiveness of the insulin that they take.

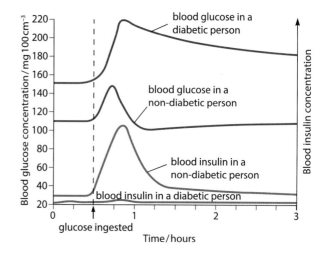

Figure 14.31: Concentrations of blood glucose and insulin following intake of glucose in a person with normal control of blood glucose and a person with diabetes.

16 Suggest the advantages of using an electronic biosensor to measure blood glucose concentration, rather than using test strips to measure glucose in urine.

14.5 Homeostasis in plants

It is as important for plants as it is for animals to maintain a constant internal environment. For example, mesophyll cells in leaves require a constant supply of carbon dioxide if they are to make best use of light energy for photosynthesis. You have seen how low concentrations of carbon dioxide limit the rate of photosynthesis (Chapter 13, Section 13.5, Limiting factors in photosynthesis). Stomata control the diffusion of gases in and out of leaves and thus control the entry of carbon dioxide into leaves. Strictly speaking, a stoma is the aperture (hole) between the guard cells, but the term is usually used to refer to the two guard cells and the aperture between them (Figure 14.32). Stomata may look very simple, but guard cells are highly specialised cells that respond to a wide range of environmental stimuli to control the internal atmosphere of the leaf (Figure 14.33).

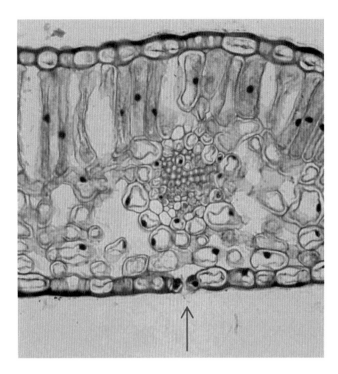

Figure 14.33: Photomicrograph of a transverse section (TS) of a leaf of *Helleborus* (×100). The arrow is pointing towards an open stoma in the lower epidermis. The sub-stomatal air space is continuous with all the intercellular air spaces in the mesophyll, as can be seen in scanning electron micrographs of the inside of leaves.

Stomata are distributed on leaves, green stems and flowers. Typically, the lower epidermis of leaves has the highest density of stomata (Figures 14.32 and 14.33). Each stomatal pore is surrounded by two guard cells that are elliptical in shape, often described as being shaped like kidneys (Figure 14.32).

Guard cells are much smaller than cells in the spongy and palisade mesophyll, but they are metabolically very active. A typical guard cell like that in thale cress (see Figure 14.34) has the following features:

- Thick cell walls that face the air outside the leaf and the stomatal pore. The outer wall has a thick waxy cuticle and is often extended into ledges. The walls facing the adjacent epidermal cells are much thinner.

- Cellulose microfibrils (see Figure 2.10) are arranged into bands around the cell as shown in Figure 14.36.

- The cell walls have no plasmodesmata.

> ### KEY WORD
>
> **guard cell:** a kidney-shaped epidermal cell found with another, in a pair surrounding a stoma and controlling its opening or closure

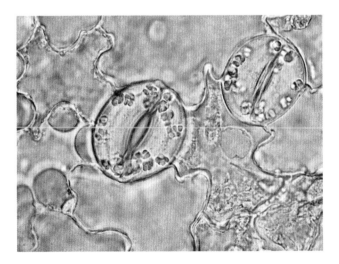

Figure 14.32: An open stoma and a closed stoma in a photomicrograph of the lower epidermis of a leaf of *Tradescantia* (×870). Chloroplasts are visible inside the guard cells and the thick internal cell wall is visible in the stoma on the left which has a narrow aperture.

- The cell surface membrane is often folded and contains many channel and carrier proteins.

- The cytoplasm has a high density of chloroplasts and mitochondria.

- Chloroplasts have thylakoids, but unlike chloroplasts in mesophyll cells they have few grana (see Figures 13.3 and 13.4). The starch grains in chloroplasts increase in size as starch is stored at night and decrease in size during the day.

- Mitochondria have many cristae.

- The nucleus is the same size as in mesophyll cells, but occupies a much larger proportion of the cell because guard cells are so much smaller than mesophyll cells.

- There are several small vacuoles rather than one large vacuole.

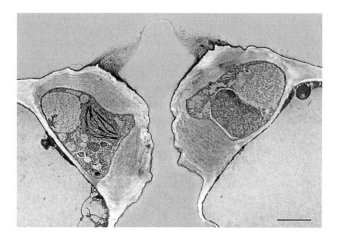

Figure 14.34: A TEM of a section through a pair of guard cells surrounding stoma of thale cress, *Arabidopsis thaliana*. The air outside the leaf is at the top and epidermal cells either side of the guard cells are on the left and right of the TEM. Scale bar = 2 μm.

Question

17 Make a labelled drawing of the pair of guard cells shown in Figure 14.34. Show in your drawing the features of guard cells as described here.

Opening and closing of stomata

Stomata show daily rhythms of opening and closing. Even when kept in constant light or constant dark, these rhythms persist (Figure 14.35). Opening during the day maintains the inward diffusion of carbon dioxide and the outward diffusion of oxygen. However, it also allows the outward diffusion of water vapour in transpiration (Chapter 7, Section 7.4, The transport of water). The closure of stomata at night when photosynthesis cannot occur reduces rates of transpiration and conserves water.

Stomata respond to changes in environmental conditions. They open in response to:

- increasing light intensity

- low carbon dioxide concentrations in the air spaces within the leaf.

When stomata are open, leaves gain carbon dioxide for photosynthesis but tend to lose much water in transpiration.

Stomata close in response to:

- darkness

- high carbon dioxide concentrations in the air spaces in the leaf

- low humidity

- high temperature

- water stress, when the supply of water from the roots is limited and/or there are high rates of transpiration.

The disadvantage of closing is that, during daylight, the supply of carbon dioxide decreases so the rate of photosynthesis decreases. The advantage is that water is retained inside the leaf, which is important in times of water stress.

Mechanisms to open and close stomata

Guard cells open when they gain water and become turgid. They close when they lose water and become flaccid. Guard cells gain and lose water by osmosis.

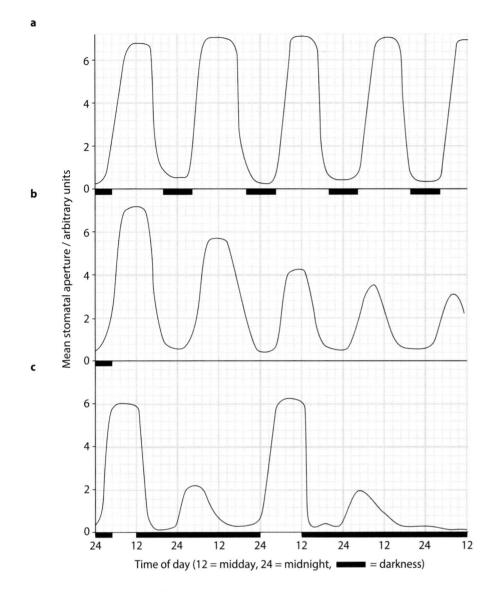

Figure 14.35: (**a**) Stomatal apertures were measured in leaves of *Tradescantia* over several days to reveal a daily rhythm of opening and closing. This rhythm persisted even when the plants were kept in constant light (**b**) and in long periods of constant dark (**c**).

Opening

A decrease in water potential is needed before water can enter the cells by osmosis. This decrease is brought about by the activities of transport proteins in the cell surface membranes. In response to light, ATP-powered proton pumps in the membrane actively transport hydrogen ions (H⁺) out of the guard cells. The decrease in the hydrogen ion concentration inside the cells causes channel proteins in the cell surface membrane to open so that potassium ions (K⁺) move into the cell. They do this because the removal of hydrogen ions has left the inside of the cell negatively charged compared with the outside. So, because potassium ions have a positive charge, they move down an electrical gradient towards the negatively charged region. The potassium ions also diffuse into the cells down a concentration gradient.

Such a combined gradient is an **electrochemical gradient** (Figure 14.36). Other ions, mainly chloride and nitrate, also enter to maintain an electrical balance.

The extra potassium ions inside the guard cells increase the concentration of solutes so decreasing the water potential. Now there is a water potential gradient between the outside and the inside of the cell, so water moves in by osmosis through aquaporins in the membrane and most enters the vacuoles, which increase in size. The turgor pressure of the guard cells increases and the stoma opens. Starch stored in chloroplasts is broken down to form negatively charged malate ions that enter the vacuoles. These ions also help maintain the electrical balance and also contribute to decreasing the water potential during opening.

Guard cells have unevenly thickened cell walls. The wall adjacent to the pore is very thick, whereas the wall furthest from the pore is thin. The bundles of cellulose microfibrils prevent the expansion of the cell

> **KEY WORD**
>
> **electrochemical gradient:** a gradient across a cell surface membrane that involves both a difference in concentrations of ions and a potential difference

in all directions. Instead cells increase in length and not diameter. Since the ends of the two guard cells are joined and the thin outer walls bend more readily than the thick inner walls, the guard cells become curved and the guard cells bulge into the adjoining cells – looking more like a pair of bananas than a pair of kidneys. This opens the pore between the two cells.

Closing

Stomata close when the hydrogen ion pump proteins stop and potassium ions leave the guard cells and enter neighbouring cells. Malate ions are returned to the

a
Stomatal aperture closed

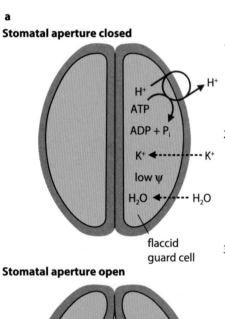

flaccid guard cell

Stomatal aperture open

stomatal aperture

turgid guard cell

1 ATP-powered proton pumps in the cell surface membrane actively transport H^+ out of the guard cell.

2 The low H^+ concentration and negative charge inside the cell causes K^+ channels to open. K^+ diffuses into the cell down an electrochemical gradient.

3 The high concentration of K^+ inside the guard cell lowers the water potential (ψ).

4 Water moves in by osmosis, down a water potential gradient.

5 The entry of water increases the volume of the guard cells, so they expand. The thin outer wall expands most, so the cells curve apart.

b

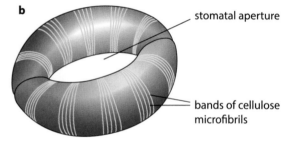

stomatal aperture

bands of cellulose microfibrils

Figure 14.36: How a stoma is opened. **a** Sequence of events that occurs during stomatal opening; **b** bundles of cellulose microfibrils restrict expansion of guard cells to the ends so cells push against each other and push outwards against the adjoining cells.

chloroplasts to be converted to starch. Now there is a water potential gradient in the opposite direction, so water leaves the guard cells so that they become flaccid and close the stoma. Closing of the stomata has significant effects on the plant. It reduces the uptake of carbon dioxide for photosynthesis and reduces the rate of transpiration. As transpiration is used for cooling the plant and also for maintaining the transpiration stream that supplies water and mineral ions to the leaves, stomatal closure only occurs when reducing the loss of water vapour and conserving water is the most important factor. In conditions of water stress, the hormone **abscisic acid** (**ABA**) is produced in plants to stimulate stomatal closure.

KEY WORD

abscisic acid (**ABA**): an inhibitory plant growth regulator that causes closure of stomata in dry conditions

---

Abscisic acid (ABA) and stomatal closure

ABA has been found in a very wide variety of plants, including ferns and mosses as well as flowering plants. ABA can be found in every part of the plant, and it is synthesised in almost all cells that possess chloroplasts or amyloplasts (organelles like chloroplasts, but that contain large starch grains and no chlorophyll).

One role of ABA is to coordinate the responses to stress; hence it is known as a stress hormone. If a plant is subjected to difficult environmental conditions, such as very high temperatures or much reduced water supplies, then it responds by secreting ABA. When water is in short supply, for example during a drought, the concentration of ABA in the leaves can rise to 40 times that which would normally be present. This high concentration of ABA stimulates the stomata to close, reducing the loss of water vapour from the leaf.

If ABA is applied to a leaf, the stomata close within just a few minutes. Although it is not known exactly how ABA achieves the closure of stomata, it seems that guard cells have ABA receptors on their cell surface membranes, and it is possible that when ABA binds with these it inhibits the proton pumps to stop hydrogen ions being pumped out. ABA also stimulates the movement of calcium ions into the cytoplasm through the cell surface membrane and the tonoplasts (membranes around the vacuoles).

Calcium ions act as second messengers to activate channel proteins to open that allow negatively charged ions to leave the guard cells. This, in turn, stimulates the opening of more channel proteins, which allows the movement of potassium ions out of the cells. At the same time, calcium ions also stimulate the closure of the channel proteins that allow potassium ions to enter. The loss of ions increases the water potential of the cells, water passes out by osmosis, the guard cells become flaccid and the stomata close.

Question

18   a   Annotate the drawing you made in answer to Question 17 to show how the guard cells are adapted for opening and closing the stomata.

      b   Draw a flow chart diagram to show the stages in opening and closing of a stoma.

      c   Explain when it is an advantage for plants to close their stomata.

      d   Outline how ABA functions to stimulate the closure of stomata.

REFLECTION

Make a list of the types of mammalian cell studied in this chapter. Search online for images of these cells. Use any images you find and the information in this chapter and Chapter 1 to make large, labelled diagrams of these cells showing as much detail as you can of the structure of each cell. Annotate your diagrams to show how each cell is adapted to carry out its functions in excretion and homeostasis. Compare your drawings with others. Use your annotated drawings to help your revision.

Final reflection

Discuss with a friend which, if any, parts of Chapter 14 you need to:

* read through again to make sure you really understand

* seek more guidance on, even after going over it again.

SUMMARY

Mammals keep their internal environment relatively constant, so providing ideal conditions for cells to carry out their activities efficiently. The maintenance of relatively constant internal conditions is known as homeostasis. Homeostatic balance requires receptors that detect external changes in conditions, such as the temperature of the surroundings, and internal changes in physiological factors such as body temperature and pH, glucose concentration and water potential of the blood. These changes in internal and external stimuli are detected by receptors, such as temperature receptors in the skin and osmoreceptors in the hypothalamus. The nervous system and the endocrine system coordinate homeostatic mechanisms. Cell signalling is involved in coordinating the activities of effectors that carry out the corrective mechanisms that restore homeostatic equilibrium.

Homeostatic control systems use negative feedback in which any change in a factor stimulates actions by effectors to restore the factor to its set point.

Effectors are the cells, tissues and organs (including muscles and glands) that carry out the functions necessary to restore physiological factors to their set points.

Excretion is the removal of waste products of metabolism, especially carbon dioxide and urea.

The deamination of excess amino acids in the liver produces ammonia, which is converted into urea, the main nitrogenous waste product. Urea is excreted in solution in water, as urine.

The kidneys regulate the concentration of various substances in the body fluids, by excreting appropriate amounts of them.

Each kidney is surrounded by a fibrous capsule and has three major regions: cortex, medulla and renal pelvis. Within each kidney are thousands of nephrons and their associated blood vessels.

The kidneys produce urine by ultrafiltration and selective reabsorption.

Blood is brought to the glomerulus in an afferent arteriole. High hydrostatic pressure in the glomerulus forces substances through the endothelium of the capillaries, the basement membrane and between the podocytes of Bowman's capsule. The basement membrane acts as a filter, allowing only small molecules through. The filtrate collects in the Bowman's capsule and then enters the proximal convoluted tubule, where most reabsorption occurs by diffusion and active transport; substances are also reabsorbed in the distal convoluted tubule and collecting duct.

Endothelial cells that line capillaries in the glomerulus have many perforations and podocytes have many slit pores that aid the filtration of small molecules from blood plasma into Bowman's capsule.

Cuboidal epithelial cells in the proximal convoluted tubules have microvilli to provide a large surface area in contact with filtrate, folded basal membrane for movement of reabsorbed substances into the blood and many mitochondria to provide energy for active transport.

The loops of Henle act to produce high concentrations of sodium and chloride ions in the tissue fluid in the medulla. The medullary tissue has a very low water potential. Water is reabsorbed from fluid in the collecting ducts by osmosis if the body is dehydrated. The water content of the blood is controlled by changing the amount of water excreted in the urine by the kidneys. This is done by regulating the permeability of the epithelial cells of the collecting ducts to water, and hence the volume of water reabsorbed from the collecting ducts into the blood. Changes in the water potential of the blood are detected by osmoreceptors in the hypothalamus. If the water potential decreases, the hormone ADH is released by the posterior pituitary gland. ADH stimulates the increase in the uptake of water from urine by collecting ducts.

The concentration of glucose in the blood is controlled by the action of the protein hormones insulin and glucagon, which are secreted by the islets of Langerhans in the pancreas.

CONTINUED

Insulin stimulates cells in the liver, muscles and adipose tissue to take up more glucose. In the liver and muscle it stimulates the formation of glycogen for short-term storage. Adipose tissue responds by converting glucose to fat for long-term storage. The overall effect of insulin is to decrease the concentration of glucose in the blood.

Glucagon stimulates cells in the liver to break down glycogen and release glucose into the blood. The effect of glucagon is to increase the concentration of glucose in the blood.

Insulin and glucagon are proteins and so cannot cross the membranes of their target cells. Both hormones bind to specific receptors in the cell surface membranes of these cells. The binding activates a series of changes in the cells that amplify the signal so that the responses of the cells are rapid.

The binding of glucagon to its receptor stimulates a G protein that activates the membrane enzyme adenylyl cyclase, which converts ATP to the second messenger cAMP or c-AMP or cAMP activates protein kinase that initiates an enzyme cascade that activates the enzyme glycogen phosphorylase that breaks down glycogen to form glucose.

Test strips are used to test urine for a variety of substances, including glucose. The presence of glucose may suggest that a person has diabetes.

Immobilised glucose oxidase is used on test strips to detect glucose. The enzyme changes glucose to gluconic acid and hydrogen peroxide, which causes a colour change in another chemical on the stick. The range of colours on the strip indicates the concentration of glucose in the urine. Biosensors use the same principle but produce a small electric current instead of a colour change, which provides a direct digital readout.

Stomata control the movement of gases between the atmosphere and the intercellular air spaces inside a leaf. They allow the inward diffusion of carbon dioxide for use in photosynthesis and the outward diffusion of water vapour in transpiration. Each stoma consists of two guard cells either side of a pore. The cell walls of guard cells have 'hoops' of cellulose fibres that restrict their increase in volume to the ends. When guard cells become turgid, the cells push on each other to open the pore. Guard cells are highly specialised cells that respond to changes in light intensity and carbon dioxide concentrations inside the leaf.

In general, guard cells open during the day and close at night although this rhythm persists in continuous light and in continuous dark. The cell surface membranes of guard cells contain proton pumps that actively transport hydrogen ions out of the cells. This stimulates the inward movement of potassium ions down their electrochemical gradient. The potassium ions decrease the water potential of the guard cells so water enters by osmosis, the cells become turgid and open the stoma. To close the stoma, the proton pumps stop working and the potassium ions flow out of the cells. This raises the water potential inside the cells, so water passes out by osmosis. The guard cells become flaccid and this closes the stoma.

Abscisic acid (ABA) is a plant hormone that is synthesised by any cells in a plant that contain chloroplasts or amyloplasts, especially in stress conditions. The presence of large concentrations of ABA in leaves stimulates stomata to close, reducing the rate of transpiration and so conserving water inside the plant.

Calcium ions act as second messengers in guard cells in response to stimulation by ABA.

EXAM-STYLE QUESTIONS

1 **a** Outline the role of the kidneys in homeostasis. [3]

b The figure is a photomicrograph of part of the kidney.

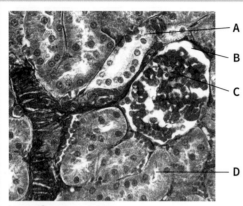

Magnification: ×180

i Name **A**, **B**, **C** and **D**. [4]

ii Identify the region of the kidney shown in the figure and **give** a reason for your identification. [2]

iii Calculate the actual maximum width of the structure labelled **A**. Show your working. [2]

[Total: 11]

2 **a** The total blood volume in a human is about $5.5\,dm^3$. At rest the kidneys receive 25% of the blood pumped out by the heart. The cardiac output at rest is $5.6\,dm^3\,min^{-1}$. In a healthy person, the glomerular filtration rate (GFR) remains constant all the time at $125\,cm^3\,min^{-1}$. The volume of urine produced each day varies between $1.2\,dm^3$ and $2.0\,dm^3$.

i Calculate the volume of blood that flows through the kidneys each minute. Show your working. [2]

ii Use the figure you have calculated in i to determine the percentage of the blood flow through the kidneys that becomes filtrate. [2]

iii A person produces $1.5\,dm^3$ of urine in a day. Calculate the percentage of the filtrate that that is lost in the urine during the course of the day. [2]

b The figure on the next page is a TEM of part of a proximal convoluted tubule.

COMMAND WORDS

Outline: set out the main points.

Give: produce an answer from a given source or recall/memory.

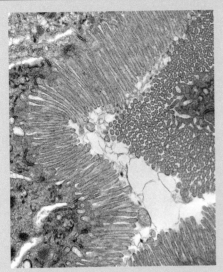

    i Explain the appearance of the parts of the cells visible in the electron micrograph. **[4]**

    ii There are many mitochondria in the cells of the proximal convoluted tubule. Explain why these cells contain many mitochondria. **[4]**

  c Explain how the cells lining collecting ducts determine the concentration of the urine that enters the renal pelvis of the kidney. **[5]**

[Total: 19]

3 The control of the water content of the blood is an example of homeostasis.

  a Name the part of the body that monitors the water potential of the blood. **[1]**

In an investigation of the factors that influence urine production, a person drank one litre of water. The person's urine was collected at half-hourly intervals for four hours after drinking. The results are shown as line **A** on the figure. On the following day, the same person drank one litre of a dilute salt solution and the urine was collected in the same way (line **B**). Dilute salt solution has about the same water potential as blood plasma.

CONTINUED

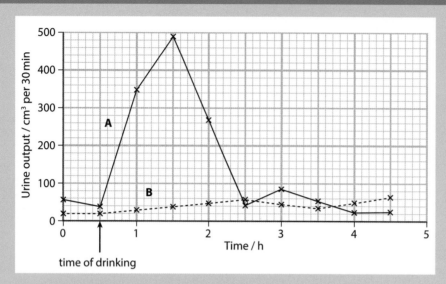

b Calculate how much urine was produced in the two hours after drinking the litre of water. [1]

c Explain why the person produced so much urine after drinking the litre of water. [4]

d Suggest why the results during the second day were so different from those on the first day. [2]

e Explain why negative feedback, and not positive feedback, is involved in homeostatic mechanisms. [5]

[Total: 13]

4 The flow chart shows some of the pathways involved in the metabolism of carbohydrate in the human body.

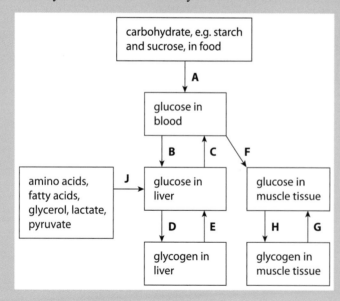

CONTINUED

   a State the letter or letters, **A** to **J**, that indicates each of the following:

      i glycogenesis

      ii glycogenolysis

      iii gluconeogenesis

      iv processes promoted by the action of insulin

      v processes promoted by glucagon.   **[5]**

   b Suggest why there is no arrow in the opposite direction to arrow **F**.   **[1]**

   c Explain why it is important to regulate the concentration of blood glucose.   **[4]**

                             [Total: 10]

5 An investigation was carried out to determine the response of pancreatic cells to an increase in the glucose concentration of the blood. A person who had been told not to eat or drink anything other than water for 12 hours then took a drink of a glucose solution. Blood samples were taken from the person at one-hour intervals for five hours, and the concentrations of glucose, insulin and glucagon in the blood were determined. The results are shown in the graph.

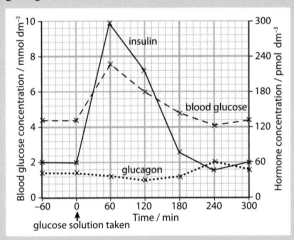

   a **i** Explain why the person was told not to eat or drink anything other than water for 12 hours before having the glucose drink.   **[3]**

      ii Use the information in the figure to describe the response of the pancreatic cells to an increase in the glucose concentration.   **[4]**

      iii Outline the role of insulin when the glucose concentration in the blood increases.   **[5]**

   b **i** Suggest how the results will change if the investigation continued longer than five hours without the person taking any food.   **[4]**

      ii Outline the sequence of events that follows the binding of glucagon to its membrane receptor on a liver cell.   **[6]**

                             [Total: 22]

CONTINUED

6 a Explain why the control of blood glucose is an example of negative feedback. **[5]**

Many processed foods eaten in modern diets contain high quantities of sucrose. It is thought that these diets are a risk factor in developing obesity and type 2 diabetes.

A study was carried out on the effect of diets high in starch and high in sucrose on the concentration of insulin in the blood of eight volunteers who were in good health.

Each volunteer fasted for 8 hours and then followed a diet high in starch for 24 hours. Sometime later the volunteers repeated the procedure but ate a diet high in sucrose. The glucose and insulin concentrations in the blood were monitored over 24 hours as shown in the graphs. The arrows indicate the times of the four meals eaten by the volunteers: breakfast, lunch, dinner and supper.

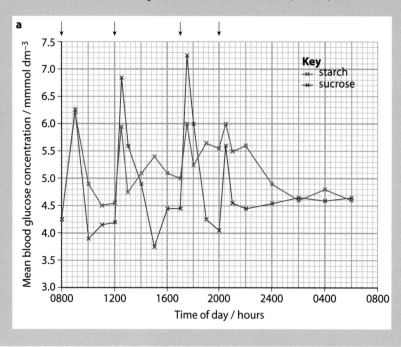

CONTINUED

b

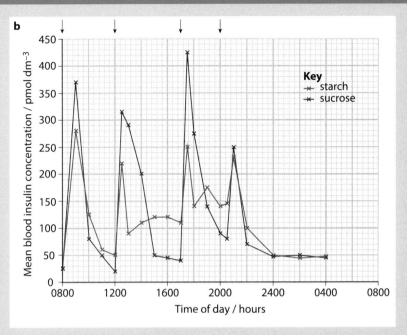

Time of day / hours

b In each diet, the carbohydrate (starch or sucrose) composed 50% of the energy. Suggest **three** other factors that should be controlled in a study such as this. **[3]**

c i State the mean fasting concentrations of glucose and insulin. **[2]**

ii Compare the effect of the two diets on the concentrations of glucose and insulin. **[6]**

iii Explain the reasons for the differences that you have identified in **c ii**. **[6]**

d Sketch a graph to show how the concentration of glucagon would change over the time period shown in the graphs. **[3]**

[Total: 25]

7 a Explain what is meant by a biosensor. **[2]**

b Copy and complete the following passage describing the action of a biosensor.

Many people with diabetes use a biosensor to measure the concentration of glucose in their blood. The biosensor uses the enzyme ...., which is .... on a pad. This enzyme converts glucose into gluconic acid and .... An electrode in the biosensor produces a tiny .... current, the size of which is .... to the concentration of glucose in the blood. The current is read by the meter, which produces a reading for blood glucose concentration. If the reading is too high, the person needs to take .... to decrease it. **[6]**

[Total: 8]

COMMAND WORDS

Compare: identify / comment on similarities and/or differences.

Sketch: make a simple drawing showing the key features.

CONTINUED

8 Abscisic acid (ABA) is a weak acid. Its structure can be represented as ABA-H. It dissociates into positively charged H^+ ions (protons) and negatively charged ABA^- ions as shown:

$$ABA\text{-}H \rightleftharpoons ABA^- + H^+$$

The following observations have been made by scientists:

- light stimulates proton (H^+ ion) uptake into the grana of chloroplasts
- ABA–H can diffuse into and out of chloroplasts, but ABA^- cannot.

This information is summarised in the diagram below.

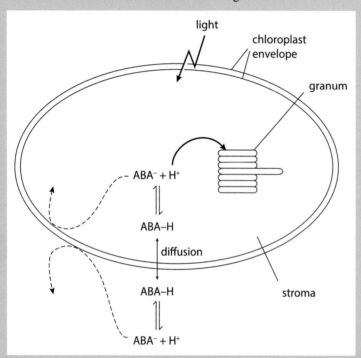

a Using all the information provided, **predict** what happens to the pH of the stroma in the light. [1]

b i When light shines on the chloroplast, dissociation of ABA–H is stimulated. Explain why this happens. [2]

ii Explain the effect that this will have on diffusion of ABA–H into or out of the chloroplast. [2]

When the mesophyll cells of leaves become dehydrated, some of the ABA stored in the chloroplasts is released into the transpiration stream in the apoplast.

c ABA travels in the apoplast pathway to the guard cells. Explain why this is an advantage when the leaf is dehydrated. [2]

[Total: 7]

COMMAND WORD

Predict: suggest what may happen based on available information.

SELF-EVALUATION CHECKLIST

After studying this chapter, complete a table like this:

I can	See section...	Needs more work	Almost there	Ready to move on
explain the meaning of the term *homeostasis* and explain why homeostasis is important for mammals	14.1			
explain the principles of homeostasis in terms of: stimuli, receptors, effectors and the way in which responses are coordinated by the nervous and endocrine systems.	14.1, 14.3, 14.4			
explain how negative feedback is involved in homeostatic mechanisms	14.1, 14.4			
state that urea is produced by deamination of excess amino acids in the liver	14.1			
describe the structure of the human kidney and identify in diagrams the parts of a nephron and its associated blood vessels	14.2			
describe and explain how urine is formed in nephrons	14.2			
describe the detailed structure of the Bowman's capsule and proximal convoluted tubule and explain how they are adapted for ultrafiltration and selective reabsorption	14.2			
describe how the kidneys control the water potential of the blood and explain how osmoregulation is coordinated	14.3			
describe the principles of cell signalling as applied to the control of blood glucose concentration by glucagon	14.4			
explain how blood glucose concentration is controlled	14.4			
explain how test strips and biosensors are used for measuring the concentration of glucose in blood and urine and explain the roles of glucose oxidase and peroxidase enzymes	14.4			
describe the structure and function of guard cells and explain how they regulate the width of the stomatal aperture	14.5			
explain that stomata control the entry of carbon dioxide by diffusion and regulate water loss by transpiration so balancing the needs for photosynthesis and conservation of water	14.5			
explain that stomata have daily rhythms of opening and closing and respond to changes in environmental conditions	14.5			
describe how abscisic acid is involved in the closure of stomata during times of water shortage	14.5			

Chapter 15

Control and coordination

LEARNING INTENTIONS

In this chapter you will learn how to:

- describe the features of the endocrine system with reference to the hormones insulin, glucagon and ADH
- compare the ways in which mammals coordinate responses to internal and external stimuli using the endocrine system and the nervous system
- describe the structure and function of sensory and motor neurones and outline how they function
- state the function of intermediate neurones
- outline the roles of sensory receptor cells using a chemoreceptor cell in a human taste bud as an example
- describe and explain the transmission of nerve impulses
- describe and explain the structure and function of cholinergic synapses
- describe the ultrastructure of striated muscle and explain how muscles contract in response to impulses from motor neurones

CONTINUED

- describe and explain the rapid response of the Venus fly trap

- explain the role of auxin in elongation growth

- describe the role of gibberellin in the germination of barley.

BEFORE YOU START

Make a list of the different roles that membrane proteins carry out. If you are unsure of any of the roles, look through the book starting with Chapter 4. Discuss your list with others.

WHERE BIOLOGY MEETS PSYCHOLOGY

Humans have five senses: touch, sight, hearing, taste and smell. It's a controversial view, but some people believe in extrasensory perception (ESP), telepathy and premonitions as a 'sixth sense'. Recent research suggests that we detect subtle changes, which we cannot put into words, so we imagine it is an extra sense. Some people also have synaesthesia – a condition where stimulation of, say, hearing also produces a visual response (Figure 15.1). Some composers have synaesthesia – the Hungarian composer György Ligeti said that to him 'major chords are red or pink, minor chords are somewhere between green and brown'. Another composer, Roxanna Panufnik, says that she hears musical notes as colours. To her the note C is white, A is bright red, D is blue.

But we do have a genuine sixth sense, which we take for granted. In his essay 'The Disembodied Lady', the neurologist Oliver Sacks relates the story of a woman who woke up one day to find she had lost any sense of having a body.* All the sensory neurones from the receptors in her muscles and joints had stopped sending impulses. She had no feedback from her muscles and could not coordinate her movements. The only way she could live without this sixth sense was to train herself to rely entirely on her eyesight for coordinating her muscles. A man with the same condition describes the efforts needed to do this as equivalent to running a marathon every day. Curiously, Oliver Sacks's patient dreamt about total loss of body awareness the night before it happened.

The Canadian neurologist Wilder Penfield treated many people with epilepsy in the middle of the 20th century by making holes in their skulls and applying

Figure 15.1: Researchers who study electrical activity in the brain have found that some people do indeed hear colour and see sound.

electrodes directly to the surface of different parts of their brains. By doing this he located the functions of different areas. For example, he was the first person to locate the areas of the brain that coordinate speech.

*The essay is published in the book *The man who mistook his wife for a hat.*

Question for discussion

Wilder Penfield made important discoveries by experimenting on his patients. Discuss the ethics of performing experiments on the nervous system of people. Think of experiments that could be carried out to discover more about people's sixth sense.

Most animals and plants are complex organisms, made up of many millions of cells. Different parts of the organism perform different functions. It is essential that information can pass between these different parts, so that their activities are coordinated. Sometimes, the purpose of this information transfer is to coordinate the regulation of substances within the organism, such as the control of blood glucose concentrations in mammals. Sometimes, the purpose may be to change the activity of some part of the organism in response to an external stimulus, such as moving away from something that may do harm.

There are communication systems within animals that coordinate the activities of receptors and effectors. The information they receive comes from the internal and the external environment. So there are receptors that detect stimuli inside the body and receptors that detect stimuli in the surrounding environment. There are examples of these in Table 15.1.

In animals, including mammals, two types of information transfer are used to coordinate the body's activities:

- nerves that transmit information in the form of electrical impulses

- hormones that are substances secreted into the blood.

In Chapter 14 you saw that hormones control some aspects of homeostasis. Glands such as the pituitary glands and the pancreas secrete these hormones into the blood. The glands that secrete hormones make up the body's endocrine system. In this chapter you will revisit some aspects of the endocrine system. After that, you will look at aspects of the nervous system.

Coordination in plants also involves the use of electrical impulses for fast responses and hormones (also known as plant growth regulators) for coordinating slower responses to stimuli. You will look at these methods of coordination at the end of this chapter.

15.1 Hormonal communication

The endocrine system

As you saw in Chapter 14, some homeostatic functions, such as the control of blood glucose concentration and the water potential of the blood, need to be coordinated all the time. However, they do not need to be coordinated rapidly. Hormones are ideal for controlling functions that do not need instant responses.

Hormones such as insulin, glucagon, ADH and adrenaline are cell-signalling molecules that are released into the blood. They are then carried long distances from the site of production to their various target organs. Hormones are made in endocrine glands. A gland is a group of cells that produces and releases one or more substances, a process known as secretion. Endocrine glands contain secretory cells that pass their products directly into the blood. As endocrine glands do not have ducts, they are often known as ductless glands (see Figure 14.22). The endocrine system consists of all the ductless glands in the body. Examples are the pituitary gland (see Figure 14.16), the islets of Langerhans in the pancreas, the adrenal glands, the testes and the ovaries.

> **KEY WORDS**
>
> **endocrine gland:** an organ that secretes hormones directly into the blood; endocrine glands are also known as ductless glands
>
> **endocrine system:** consists of all the endocrine glands in the body together with the hormones that they secrete

The hormones you considered in Chapter 14 are peptides or small proteins. They are water-soluble, so they cannot cross the phospholipid bilayer of cell surface membranes. These hormones bind to receptors on their target cells that in turn activate second messengers to transfer the signal throughout the cytoplasm (see Figure 14.26).

The testes and ovaries secrete the steroid hormones – testosterone, oestrogen and progesterone. Steroids are lipid-soluble, so they can pass through the phospholipid bilayer. Once they have crossed the cell surface membrane, they bind to receptor molecules inside the cytoplasm or the nucleus and activate processes such as transcription (Chapter 6, Section 6.5, Protein synthesis).

Questions

1   a   Make an outline drawing of the human body and indicate the positions of the pituitary gland, pancreas, adrenal glands, testes and ovaries. Annotate your drawing to show the roles of the endocrine system.

    b   Glucagon and ADH are both hormones that are transported around the whole body in the blood. The two hormones use the same intracellular signalling cascade (see Chapter 14). Explain why ADH does not stimulate the signalling cascade that promotes glycogenolysis in liver cells.

c Explain why steroid hormones, such as progesterone and oestrogen, can pass easily through the cell surface membrane whereas other hormones cannot.

2 Insulin, glucagon and ADH coordinate aspects of homeostasis. Make a table to summarise everything you have already learnt from Chapter 14 about these three hormones.

15.2 Nervous communication

The mammalian nervous system is made up of:

- the brain and spinal cord, which form the central nervous system (CNS)

- the cranial and spinal nerves, which form the peripheral nervous system (PNS) (Figure 15.2).

Nerves contain many nerve cells. Cranial nerves are attached to the brain and spinal nerves to the spinal cord. Information is transferred in the form of nerve impulses, which travel along nerve cells at very high speeds. Nerve cells are also known as neurones,

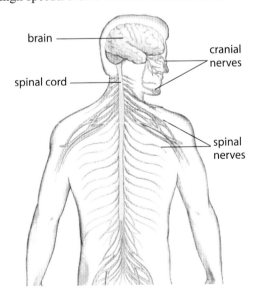

Figure 15.2: The human nervous system. Each nerve contains many neurones. Most of the nerves shown in the drawing contain both sensory and motor neurones.

and they carry information directly to their target cells. Neurones coordinate the activities of sensory receptors (e.g. those in the eye), decision-making centres in the CNS, and effectors such as muscles and glands.

Neurones

There are three types of neurone (Figure 15.3), each with a different function:

- **sensory neurones** transmit impulses from receptors to the CNS

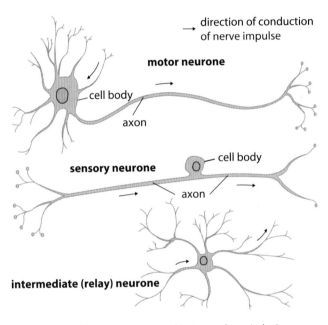

Figure 15.3: Motor, sensory and intermediate (relay) neurones.

KEY WORDS

nerve impulse: (usually shortened to **impulse**) a wave of electrical depolarisation that is transmitted along neurones

neurone: a nerve cell; a cell which is specialised for the conduction of nerve impulses

sensory neurone: a neurone that transmits nerve impulses from a receptor to the central nervous system (CNS)

- intermediate neurones (also known as relay or connector neurones) transmit impulses from sensory neurones to motor neurones

- **motor neurones** transmit impulses from the CNS to effectors.

Motor neurones

Figure 15.4 shows the detailed structure of a mammalian motor neurone, which transmits impulses from the brain or spinal cord to a muscle or gland.

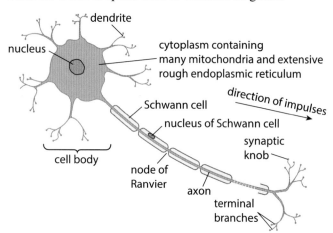

Figure 15.4: A longitudinal section (LS) of a motor neurone. The axon may be over a metre long.

The cell body of a motor neurone lies within the spinal cord or brain. The nucleus of a neurone is always in its cell body. Often when viewed in the light microscope, dark specks can be seen in the cytoplasm (Figure 15.5). These are small regions of rough endoplasmic reticulum that synthesise proteins.

Thin cytoplasmic processes extend from the cell body. Some are very short and often have many branches – these are dendrites. A motor neurone has many highly branched dendrites. These provide a large surface area for the axon terminals of other neurones. The axon is much longer and conducts impulses over long distances. A motor neurone with its cell body in your spinal cord might have its axon running all the way to one of your toes, so axons may be extremely long. Within the cytoplasm of an axon there are some organelles such as mitochondria. The ends of the branches of the axon have mitochondria, together with many vesicles containing chemicals called transmitter substances. These vesicles are

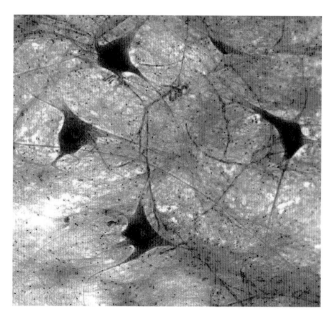

Figure 15.5: A photomicrograph of four motor neurones from the spinal cord. The cell bodies, nuclei and cell extensions are visible. In each case, one of the extensions is an axon (×130).

involved in passing impulses to an effector cell such as a muscle cell or a gland.

Sensory neurones

A sensory neurone has the same basic structure as a motor neurone, but it has one long axon with a cell body that may be near the source of stimuli or in a swelling of a spinal nerve known as a ganglion (Figure 15.6). (Note that the term *dendron* should not be used.)

Relay neurones

Relay neurones are found entirely within the CNS.

Question

3   Make a table to compare the structure and function of motor and sensory neurones.

KEY WORDS
motor neurone: a neurone whose cell body is in the brain, spinal cord or a ganglion (a swelling on a nerve), and that transmits nerve impulses to an effector such as a muscle or gland

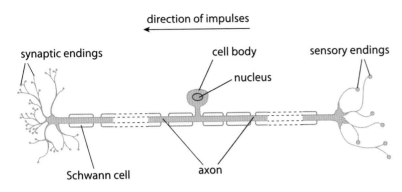

Figure 15.6: Longitudinal section of a sensory neurone.

Myelin

For most of their length, the axons of motor and sensory neurones are protected within nerves. Figure 15.7 shows a cross section of a nerve full of neurones. You can see that some of these are surrounded by thick dark rings. This darkly stained material is **myelin**, which is made by specialised cells – Schwann cells – that surround the axons of some neurones. You can see these Schwann cells surrounding a motor neurone in Figures 15.4 and 15.8.

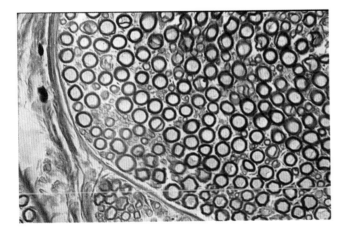

Figure 15.7: A photomicrograph of a transverse section (TS) of a nerve (×1600). The circles are axons of sensory and motor neurones in cross section. Most of these are myelinated (the ones with dark lines around) and some are not. Each group of axons is surrounded by a perineurium (red) composed of connective tissue with collagen fibres. Several such groups make a complete nerve, such as a spinal nerve.

KEY WORDS

myelin: insulating material that surrounds the axons of many neurones; myelin is made of layers of cell surface membranes formed by Schwann cells so that they are very rich in phospholipids and therefore impermeable to water and ions in tissue fluid

node of Ranvier: a very short gap between Schwann cells where myelinated axons are not covered in myelin so are exposed to tissue fluid

Not all axons are protected by myelin. You can see in Figure 15.7 that there are some neurones without dark rings; these are unmyelinated neurones. About two-thirds of your motor and sensory neurones are unmyelinated.

Myelin is made when Schwann cells wrap themselves around the axon all along its length. Figure 15.8a shows an axon in cross section surrounded by myelin. Figure 15.8b shows how a Schwann cell spirals around, enclosing an axon in many layers of its cell surface membrane. This enclosing sheath, called the myelin sheath, is made largely of lipid, together with some proteins. The sheath affects the speed of conduction of the nerve impulse. The small, uncovered areas of axon between Schwann cells are called **nodes of Ranvier**. They occur about every 1–3 mm in human neurones. The nodes themselves are very small, around 2–3 µm long.

a

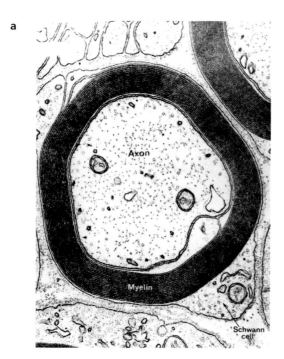

b

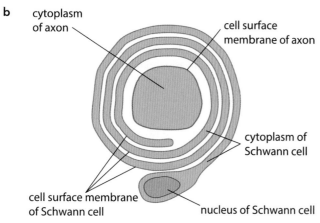

Figure 15.8: a A transmission electron micrograph (TEM) of a cross section of a myelinated axon (x24 000); **b** a diagram of a cross section of the axon of a myelinated neurone showing how myelin is made by a Schwann cell.

Questions

4   Use any readily available materials to make a 3D model of a myelinated neurone to show the relationship between an axon, the myelin sheath and the nodes of Ranvier.

5   What are the advantages of neurones being arranged in series as shown in Figure 15.9?

How neurones work together

Figure 15.9 shows how a sensory neurone, an intermediate neurone and a motor neurone work together to bring about a response to a stimulus. A reflex arc is the pathway along which impulses are transmitted from a receptor to an effector without involving 'conscious' regions of the brain. Examples of simple reflex actions that are coordinated by these pathways are:

- removing the hand rapidly from a sharp or hot object
- blinking
- focusing
- controlling how much light enters the eye.

Some reflex arcs have no intermediate neurone and the impulse passes directly from the sensory neurone to the motor neurone. An example is the knee-jerk (patellar) reflex that health professionals use to test the nervous system. Within the CNS, the sensory neurone and the relay neurone have extensions that branch to connect with other neurones in the CNS. These connections allow the information from sensory neurones to be integrated so that complex forms of behaviour can be coordinated. The gaps between the neurones are called synapses; they allow impulses to travel from one neurone to the next in the neuronal pathway.

Transmission of nerve impulses

Neurones transmit electrical impulses. These impulses travel very rapidly along the cell surface membrane from one end of the cell to the other; they are *not* a flow of electrons like an electric current. The signals are very brief changes in the distribution of electrical charge *across* the cell surface membrane. These signals are called **action potentials**. They are caused by very rapid movement of sodium ions and potassium ions across the axon membrane between the tissue fluid and the cytoplasm of the axon.

> **KEY WORD**
>
> **action potential:** a brief change in the potential difference from −70 mV to +30 mV across the cell surface membranes of neurones and muscle cells caused by the inward movement of sodium ions

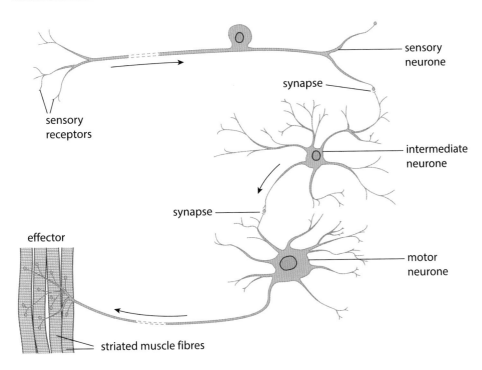

Figure 15.9: A simple diagram of a reflex arc – the arrangement of three neurones in series that coordinates a fast response to a particular stimulus. The arrows show the direction of impulses in the neurones.

Resting potential

Some axons in animals such as squids and earthworms are unmyelinated and very wide; it is possible to insert tiny electrodes into their cytoplasm to measure the changes in electrical charge. Figure 15.10 shows part of one of these axons. In a resting axon that is not transmitting impulses, the inside of the axon always has a slightly negative electrical potential compared with the outside (Figures 15.10 and 15.11). The difference between these potentials is called the **potential difference**, and is often between $-60\,mV$ and $-70\,mV$. In other words, the electrical potential of the inside of the axon is between $60\,mV$ and $70\,mV$ *lower* than the outside. This difference is called the **resting potential**. There are several factors that contribute to a resting potential of a neurone.

- Sodium–potassium pumps in the cell surface membrane (Figure 15.11b and Chapter 4, Section 4.5, Movement of substances across membranes). These constantly move sodium ions (Na^+) out of the axon, and potassium ions (K^+) into the axon. The sodium–potassium pumps are membrane proteins that use energy from the hydrolysis of ATP to move both of these ions against their concentration gradients. Three sodium ions are removed from the axon for every two

> **KEY WORDS**
>
> **potential difference:** the difference in electrical potential between two points; in the nervous system, between the inside and the outside of a cell surface membrane such as the membrane that encloses an axon
>
> **resting potential:** the difference in electrical potential that is maintained across the cell surface membrane of a neurone when it is not transmitting an action potential; it is normally about $-70\,mV$ inside and is partly maintained by sodium–potassium pumps

potassium ions brought in for every one molecule of ATP hydrolysed.

- The presence of many organic anions inside the cell, such as negatively charged proteins.

- The impermeability of the membrane to ions; sodium ions cannot diffuse through the axon membrane when the neurone is at rest. Remember from Chapter 4 that the phospholipid bilayer has a hydrophobic core which does not permit the movement of ions.

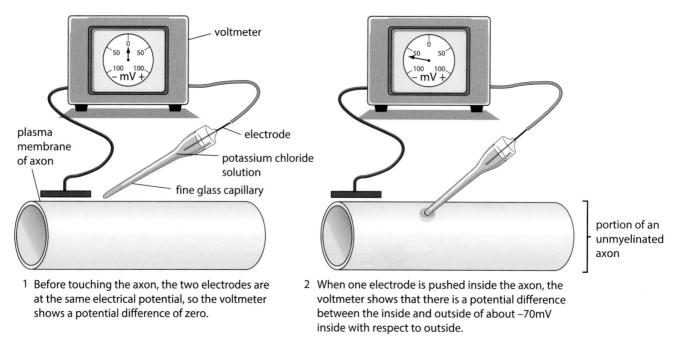

1 Before touching the axon, the two electrodes are at the same electrical potential, so the voltmeter shows a potential difference of zero.

2 When one electrode is pushed inside the axon, the voltmeter shows that there is a potential difference between the inside and outside of about −70mV inside with respect to outside.

Figure 15.10: Measuring the resting potential of an axon.

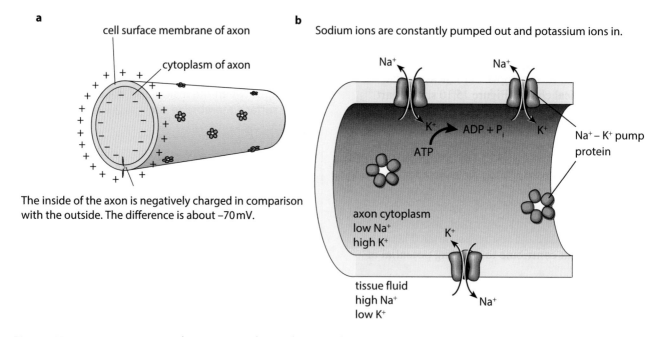

The inside of the axon is negatively charged in comparison with the outside. The difference is about −70mV.

b Sodium ions are constantly pumped out and potassium ions in.

Figure 15.11: a At rest, an axon has negative electrical potential inside. **b** The sodium–potassium pump maintains the resting potential by keeping more sodium ions outside in the tissue fluid than there are potassium ions inside.

Channel proteins that respond to changes in the potential difference across the membrane are closed so sodium and potassium ions cannot diffuse through them. These proteins are described later and are known as voltage-gated channel proteins.

The membrane has protein channels for potassium and for sodium which are open all the time. There are far more of these for potassium than for sodium. Therefore, more potassium ions could diffuse out compared with the sodium ions diffusing in. However, there are many large, negatively charged molecules inside the cell that attract the potassium ions reducing the chance that they will diffuse out. The result of these effects is an overall excess of negative ions inside the membrane compared with outside.

The axon membrane is relatively impermeable to sodium ions but there are two things that influence the inward movement of sodium ions during an action potential: there is a steep concentration gradient, and also the inside of the membrane is negatively charged, which attracts positively charged ions. A 'double' gradient like this is known as an electrochemical gradient (see Chapter 14).

Action potentials

With a small addition to the apparatus shown in Figure 15.10, it is possible to stimulate the axon with a very brief, small electric current (Figure 15.12). If the axon is stimulated in this way, the steady trace on the computer screen suddenly changes. The potential difference across the cell surface membrane of the axon suddenly switches from −70 mV to +30 mV. It swiftly returns to normal after a brief 'overshoot' (Figure 15.13). The whole process takes about 3 milliseconds (ms).

This rapid, fleeting change in potential difference across the membrane is the action potential. It is caused by changes in the permeability of the cell surface membrane to sodium ions and potassium ions.

As well as the channel proteins that are open all the time, there are other channel proteins in the cell surface membrane that allow sodium ions or potassium ions to pass through. These open and close depending on the electrical potential (or voltage) across the membrane, and are called **voltage-gated channel proteins**. When the membrane is at its resting potential, these channels are closed.

> ### KEY WORD
>
> **voltage-gated channel protein:** a channel protein through a cell membrane that opens or closes in response to changes in electrical potential across the membrane

First, the electric current used to stimulate the axon causes the opening of the voltage-gated channels in the cell surface membrane. This allows sodium ions to pass through. Because there is a much greater concentration of sodium ions outside the axon than

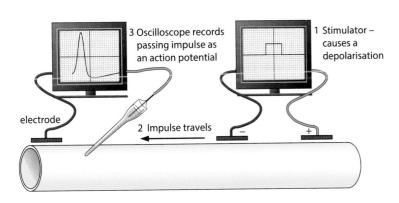

Figure 15.12: Recording action potentials. The changes in potential difference across an axon membrane are displayed as an impulse passes the electrode.

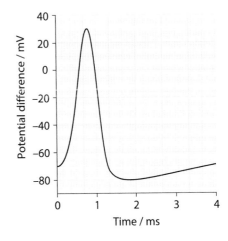

Figure 15.13: An action potential recorded at one position on an axon (as shown in Figure 15.12).

inside, sodium ions enter through the open channels. To begin with, only a few channels open. The inward movement of sodium ions changes the potential difference across the membrane, which becomes less negative on the inside. This is called depolarisation. It triggers some more channels to open so that more sodium ions enter. There is more depolarisation. If the potential difference reaches about –50 mV, then many more channels open and the inside reaches a potential of +30 mV compared with the outside. This is an example of a positive feedback because a small depolarisation leads to a greater and greater depolarisation (Section 14.1, Homeostasis). Action potentials are only generated if the potential difference reaches a value between –60 mV and –50 mV. This value is the threshold potential. If this value is not reached, an action potential does not occur.

After about 1 ms, all the sodium ion voltage-gated channels close, so sodium ions stop diffusing into the axon. At the same time, another set of voltage-gated channel proteins open to allow the diffusion of potassium ions *out* of the axon, down their concentration gradient. The outward movement of potassium ions removes positive charge from inside the axon to the outside, thus returning the potential difference to normal (−70 mV). This is called repolarisation. In fact, the potential difference across the membrane briefly becomes even more negative than the normal resting potential (Figure 15.13). The potassium ion channel proteins then close and the sodium ion channel proteins become responsive to depolarisation again. The sodium–potassium pump continues pumping sodium ions out and potassium ions in all the time.

> ### KEY WORDS
>
> depolarisation: the reversal of the resting potential across the cell surface membrane of a neurone or muscle cell, so that the inside becomes positively charged compared with the outside
>
> threshold potential: the critical potential difference across the cell surface membrane of a sensory receptor or neurone which must be reached before an action potential is initiated
>
> repolarisation: returning the potential difference across the cell surface membrane of a neurone or muscle cell to normal following the depolarisation of an action potential

These pumps maintain the distribution of sodium ions and potassium ions across the membrane so that action potentials can continue to occur.

Use your finger to tap on one place on a hard surface such as a table. Tap faster and see how many times you can tap your finger in 15 seconds. Calculate your frequency in taps per second. Compare this with the frequency of impulses in a neurone. Remember that each impulse is the movement of an action potential (a finger tap) along a neurone and that information about the strength of stimuli can be encoded as the frequency of impulses.

Figure 15.13 shows what happens at one particular point in an axon membrane. However, the function of a neurone is to transmit information *along* itself. How do action potentials help to transmit information along a neurone?

An action potential at any point in an axon's cell surface membrane triggers the production of an action potential in the membrane on either side of that point. Figure 15.14 shows how this happens. The temporary depolarisation of the membrane at the site of the action potential causes current to flow in both directions between the depolarised region and the resting regions on either side of it. These local circuits depolarise the resting regions where voltage-gated sodium ion channel proteins open and the membrane potential reaches the threshold potential so that action potentials pass along the membrane.

Current flows because there is a difference in charge between the inside and the outside of the axon membrane. It is a convention to show the direction of current flow with arrows pointing from positive to negative, as shown in Figure 15.14.

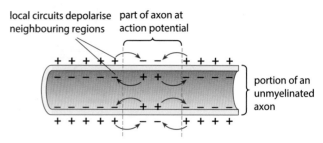

Figure 15.14: How an action potential passes along a neurone. The central part has been stimulated with an electrode to depolarise. The parts of the axon to left and right are at resting potential. Current flow (shown by arrows) depolarises the adjacent parts so impulses will pass along the axon in both directions away from the part stimulated.

The depolarisation on both sides of the action potential only happens in an experimental situation when a stimulus is applied somewhere along an axon, as in Figure 15.14. In the body, action potentials begin at one end of an axon, such as the junction between the axon and the cell body. 'New' action potentials are generated *ahead* and not behind. This is because the region behind is recovering from the action potential that has just occurred, so the sodium ion voltage-gated channels are closed. These channels are so tightly closed that they cannot open. This period of recovery, when the axon is unresponsive, is called the **refractory period**. This means:

- action potentials are discrete events; they do not merge into one another

- there is a minimum time between action potentials occurring at any one place on a neurone

- the length of the refractory period determines the maximum frequency at which impulses are transmitted along neurones; for many neurones this is between 200 and 300 impulses per second

- the impulse can only travel in one direction along the neurone.

Question

6 Make a copy of Figure 15.13.

a On your graph, draw a horizontal line right across it to represent the resting potential.

b The resting potential is said to be –70 mV inside. What does this mean?

c Describe how a neurone maintains this resting potential.

d As an action potential begins, the potential difference changes from –70 mV to +30 mV inside.

   i Why is this called *depolarisation*?

   ii Annotate your graph to describe what is happening in the axon membrane to cause this depolarisation.

e Annotate your graph to describe what is happening between 1 ms and 2 ms.

f If the action potential starts at time 0, how long does it take for the resting potential to be restored?

g i Indicate the refractory period on your graph.

   ii What are the roles of the refractory period?

h Ouabain is a poison that stops the activity of sodium–potassium pumps. If ouabain is added to part of an axon at a specific place along an axon, action potentials can continue to pass that region for about 1000 impulses. Suggest why they do not stop immediately

How action potentials carry information

Action potentials do not change in size as they travel, nor do they change in size according to the intensity of the stimulus. Action potentials continue to reach a peak value of +30 mV inside for the whole length of an axon. A very strong light shining in your eyes produces action potentials of precisely the same size as a dim light. The speed at which action potentials travel does not vary according to the size of the stimulus. In any one axon, the speed of impulse transmission is always the same.

What is different about the action potentials resulting from a strong and a weak stimulus is their frequency. A strong stimulus produces a rapid succession of action potentials, each one following along the axon just behind its predecessor. A weak stimulus results in fewer action potentials per second (Figure 15.15).

A strong stimulus is likely to stimulate more neurones than a weak stimulus. Whereas a weak stimulus might result in action potentials passing along just one or two neurones, a strong stimulus could produce action potentials in many more.

The brain interprets the *frequency* of action potentials arriving along the axon of a sensory neurone, and the *number* of neurones carrying action potentials, to get information about the *strength* of the stimulus being detected. The *nature* of the stimulus, whether it is light, heat, touch or so on, is deduced from the *position* of the sensory neurone bringing the information. If the neurone is from the retina of the eye, then the brain will interpret the information as meaning 'light'. If for some reason a different stimulus, such as pressure, stimulates a receptor cell in the retina, the brain will still interpret the action potentials from this receptor as meaning 'light'.

KEY WORD

refractory period: a period of time during which a neurone is recovering from an action potential, and during which another action potential cannot be generated

---

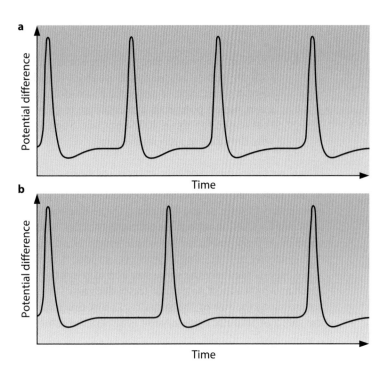

Figure 15.15: Action potentials resulting from **a** a strong stimulus and **b** a weak stimulus. Note that the amplitude of each action potential remains the same, only its frequency changes. **a** A high frequency of impulses is produced when a receptor is given a strong stimulus. This high frequency carries the message 'strong stimulus'. **b** A lower frequency of impulses is produced when a receptor is given a weaker stimulus. This lower frequency carries the message 'weak stimulus'.

This is why rubbing your eyes when they are shut can cause you to 'see' patterns of light.

Speed of conduction of impulses

Two factors determine the speed of conduction:

- the presence or absence of myelin

- the diameter of axons.

In unmyelinated neurones, the speed of conduction is slow, being as low as $0.5\,\mathrm{m\,s^{-1}}$ in some cases. In myelinated mammalian neurones, action potentials travel at speeds of up to $100\,\mathrm{m\,s^{-1}}$. Myelin speeds up the rate at which action potentials travel, by insulating the axon membrane. Sodium and potassium ions cannot flow through the myelin sheath, so it is not possible for depolarisation or action potentials to occur in parts of the axon which are surrounded by the myelin sheath. Action potentials can only occur at the nodes of Ranvier, where all the channel proteins and pump proteins are concentrated.

Figure 15.16 shows how an action potential is transmitted along a myelinated axon. The local circuits exist from one node to the next. Thus action potentials 'jump' from one node to the next, a distance of 1–3 mm. This is called **saltatory conduction**. In a myelinated axon, saltatory conduction can increase the speed of transmission by up to 50 times that in an unmyelinated axon of the same diameter.

> **KEY WORD**
>
> **saltatory conduction:** movement of an action potential along a myelinated axon, in which the action potential 'jumps' from one node of Ranvier to the next

Diameter also affects the speed of transmission (Figure 15.17). Thick axons transmit impulses faster than thin ones. This is because they have a greater surface area over which diffusion of ions can occur, which increases the rate of diffusion. Earthworms, which have no myelinated axons, have a small number of very thick unmyelinated ones that run all along their body.

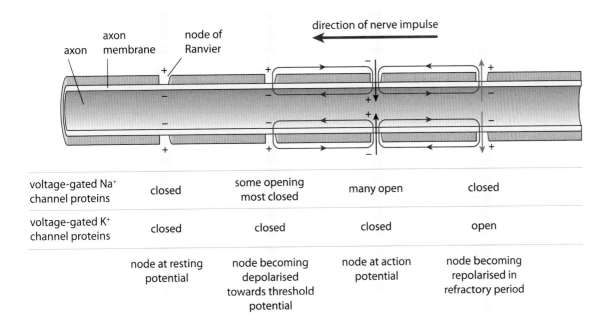

voltage-gated Na⁺ channel proteins	closed	some opening most closed	many open	closed
voltage-gated K⁺ channel proteins	closed	closed	closed	open
	node at resting potential	node becoming depolarised towards threshold potential	node at action potential	node becoming repolarised in refractory period

Figure 15.16: Transmission of an action potential in a myelinated axon. The myelin sheath acts as an insulator, preventing changes in membrane potential across the parts of the axon membrane surrounded by the sheath. Changes in membrane potential differences only occur at the nodes of Ranvier. The action potential therefore 'jumps' from one node to the next, travelling much faster than in an unmyelinated axon.

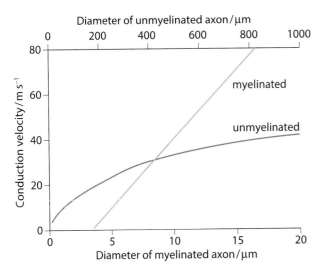

Figure 15.17: Speed of transmission in myelinated and unmyelinated axons of different diameters.

Question

7   If myelinated neurones conduct impulses so fast, why do mammals have unmyelinated neurones? What is the likely function of giant axons in earthworms?

What starts an action potential?

The stimulus for the action potential described earlier was a small electric current. In life, action potentials are generated by a wide variety of stimuli, such as light, pressure (touch), sound, temperature or chemicals.

A cell that responds to one such stimulus by initiating an action potential is called a receptor cell. Receptor cells are transducers: they convert the energy of stimuli – such as light, heat or sound – into electrical impulses in neurones (Table 15.1).

Receptor cells are often found in sense organs; for example, light receptor cells are found in the eye, and sound receptor cells are found in the ear. Some receptors, such as light receptors in the eye and **chemoreceptors** in the taste buds, are specialised cells

---

KEY WORD

chemoreceptor: a receptor cell that responds to chemical stimuli; chemoreceptors are found in taste buds on the tongue, in the nose and in blood vessels where they detect changes in oxygen and carbon dioxide concentrations

---

Receptor	Sense	Energy of stimulus
rod or cone cells in retina	sight	light
taste buds on tongue	taste	chemical potential
olfactory cells in nose	smell	chemical potential
Pacinian corpuscles in skin	pressure	movement and pressure
Meissner's corpuscles in skin	touch	movement and pressure
Ruffini's endings in skin	temperature	heat
proprioceptors (stretch receptors) in muscles	placement of limbs	mechanical displacement – stretching
hair cells in semicircular canals in ear	balance	movement
hair cells in cochlea	hearing	sound

Table 15.1: Some examples of receptors. Each receptor is a transducer converting the energy of the stimulus to impulses in sensory neurones. All of the receptors in the table except for stretch receptors respond to external stimuli. Stretch receptors respond to changes inside the muscles. There are many other receptors that respond to internal stimuli.

which detect a specific type of stimulus and influence the electrical activity of a sensory neurone. Other receptors, such as some kinds of touch receptors, are simply the ends of the sensory neurones themselves (Figure 15.18 and Exam-style question 3).

Your tongue is covered in many small bumps or papillae. Each papilla has many taste buds over its surface (Figure 15.19). Within each taste bud are between 50 and 100 receptor cells that are sensitive to chemicals in the liquids that you drink or chemicals from your food that dissolve in saliva. Each chemoreceptor is covered with receptor proteins that detect these different

chemicals. There are several types of receptor proteins, each detecting a different type of chemical and giving you a different sensation. There are five tastes: sweet, sour, salt, bitter and umami (savoury).

Chemoreceptors in the taste buds that detect salt are directly influenced by sodium ions (Figure 15.19d). These ions diffuse through highly selective channel proteins in the cell surface membrane of the microvilli leading to depolarisation of the membrane. The increase in positive charge inside the cell is the **receptor potential**. If there is sufficient stimulation by sodium ions in the mouth, the receptor potential becomes

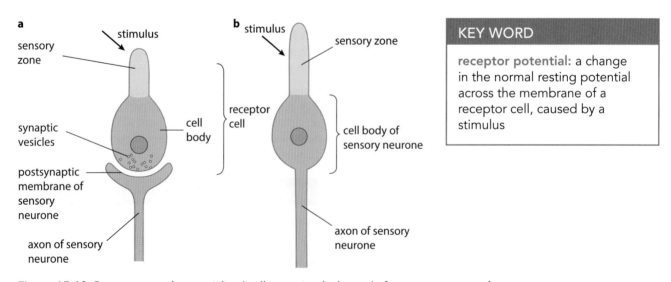

KEY WORD

receptor potential: a change in the normal resting potential across the membrane of a receptor cell, caused by a stimulus

Figure 15.18: Receptors can be specialised cells **a** or simply the end of a sensory neurone **b**.

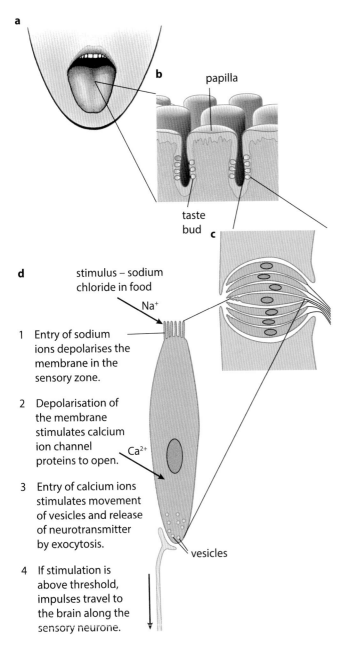

d stimulus – sodium chloride in food

Na⁺

1   Entry of sodium ions depolarises the membrane in the sensory zone.

2   Depolarisation of the membrane stimulates calcium ion channel proteins to open.

Ca²⁺

3   Entry of calcium ions stimulates movement of vesicles and release of neurotransmitter by exocytosis.

vesicles

4   If stimulation is above threshold, impulses travel to the brain along the sensory neurone.

Figure 15.19: a Taste buds are in papillae that are distributed across the tongue; **b** a cross section through a papilla showing the distribution of taste buds; **c** a taste bud; **d** details of one chemoreceptor cell.

large enough to stimulate the opening of voltage-gated calcium ion channel proteins. Calcium ions enter the cytoplasm and lead to exocytosis of vesicles containing neurotransmitter from the basal membrane of the chemoreceptor. The neurotransmitter stimulates an action potential in the sensory neurone that transmits impulses to the taste centre in the cerebral cortex of the brain.

When receptors are stimulated, they are depolarised. If the stimulus is very weak and below the threshold, the cells are not depolarised very much and the sensory neurone is not activated to send impulses (Figure 15.20). If the receptor potential is above the threshold, then the receptor cell stimulates the sensory neurone to send impulses. This is an example of the **all-or-none law**: neurones either transmit impulses from one end to the other or they do not. As you have already seen, the action potentials always have the same amplitude. As the stimuli increase in intensity, the action potentials are produced more frequently. The action potentials do not become bigger; they have the same amplitudes.

> ### KEY WORD
>
> **all-or-none law:** neurones and muscle cells only transmit impulses if the initial stimulus is sufficient to increase the membrane potential above a threshold potential

Threshold levels in receptors rarely stay constant. With continued stimulation, they often increase so that it requires a greater stimulus before receptors send impulses along sensory neurones.

Question

8   Use Figure 15.20 to answer these questions.

   a   Explain what is meant by the terms:

      i   *receptor potential*

      ii   *threshold receptor potential*

      iii   the *all-or-none law*.

   b   Describe the relationship between the strength of the stimulus and the size of the receptor potential that is generated.

   c   Describe the relationship between the strength of the stimulus applied and the frequency of action potentials generated in the sensory neurone.

   d   What determines the maximum frequency of action potentials in a neurone?

   e   Threshold potentials in receptor cells can increase and decrease. Suggest the likely advantages of this.

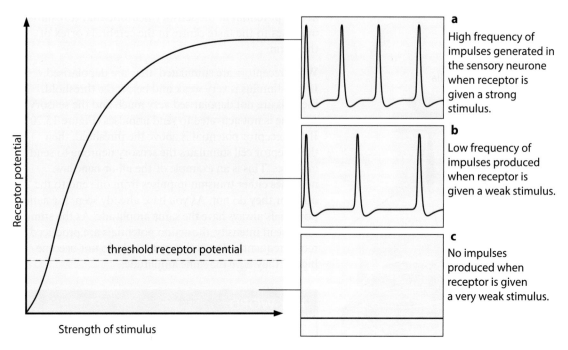

Figure 15.20: **a** Below the threshold receptor potential, depolarisation does not result in any impulses. As the strength of a stimulus increases, the receptor potential also increases. **b** If the receptor potential reaches the threshold, then impulses are sent along the sensory neurone at low frequency. **c** Increasing the strength of the stimulus above the threshold increases the frequency of the impulses; it does not change their amplitude.

Synapses

Where two neurones meet, they do not quite touch. There is a very small gap, about 20 nm wide, between them. This gap is called the **synaptic cleft**. The parts of the two neurones near to the cleft, plus the cleft itself, make up a **synapse** (Figure 15.21).

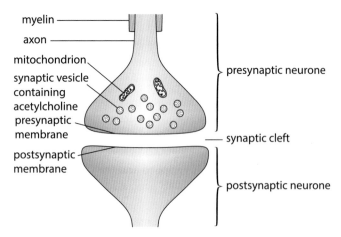

Figure 15.21: A cholinergic synapse between two neurones (see Figure 15.9).

The mechanism of synaptic transmission

Impulses cannot 'jump' across the type of synapse shown in Figure 15.21. Instead, molecules of a transmitter substance, or **neurotransmitter**, are released to stimulate the next neurone.

KEY WORDS

synaptic cleft: a very small gap between two neurones at a synapse; nerve impulses are transmitted across synaptic clefts by neurotransmitters

synapse: a point at which two neurones meet but do not touch; the synapse is made up of the end of the presynaptic neurone, the synaptic cleft and the end of the postsynaptic neurone

neurotransmitter: a chemical released at synapses to transmit impulses between neurones or between a motor neurone and a muscle fibre

Here is an outline of the sequence of events that occurs.

1 An action potential occurs at the cell surface membrane of the first neurone, or **presynaptic neurone**.

2 The action potential causes the release of molecules of transmitter substance into the cleft.

3 The molecules of transmitter substance diffuse across the cleft and bind temporarily to receptors on the **postsynaptic neurone**.

4 The postsynaptic neurone responds to all the impulses arriving at any one time by depolarising; if the overall depolarisation is above its threshold, then it will send impulses.

Let's look at these processes in more detail. The cytoplasm of the presynaptic neurone contains vesicles of transmitter substance (Figure 15.22). More than 40 different transmitter substances are known; **noradrenaline** and **acetylcholine (ACh)** are found throughout the nervous system, whereas others such as dopamine, glutamic acid and gamma-aminobutyric acid (GABA) occur only in the brain. You will concentrate on the synapses that use ACh as the transmitter substance. These are known as **cholinergic synapses**.

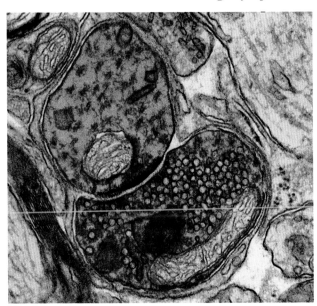

Figure 15.22: False-colour TEM of a synapse (×52 000). The presynaptic neurone (at the bottom) has mitochondria (shown in green) and numerous vesicles (blue), which contain molecules of neurotransmitter.

You will remember that, as an action potential occurs at one place on an axon, local circuits depolarise the next piece of membrane, stimulating the opening of sodium ion voltage-gated channel proteins. In the part of the membrane of the presynaptic neurone that is next to the synaptic cleft, the arrival of the action potential also causes **voltage-gated calcium ion channel proteins** to open (Figure 15.23). Thus, the action potential causes not only sodium ions but also calcium ions to diffuse into the cytoplasm of the presynaptic neurone. There are virtually no calcium ions in the cytoplasm but many in the tissue fluid surrounding the synapse. This means that there is a very steep electrochemical gradient for calcium ions.

The influx of calcium ions stimulates vesicles containing ACh to move to the presynaptic membrane and fuse with it, emptying their contents into the synaptic cleft. The attachment of vesicle to membrane is helped by SNARE proteins which are on the vesicles and the presynaptic membrane. Each action potential causes just a few vesicles to do this, and each vesicle contains up to 10 000 molecules of ACh. The ACh diffuses across the synaptic cleft, usually in less than 0.5 ms.

The cell surface membrane of the postsynaptic neurone contains **receptor proteins**. Part of the receptor protein molecule has a complementary shape to part of the ACh

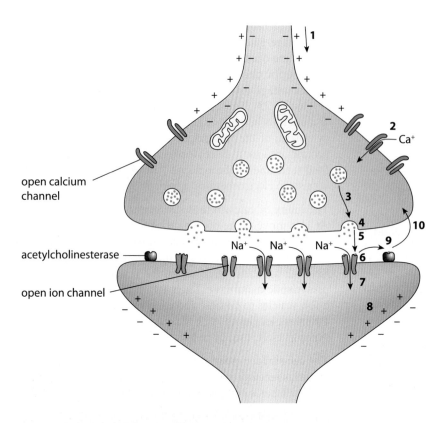

1 An action potential arrives.
2 Depolarisation of the synaptic terminal stimulates the opening of voltage-gated calcium ion channel proteins. Calcium ions diffuse in.
3 Synaptic vesicles move towards the presynaptic membrane.
4 Synaptic vesicles fuse with presynaptic membrane and empty ACh into synaptic cleft.
5 ACh diffuses across the synaptic cleft.
6 ACh molecules bind to receptors in the postsynaptic membrane.
7 Receptors go through conformational change and open to allow sodium ions to diffuse into the postsynaptic neurone.
8 Postsynaptic membrane is depolarised.
9 Acetylcholinesterase breaks down ACh.
10 Choline is absorbed by presynaptic neurone and recycled into ACh

Figure 15.23: Synaptic transmission.

molecule, so that the ACh molecules can temporarily bind with the receptors. The binding changes the shape of the protein, opening channels through which sodium ions can pass (Figure 15.24). Sodium ions diffuse into the cytoplasm of the postsynaptic neurone down the electrochemical gradient and depolarise the membrane. These receptor proteins with their channels are ligand-gated ion channels as they are stimulated to open by a ligand (a chemical) and not by a voltage change.

If ACh remained bound to the postsynaptic receptors, these sodium ion channels would remain open, and the postsynaptic neurone would be permanently depolarised. The ACh is recycled to prevent this from happening and also to avoid wasting it. The synaptic cleft contains an enzyme, **acetylcholinesterase**, which catalyses the hydrolysis of each ACh molecule into acetate and choline.

> **KEY WORD**
>
> **acetylcholinesterase:** an enzyme in the synaptic cleft and on the postsynaptic membrane that hydrolyses ACh to acetate and choline

The choline is taken back into the presynaptic neurone, where it reacts with acetyl coenzyme A to form ACh once more. The ACh is then transported into the presynaptic vesicles, ready for the next action potential. The entire sequence of events, from initial arrival of the action potential to the re-formation of ACh, takes about 5–10 ms.

Question

9 a Name the process by which vesicles release their contents at the presynaptic membrane.

 b Describe the role of acetylcholinesterase.

The depolarisation of the postsynaptic neurone leads to the generation of an action potential when the potential difference is above the threshold for that neurone. If not, then there is no action potential. The chance that an action potential is generated and an impulse sent in the postsynaptic neurone is increased if more than one presynaptic neurone releases ACh at the same time or over a short period of time.

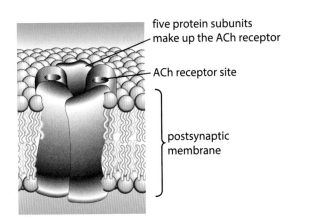

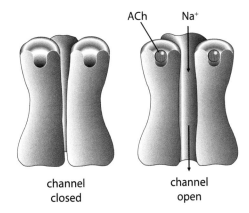

Figure 15.24: Detail of how the ACh receptor works. The receptor is made of five protein subunits spanning the membrane arranged to form a cylinder. Two of these subunits contain ACh receptor sites. When ACh molecules bind with both of these receptor sites, the proteins change shape, opening the channel between the units. Parts of the protein molecules around this channel contain negatively charged amino acids, which attract positively charged sodium ions so they pass through the channel.

Much of the research on synapses has been done at synapses between a motor neurone and a muscle, not those between two neurones. The motor neurone forms a motor end plate with each muscle fibre and the synapse is called a neuromuscular junction (Figure 15.25). Such synapses function in the same way as described above. An action potential is produced in the muscle fibre, which may cause it to contract (Section 15.3).

KEY WORD

neuromuscular junction: a synapse between a motor neurone and a muscle

---

The roles of synapses

Synapses slow down the rate of transmission of a nerve impulse that has to travel along two or more neurones. Responses to a stimulus would be much quicker if action potentials generated in a receptor travelled along an unbroken neuronal pathway from receptor to effector, rather than having to cross synapses on the way. So why have synapses?

- **Synapses ensure one-way transmission.** Impulses can only pass in one direction at synapses. This is because neurotransmitter is released on one side and its receptors are on the other. There is no way that chemical transmission can occur in the opposite direction.

- **Synapses allow the interconnection of nerve pathways.** Synapses allow a wider range of

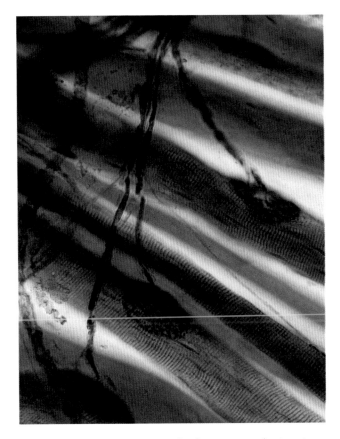

Figure 15.25: Photomicrograph of neuromuscular junctions (×200). The red tissue is muscle fibres, whereas the axons show as dark lines. The end of the axon of a motor neurone branches to supply different muscle fibres. The oval structure on each muscle fibre is a neuromuscular junction. Action potentials are passed from the axon to the muscle, across a synaptic cleft, at these neuromuscular junctions.

behaviour than could be generated in a nervous system in which neurones were directly 'wired up' to each other. They do this by allowing the interconnection of many nerve pathways. This happens in two ways:

- Individual sensory and relay neurones have axons that branch to form synapses with many different neurones; this means that information from one neurone can spread out throughout the body to reach many motor neurones and many effectors as happens when you respond to dangerous situations.

- There are many neurones that terminate on each relay and motor neurone as they have many dendrites to give a large surface area for many synapses; this allows one neurone to integrate the information coming from many different parts of the body – something that is essential for decision-making in the brain.

Questions

10 Suggest why:

   a impulses travel in only one direction at synapses

   b if action potentials arrive repeatedly at a synapse, the synapse eventually becomes unable to transmit the impulse to the next neurone.

11 Make a table to compare coordination in mammals by the nervous system and by the endocrine system.

15.3 Muscle contraction

This section concerns the contraction of striated muscle (Figure 15.26). This type of muscle tissue makes up the many muscles in the body that are attached to the skeleton. Striated muscle only contracts when it is stimulated to do so by impulses that arrive via motor neurones. Muscle tissue like this is described as being neurogenic. You have already seen how the cardiac muscle in the heart is myogenic – it contracts and relaxes automatically, with no need for impulses arriving from neurones (Chapter 8, Section 8.6, The heart). There is also a third type of muscle tissue, smooth muscle, which is found throughout the body in organs, such as in the gas exchange

system (Chapter 9, Section 9.3, Trachea, bronchi and bronchioles), alimentary canal and in the walls of the arteries, arterioles and veins (Chapter 8, Section 8.3, Blood vessels). Most smooth muscle only contracts when it receives impulses in motor neurones. However, smooth muscle in arteries also contracts when it is stretched by the pressure of blood surging through them. This happens without any input from the nervous system. This type of muscle is called smooth because, unlike the other two types of muscle tissue, it has no striations. Smooth muscle does *not* form smooth linings of tubular structures, such as the trachea and arteries; the lining of these structures is always formed by an epithelium. The structures and functions of the three types of muscle tissue are compared in Table 15.2.

It is important that the activities of the different muscles in your body are coordinated. When a muscle contracts, it exerts a force on a particular part of the body, such as a bone. This results in a particular response. The nervous system ensures that the behaviour of each muscle is coordinated with all the other muscles, so that together they can bring about the desired movement without causing damage to any parts of the skeletal or muscular system.

The structure of striated muscle

A muscle such as a biceps is made up of thousands of muscle fibres (Figure 15.26). Each muscle fibre is a highly specialised 'cell' with a highly organised arrangement of contractile proteins in the cytoplasm, surrounded by a cell surface membrane. Some biologists prefer not to call it a cell because it contains many nuclei. Instead, they prefer the term *syncytium* to describe the multinucleate muscle fibre. The parts of the fibre are known by different terms. The cell surface membrane is the sarcolemma, the cytoplasm

KEY WORDS

striated muscle: type of muscle tissue in skeletal muscles; the muscle fibres have regular striations that can be seen under the light microscope

sarcolemma: the cell surface membrane of a muscle fibre

sarcoplasm: the cytoplasm of muscle cells

Features	Type of muscle		
	Striated	Cardiac	Smooth
Appearance in the light microscope	stripes (striations) at regular intervals	stripes (striations) at regular intervals	no striations
Cell structure	multinucleate (syncytium)	uninucleate cells joined by intercalated discs (Figure 8.22)	uninucleate cells
Shape of cells	long, unbranched cylinder	cells are shorter with branches that connect to adjacent cells	long, unbranched cells that taper at either end
Organisation of contractile proteins inside the cell	organised into parallel bundles of myofibrils	organised into parallel bundles of myofibrils	contractile proteins not organised into myofibrils
Distribution in the body	muscles attached to the skeleton	heart	tubular structures, e.g. blood vessels (arteries, arterioles and veins), airways, gut, Fallopian tubes (oviducts), uterus
Control	neurogenic	myogenic	neurogenic

Table 15.2: Mammals have three types of muscle tissue: striated, cardiac and smooth.

is sarcoplasm and the endoplasmic reticulum is sarcoplasmic reticulum (SR). The sarcolemma has many deep infoldings into the interior of the muscle fibre, called transverse system tubules (also known as T-system tubules or T-tubules for short) (Figure 15.27). These run close to the SR. The membranes of the SR have huge numbers of protein pumps that transport calcium ions into the lumen (cisternae) of the SR. The sarcoplasm often contains a large number of mitochondria, often packed tightly between the myofibrils. These carry out aerobic respiration, generating the ATP that is required for muscle contraction.

The most striking thing about a muscle fibre is its stripes, or striations. These are produced by a very regular arrangement of many myofibrils in the sarcoplasm. Each myofibril is striped in exactly the same way, and is lined up precisely against the next one, so producing the pattern you can see in Figures 15.26 and 15.27.

This is as much as you can see using a light microscope, but with an electron microscope it is possible to see that each myofibril is itself made up of yet smaller components, called filaments. Parallel groups of thick filaments lie between groups of thin ones. Both thick and thin filaments are made up of protein. The thick filaments are made mostly of myosin, while the thin ones are made mostly of actin. Now you can understand what causes the stripes. The darker parts of the stripes, the A bands, correspond to the thick (myosin) filaments.

> ## KEY WORDS
>
> **sarcoplasmic reticulum (SR):** the endoplasmic reticulum of a muscle fibre
>
> **transverse system tubule (or T-system tubule or T-tubule):** infolding of the sarcolemma that go deep into a muscle fibre and conducts impulses to the SR
>
> **myofibril:** one of many cylindrical bundles of thick (myosin) and thin (actin) filaments inside a muscle fibre
>
> **myosin:** the protein that makes up the thick filaments in striated muscle; the globular heads of each molecule break down ATP (they act as an ATP-ase)
>
> **actin:** the protein that makes up the thin filaments in striated muscle

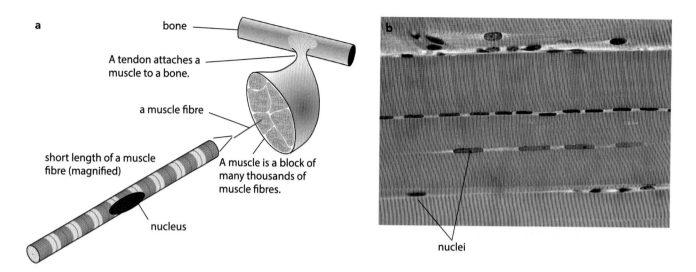

a

bone

A tendon attaches a muscle to a bone.

a muscle fibre

short length of a muscle fibre (magnified)

A muscle is a block of many thousands of muscle fibres.

nucleus

b

nuclei

Figure 15.26: a The structure of a muscle. As each muscle is composed of several tissues (striated muscle tissue, blood, nerves and connective tissue), it is an example of an organ. **b** A photomicrograph of several muscle fibres showing the striations that can be seen with a light microscope. Many nuclei are also visible (×300).

a Short length of muscle fibre

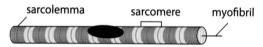

sarcolemma   sarcomere   myofibril

b Highly magnified edge of muscle fibre

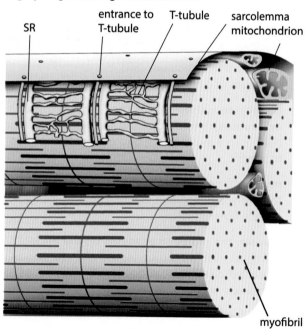

SR   entrance to   T-tubule   sarcolemma
             T-tubule   mitochondrion

myofibril

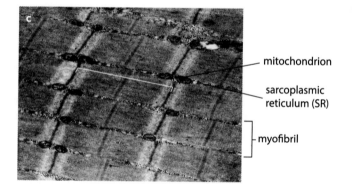

c

mitochondrion

sarcoplasmic reticulum (SR)

myofibril

Figure 15.27: Ultrastructure of part of a muscle fibre: **a** a short length of a muscle fibre showing the relative size of a myofibril; **b** a diagram made from scanning electron micrographs showing the edge of a muscle fibre; **c** a TEM of a LS of a muscle fibre showing parts of seven myofibrils. The white bracket indicates a sarcomere.

The lighter parts, the I bands, are where there are no thick filaments, only thin (actin) filaments (Figure 15.28). The very darkest parts of the A band are produced by the overlap of thick and thin filaments, while the lighter area within the A band, known as the H band, represents the parts where only the thick filaments are present. A line known as the Z line provides an attachment for the actin filaments, and the M line does the same for the myosin filaments. The part of a myofibril between two Z lines is called a **sarcomere**. Myofibrils are cylindrical in shape, so the Z line is a disc separating one sarcomere from another and is also called the Z disc.

> **KEY WORD**
>
> **sarcomere:** the part of a myofibril between two Z discs

Question

12 a Name the type of muscle tissue shown in Figure 15.26. Explain your answer.

    b Use Figure 15.28 to make a simple diagram to show the arrangement of the thick and thin filaments in a sarcomere of a resting muscle. In your diagram, show and label the following: one thick filament, four thin filaments and two Z lines. You may find it a good idea to draw on squared paper (e.g. graph paper).

    c Indicate and label the following on your diagram: A band, I band and H band.

    d The average length of a sarcomere in a resting muscle is 2.25 μm. Calculate the magnification of your diagram and state the steps you took in making the calculation. Show your answer to the nearest whole number. Ask someone to make sure your answer is correct.

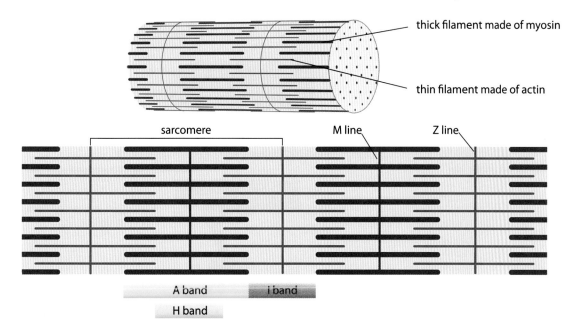

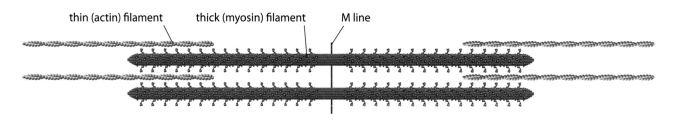

Figure 15.28: The structure of a myofibril.

Structure of thick and thin filaments

Thick filaments are composed of many molecules of myosin, which is a fibrous protein with a globular head. The fibrous portion helps to anchor the molecule into the thick filament. Within the thick filament, many myosin molecules all lie together in a bundle with their globular heads all pointing away from the M line.

The main component of thin filaments, actin, is a globular protein. Many actin molecules are linked together to form a chain. Two of these chains are twisted together to form a thin filament. Also twisted around the actin chains is a fibrous protein called **tropomyosin**. Another protein, **troponin**, is attached to the actin chain at regular intervals (Figure 15.29).

How muscles contract

Muscles cause movement by contracting. The sarcomeres in each myofibril get shorter as the Z discs are pulled closer together. Figure 15.29 shows how this

> ### KEY WORDS
>
> **tropomyosin:** a fibrous protein that is part of the thin filaments in myofibrils in striated muscle; tropomyosin blocks the attachment site on the thin filament for myosin heads so preventing the formation of cross-bridges
>
> **troponin:** a calcium-binding protein that is part of the thin filaments in myofibrils in striated muscle

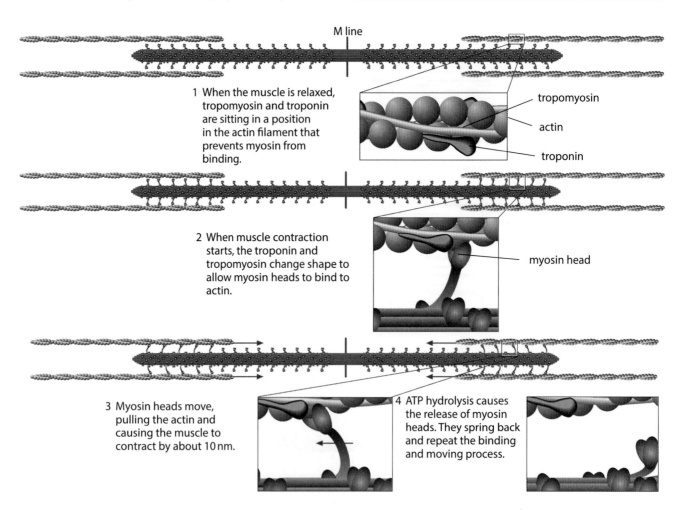

1 When the muscle is relaxed, tropomyosin and troponin are sitting in a position in the actin filament that prevents myosin from binding.

2 When muscle contraction starts, the troponin and tropomyosin change shape to allow myosin heads to bind to actin.

3 Myosin heads move, pulling the actin and causing the muscle to contract by about 10 nm.

4 ATP hydrolysis causes the release of myosin heads. They spring back and repeat the binding and moving process.

Figure 15.29: The sliding filament model of muscle contraction. Find some animations of the sliding filament model online to see the movement of the thin filaments during muscle contraction.

happens. It is known as the **sliding filament model** of muscle contraction.

The energy for the movement comes from ATP molecules that are attached to the myosin heads. Each myosin head is an ATPase.

When a muscle contracts, calcium ions are released from stores in the SR and bind to troponin. This stimulates troponin molecules to change shape (Figure 15.29). The troponin and tropomyosin proteins move to a different position on the thin filaments, so exposing parts of the actin molecules, which act as binding sites for myosin. The myosin heads bind with these sites, forming cross-bridges between the two types of filament.

Next, the myosin heads move, pulling the actin filaments along towards the centre of the sarcomere. The heads then hydrolyse ATP molecules, which provide enough energy to enable the heads to let go of the actin. The heads move back to their previous positions and bind again to the exposed sites on the actin. The thin filaments have moved as a result of the previous power stroke, so myosin heads now bind to actin further along the thin filaments closer to the Z disc. The myosin heads move again, pulling the actin filaments even further along, then hydrolyse more ATP molecules so that they can let go again. This continues for as long as the troponin and tropomyosin molecules are not blocking the binding sites, and the muscle has a supply of ATP.

Question

13 LSs and TSs of striated muscle fibres were examined in an electron microscope. Figure 15.30 shows drawings of the structures visible in a sarcomere in LS and TS as seen in a TEM.

   a Explain why an electron microscope rather than a light microscope was used to study these sections.

   b i Name the structures **A**, **B** and **C**.

      ii Name the regions of the sarcomere labelled **D**, **E** and **F**.

   c State the region of the sarcomere where the TS was taken.

   d Make a model of a sarcomere and use it to explain how the sliding of filaments in a sarcomere leads to the contraction of a muscle fibre. Use the model you have made to explain the sliding filament model of muscle contraction to someone else.

longitudinal section (LS)

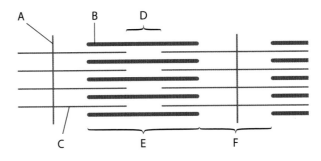

transverse section (TS)

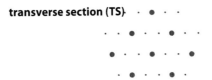

Figure 15.30: LS and TS of striated muscle fibre.

Stimulating muscle to contract

Skeletal muscle contracts when it receives an impulse from a neurone. An impulse moves along the axon of a motor neurone and arrives at the presynaptic membrane (Figure 15.31). A neurotransmitter, generally ACh, diffuses across the neuromuscular junction and binds to receptor proteins on the postsynaptic membrane – which is the sarcolemma (the cell surface membrane of the muscle fibre). The binding of ACh stimulates the ion channels to open, so that sodium ions enter to depolarise the membrane and generate an action potential in the sarcolemma.

Impulses pass along the sarcolemma and along the T-tubules towards the centre of the muscle fibre. The membranes of the SR are very close to the T-tubules. The arrival of the impulses causes voltage-gated calcium ion channel proteins in the membranes to open. Calcium ions diffuse out of the SR, down a very steep concentration gradient, into the sarcoplasm surrounding the myofibrils.

The calcium ions bind with troponin molecules that are part of the thin filaments. This changes the shape of the troponin molecules, which causes the troponin and tropomyosin to move so exposing the binding sites for the myosin heads. The myosin heads attach to the binding sites on the thin filaments and form cross-bridges (Figures 15.29 and 15.31). When there is no longer any stimulation from the motor neurone, there are no impulses conducted along the T-tubules. Released from stimulation, the calcium ion channels in the SR close and carrier proteins pump calcium ions back into stores in the SR. As calcium ions leave their binding sites on troponin, tropomyosin moves back to cover the myosin-binding sites on the thin filaments.

When there are no cross-bridges between thick and thin filaments, the muscle is in a relaxed state. There is nothing to hold the filaments together so any pulling force applied to the muscle will lengthen the sarcomeres so that they are ready to contract (and shorten) again. Each skeletal muscle in the body has an antagonist – a muscle that restores sarcomeres to their original lengths when it contracts. For example, the triceps is the antagonist of the biceps.

Question

14 Interneuronal synapses are those found between neurones, such as those in a reflex arc (Figures 15.9 and 15.21). Describe the similarities and differences between the structure and function of interneuronal synapses and neuromuscular junctions.

Events at the neuromuscular junction

1 An action potential arrives.

2 The action potential causes the diffusion of calcium ions into the neurone.

3 The calcium ions cause vesicles containing ACh to fuse with the presynaptic membrane.

Events in muscle fibre

7 The depolarisation of the sarcolemma spreads down T-tubules.

8 Channel proteins for calcium ions open and calcium ions diffuse out of the sarcoplasmic reticulum.

9 Calcium ions bind to troponin. Tropomyosin moves to expose myosin-binding sites on the actin filaments. Myosin heads form cross-bridges with thin filaments and the sarcomere shortens.

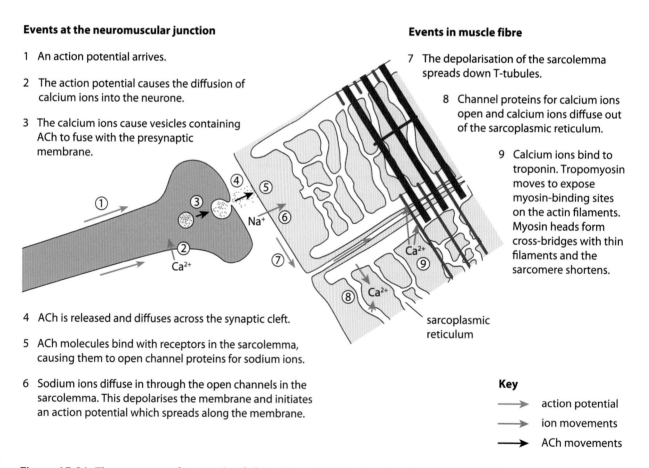

4 ACh is released and diffuses across the synaptic cleft.

5 ACh molecules bind with receptors in the sarcolemma, causing them to open channel proteins for sodium ions.

6 Sodium ions diffuse in through the open channels in the sarcolemma. This depolarises the membrane and initiates an action potential which spreads along the membrane.

sarcoplasmic reticulum

Key

→ action potential

→ ion movements

→ ACh movements

Figure 15.31: The sequence of events that follows the arrival of an impulse at a motor end plate.

Providing energy for muscle contraction

Muscle contraction is one of the uses of energy in animals (Chapter 12). A contracting muscle uses a lot of ATP. The very small quantity of ATP in the muscle fibres in a resting muscle is used up rapidly once the muscle starts to contract. More ATP is produced by respiration – both aerobic respiration inside the mitochondria and, when that cannot supply ATP fast enough, by lactate fermentation in the sarcoplasm (Chapter 12, Section 12.4, Respiration without oxygen).

Question

15 Explain why striated muscle tissue produces lactate during strenuous exercise. Look back to Chapter 12 if you are unsure.

15.4 Control and coordination in plants

Plants, like animals, have communication systems that allow coordination between different parts of their bodies. They respond to changes in their external and internal environments, as you saw in Chapter 14. Most plant responses involve changing some aspect of their growth to respond to factors such as gravity, light and water availability. Plants can also respond fairly quickly to changes in carbon dioxide concentration, lack of water, grazing by animals and infection by fungi and bacteria. Some of these responses are brought about by quick changes in turgidity, as happens when stomata respond to changes in humidity, carbon dioxide concentration and water availability (Chapter 14, Section 14.5, Homeostasis in plants).

Electrical communication in plants

Like animal cells, plant cells have electrochemical gradients across their cell surface membranes. They also have resting potentials. As in animals, plant action potentials are triggered when the membrane is depolarised. In at least some species, some responses to stimuli are coordinated by action potentials. The 'sensitive plant', *Mimosa*, responds to touch by folding up its leaves. Microelectrodes inserted into leaf cells detect changes in potential difference that are very similar to action potentials in animals. The depolarisation results not from the influx of positively charged sodium ions but from the outflow of negatively charged chloride ions. Repolarisation is achieved in the same way as in neurones, by the outflow of potassium ions. Plants do not have specific nerve cells, but many of their cells transmit waves of electrical activity that are very similar to those transmitted along the neurones of animals. The action potentials travel along the cell membranes of plant cells and from cell to cell through plasmodesmata that are lined by cell membrane (see Figure 1.21). The action potentials generally last much longer and travel more slowly than in animal neurones.

Many different stimuli trigger action potentials in plants. Chemicals coming into contact with a plant's surface trigger action potentials. For example, dripping a solution of acid on soya bean leaves causes action potentials to sweep across them. In potato plants, Colorado beetle larvae feeding on leaves have been shown to induce action potentials. It is thought that these electrical signals are used to coordinate the responses to damage and other stresses.

The Venus fly trap, *Dionaea muscipula*, is a carnivorous plant that obtains a supply of nitrogen compounds by trapping and digesting small animals, mostly insects (Figure 15.32a). Charles Darwin made the first scientific study of carnivorous plants describing Venus fly traps as 'one of the most wonderful plants in the world'. The specialised leaf is divided into two lobes either side of a midrib. The inside of each lobe is often red and has nectar-secreting glands around the edge to attract insects. Each lobe has three stiff sensory hairs that respond to being deflected. The outer edges of the lobes have stiff hairs that interlock to capture the insect inside. The surface of the lobes has many glands that secrete enzymes for the digestion of trapped insects. The touch of a fly or other insect on the sensory hairs on the inside of the folded leaves of the Venus fly trap stimulates action potentials that travel very fast across the leaf causing it to fold over and capture the insect (Figure 15.32b).

The deflection of a sensory hair activates calcium ion channels in cells at the base of the hair. These channels open so that calcium ions flow in to generate a receptor potential. If two of these hairs are stimulated within a period of 20−35 seconds, or one hair is touched twice within the same time interval, action potentials travel

Figure 15.32: a The Venus fly trap, *Dionaea muscipula,* is a carnivorous plant that grows in poor, acidic soils in the Carolinas in the USA. **b** Some of the leaves are adapted for trapping and digesting small animals, mainly insects. After digesting several insects, the traps die and turn black.

across the trap. When the second trigger takes too long to occur after the first, the trap will not close, but a new time interval starts again. If a hair is deflected a third time, the trap will still close. The time between stimulus and response is about 0.5 s. It takes the trap less than 0.3 s to close and capture the insect.

The lobes of the leaf bulge upwards when the trap is open. They are convex in shape. No one is quite sure how the trap closes but, as Darwin noticed, the lobes rapidly change into a concave shape, bending downwards so the trap snaps shut. This happens too fast to be simply the result of water movement from the cells on the top of the lobes to cells underneath. Instead, it is likely that the rapid change occurs as a result of a release of elastic tension in the cell walls.

However, the trap is not completely closed at this moment. To seal the trap, it requires ongoing activation of the trigger hairs by the captured prey. Unless the prey is able to escape, it will further stimulate the inner surface of the lobes, thereby triggering further action potentials. This forces the edges of the lobes together, sealing the trap so that the prey can be digested. Further deflections of the sensory hairs by the insect stimulate the entry of calcium ions into gland cells (Figure 15.33). Here, calcium ions stimulate the exocytosis of vesicles containing digestive enzymes in a similar way to their role in synapses (Section 15.2, Nervous communication). The traps stay shut for up to a week for digestion to take place. Once the insect is digested, the cells on the upper

surface of the midrib grow slowly so the leaf reopens and tension builds in the cell walls of the midrib and the trap is set again.

Venus fly traps have two adaptations to avoid closing unnecessarily and wasting energy. First, the stimulation

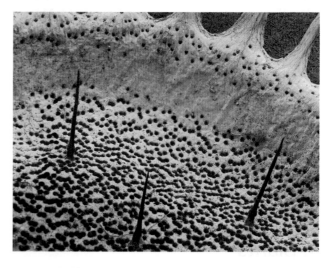

Figure 15.33: False-colour SEM of a leaf of a Venus fly trap with a group of stiff, sensitive hairs (black). When these are touched, the leaves respond by closing, capturing whatever was crawling over them. Enzymes are then secreted by glands (red) to digest the enclosed organism. Soluble products are absorbed by the leaf cells (×25).

of a single hair does not trigger closure. This prevents the traps closing when it rains or when a piece of debris falls into the trap. Second, the gaps between the stiff hairs that form the 'bars' of the trap allow very small insects to crawl out. The plant would waste energy digesting a very small 'meal'.

Chemical communication in plants

Chemicals known as plant hormones or **plant growth regulators** are responsible for most communication within plants. Unlike animal hormones, plant growth regulators are not produced in specialised cells within glands but in a variety of tissues. They move in the plant either directly from cell to cell (by diffusion or active transport) or are carried in the phloem sap or xylem sap. Some may not move far from their site of synthesis and may have their effects on nearby cells.

You are going to consider two types of plant growth regulator:

- **auxins**, which influence many aspects of growth including elongation growth which determines the overall length of roots and shoots

- **gibberellins**, which are involved in seed germination (discussed later in this chapter) and controlling stem elongation (Chapter 16, Section 16.7, Genes, proteins and phenotype).

> ## KEY WORDS
>
> **plant growth regulator (plant hormone):** any chemical produced in plants that influences their growth and development (e.g. auxins, gibberellins, cytokinins and ABA)
>
> **auxin:** a plant growth regulator (plant hormone) that stimulates cell elongation
>
> **gibberellin:** a plant growth regulator (plant hormone) that stimulates seed germination and regulates plant height (stem growth); a lack of gibberellin causes dwarfness

Abscisic acid (ABA) is another plant hormone, which controls the response of plants to environmental stresses such as shortage of water (Chapter 14, Section 14.5, Homeostasis in plants).

Plant hormones interact with receptors on the surface of cells or in the cytoplasm or nucleus. These receptors usually initiate a series of chemical or ionic signals that amplify and transmit the signal within the cell in much the same way that you saw in Chapters 4 and 14.

Question

16 In Chapter 14 you learnt about the plant hormone abscisic acid (ABA). Plant physiologists have found that solutions of ABA with concentrations as low as $5.0 \, \mu mol \, dm^{-3}$ will cause stomata to close. Decide how you will prepare a range of solutions of ABA from a stock solution of $1.0 \, mmol \, dm^{-3}$ and use the solutions to find the lowest concentration that stimulates stomatal closure in leaves of a *Arabidopsis thaliana*. Discuss with others the strategy that you have devised.

Auxins

Plants make several chemicals known as auxins, of which the principal one is IAA (indole 3-acetic acid, Figure 15.34). This is often simply referred to as 'auxin'. IAA is synthesised in the growing tips (meristems) of shoots and roots, where the cells are dividing. IAA is transported back down the shoot, or up the root, by active transport from cell to cell, and also to a lesser extent in phloem sap.

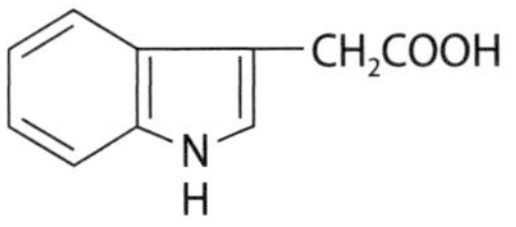

Figure 15.34: The molecular structure of indole 3-acetic acid, IAA.

Growth in plants occurs at meristems, such as those at shoot tips and root tips (see Chapter 5, Section 5.4, Mitosis). Growth occurs in three stages: cell division by mitosis, cell elongation by absorption of water, and cell differentiation. Auxin is involved in controlling growth by elongation (Figure 15.35).

Auxin stimulates cells to pump hydrogen ions (protons) into the cell wall. The cell walls become acidified, which leads to a loosening of the bonds between cellulose microfibrils and the matrix that surrounds them. The cells absorb water by osmosis and the increase in the internal pressure causes the walls to stretch so that these cells elongate (become longer).

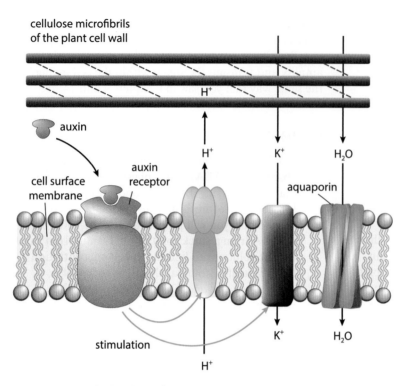

cellulose microfibrils
of the plant cell wall

auxin

cell surface membrane

auxin receptor

aquaporin

stimulation

Figure 15.35: The binding of auxin to its receptor is thought to activate a membrane protein, which stimulates the pumping of protons out of the cell into the cell wall where they lower the pH and break bonds. Potassium ion channels are also stimulated to open leading to an increase in potassium ion concentration in the cytoplasm. This decreases the water potential so water enters through aquaporins.

The details of this process are shown in Figure 15.35. Molecules of auxin bind to a receptor protein on the cell surface membrane. The binding of auxin stimulates ATPase proton pumps to move hydrogen ions across the cell surface membrane from the cytoplasm into the cell wall. In the cell walls, proteins known as **expansins** are activated by the decrease in pH. The expansins loosen the linkages between cellulose microfibrils. It is not known exactly how they do this, but it is thought that expansins disrupt hydrogen bonds between the cellulose microfibrils and surrounding substances, such as hemicelluloses, in the cell wall. This disruption occurs briefly so that microfibrils can move past each other allowing the cell to expand without losing much of the overall strength of the wall.

Gibberellins

Gibberellins are plant growth regulators that are synthesised in most parts of plants. They are present in especially high concentrations in young leaves and in seeds, and are also found in stems, where they have an important role in determining their growth.

Gibberellins promote cell extension in stems in a different way to auxins. Gibberellins stimulate enzymes known as XET in the cell walls of stems. XET breaks bonds within hemicellulose molecules so that cellulose microfibrils can move further apart, so allowing cell walls to expand. You can read more about the action of gibberellins in Chapter 16 (Section 16.7, Genes, proteins and phenotype).

Gibberellins are involved in the control of germination of cereal seeds, such as those of wheat and barley. Figure 15.36 shows the structure of a barley seed. When the seed is shed from the parent plant, it is in a state of dormancy; that is, it contains very little water and is metabolically inactive. This is useful because it allows the seed to survive in adverse conditions, such as through a cold winter, only germinating when the temperature rises in spring.

> ### KEY WORD
>
> **expansins:** proteins in the cell walls of plants that loosen the attachment of microfibrils of cellulose during elongation growth

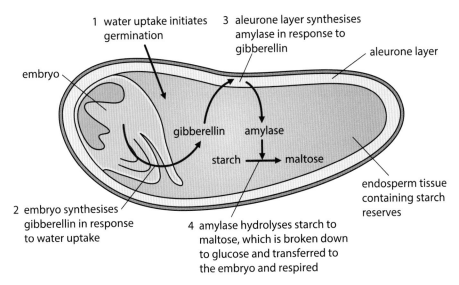

Figure 15.36: LS through a barley seed, showing how secretion of gibberellins by the embryo results in the breakdown of starch in the endosperm during germination.

The seed contains an embryo, which will grow to form the new plant when the seed germinates. The embryo is surrounded by endosperm, which is an energy store containing the polysaccharide starch. On the outer edge of the endosperm is a protein-rich aleurone layer. The whole seed is covered by a tough, waterproof, protective layer (Figure 15.36).

> ## KEY WORDS
>
> endosperm: a tissue in some seeds, such as barley, that is a store of starch and other nutrients
>
> aleurone layer: a layer of tissue around the endosperm that synthesises amylase during germination

The absorption of water at the beginning of germination stimulates the embryo to produce gibberellins. These gibberellins diffuse to the aleurone layer and stimulate the cells to synthesise amylase. The amylase mobilises energy reserves by hydrolysing starch molecules in the endosperm, converting them to soluble maltose molecules. These maltose molecules are converted to glucose and transported to the embryo,

providing a source of carbohydrate that can be respired to provide energy as the embryo begins to grow.

Gibberellins cause these effects by regulating genes that are involved in the synthesis of amylase. In barley seeds, it has been shown that application of gibberellin causes an increase in the transcription of mRNA coding for amylase. It has this action by promoting the destruction of DELLA proteins that inhibit factors that promote transcription (Chapter 16, Section 16.8, Control of gene expression). (DELLA stands for the first five amino acids in the primary sequence of these proteins.)

Question

17 a   i   Explain the advantages to plants of having fast responses to stimuli.

     ii   The closure of a leaf of the Venus fly trap is an example of the all-or-none law. Explain why.

     iii   Suggest the advantage to Venus fly traps of digesting insects.

  b   Outline how auxin stimulates elongation growth.

REFLECTION

Summarise the various ways in which cells in multicellular organisms communicate with each other. Write revision notes for someone who has to learn the topic of cell communication by self study.

What were some of the most interesting discoveries that you made while working on this activity?

Final reflection

Discuss with a friend which, if any, parts of Chapter 15 you need to:

* read through again to make sure you really understand
* seek more guidance on, even after going over it again.

SUMMARY

Endocrine glands are ductless glands that secrete hormones in the blood. The endocrine glands and the hormones that they secrete comprise the endocrine system.

Hormones are chemicals that are made in endocrine glands and transported in blood plasma to their target cells, where they bind to specific receptors and so affect the behaviour of the cells.

Animals and plants have internal communication systems that allow information to pass between different parts of their bodies and so help them to respond to changes in their external and internal environments.

Neurones are cells adapted for the rapid transmission of electrical impulses; to do this, they have long, thin processes called axons. Sensory neurones transmit impulses from receptors to the CNS (brain and spinal cord). Motor neurones transmit impulses from the CNS to effectors. Intermediate (relay) neurones transmit impulses within the CNS.

Receptors are either specialised cells or the endings of sensory neurones; they act as transducers converting the energy of stimuli into electrical impulses. There are receptors that detect external stimuli and receptors that detect internal changes.

Neurones have a resting potential, which is a potential difference across their membranes, with the inside having a negative potential compared with the outside; this potential difference is about $-70\,mV$.

An action potential is a rapid reversal of this potential, caused by an increase in permeability of the cell surface membrane to sodium ions. Action potentials always have the same amplitude. Information about the strength of a stimulus is given by the frequency of action potentials produced. Action potentials are propagated along axons by local circuits that depolarise regions of membrane ahead of the action potential. This depolarisation stimulates voltage-gated sodium ion channel proteins to open, so that the permeability to sodium ions increases and the action potential occurs further down the axon.

Axons are repolarised by the opening of voltage-gated potassium ion channels that allow potassium ions to diffuse out of the axon. After a short refractory period when the voltage-gated sodium ion channels cannot open, the membrane is able to respond again.

Refractory periods determine the maximum frequency of impulses. In mammals, the axons of many neurones are insulated by a myelin sheath. In myelinated neurones, action potentials only occur at nodes of Ranvier which are gaps between the myelin sheaths of adjacent Schwann cells. Saltatory transmission occurs in myelinated neurones and is much faster than transmission in unmyelinated neurones of the same axon diameter.

CONTINUED

A synapse is a junction between two neurones or between a motor neurone and a muscle cell. At cholinergic synapses, a transmitter substance, ACh, is released when action potentials arrive. Impulses pass in one direction only, because transmitter substances are released by exocytosis by the presynaptic neurone to bind to receptor proteins that are only found on the postsynaptic neurone. The receptor proteins are ligand-gated sodium ion channel proteins. When ACh binds to them they open to allow sodium ions to diffuse into the postsynaptic neurone so causing depolarisation.

At least several hundred neurones are likely to have synapses on the dendrites and cell body of each neurone within the CNS. The presence of many synapses on the cell body of a neurone allows integration within the nervous system.

The nervous system and the endocrine system coordinate the activities of the body in different ways. Signalling in the nervous system is very fast as impulses are transmitted directly along neurones, whereas signalling in the endocrine system is slower as hormones are transported around the body in the blood.

Striated (skeletal) muscle is made of many multinucleate cells called muscle fibres, which contain many myofibrils. Myofibrils contain regularly arranged thick (myosin) and thin (actin) filaments which give the striations seen in the muscle. Thick filaments are made of myosin molecules that have a globular head and fibrous tail; the head is an ATPase. Thin filaments are composed of actin, troponin and tropomyosin. Each myofibril is divided into sarcomeres by Z discs; the thin filaments are attached to the Z discs and the thick filaments can slide between the thin filaments.

The arrival of an action potential at a neuromuscular junction causes the release of ACh, which diffuses across the synaptic gap and binds to receptor proteins on the sarcolemma. The binding of ACh causes the opening of ligand-gated sodium ion channel proteins so the sarcolemma is depolarised by the entry of sodium ions. An action potential passes across the sarcolemma and down T-tubules where it leads to SR becoming permeable to calcium ions that are stored within it. Calcium ions diffuse out of the SR to bind to troponin causing tropomyosin to move so exposing binding sites on the actin in the thin filaments.

Myosin heads bind to thin filaments to form cross-bridges; the myosin heads then tilt pulling the thin filaments together so that each sarcomere decreases in length as the filaments slide over each other. The myosin ATPase then hydrolyses ATP, providing the energy for myosin heads to detach from the thin filament and flip back ready to bind with actin again. This process is repeated many times during a contraction, but it can only be reversed by the relaxation of the muscle (with no cross-bridges) and the contraction of an antagonist muscle that pulls the filaments further away lengthening each sarcomere.

Muscles rely on energy from the small quantity of ATP in the sarcoplasm, small stores of creatine phosphate, aerobic respiration in mitochondria and, if oxygen is in short supply, lactate fermentation in the sarcoplasm.

Plants make limited use of action potentials, but they are used to coordinate fast responses (e.g. the closing of Venus fly traps).

Plants produce several chemicals known as plant growth regulators that are involved in the control of growth and responses to environmental changes. The auxin indole 3-acetic acid (IAA) is synthesised mainly in growing tips of shoots and roots, and it stimulates cells to pump protons into the cell wall to lower the pH. Proteins in the cell wall known as expansins respond to a low pH by loosening the links between cellulose microfibrils and the matrix of the cell wall so allowing microfibrils to slide apart. Plant cells absorb water by osmosis and the internal hydrostatic pressure causes the walls to stretch and the cells to elongate.

Gibberellin is synthesised in young leaves and in seeds. It stimulates growth of stems and germination of seeds such as those of barley. In germinating seeds, gibberellins activate the synthesis of amylase enzymes for the breakdown and mobilisation of starch.

EXAM-STYLE QUESTIONS

1 ADH, insulin and glucagon are hormones that control aspects of homeostasis.

ADH is a short peptide, glucagon is a single polypeptide and insulin is composed of two polypeptides. The target cells for these hormones only respond if they have specific cell surface receptors.

a i   Explain why the target cells for ADH, insulin and glucagon must have cell surface receptors in order for them to respond. [2]

ii State the target cells for each of these hormones. [3]

b Two intracellular enzymes that are involved with the synthesis and breakdown of glycogen in liver cells are glycogen synthase and glycogen phosphorylase. Liver cells were exposed to a solution with a high concentration of glucose. The activity of the two enzymes was determined at intervals for 10 minutes. The graph shows the results.

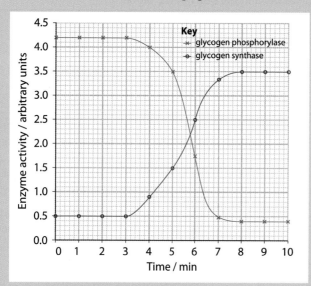

i   With reference to the graph, describe the changes in activity of the two enzymes. [2]

ii State what happens to the quantity of glycogen stored in a liver cell between 4 minutes and 10 minutes. [1]

c Similar results are recorded when the activity of the two enzymes is determined in liver cells in the body of a mammal following a meal rich in starch.

Explain why these two enzymes change in activity following the meal. [4]

d Cells can control the activity of these enzyme. Describe how the activity of the glycogen phosphorylase is controlled. [2]

e Explain the advantages of using the endocrine system rather than the nervous system for coordinating the effectors that control the composition of the blood. [3]

[Total: 17]

CONTINUED

2 The drawing was made from a TEM of an LS through a myelinated neurone.

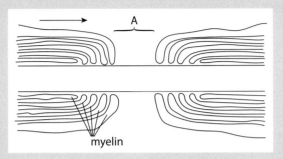

a **i** Name the region of the neurone labelled **A**. [1]

ii State the name of the cell that makes myelin. [1]

b Explain the role of myelin in impulse transmission. [4]

c Outline the changes that occur at region **A** during the passage of an impulse in the direction shown by the arrow. [5]

[Total: 11]

3 The Pacinian corpuscle is a type of receptor found in the dermis of the skin. Pacinian corpuscles contain an ending of a sensory neurone, surrounded by several layers of connective tissue called a capsule. The activity of a Pacinian corpuscle was investigated by inserting microelectrodes into the axon at the positions shown in the diagram.

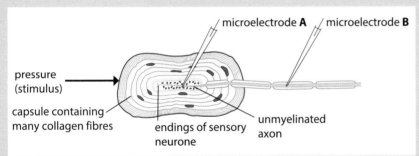

Pressure was applied to the Pacinian corpuscle and recordings made of the electrical activity in the axon at microelectrodes **A** and **B**. The results are shown in the diagram.

CONTINUED

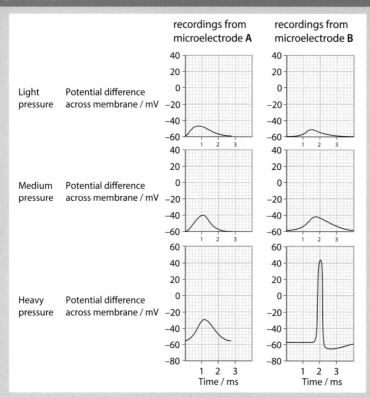

a   Suggest what happened in the unmyelinated region of the axon as pressure
    was applied to the Pacinian corpuscle.   [4]

b   Explain the pattern of recordings from microelectrode **B** as the pressure
    applied to the corpuscle was increased.   [4]

c   Explain why sensory neurones from Pacinian corpuscles are myelinated
    and not unmyelinated.   [3]

[Total: 11]

4 a Outline the events that occur when an impulse crosses a synapse between
      two neurones.   [6]

   b The table shows the properties of four compounds that act at cholinergic
      synapses.

Compound	Effect at cholinergic synapses
curare	competes with ACh for its receptor site on ligand-gated sodium ion channel proteins
eserine	competes with ACh for the active site of acetylcholinesterase
methylmercury	inhibits the enzyme that synthesises ACh
nicotine	activates some ligand-gated sodium ion channels on postsynaptic membranes

CONTINUED

    i State and explain the effect of each compound on transmission across cholinergic synapses. **[8]**

    ii Eserine can be used to counteract the effect of curare. Explain how eserine has this effect. **[3]**

                                                            [Total: 17]

5 The electron micrograph shows parts of some myofibrils in a striated muscle that is in a relaxed state.

  a **i** Name the parts labelled **K**, **L** and **M**. **[3]**

      ii How many myofibrils are visible in the electron micrograph? Explain your answer. **[2]**

  b **i** There are many glycogen granules and mitochondria visible in the electron micrograph. Explain why they are both there. **[2]**

      ii Describe how you can tell that this electron micrograph is from relaxed muscle and not contracted muscle. **[3]**

  c The electron micrograph is magnified 16 000 times. Calculate the actual length of the sarcomere which includes the region labelled **K**. Give your answer in micrometres (μm). **[2]**

                                                            [Total: 12]

6 The diagrams show part of a sarcomere in different states of contraction.

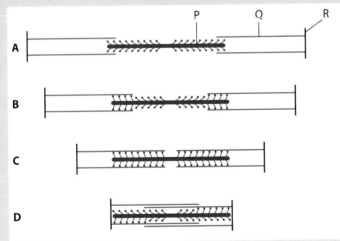

CONTINUED

a Name the parts labelled **P**, **Q** and **R**. [3]

b Explain why there are no actin–myosin cross-bridges visible in diagram **A**. [2]

c Muscle fibres are able to contract with more force in some states of contraction than others. Suggest which of the diagrams shows the state that can develop the greatest force, and explain the reasons for your answer. [4]

d Explain why the sarcomere shown in diagram **D** would not be able to contract any further. [1]

e A muscle can contract with force, but it cannot pull itself back to its original relaxed length.

   i With reference to the mechanism of muscle contraction, explain why this is so. [2]

   ii Suggest how the sarcomere in diagram **D** could be returned to the state shown in diagram **A**. [2]

[Total: 14]

7 A biopsy was taken from a leg muscle of a healthy racehorse. The muscle fibres were teased apart and cross sections were taken from one of the muscle fibres. These cross sections were examined with a TEM. The figure shows drawings made from three different cross sections of a myofibril from the muscle fibre.

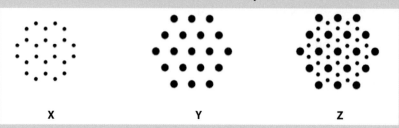

a Explain the differences between the sections **X**, **Y** and **Z**. You may draw a labelled diagram to illustrate your answer. [4]

b The sections were taken from a relaxed muscle fibre. Suggest how the sections would appear if taken from a fibre that had contracted to its maximum extent. Explain your answer. [3]

c Muscle weakness in racehorses may sometimes be related to a deficiency of calcium. Outline the roles of calcium ions in the coordination of muscle contraction. [6]

[Total: 13]

8 Expansins are proteins that are found in plant cell walls and are believed to have a role in cell growth. Plant physiologists investigated the effects of expansins and the auxin IAA on shoot growth in thale cress, *Arabidopsis thaliana*.

Shoots from seedlings of *A. thaliana* were cut into sections and divided into six groups of ten (**A** to **F**). The sections in each group were placed in a Petri dish and treated as follows:

- group **A** was the control group
- groups **B** to **D** were treated with different concentrations of the auxin, IAA
- group **E** was treated with a solution of expansins isolated from cell walls
- group **F** was treated with expansins and the highest concentration of IAA.

CONTINUED

The lengths of the sections were measured at 4 hours and at 18 hours after the treatments started. The results are shown in the bar chart.

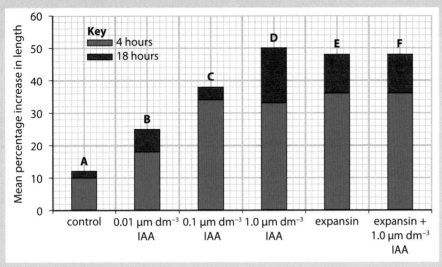

a   Suggest a suitable treatment for group **A**. [1]

b   Suggest why the results are shown as percentage increases in length rather than actual increases. [1]

c   Use the data in the bar chart to describe the effect of different concentrations of IAA on the increase in length of the shoots (groups **B** to **D**). [3]

d   The results show that there is no difference between the mean percentage increase of the sections in group **E** and in group **F**.

Suggest why the results are the same even though both IAA and expansins stimulate elongation growth. [3]

[Total: 8]

9   Barley grains are used to provide maltose in the making of beer. During the malting stage, gibberellin is often sprayed on the grains to increase the production of maltose. The natural concentration of gibberellin in barley grains is stated to be approximately $346 \times 10^{-6}\,g\,dm^{-3}$ which is equivalent to $1.0\,\mu mol\,dm^{-3}$.

Outline a strategy that you could follow to investigate the effect of different concentrations of gibberellin on the activity of amylase in germinating barley grains.

[Total: 8]

SELF-EVALUATION CHECKLIST

After studying this chapter, complete a table like this:

I can	See section...	Needs more work	Almost there	Ready to move on
describe the features of the endocrine system with reference to the hormones insulin, glucagon and ADH	15.1			
compare the ways in which mammals coordinate responses to internal and external stimuli using the endocrine system and the nervous system	15.1, 15.2			
describe the structure and function of sensory and motor neurones and outline how they function	15.2			
state the function of intermediate neurones	15.2			
outline the roles of sensory receptor cells using a chemoreceptor cell in a human taste bud as an example	15.2			
describe and explain the transmission of nerve impulses	15.2			
describe and explain the structure and function of cholinergic synapses	15.2			
describe the ultrastructure of striated muscle and explain how muscles contract in response to impulses from motor neurones	15.3			
describe and explain the rapid response of the Venus fly trap	15.4			
explain the role of auxin in elongation growth	15.4			
describe the role of gibberellin in the germination of barley	15.4			

Inheritance

BEFORE YOU START

Explain why mitosis produces cells that have the same structure and functions as their parent cell.

Think about:

- what determines the structure and function of a cell

- how the information about this is passed on from one cell to another during mitosis.

OCICATS

In the early 1960s a cat breeder in the USA crossed a Siamese cat with an Abyssinian cat. These two breeds have been around for a very long time. The breeder was trying to produce a new type of cat with the Siamese coat pattern and Abyssinian colouring. She was therefore not especially interested in one of the kittens that had a spotted coat. She named him Tonga and sold him, asking the buyer to have him neutered and not breed from him.

Shortly after this, another cat breeder heard about Tonga. He was very excited, as he wanted to breed a spotted cat. He encouraged the original breeder to try to produce more of them. So the Siamese and Abyssinian were crossed again, and another spotted kitten was produced. Over time, more breeders became involved, and they gradually learnt which crosses were likely to produce the spotted cats. They called them ocicats, because the spotted coat looked a little like the coat of a wild ocelot.

Today, ocicats are bred in many different countries. Breeders have chosen the parents carefully and have now produced ocicats with several different colours. There is better understanding of the genes that produce the spotted coat, so that breeders are able to predict the chances of any particular coat colour appearing in the offspring of a cross. But, as always

Figure 16.1: A young ocicat. This breed, with its spotted coat, was first developed in the 1960s.

in genetics, nothing is ever certain, and a surprise is always possible.

Questions for discussion

- Using your knowledge of how genes function, suggest how different forms of a gene can produce different coat colours in a cat or other animal.

- Thinking about genes and the way they work, how do you think two cats with no spots might produce a kitten with spots?

16.1 Gametes and reproduction

Cats and humans, like many animals, reproduce only by **sexual reproduction**. Many plants also reproduce in this way. Sexual reproduction involves the production of special sex cells, called **gametes**. The nuclei of two

KEY WORDS

sexual reproduction: reproduction involving the fusion of gametes (fertilisation) to produce a zygote

gamete: a sex cell; during sexual reproduction, two gametes fuse together to form a zygote; gametes are usually haploid

gametes fuse together, in a process called fertilisation. The cell produced by this fusion is called a zygote. The zygote then divides repeatedly by mitosis, producing a multicelled organism. This is how you and every other human began their life.

You have seen that DNA, carried in chromosomes, contains instructions for making proteins in a cell. Each cell needs a complete set of these instructions. Each chromosome contains a DNA molecule, which in turn contains the code for the synthesis of many different polypeptides or proteins. A length of DNA coding for one protein or polypeptide is called a gene. When a cell divides, it is important that each new (daughter) cell obtains a complete set of genes. In Chapter 5 you saw how this is achieved in mitosis. During sexual reproduction, however, something a little different is required.

Haploid and diploid cells

In most of your body cells there are two complete sets of chromosomes in the nucleus. (Red blood cells are an exception, because they do not have a nucleus at all.) A cell that has two complete sets of chromosomes is said to be diploid. One complete set of chromosomes contains one complete set of genes and therefore one complete set of instructions for making all the proteins that the organism needs. In humans, there are 23 chromosomes in one complete set. There are therefore 46 chromosomes in a diploid cell.

Figure 16.2 shows these two sets of chromosomes, taken from a human cell. Their individual photographs have been moved around so that the chromosomes are arranged in their matching pairs. Each chromosome has a number. The chromosomes with the same number contain the same genes in the same positions. These are said to be homologous chromosomes.

Questions

1   Suggest why the chromosomes in Figure 16.2 have been arranged in the order shown.

2   The karyogram is made by manipulating the photographs of the chromosomes – they never do actually line up neatly like this. Suggest at what stage of the cell cycle the photographs are taken. Give a reason for your suggestion.

During sexual reproduction, each gamete contributes one set of chromosomes to form the zygote. You, for example, began your life when a set of chromosomes

from your father's sperm was joined with a set of chromosomes from your mother's egg cell, as the nuclei of these two gametes fused. It is therefore important that gametes have only one set of chromosomes. A cell with a single set of chromosomes is said to be haploid.

You can use the letter n to signify the number of chromosomes in one set. A haploid cell has n number of chromosomes, and a diploid cell has $2n$. The number of chromosomes in a complete set varies in different species. In humans, n is 23. In a mosquito, it is 3. In an avocado tree, it is 12.

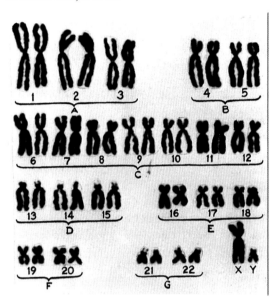

Figure 16.2: The chromosomes in a nucleus of a human male, arranged in their homologous pairs. A photograph like this is called a karyogram.

KEY WORDS

fertilisation: the fusing of the nuclei of two gametes, to form a zygote

zygote: a cell formed by the fusion of the nuclei of two gametes; most zygotes are diploid

diploid: containing two complete sets of chromosomes; can be signified by the symbol $2n$

homologous chromosomes: two chromosomes that carry the same genes in the same positions

haploid: containing one complete set of chromosomes; can be signified by the symbol n

Gametes need to be haploid so that, when their nuclei fuse, a zygote is formed with the diploid number of chromosomes. This is shown in Figure 16.3.

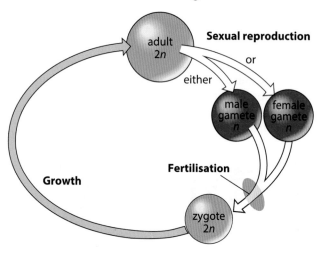

Figure 16.3: An outline of the life cycle of a mammal.

Question

3   Look at the diagram in Figure 16.3. At what stage or stages does nuclear division by mitosis occur?

Meiosis

Meiosis is a type of nuclear division that produces haploid cells from a diploid cell. It is used in the production of gametes in animals and plants.

You have already studied the events that take place in mitosis. You may like to look back at Chapter 5 to remind yourself of these, before you read further in this chapter.

Figure 16.4 summarises the events that take place during meiosis. Keep looking at that series of diagrams as you read the description in the next few paragraphs.

Meiosis has two divisions, not one as in mitosis. These are called meiosis I and meiosis II. Each division has the same sequence of stages as in mitosis – prophase, metaphase, anaphase and telophase.

Prophase I

Meiosis begins, as in mitosis, as the chromosomes condense and become visible. Each chromosome has already been copied, so that each one is made up of two identical 'sister' chromatids joined at the centromere. Unlike mitosis, however, the chromosomes now arrange themselves in homologous pairs. The two chromosomes 1s, for example, line up side by side. Each pair of homologous chromosomes is called a **bivalent**.

The chromosomes in a bivalent are very closely associated. A chromatid of one of these chromosomes intertwines with a chromatid of the other. Each crossing point is called a **chiasma** (plural: **chiasmata**). There is almost always at least one, and often several, chiasmata in each pair (Figure 16.5). The chiasmata help to hold the chromosomes together in their pair, as they move through the next stages. Part of a chromatid from one chromosome may break and rejoin with the chromatid from the other chromosome. This is called **crossing over**, and you will learn about its significance later in this chapter.

Just as in mitosis, the centrioles migrate to opposite ends of the cell during prophase I, and form spindle fibres made from microtubules. These begin to attach themselves to the centromeres of the homologous pairs of chromosomes. The nuclear envelope breaks down, and the nucleolus disappears.

Metaphase I

The spindle fibres, attached to the centromeres, now move the bivalents to the equator of the cell. The homologous chromosomes in each bivalent remain attached to each other at the chiasmata.

KEY WORDS

meiosis: nuclear division that results in the production of four daughter cells with half the chromosome number of the parent cell and with reshuffled alleles; in animals and plants it results in the formation of gametes

bivalent: two homologous chromosomes lying alongside each other during meiosis I

chiasma (plural: **chiasmata**): a position at which non-sister chromatids of homologous chromosomes cross over each other

crossing over: the exchange of alleles between non-sister chromatids of homologous chromosomes during meiosis I

Meiosis I

1 Early prophase I
– as mitosis early prophase

2 Middle prophase I
Homologous chromosomes pair up. This process is called synapsis. Each pair is called a bivalent.

centrosomes moving to opposite ends of nucleus, as in mitosis

4 Metaphase I (showing crossing over of long chromatids)

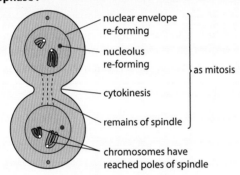

bivalents line up across equator of spindle, attached by centromeres

spindle formed, as in mitosis

6 Telophase I

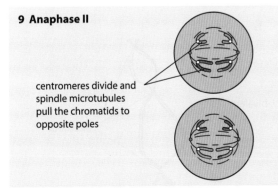

nuclear envelope re-forming

nucleolus re-forming

cytokinesis — as mitosis

remains of spindle

chromosomes have reached poles of spindle

Animal cells usually divide before entering meiosis II. Many plant cells go straight into meiosis II with no reformation of nuclear envelopes or nucleoli. During meiosis II, chromatids separate as in mitosis.

3 Late prophase I

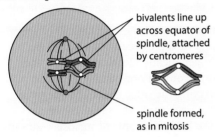

nuclear envelope breaks up as in mitosis

crossing over of chromatids may occur

nucleolus 'disappears' as in mitosis

Bivalent showing crossing over:

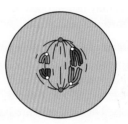

chromatids may break and may reconnect to another chromatid

centromere

chiasma = point where crossing over occurs (plural: chiasmata)

one or more chiasmata may form, anywhere along length

At the end of prophase I a spindle is formed.

5 Anaphase I

Centromeres do not divide, unlike in mitosis.

Whole chromosomes move towards opposite ends of spindle, centromeres first, pulled by microtubules.

Meiosis II

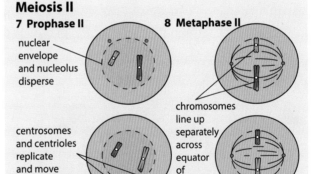

7 Prophase II

nuclear envelope and nucleolus disperse

centrosomes and centrioles replicate and move to opposite poles of the cell

8 Metaphase II

chromosomes line up separately across equator of spindle

9 Anaphase II

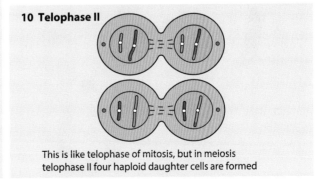

centromeres divide and spindle microtubules pull the chromatids to opposite poles

10 Telophase II

This is like telophase of mitosis, but in meiosis telophase II four haploid daughter cells are formed

Figure 16.4: Meiosis and cytokinesis in an animal cell.

Anaphase I

The spindle fibres begin to pull on the centromeres. This is where the next big difference from mitosis occurs. Instead of each chromosome being pulled apart into its two chromatids, it is the two whole chromosomes in each bivalent that are pulled apart. The centromeres remain intact, continuing to hold the two chromatids of one chromosome firmly together.

Telophase I

The chromosomes now arrive at opposite ends of the dividing cell. The spindle fibres have completed their task of pulling the chromosomes apart, and the fibres now break down. In most animals, a nuclear envelope forms around each set, and the nucleolus generally reforms. This may not happen in plant cells, which may go straight into the next stage.

What has taken place up to this point is called a **reduction division**. Each new cell contains one complete set of chromosomes – one from each homologous pair. The original cell was diploid, with two sets of chromosomes. The new cells are haploid.

Cytokinesis

Usually, the cytoplasm now splits into two, forming two complete cells, each with the haploid number of chromosomes.

Prophase II, metaphase II, anaphase II and telophase II

Next, each of the newly formed haploid cells undergoes a division almost identical to mitosis. This is called the second division of meiosis. Look carefully at Figure 16.4, which will remind you of the sequence of events that takes place.

The overall result of meiosis is the formation of four haploid cells from one diploid cell. As you will see, these cells are not genetically identical to each other. Although they each contain one complete set of chromosomes carrying the same genes, the alleles of these genes are not necessarily the same. In the next section you will see how the events of meiosis result in genetic variation among the daughter cells.

KEY WORD

reduction division: nuclear division that results in a reduction in chromosome number; the first division of meiosis is a reduction division

---

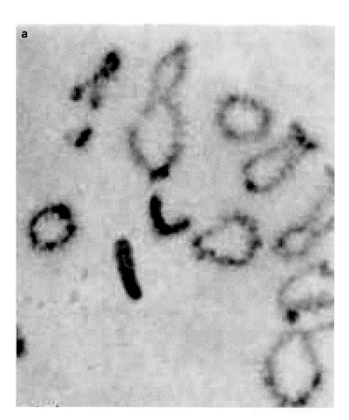

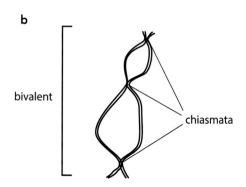

Figure 16.5: a Photomicrograph of bivalents in prophase I of meiosis, showing chiasmata. A chiasma shows that crossing over has occurred between two non-sister chromatids. **b** Interpretive drawing of one bivalent.

Questions

4 Name the stage of meiosis at which each of the following occurs. Remember to state whether the stage you name is during division I or division II.

   a Homologous chromosomes pair to form bivalents.

   b Crossing over between chromatids of homologous chromosomes takes place.

   c Homologous chromosomes separate.

   d Centromeres split and chromatids separate.

   e Haploid nuclei are first formed.

5 A cell with three sets of chromosomes is said to be triploid, 3*n*. A cell with four sets of chromosomes is said to be tetraploid, 4*n*. Could meiosis take place in a 3*n* or a 4*n* cell? Explain your answer.

6 The diploid (2*n*) chromosome number of *Drosophila* is 8. Copy and complete Table 16.1 to show the different outcomes of mitotic and meiotic division of a *Drosophila* cell.

	Mitosis	Meiosis
number of division cycles		
number of daughter cells		
number of chromosomes per nucleus in daughter cells		

Table 16.1: Table for Question 6.

16.2 The production of genetic variation

You have seen that each chromosome in a homologous pair contains the same genes, in the same positions. The position of a gene on a chromosome is called its locus (plural: loci). For example, the fruit fly *Drosophila melanogaster* has 5 pairs of chromosomes. On each chromosome 2, there are genes that help to determine the formation of antennae on the fly's head, the colour of its body, the colour of its eyes, and its wing length. Figure 16.5a shows the loci of these genes. Note that there are many more genes on this chromosome than are shown.

You may remember that genes can exist in different forms, called alleles. For example, a gene that determines the colour of a fruit fly's eyes may have different alleles that code for red eyes or brown eyes. Figure 16.6b shows two alleles of each of the four genes shown in Figure 16.6a.

> **KEY WORDS**
>
> locus (plural: loci): the position of a gene on a chromosome
>
> allele: a variety of a gene

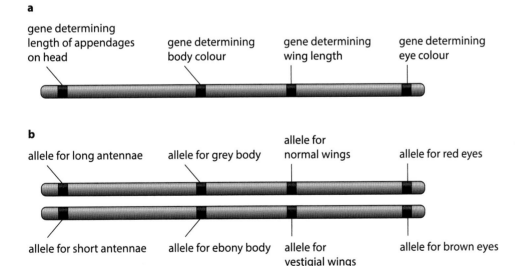

Figure 16.6: a The loci of four genes on a chromosome in the fruit fly, *Drosophila melanogaster;* **b** some of the possible alleles of these four genes.

So, in a diploid cell, each member of a pair of homologous chromosomes may contain different alleles of the same gene. The two homologous chromosomes are not genetically identical.

Two processes that happen during meiosis I result in a mixture of these alleles that is not the same in every daughter cell. These processes are crossing over and independent assortment.

Genetic variation arising from crossing over

You have seen how, during meiosis I, pieces of chromatids from one chromosome in a bivalent can exchange places with the equivalent piece on the other chromosome. This is called crossing over, and it produces different combinations of alleles on the two chromosomes.

Let's think, for example, about two of the genes shown in Figure 16.6 – the one that determines the length of the head appendages, and the one that determines eye colour. The gene for antenna length has two alleles. Allele **E** gives long antennae, and allele **e** gives short ones (a condition called aristopedia). The gene for eye colour also has two alleles, **R** which gives red eyes, and **r** which gives brown eyes (Figure 16.7).

The original cell has all four of these alleles. You can see that, on one of the homologous pairs of chromosomes, the alleles for these two genes are **E** and **A**. On the other homologous chromosome, the alleles are **e** and **a**.

Now look at what happens when these chromosomes pair up during meiosis. In some of the cells undergoing meiosis, crossing over between these two gene loci does *not* happen. The alleles stay on their own chromosome. But in some of the cells, crossing over switches the positions of the alleles. Now the alleles on one chromosome are **E** and **a**, and on the other they are **e** and **A**.

At the end of meiosis, when the new daughter cells (gametes) are finally formed, each one gets just one chromatid from each chromosome. Some will get the non-crossed-over chromatids, so will have either **E** and **A** or **e** and **a.** But some will get crossed-over chromatids, and they will have either **E** and **a** or **e** and **A**.

This means that there are four different kinds of gamete:

alleles **E** and **A**, coding for long antennae and red eyes

alleles **e** and **a**, coding for short antennae and brown eyes

alleles **E** and **a**, coding for long antennae and brown eyes

alleles **e** and **A**, coding for short antennae and red eyes

Later in this chapter you will see how this affects the offspring (young) of an organism in which crossing over takes place.

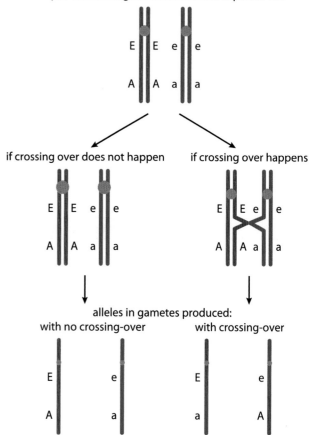

Figure 16.7: How crossing over produces genetic variation in daughter cells.

Genetic variation arising from independent assortment

So far, you have looked at how the swapping of alleles between two homologous chromosomes can produce genetic variation in the daughter cells. Now you need to think about how the combinations of different chromosomes can also cause genetic variation.

Think about the events that lead up to metaphase I in meiosis. You will remember that the chromosomes have already paired up, and are now pulled to the equator of the cell by the spindle fibres. Each pair can be either way up (Figure 16.8). Their orientation (arrangement) is entirely random. The orientation of one pair has no effect on the orientation of any other pair.

As the homologous chromosomes are pulled apart, the combination of alleles that ends up in the daughter cells depends on how these chromosomes were lined up. Looking at just two pairs of chromosomes, each with one gene, you can see that four different combinations of alleles are possible. Now imagine how many combinations of alleles you can get with 23 pairs of chromosomes, each with hundreds or thousands of genes on them. It would seem to be almost limitless. The ability of any allele to find itself in the same cell as any other allele is called independent assortment.

Thinking about the combinations of chromosomes alone, there are actually 8 324 608 different possibilities. You can work this out by calculating 2^n, where n is the haploid number of chromosomes. Then factor in all the different alleles of all the different genes on these chromosomes and you can see that the possible variations are enormous.

> **KEY WORD**
>
> **independent assortment:** the production of different combinations of alleles in daughter cells, as a result of the random alignment of bivalents on the equator of the spindle during metaphase I of meiosis

Genetic variation arising from random fertilisation

The two sources of genetic variation you have looked at so far – crossing over and independent assortment – both result in different combinations of alleles in gametes. If you assume that any male gamete can fuse with any female gamete, each with these potentially large amounts of variation between them, you can see that the new individuals produced as a result of sexual reproduction have almost no chance of being genetically identical. They will inevitably have different combinations of alleles.

Table 16.2 summarises the causes and effects of these three sources of genetic variation.

16.3 Genetics

Genetics is the study of how characteristics that are determined by genes are passed down from a parent or parents to their offspring.

You will remember that a gene is a length of DNA that codes for the production of a polypeptide molecule. The code is held in the sequence of nucleotide bases in the DNA. A triplet of three bases codes for one amino acid in the polypeptide that will be constructed on the ribosomes in the cell (Chapter 6, Section 6.5, Protein synthesis). One chromosome contains enough DNA to code for many polypeptides.

The cell that is about to divide has two pairs of chromosomes. These carry alleles **A**, **a**, **D** and **d**.

At metaphase of meiosis I, the pairs of homologous chromosomes line up on the equator independently of each other. For two pairs of chromosomes, there are two possible orientations.

At the end of meiosis II, each orientation gives two types of gamete. There are therefore four types of gamete altogether.

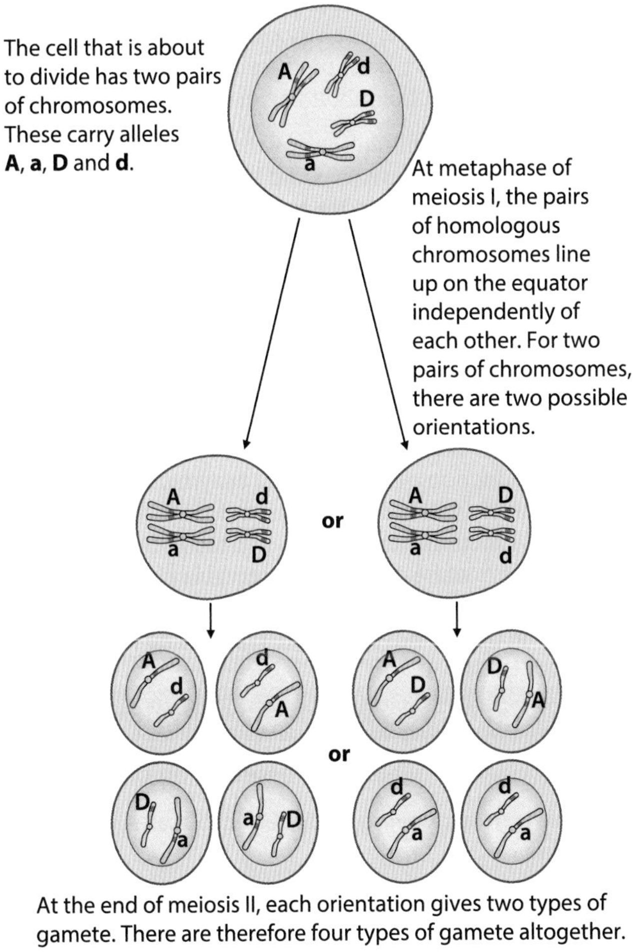

Figure 16.8: How independent assortment produces genetic variation in daughter cells.

Source of genetic variation	How it causes variation	Effect
crossing over during prophase I of meiosis	changes the combination of alleles of one or more genes that are carried on a chromosome, and therefore the overall combination of alleles on that chromosome	genetic variation between gametes produced by an individual
independent assortment during metaphase I of meiosis	random orientation of bivalents results in many different combinations of chromosomes and therefore many different combinations of alleles	genetic variation between gametes produced by an individual
random fusion of gametes	any male gamete can fuse with any female gamete	genetic variation between resulting individual organisms

Table 16.2: The causes and effects of the three sources of genetic variation.

The next sections describe basic genetics, including monohybrid crosses, which you may already have studied at IGCSE or O Level. If so, these sections will be revision for you, and you may like to skim quickly through them and then concentrate on Section 16.5, Dihybrid inheritance.

Genes and alleles

Let's imagine a gene that determines coat colour in a species of mammal – let's say a type of rabbit. This gene codes for an enzyme. The enzyme catalyses a step in a metabolic pathway that produces a pigment.

This gene is found at the same locus (position) on the same chromosome in all members of this species of rabbit. However, there are several slightly different forms of this gene, each with a very slightly different sequence of nucleotide bases. As you have seen, these different forms of the same gene are called alleles.

Let's say that there are just two alleles of this coat colour gene. One allele codes for an enzyme that results in the production of a brown pigment, and therefore a brown coat. You can use the symbol **B** to stand for this allele. The other allele codes for an enzyme that cannot function properly. No pigment is produced, and the rabbit has a white coat. You can use the symbol **b** for this allele.

Genotype and phenotype

You have seen that every body cell contains two copies of each type of chromosome. This means that every cell contains two copies of every gene. A rabbit therefore has two copies of the coat colour gene in each of its cells. These will be the same in every cell, because all of the cells in its body have been produced by mitosis from the zygote from which the rabbit began its life.

There are three combinations of the alleles of this gene that a rabbit could have. It could have two copies of the **B** allele, or two copies of the **b** allele, or one of each. You can write these as **BB**, **bb** or **Bb**. These are the possible genotypes of the rabbit – the combination of alleles that it has. A genotype in which both alleles are the same is said to be homozygous. A genotype in which the two alleles are different is heterozygous.

Now let's think about the effect that these genotypes will have on the coat colour of the rabbit. The allele **B** codes for the production of a functional enzyme, so any rabbit with this allele will have a brown coat. The allele **b** codes for a non-functional enzyme, so if a rabbit has only this allele, it has a white coat. The observable characteristics of an organism are called its phenotype, so these colours are part of the phenotype of the rabbit. The relationship

---

KEY WORDS

genotype: the alleles possessed by an organism

homozygous: having two identical alleles of a gene

heterozygous: having two different alleles of a gene

phenotype: the observable features of an organism; it is affected by genes and also by environment

between genotype and phenotype can be summarised like this:

genotype	phenotype
BB	brown coat
Bb	brown coat
bb	white coat

In this example, the coat colour of a rabbit with the genotype **BB** is the same as one with the genotype **Bb**. Allele **B** is dominant, and allele **b** is recessive. Allele **b** only affects the phenotype when no allele **B** is present.

This is not true for all alleles of genes. For example, in humans, blood groups are coded for by a gene that has three alleles (multiple alleles). Allele **A** gives blood group A, and allele **B** gives blood group B. However, if a person has one copy of **A** and one of **B**, they have the blood group AB. These alleles are codominant – they both have an effect in a heterozygous person.

When you are dealing with codominant alleles, it is generally a good idea to show them in a slightly different way from that used for the dominant / recessive coat colour genes. For codominance, you use a capital letter for the gene, and then superscripts for the different alleles. So, for the blood group alleles, the symbols are I^A for the group A allele and I^B for the group B allele.

The blood group gene also has a third allele, which codes for blood group O. This allele is recessive to the group A and group B alleles. Its symbol is therefore I^o, where the superscript o is a small letter (not a capital letter). To summarise:

genotype	phenotype
$I^A I^A$	blood group A
$I^A I^B$	blood group AB
$I^A I^o$	blood group A
$I^B I^B$	blood group B
$I^B I^o$	blood group B
$I^o I^o$	blood group O

When you are answering genetics questions, it is usually a very good idea to write down all the possible combinations of alleles – all the different genotypes – and the phenotypes that they produce. This will help you a lot as you work through the genetics problem.

16.4 Monohybrid inheritance and genetic diagrams

In this section you look at how the alleles for a single gene are passed from one generation to the next. This is known as monohybrid inheritance.

Imagine that a heterozygous brown rabbit and a white rabbit are crossed. You can use your knowledge of genotypes, phenotypes and what happens during meiosis to predict the probable coat colours of their offspring.

You will remember that meiosis produces gametes, and that these gametes have only a single set of chromosomes – they are haploid. This means that each gamete has only *one* copy of each gene, rather than two.

In this example, the heterozygous brown rabbit is male. His genotype is **Bb**. In his testes, sperm are produced by meiosis. Half of the sperm receive a **B** allele, and half receive a **b** allele. The white female rabbit, with genotype **bb**, produces eggs which all have the allele **b**.

When the rabbits mate, the sperm swim through the female's reproductive system towards her eggs. It is pure chance whether a sperm with a **B** allele or one with a **b** allele reaches each egg first. There is therefore an equal chance that a zygote will have the genotype **Bb** or the genotype **bb**. You would therefore expect roughly half of the offspring to be **Bb**, with brown coats, and half to be **bb**, with white coats.

KEY WORDS

dominant: a dominant allele has the same effect on phenotype, whether or not another allele is present

recessive: a recessive allele only affects phenotype if no dominant allele is present

multiple alleles: the existence of three or more alleles of a gene, as, for example, in the determination of A,B,O blood groups

codominant: codominant alleles each affect phenotype when both of them are present

monohybrid inheritance: inheritance of one gene

You can show all of this in a **genetic diagram**. This is a standard way of predicting what you would expect happen as the result of a genetic cross.

parental phenotypes	brown coat	×	white coat
parental genotypes	**Bb**		**bb**
parental gametes	Ⓑ or ⓑ		all ⓑ

			male gametes	
			Ⓑ	ⓑ
offspring genotypes and phenotypes	female gametes	ⓑ	**Bb** brown coat	**bb** white coat

predicted offspring ratio: 1 brown coat : 1 white coat

Now consider what you would expect to happen if two heterozygous rabbits are crossed. The genetic diagram for this cross is as follows.

parental phenotypes	brown coat	×	brown coat
parental genotypes	**Bb**		**Bb**
parental gametes	Ⓑ or ⓑ		Ⓑ or ⓑ

			male gametes	
			Ⓑ	ⓑ
offspring genotypes and phenotypes	female gametes	Ⓑ	**BB** brown coat	**Bb** brown coat
		ⓑ	**Bb** brown coat	**bb** white coat

predicted offspring ratio: 3 brown coat : 1 white coat

There are several important things to notice and remember about genetic diagrams.

- Always show the complete genetic diagram, including the headings at the left-hand side. This makes clear to someone looking at your work exactly what you are showing – and it also helps you to remember what you are doing!

- The grid that is drawn part way through the genetic diagram is called a **Punnett square**. A Punnett square is *not* a genetic diagram! It is a *part* of a genetic diagram.

KEY WORDS

genetic diagram: a standard format in which the results of a genetic cross are predicted and explained

Punnett square: part of a genetic diagram in which the genotypes of the offspring are worked out from the genotypes of the gametes

- In the *parental gametes* line you are showing the different types of gamete that each parent can produce. If the parent is homozygous, as for the white parent in the first genetic diagram, there is only one type of gamete that can be produced. So you need only show this one type. There is no need to write down ⓑ and ⓑ. If you do that, you will still get the right answer at the end, but your diagram will be unnecessarily complicated.

- You will usually be expected to show which phenotype is associated with which genotype, in the offspring. The easiest way to do this is to write the phenotype just underneath the genotype in the Punnett square.

- It is important to remember that the predicted genotypes are all based on chance. You cannot be sure which sperm will fertilise which egg. In the cross between the two heterozygous rabbits above, the prediction is that there will be three times as many brown offspring as white offspring. However, you should not be surprised if this does not work out exactly. For example, if only two baby rabbits are born, they could both be brown. They could even both be white.

- Genetic diagrams involving codominant alleles are constructed in exactly the same way as in the example above, but of course using the correct symbols for these alleles.

Questions

7 Construct a genetic diagram to predict the chance that a child born to two parents, both with blood group AB, will have blood group B. Use the symbols I^A and I^B to represent the alleles.

8 A woman with blood group A and a man with blood group B have a child with blood group O. Use this information to determine the genotypes of the woman and the man, and then construct a genetic diagram to explain how the child inherited her blood group. Use the symbols I^A, I^B and I^O to represent the alleles.

F_1, F_2 and test crosses

You now know enough to be able to answer most questions about crosses involving different alleles of one gene. These are called monohybrid crosses. However, there are three more terms that you need to be familiar with.

If two homozygous individuals are crossed – for example, a homozygous brown rabbit, **BB**, with a homozygous white rabbit, **bb** – the offspring are known as the F_1 generation. They are, of course, always all heterozygous.

If two of the F_1 generation are crossed, their offspring are known as the F_2 generation.

Questions

9 Construct a genetic diagram to show that all of the offspring of a cross between a homozygous brown rabbit and a white rabbit are heterozygous brown rabbits.

10 Construct a genetic diagram to predict the ratios of phenotypes in the F_2 generation.

You will probably have noticed by now that, if an individual shows the recessive phenotype, it must be homozygous for the recessive allele. A white rabbit always has the genotype **bb**. However, the genotype of a brown rabbit is unknown. It could be **Bb**, or it could be **BB**.

In order to determine the genotype of an individual showing the dominant characteristic in its phenotype, you can do a test cross. This involves crossing the unknown individual with one showing the recessive phenotype. By looking at the phenotypes of the offspring, you can obtain information about the genotype of the parent.

KEY WORDS

F_1 generation: the offspring resulting from the cross between individuals with a homozygous recessive and a homozygous dominant genotype

F_2 generation: the offspring resulting from a cross between two F_1 individuals

test cross: a genetic cross in which an organism showing the dominant characteristic is crossed with a homozygous recessive organism; the phenotypes of the offspring can indicate whether the original organism is homozygous or heterozygous

Question

11 a A test cross was carried out between a brown rabbit and a white rabbit. Five brown offspring and one white offspring were produced. Use a genetic diagram to show how this indicates that the brown rabbit must be heterozygous.

b A test cross using a different brown rabbit produced four offspring, all of which were brown. Explain why this indicates that the brown rabbit may be homozygous but does not allow you to be sure about this.

Sex linkage

If you look back at Figure 16.2, you can see that the last two chromosomes in the karyogram are not the same as each other. These chromosomes are from a human male. These chromosomes are the sex chromosomes. In men, one of these is a short chromosome with very few genes on it, called the Y chromosome. The other is much longer, and contains many genes that are not found on the Y chromosome. This is called the X chromosome. Men have one of each of these chromosome (XY) while women have two X chromosomes (XX).

One of the genes on the X chromosome codes for the production of a factor necessary for blood clotting, called factor VIII. There are two alleles, a dominant one that codes for the normal factor VIII, and a recessive one which results in the lack of factor VIII. You can use the symbols **F** and **f** for these two alleles. A person with only this recessive allele, and no dominant allele, does not make factor VIII. Their blood does not clot normally, and they have haemophilia.

A woman has two X chromosomes, each with one copy of this gene. She therefore has three possible genotypes. Because the genes are on the X chromosome, they are shown like this:

genotype	phenotype
$X^F X^F$	normal blood clotting
$X^F X^f$	normal blood clotting
$X^f X^f$	haemophilia

A man, however, has only one X chromosome. There are therefore only two genotypes that he can have:

genotype	phenotype
$X^F Y$	normal blood clotting
$X^f Y$	haemophilia

> **KEY WORD**
>
> **sex chromosomes:** the chromosomes that determine sex; in humans, these are the X and Y chromosomes

parental phenotypes	normal female	×	normal male
parental genotypes	$X^F X^f$		$X^F Y$
parental gametes	(X^F) or (X^f)		(X^F) or (Y)

		male gametes	
		(X^f)	(Y)
female gametes	(X^F)	$X^F X^F$ female with normal blood clotting	$X^F Y$ male with normal blood clotting
	(X^f)	$X^F X^f$ female with normal blood clotting	$X^f Y$ male with haemophilia

offspring genotypes and phenotypes

predicted offspring ratios: 2 females with normal blood clotting : 1 male with normal blood clotting : 1 male with haemophilia

This gene is said to be **sex-linked**. Because it is found only on the X chromosome, its inheritance is affected by the sex of an individual. For example, the genetic diagram on the previous page shows the possible offspring born to a heterozygous woman and a man with normal blood clotting.

Neither parent had haemophilia, yet there is a one in four chance that they will have a boy child with haemophilia. The haemophilia allele comes from the mother. She is a symptomless **carrier** for haemophilia.

Questions

12 Explain why a boy cannot inherit haemophilia from his father.

13 There is a gene on the human X chromosome that determines the ability to see the colours red and green. A common recessive allele prevents this, so that the person cannot tell the difference between red and green. They are said to be red–green colour-blind.

   a Suggest suitable symbols for the two alleles of this gene.

   b Using your chosen symbols, construct a genetic diagram to predict the chance that a child born to a man with normal vision and a woman who is heterozygous will be a colour-blind boy. (Remember to show the X and Y chromosomes, as well as the symbols for the alleles.)

14 One of the genes for coat colour in cats is sex linked. The allele C^O gives orange fur, whereas C^B gives black fur. The two alleles are codominant and, when both are present, the cat has patches of orange and black, which is known as tortoiseshell.

   a Explain why male cats cannot be tortoiseshell.

   b Draw a genetic diagram to show the expected genotypes and phenotypes of the offspring from a cross between an orange male and a tortoiseshell female cat.

16.5 Dihybrid inheritance

So far, you have looked at the inheritance of the alleles of just one gene. Now you will consider the inheritance of two different genes. This is called **dihybrid inheritance**.

Let's return to the example of rabbit coat colour (alleles **B** and **b** for brown and white fur) and now consider ear length as well. Imagine that there are two alleles for

ear length, **E** for long ears and **e** for short ears, where allele **E** is dominant and **e** is recessive. The gene for coat colour and the gene for ear length are on different chromosomes.

There are now several different genotypes and phenotypes to consider:

genotype	phenotype
BBEE	brown fur, long ears
BBEe	brown fur, long ears
BBee	brown fur, short ears
BbEE	brown fur, long ears
BbEe	brown fur, long ears
Bbee	brown fur, short ears
bbEE	white fur, long ears
bbEe	white fur, long ears
bbee	white fur, short ears

Notice how the genotypes are written. First you write the genotype for one gene, immediately followed by the genotype for the second gene. Do not mix up **B**s with **E**s.

Now consider the gametes that can be produced by a rabbit with the genotype **BbEe**. During meiosis, the chromosome with the **B/b** gene and the one with the **E/e** gene behave entirely independently of one another. At the end of meiosis, this rabbit will produce four types of sperm or eggs. Half will have allele **B** for coat colour, and half will have allele **b**. Of these, half of those with allele **B** will have allele **E** for ear length and half will have allele **e**. The same is true for those with allele **b**. So the genotypes of this rabbit's gametes are:

KEY WORDS

sex-linked gene: a gene found on a region of a sex chromosome that is not present on the other sex chromosome; in humans, most sex-linked genes are found on the X chromosome

carrier: an individual that possesses a particular allele as a single copy whose effect is masked by a dominant allele, so that the associated characteristic (such as a hereditary disease) is not displayed but may be passed to offspring

dihybrid inheritance: the inheritance of two genes

Notice:

- Just as for monohybrid crosses, the gametes have only one copy of each gene.

- You write the alleles of the two genes next to each other.

- It is a good idea to always put the same gene first – don't swap the **B**s and **E**s around.

Let's consider what happens if a rabbit with genotype **BbEe** is crossed with a rabbit with genotype **Bbee**.

parental phenotypes	brown coat, long ears		brown coat, short ears
parental genotypes	**BbEe**	×	**Bbee**
parental gametes	(BE) (Be) (bE) (be)		(Be) (be)

offspring genotypes and phenotypes

gametes from the other parent		gametes from one parent	
		(Be)	(be)
	(BE)	**BBEe** brown coat, long ears	**BbEe** brown coat, long ears
	(Be)	**BBee** brown coat, short ears	**Bbee** brown coat, short ears
	(bE)	**BbEe** brown coat, long ears	**bbEe** white coat, long ears
	(be)	**Bbee** brown coat, short ears	**bbee** white coat, short ears

predicted ratio of phenotypes in offspring: 3 brown coat, long ears : 3 brown coat, short ears : 1 white coat, long ears : 1 white coat, short ears

Notice:

- For the parent with genotype **Bbee**, only two types of gamete can be produced. You therefore need only show these two types – you do not need to write each one down twice. (If you do that, you will not go wrong, but your Punnett square will be twice as big as it needs to be and will take you twice as long to complete.)

- Take great care when writing the genotypes in the Punnett square. Always write the two alleles of one of the genes, followed by the two alleles of the second gene. Do not mix up **B**s and **E**s.

Another example of a dihybrid cross is shown on the next page.

In tomato plants there is a gene that codes for stem colour. This gene has two alleles:

stem colour gene

    A = allele for purple stem

    a = allele for green stem

where **A** is dominant and **a** is recessive.

A different gene, at a different locus on a different chromosome, codes for leaf shape. Again, there are two alleles:

leaf shape gene

    D = allele for cut leaves (jagged edges)

    d = allele for potato leaves (smooth edges)

where **D** is dominant and **d** is recessive.

parental phenotypes	purple stem, cut leaves		green stem, potato leaves
parental genotypes	**AaDd**	×	**aadd**
parental gametes	(AD) (Ad) (aD) (ad)		(ad)

		gametes from one parent	
		(ad)	
offspring genotypes and phenotypes	gametes from the other parent	(AD)	**AaDd** purple stem, cut leaves
		(Ad)	**Aadd** purple stem, potato leaves
		(aD)	**aaDd** green stem, cut leaves
		(ad)	**aadd** green stem, potato leaves

predicted ratio of phenotypes in offspring:

four different phenotypes in a ratio of 1 : 1 : 1 : 1

This is an example of a dihybrid test cross. If you cross an individual showing the dominant characteristics in their phenotype with one showing the recessive characteristics, you can use the phenotypes of the offspring to work out the genotype of the unknown parent.

If you cross two tomato plants that are both heterozygous at both loci, you get a 9 : 3 : 3 : 1 ratio in the offspring. This genetic diagram on the next page shows why.

parental phenotypes   purple stem, cut leaves   purple stem, cut leaves

parental genotypes   **AaDd**   ×   **AaDd**

parental gametes   (AD) (Ad) (aD) (ad)   (AD) (Ad) (aD) (ad)

offspring genotypes and phenotypes

		gametes of one parent			
		(AD)	(Ad)	(aD)	(ad)
gametes of the other parent	(AD)	**AADD** purple stem, cut leaves	**AADd** purple stem, cut leaves	**AaDD** purple stem, cut leaves	**AaDd** purple stem, cut leaves
	(Ad)	**AADd** purple stem, cut leaves	**AAdd** purple stem, potato leaves	**AaDd** purple stem, cut leaves	**Aadd** purple stem, potato leaves
	(aD)	**AaDD** purple stem, cut leaves	**AaDd** purple stem, cut leaves	**aaDD** green stem, cut leaves	**aaDd** green stem, cut leaves
	(ad)	**AaDd** purple stem, cut leaves	**Aadd** purple stem, potato leaves	**aaDd** green stem, cut leaves	**aadd** green stem, potato leaves

The expected phenotype ratios are therefore 9 purple stem, cut leaves : 3 purple stem, potato leaves : 3 green stem, cut leaves : 1 green stem, potato leaves.

This 9 : 3 : 3 : 1 ratio is typical of a dihybrid cross where both parents are heterozygous at both gene loci.

Questions

15 The allele for grey body colour in a species of animal is dominant to white, and the allele for dark eyes is dominant to the allele for pale eyes.

   a   Using the symbols **G** and **g** for the alleles for coat colour, and **D** and **d** for the alleles for eye colour, draw a genetic diagram to show the genotypes and phenotypes of the offspring you would expect from a cross between a homozygous grey animal with dark eyes and a homozygous white animal with pale eyes.

   b   If this first generation of offspring were bred together, what would be the expected phenotypes in the second generation of offspring, and in what ratios would they occur? Use a genetic diagram to explain your answer.

16 In a species of plant, the allele for tall stem is dominant to short. The two alleles for leaf colour, giving green or white in the homozygous condition, are codominant, producing variegated leaves in the heterozygote.

   A plant with tall stems and green leaves was crossed with a plant with short stems and variegated leaves. The offspring from this cross consisted of plants with tall stems and green leaves and plants with tall stems and variegated leaves in the ratio of 1 : 1. Construct a genetic diagram to explain this cross.

17 In a species of mammal, it is known that the allele for black eyes, **B**, is dominant to the allele for red eyes, **b**, and that the allele for long fur, **F**, is dominant to the allele for short fur, **f**.

   a   What are the possible genotypes for an animal with black eyes and long fur?

   b   How could you find out which genotype this animal had?

Epistasis

Sometimes, two different genes on different chromosomes affect the same feature. The alleles of one gene affect the expression of the other. This is called epistasis.

For example, in the inheritance of feather colour in chickens, there is an interaction between two gene loci on different chromosomes, **F/f** and **G/g**. The gene **G/g** determines whether or not the bird produces coloured feathers – allele **G** codes for a pigment that produces coloured feathers, whereas allele **g** does not produce a pigment, so the chicken has white feathers. However, this is also affected by the gene **F/f**. The dominant allele, **F**, prevents the production of coloured feathers, even if the bird has allele **G**.

The possible genotypes and phenotypes are:

genotype	phenotype
FFGG	white feathers
FFGg	white feathers
FFgg	white feathers
FfGG	white feathers
FfGg	white feathers
Ffgg	white feathers
ffGG	coloured feathers
ffGg	coloured feathers
ffgg	white feathers

Questions

18 Refer to the box above. A breed of chickens called White Leghorn have the genotype **FFGG**. Another breed, White Wyandotte, have the genotype **ffgg**.

   a Construct a genetic diagram to show that the F_1 offspring of a cross between a White Leghorn and a Wyandotte chicken will have white feathers.

   b Construct a second genetic diagram to predict the offspring phenotypes of a cross between two of these F_1 chickens.

19 In the plant *Salvia* the colour of the flowers is affected by two genes, **A/a** and **B/b**. Allele **B** gives purple flowers and is dominant to allele **b**, which gives pink flowers. However, neither of these colours can be produced unless allele **A** is also present.

   a List the nine possible genotypes and the phenotypes that each will produce.

   b Construct a genetic diagram to show how a cross between a homozygous pink-flowered *Salvia* and a homozygous white-flowered *Salvia* can produce offspring that all have purple flowers.

   c Construct a second genetic diagram to explain why interbreeding these offspring produces an F_2 generation with purple-, pink- and white-flowered plants in the ratio of 9 : 3 : 4.

Autosomal linkage

When two or more gene loci are on the same chromosome, they do not assort independently in meiosis as they would if they were on different chromosomes. The genes are said to be linked. They stay together in the same combinations as in the parents, and are said to be linked.

Autosomal linkage involves the autosomes – that is, all of the chromosomes except the sex chromosomes.

The fruit fly, *Drosophila*, normally has a striped body and antennae with a feathery arista (Figure 16.9). The gene for body colour and the gene for antennal shape are close together on the same chromosome and so are linked.

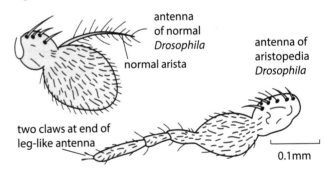

Figure 16.9: Normal and aristopedia *Drosophila* antennae.

KEY WORDS

epistasis: the interaction of two genes at different loci; one gene may affect the expression of the other

autosomal linkage: the presence of two genes on the same autosome, (any chromosome other than a sex chromosome) so that they tend to be inherited together and do not assort independently

A black body with no stripes results from a recessive allele called 'ebony'. A recessive allele for antennal shape, called 'aristopedia', gives an antenna looking rather like a *Drosophila* leg, with two claws on the end.

The alleles of these two genes that affect body colour and antenna shape are:

body colour gene

> **E** = allele for striped body
>
> **e** = allele for ebony body

antennal shape gene

> **A** = allele for normal antennae
>
> **a** = allele for aristopedia antennae

A fly homozygous for striped body and normal antennae was crossed with a fly homozygous for ebony body and aristopedia antennae. All the offspring had striped bodies and normal antennae. You can use a genetic diagram to show this.

To help keep track of linked alleles in a genetic diagram, it is best to bracket each linkage group. So, where you would write **EEAA** for the genotype if there was no linkage, here you write **(EA)(EA)**.

parental phenotypes	male, striped body, normal antennae		female, ebony body, aristopedia antennae
parental genotypes	**(EA)(EA)**	×	**(ea) (ea)**
parental gametes	(EA)		(ea)

			male gametes
			(EA)
offspring genotypes and phenotypes	female gametes	(ea)	**(EA)(ea)** striped body, normal antennae

predicted phenotypes of offspring: all striped body, normal antennae

Now consider what will happen if a male from this F_1 generation is crossed with a female with ebony body and aristopedia antennae.

parental phenotypes	male, striped body, normal antennae		female, ebony body, aristopedia antennae
parental genotypes	**(EA)(ea)**	×	**(ea) (ea)**
parental gametes	(EA) (ea)		(ea)

			male gametes	
			(EA)	(ea)
offspring genotypes and phenotypes	female gametes	(ea)	**(EA)(ea)** striped body, normal antennae	**(ea)(ea)** ebony body, aristopedia antennae

predicted phenotype ratios of offspring:

1 striped body, normal antennae : 1 ebony body, aristopedia antennae

Question

20 What ratio of phenotypes would you expect from the cross of a male *Drosophila* from the F_1 generation discussed with a female with ebony body and aristopedia antennae if the genes for body colour and antenna shape were *not* linked – that is, they were on different chromosomes? (You may like to use a genetic diagram to work out your answer.)

Autosomal linkage and crossing over

Complete linkage between genes on the same chromosome is very rare. You have seen that, during prophase I of meiosis, homologous chromosomes swap pieces of chromatids. Alleles from one homologous chromosome can therefore change places with alleles from the other. You may remember that this is called crossing over.

Crossing over breaks the linkage between genes on the same chromosomes.

Unusually, in male *Drosophila*, no crossing over takes place. (No one really knows why!) Crossing over does, however, take place in female *Drosophila*. Let's return to the *Drosophila* cross described above and test cross the female offspring. These have the genotype **(EA)(ea)**.

Figure 16.10 will help you to see how this results in four different kinds of gametes, rather than the two types you would expect if no crossing over takes place.

Phenotype	female, striped body, normal antennae	male, ebony body, aristopedia antennae
Genotype	(EA)(ea)	(ea)(ea)

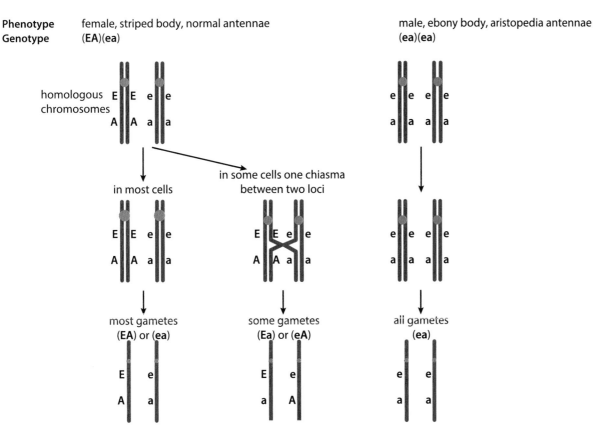

Figure 16.10: Crossing over in a female *Drosophila* (on the left). No crossing over occurs in male *Drosophila* (on the right).

Most of the offspring of this cross have their parents' combinations of characteristics – that is, either striped body, normal antennae or ebony body, aristopedia antennae. These are called **parental types**. They are in a 1 : 1 ratio. If linkage is complete, you would expect *all* of the offspring to be like this – which is exactly what happened with the test cross involving the male *Drosophila*.

But when the female is involved in this test cross, some flies are produced that have different combinations of characters. Some have striped body and aristopedia antennae, and some have ebony body with normal antennae. These are called **recombinants**. They result from crossing over, which 'recombines' the characteristics of the original parents. The two recombinant classes themselves are in a 1 : 1 ratio.

The actual results of the cross are:

striped body, normal antennae	44%
ebony body, aristopedia antennae	44%
striped body, aristopedia antennae	6%
ebony body, normal antennae	6%

You can show this with a genetic diagram:

parental phenotypes	female, striped body, normal antennae		male, ebony body, aristopedia antennae
parental genotypes	(EA)(ea)	×	(ea)(ea)
parental gametes	large numbers of (EA) (ea)		(ea)
	small numbers of (Ea) (eA)		

offspring genotypes and phenotypes

		male gametes
		(ea)
female gametes in large numbers	(EA)	**(EA)(ea)** striped body, normal antennae
	(ea)	**(ea)(ea)** ebony body, aristopedia antennae
female gametes in small numbers	(Ea)	**(Ea)(ea)** striped body, aristopedia antennae
	(eA)	**(eA)(ea)** striped body, normal antennae

Crossing over between two gene loci is more likely to take place if the genes are further apart, because there is more length of chromosome between them that can cross over. You can use this to get an idea of the positions of genes on a chromosome. The more recombinants you get in the offspring, the more crossing over has taken place, and the further apart the genes are.

Questions

21 (As you will quickly realise, this is a completely imaginary example!)

The Rainbow family only marry within their family. They have either yellow or blue hair and either green or orange toenails.

The allele for yellow hair, **Y**, is dominant, as is the allele **G** for green toenails.

KEY WORDS

parental type: offspring that show the same combinations of characteristics as their parents

recombinant: offspring that show different combinations of characteristics from their parents

a A couple with genotypes **YyGg** and **yygg** have a child. Predict the possible genotypes and phenotypes of the child, if the genes are on different chromosomes.

b Predict the possible genotypes and phenotypes of the child, if the genes are on the same chromosome and no crossing over occurs between the gene loci.

c Explain how one of the children of this couple could have a different combination of hair colour and toenail colour from either of their parents, even if the genes for these two characteristics are on the same chromosome.

22 Homozygous *Drosophila* with straight wings and grey bodies were crossed with homozygous curled-wing, ebony-bodied flies. All the offspring were straight-winged and grey-bodied. Female offspring were then test crossed with curled-wing, ebony-bodied males, giving the following results:

straight wing, grey body   113

straight wing, ebony body   30

curled wing, grey body   29

curled wing, ebony body   115

a State the ratio of phenotypes expected in a dihybrid test cross such as this, if there was no linkage and no crossing over.

b Explain the discrepancy between the expected result and the results given.

c Calculate the percentage of offspring that are recombinants.

16.6 The chi-squared (χ^2) test

If you look back at the cross between the two heterozygous tomato plants in Section 16.5, Dihybrid inheritance, you will see that a $9:3:3:1$ ratio of phenotypes is expected in the offspring. It is important to remember that this ratio represents the *probability* of getting these phenotypes, and it would be surprising if the numbers came out absolutely precisely to this ratio.

But just how much difference might scientists be happy with, before they began to worry that perhaps the situation was not quite what they had thought? For example, imagine that the two plants produced a total of 144 off spring. If the parents really were both heterozygous, and if the purple stem and cut leaf alleles

really are dominant, and if the alleles really do assort independently, then you would expect the following numbers of each phenotype to be present in the offspring:

$$\text{purple, cut} \quad = \frac{9}{16} \times 144 = 81$$

$$\text{purple, potato} = \frac{3}{16} \times 144 = 27$$

$$\text{green, cut} \quad = \frac{3}{16} \times 144 = 27$$

$$\text{green, potato} \quad = \frac{1}{16} \times 144 = 9$$

But imagine that the results actually observed among these 144 offspring were:

purple, cut   86

purple, potato   26

green, cut   24

green, potato   8

You might ask: are these results sufficiently close to the expected results that the differences could have arisen by chance, or are they so different that something unexpected must be going on?

To answer this question, you can use a statistical test called the **chi-squared** (χ^2) **test**. This test allows you to compare the observed results with the expected results and decide whether or not there is a significant difference between them.

> **KEY WORD**
>
> **chi-squared (χ^2) test:** a statistical test that is used to determine whether differences between observed and expected results are significant

The first stage in carrying out this test is to work out the expected results. These and the observed results are then recorded in a table like the one in Table 16.3. You can then calculate the difference between each set of results, and square each difference. (Squaring gets rid of any minus signs – it is irrelevant whether the differences are negative or positive.) Then you divide each squared difference by the expected value, and add up all of these answers:

$$\chi^2 = \sum \frac{(O - E)^2}{E}$$

where: Σ = sum of

       O = observed value

       E = expected value

	Phenotypes of plants			
	purple stems, cut leaves	purple stems, potato leaves	green stems, cut leaves	green stems, potato leaves
Observed number (O)	86	26	24	8
Expected ratio	9 : 3 : 3 : 1			
Expected number (E)	81	27	27	9
$O-E$	+5	−1	−3	−1
$(O-E)^2$	25	1	9	1
$(O-E)^2/E$	0.31	0.04	0.33	0.11
$\chi^2 = \sum \dfrac{(O-E)^2}{E} = 0.79$				

Table 16.3: Table of observed and expected results.

So now you have a value of χ^2. Next you have to work out what it means. To do this, you look in a table that relates χ^2 values to probabilities (Table 16.4). The probabilities given in the table are the probabilities that the differences between the expected and observed results are due to chance.

For example, a probability of 0.05 means that you would expect these differences to occur in 5 out of every 100 experiments, or 1 in 20, just by chance. A probability of 0.01 means that you would expect these differences to occur in 1 out of every 100 experiments, just by chance.

In this example, a probability of 0.05 is taken as being the critical one. If your χ^2 value represents a probability of 0.05 or larger, then you can be fairly certain that the differences between your observed and expected results are due to chance – the differences between them are not significant. However, if the probability is smaller than 0.05, then it is likely that the difference is significant, and you must reconsider assumptions about what was going on in this cross.

There is one more aspect of the results to consider before you can look up the value of χ^2 in Table 16.4.

This is the number of degrees of freedom in the results. The degrees of freedom take into account the number of comparisons made. (Remember that to get your value for χ^2, you added up all the calculated values. So, the larger the number of observed and expected values, the larger χ^2 is likely to be. You need to compensate for this.) To work out the number of degrees of freedom, simply calculate the number of classes of data minus 1. Here you have four classes of data (the four possible sets of phenotypes), so the degrees of freedom are: $4-1=3$.

Now, at last, you can look at Table 16.4 to determine whether the results show a significant deviation from what was expected. The numbers in the body of the table are χ^2 values. You look at the third row in the table (because that is the one relevant to 3 degrees of freedom), and find the χ^2 value that represents a probability of 0.05. You can see that this is 7.82. The calculated value of χ^2 was 0.79. So your value is a much, much smaller value than the one you have read from the table. In fact, there is nothing like this number in the table – it would be way off the left-hand side, representing a probability of much more than 0.1 (1 in 10) that the difference in your results is just due to

Degrees of freedom	Probability that the difference between observed and expected results is due to chance			
	0.1	0.05	0.01	0.001
1	2.71	3.84	6.64	10.83
2	4.60	5.99	9.21	13.82
3	6.25	7.82	11.34	16.27
4	7.78	9.49	13.28	18.46

Table 16.4: Table of χ^2 values.

chance. So you can say that the difference between the observed and expected results is very likely to be due to chance, and there is no significant difference between what was expected and what actually happened.

As in other statistical tests, you often use a null hypothesis when using χ^2. The null hypothesis is that there is no difference between your observed and expected results. In other words, the null hypothesis says that any difference between the observed and expected results is due to chance. In this example, the χ^2 value you have calculated supports the null hypothesis.

Question

23 Look back at your answer to Question 15b. In the actual cross between the animals in this generation, the numbers of each phenotype obtained in the offspring were:

grey body, dark eyes	54
grey body, pale eyes	4
white body, dark eyes	4
white body, pale eyes	18

Use a χ^2 test to determine whether the difference between these observed results is significant.

16.7 Genes, proteins and phenotype

So far in the study of genetics, you have looked at the effect that genes have on phenotype, without looking into the mechanisms that cause these effects. In this section you will look at four genes that affect human phenotypes, and consider how the genes have these effects.

In this section a different convention is used for symbols for alleles of human genes. Previously, you have used a single letter, but now you will use the general convention for most human genes of a three-letter abbreviation, written in italics. The same abbreviations are used by all scientists whose work involves these genes. For example, the gene for producing tyrosinase is shown as *TYR*. The same three-letter code shown in normal type (not italics), TYR, represents the protein or polypeptide that the gene codes for.

IMPORTANT

When you are writing gene abbreviations by hand, you can underline the symbol for the gene to indicate italics, like this: TYR.

The *TYR* gene, tyrosinase and albinism

Albinism provides a good example of the relationship between a gene, an enzyme and a human phenotype.

In albinism the dark pigment melanin is totally or partially missing from the eyes, skin and hair. In humans this results in pale blue or pink irises in the eyes and very pale skin and hair (Figure 16.11). The pupils of the eyes appear red. The condition is often accompanied by poor vision, rapid, jerky movements of the eyes and a tendency to avoid bright light.

Figure 16.11: A boy with albinism with his classmates in South Africa.

The *TYR* gene is found on the long arm of chromosome 11 (Figure 16.12). There is a faulty recessive allele that results in albinism. About 1 in 17000 children born worldwide are homozygous recessive for this allele and therefore show albinism. However, the condition is relatively common in some populations, such as the Hopi in Arizona and the Kuna San Blas Indians in Panama.

Figure 16.12: The loci of the *TYR* and *HBB* genes on chromosome 11.

Melanin is produced by this metabolic pathway:

tyrosinase

tyrosine → DOPA → dopaquinone → melanin

A recessive allele of the gene for the enzyme tyrosinase results in either the absence of tyrosinase or the presence of inactive tyrosinase in the cells where melanin is made. Tyrosine cannot be converted into DOPA and dopaquinone. The first two steps of the conversion of the amino acid, tyrosine, into melanin therefore cannot take place.

Tyrosinases occur in plant as well as in animal tissues. The action of the enzyme can be seen in the blackening of a slice of potato left exposed to the air.

The *HBB* gene, haemoglobin and sickle cell anaemia

HBB is the gene that codes for the amino acid sequence in the β-globin polypeptide in haemoglobin. It is found on the short arm of chromosome 11.

In most people, the β-globin polypeptide begins with the amino acid sequence coded from the normal allele:

Val–His–Leu–Thr–Pro–Glu–Glu–Lys–

But in people with an abnormal form of allele, the base sequence CTT is replaced by CAT, and the amino acid sequence becomes:

Val– His–Leu–Thr–Pro–Val–Glu–Lys–

This small difference in the amino acid sequence makes little difference to the haemoglobin molecule when it is combined with oxygen. But when it is not combined with oxygen, the 'unusual' β-globin polypeptides make the haemoglobin molecule much less soluble. The molecules tend to stick to each other, forming long fibres inside the red blood cells. The red cells are pulled out of shape, into a half-moon or sickle shape. When this happens, the distorted cells become useless at transporting oxygen. They also get stuck in small capillaries, stopping any unaffected cells from getting through.

A person with this unusual β-globin can suffer severe anaemia (lack of oxygen transported to the cells) and may die. Sickle cell anaemia is especially common in some parts of Africa and in India.

A person with one copy of the normal *HBB* allele and one copy of the sickle cell allele makes some normal haemoglobin and some sickle cell haemoglobin. They generally show no symptoms unless they are in conditions where there is excessive oxygen demand by their muscles – for example, exercising very vigorously.

The *F8* gene, factor VIII and haemophilia

The *F8* gene contains the code for synthesising a protein called coagulation factor VIII. The protein is synthesised in liver cells. It is secreted into blood plasma and plays an important role in the sequence of events that takes place during blood clotting.

Abnormal alleles of this gene result in the production of abnormal forms of factor VIII protein, less factor VIII than usual, or even no factor VIII at all. This means that blood does not clot normally, and excessive bleeding can follow from even a small injury. The condition is called haemophilia.

The *F8* gene is found on a non-homologous region of the X chromosome. This means that it is a sex-linked gene. Males have only one copy and cannot therefore mask the effect of the faulty allele with a normal one. Females can be heterozygous for this condition without showing any symptoms at all, as only one copy of the normal gene is required to result in the synthesis of enough factor VIII.

The *HTT* gene, huntingtin and Huntington's disease

The locus of the *HTT* gene is on chromosome 4. This gene codes for the production of a protein called huntingtin. Scientists still do not know exactly what this protein does, but it is known to be important in the development of neurones, particularly in the brain.

In some people, the nucleotide sequence of this gene contains a large number of repeated CAG triplets. (This is sometimes called a 'stutter'.) If the number of repeats is over 40, neurone development is abnormal and the person develops Huntington's disease. (If repeats number between 36 and 39, the disease sometimes develops but sometimes not.) The condition develops gradually as a person gets older, and often no symptoms show until the person is 30–40 years old. They begin to lose their ability to control movements and to walk, talk or think clearly. The condition is fatal, with death occurring within 15–20 years after symptoms first appear.

This faulty allele is dominant. There is therefore a one in two chance that a person with a parent with the allele will inherit the condition. As the condition may not be noticed until the person is adult, they may have had children before they knew of the possibility of passing on Huntington's.

The *Le* gene, gibberellin and stem elongation

You are now going to look at the relationship between genes and phenotype that occurs in some types of plant. In plants, the three-letter style used for most human genes is not always used. Traditionally, plant genes have been given a two-letter abbreviation. As in humans, the symbol is shown in italics.

The height of some plants is partly controlled by their genes. For example, tallness in pea plants is affected by a gene with two alleles, *Le* and *le*. If the dominant allele, *Le*, is present, the plants can grow tall, but plants homozygous for the recessive allele, *le*, always remain short. The dominant allele of this gene regulates the synthesis of the last enzyme in a pathway that produces an active form of gibberellin, GA_1. (You learnt about gibberellin in Chapter 15, Section 15.4, Control and coordination in plants.) Active gibberellin stimulates cell division and cell elongation in the stem, so the plant grows tall.

A recessive allele of this gene has one nucleotide that differs from the normal allele. This allele codes for alanine instead of threonine at one position in the primary structure of the enzyme near its active site, producing a non-functional enzyme. Homozygous plants, *lele*, are genetically dwarf as they do not have the active form of gibberellin. Applying active gibberellin to plants which would normally remain short, such as cabbages, can stimulate them to grow tall.

16.8 Control of gene expression

A gene is said to be expressed when it is transcribed to mRNA and then the mRNA is translated to produce a protein. Only a tiny proportion of the genes present in the nucleus of a cell are actually expressed at any one time. For example, the gene for melanin production will never be expressed in your heart muscle cells.

In this section you will look first at how the expression of a gene is controlled in a prokaryote organism, the bacterium *Escherichia coli*. You will then consider the control of gene expression in eukaryotes.

Gene control in prokaryotes

An understanding of how genes are 'switched on and off' first came from studies in bacteria. One of the most-studied genes is the one that codes for the production of the enzyme β-galactosidase (also known as lactase). This enzyme is used by some bacteria to hydrolyse lactose in the bacterium's environment to glucose and galactose, which can then be absorbed and used as an energy source by the cell.

The gene that codes for the production of β-galactosidase is an example of a **structural gene**. A structural gene is one that codes for the production of a protein that is used by the cell. Some structural genes live up to their name by coding for proteins that become part of a structure in the cell, but many structural genes have other roles, such as coding for enzymes.

The expression of the lactase gene is controlled by other genes that lie close to it on the circular DNA (DNA molecule). These are called **regulatory genes**.

> **KEY WORDS**
>
> **β-galactosidase:** an enzyme that catalyses the hydrolysis of lactose to glucose and galactose
>
> **structural gene:** a gene that codes for a protein that has a function within a cell
>
> **regulatory gene:** a gene that codes for a protein that helps to control the expression of other genes

Structural and regulatory genes that work together are generally found in a group, and this cluster of genes is called an **operon**. The operon that is responsible for the production of lactase in bacteria is called the *lac* operon. The structure of the lac operon is shown in Figure 16.13.

In the bacterium *Escherichia coli*, the number of molecules of β-galactosidase present in a cell varies according to the concentration of lactose in the medium in which the bacterium is growing. The quantity of the enzyme is altered by switching the transcription of the β-galactosidase gene on or off.

The *lac* operon also contains other structural genes, besides the one that codes for β-galactosidase. There are three structural genes altogether:

- *lacZ*, coding for β-galactosidase

- *lacY*, coding for permease (which allows lactose to enter the cell)

- *lacA*, coding for transacetylase.

Transcription of all of these genes is controlled by the same promoter, and they are all transcribed at the same time.

The sequence of events when there is no lactose in the medium in which the bacterium is growing is as follows.

KEY WORDS

operon: a functional unit of transcription; a cluster of genes that are controlled by the same promoter

lac **operon:** an operon (see above) found in some bacteria that controls the production of β-galactosidase and two other structural proteins

- The regulatory gene codes for a protein called a repressor.

- The repressor binds to the operator region, close to the gene for β-galactosidase.

- Because the repressor is attached to the operator, RNA polymerase cannot bind to DNA at the promoter region.

- As a result, there is no transcription of the three structural genes.

The repressor protein has two binding sites. This repressor protein can bind to DNA at one site and to lactose at the other. When lactose binds to its site, the shape of the repressor protein changes so that the DNA-binding site is closed.

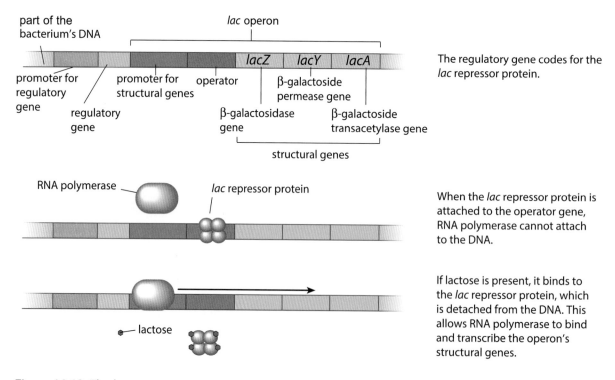

The regulatory gene codes for the *lac* repressor protein.

When the *lac* repressor protein is attached to the operator gene, RNA polymerase cannot attach to the DNA.

If lactose is present, it binds to the *lac* repressor protein, which is detached from the DNA. This allows RNA polymerase to bind and transcribe the operon's structural genes.

Figure 16.13: The *lac* operon.

When lactose is present in the medium in which the bacterium is growing, the following processes occur.

- Lactose is taken up by the bacterium.

- Lactose binds to the repressor protein, distorting its shape and preventing it from binding to DNA at the operator site.

- Transcription is no longer inhibited and messenger RNA is produced from the three structural genes.

The genes have been switched on and are transcribed together. The bacterium can now absorb and break down lactose.

This mechanism allows the bacterium to produce β-galactosidase, permease and transacetylase only when lactose is available in the surrounding medium and to produce them in equal amounts. It avoids the waste of energy and materials in producing enzymes for taking up and hydrolysing a sugar that the bacterium may never meet. However, the sugar can be hydrolysed when it is available.

The enzyme β-galactosidase is an **inducible enzyme**. This means that it is synthesised only when its substrate is present. The presence of the substrate induces (causes) the transcription of the gene for the enzyme. The binding of the effector molecule (which in this case is lactose) to the repressor prevents the repressor from binding to the operator, the repressor is released and transcription proceeds.

The production of other enzymes, called **repressible enzymes**, is controlled in a slightly different way. Here, the binding of the effector molecule to the repressor helps it to bind to the operator. So the repressor attaches to the operator region, which stops transcription.

Transcription factors in eukaryotes

Eukaryotes do not have operons as prokaryotes do. Instead, the expression of genes in eukaryotes is controlled by **transcription factors**.

A transcription factor is a protein that binds to DNA and affects whether or not a gene is transcribed. The role of transcription factors is to make sure that genes are expressed in the correct cell at the correct time and to the correct extent.

In humans, for example, about 10% of genes are thought to code for proteins that act as transcription factors.

Some transcription factors bind to the promoter region of a gene, either allowing or preventing its transcription. Their presence either increases or decreases the rate of transcription of a gene.

There are many different types of transcription factors, which have different effects. Scientists have probably discovered only a small proportion of them so far, and research continues to find new ones and increase understanding of how they work. Some examples of the effects of transcription factors include the following. You do not need to know any details of these but, if any of the bullet points in the list make you want to know more, try an internet search for more information.

- General transcription factors are necessary for transcription to occur. They form part of the protein complex that binds to the promoter region of the gene concerned.

- Other transcription factors help to ensure that a number of different genes are activated in the correct sequence. This is important to allow the correct pattern of development of body regions as a zygote gradually becomes an embryo and then a fetus.

- A transcription factor is responsible for the determination of sex in mammals.

- Transcription factors allow responses to environmental stimuli, such as switching on the correct genes to respond to high environmental temperatures.

- Some transcription factors, including the products of proto-oncogenes and tumour suppressor genes, regulate the cell cycle, growth and apoptosis (programmed cell death).

- Many hormones, such as testosterone, have their effect through transcription factors.

KEY WORDS

inducible enzyme: an enzyme that is synthesised only when its substrate is present

repressible enzyme: an enzyme that is normally produced, and whose synthesis is prevented by the presence of an effector

transcription factor: a molecule that affects whether or not a gene is transcribed

---

Transcription factors act in similar ways in plants and animals. In Chapter 15, you saw that the plant hormone gibberellin controls seed germination in plants such as wheat and barley by stimulating the synthesis of amylase. This is a good example of how a hormone can influence transcription. If gibberellin is applied to barley seeds, there is an increase in the transcription of mRNA coding for amylase.

Gibberellin has this effect by causing the breakdown of DELLA proteins (Figure 16.14). A molecule known as a DELLA protein is a repressor protein. DELLA proteins normally inhibit the binding of a transcription factor, such as phytochrome-interacting protein (PIF), to a gene promoter. Gibberellin causes the breakdown of the DELLA protein, which allows PIF to bind to its target promoter. Transcription of the gene can then take place, resulting in an increase in amylase production.

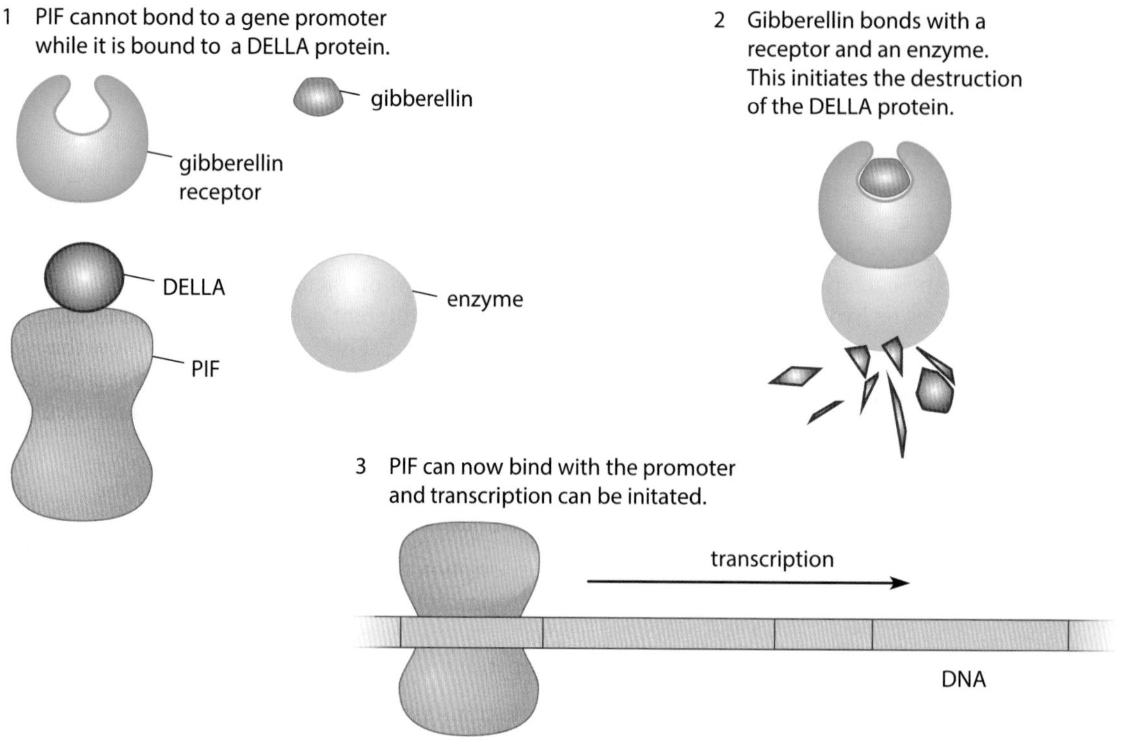

1 PIF cannot bond to a gene promoter while it is bound to a DELLA protein.

gibberellin

gibberellin receptor

DELLA

enzyme

PIF

2 Gibberellin bonds with a receptor and an enzyme. This initiates the destruction of the DELLA protein.

3 PIF can now bind with the promoter and transcription can be initated.

transcription

DNA

Figure 16.14: How gibberellin activates the transcription of the amylase gene.

REFLECTION

In 2009 biological researchers developed the technology that allowed them to analyse the RNA of a single cell. This has led to the identification of different types of cell in human tissues that were previously unknown. The cells look identical to other cells, but their RNA shows that they are actually doing something different.

For example, in 2018 a previously unknown type of cell was found in the lining of the trachea in mice. Now named pulmonary ionocytes, these cells produce more of a protein called CFTR than do other cells in the tracheal lining. This protein controls the movement of chloride ions out of cells. Water follows by osmosis, and this helps to thin the mucus secreted by other cells in the lining.

Thinking about your knowledge of DNA and protein synthesis (Chapter 6, Section 6.5, Protein synthesis), the functions of the cells in the lining of the trachea (Chapter 9, Section 9.3, Trachea, bronchi and bronchioles) and the control of gene expression, consider:

- how cells that look identical and possess identical sets of genes can have different functions

- how analysing RNA, rather than DNA, from a single cell can help to identify a new type of cell

- how this newly discovered type of cell can help to prevent infections developing in the lungs.

What problems did you encounter when you were working on these questions? How did you solve them?

Final reflection

Discuss with a friend which, if any, part of Chapter 16 you need to:

- read through again to make sure you really understand

- seek more guidance on, even after going over it again.

SUMMARY

Homologous chromosomes are pairs of chromosomes in a diploid cell that have the same structure and the same genes at the same loci, but not necessarily the same varieties of those genes.
Meiosis consists of two divisions. The first division, meiosis I, is a reduction division that separates the homologous chromosomes, so that each cell now has only one of each pair. The second division, meiosis II, separates the chromatids of each chromosome. Meiotic division therefore produces four cells, each with one complete set of chromosomes.
Diploid cells contain sets of chromosomes and therefore two copies of each gene. In sexual reproduction, haploid gametes are formed containing one set of chromosomes and therefore one copy of each gene. Each offspring receives two copies of each gene, one from each of its parents.
The cells produced by meiosis are genetically different from each other and from their parent cell. This results from independent assortment of the chromosomes as the bivalents line up on the equator during metaphase I, and also from crossing over between the chromatids of homologous chromosomes during prophase I. Genetic variation also results from random fertilisation, as gametes containing different varieties of genes fuse together to form a zygote.
An organism's genetic constitution is its genotype. Its observable characteristics are its phenotype, which is influenced by the expression of its genes. Different varieties of a gene are called alleles. Alleles may show dominance, codominance or recessiveness. An organism possessing two identical alleles of a gene is homozygous; an organism possessing two different alleles of a gene is heterozygous. If a gene has several different alleles, such as the gene for human blood groups, these are known as multiple alleles.
A gene found on the X chromosome but not on the Y chromosome is known as a sex-linked gene. Genes that are close together on a chromosome that is not a sex chromosome are said to be autosomally linked.
The genotype of an organism showing dominant characteristics can be determined by looking at the offspring produced when it is crossed with an organism showing recessive characteristics. This is called a test cross. Monohybrid crosses consider the inheritance of one gene. Dihybrid crosses consider the inheritance of two different genes. Different genes may interact to affect the same phenotypic character, a situation known as epistasis.

CONTINUED

The chi-squared (χ^2) test can be used to find out whether any differences between expected results and observed results of a genetic cross are due to chance or whether the difference is significant.

The *HBB* gene codes for the beta globin polypeptides in haemoglobin. An allele of this gene with a different base sequence produces sickle cell haemoglobin. The allele of the *HTT* gene that is responsible for Huntington's disease includes a repeated triplet of nucleotides called a 'stutter'. Albinism and haemophilia show the effect on the phenotype of missing or inactive polypeptides.

The *lac* operon provides an example of how a prokaryote can alter the transcription of a cluster of structural genes coding for enzymes concerned with lactose uptake and metabolism, depending on whether or not lactose is present. 'Structural' genes code for the proteins required by a cell for its structure or metabolism, whereas 'regulatory' genes control the expression of other genes. A repressor protein can block the synthesis of a 'repressible' enzyme, by binding to the gene's operator site. An 'inducible' enzyme is synthesised only when its substrate is present.

Transcription factors in eukaryotes make sure that genes are expressed in the correct cell, at the correct time and to the correct extent. In plants, gibberellins allow gene transcription by causing the breakdown of DELLA proteins which inhibit the binding of transcription factors.

EXAM-STYLE QUESTIONS

1 a Distinguish between the terms *genotype* and *phenotype*. [2]

b Distinguish between the terms *homozygous* and *heterozygous*. [2]

c In sweet-pea plants, the gene **A/a** controls flower colour. The dominant allele gives purple flowers and the recessive allele red flowers.

A second gene, **B/b**, controls the shape of the pollen grains. The dominant allele gives elongated grains and the recessive allele spherical grains.

A plant with the genotype **AaBb** was test crossed by interbreeding it with a plant with red flowers and spherical pollen grains.

Copy and complete the table to show the expected ratio of phenotypes of the offspring of this cross. The gametes from one parent are already in the table.

		Gametes of the other parent
Gametes of one parent	(AB) genotype: phenotype:	
	(Ab) genotype: phenotype:	
	(aB) genotype: phenotype:	
	(ab) genotype: phenotype:	

[5]

[Total: 9]

CONTINUED

2 a The fruit fly, *Drosophila melanogaster*, feeds on sugars found in damaged fruits. A fly with normal features is called a wild type. It has a grey striped body and its wings are longer than its abdomen. Some flies have an ebony-coloured body or vestigial wings. These three types of fly are shown in the diagrams.

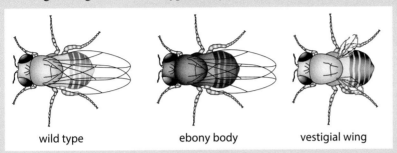

| wild type | ebony body | vestigial wing |

Wild-type features are coded for by dominant alleles: **A** for wild-type body and **B** for wild-type wings.

Explain what is meant by the terms *allele* and *dominant*.   **[2]**

b Two wild-type fruit flies were crossed. These were heterozygous at both gene loci.

Draw a genetic diagram to show the possible offspring of this cross.   **[6]**

c When the two heterozygous flies in **b** were crossed, 384 eggs hatched and developed into adult flies. A chi-squared (χ^2) test was carried out to test the significance of the differences between observed and expected results:

$$\chi^2 = \Sigma \frac{(O - E)^2}{E}$$

where: Σ = sum of

O = observed value

E = expected value.

i Copy and complete the table.

	Phenotypes of *Drosophila melanogaster*			
	grey body long wing	grey body vestigial wing	ebony body long wing	ebony body vestigial wing
Observed number (O)	207	79	68	30
Expected ratio	9	3	3	1
Expected number (E)	216	72	72	24
O−E	−9		−4	6
(O−E)²	81		16	36
(O−E)²/E	0.38		0.22	1.50

[3]

CONTINUED

ii   Calculate the value for χ^2.   [1]

The table below relates χ^2 values to probability values.

As four classes of data were counted, the number of degrees of freedom was $4-1=3$. The table gives values of χ^2 where there are three degrees of freedom.

Probability greater than	0.50	0.20	0.10	0.05	0.01	0.001
Values for χ^2	2.37	4.64	6.25	7.82	11.34	16.27

iii   Using your value for χ^2 and the table above, explain whether or not the observed results were significantly different from the expected results.   [2]

[Total: 14]

Cambridge International AS & A Level Biology (9700/41), Question 7, October/November 2009

3   Feather colour in budgerigars is affected by many different genes. One of these genes is **G/g**, which determines whether the feathers are green or blue. Allele **G** is dominant and gives green feathers, and allele **g** gives blue feathers.

A second gene, on a different chromosome, affects the intensity of the colouring. It has two codominant alleles. $\mathbf{C^P}$ produces a pale colour and $\mathbf{C^D}$ gives a dark colour.

The table shows the six colours produced by various combinations of the alleles of these two genes.

Colour	Intensity of colour		
	pale	medium	dark
green	light green	dark green	olive green
blue	sky blue	cobalt blue	mauve

a   State the genotype of:

i   a dark green bird that is homozygous at the **G/g** locus   [1]

ii   a sky blue bird   [1]

b   Construct a genetic diagram to show the possible offspring produced from a cross between the dark green bird in **a i** and a cobalt blue bird.   [5]

[Total: 7]

4   a   With reference to the control of expression of the gene for β-galactosidase in *Escherichia coli*, explain the meaning of each of the following terms.

i   operon   [2]

ii   structural gene   [1]

iii   inducible enzyme   [1]

CONTINUED

    b Explain how the presence of lactose in the environment causes the synthesis of β-galactosidase.   **[5]**

    c Explain why it is advantageous to the bacterium to secrete β-galactosidase only when lactose is present.   **[2]**

    [Total: 11]

5 Thyroid hormones have various functions in the body, including increasing metabolic rate, stimulating growth in young people and increasing the ability of heart muscle to contract. Thyroid hormones are small molecules, based on the amino acid tyrosine, that enter their target cells through carrier proteins.

    a Explain why thyroid hormones enter cells through carrier proteins, rather than diffusing through the lipid bilayer.   **[2]**

    b Thyroid hormones move into the nucleus of the target cell, where they bind to a receptor. These hormone receptors are normally already bound to DNA, close to a particular gene, where they inhibit its transcription. When the hormone binds to the receptor, transcription of the gene is stimulated.

        i State the name for a molecule, such as the thyroid hormone receptor, which affects the transcription of a gene.   **[1]**

        ii One gene whose transcription is affected by thyroid hormones codes for the synthesis of myosin.
            Suggest how the effect of thyroid hormones on the myosin gene could affect cardiac muscle.   **[3]**

    c The gene *THBR* codes for one type of thyroid hormone receptor. Its locus is on chromosome 3. Some people have a faulty allele of this gene on one of their chromosome 3s. They have a condition called thyroid resistance, in which thyroid hormones are produced normally but do not have their usual effects on target cells.

        i Use the information to determine whether the faulty allele is dominant or recessive. Explain your answer.   **[1]**

        ii Explain how the faulty allele can result in a lack of ability of cells to respond to thyroid hormones.   **[3]**

    [Total: 10]

SELF-EVALUATION CHECKLIST

After studying this chapter, complete a table like this:

I can	See section...	Needs more work	Almost there	Ready to move on
describe the process of meiosis, and explain its significance in terms of maintaining chromosome number in sexual reproduction and producing genetically different offspring	16.1, 16.2			
describe and explain how different alleles of genes affect phenotype	16.2, 16.3			
construct and interpret genetic diagrams showing monohybrid crosses, including the involvement of dominant, recessive and codominant alleles and sex linkage	16.4			
construct and interpret genetic diagrams showing dihybrid crosses, including the involvement of dominant, recessive and codominant alleles, autosomal linkage and epistasis	16.5			
use the chi-squared test to determine the significance of differences between observed and expected results in genetic crosses	16.6			
explain the relationship between genes, proteins and phenotype, using the genes *TYR*, *HBB*, *F8* and *HTT* as examples	16.7			
explain how the alleles *Le* and *le* control gibberellin production and hence stem elongation	16.7			
use the *lac* operon to explain how gene expression is controlled in prokaryotes	16.8			
describe how transcription factors are involved in the control of gene expression in eukaryotes, including the role of gibberellin and DELLA protein repressors in plants	16.8			

> Chapter 17
Selection and evolution

LEARNING INTENTIONS

In this chapter you will learn how to:

- explain that genetic and environmental factors affect phenotypic variation
- explain the differences between continuous and discontinuous variation
- explain how natural selection takes place, including reference to the development of antibiotic resistance in bacteria
- explain the differences between stabilising, disruptive and directional selection
- explain how the founder effect and genetic drift may affect allele frequencies
- use the Hardy–Weinberg equations
- describe the principles of selective breeding, including examples
- outline the theory of evolution in terms of changes to gene pools
- discuss the use of DNA sequencing to determine relationships between species
- explain how new species can be formed by allopatric and sympatric processes

BEFORE YOU START

Some breeds of cow tend to produce more milk than others. Cows that are fed on a high-quality diet tend to produce more milk than cows fed on a low-quality diet.

A farmer wants to breed a herd of cows that produce large quantities of milk. With a partner, discuss whether the farmer should choose cows from a particular breed or cows that have been fed on a high-quality diet to start off his herd.

Be ready to explain your ideas.

DECEPTIVE FLOWERS

Coevolution is the evolution of two species as a result of interactions between them. A good example of coevolution is found in the adaptations that have evolved in the flowers of orchids, and the behaviour of their pollinators. Most orchids have flowers that are adapted for pollination by a very specific type of insect. Often, the orchid is pollinated by only this species of insect, and the insect is attracted to the flower of only this species of orchid.

An orchid flower has three outer sepals, two petals and a conspicuously shaped and coloured 'lip' (labellum), which is the third petal. In the centre of the flower is the 'column', which carries packages of pollen on its upper side and the surface of the stigma on its lower side. This arrangement encourages cross-pollination and avoids self-pollination.

In bee orchids and fly orchids, the lip looks and smells like a female of the species of pollinating insect (Figure 17.1). Male insects, attempting to mate with the 'decoy female', collect pollen on their backs and deliver it to the stigma of another flower.

The flowers of this species of orchid are not all exactly alike. However, as a result of natural selection, over many generations of orchids, the lip has become more and more like a female insect. The male insect receives his reward of nectar or wax so long as he is attracted by the decoy female.

Questions for discussion

The shape and colour of flowers is controlled by genes.

Figure 17.1: A fly orchid. You can imagine how a fly might mistake this flower for its own species, and attempt to mate with it.

- What could cause variation in shape and colour between different individuals of the same species of orchid?

- Suggest why some individuals of this species of orchid might be more likely to be pollinated than other individuals of the same species.

17.1 Variation

In Chapter 16 you saw how sexual reproduction produces **genetic variation** among the individuals in a population. Genetic variation is caused by:

- independent assortment of chromosomes, and therefore alleles, during meiosis

- crossing over between chromatids of homologous chromosomes during meiosis

- random fusion of gametes, and random mating between organisms within a species

- mutation.

The first four of these processes reshuffle existing alleles in the population. Offspring have combinations of alleles which differ from those of their parents and from each other. This genetic variation produces **phenotypic variation**.

Mutation, however, does not reshuffle alleles that are already present. Mutation, which is described in Chapter 6 (Section 6.6, Gene mutations), can produce completely new alleles. This may happen, for example, if a mistake occurs in DNA replication, so that a new base sequence occurs in a gene. This is probably how the sickle cell allele of the gene for the production of the β-globin polypeptide first arose. Such a change in a gene, which is quite unpredictable, is called a gene mutation. The new allele is very often recessive, so it frequently does not show up in the population until some generations after the mutation actually occurred, when by chance two descendants of organisms in which the mutation happened mate and produce offspring.

Genes are not the only cause of differences between the phenotypes of organisms of the same species. The environment also affects phenotype. For example, a plant that has a genotype that allows it to grow tall will only be able to grow tall if it has plenty of sunlight and a good supply of minerals and water in the soil. If these are lacking, then it will not grow to the potential size determined by its genotype. The phenotype of an organism is a result of interaction between genetic and environmental factors.

Question

1   Explain why variation caused by the environment cannot be passed from an organism to its offspring.

Genetic variation

Mutations that occur in body cells often have no effects at all on the organism. If only one cell is affected, then the overall function of the tissue of which the cell is part continues as normal. An exception is if the mutation affects the control of the mitotic cell cycle, allowing the cell to divide uncontrollably, which can lead to the development of a tumour.

However, mutations in cells in the ovaries or testes of an animal, or in the ovaries or anthers of a plant, may be inherited by offspring. If a cell containing a mutation divides to form gametes, then the gametes may also contain the mutated allele. If such a gamete is one of the two which fuse to form a zygote, then the mutated allele will also be in the zygote. This single cell then divides repeatedly to form a new organism, in which all the cells will contain the mutated allele.

So genetic variation, whether caused by the reshuffling of alleles during meiosis and sexual reproduction or by the introduction of new alleles by mutation, can be passed on by parents to their offspring, producing differences in phenotype. But variation caused by the environment is not passed on by parents to their offspring.

Continuous and discontinuous variation

Phenotypic differences between you and your friends include qualitative differences such as blood groups and quantitative differences such as height and mass.

Qualitative differences fall into clearly distinguishable categories, with no intermediates – for example, you have one of four possible ABO blood groups: A, B, AB or O (Figure 17.2). This is an example of **discontinuous variation**.

> **KEY WORDS**
>
> **genetic variation:** differences between the DNA base sequences of individuals within a species
>
> **phenotypic variation:** differences between the observable characteristics of individuals within a species
>
> **discontinuous variation:** differences between individuals of a species in which each one belongs to one of a small number of distinct categories, with no intermediates

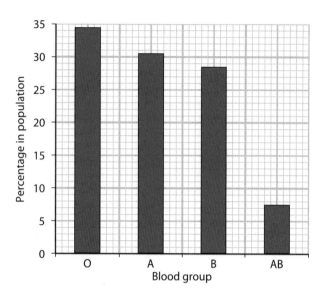

Figure 17.2: A bar chart showing variation in blood groups in a population.

In contrast, the quantitative differences between your individual heights or masses do not fall into distinct categories. When the heights of a large number of people are measured, there are no distinguishable height classes. Instead, there is a range of heights between two extremes (Figure 17.3). This is **continuous variation**.

The genetic basis of continuous and discontinuous variation

Discontinuous variation is caused entirely by genes, with the environment having no effect. Your ABO blood group depends on your genotype – the combination of the I^A, I^B or I^o alleles that you have in your cells.

Continuous variation is also affected by genes, but environment can also have an effect. For example, your height is a result of the genes affecting growth that you inherited from your parents, interacting with lifestyle factors as you grew up – for example, the type of diet that you had.

So both discontinuous variation and continuous variation are affected by genes. Both may involve several different genes. However, there are important differences between them.

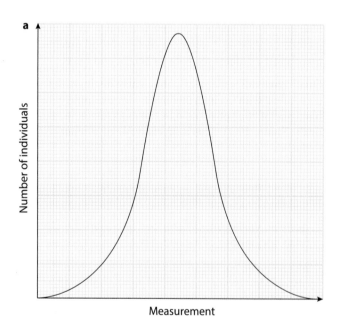
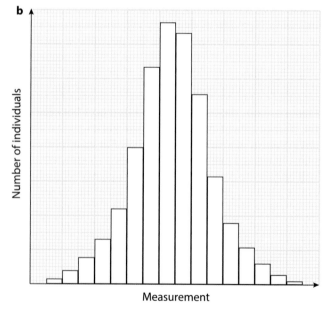

Figure 17.3: a A distribution curve and **b** a frequency diagram (histogram) showing continuous variation.

In discontinuous variation:

- different alleles at a single gene locus have large effects on the phenotype.

In continuous variation:

- different alleles at a single gene locus have small effects on the phenotype

- different genes have the same, often additive, effect on the phenotype

- a large number of genes may have a combined effect on a particular phenotypic trait; these genes are known as **polygenes**.

KEY WORD

polygenes: a number of different genes at different loci that all contribute to a particular aspect of phenotype

In Chapter 16 you met a number of examples of discontinuous variation where different alleles of a single gene had a large effect on phenotype (Section 16.2, The production of genetic variation). You also saw how two different genes, at different loci, can interact to produce phenotypic differences, a situation known as epistasis. The inheritance of sickle cell anaemia and haemophilia are examples of discontinuous variation in humans, caused by variants of the alleles *HBB* and *F8* respectively. Flower colour in *Salvia*, stem colour of tomato plants and feather colour of chickens are examples of discontinuous variation in other species.

It is actually very difficult to find good examples of large effects of a single gene in an organism, such as those that you looked at in Chapter 16. It is much more common to see a large number of different genes affecting a particular characteristic. Moreover, most genes have many more than the two alleles that you considered in almost all of the examples in Chapter 16. Multiple alleles, such as those involved in the determination of blood group, are the norm – and usually there are many more than three possible alleles for any one gene.

Two of the typical effects of the inheritance of continuous variation – the small effects of the different alleles of one gene on the phenotype and the additive effect of different genes on the same phenotypic character – can be seen in a hypothetical example of the inheritance of an organism's height.

Suppose that the height of an organism is controlled by two unlinked (that is, on different chromosomes) genes: **A/a** and **B/b**. The recessive alleles of both genes (**a** and **b**) each contribute x cm to the height of the organism. The dominant alleles (**A** and **B**) each add $2x$ cm.

Since the effect of such genes is additive, the homozygous recessive (**aabb**) is therefore potentially $4x$ cm tall and the homozygous dominant (**AABB**) is potentially $8x$ cm tall. The other genotypes will fall between these extremes.

Consider, for example, what might happen if these two homozygous individuals interbreed, and if their offspring (the F_2 generation) also interbreed.

The number of offspring and their potential heights according to their genotypes are summarised in the histogram in Figure 17.4. These results fall approximately on a normal distribution curve.

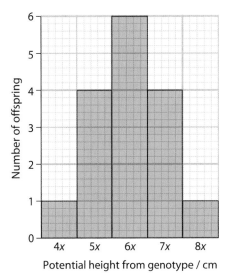

Figure 17.4: The added effects of alleles of two different genes affecting height.

Now imagine what the variation might be if the effects of the dominant alleles of the two genes were not the same – for example, if allele **A** added $3x$ cm to the potential height, rather than 2. (You might like to work that out, using the genotypes in the Punnett square above.) In fact, there are many more than two genes that affect height in humans, and in most plants. It is common for a large number of genes to be involved, each of them having a small effect and all of these effects adding together. The control of height is therefore a polygenetic effect.

| parental phenotypes | $8x$ cm tall | × | $4x$ cm tall |

| parental genotypes | **AABB** | | **aabb** |

| parental gametes | (AB) | | (ab) |

| F_1 offspring genotypes | | **AaBb** |
| and phenotypes | | $6x$ cm tall |

parental phenotypes	$6x$ cm tall	×	$6x$ cm tall
parental genotypes	**AaBb**		**AaBb**
parental gametes	(AB) (Ab) (aB) (ab)		(AB) (Ab) (aB) (ab)

offspring genotypes and phenotypes

		gametes of one parent			
		(AB)	(Ab)	(aB)	(ab)
gametes of the other parent	(AB)	**AABB** $8x$ cm	**AABb** $7x$ cm	**AaBB** $7x$ cm	**AaBb** $6x$ cm
	(Ab)	**AABb** $7x$ cm	**AAbb** $6x$ cm	**AaBb** $6x$ cm	**Aabb** $5x$ cm
	(aB)	**AaBB** $7x$ cm	**AaBb** $6x$ cm	**aaBB** $6x$ cm	**aaBb** $5x$ cm
	(ab)	**AaBb** $6x$ cm	**Aabb** $6x$ cm	**aaBb** $5x$ cm	**aabb** $4x$ cm

Moreover, each of these many genes may have many more than two alleles, adding to the potential for different heights. Now add in the effects of the environment, and it is easy to see why height shows continuous variation. Any value of height can be seen, lying between the two possible extremes.

In a classic experiment, the American geneticists Ralph Emerson and Edward East crossed two varieties of maize which had distinctively different cob lengths. Both of the parental varieties (Black Mexican and Tom Thumb) were homozygous for most of their genes. The cob lengths of the plants used as parents and the first and second

generations of offspring resulting from the cross were measured to the nearest centimetre. The number of cobs in each length category was counted. The results are shown in Table 17.1.

Question

2 a In the classic experiment by Emerson and East, the Black Mexican parents were homozygous at all gene loci affecting cob length. What caused the variation in their cob length?

Cob length / cm	5	6	7	8	9	10	11	12	13	14	15	16	17	18	19	20	21
Number of Black Mexican parent cobs									3	11	12	14	26	15	10	7	2
Number of Tom Thumb parent cobs	4	21	24	8													
Number of F_1 cobs				1	12	12	14	17	9	4							
Number of F_2 cobs			1	10	19	26	47	73	68	68	39	25	15	9	1		

Table 17.1: Variation in cob length of two varieties of maize and of the F_1 and F_2 generations.

b Was the variation in cob length of the F$_1$ generation caused by genes, environment or both? Explain your answer.

c Was the variation in cob length of the F$_2$ generation caused by genes, environment or both? Explain your answer.

Where you see variation in the same feature in different populations, you can use the *t*-test to compare the means of the two populations – for example, the mean length of the cobs of the Tom Thumb and Black Mexican parents. The results of the test tell you whether the difference between the means is significant or could just be due to chance. The *t*-test is explained in Chapter P2 (Section P2.8, Analysis, conclusions and evaluation).

17.2 Natural selection

All organisms have the reproductive potential to increase their populations. Rabbits, for example, produce several young at a time, and each female may reproduce several times each year. If all the young rabbits survived to adulthood and reproduced, then the rabbit population would increase rapidly. Figure 17.5 shows what might happen.

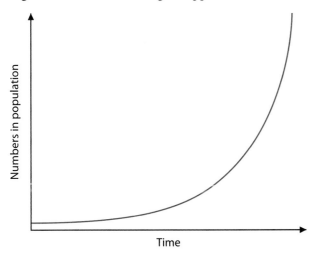

Figure 17.5: The numbers in a population may increase exponentially, if they are not checked by environmental factors.

This sort of population growth actually did happen in Australia in the 19th century. In 1859, 12 pairs of rabbits from Britain were released on a ranch in Victoria, as a source of food. The rabbits bred rapidly, as there was an abundance of food and there were very few predators. The number of rabbits soared. Their numbers became

so great that they seriously affected the availability of grazing for sheep (Figure 17.6).

Such population explosions are rare in normal circumstances. Although rabbit populations have the potential to increase at such a tremendous rate, they do not usually do so.

As a population of rabbits increases, various **environmental factors** come into play to keep down the rabbits' numbers. These factors may be **biotic factors** – caused by other living organisms such as through predation, **competition** for food, or infection by pathogens – or they may be **abiotic factors** – caused by non-living components of the environment such as water supply or nutrient levels in the soil.

For example, an increasing number of rabbits will eat an increasing amount of vegetation, until food is in short supply. The larger population of rabbits may allow the populations of predators such as foxes, stoats and weasels to increase. Overcrowding may occur, increasing the ease with which diseases such as myxomatosis may spread. This disease is caused by a virus that is transmitted by fleas, and it is fatal. The closer together the rabbits live, the more easily fleas, and therefore viruses, will pass from one rabbit to another.

These environmental factors act to reduce the rate of growth of the rabbit population. Of all the rabbits born, many will die from lack of food, or be killed by predators, or die from myxomatosis. Only a small proportion of young will grow to adulthood and reproduce, so population growth slows.

This is true for most populations of organisms in the wild. The number of young produced is far greater than the number which will survive to adulthood. Many young die before reaching reproductive age.

KEY WORDS

environmental factor: a feature of the environment of an organism that affects its survival

biotic factor: an environmental factor that is caused by living organisms (e.g. predation, competition)

competition: the need for a resource by two organisms, when that resource is in short supply

abiotic factor: an environmental factor that is caused by non-living components (e.g. soil pH, light intensity)

Figure 17.6: Attempts to control the rabbit population explosion in Australia in the mid- to late-19th century included 'rabbit drives', in which huge numbers were rounded up and killed. Eventually, myxomatosis brought numbers down.

Selection pressures and survival

What determines which will be the few rabbits to survive and which will die? It may be just luck. However, some rabbits will be born with a better chance of survival than others. Variation within a population of rabbits means that some will have features which give them an advantage in the 'struggle for existence'.

One feature that can vary is coat colour. Most rabbits have alleles which give the normal agouti (brown) colour. A few, however, may be homozygous for the recessive allele which gives white coat. Such white rabbits will stand out distinctly from the others, and are more likely to be picked out by a predator such as a fox. They are less likely to survive than agouti rabbits.

The chances of a white rabbit reproducing and passing on its alleles for white coat to its offspring are therefore very small. The term **fitness** is often used to refer to the extent to which organisms are adapted to their environment. Fitness is the capacity of an organism to survive and transmit its alleles to its offspring.

In this example, predation by foxes is an example of a **selection pressure**. Selection pressures increase the chances of some alleles being passed on to the next generation and decrease the chances of others. In this case, rabbits with at least one allele for agouti coat have a selective advantage over rabbits with the alleles for white. The agouti rabbits have a better chance of reproducing and passing on their alleles to their offspring. The alleles for agouti will remain the commoner alleles in the population, while the alleles for white will remain

very rare. As this selection continues to act over many generations, the frequency of agouti alleles is likely to increase, while the frequency of the alleles for white coat will decrease and they may even disappear completely.

The effect of such selection pressures on the frequency of alleles in a population is called **natural selection**. Natural selection increases the frequency of alleles conferring an advantage, and reduces the frequency of alleles conferring a disadvantage.

> ### KEY WORDS
>
> **fitness:** the ability of an organism to survive and reproduce
>
> **selection pressure:** an environmental factor that affects the chance of survival of an organism; organisms with one phenotype are more likely to survive and reproduce than those with a different phenotype
>
> **natural selection:** the process by which individuals with a particular set of alleles are more likely to survive and reproduce than those with other alleles; over time and many generations, the advantageous alleles become more frequent in the population

Question

3   Skomer is a small island off the coast of Wales. Rabbits have been living on the island for many years. There are no predators on the island.

a Rabbits on Skomer are not all agouti. There are quite large numbers of rabbits of different colours, such as black and white. Suggest why this is so.

b Suggest what might be important selection pressures acting on rabbits on Skomer.

Stabilising, disruptive and directional selection

Usually, natural selection keeps things the way they are. This is **stabilising selection** (Figure 17.7a and b). Agouti rabbits are the best-adapted rabbits to survive predation, so the agouti allele remains the most common coat colour allele in rabbit populations. Unless something changes,

natural selection will ensure that this continues to be the case.

However, if a new environmental factor or a new allele appears, then natural selection may cause allele frequencies to change over successive generations. This is called **directional selection** (Figure 17.7c).

KEY WORDS

stabilising selection: natural selection that tends to keep allele frequencies relatively constant over many generations

directional selection: natural selection that causes a gradual change in allele frequency over many generations

---

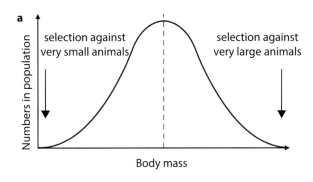

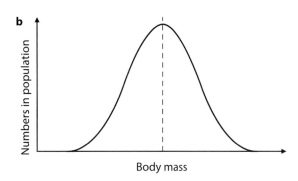

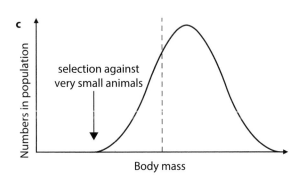

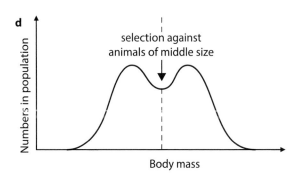

Figure 17.7: If a characteristic in a population, such as body mass, shows wide variation, selection pressures often act against the two extremes (graph **a**). Very small or very large individuals are less likely to survive and reproduce than those whose size lies nearer the centre of the range. This results in a population with a narrower range of body size (graph **b**). This type of selection, which tends to keep the variation in a characteristic centred around the same mean value, is called *stabilising selection*. Graph **c** shows what would happen if selection acted against smaller individuals but not larger ones. In this case, the range of variation shifts towards larger size. This type of selection, which results in a change in a characteristic in a particular direction, is called *directional selection*. Graph **d** shows the result of selection that favours both large and small individuals but acts against those whose size is in the middle of the range. This is *disruptive selection*.

A third type of selection, called **disruptive selection**, can occur when conditions favour both extremes of a population. This type of selection maintains different phenotypes (**polymorphism**) in a population (Figure 17.7d).

Directional selection leading to change in allele frequency

Directional selection can happen when there is a change in selection pressures, or when a new allele arises by mutation.

Imagine that the climate where the hypothetical population of rabbits lives becomes much colder, so that snow covers the ground for almost all of the year. Assuming that rabbits can survive in these conditions, white rabbits now have a selective advantage during seasons when snow lies on the ground, as they are better camouflaged (like the hare in Figure 17.8). Rabbits with white fur are more likely to survive and reproduce, passing on their alleles for white fur to their offspring.

Figure 17.8: The white winter coat of a mountain hare provides excellent camouflage from predators when viewed against snow.

The frequency of the allele for white coat increases at the expense of the allele for agouti. Over many generations, almost all rabbits will come to have white coats rather than agouti. There is a directional change in the population, with a decrease in frequency of the agouti allele, and an increase in frequency of the white allele, as a result of a change in selection pressure.

Mutation may also happen in an individual in the rabbit population. Mutations are random events, and the type of mutation that occurs is not affected in any way by the environment. As most organisms are already well adapted to their environment, most mutations are likely to produce features that are harmful. That is, they produce organisms that are less well adapted to their environment than 'normal' organisms. Other mutations may be neutral, conferring neither an advantage nor a disadvantage on the organisms within which they occur. Very occasionally, mutations may produce useful features.

Imagine that a mutation occurs in the coat colour gene of a rabbit, producing a new allele which gives a better-camouflaged coat colour than agouti. Rabbits possessing this new allele will have a selective advantage. They will be more likely to survive and reproduce than agouti rabbits, so the new allele will become more common in the population. Over many generations, almost all rabbits will come to have the new allele.

Antibiotic resistance in bacteria

The development of antibiotic resistance in a population of pathogenic bacteria is an example of directional selection. As you saw in Chapter 10 (Section 10.2, Antibiotics), antibiotics are chemicals produced by living organisms that inhibit or kill bacteria but do not normally harm human tissue.

When someone takes the antibiotic penicillin to treat a bacterial infection, bacteria that are sensitive to penicillin die. In most cases, this is the entire population of the disease-causing bacteria. However, by chance, there may be among them one or more individual bacteria with an allele giving resistance to penicillin. This allele arises by random mutation. One example of such an allele occurs in some populations of the bacterium *Staphylococcus*, where some individual bacteria have an allele that codes for the production of an enzyme, penicillinase, which inactivates penicillin.

As bacteria have only a single loop of DNA, they have only one copy of each gene, so the mutant allele will have an immediate effect on the phenotype of any bacterium possessing it. These individuals have a tremendous selective advantage in an environment where penicillin is present. The bacteria without this allele will be killed, while those bacteria with resistance to penicillin can survive and reproduce. Bacteria reproduce very rapidly in ideal conditions and, even if there was initially only one resistant bacterium, it might produce 10 000 million descendants within 24 hours. A large population of a penicillin-resistant strain of *Staphylococcus* would result.

Such antibiotic-resistant strains of bacteria are continually appearing (Figure 17. 9). By using antibiotics, humans change the selection pressures on bacteria. A constant race is on to find new antibiotics against new resistant strains of bacteria.

Question

4 These questions are about the bar chart in Figure 17.9.

 a Describe the trends in deaths from all types of *S. aureus* between 1993 and 2012.

 b Describe the differences between the trends in deaths from meticillin-resistant *S. aureus* (MRSA) and non-resistant *S. aureus*.

 c Many cases of MRSA develop in hospitals. Suggest why this is so.

 d In the mid-2000s, healthcare professionals were asked not to prescribe antibiotics unless strictly necessary. Suggest how this could explain the pattern shown by the graph between 2007 and 2012.

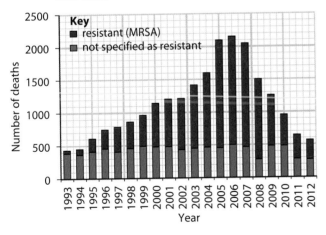

Figure 17.9: Meticillin is an antibiotic that is used to cure infections caused by *Staphylococcus aureus*. However, many populations of this bacterium have become resistant to this antibiotic and are known as meticillin-resistant *Staphyloccus aureus*, MRSA. The graph shows changes in cases and deaths from MRSA in a European country between 1993 and 2012.

Alleles for antibiotic resistance often occur on plasmids (Chapter 1, Section 1.7, Bacteria). Plasmids are quite frequently transferred from one bacterium to another, even between different species. So it is possible for resistance to a particular antibiotic to arise in one species of bacterium and be passed on to another. The more humans use antibiotics, the greater the selection pressure we exert on bacteria to evolve resistance to them.

Industrial melanism

Another well-documented example of directional selection producing changes in allele frequencies is the peppered moth, *Biston betularia* (Figure 17.10), in the UK and Ireland. This is a night-flying moth which spends the day resting underneath the branches of trees. It relies on camouflage to protect it from insect-eating birds that hunt by sight.

Until 1849, all specimens of this moth in collections had pale wings with dark markings, giving a speckled appearance. In 1849, however, a black (melanic) individual was caught near Manchester (Figure 17.11). During the rest of the 19th century, the numbers of black *Biston betularia* increased dramatically in some areas, whereas in other parts of the country the speckled form remained the more common.

The difference between the black and speckled forms of the moth is caused by a single gene. The normal speckled colouring is produced by a recessive allele of this gene, **c**, while the black colour is produced by a dominant allele, **C**. Up until the late 1960s, the frequency of the allele **C** increased in areas near industrial cities. In non-industrial areas, the allele **c** remained the more common allele.

The selection pressure causing the change of allele frequency in industrial areas was predation by birds. In areas with unpolluted air, tree branches are often covered with grey, brown and green lichen. On such tree branches, speckled moths are superbly camouflaged.

However, lichens are very sensitive to pollutants such as sulfur dioxide, and do not grow on trees close to or downwind of industries releasing pollutants into the air. Trees in these areas therefore have much darker bark, against which the dark moths are better camouflaged. Experiments have shown that pale moths have a much higher chance of survival in unpolluted areas than dark moths, while in polluted areas the dark moths have the selective advantage. As air pollution from industry

Figure 17.10: The dark and light forms of the peppered moth, resting on dark and pale tree bark.

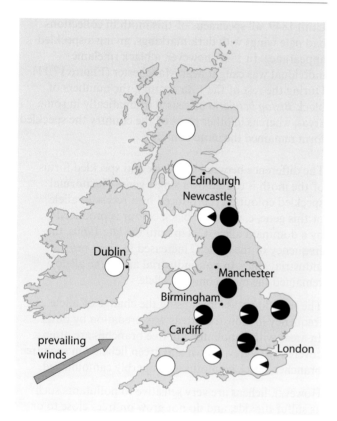

Figure 17.11: The distribution of the pale and dark forms of the peppered moth, *Biston betularia*, in the UK and Ireland during the early 1960s. The ratio of dark to pale areas in each circle shows the ratio of dark to pale moths in that part of the country.

is reduced, the selective advantage swings back in favour of the speckled variety. So you would expect the proportion of speckled moths to increase if there was a reduction in the output of certain pollutants. This is, in fact, what has happened since the 1970s.

It is important to realise that mutations to the **C** allele have probably always been happening in *B. betularia* populations. The mutation was not caused by pollution. Until the 19th century there was such a strong selection pressure against the **C** allele that it remained exceedingly rare. Mutations of the **c** allele to the **C** allele may have occurred quite frequently, but moths with this allele would almost certainly have been noticed and eaten by birds before they could reproduce. Changes in environmental factors only affect the likelihood of an allele surviving in a population; they do not affect the likelihood of such an allele arising by mutation.

17.3 Genetic drift and the founder effect

Selection pressures are not the only factor that determines which individuals survive and reproduce. Chance can come into the equation, too. Chance is most likely to have a significant effect if the population is small. Imagine a very small population of plants in which two plants have white flowers and three plants have yellow flowers. It could happen that, just by chance, the seeds from the white flowers fall on unsuitable ground, while a few seeds from the yellow flowers fall in a better area where they can germinate and grow into adult plants. Over several generations, the alleles for white flowers could be completely lost, just by chance. This is called **genetic drift**. Genetic drift is a change in allele frequency that occurs by chance, not as a result of natural selection. It is most likely to happen when a small number of individuals are separated from the rest of a large population.

KEY WORD
genetic drift: the gradual change in allele frequencies in a small population, where some alleles are lost or favoured just by chance and not by natural selection

Indeed, in the small population, some alleles may not be present at all. The **gene pool** – the complete set of genetic information in a population – may be smaller than that of the original population. Consequently, changes in the allele frequencies of this population may take a different direction from that of the larger parent population, just because of this chance effect, and not because of the selection pressures acting on them.

This process, occurring in a recently isolated small population and resulting from only part of the gene pool being present in this small population, is called the **founder effect**.

KEY WORDS

gene pool: the complete range of DNA base sequences in all the organisms in a species or population

founder effect: the reduction in a gene pool compared with the main populations of a species, resulting from only two or three individuals (with only a selection of the alleles in the gene pool) starting off a new population

---

For example, there is a very large number of small islands in the Caribbean, and anole lizards live on most of them. Lizards can be carried from one island to another on floating vegetation. It is just chance which individual lizards land on an island and which combination of alleles they will carry. There will be many other alleles in the gene pool of the population on the original island but only a small selection of them in the small number of lizards that arrive on the new island. If the original population of lizards had a range of colouration from green to brown, but the only two that floated to the new island were both green, then the population that develops on the new island might all be green, with no brown individuals. This difference between the two populations is not the result of natural selection but of a chance event that meant the alleles for brown colour never arrived in the population.

It is difficult to study the founder effect, because people are not often in the right place at the right time to see the individuals arriving in their new habitat. But in 2004 a hurricane resulted in several islands off the Bahamas becoming completely submerged in water for a time. When the water subsided, scientists found that all of the lizards on seven small islands had been killed. Not one living lizard was found.

The scientists decided that this was a good opportunity to study the founder effect. They collected lizards belonging to the species *Anolis sagrei* from a larger island nearby, where the lizards had survived. This island had quite large shrubs and trees. These individuals showed variation in their leg length, but overall had quite long legs – it is known that lizards living on large shrubs and trees have an advantage if they have long legs, because it is easier to grip the large branches. In 2005 the researchers selected one male and one female lizard from this island randomly, measured their leg lengths, and placed them on one of the seven previously flooded islands. This was repeated for the other six islands.

Figure 17.12: *Anolis sagrei* lives in bushes and trees. Lizards with longer legs have a selective advantage when the trees have large branches because they are better able to grip. In lower vegetation, lizards with shorter legs are more likely to survive and reproduce.

The two lizards placed on each island reproduced, so that the population on each island grew. The researchers collected lizards from each of the islands over the next four years. They measured their leg lengths, and they also measured the sizes of plants on the islands. They found that the mean leg lengths of the lizards on each of the small islands gradually got less. This is what you would expect. The original lizards came from an island with large vegetation, and were now living on an island where the vegetation was still small, as it had not had time to grow back after the hurricane had damaged it.

However, the researchers also found that the mean leg length of the lizards was correlated with the leg lengths of the two randomly selected lizards that had been placed on each island. For example, if the pair of lizards placed on island A had relatively long legs, and those placed on island B had relatively short legs, then after four years the mean leg length on island A was more than on island B. The leg length of the lizards had been affected not only by the selection pressure exerted by the small size of the vegetation on the islands, but also by the set of alleles brought to the island by the original parents – the founder effect.

The bottleneck effect

Something similar to the founder effect can happen if a population that was originally large suffers a significant fall in numbers.

The cheetah, *Acinonyx jubatus*, is a species that is in danger of extinction. Today, all cheetahs are genetically very similar to each other. They show little phenotypic or genotypic variation. Many cheetahs are homozygous at a very high proportion of their gene loci – in other words, there are not many different alleles present in a population. They have less than 5% of the genetic variation that is normal within animal species. This lack of genetic variation is of concern to conservationists, as it puts cheetahs at a relatively high risk of extinction. Without genetic variation, the species is unlikely to be able to adapt to changes in its environment, such as climate change.

What could be the reason for this lack of genetic variation in cheetahs? Scientists believe it results from a period about 10 000 years ago, when all but a few cheetahs were killed as a result of climate changes at the end of the last Ice Age. Cheetahs found themselves living in small populations, where the only mates available were close relatives. Over time, much of the genetic variation that was probably present in the earlier populations was lost. An event like this is called an **evolutionary bottleneck**. This is a situation where the population falls so low that the gene pool is greatly reduced.

Figure 17.13: The cheetah is supremely adapted as a fast-running predator, but its gene pool is so small that it is at high risk of extinction.

KEY WORD

evolutionary bottleneck: a period when the numbers of a species fall to a very low level, resulting in the loss of a large number of alleles and therefore a reduction in the gene pool of the species

17.4 The Hardy–Weinberg principle

So far, you have considered allele frequencies qualitatively. The Hardy–Weinberg equations allow you to calculate allele frequencies, and to predict how these might change in future generations.

When a particular phenotypic trait is controlled by two alleles of a single gene, **A/a**, the population will be made up of three genotypes: **AA**, **Aa** and **aa**. Calculations based on the Hardy–Weinberg principle allow the proportions of each of these genotypes in a large, randomly mating population to be calculated.

The frequency of a genotype is its proportion of the total population. The total is the whole population (that is 1) and the frequencies are given as decimals (e.g. 0.25) of the total.

Use the letter p to represent the frequency of the dominant allele, **A**, in the population and the letter q to represent the frequency of the recessive allele, **a**. Then, since there are only two alleles of this gene:

$$p + q = 1 \qquad \textbf{Equation 1}$$

You can also say that:

- the chance of an offspring inheriting a dominant allele from both parents $= p \times p = p^2$

- the chance of an offspring inheriting a recessive allele from both parents $= q \times q = q^2$

- the chance of an offspring inheriting a dominant allele from the father and a recessive allele from the mother $= p \times q = pq$

- the chance of an offspring inheriting a dominant allele from the mother and a recessive allele from the father $= p \times q = pq$

As these are the only possible combinations of alleles that can be inherited, you can say that:

$$p^2 + 2pq + q^2 = 1 \qquad \textbf{Equation 2}$$

Note that you do not need to remember these two equations. They are given to you if you are asked a question on this topic in your examination.

Worked example 1 shows you how to use these two equations to calculate the frequency of the dominant and recessive allele, and of the different genotypes, in a population.

These Hardy–Weinberg calculations do not apply when the population is small or when there is:

- significant selective pressure against one of the genotypes

- migration of individuals carrying one of the two alleles into, or out of, the population

- non-random mating.

WORKED EXAMPLE

1 Imagine a population in which 1% of the individuals show the recessive phenotype. Another way of stating this is to say that the frequency of these individuals is 0.01.

These individuals must have the genotype **aa**. You therefore know that the frequency of **aa** individuals, which is represented by q^2, is 0.01.

Therefore, $q = \sqrt{0.01} = 0.1$

Using Equation 1:

$p + q = 1$

so, $p = 1 - q$

$= 1 - 0.1$

$= 0.9$

In other words, you know that the frequency of the dominant allele is 0.9 and the frequency of the recessive allele is 0.1.

You can calculate the frequency of the homozygous dominant and heterozygous genotypes:

frequency of homozygous dominant genotype $= p^2 = 0.9^2 = 0.81$

frequency of heterozygous genotype $= 2pq = 2 \times 0.9 \times 0.1 = 0.18$

You can check your calculations by adding up the frequencies of the three genotypes, which should come to 1.

What is the use of these calculations? When the ratios of the different genotypes in a population have been determined, their predicted ratios in the next generation can be compared with the observed values. Any differences can be tested for significance using the χ^2 test (Chapter 16, Section 16.6, The chi-squared (χ^2) test). If the differences are significant and migration and non-random mating can be discounted, this suggests that directional selection is occurring in the population.

Question

5 **a** A phenotypic trait is controlled by two alleles of a single gene **D/d**. Explain why only the homozygous recessives, **dd**, can be recognised.

 b Calculate the proportions of homozygous dominant and of heterozygous individuals in a population in which the proportion of homozygous recessives is 16%.

17.5 Artificial selection

Artificial selection is a process in which humans determine which individuals survive and reproduce. Artificial selection has been taking place for thousands of years and, for most of that time, people knew nothing at all about genetics. Today, scientists have a better understanding of the mechanisms that determine inheritance of desirable phenotypes.

KEY WORD

artificial selection: the selection by humans of organisms with desired traits to survive and reproduce; also known as selective breeding

Artificial selection is done for many reasons. For example, horse breeders may want to breed horses that can run fast or have the strength to pull heavy loads. Cattle may be bred to produce more milk or more meat. Maize may be bred to produce a variety with heavier yields, or to survive in conditions where water is scarce, or to be resistant to attack from parasitic fungi. In every case, the principles are the same.

1 The population that is to be used for artificial selection must show some variation. For example, some individuals in a variety of wheat may have resistance to a disease, while others are killed by it.

2 The breeder selects an individual that has the feature that she wants future generations to have. In this case, she would select a plant that has better resistance to the disease than other individuals.

3 She then selects another parent plant. This could be from the same variety and also have good resistance to disease. However, in some cases, the breeder might select a parent from a different variety that shows another beneficial characteristic, such as high yield, if she wants to produce a new variety with a good combination of disease resistance and high yield.

4 The two chosen parents are then bred together.

5 The resulting offspring are grown to adulthood and tested. For example, if the breeder is trying to produce a variety of wheat with good resistance to a disease, she will ensure that all of the offspring are exposed to the disease. She will then select the ones that show the greatest resistance. Alternatively, if she is looking for both resistance and high yield, she will select the ones that show the best combination of these two characteristics.

6 This process continues for many generations, each time selecting the 'best' individuals for breeding, until all individuals show the desired characteristic or characteristics.

Generally, at the end of this process, the breeder will have produced a population of individuals that all show the desired characteristics and that can be interbred among themselves to produce offspring that also show these characteristics. This means that they are all homozygous at all the gene loci that control these features. The breeder does not have to know anything about the genetics of this – she simply keeps selecting individuals according to their phenotype, without knowing their genotype. This makes it possible to work with characteristics that are controlled by a large number of genes, where no one fully understands exactly which genes are affecting the phenotype.

The breeding process outlined in steps 1 to 6 above can be varied according to the breeder's requirements. For example, she could breed two individuals from one generation with each other, or bring in an individual from a different variety – perhaps from the original variety with high yield or from a third variety that has another desirable feature.

Introduction of disease resistance to varieties of wheat and rice

Most modern varieties of wheat belong to the species *Triticum aestivum*. Selective breeding has produced many different varieties of wheat. Much of it is grown to produce grains rich in gluten, which makes them good for making bread flour. For making other food products such as pastry, varieties that contain less gluten are best.

Breeding for resistance to various fungal diseases, such as head blight, caused by *Fusarium*, is important, because of the loss of yield resulting from such infections.

Successful introduction of an allele giving resistance takes many generations, especially when it comes from a wheat grown in a different part of the world. To help with such selective breeding, the Wheat Genetic Improvement Network was set up in the UK in 2003 to bring together research workers and commercial plant breeders. Its aim is to support the development of new varieties by screening seed collections for plants with traits such as disease resistance, or climate resilience (Figure 17.14). Any plant with a suitable trait is grown in large numbers and passed to the commercial breeders.

Figure 17.15: Sheath rot, caused by *Sarocladium oryzae*, can greatly reduce the yields of rice plants. Breeders are attempting to produce rice varieties that have natural resistance to this disease.

Figure 17.14: Selective breeding of wheat and rice takes place in closely controlled conditions, to prevent accidental pollination between individuals that have not been selected to breed together.

Rice, *Oryza sativa*, is also the subject of much selective breeding. The International Rice Research Institute, based in the Philippines, holds the rice gene bank and together with the Global Rice Science Partnership coordinates research aimed at improving the ability of rice farmers to feed growing populations. (You can read about seed banks in Chapter 18, Section 18.4, Protecting endangered species.)

The yield of rice can be reduced by bacterial diseases such as bacterial blight, and by a range of fungal diseases including various 'spots' and 'smuts'. The most significant fungal disease is rice blast, caused by the fungus *Magnaporthe*. Researchers are using selective breeding to try to produce varieties of rice that show some resistance to all these diseases.

Inbreeding and hybridisation in maize

Maize, *Zea mays*, is also known as corn in some parts of the world. It is a tall grass with broad, strap-shaped leaves (Figure 17.16). Maize grows best in climates with long, hot summers, which provide plenty of time for its cobs (seed heads) to ripen. It was originally grown in Central and South America, but now it forms the staple crop in some regions of Africa and is grown as food for people or animals in Europe, America, Australia, New Zealand, China and Indonesia.

If maize plants are inbred (crossed with other plants with genotypes like their own), the plants in each generation become progressively smaller and weaker (Figure 17.17). This **inbreeding depression** occurs because repeated **inbreeding** produces homozygosity.

KEY WORDS

inbreeding depression: a loss of the ability to survive and grow well, due to breeding between close relatives; this increases the chance of harmful recessive alleles coming together in an individual and being expressed

inbreeding: breeding between organisms with similar genotypes, or that are closely related

In maize, homozygous plants are less vigorous than heterozygous ones. **Outbreeding** – crossing with other, less closely related plants – produces heterozygous plants that are healthier, grow taller and produce higher yields. They show **hybrid vigour**.

> ### KEY WORDS
>
> **outbreeding:** breeding between individuals that are not closely related
>
> **hybrid vigour:** an increased ability to survive and grow well, as a result of outbreeding and therefore increased heterozygosity

However, if outbreeding is done at random, the farmer would end up with a field full of maize in which there was a lot of variation between the individual plants. This would make things very difficult. To be able to harvest and sell the crop easily, a farmer needs the plants to be uniform. They should all be about the same height and all ripen at about the same time.

So the challenge when growing maize is to achieve both heterozygosity and uniformity. Farmers buy maize seed from companies that specialise in using inbreeding to produce homozygous maize plants and then crossing them. This produces F_1 plants that all have the same genotype. There are many different homozygous maize varieties, and different crosses between them can produce a large number of different hybrids, suited for different purposes. Every year, thousands of new maize hybrids are trialled, searching for varieties with characteristics such as high yields, resistance to more

Figure 17.16: Maize plants in flower.

pests and diseases, and good growth in nutrient-poor soils or where water is in short supply.

Figure 17.17: The effects of inbreeding depression in maize over eight generations.

Question

6 Explain why farmers need to buy maize seed from commercial seed producers each year, rather than saving their own seed to plant.

Improving milk yield of dairy cattle

In some countries, particularly in Europe, America and some parts of Africa, cattle are kept to produce milk. For people who can digest lactose, milk is a valuable food, rich in protein and calcium.

Milk production, like most characteristics of the crop plants that humans grow and the farmed animals that we keep, is influenced by both environment and genotype. We still do not know which genes, let alone which alleles of genes, contribute to the ability of cows to produce large quantities of high-quality milk. But, for selective breeding to be successful, we do not need to know this. We simply choose the cows with the highest milk yield – and the bulls with female relatives with high milk yield – and breed them together, continuing to do this over many generations.

Unlike natural selection, artificial selection (selective breeding) often concentrates on just one or two characteristics. So, whereas natural selection tends to result in a species that is well-adapted to its environment in many different ways, artificial selection risks producing varieties that show one characteristic to an extreme, while other characteristics are retained (or even accidentally enhanced) that would be positively disadvantageous in a natural situation.

An example of this is shown by a breeding experiment that was carried out with Holstein cattle in the USA (Figure 17.18). A large number of cows were used, and they were divided into two groups. In the first group, only the cows that produced the highest milk yields were allowed to breed, and they were fertilised with sperm from bulls whose female relatives also produced high milk yields. This was called the 'selection line'. The second group was a control, in which all the cows were allowed to breed, and they were fertilised by bulls chosen more randomly. The selection was carried out in each generation for 25 years. All the cattle were kept in identical conditions and fed identical food. The results are shown in Table 17.2 and Figure 17.19.

Figure 17.18: A Holstein cow. Her large udder shows that she can produce large quantities of milk.

The graph in Figure 17.19 shows the large increase in milk yield that was produced in the selection line. The results for the control line show that this increase must be due to genetic differences between the two groups, because environmental conditions were the same for both. It is interesting to see that the milk yield in the control line actually went down. Why could this be? Perhaps there is a selective disadvantage to having high milk yields, so that the cows with lower milk yields were more likely to have more offspring, all other factors being equal. Or perhaps this is just the result of random variation or genetic drift.

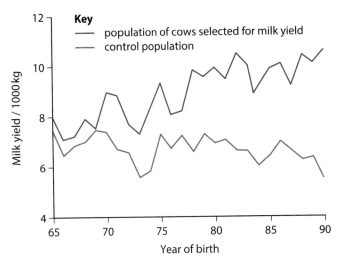

Figure 17.19: The results of selection for milk yield in Holstein cattle, over a 25-year period.

The data in Table 17.2 support the hypothesis that very high milk yields would be disadvantageous in a natural situation. Health costs for every kind of ailment were greater in the selection line than in the control line. Again, we do not know exactly why this is, but we can make informed suggestions. Mastitis is inflammation of the udder, the organ in which milk is produced and

Health costs per year from treatment for:	Selection line / USD	Control line / USD
mastitis	43	16
ketosis and milk fever	22	12
reproductive issues	18	13
lameness	10	6
respiratory problems	4	1

Table 17.2: Health costs in the selection line and control line in Holstein cattle.

stored. Very large quantities of milk in the udder could make it more likely to become inflamed. Heavier udders could also put more strain on legs, so increasing the incidence of lameness. Perhaps, too, there are alleles that confer a greater likelihood of suffering these conditions, and these were accidentally selected for along with the selection for high milk yields.

17.6 Evolution

Evolution is the change of characteristics of species over time, due to changes in allele frequency. It can lead to the formation of new species from pre-existing ones, as a result of changes to the gene pools of populations over many generations.

You have seen how natural selection, the founder effect and genetic drift can bring about changes in allele frequencies in a population within a species. This section takes these arguments further, to see how these changes could become so great that a new species is produced.

Species and speciation

It is not easy to define the term *species*. One definition of a species that is quite widely accepted by biologists is a group of organisms, with similar morphological, physiological, biochemical and behavioural features, which can interbreed to produce fertile offspring, and are reproductively isolated from other species.

Morphological features are structural features, while **physiological** features are the way that the body works. Biochemical features include the sequences of bases in DNA molecules and the sequences of amino acids in proteins.

> ### KEY WORDS
>
> **evolution:** a process leading to the formation of new species from pre-existing species over time
>
> **morphological:** relating to structural features
>
> **physiological:** relating to metabolic and other processes in a living organism

Thus, all donkeys look and behave like donkeys, and they can breed with other donkeys to produce more donkeys, which themselves can interbreed. All donkeys belong to the same species. Donkeys can interbreed with organisms of another similar species, horses, to produce offspring called mules. However, mules are infertile; they cannot breed and are effectively a 'dead-end'. So, using the definition above, donkeys and horses do not belong to the same species.

When a decision needs to be made as to whether two organisms belong to the same species or to two different species, the organisms should ideally be tested to find out if they can interbreed successfully, producing fertile offspring. However, as you can imagine, this is not always possible. Perhaps the organisms are dead; they may even be museum specimens or fossils. Perhaps they are both of the same sex. Perhaps the biologist making the decision does not have the time or the facilities to attempt to interbreed them. Perhaps the organisms will not breed in captivity. Perhaps they are not organisms which reproduce sexually, but only asexually. Perhaps they are immature and not yet able to breed.

As a result of all of these problems, it is quite rare to test the ability of two organisms to interbreed. Biologists frequently rely only on morphological, biochemical, physiological and behavioural differences to decide whether two organisms belong to the same species or to two different species. In practice, it may be only morphological features which are considered, because physiological and biochemical ones, and to some extent behavioural ones, are more time-consuming to investigate. Sometimes, however, detailed studies of DNA sequences may be used to assess how similar two organisms are to each other.

It can be extremely difficult to decide when these features are sufficiently similar or different to define two organisms as belonging to the same or different species.

This leads to great uncertainty and disagreement about whether to classify many slightly different varieties of organisms together into one species, or whether to split them up into many different species. You can find more discussion about the various ways of defining the term *species* in Chapter 18 (Section 18.1, Classification).

Genetic isolation

Despite the problems described above, many biologists would agree that the feature which really decides whether two organisms belong to different species is their inability to interbreed successfully. In explaining how natural selection can produce new species, therefore, it is necessary to consider how a group of interbreeding organisms (that is, all of the same species) can produce another group of organisms which cannot interbreed successfully with the first group. The two groups must undergo **reproductive isolation** from one another. This also means that they are **genetically isolated** – there is no interchange of genes between the two groups because they can no longer interbreed.

Reproductive and genetic isolation can take very different forms. Reasons for an inability to interbreed successfully include:

- individuals not recognising one another as potential mates or not responding to mating behaviour

- animals being physically unable to mate

- incompatibility of pollen and stigma in plants

- inability of a male gamete to fuse with a female gamete

- failure of cell division in the zygote

- non-viable offspring (offspring that soon die)

- viable but sterile offspring.

So how can this happen? How can a species somehow become split into two groups that are no longer able to interbreed with one another? In other words, how does **speciation** happen? The next sections describe how this might occur in two types of situation:

- where a geographical barrier separates the species into two groups

- where the reproductive isolation happens while the species is still living in the same place.

Allopatric speciation

Geographical isolation has played a major role in the evolution of many species. Many islands have their own unique groups of species. The Hawaiian and Galapagos islands, for example, are famous for their spectacular arrays of species of all kinds of animals and plants found nowhere else in the world (Figure 17.20).

Geographical isolation requires a barrier of some kind to arise between two populations of the same species, preventing them from mixing. This barrier might be a stretch of water. You can imagine that a group of organisms, perhaps a population of a species of bird, somehow arrived on one of the Hawaiian islands from mainland America. The birds might have been blown off course by a storm. Here, separated by hundreds of miles of ocean from the rest of their species on mainland America, the group interbred with each other.

> ### KEY WORDS
>
> **reproductive isolation:** the inability of two groups of organisms to breed with one another; two populations of the same species may be geographically separated, or two different species are unable to breed to produce fertile offspring
>
> **genetically isolated:** no longer able to breed together; there is no exchange of genes
>
> **speciation:** the production of new species
>
> **geographical isolation:** separation by a geographical barrier, such as a stretch of water or a mountain range

They could not, of course, breed with the mainland population, so all gene flow between the island and mainland populations stopped. The island population was genetically isolated from its parent population.

The selection pressures on the island were very different from those on the mainland, resulting in different alleles being selected for. Over time, the morphological, physiological and behavioural features of the island population became so different from the mainland population that the two populations could no longer interbreed even if they were brought together. A new species had evolved.

Figure 17.20: *Hibiscus clayi* is found only on Hawaii.

If the number of individuals that arrived on the island was small, then genetic drift and the founder effect, as well as natural selection, could also contribute to differences between the gene pools of this new population and their parent population.

This method of speciation, as a result of geographical separation, is called **allopatric speciation**.

Sympatric speciation

Although allopatric speciation is probably the most common way in which new species arise, there is increasing evidence that it is also possible for speciation to happen without geographical isolation. This is called **sympatric speciation**.

> ### KEY WORDS
>
> **allopatric speciation:** the development of new species following geographical isolation
>
> **sympatric speciation:** the development of new species without any geographical separation

For sympatric speciation to happen, something must take place that splits a population into two groups, with no gene flow between them, while they are living in the same place. How might this happen?

Two species of palm trees, *Howea forsteriana* and *H. belmoreana*, provide an example. These palms are endemic to Lord Howe Island. ('Endemic' means that they are found in no other place.) You may have seen

one or both of them, as they are both widely grown as house plants (Figure 17.21).

The two species of palm look different from one another – that is, there are morphological differences between them. *H. forsteriana* has many flower spikes and straight leaves, whereas *H. belmoreana* has only one flower spike and curved leaves. The palms also grow on different soils on the island. *H. forsteriana* tends to grow on calcareous (alkaline) soil, while *H. belmoreana* grows on volcanic soils, which are more acidic.

The flowering times of the two species are also different (Figure 17.22.) There is so little overlap between them that it is almost impossible for one to be pollinated by the other. The two species are reproductively isolated from one another.

Scientists have studied how this situation might have arisen. There is evidence that the island was first colonised by an ancestor of these two species of palm about 5 million years ago, from Australia. This species grew on neutral and acidic soils on the island. However, at some point in time, some seeds germinated on the more calcareous soils. The high pH of these soils affects flowering time, making it occur earlier. So these trees were unable to pollinate, or be pollinated by, the trees growing on volcanic soils. They became genetically isolated. Over time, the different selection pressures imposed on them in their slightly new environment resulted in differences in their morphology and physiology, so that they became better adapted to growing in the calcareous soil.

Figure 17.21: a *Howea forsteriana*, the kentia or thatch palm; **b** *H. belmoreana*, the Belmore sentry palm.

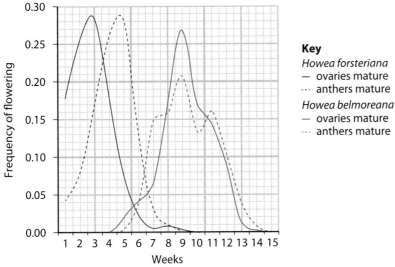

Key
Howea forsteriana
— ovaries mature
··· anthers mature
Howea belmoreana
— ovaries mature
··· anthers mature

Figure 17.22: Flowering times of *Howea forsteriana* and *H. belmoreana*.

This is an example of **ecological separation**. The two types of soil provide different ecological conditions, which results in a difference in flowering time. As a result, the plants growing on the two types of soil became genetically isolated and developed into two different species.

Sympatric speciation can also happen in animals. One example is two species of cichlid fish, *Amphilophus citrinellus* and *A. zaliosus* that live in Lake Apoyo in Nicaragua (Figure 17.23). It is thought that *A. citrinellus* colonised this lake at least 10 000 years ago. Within the lake, some individuals tended to feed on the bottom, while others spent most of their time in the open water. Scientists think that disruptive selection may have occurred, with selection pressures resulting in advantages both for fish with features adapting them for bottom feeding (such as long jaws) and fish with features adapting them for feeding in mid-water (such as

shorter jaws). Over time, the two groups of fish became so different that today they no longer interbreed. They have different courtship behaviours and will not mate with each other.

This example shows a combination of **behavioural separation** and ecological separation. The original

> **KEY WORDS**
>
> **ecological separation:** the separation of two populations because they live in different environments in the same area and so cannot breed together
>
> **behavioural separation:** the separation of two populations because they have different behaviours which prevent them breeding together

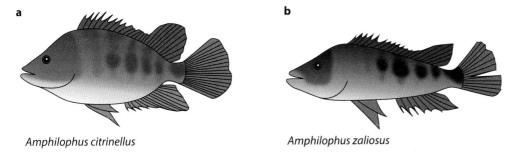

a
Amphilophus citrinellus

b
Amphilophus zaliosus

Figure 17.23: a *Amphilophus citrinellus* and **b** *A. zaliosus*. *A. zaliosus* is thought to have split off from *A. citrinellus* as a result of behavioural and ecological separation.

species split apart because some fish had different behaviour, tending to feed on the bottom of the lake rather than in the open water. This also meant that they were living in different ecological conditions. This prevented gene flow between the two groups, resulting in the evolution of the two species that are present in the lake today.

When thinking about how one species might split into two, it is important not to confuse the original factors that *caused* the separation with the factors that prevent the two species from breeding after they have become genetically separated. These fish, for example, are now prevented from interbreeding because they have different courtship displays, so will not mate with one another. But this is not what caused the new species to form in the first place. This difference in mating behaviour has arisen *after* the two groups became separated, as a result of the genetic isolation brought about by the differences in feeding behaviour of two groups of fish in the original *A. citrinellus* population that colonised the lake.

17.7 Identifying evolutionary relationships

Molecular evidence from comparisons of the nucleotide sequences of DNA can be used to reveal similarities between related species.

DNA is mostly found in the nucleus, but there are also small circles of DNA in mitochondria and chloroplasts. All of these sources of DNA can give information about the relationships between species.

The more similar DNA nucleotide sequences of two species are, the more closely related the species. In other words, two species with very similar DNA split apart more recently than two species with less similar DNA. Differences in the nucleotide sequences of DNA can be used to study the origin and spread of our own species, *Homo sapiens*. For example, humans share about 98% of our DNA with chimpanzees, suggesting that we are quite closely related to them in evolutionary terms. It is not possible to determine exactly how long ago our common ancestor lived, but these DNA sequence differences suggest that it was a few million years ago. The DNA sequences of modern humans and DNA extracted from the remains of Neanderthal people

are more similar than this, and they suggest that the Neanderthal and the modern human evolutionary lines split apart about 500 000 years ago.

Human mitochondrial DNA (mtDNA) is inherited through the female line. A zygote contains the mitochondria of the egg but not of the sperm. Since the mtDNA is circular and therefore cannot undergo any form of crossing over, changes in the nucleotide sequence can arise only by mutation. Mitochondrial DNA mutates faster than nuclear DNA, acquiring one mutation every 25 000 years.

Different human populations show differences in mitochondrial DNA sequences. These provide evidence for the origin of *H. sapiens* in Africa and for the subsequent migrations of the species around the world. These studies have led to the suggestion that all modern humans, of whatever race, are descendants from one woman, called Mitochondrial Eve, who lived in Africa between 150 000 and 200 000 years ago. This date is derived from the 'molecular clock' hypothesis, which assumes a constant rate of mutation over time and that the greater the number of differences in the sequence of nucleotides, the longer ago those individuals shared a common ancestor. The 'clock' can be calibrated by comparing nucleotide sequences of species whose date of speciation can be estimated from fossil evidence. Fossils can be dated by methods such as carbon dating, which can provide a good idea of how long ago the organism lived.

In Section 17.3, Genetic drift and the founder effect, you looked at how the founder effect and genetic drift could affect the phenotypes of lizards isolated on different islands on the Caribbean. Analysis of mtDNA of the different species of anole lizards that are found throughout the Caribbean and the adjacent mainland provides evidence of their relationships (Figure 17.24). Each island species of lizard is found only on one island or a small group of islands. Table 17.3 shows the results of comparing part of the mtDNA of four of the species. These results show that the three species *Anolis brunneus*, *A. smaragdinus* and *A. carolinensis* are more closely related to *A. porcatus* than they are to each other. This suggests that these species have each originated from separate events in which a few individuals of *A. porcatus* spread from Cuba to three different places. The mtDNA analysis shows that allopatric speciation has occurred.

	A. brunneus			
A. brunneus		A. smaragdinus		
A. smaragdinus	12.1		A. carolinensis	
A. carolinensis	16.7	15.0		A. porcatus
A. porcatus	11.3	8.9	13.2	

Table 17.3: The results of comparing part of the mitochondrial DNA of four of the species of anole lizards. The smaller the number, the smaller the differences between the base sequences of the two species.

Figure 17.24: Distribution of different *Anole* lizard species in the Caribbean.

We can use the results of DNA analysis, and a comparison of base sequences in different species, to draw a 'family tree' showing the relationships between different species, genera or even larger classification groups. The family tree in Figure 17.25 shows how *Anolis* lizards are thought to be related to five other genera of lizards.

Work from left to right to think about the tree. Starting at the left, the diagram indicates that all these six genera had a common ancestor (whose name we do not know), whose population then split to form two species. One species gave rise to the genus *Sphenodon* – a lizard with

some very 'primitive' features, called the tuatara, which now lives only in New Zealand (see Figure 17.26). The other branch splits again, giving rise to the genus *Heloderma*, which contains species such as the Gila monster (see Figure 17.27).

The remaining branches split again, producing the genera *Agama* (agama lizards), *Chamaleo* (chameleons), *Oplurus* (which all live in Madagascar) and, of course, *Anolis*.

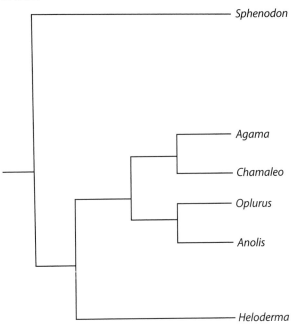

Figure 17.25: Family tree showing the evolutionary relationships of six general of lizards.

Figure 17.26: A tuatara lizard, one of two living species belonging to the genus *Sphenodon*

Figure 17.27: A Gila monster, *Heloderma suspectum*

REFLECTION

When describing natural selection, the term *struggle for existence* is often used.

- Using what you have learnt in this chapter, do you think this is a useful term or is it misleading?

- What did you learn about yourself as you worked on this question?

Final reflection

Discuss with a friend which, if any, parts of Chapter 17 you need to:

- read through again to make sure you really understand

- seek more guidance on, even after going over it again.

SUMMARY

Phenotypic variation may be continuous (as in the height or mass of an organism) or discontinuous (as in the human ABO blood groups). The genotype of an organism gives it the potential to show a particular characteristic. In many cases, the degree to which this characteristic is shown is also influenced by the organism's environment. Genetic variation within a population is the raw material on which natural selection can act.

Meiosis, random mating and the random fusion of gametes produce genetic variation within populations of sexually reproducing organisms. Variation is also caused by the interaction of the environment with genetic factors, but such environmentally induced variation is not passed on to an organism's offspring. The only source of new alleles is mutation.

All species of organisms have the reproductive potential to increase the sizes of their populations but, in the long term, this rarely happens. This is because environmental factors come into play to limit population growth. Such factors decrease the rate of reproduction or increase the rate of mortality so that many individuals die before reaching reproductive age.

CONTINUED

Within a population, certain alleles may increase the chance that an individual will survive long enough to be able to reproduce successfully. These alleles are, therefore, more likely to be passed on to the next generation than others. This is known as natural selection. Normally, natural selection keeps allele frequencies as they are; this is stabilising selection. However, if environmental factors that exert selection pressures change, or if new alleles appear in a population, then natural selection may cause a change in the frequencies of alleles; this is directional selection. Over many generations, directional selection may produce large changes in allele frequencies. This is how evolution occurs.

The evolution of antibiotic resistance in bacteria and the spread of industrial melanism in moths are examples of changes in allele frequencies.

Allele frequencies in a small population may change thanks to a random process called genetic drift. The number of alleles in an isolated population may be much smaller than in the parent population, as a result of the isolated population having begun with only a few individuals; this is known as the founder effect. The allele frequencies and the proportions of genotypes of a particular gene in a population can be calculated using the Hardy–Weinberg equations.

Artificial selection involves the choice by humans of which organisms to allow to breed together, in order to bring about a desirable change in characteristics. Thus, artificial selection, like natural selection, can affect allele frequencies in a population.

A species can be defined as a group of organisms with similar morphology, behaviour, physiology and biochemistry that are capable of interbreeding to produce fertile offspring. However, in practice, it is not always possible to determine whether or not organisms can interbreed.

New species arise by a process called speciation. In allopatric speciation, two populations become isolated from one another, perhaps by some geographical feature, and then evolve along different lines until they become so different that they can no longer interbreed. In sympatric speciation, new species may arise through ecological or behavioural separation. In both allopatric and sympatric speciation, the gene pools of the two groups change over time, so that the two groups become genetically isolated from one another, with no gene flow between them.

Comparisons of the DNA nucleotide sequences of two species can give information about how closely they are related to each other.

EXAM-STYLE QUESTIONS

1   a   With reference to the evolution of antibiotic resistance in bacteria, explain
        the meaning of the term *directional selection*.   [3]

    b   List the numbers of the following statements in the correct order, to explain
        the evolution of resistance to the antibiotic streptomycin by the bacterium
        Escherichia coli.

        1   Most of the population of *E. coli* is resistant to streptomycin.

        2   A random mutation in a DNA triplet of a plasmid, changing TTT to
            TTG, gives an *E. coli* bacterium resistance to streptomycin.

        3   The resistant bacterium divides and passes copies of the R plasmid
            (plasmid with gene for resistance to antibiotic) to its offspring.

        4   Sensitive bacteria die in the presence of streptomycin as a selective
            pressure.

CONTINUED

5 The frequency of the mutated allele in the population increases.

6 The resistant bacterium has a selective advantage and survives. **[5]**

[Total: 8]

2 Hybrids produced by crossing two different inbred (homozygous) varieties are often more vigorous in their growth than either of their parents. Copy and complete the flow diagram to show how breeders of maize produce plants that show hybrid vigour.

Inbred line 1
Genotype: homozygous
Phenotype: uniform
Yield: low

Inbred line 2
Genotype: ....
Phenotype: ....
Yield: ....

Hybrid
Genotype: ....
Phenotype: ....
Yield: ....

[6]

3 a Copy and complete the table to compare artificial selection with natural selection.

Natural selection	Artificial selection
the selective agent is the total environment of the organism	
adaptations to the prevailing conditions are selected	
many different traits contributing to fitness are selected	

[3]

b Pale and dark peppered moths were collected and placed on pale and dark areas of bark on trees in a park in a city in England. Some of the moths were predated by birds. The results of the investigation are shown in the table.

Colour of moth	Percentage of moths taken by birds	
	from pale bark	from dark bark
pale	20	44
dark	40	15

i Forty dark moths were placed on pale bark. Calculate the number of moths taken by birds. Show your working. **[2]**

ii Suggest an explanation for the differences in the numbers of moths taken by birds. **[4]**

[Total: 9]

4 The table shows the changes in milk yield and nutrient content in a herd of Jersey cattle in which artificial selection for high yields of high-quality milk was carried out. The figures in the table are the mean results per cow for one year.

Year	Mean milk yield per cow/kg	Percentage protein content	Percentage fat content
1989	4104	3.83	5.40
1990	4104	3.84	5.40
1991	4123	3.84	5.42
1992	4151	3.84	5.41
1993	4182	3.83	5.40
1994	4245	3.82	5.37
1995	4281	3.81	5.35
1996	4311	3.81	5.35
1997	4370	3.80	5.35
1998	4412	3.79	5.33
1999	4470	3.79	5.32

a Outline how the selection programme could be carried out. [3]

b Calculate the mean change in milk yield per year over the ten-year period of the breeding experiment. [2]

c Describe the trends in the nutrient content of the milk over the ten-year period. [3]

d It was found that the herd of cows in 1999 had more health problems than those in 1989. Suggest why this happened. [3]

[Total: 11]

5 The snail *Cepaea nemoralis* may have a yellow, pink or brown shell. Each colour shell may have up to five dark bands or have no bands. Both shell colour and number of bands are genetically controlled and are not affected by the environment. The snails are eaten by birds such as thrushes, which hunt by sight.

The following observations were made.

• Most snails living on a uniform background, such as short grass, have no bands.

• Most snails living on a green background, such as grass, are yellow.

• Most snails living on a non-uniform background, such as rough vegetation, have bands.

a Suggest an explanation for these observations. [4]

b Predict the phenotype of snails living on a dark background of dead leaves. [2]

c   Suggest what will happen, during the course of a year, to the frequencies of the different alleles controlling shell colour and banding in a snail population living in deciduous woodland. (Deciduous trees shed their leaves in autumn. The background for the snails will be made up of dead leaves in the autumn and winter, and green vegetation in the spring and summer.)   [4]

[Total: 10]

6   The common froghopper, *Philaenus spumarius*, is found in two colour forms, striped and melanic. The diagram shows the frequencies of the two colour forms on different islands in the Isles of Scilly in the Atlantic Ocean.

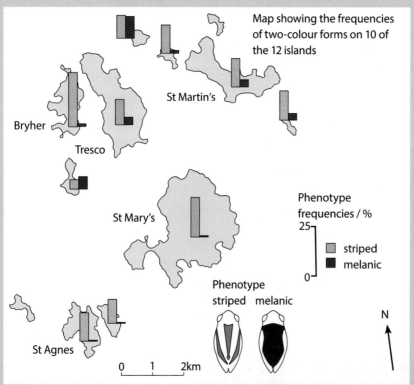

a   Outline how the information in the diagram suggests that the phenotypic variation is caused by genes and not by environment.   [2]

b   Compare the phenotypic frequencies of the two colour forms on Bryher and Tresco.   [2]

c   The colours of this species are determined by seven different alleles of a single gene. The differences between the phenotypic frequencies on the different islands are thought to be a result of genetic drift, and not natural selection.

Explain how genetic drift could cause the differences in phenotypic frequencies that you have described in your answer to **b**.   [4]

[Total: 8]

CONTINUED

7 The heliconid butterflies of South America have brightly coloured patterns on their wings. A hybrid between two species, *Heliconius cydno* and *H. melpomene*, has wing patterns that are different from both parental species.

An investigation was carried out to see whether the hybrid was a new species.

Separate groups of four butterflies, each consisting of a male and female of one of the parental species and a male and female of the hybrid, were placed together and their choices of mates recorded. The results are shown in the table.

	Number of matings	
	H. melpomene male	hybrid male
H. melpomene female	15	0
hybrid female	0	15
	H. cydno male	hybrid male
H. cydno female	5	3
hybrid female	0	5

a With reference to the information in the table, explain whether or not the results of the investigation suggest that the hybrid butterfly is a separate species. [4]

b Suggest how the hybrid could be reproductively isolated from the two parent species of butterfly. [2]

c Outline how allopatric speciation can occur. [4]

[Total: 10]

SELF-EVALUATION CHECKLIST

After studying this chapter, complete a table like this:

I can	See section...	Needs more work	Almost there	Ready to move on
explain that genetic and environmental factors affect phenotypic variation	17.1			
explain the differences between continuous and discontinuous variation	17.1			
explain how natural selection takes place, including reference to the development of antibiotic resistance in bacteria	17.2			
explain the differences between stabilising, disruptive and directional selection	17.2			
explain how the founder effect and genetic drift may affect allele frequencies	17.3			
use the Hardy–Weinberg equations	17.4			
describe the principles of selective breeding, including examples	17.5			
outline the theory of evolution in terms of changes to gene pools	17.6			
explain how new species can be formed by allopatric and sympatric processes	17.6			
discuss the use of DNA sequencing to determine relationships between species	17.7			

> Chapter 18
Classification, biodiversity and conservation

LEARNING INTENTIONS

In this chapter you will learn how to:

- discuss the meaning of the term *species* and explain how species are classified
- outline the characteristic features of the three domains and of the four kingdoms of eukaryotic organisms
- outline how viruses are classified
- explain the importance of biodiversity in terms of ecosystems, habitats, species and the genetic diversity within each species
- investigate ecosystems using techniques for assessing the occurrence, abundance and distribution of species
- explain how species may become extinct

CONTINUED

- calculate Simpson's index of diversity and use it to compare the biodiversity of different areas
- use statistical methods to analyse the relationships between the distribution and abundance of species and abiotic or biotic factors
- discuss the reasons for maintaining biodiversity and outline the ways in which biodiversity is conserved
- describe methods of assisted reproduction used in the conservation of endangered mammal species
- explain why it is necessary to control invasive alien species
- discuss the roles of the International Union for Conservation of Nature (IUCN) and the Convention on International Trade in Endangered Species of Wild Fauna and Flora (CITES) in global conservation.

BEFORE YOU START

Summarise the causes of genetic variation in populations of animals and plants. Compare the causes that you have listed with others. Make a presentation on genetic diversity to use for revision. Include some examples to illustrate your presentation.

MOCKINGBIRDS

Mockingbirds are found throughout the Americas. There are four species of mockingbird in the Galapagos Islands in the Pacific of which the Floreana mockingbird is the rarest (Figure 18.1). The population of this species became extinct on the island of Floreana in the second half of the 19th century, mainly because people colonised the island and introduced species such as rats that destroyed its nests. People also cut down the prickly pear cactus that is the bird's source of food and a favourite nesting site. Two small populations of several hundred individuals remain on two nearby tiny islands, Champion and Gardner-by-Floreana. Conservation programmes have had some success at increasing the numbers of this species and there are plans to reintroduce the species to Floreana. Progress of the project can be followed on the web site of the Galapagos Conservation Trust. One of the rarest birds in the world, it is worth saving from extinction not least because this was the first mockingbird species that Charles Darwin saw on his visit to the Galapagos Islands in 1835. He went on to notice that the mockingbirds on different islands within the Galapagos were not all alike and all differed from the species he had seen in South America. This helped him devise his theory about how organisms change over time.

Figure 18.1: One of the world's rarest birds – the Floreana mockingbird, *Nesomimus trifasciatus.*

Question for discussion

The mockingbirds of the Galapagos Islands played an important part in Charles Darwin's thinking about how organisms change over time. Discuss what Darwin observed about these birds as he travelled through the islands and how those observations influenced his thinking.

18.1 Classification

The species concept

So far in this book, you have looked at evidence for the unity of life. In this chapter you will consider the diversity of life on Earth. At its simplest, diversity can be thought of as a catalogue of all the different species.

The term *species* is often used to mean a group of organisms that appear similar to each other, and that can breed together successfully to produce fertile offspring. This definition describes the **biological species** concept, also known as the biospecies concept. When many species are described for the first time, it is impossible to apply this definition because most are described using physical features, such as morphology (outward appearance) and anatomy. In these circumstances biologists are using the **morphological species** concept. Biologists also apply the **ecological species** concept when they find a **population** of organisms that share the same features and all live in the same habitat at the same time.

New species are discovered and named all the time. You will have noticed that some species are given both their common and scientific names. When a new species is discovered, it is given a scientific name using the binomial system that was developed by the Swedish scientist Linnaeus in the 18th century. The first name is the genus (or generic) name. This indicates a rank higher than species in the classification system. Species that show many similarities and are closely related are classified together in the same genus. The second name is the specific epithet or trivial name. The generic name is one word (e.g. *Nesomimus*); the species name is both words (e.g. *Nesomimus trifasciatus*). *Nesomimus trifasciatus* is one species within the genus *Nesomimus*, which includes all four mockingbird species of the Galapagos. If you have already used the name once, then it is permissible to abbreviate it when you use it again. The abbreviated form is the first letter of the generic name followed by the specific epithet (e.g. *N. trifasciatus*). If there is any ambiguity about doing this (e.g. you might be writing about two species with generic names both beginning with A), then you have to write out the name in full. If asked for a species name, then always give two names: genus followed by the specific epithet.

KEY WORDS

biological species: a group of organisms with similar morphology and physiology, which can breed together to produce fertile offspring and are reproductively isolated from other species

morphological species: a group of organisms that share many physical features that distinguish them from other species

ecological species: a population of individuals of the same species living in the same area at the same time

population: all of the organisms of the same species present in the same place and at the same time that can interbreed with one another

---

Figure 18.2: Appearances can be deceptive. These mammals look very similar, but they are two different species, classified in two different orders. **a** This is a mouse from southern Africa; **b** this is an antechinus from Australia. The mouse is a placental mammal and the antechinus is a marsupial.

No one knows for certain how many different species there are on Earth (Figure 18.2). More than 1.5 million species of animals have been described and named to date. Estimates of the total number of species range up to 100 million species.

Hierarchical classification

With such a huge number of different kinds of organisms living on Earth, biologists have always wanted to arrange them into groups, a process called classification. We find it difficult to memorise or absorb information about thousands of different unrelated objects. By grouping them into different categories, it is much easier to understand them and to remember their key features.

Taxonomy is the study and practice of classification, which involves placing organisms in a series of taxonomic units, or **taxa** (singular: **taxon**). In **biological classification**, these taxa form a hierarchy. Each kind of organism is assigned to its own species, and similar species are grouped into a genus (plural: genera). Similar genera are grouped into a family, families into an order, orders into a class, classes into a phylum (plural: phyla) and phyla into a **kingdom**. The **domain** is at the highest **taxonomic rank** in this **hierarchical classification** system. Table 18.1 shows how African bush elephants and hibiscus plants (Figure 18.3) are classified.

Taxonomic rank	African bush elephant	Hibiscus
domain	Eukarya	Eukarya
kingdom	Animalia	Plantae
phylum	Chordata	Angiospermae
class	Mammalia	Dicotyledonae
order	Proboscidea	Malvales
family	Elephantidae	Malvaceae
genus	*Loxodonta*	*Hibiscus*
species	*Loxodonta africana*	*Hibiscus rosa-sinensis*

Table 18.1: The classification of African bush elephants and hibiscus plants.

KEY WORDS

biological classification: the organisation of living and extinct organisms into systematic groups based on similarities and differences between species

taxonomy: the study and practice of naming and classifying species and groups of species within the hierarchical classification scheme

hierarchical classification: the arrangement of organisms into groups of different rank. The lowest rank is the species; similar species are grouped together into the next rank, which is the genus; this continues to the highest rank, which is the domain where many species are grouped together

taxonomic rank: one of the groups used in the hierarchical classification system for organisms, e.g. species, genus, family, order, class, phylum, kingdom and domain

taxon (plural: taxa): a taxonomic group of any rank, such as a particular species (e.g. *Giraffa camelopardalis*), a family (e.g. Elephantidae), a class (e.g. Mammalia) or a kingdom (e.g. Plantae)

domain: the highest taxonomic rank

kingdom: the taxonomic rank below domain

Figure 18.3: *Hibiscus rosa-sinensis* is a plant that has spread from Asia to much of the tropics and sub-tropics. Flower colour is a good example of the genetic diversity in this species.

Question

1 **a** The giraffe, *Giraffa camelopardalis,* is a mammal that belongs to the order Artiodactyla and the family Giraffidae. Make a table to show how the giraffe is classified.

  b Use examples from Table 18.1 to explain:

  i   the term *taxonomic rank*

  ii why the classification system is hierarchical.

Three domains

Biologists used to divide organisms into two large groupings based on their cell structure. In Chapter 1 you saw that prokaryotes and eukaryotes have significantly different cellular structures. In the 1970s prokaryotes were discovered living in extreme environments, such as hot springs where temperatures often exceed 100 °C. These organisms are called extremophiles and are not like typical bacteria. Studies revealed that the genes coding for the RNA that makes up their ribosomes were more like those of eukaryotes. The extremophiles were found to share features with both typical bacteria and eukaryotes. At this time, studies of molecular biology assumed a much greater significance in taxonomy. This meant that a new taxon, the domain, had to be introduced to reflect the differences between these extremophiles and typical bacteria. The domain is the taxon at the top of the hierarchy (Table 18.1). The prokaryotes are divided between the domains **Bacteria** and **Archaea** and all the eukaryotes are placed into the domain **Eukarya**.

Many Archaea live in extreme environments, such as hot springs, around deep volcanic vents (black smokers) in the oceans (Figure 18.4) and in lakes where there is a very high concentration of salt. Some of them produce methane, cannot survive where there is oxygen and have many unusual enzymes. Since they were discovered in extreme environments, they also have been found in many less extreme environments; for example, they form an important part of the plankton in the oceans.

Figure 18.4: A deep-sea hydrothermal vent (black smoker) surrounded by giant tubeworms. The community relies on energy made available by bacteria and archaeans.

In several ways, the Archaea appear to have more in common with the Eukarya than with Bacteria. It is thought that Bacteria and Archaea separated from each other very early in the evolution of life. The Archaea and Eukarya probably diverged later.

Domain Bacteria

Bacteria are prokaryotic as their cells have no nucleus. They are all small organisms that vary in size between that of the largest virus and the smallest single-celled eukaryote.

Look back at Figure 1.30 to remind yourself of these features and to see how prokaryotic cell structure differs from that of eukaryotes. There are electron micrographs of two pathogenic species of bacteria in Chapter 10 (see Figures 10.2 and 10.12). Figure 18.5 shows the cyanobacterium *Nostoc*.

Domain Archaea

Archaeans are also prokaryotic as their cells have no nucleus. Their range of size is similar to that of bacteria. Many inhabit extreme environments (Figures 18.4 and 18.6).

KEY WORDS

Bacteria: the domain that contains all prokaryotic organisms except those classified as Archaea

Archaea: the domain of prokaryotic organisms that resemble bacteria but share some features with eukaryotes

Eukarya: the domain that contains all eukaryotic organisms: protoctists, fungi, plants and animals

---

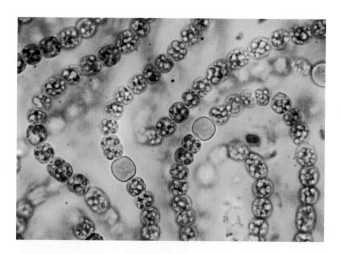

Figure 18.5: The filamentous cyanobacterium *Nostoc*. This species fixes carbon dioxide in photosynthesis; it also fixes nitrogen by converting N_2 into organic forms of nitrogen in the wider, lighter green cells in its filaments (×600).

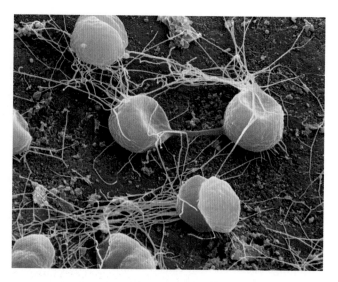

Figure 18.6: A scanning electron micrograph (SEM) of the archaean *Pyrococcus furiosus* (×12 500). Although they look like bacteria, archaeans have differences in structure, metabolism and genetics. *P. furiosus* is only found in near-boiling water; if the temperature falls below 70 °C, it freezes and dies. It respires in anaerobic conditions using sulfur instead of oxygen as the final electron acceptor.

IMPORTANT

Characteristic features of bacteria

- Cells with no nucleus
- DNA is circular and does not have histone proteins associated with it
- Smaller circular molecules of DNA called plasmids are often present
- No membrane-bound organelles (such as mitochondria, endoplasmic reticulum, Golgi body, chloroplasts) are present
- Ribosomes (70S) are smaller than in eukaryotic cells
- Cell walls are always present and contain peptidoglycans (not cellulose)
- Cells divide by binary fission, not by mitosis
- Usually exist as single cells or small groups of cells.

The metabolism of archaeans is similar to that of bacteria, but the way in which transcription occurs has much in common with eukaryotes.

Domain Eukarya

All the organisms classified into this domain have cells with nuclei and membrane-bound organelles.

IMPORTANT

Characteristic features of archaeans

- Cells with no nucleus
- DNA exists as a circular 'chromosome' and does have histone proteins associated with it
- Smaller circular molecules of DNA called plasmids are often present
- Cells with no membrane-bound organelles
- Ribosomes (70S) are smaller than in eukaryotic cells, but the small subunit has features that are similar to those in eukaryotic ribosomes but not to bacterial ribosomes; the base sequences of rRNA and the primary structure of ribosomal proteins are more like those in eukaryotes rather than bacteria
- Membrane lipids are unique – they are not found in membranes of bacteria or eukarya
- Cell walls are always present but do not contain peptidoglycans
- Cells divide by binary fission, not by mitosis
- Usually exist as single cells or small groups of cells

Characteristic features of eukaryotes

- Cells with a nucleus and membrane-bound organelles
- DNA in the nucleus arranged as linear chromosomes with histone proteins
- Ribosomes (80S) in the cytosol are larger than in prokaryotes; chloroplasts and mitochondria have 70S ribosomes, like those in bacteria
- Chloroplast and mtDNA is circular as in prokaryotes
- A great diversity of forms: there are unicellular (Figure 18.7), colonial (Figure 18.8) and multicellular organisms
- Cell division is by mitosis
- Cell walls are present in some eukaryotes
- Many different ways of reproducing – asexually and sexually

Questions

2   Make a table to compare the features of the three domains: Bacteria, Archaea and Eukarya.

3   State **three** ways in which organisms classified as Archeans differ from organisms classified in the domain Bacteria.

Kingdoms

The three domains are each divided into kingdoms. This section describes the features of the four kingdoms of the domain Eukarya:

- Protoctista
- Fungi
- Plantae
- Animalia.

Kingdom Protoctista

The **Protoctista** is made up of a very diverse range of eukaryotic organisms, which includes those that are often called protozoans ('simple animals') and algae, such as seaweeds. Any eukaryote that is not a fungus, plant or animal is classified as a **protoctist** (Figures 18.7 and 18.8).

KEY WORDS

Protoctista: kingdom of eukaryotic organisms which are single-celled or made up of groups of similar cells

protoctist: a member of the Protoctista kingdom

IMPORTANT

Characteristic features of protoctists

- Eukaryotic
- Mostly single-celled, or exist as groups of similar cells
- Some have animal-like cells (no cell wall) and are sometimes known as protozoa
- Others have plant-like cells (with cellulose cell walls and chloroplasts) and are sometimes known as algae

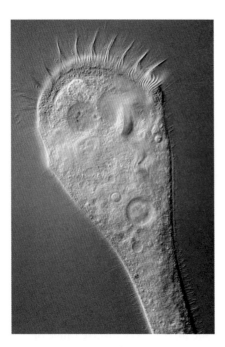

Figure 18.7: *Stentor roseli*, a protoctist covered in many cilia which it uses for movement and for feeding. Although unicellular, it has considerable specialisation of regions within its body (×240).

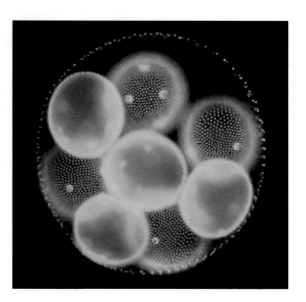

Figure 18.8: *Volvox globator* is a spherical colonial green protoctist. The body is composed of thousands of cells with flagella. These cells work together in a coordinated way but there is little specialisation of cells. Cells at one pole detect light so the colony swims towards the light. Cells at the other pole are specialised for reproduction. Inside there are new colonies that are just about to be released (×60).

Many organisms in this kingdom may actually be more closely related to organisms in other kingdoms than they are to each other. For example, there are strong arguments for classifying algae as plants.

Kingdom Fungi

Fungi have some similarities with plants, but no fungus is able to photosynthesise. Fungi are all heterotrophic, obtaining energy and carbon from dead and decaying matter or by feeding as parasites on living organisms. There is a vast range in size from the microscopic yeasts to what may be the world's largest organism. A specimen of the honey fungus, *Armillaria bulbosa*, grows in a forest in Wisconsin, USA, and spreads over 160 000 m². Not only is it possibly the largest organism in the world, but it may also be the oldest at 1500–10 000 years old; its estimated mass is 100 tonnes.

> ### KEY WORD
>
> **Fungi:** kingdom of eukaryotic organisms which do not photosynthesise and have cell walls but without cellulose

> ### IMPORTANT
>
> **Characteristic features of fungi**
>
> - Eukaryotic
> - Do not have chlorophyll and do not photosynthesise
> - Heterotrophic nutrition – they use organic compounds made by other organisms as their source of energy and source of molecules for metabolism
> - Reproduce by means of spores (Figure 18.9)
> - Simple body form, which may be unicellular or made up of long threads called hyphae (with or without cross walls) (Figure 18.10); all the hyphae that grow from a single spore form the mycelium (body of the fungus); large fungi such as mushrooms produce large compacted masses of hyphae known as 'fruiting bodies' to release spores
> - Cells have cell walls made of chitin or other substances, not cellulose
> - Never have cilia

Figure 18.9: Fruiting bodies of the puffball fungus, *Lycoperdon perlatum*, releasing millions of microscopic spores. Their method of feeding on dead and decaying matter means that eventually the food is all used up. A few of these spores may land on a suitable food source and be able to grow.

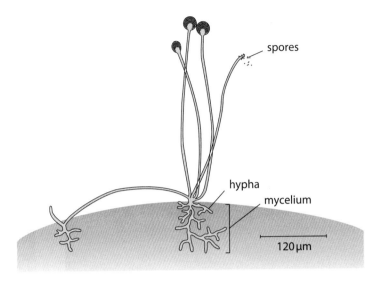

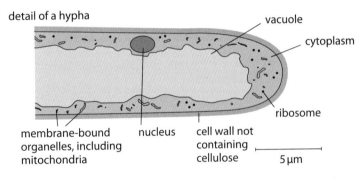

Figure 18.10: The bread mould fungus, *Rhizopus nigricans*, and a detail of the end of one hypha.

Kingdom Plantae

Plantae (plants) are all multicellular photosynthetic organisms (Figures 18.11 and 18.12). They have complex bodies that are often highly branched both above and below ground.

> **KEY WORD**
>
> **Plantae:** kingdom of eukaryotic organisms which are multicellular, have cell walls that contain cellulose and can photosynthesise

> **IMPORTANT**
>
> **Characteristic features of plants**
>
> - Multicellular eukaryotes with cells that are differentiated to form tissues and organs
> - Few types of specialised cells
> - Some cells have chloroplasts and photosynthesise (see Figures 1.21 and 1.34)
> - Autotrophic nutrition
> - Cells have large, often permanent vacuoles for support
> - Cell walls are always present and are made of cellulose
> - Cells may occasionally have flagella (e.g. male gametes in ferns)

Figure 18.11: Tree ferns, *Cyathea* sp., growing in Whirinaki Conservation Park, New Zealand.

Kingdom Animalia

The **Animalia** are multicellular organisms that are all heterotrophic with many ways of obtaining their food. There is a great diversity of forms within this kingdom (Figure 18.13). The nervous system is unique to the animal kingdom.

Figure 18.12: Bristlecone pines are some of the oldest trees on Earth, many estimated to be between 2000 and 3000 years old. The trees in the photograph grow at over 2900 metres in the Twisted Forest in the Ashdown Gorge Wilderness area of Dixie National Forest, Utah, USA.

KEY WORD

Animalia: kingdom of eukaryotic organisms which are multicellular and heterotrophic and have a nervous system

IMPORTANT

Characteristic features of animals

- Multicellular eukaryotes with many different types of specialised cells
- Cells that are differentiated to form tissues and organs
- Cells do not have chloroplasts and cannot photosynthesise (although some, e.g. coral polyps, have photosynthetic protoctists living within their tissues)
- Cell vacuoles are small and temporary (e.g. lysosomes and food vacuoles)
- Heterotrophic nutrition
- Cells do not have cell walls
- Communication is by the nervous system and chemical signalling (Chapter 15)
- Some specialised cells have cilia

Figure 18.13: The crown-of-thorns starfish, *Acanthaster planci*, feeds on coral in the Great Barrier Reef. It has been through several population explosions over recent years, causing destruction of much of the coral on parts of the reef (see Section 18.2).

Question

4 a Which eukaryotic kingdoms contain:

    i autotrophic organisms

    ii heterotrophic organisms?

  b Make a table to compare the features of the four kingdoms of eukaryotes.

Viruses

Viruses are microorganisms whose structure is only visible with electron microscopes (Figures 18.14 and 18.15). Viruses are acellular – they do not have a cellular structure like bacteria and fungi. In Chapter 1 you looked at their structure (see Figure 1.36); in Chapters 10 and 11 you considered some human viral pathogens, and in Chapter 19 you will see that they have important roles in gene technology.

Viruses are not in the three-domain classification system. This is because viruses have none of the features traditionally used for classification. When viruses are free in the environment, they are infectious but they have no metabolism. When they infect cells, they make use of the biochemical machinery of the host cell to copy the viral nucleic acids and to make viral proteins. This often leads to destruction of the host cells. The energy for these processes is provided by respiration in the host cell.

The taxonomic system for classifying viruses is based on the type of nucleic acid they contain (DNA or RNA) and whether the nucleic acid is single-stranded or

a

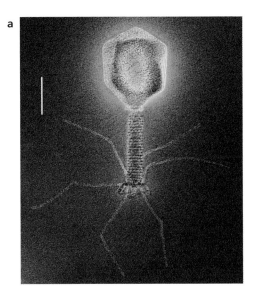

b

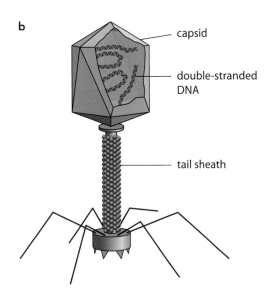

capsid

double-stranded DNA

tail sheath

Figure 18.14: a A transmission electron micrograph (TEM) of a T4 bacteriophage – a virus that infects *Escherischia coli* bacteria and is used as a vector in genetic modification. The scale bar represents 50 nm. **b** A diagram of a T4 bacteriophage.

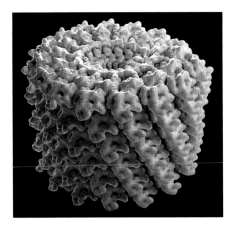

Figure 18.15: A model showing the structure of part of the tobacco mosaic virus, TMV. The blue strand is the single strand of RNA and the rest is composed of proteins. In a survey of plant pathologists in 2011, TMV was voted the most important plant virus.

Nucleic acid	Number of strands	Example	Host organism	Disease
DNA	1	canine parvovirus type 2	dogs	canine parvovirus
		African cassava mosaic virus	cassava plants	mosaic disease
	2	varicella zoster virus (VZV)	humans	chickenpox
		T4 bacteriophage (Figure 18.14)	*Escherischia coli*	
RNA	1	rotavirus	humans	gastroenteritis
		morbillivirus	humans	measles
		tobacco mosaic virus (TMV) (Figure 18.15)	tobacco, tomato, pepper	mosaic disease (Figure 18.16)
	2	human immunodeficiency virus (Figures 10.9 and 10.10)	humans	HIV/AIDS

Table 18.2: Viruses are classified into four groups according to the type and structure of their nucleic acid.

double-stranded. In cellular organisms, DNA is double-stranded and RNA is single-stranded. But in viruses, both DNA and RNA can be either single-stranded or double-stranded. This means there are four groups of viruses. Some examples of viruses in these four groups are shown in Table 18.2.

Question

5 a Explain why viruses are not included in the three-domain classification system described in this chapter.

b State the features that are used in the classification of viruses.

c Should viruses be considered as living organisms or not?

Figure 18.16: Viruses are the ultimate in parasitism – they can only reproduce inside the cells of their host. This tobacco plant is showing signs of infection by the tobacco mosaic virus. TMV severely reduces plant growth and spreads rapidly through crops such as tobacco and tomato.

18.2 Biodiversity

Biodiversity can be defined as the degree of variation of life forms in an ecosystem. However, the concept is considered much wider than just a list of species and is usually taken to include diversity at three levels:

- the number and range of ecosystems and habitats
- the number of different species in the ecosystem and their relative abundance
- the genetic variation within each species.

Some areas of the world have very high biodiversity. Examples of these include the Congo basin in Africa, South East Asia, the Caribbean and Central America, Amazonia and south-west Australia. These areas have many **endemic** species – that is, species that are only found in these areas and nowhere else (Figure 18.17).

Figure 18.17: Because New Zealand was isolated for many millions of years, it has many endemic species and also some, like this tuatara, *Sphenodon* sp., that have become extinct elsewhere.

Ecosystems and habitats

Species do not live in isolation; they share their living space with others to form communities like that in a forest (Figure 18.18). These communities of organisms interact with each other and with their environment.

Figure 18.18: Trees in tropical forests, as here in Costa Rica, are often covered with epiphytes – plants that grow on other plants. These provide far more habitats for small animals, such as beetles, than does the bare bark of trees in temperate forests. One tree in a tropical rainforest can contain up to 1200 species of beetle.

An **ecosystem** is a relatively self-contained, interacting **community** of organisms, and the environment in which they live and with which they interact. A forest ecosystem includes the community of organisms and the soil, the dead leaves that form leaf litter, water in the rain and in streams, the air, the rocks and all the physical and chemical factors which influence

KEY WORDS

biodiversity: the variety of ecosystems and species in an area and the genetic diversity within each species

endemic: of species, a species that is only found in a certain area and nowhere else

ecosystem: a relatively self-contained, interacting community of organisms, and the environment in which they live and with which they interact

community: all of the living organisms, of all species, that are found in a particular ecosystem at a particular time

organisms. No ecosystem is entirely self-contained; organisms in one ecosystem interact with those from others. Many birds, for example, migrate from one ecosystem to another, often over very great distances, to find food and to breed.

You can think of ecosystems on different scales: a small pond is an ecosystem because the water provides a very different environment from the soil and air around it. The organisms in the pond community are therefore very different from those of the surrounding ecosystem. At the other end of the scale is the open ocean, which is a huge ecosystem. Some ecosystems (e.g. tropical rainforests and coral reefs) are very complex; others (e.g. sandy deserts) are very simple.

A **habitat** describes the place where a species lives within an ecosystem. The **niche** occupied by a species is more than a physical description of a place. A niche is the role of an organism in an ecosystem; it is how the organism 'fits into' the ecosystem (Figure 18.19). An organism's niche describes where it is, how it obtains energy, how it interacts with both its physical environment and with other species. Organisms require resources from their surroundings and they have special adaptations for obtaining them.

Figure 18.19: The niche of this great egret includes the freshwater ecosystem where it spends much of its time feeding. It also includes the nearby trees where it roosts and nests.

It is almost impossible to provide a complete description of the niche of any organism, because there are so many ways in which one organism interacts with other components of the ecosystem of which it is a part.

Question

6   Distinguish between the terms *ecosystem* and *niche*.

Species diversity

The number of species in a community is known as species richness. **Species diversity** takes species richness into account, but it also includes a measure of the evenness of the abundance of the different species. The more species there are and the more evenly the number of organisms is distributed among the different species, the greater the species diversity. Table 18.3 shows the number of trees of different species that were recorded in two similar ecosystems.

> **KEY WORDS**
>
> **habitat:** the place where an organism, a population or a community lives
>
> **niche:** the role of an organism in an ecosystem
>
> **species diversity:** all the species in an ecosystem

Tree species	Ecosystem 1	Ecosystem 2
A	45	65
B	23	10
C	55	20
D	14	0
E	19	5
F	23	4

Table 18.3: These two ecosystems have the same species richness, but Ecosystem 1 has a higher diversity as its species evenness is greater than Ecosystem 2.

Coral reefs have a very high biodiversity. Such an ecosystem offers many different ecological niches, which are exploited by different species. Species diversity is considered important because ecosystems with high species diversity tend to be more stable than ones with limited diversity. Highly diverse ecosystems have greater resilience because they are able to resist changes in environmental factors.

Some ecosystems are dominated by one or two species and other species may be rare. This is the case in the natural pine forests in Florida and temperate forests in Canada, which are dominated by a few tree species.

The tropics are important centres for biodiversity. This may be because living conditions are not too extreme (no frost, snow or ice), there is light of high intensity all year round, and birds and mammals do not need to use energy keeping warm. For example, there are about 1500 species of bird in Central America, but only 300 in the Northwest Territories of Canada.

Genetic diversity

Genetic diversity is the diversity of alleles within the genes in the genome of a single species. All the individuals of a species have the same genes, but they do not all have the same alleles of those genes. Genetic diversity within a species can be assessed by finding out what proportion of genes have different alleles and how many alleles there are of each gene.

> **KEY WORD**
>
> **genetic diversity:** all the alleles of all the genes in the genome of a species

The genetic diversity that exists between varieties of cultivated plants and domesticated animals is obvious because we can see the differences (e.g. between types of garden rose or breeds of dog). Similar genetic diversity, although not always so obvious, exists in natural populations (Figure 18.20). The genetic differences between populations of the same species exist because populations may be adapted slightly differently in different parts of their range. There is also genetic diversity within each population. This diversity is important in providing populations with the ability to adapt to changes in biotic and abiotic factors. Such factors include competition with other species, evading new predators, resisting new strains of disease and changes in temperature, salinity, humidity and rainfall.

Question

7   a   The snails in Figure 18.20 look very different from one another. Explain why they are all members of the same species.

   b   One measure of the genetic diversity in a population is the frequency of different alleles and the proportion of heterozygous individuals. Suggest how you would investigate these in a population of the snails shown in Figure 18.20.

   c   Suggest and explain the effect of the following on genetic diversity: artificial selection (selective breeding), habitat destruction and the release of farmed fish into the wild.

Figure 18.20: Phenotypic variation in shells of the land snail *Cepaea nemoralis*. The differences between them are the result of different alleles for the genes that control shell colour and number of bands on the shells.

Assessing species diversity

Collecting organisms and making species lists

Imagine you are in an ecosystem like that in Figure 18.21. The most obvious species are the large plants and maybe some of the larger animals, particularly bird species. The first task when assessing species diversity is to identify and catalogue the types of organism present and build a species list.

Biologists use identification keys to name the organisms that they find. There are different forms of key: some have drawings or photographs with identifications; others ask a series of questions. The most common of these is a dichotomous key. In your own fieldwork, you may use one of these to identify some plant species. Identification requires good skills of observation.

At first, it is a good idea to do a timed search throughout the area you are studying to see how many species you can collect and then identify. If you cannot identify particular species, take photographs of them and name them as species **A**, species **B**, and so on. Some animals will be hard to find and collect, especially small ones such as tiny beetles. A pooter is a simple piece of apparatus that is used to collect these animals (Figure 18.22). Breathing air into the mouth sucks up small animals into a plastic container. They can be removed and studied and identified using a hand lens, and then returned to their habitat.

It is rare to try to catalogue everything. In an area of grassland or woodland, you might choose to concentrate on just one or two groups, such as flowering plants and insects. On a rocky shore, a study may involve the most obvious organisms such as seaweeds and molluscs (see Worked Example 3).

Figure 18.21: How would you start to investigate and catalogue the biodiversity of an area like this?

Figure 18.22: This ecologist is using a pooter to collect small animals from high in the tree canopy in a Yungas forest, along the eastern slopes of the Andes in Argentina.

There are now two questions to ask:

* How are the different species spread throughout the ecosystem?

* How many individuals of each species are there?

The answers to these questions describe *distribution* and *abundance*.

Question

8 Some students surveyed the species diversity of an area of woodland and some grassland nearby. The students used a 20-minute timed search.

    a Explain why they used the same technique for the two areas.

    b The students found 56 species in the woodland and 12 in the grassland. What other data could they have collected to compare the biodiversity of the two ecosystems?

Sampling

How would you find out which species are present in an ecosystem and the population size of each of them? Ideally, you would find, identify and count every organism that lives there. This is sometimes possible if the area is very small or the species are very large. But usually you take samples from the area you are interested in, and use them to make an estimate of the total numbers in the area.

Sampling can be **random sampling** or **systematic sampling**. If an area looks reasonably uniform or if there is no clear pattern to the way species are distributed, it is best to use random sampling.

KEY WORDS

random sampling: method of investigating the abundance and/or distribution of populations which is determined by chance and shows no bias on the part of the person carrying out the sampling

systematic sampling: a non-random method of investigating the abundance and/or distribution of populations in which the position of sampling points are determined by the person carrying out the sampling (e.g. at every 2 m along a transect)

quadrat: a square frame which is used to mark out an area for sampling populations of organisms

---

Random sampling using quadrats

A **quadrat** is a square frame that marks off an area of ground or water where you can identify the different species present and take a measurement of their abundance. You need to decide on a suitable size for the quadrat and how many samples you will take.

Samples must be taken randomly to avoid any bias. For example, you might choose to take all of your samples from the place with fewest species simply because it is the easiest to do. This would not be representative of the whole area. The usual way to ensure that a sample is random is to mark out an area with measuring tapes and use a random number generator, such as an app on a mobile phone. The random numbers give you the coordinates of the sampling points in relation to the two tapes you have used to mark out the area (Figure 18.23).

Figure 18.23: In random sampling, quadrats are positioned randomly in an area marked off by measuring tapes. This reduces the chances of bias in sampling the ecosystem.

You can use your results in two different ways: to calculate species frequency and species density. Species frequency is a measure of the chance of a particular species being found within any one quadrat. You simply record whether the species was present in each quadrat that you analyse. For example, if you placed your quadrat 50 times and found daisy plants in 22 of your samples, then the species frequency for daisies is:

$$\frac{22}{50} \times 100 = 44\%$$

Species density is a measure of how many individuals there are per unit area – for example, per square metre. The number of individuals that you have counted is divided by the total area of all your quadrats.

It is not always possible to count individual plants and animals because of the way that they grow. For example, many animals and plants grow over surfaces forming a covering and it is almost impossible to count individuals. How do you decide how many grass plants there are in a quadrat that you have placed on a lawn? In this case, you can estimate the percentage cover of the species within your quadrat (Figure 18.24). To help with this, you can use a 100 cm × 100 cm quadrat with wires running across it at 10 cm intervals in each direction, dividing the quadrat into 100 smaller squares. You then decide approximately what percentage of the area inside the quadrat is occupied by each species. These percentages may not add up to 100%. For example, there might be

bare ground in the quadrat, so the numbers will come to less than 100%. Or there may be plants overlying one another, in which case the numbers may add up to more than 100%. An alternative to estimating percentage cover of each species is to use an abundance scale, such as

the Braun–Blanquet scale for number and plant cover (Table 18.4).

Braun–Blanquet Cover Scale	
Description	Value
Very few plants, cover is less than 1%	+
Many plants, but cover is 1–5%	1
Very many plants or cover is 6–25%	2
Any number of plants; cover is 26–50%	3
Any number of plants; cover is 51–75%	4
Cover is greater than 75%	5

Table 18.4: The Braun–Blanquet scale for recording vegetation within quadrats.

Questions

9   A survey gave the results shown in Table 18.5 for a species of the red sea anemone, *Isactinia tenebrosa* (Figure 18.25), on a rocky shore in New Zealand, using a quadrat with an area of 0.25 m².

   a   Calculate **i** the species frequency, and **ii** the species density of *I. tenebrosa* from the results of this survey.

   b   Suggest when it might be more appropriate to use species frequency rather than species density to record the abundance of a species.

Figure 18.24: Estimating percentage cover. This 1 m² quadrat is divided into 100 small squares to make it easier to make the estimation for each species.

Figure 18.25: A red sea anemone that lives between the tides on rocky shores.

Quadrat	1	2	3	4	5	6	7	8	9	10
Number of red sea anemones	0	3	0	1	0	0	5	2	0	1

Table 18.5: Survey results of *Isactinia tenebrosa* using a quadrat with an area of 0.25 m².

Quadrat	1	2	3	4	5	6	7	8	9	10
Number of dayflowers on lawn	0	0	4	3	0	1	2	4	0	3
Number of dayflowers in field	0	0	0	2	5	0	0	1	0	0

Table 18.6: Survey results of *Commelina benghalensis* using ten 1.0 m² quadrats.

10 A survey was made of the Benghal dayflower, *Commelina benghalensis*, growing on a lawn and in a field of young soybean plants. Ten 1.0 m² quadrats were placed randomly in each area, and the number of dayflower plants in each quadrat was counted. The results are shown in Table 18.6.

a Calculate **i** the species frequency, and **ii** the species density of dayflower plants in each of the two areas.

b Explain why it was important to use randomly placed quadrats for this survey.

c Suggest two disadvantages with calculating percentage cover or using an abundance scale, such as the Braun–Blanquet scale.

Estimating abundance of mobile animals

Quadrats are obviously no use for finding or counting mobile animals, so different methods have to be used for these.

A good method of estimating the population size of mobile organisms is to use the Lincoln Index that is based on the **mark–release–recapture** technique. First, as many individuals as possible are caught. Each individual is marked, in a way that will not affect its future chance of survival. The marked individuals are counted, returned to their habitat and left to mix randomly with the rest of the population.

When enough time has elapsed for the mixing to take place, another large sample is captured. The numbers of marked and unmarked individuals are counted. The proportion of marked to unmarked individuals is then used to calculate an estimate of the total number in the population (Worked Example 1). For example, if you find that one-tenth of the second sample was marked, then you presume that you originally caught one-tenth of the population in your first sample. Your best estimate is therefore that the number in the population is ten times the number you caught and marked in your first sample.

The formula for calculating the estimated number in a population is:

$$N \text{ (population size)} = \frac{n_1 \times n_2}{m_2}$$

N = population estimate

n_1 = number of marked individuals released

n_2 = number of individuals (both marked and unmarked) captured

m_2 = number of marked individuals recaptured

KEY WORD

mark–release–recapture: a method of estimating the numbers of individuals in a population of mobile animals

Simpson's index of diversity

When you have collected information about the abundance of the species in the area you are studying, you can use your results to calculate a value for the species diversity in that area. You can do this using **Simpson's index of diversity** (*D*). The formula for this is:

$$D = 1 - \left(\sum \left(\frac{n}{N} \right)^2 \right)$$

where *n* is the total number of organisms of a particular species, and *N is* the total number of organisms of all species (see Worked Example 2).

Values of *D* range from 0 to 1. A value near 0 represents a very low species diversity. A value near 1 represents a very high species diversity.

KEY WORD

Simpson's index of diversity (*D*): used to calculate the biodiversity of a habitat; the range of values is 0 (low biodiversity) to 1 (high biodiversity)

WORKED EXAMPLES

The mark–release–recapture technique

1   Brown planthoppers are a serious insect pest of rice. Some students used sweep nets to catch a large sample of planthoppers in a field of rice. Each animal was marked with a very small spot of non-toxic waterproof paint and then they were released across the field. The next day, a second large sample was caught.

Number caught and marked in first sample   = 247

Number caught in second sample   = 259

Number in the second sample that had been marked   = 16

So the estimated number in the population $= \dfrac{247 \times 259}{16}$

= 399

Simpson's index of diversity

2   A sample was made of the animals living on two rocky shores. Ten quadrats were placed on each shore, and the number of animals of each species in each quadrat was counted. The results are shown in Table 18.7.

Species	Number of individuals, *n*	
	Shore A	Shore B
painted topshells	24	51
limpets	367	125
dogwhelks	192	63
snakelocks anemones	14	0
beadlet anemones	83	22
barnacles	112	391
mussels	207	116
periwinkles	108	93
total number of individuals, *N*	1107	861

Table 18.7: Sample of animals living on two rocky shores.

CONTINUED

To determine Simpson's index for shore **A**, calculate $\frac{n}{N}$ for each species, square each value, add them up and subtract from 1 (as shown in Table 18.8). Repeat the procedure for shore **B**. The working is rounded to three decimal places in columns 3 and 4.

Species	Shore A		
	n	$\frac{n}{N}$	$\left(\frac{n}{N}\right)^2$
painted topshells	24	0.022	0.000
limpets	367	0.332	0.110
dogwhelks	192	0.173	0.030
snakelocks anemones	14	0.013	0.000
beadlet anemones	83	0.075	0.006
barnacles	112	0.101	0.010
mussels	207	0.187	0.035
periwinkles	108	0.098	0.010
total number of individuals, N	1107		$\Sigma\left(\frac{n}{N}\right)^2 = 0.201$

Table 18.8: Calculating Simpson's index for shore **A**.

For shore **A**, Simpson's index of diversity $(D) = 1 - 0.201 = 0.799$

Question

11 Look at the figures in Table 18.7 and the working in Table 18.8 in Worked Example 2.

   a   Calculate D for shore **B**. Show all your working as in Table 18.8. The easiest way to do this is to use a spreadsheet. Once you have set up a spreadsheet, you can use it for calculating this index of diversity for data from other ecosystems.

   b   Compare the diversity of the two shores.

One advantage of using Simpson's index of diversity is that you do not need to identify all, or even any, of the organisms present to the level of species. You can, for example, just decide to call the species of anemone that has short tentacles 'anemone **A**', and the species that has a few long tentacles 'anemone **B**'. So long as you can recognise that they are different species, you do not need to find their scientific names. But beware: some species have many phenotypic forms (Figure 18.20).

The higher the number you get for D, the greater the diversity. You can probably see that the diversity depends on the number of different species there are and the abundance of each of those species. A community with ten species where one species is present in large numbers and nine are very rare is less diverse than a community with ten species where several species have a similar abundance. Comparisons using this diversity index should be between similar communities and organisms. For example, this index should not be used to compare the diversity of fish in a lake with the diversity of moths in a forest.

Systematic sampling

Random sampling is not suitable for every place that you may wish to survey. You might want to investigate how species are distributed in an area where the physical conditions change. Such conditions are: altitude, soil moisture content, soil type, soil pH, exposure or light intensity. For example, suppose you want to investigate the change at the edge of a field where it becomes very marshy. In this case, you should select at random a starting point in the field and lay out a measuring tape in a straight line to the marshy area. You then sample the organisms that are present along the line, which is called a **transect**. The simplest way to do this is to record the identity of the organisms that touch the line at set distances – for example, every two metres (Figure 18.26). This line transect will give you qualitative data that can be presented as a drawing (Figure 18.27a). You can also use the belt transect technique by placing a quadrat at regular intervals along the line and recording the abundance of each species within the quadrat (Figure 18.27b). Data from a belt transect can be plotted as a set of bar charts or as a kite diagram (Worked Example 3).

KEY WORD

transect: a line marked by a tape measure along which samples are taken, either by noting the species at equal distances (line transect) or placing quadrats at regular intervals (belt transect)

Figure 18.26: Using a line transect to record changes in distribution of plants with increasing altitude in the Sierra de Gredos in Spain.

a Line transect – a line across one or more habitats

The organisms found at regular points along a line are noted. Transects are used to detect changes in community composition along a line across one or more habitats.

b Interrupted belt transect

The abundance of organisms within quadrats placed at regular points along a line is noted.

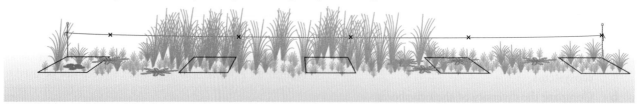

Figure 18.27: Systematic sampling using transects: **a** a line transect; **b** an interrupted belt transect.

Drawing kite diagrams to display data on species abundance

3   Some students used an interrupted belt transect to investigate the distribution and abundance of seaweeds and molluscs on a rocky shore placing a quadrat every 20m. The students began sampling at 20m below mean sea level, when the tide was out, and worked their way up the shore (Figure 18.28). They used two different scales for assessing the abundance of seaweeds and molluscs. On these scales, 5 indicates the highest level of abundance and 1 the lowest. If a species is not present in a quadrat, it is obviously recorded as 0. Table 18.9 shows the data collected from an interrupted belt transect on a rocky shore. The data are presented in the kite diagram in Figure 18.29.

Figure 18.28: A quadrat placed over part of a rocky shore covered in green and brown seaweeds. Some molluscs are visible at the bottom of the photograph.

Distance on the shore / m	Seaweeds (algae)				Molluscs				
	Kelp	Serrated wrack	Bladder wrack	Spiral wrack	Dog whelk	Edible periwinkle	Limpet	Flat periwinkle	Rough periwinkle
200	0	0	0	0	0	0	0	0	0
180	0	0	0	0	0	0	0	0	5
160	0	0	0	0	0	0	0	0	5
140	0	0	5	5	0	0	0	0	0
120	0	0	1	4	0	0	0	0	0
100	0	5	5	0	0	0	0	0	0
80	0	5	5	0	0	0	5	4	5
60	0	5	5	0	0	1	4	0	4
40	0	5	5	0	0	4	4	0	0
20	0	4	5	0	1	4	5	0	0
0	3	5	0	0	0	0	0	0	0

Table 18.9: Data collected from an interrupted belt transect on a rocky shore.

CONTINUED

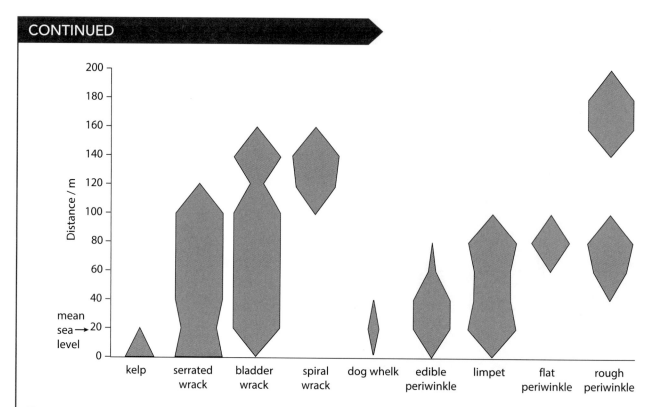

Figure 18.29: A kite diagram shows the data from a belt transect. The distribution of seaweeds and molluscs from low tide to the top of the rocky shore is shown by the lengths of the 'kites' and the abundance by their widths. This gives a representation of the ecosystem in a way that is easy to see.

Question

12 In a survey of trees in a dry tropical forest, some students identified five tree species (**A** to **E**). They counted the numbers of trees in an area $100\,\text{m} \times 100\,\text{m}$. Their results are as follows:

A 56   **B** 48   **C** 12   **D** 6   **E** 3

a Calculate the Simpson's index of diversity for the trees within the area sampled.

b Explain the advantage of using Simpson's index of diversity rather than a species list as a way to represent the biodiversity of an area.

c The Simpson's index of diversity for the vegetation in an area of open grassland was 0.8; for a similar sized area of vegetation beneath some conifer trees it was 0.2. What do you conclude from these results?

d Looking at Table 18.9 and Figure 18.29, write a set of instructions for making a kite diagram.

Correlation

While doing random sampling or carrying out a belt transect, you may observe that two plant species always seem to occur together. Is there an association between them? Or you might want to know if there is any relationship between the distribution and abundance of a species and an abiotic factor, such as exposure to light, temperature, soil water content or salinity (saltiness). To decide if there is an association, you can plot scatter graphs and make a judgement by eye (Figure 18.30).

The strongest correlation you can have is when all the points lie on a straight line: there is a perfect linear correlation. This has a correlation coefficient of 1. If as variable **A** increases so does variable **B**, the relationship is a positive linear correlation (Figure 18.30a). If as variable **A** increases, variable **B** decreases, then the relationship is a negative linear correlation (Figure 18.30c). A correlation coefficient of 0 means there is no correlation at all (Figure 18.30b).

You can calculate a correlation coefficient (*r*) to determine whether there is indeed a linear relationship and also to find out the strength of that relationship. The strength means how close the points are to the straight line.

Pearson's linear correlation coefficient can only be used where you can see that there might be a linear correlation (a and c in Figure 18.30) and when you have collected quantitative data as measurements (e.g. length, height, depth, light intensity, mass) or counts (e.g. number of plant species in quadrats). The data must be distributed normally, or you must be fairly sure that this is the case.

Sometimes you may not have collected quantitative data but used an abundance scale (Table 18.4) or you may not be sure if your quantitative data is normally distributed. It might also be possible that a graph of your results shows that the data is correlated but not in a linear fashion. If so, you can calculate **Spearman's rank correlation** coefficient, which involves ranking the data recorded for each variable and assessing the difference between the ranks.

KEY WORDS

Pearson's linear correlation: a statistical test used to determine if there is a linear correlation between two variables that are normally distributed

Spearman's rank correlation: a statistical test to determine if there is a correlation between two variables when one or both of them are not normally distributed

---

You should always remember that correlation does not mean that changes in one variable *cause* changes in the other variable. These correlation coefficients are used to test relationships that you have recorded to see if the variables are correlated and, if so, to find the strength of that correlation.

Before going any further, you should read Section P2.8, Analysis, conclusions and evaluation, in Chapter P2, which shows you how to calculate and interpret these correlation coefficients.

Spearman's rank correlation

An ecologist was studying the composition of vegetation on moorland following a reclamation scheme. He observed that common heather, *Calluna vulgaris*, and bilberry, *Vaccinium myrtillus*, appeared to be growing together. He assessed the abundance of these two species by recording the percentage cover in 11 quadrats as shown in Table 18.10.

Quadrat	Percentage cover	
	C. vulgaris	*V. myrtillus*
1	30	15
2	37	23
3	15	6
4	15	10
5	20	11
6	9	10
7	3	3
8	5	1
9	10	5
10	25	17
11	35	30

Table 18.10: Results from a study of the composition of vegetation on a moorland ecosystem.

To find out if there is a relationship between the percentage cover of these two species, the first task is to make a null hypothesis that there is no correlation between the percentage cover of the two species.

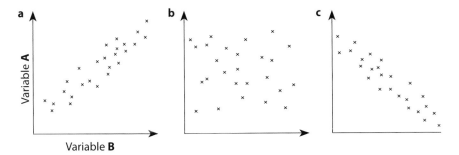

Variable **A**

Variable **B**

Figure 18.30: Three types of association: **a** a positive linear correlation; **b** no correlation; **c** a negative linear correlation.

The equation to calculate the Spearman's rank correlation coefficient, r_s, is:

$$r_s = 1 - \left(\frac{6 \times \sum D^2}{n^3 - n} \right)$$

where n is the number of pairs of items in the sample and D is the difference between each pair of ranked measurements and $\sum$ is the 'sum of'.

The next step is to draw a scatter graph to see if it looks as if there is a correlation between the abundance of the two species. This can be done very quickly using the graphing facility of a spreadsheet program. You can now follow the steps shown in Chapter P2, Section P2.8, Analysis, conclusions and evaluation, to calculate the value for r_s. Again, the quickest way to do this is to set up a spreadsheet that will do the calculations.

The ecologist calculated the value of r_s to be +0.930. A correlation coefficient of +0.930 is very close to +1, so we can conclude that there is a positive correlation between the two species and that the strength of the association is very high. The ecologist was able to reject the null hypothesis and accept the alternative hypothesis that there is a correlation between the abundance of *C. vulgaris* and *V. myrtillus* on this reclaimed moorland.

Question

13 a   Draw a scatter graph to show the data in Table 18.10.

b   Follow the example in Chapter P2 to calculate the Spearman's rank correlation coefficient (r_s) for the data in Table 18.10. Show all the steps in your calculation.

c   Explain why the ecologist was able to reject the null hypothesis.

d   State the conclusion that the ecologist could make from this investigation.

e   The ecologist thinks that the relationship is the result of habitat preference, that both species prefer drier soil. Describe an investigation that he could carry out to test this hypothesis.

Pearson's linear correlation

In many investigations, the data collected are for two continuous variables and the data within each variable show a normal distribution. When this is the case, Pearson's linear correlation coefficient can be used. This also calculates numbers between +1 and −1 and

the result is interpreted in the same way. The method of calculation looks more complex, but the test can be done easily with a spreadsheet.

The first step is to check whether the relationship between the two continuous variables appears to be linear by drawing a scatter graph. The variables can be plotted on either axis, it makes no difference. The correlation coefficient should not be calculated if the relationship is not linear. The nearer the scatter of points is to a straight line, the higher the strength of association between the variables. Before using this test you must also be satisfied that the data for the variables you are investigating show a normal distribution.

As trees grow older, they tend to get cracks in their bark. A student measured the width of cracks on many pine trees in a plantation and found that they varied considerably. The data she collected showed a normal distribution. She noticed that the larger, and presumably older, trees tended to have wider cracks in their bark than the smaller trees. She wanted to see if there was a correlation between the size of the trees and the size of these cracks. She chose to measure the circumference of each tree as a measure of their overall size. She measured the width of the cracks in the bark. This means that she collected continuous data for each of the two variables – tree circumference and crack width. She investigated this by selecting twelve trees at random and measuring the circumference of each trunk and the widths of three cracks on the bark at head height. Her results are in Table 18.11.

Number of tree	Circumference of tree / metres	Mean width of crack / mm
1	1.77	50
2	1.65	28
3	1.81	60
4	0.89	24
5	1.97	95
6	2.15	51
7	0.18	2
8	0.46	15
9	2.11	69
10	2.00	64
11	2.42	74
12	1.89	69

Table 18.11: Widths of cracks on pine trees in a plantation.

The student plotted these results on a scatter graph and found that they look as if there might be a linear correlation between them. She then used the following formula to calculate Pearson's correlation coefficient, r.

$$r = \frac{\sum xy - n\bar{x}\bar{y}}{(n-1)s_x s_y}$$

The student calculated the correlation coefficient as $r = 0.79$.

Question

14 a Draw a scatter graph of the data in Table 18.11.

   b Use the worked example in Chapter P2 to help you calculate the Pearson's linear correlation coefficient (r) for the data.

   c Explain why the student was able to reject the null hypothesis.

   d State the conclusion that the student could make from this investigation.

18.3 Maintaining biodiversity

Extinctions

Many species are all under threat of extinction – of disappearing forever from the Earth. Millions of species have become extinct in the past, sometimes huge numbers at one time in so-called mass extinctions. However, these events were all natural, and at least some are thought to have been caused by sudden changes in the environment, such as a large asteroid colliding with the Earth, which may have led to the extinction of the dinosaurs 65 million years ago.

The Earth is currently facing the likelihood of another mass extinction, this time caused by humans. The main reason for this is the loss of habitats (Figure 18.31). Many species are adapted for survival in a particular habitat with a particular range of environmental conditions. Humans are destroying habitats by draining wetlands, cutting down rainforests, and polluting the air, water and soil. Another reason for a species to become extinct is if we kill too many of

them, perhaps for sport or for food. Climate change is also predicted to cause extinctions, as mean global temperature increase. For example, increases in sea level, in ocean temperatures and in ocean acidity – all the result of increased carbon dioxide concentration in the atmosphere – are causing damage to coral reefs in many parts of the world. These are areas of very high biodiversity, and it is likely that some species of corals, invertebrates and fish that live on these reefs will eventually become extinct.

Figure 18.31: Orangutans live only in dense tropical forest in Borneo. Deforestation is threatening their survival.

Another reason for extinction is the introduction of a new species to a habitat. In New Zealand, for example, the arrival of Europeans in the 17th and 18th centuries brought predators such as cats and rats to an ecosystem in which there were no ground-dwelling predators. Fifty-three species of flightless birds that had evolved on these islands have since become extinct as a result of predation by introduced animals.

Competition can also cause extinctions. Interspecific competition occurs when two species both require a resource that is in short supply. For example, fossils show that a large number of different species of dog lived in North America around 30 million years ago. Today, there are only nine species of dog in North America (Figure 18.32). Several possible reasons have been suggested for the extinction of so many dog species, one of which is the spread of several cat species from Asia into North America. Both cats and dogs are carnivores, and it seems as though many cat species

Figure 18.32: a The coyote, *Canis latrans*, is one of the few species of dog now living in North America. **b** At least part of the reason for extinction of many dog species in North America over the past few million years is competition with cat species that arrived from Asia. This is a North American bobcat, *Lynx rufus*.

were able to out-compete dogs for a limited amount of prey. And, of course, many species now find themselves in competition with our own species, *Homo sapiens*, for resources such as habitat, water or food supplies.

Reasons for maintaining biodiversity

Moral and ethical reasons

For many people, the loss of biodiversity is a simple moral or ethical issue: we share our planet with a huge range of other organisms and we have no right to drive them to extinction. Some people believe that humans have custody of the Earth and should therefore value and protect the organisms that share the planet with us.

Ecological reasons

There are ecological reasons why biodiversity matters. In general, the higher the diversity of an ecosystem, the less likely it is to be unbalanced by changes in conditions or threats such as pollution. The loss of a single species can have devastating effects on the rest of its community. The Pacific sea otter, *Enhydra lutris*, is a predator of sea urchins in kelp forests (Figures 18.33 and 18.34). In the 19th century, sea otters were hunted for their fur. The decrease in population numbers of sea otters meant numbers of sea urchins increased rapidly. The sea urchins ate their way through the stipes ('stems') of the kelp forests, causing a change to the whole of the food web as organisms that depended on the kelp declined. The loss of one species, the sea otter, led to catastrophic loss of many others. Organisms like the sea otter that play a central role in an ecosystem are known as keystone species. Sea otters are now protected and their numbers increased in the latter half of the 20th century. However, they are now preyed on by killer whales because overfishing may be reducing the whales' food sources.

Figure 18.33: A sea otter, *Enhydra lutris*.

The African bush elephant, *Loxodonta africana*, is a keystone species of the savannah grasslands of East and Southern Africa. Bush elephants are very destructive of vegetation as they push over and eat many tree species. This extreme form of grazing helps to maintain this ecosystem, which is renowned for its diversity of large mammals as well as many other species. Elephant dung provides a very rich habitat – almost an ecosystem in itself – for many organisms including fungi and dung beetles. Elephants were once hunted widely for their ivory and their populations decreased considerably. Now protected by international agreements, they are still at risk of poaching to supply the illegal trade in ivory.

Figure 18.34: A kelp forest in the Pacific Ocean off the coast of California. The giant seaweeds provide habitats for many species including sea urchins, fish and sea otters.

Economic reasons

Ecosystems are of direct value to humans. Many of the drugs that we use originate from living organisms. Antibiotics are isolated from fungi and bacteria. Anti-cancer drugs have been isolated from plants such as the Madagascan periwinkle, *Catharanthus roseus*, and the Pacific yew tree, *Taxus brevifolia*, which is the source of the drug paclitaxel (Taxol®). The natural habitat of the Madagascan periwinkle has been almost lost, largely because of slash-and-burn agriculture. Fortunately, the plant is able to survive in artificial habitats, such as along roadsides, and is now cultivated in many countries. The Himalayan yew, which is also a source of paclitaxel, is threatened by over-harvesting for medicinal use and collection for fuel.

There is currently much interest in cataloguing plants used in traditional Chinese and Indian medicines to see if they can provide drugs that can be mass-produced. There are doubtless many more that we do not know about. If we allow tropical forests with their great biodiversity to disappear, then we are undoubtedly losing species that could be beneficial to us.

Wildlife is a source of income for many countries as ecotourism has increased in popularity. Countries such as Belize, Malaysia, the Maldives and Costa Rica encourage tourists to visit their National Parks. This form of tourism provides employment and contributes to the economies of these nations.

Few give any thought to the contribution of microorganisms, which are the source of many useful products, not least antibiotics. The heat-stable enzyme *Taq* polymerase was discovered in a thermophilic bacterium, *Thermus aquaticus*, from a hot spring in Yellowstone National Park in the USA. This enzyme is mass-produced by genetically modified bacteria for use in the polymerase chain reaction which is used by forensic and other scientists to increase quantities of DNA for analysis. (Chapter 19, Section 19.4, Separating and amplifying DNA.) There are likely to be many other such compounds, especially enzymes, in archaeans that live in extreme conditions not unlike those in some industrial processes.

Aesthetic reasons

Aesthetics is concerned with our appreciation of beauty. There is an aesthetic argument for maintaining biodiversity. Many people gain pleasure from studying or just appreciating the natural world, which continues to provide much inspiration for artists, photographers, poets, writers and other creative people.

Agricultural reasons

Our crop plants do not have as much genetic diversity as their wild relatives This is because diversity has been lost by selective breeding for uniform, high-yielding crops. The wild relatives of maize grow in the states of Oaxaca and Puebla in Mexico. These plants can provide the genetic resources we will need to widen the genetic diversity of cultivated maize if it is affected by disease or by other catastrophes. Many of these wild relatives are threatened by climate change, habitat destruction and perhaps the spread of genetically modified crops.

A species of rice, *Oryza longistaminata*, which grows wild in Mali in North Africa, is not suitable for cultivation as a crop plant because of its low yield and poor taste. However, it is resistant to many different strains of the organism causing bacterial blight of rice. It has been successfully interbred with cultivated rice, *O. sativa*, to give varieties of rice with resistance to the disease.

Another plant example is the potato. There are about 150 species of potato growing in the Andes. Outside that region, the world's crop comes from a single species, *Solanum tuberosum*. This means that the crop is vulnerable to diseases, such as potato blight. The International Potato Center (CIP) in Peru has used the Andean species as a source of alleles for resistance. These alleles have been introduced into the crop species both by interbreeding and by genetic technology (Chapter 19). Obviously, it is important to conserve all the Andean potato species.

Environmental reasons

Ecosystems provide environmental services for us. Forests and peat bogs absorb carbon dioxide and may help to reduce the effect of increases in carbon dioxide in the atmosphere.

Organic waste material added to waters, such as lakes and rivers, is broken down by microorganisms. The transpiration of plants contributes to the water cycle providing us with drinking and irrigation water. Termites and ants along with many species of fungi and bacteria recycle elements, such as carbon, nitrogen, sulfur and phosphorus. Without this recycling, the supply of nitrates, sulfates and phosphates for plants would become limiting. Plant growth would slow and there would be less food available for organisms in other trophic levels.

Question

15　a　List some of the threats to ecosystems.

　　b　State **five** reasons why it is important to maintain biodiversity.

18.4 Protecting endangered species

An endangered species is one that is threatened with extinction. There are a variety of ways to protect endangered species.

The best way to conserve any species is to keep it in its natural habitat. Maintaining the natural habitat means that all the 'life support systems' are provided. Members of the public tend to think about conservation in terms of high-profile programmes centred on mammals, such as giant pandas and whales. The protection of whole ecosystems threatened by development is equally important. The most popular of these is the tropical rainforest. However, there are many other, less well-known ecosystems that should be conserved (e.g. karst limestone) because they are very vulnerable to pollution.

National parks

Most countries now set aside areas where wildlife and the environment have some form of protection, and where the activities of humans are limited. For example, conservation areas may be set up where there are strict limits on building, grazing farm animals, hunting or other activities that might adversely affect animals and plants that live there.

National parks are areas of land that are controlled by the government of a country and protected by legislation. Agriculture, building, mining and other industrial activities are strictly controlled. In some countries, such as Kenya, national parks act as conservation areas where populations of wild animals are maintained (Figure 18.35).

The world's first national park, Yellowstone National Park in the USA, was set up in 1872. It is the last remaining nearly intact ecosystem of the northern temperate climatic zone and serves as both a recreational and a conservation area. Three of the animal species that can be found there are listed in the USA as threatened (bald eagle, grizzly bear and lynx) and two as endangered (whooping crane and grey wolf).

Much of the Galapagos Islands, which belong to Ecuador, is a national park. Since its establishment over 50 years ago, the park authorities have done much active conservation. They have restricted access to the uninhabited islands and limited access to other areas which are sensitive to human interference. A marine reserve of $133\,000\,km^2$ has been

Figure 18.35: Elephants in the Amboseli National Park, Kenya. Elephants throughout Africa are exposed to numerous threats, not least poaching. Biodiversity suffers if their numbers increase or decrease. There is a delicate balance to achieve and this needs careful management by park authorities.

set up to protect the environment from the destructive activities of fishing. The reserve is cared for by local people as well as by conservation organisations. Alien animal species, such as rats and goats, are being removed, and invasive plants, such as elephant grass, are dug up and destroyed. There are captive breeding and reintroduction programmes, notably for giant tortoises, coordinated by the Charles Darwin Research Station.

There are restrictions on human activities in national parks. Tourism brings in money to pay for the maintenance of the parks, and also helps to inform people about how conservation takes place. This raises awareness of important issues and can elicit support from the public. This works best if local people are involved in some way, so they feel that the park is 'theirs' and can obtain benefits from it. This may involve allowing them to use some areas of the park for herding their animals or growing crops, employing them as wardens or rangers, or using some of the money raised from tourism to improve local health or education facilities.

Marine parks, such as that in the Galapagos Islands, have been set up in many places to conserve fragile ecosystems and areas at risk of overfishing, dredging and pollution. The marine reserve off the coast of Little Cayman in the Caribbean is a 'no-take' reserve that protects one of the last spawning grounds of an endangered fish, the Nassau grouper, *Epinephelus striatus*. The establishment of marine parks and reserves around the coast of New Zealand has increased biodiversity and also led to an increase in fish catches.

The standard of management of parks and reserves varies throughout the world. Some countries have the resources and the national will to provide excellent protection and careful management. Others do not.

Question

16   Explain the importance of management of national parks and other similar protected areas.

Zoos

Zoos have a variety of functions in addition to providing enjoyment and interest for visitors who can see and study animals that they would not otherwise be able to see.

Zoos provide protection for endangered and vulnerable species, and they have had success with captive breeding programmes, often with the long-term aim of reintroducing the animals to their natural habitat. For example, The Durrell Wildlife Conservation Trust at Jersey Zoo in the Channel Islands has been involved with the captive breeding of various species of tamarins from Brazil (Figure 18.36).

Figure 18.36: Golden lion tamarin, *Leontopithecus rosalia*, from the coastal forests of Brazil. As their habitat has been destroyed, they have been rescued, bred in captivity and reintroduced to protected reserves.

A problem with breeding animals from small populations is inbreeding. The cheetah, *Acinonyx jubatus*, is a species classified by the IUCN as vulnerable. Genetic diversity among cheetahs is very low because they nearly became extinct 10 000 years ago and only a few survived. Maintaining the genetic diversity is an aim in the conservation of many species, including the cheetah. In the wild, female cheetahs tend to mate with many different males, which helps to increase genetic diversity in the population.

Zoos also have an important role in research, especially in trying to gain a better understanding of breeding habits, habitat requirements and ways to increase genetic diversity. The Zoological Society of London (ZSL), like many large zoos, has an important programme of research.

The major goal of captive breeding is to reintroduce animals to their natural habitat. This can prove extremely difficult as there are many factors that affect the success of these schemes. The scimitar-horned oryx, *Oryx dammah*, was hunted for its meat and skin and was driven almost to extinction in its habitat, the semi-deserts in northern Africa (Figure 18.37). During the 1960s and 1970s, it was recognised that the oryx would become extinct if nothing was done. A few oryx were caught and transported to zoos in several places around the world. A captive breeding programme was successful and breeding herds of these animals have been established in reserves in North Africa.

Figure 18.37: A conservation success story: the scimitar-horned oryx, *Oryx dammah*, saved from extinction and bred in captivity, is now protected in reserves in Senegal, Tunisia and Morocco.

However, not every conservation attempt has been a success story. Some animals simply refuse to breed in captivity. Often, it is not possible to create suitable habitats for them, so they cannot be returned to the wild. Sometimes, even if a habitat exists, it is very difficult for the animals to adapt to living in it after being cared for in a zoo. The giant panda is a good example. In 2011 there were more than 300 pandas in zoos and research centres in their native China and others on loan to zoos around the world. A captive breeding programme was started in 1963, and since then about 300 pandas have been born in captivity, but so far no panda has successfully been returned to the wild. The first captive-bred panda to be

released was killed, aged five years, probably by other pandas. Female golden lion tamarins released into forest reserves in Brazil often die before breeding because they do not have the climbing and foraging skills that they need to survive. Some captive-bred animals do not know how to avoid predators, find food or rear their own young.

Assisted reproduction

Assisted reproduction is a solution to the problem of inbreeding. Zoos used to transport large mammals from one zoo to another as part of their captive breeding programmes. Movement of large mammals is difficult and expensive, and breeding did not always happen. A much cheaper option is to collect semen and keep it frozen in a sperm bank. Samples are collected from males, checked for sperm activity and then diluted with a medium containing a buffer solution and albumen. Small volumes of semen are put into thin tubes known as straws, which are stored in liquid nitrogen at − 196 °C.

Different methods of assisted reproduction solve the problem of males and females who do not show any courtship behaviour and will not mate. In **artificial insemination (AI)**, a straw is withdrawn from the sperm bank and placed into warm water so that sperm become active. The straw with active sperm is then put into a catheter, which is inserted into the vagina, through the cervix and into the uterus of a female. AI may happen when the female is naturally ready to mate, but it also may follow hormone treatment so she ovulates at the same time. Following AI, the resulting embryos may be 'flushed out' of the uterus and transferred to other females that have had hormonal treatment to prepare them for pregnancy. These females need not be of the same species – they could be a related but not endangered species. This process of **embryo transfer** protects the endangered

---

KEY WORDS

assisted reproduction: any technique that is involved in treating infertility or protecting a female mammal of an endangered species from the health risks of pregnancy

artificial insemination (AI): injection of semen collected from a male into the uterus

embryo transfer: embryos are removed from the uterus of a female mammal of an endangered species shortly after fertilisation and transferred to surrogate females to bring to full term

animal from the risks of pregnancy and means that she can be a source of many offspring. Females that receive embryos like this are **surrogate** mothers. This technique of embryo transfer has been used for many mammal species including wild ox and different species of African antelope.

In order to carry out *in vitro* **fertilisation (IVF)**, eggs (oocytes) are collected by inserting a needle into the female's ovaries and withdrawing some mature follicles. The oocytes are kept in a culture medium for a short time and then mixed with semen. The resulting zygotes divide to form embryos, which are cultured for several days and then placed into the mother or into several females of the same or different species.

Eggs and embryos can also be stored in much the same way as sperm. Eggs are more difficult to freeze as they are more likely to be damaged by the freezing or thawing processes. Eggs are large cells with lots of water which tends to form ice crystals that damage internal membranes. Eggs are fertilised *in vitro* and then frozen until such time as a surrogate mother becomes available. A 'frozen zoo', such as the one at the San Diego Zoo in the USA, holds genetic resources in the form of sperm, eggs, embryos and tissue samples from many endangered and vulnerable species until they might be needed. Frozen zoos can hold much more genetic diversity than a normal zoo and the material can be kept for very long periods of time.

Questions

17 a Suggest why some animals do not breed in captivity.

b Explain the following terms: artificial insemination, *in vitro* fertilisation, sperm bank, embryo transfer, surrogacy and 'frozen zoo'.

c Explain why it is important that zoos do not keep small, reproductively isolated populations of animals for breeding purposes.

18 Many people think that keeping animals in zoos should be banned. Outline the arguments for zoos.

Botanic gardens and seed banks

Botanic gardens play similar roles for endangered plants as zoos do for endangered animals. Seeds or cuttings are collected from species in the wild and then used to build up a population of plants from which some plants may be reintroduced to their natural habitats in the future.

It is also possible to take small samples of cells and grow them on agar in sterile conditions. The cells divide by mitosis to give a mass of cells that can be cloned by subdividing them. When the cells are transferred to a medium containing an appropriate mixture of plant hormones, they grow stems and roots and can then be transferred to grow in soil. These techniques of tissue culture and cloning are used to produce large numbers of plants from a few original specimens.

The roles of botanic gardens are to:

- protect endangered plant species; the world's botanic gardens already cultivate around one-third of the world's known plant species, many of which are increasingly threatened in the wild by environmental degradation and climate change

- research methods of reproduction and growth so that species cultivated in botanic gardens can be grown in appropriate conditions and be propagated

- research conservation methods so plants can be introduced to new habitats if their original habitat has been destroyed

- reintroduce species to habitats where they have become very rare or extinct

- educate the public in the many roles of plants in ecosystems and their economic value.

It often takes a long time to reintroduce a plant species and ensure its survival. This is especially true with slow-growing plants, such as Sargent's cherry palm, *Pseudophoenix sargentii*. Specimens of this species were grown at the Fairchild Tropical Botanical Gardens in Miami before being reintroduced to its natural habitat in the Florida Keys.

KEY WORDS

surrogacy: a female becomes pregnant with an embryo from another female and carries it to full term; embryos can be conceived naturally, by AI or by IVF

in vitro **fertilisation (IVF):** the fertilisation of an egg that occurs outside the body of a female (e.g. in a Petri dish)

frozen zoo: a facility where genetic materials taken from animals are stored at very low temperatures (−196 °C); sperm, eggs, embryos and tissue samples are examples of these genetic materials

Seed banks

As well as cultivating plants, botanic gardens may store seeds in a **seed bank**. The Royal Botanic Gardens at Kew, UK, runs a hugely ambitious project called the Millennium Seed Bank (MSB), which began in 2000 (Figures 18.38 and 18.39). The bank's ambition is to collect and store seeds from at least 25% of the world's plants by 2020. Thus, if the plants become extinct in the wild, there will be seeds from which they can be grown. If possible, seeds of the same species are collected from different sites, so that the stored samples contain a good proportion of the total gene pool for that species.

> **KEY WORD**
>
> **seed bank:** facility where seeds are dried and kept in cold storage to conserve plant biodiversity

Figure 18.39: A botanist with one of the seed collections in a cold vault at the MSB.

The Svalbard Global Seed Vault is a seed bank run by the government of Norway. The vault is at the end of a 120-metre tunnel cut into the rock of a mountain on the island of Spitsbergen, within the Arctic Circle. The vault is thought to have ideal storage conditions, and it is only opened in winter when the environmental temperature falls close to the operating temperature of –18 °C. Its first seed samples went into storage in January 2008, and by 2018 the vault held over 900 000 different seed samples of crop varieties from all over the world.

Many national and international organisations collect and store seeds so that the genetic diversity in our crop plants is not lost. Seeds from each of these samples are stored in the Svalbard Global Seed Vault. If seeds stored elsewhere are lost for any reason – from an environmental disaster to mismanagement to loss of funding or accidents or failure of equipment – then there will always be duplicate samples available from Svalbard. The depositing seed bank owns its seeds and no other organisation has access to them. Any research organisation wishing to use any of the seeds has to apply to the original seed bank. The storage of the seeds is free of charge, as the costs of the upkeep of the vault are covered by the Norwegian government and by the Global Crop Diversity Trust. This trust also helps developing countries to select and package seeds that can then be sent to Svalbard to be stored.

Figure 18.38: The Millennium Seed Bank, Wakehurst, UK. Seeds arriving at the seed bank are checked for pests and diseases, assessed for viability, dried, and then stored in airtight jars (Figure 18.37) and kept in the seed-storage vault at –20 °C.

Another important seed bank is that of the International Rice Institute in the Philippines, which holds all rice varieties.

Many plants produce seeds that remain viable for at least 15 years if they are carefully dehydrated until they contain about 5% water and are stored at around –15 to –20 °C. With this small water content, there is little danger that cells in the seed will be damaged by ice crystals during freezing and thawing.

The only way to find out whether or not stored seeds are still viable is to try to germinate them. Seed banks carry out germination tests at five-year intervals. When fewer than 85% of the seeds germinate successfully, plants are grown from these seeds so that fresh seed can be collected and stored.

When such plants are grown from samples of stored seed, there is the possibility of altering the genetic diversity that was originally stored. Small samples of seeds from rare plants present a particular problem. This is because even fewer seeds of the original are taken to test for viability or to grow into plants to increase the number of seeds in store. Such samples are unlikely to contain all the genetic diversity of the original sample. The only answer to this problem is to put as large and diverse a sample as possible into store in the first place.

Most seeds are easy to store, but some plants have seeds that cannot be dried and frozen. These are called 'recalcitrant seeds' and include seeds of economically important tropical species such as rubber, coconut palm, coffee and cocoa (Figure 18.40). The only ways to keep the genetic diversity of these species is to collect seeds and grow successive generations of plants or to keep them as tissue culture. Cocoa is banked as trees. The International Cocoa Genebank in Trinidad has about 12 000 trees – examples of all the cocoa varieties found in Latin America and the Caribbean. Selected material from the Trinidad collection is distributed to other cocoa-producing countries after it has been through quarantine at the University of Reading in the UK.

Figure 18.40: Cocoa, *Theobroma cacao*. The future of this crop is threatened by disease, climate change, natural disasters, limited genetic diversity and the failure to manage plantations by replacing old trees. Between 30% and 40% of the world's production is lost to pests and disease.

Questions

19 a Why is it important to keep seeds in seed banks?

   b Explain why it is not possible to keep the seeds of all species in seed banks, such as the Millennium Seed Bank and the Svalbard Seed Bank.

20 It has been suggested that seed banks put selection pressures on the seeds that are different from those that the plants would experience in the wild.

   a How might these selection pressures differ?

   b How might this affect the chances of success in returning the plants to the wild?

   c Suggest some particular problems that face gene banks for plants with recalcitrant seeds, such as cocoa and coconut.

18.5 Controlling alien species

Alien species (invasive species) are those that have moved from one ecosystem to another where they were previously unknown. People have been responsible for the movement of species about the globe by trading animals and plants or unwittingly carrying them on ships. Some species have been introduced as biological control agents to control pests. The small Indian mongoose, *Herpestes auropunctatus*, was introduced to Jamaica in 1872 and proved so successful at controlling rats in the cane fields that it was introduced elsewhere. Unfortunately, it then became a predator of other animals.

> ## KEY WORD
>
> **alien species:** a species that has moved into a new ecosystem where it was previously unknown; also known as invasive species

Perhaps the most notorious introduction is the cane toad, introduced to Queensland, Australia, from Hawaii in 1935 to control an insect pest of sugar cane. In Australia, the cane toad has become a pest as it breeds rapidly and has spread across the eastern, northern and western parts of the country. The cane toad has few predators in Australia, mainly because it produces a powerful toxin that kills most animals that eat it. The species known to be most at risk from invasion by cane toads is the northern quoll, *Dasyurus hallucatus*, which tries to eat the toads. Numbers of this endangered marsupial carnivore decrease steeply after cane toads invade its habitat. Cane toads probably compete with some other amphibian species for food and are known to eat the chicks of a ground-nesting bird, the rainbow bee-eater, *Merops ornatus*.

The red lionfish, *Pterois volitans*, is native to the seas of South East Asia. No one knows how it came to invade the waters of the Caribbean, but it seems likely to have escaped from aquaria in the United States. It has spread throughout the Caribbean, eating its way through many local species on coral reefs. Again, there is no natural predator of the animal in its new environment. In Belize, divers are encouraged to spear them to reduce their populations. The Jamaican government believes that, if it encourages people to develop a taste for them,

fishermen will catch more of them and their population will soon decrease (Figure 18.41).

Figure 18.41: The red lionfish, *Pterois volitans*, is an alien species that escaped into the Caribbean and is causing havoc on coral reefs as it eats many reef animals and has no natural predator.

Invasive species have a variety of effects on their new environments. As well as being successful predators with few controls, they may compete effectively with native organisms that occupy the same niche, pushing them to extinction. They may also introduce diseases that spread to similar organisms that have never been exposed to the pathogens. Some invasive plants grow so successfully that they cover huge areas of land or water. The water hyacinth, *Eichhornia crassipes*, is a floating aquatic plant that spreads rapidly when introduced to new habitats. It blocks sunlight from reaching native aquatic plants and reduces the oxygen concentration of the water, so killing fish. Water hyacinth also provides a habitat for mosquito larvae so its control is important for the sake of human health too. Japanese knotweed, *Fallopia japonica*, has a very vigorous root system and its growth is so strong that it can damage buildings, roads and walls. It also outcompetes native species simply by reducing the space where they can grow.

Question

21 a Explain the damage that alien species may have on an ecosystem.

   b Suggest how you might investigate the effect of an alien plant species on the biodiversity of an ecosystem.

18.6 International conservation organisations

CITES

In 1973, 145 countries signed an agreement to control the trade in endangered species and any products from them, such as furs, skins and ivory. More countries have joined since. This agreement is called the Convention on International Trade in Endangered Species of Wild Flora and Fauna (CITES).

CITES considers the evidence presented to it about endangered and vulnerable species and assigns them to one of three Appendices (Table 18.12). The species listed in the CITES appendices are reviewed by expert committees and the list is growing. However, there is concern that a CITES listing does not always benefit a species (Figure 18.42). If trade in a species or its products becomes illegal, then the price that can be obtained for those products rises, and this is likely to make it worthwhile for people to break the law. Particular problems arise when it is announced in advance that a species will go on the list; in the months between the announcement and the introduction of the new law, trade in that species tends to increase.

You can learn a lot more about CITES and see photographs and information about the species that are listed on their website.

Figure 18.42: Policemen in Malaysia examine dead sea turtles from a boat stopped on its way to the souvenir market. All sea turtles are listed in CITES Appendix I. Poaching, fishing nets, pollution and habitat destruction are all serious threats to sea turtle populations.

IUCN

The International Union for Conservation of Nature (IUCN) is the 'global authority on the status of the natural world and the measures needed to safeguard it'. As part of its work, the IUCN assesses the status of many of the world's species of animal and plant. Figure 18.46 shows the IUCN classification system for the conservation status of plant and animal species. The information is made available online in the IUCN Red List of Threatened Species™. Scientists monitor populations and evaluate the risks of species becoming extinct. They then apply certain criteria to the information that they have available before assigning each species to one of the categories shown in Figure 18.43.

Information in the Red List is available to governments, planners, conservationists and environmental campaigners around the world.

Question

22 Use the IUCN database to find information about examples of plant and animal species in your country that are endangered or critically endangered and then find out what is being done to conserve them.

CITES Appendix	Criteria	Trading regulations	Animal examples	Plant examples
I	Species that are the most endangered and threatened with extinction	All trade in species or their products is banned	Orangutans, *Pongo abelii* and *P. pygmaeus* (Borneo, Indonesia)	Kinabulu pitcher plant, *Nepenthes kinabaluensis* (Malaysia)
II	Species that are not threatened with extinction, but will be unless trade is closely controlled	Trade is only allowed if an export permit is granted by the countries concerned	Sir David's long-beaked echidna, *Zaglossus attenboroughi* (Papua, Indonesia)	All species in the genus *Nepenthes*; Venus fly trap, *Dionaea muscipula*
III	Species included at the request of a country that regulates trade in the species and needs the cooperation of other countries to prevent unsustainable or illegal exploitation	Trade in these species is regulated; permits are required, but they are easier to obtain than for species in Appendix II	Mauritian pink pigeon, *Columba mayeri*	Spur tree from Nepal, *Tetracentron sinense*

Table 18.12: CITES Appendices I, II and III.

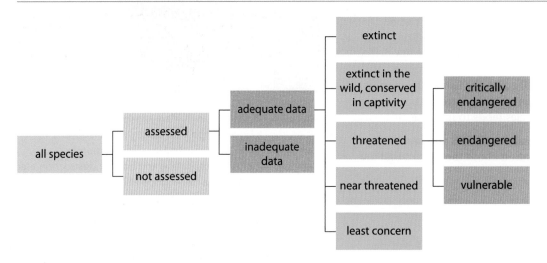

Figure 18.43: The IUCN classification of species. The Floreana mockingbird (Figure 18.1) is classified as endangered.

REFLECTION

This chapter has discussed the conservation of plants and animals.

- Why is it just as important to be concerned about the biodiversity of microorganisms and their conservation?
- What resources did you use while working on this activity? Which resources were especially helpful and would you use again?

Final reflection

Discuss with a friend which, if any, parts of Chapter 18 you need to:

- read through again to make sure you really understand
- seek more guidance on, even after going over it again.

SUMMARY

There are three difference species concepts. A biological species is a group of organisms that have many features in common and are able to interbreed and produce fertile offspring. A morphological species is a group of organisms that share many physical features that distinguish them from other species. An ecological species is a population of individuals of the same species living in the same area at the same time.

Species are classified into a taxonomic hierarchy comprising: domain, kingdom, phylum, class, order, family, genus and species. There are three domains: Bacteria, Archaea and Eukarya.

Archaea and Bacteria are prokaryotes. Archaea differ from Bacteria in the lipids in their membranes, their ribosomal RNA and the composition of their cell walls.

All eukaryotic organisms are classified in the Eukarya, which is divided into four kingdoms: Protoctista, Fungi, Plantae and Animalia.

Viruses are not included in this classification because they are acellular; they have no cells and are composed of only nucleic acid (DNA or RNA) surrounded by a protein coat. Viruses are classified according to the type of nucleic acid that they have and whether it is single-stranded or double-stranded.

An ecosystem is a relatively self-contained, interacting community of organisms, and the environment in which they live and with which they interact. A niche is the role of an organism in an ecosystem; it is how it 'fits into' the ecosystem.

Biodiversity is considered at three different levels: variation in ecosystems or habitats, the number of species and their relative abundance, and genetic variation within each species.

Random sampling in fieldwork is important to collect data that is representative of the area being studied and to avoid bias in choice of samples. Random sampling is appropriate for habitats where species are distributed uniformly across the whole area and all are exposed to the same environmental conditions.

Frame quadrats are used to assess the abundance of organisms. Abundance can be recorded as species frequency, species density and percentage cover. Line and belt transects are used to investigate the distribution of organisms in a habitat where conditions are not uniform (e.g. from low to high altitude). Line transects show qualitative changes in species distribution; belt transects show changes in abundance as well as distribution.

The Lincoln index is a way to estimate the number of organisms in populations of motile animals in a particular place. Population size is determined by the mark–release–recapture method.

Simpson's index of diversity (D) is used to calculate the biodiversity of a habitat. The range of values is 0 (low biodiversity) to 1 (high biodiversity). Spearman's rank correlation and Pearson's linear correlation are used to see whether there is a relationship between two features.

There are many threats to the biodiversity of ecosystems; these include climate change, competition, especially with alien species, hunting by humans and degradation of ecosystems leading to habitat loss. These factors are responsible for local extinction of populations and the total extinction of species.

There are moral and ethical reasons for maintaining biodiversity, and also more practical ones; for example, plants may be sources of future medicines and animals may provide alleles to use in animal breeding.

Conservation of an endangered animal species may involve captive breeding programmes, in which viable populations are built up in zoos and wildlife parks. These programmes try to ensure that the gene pool is maintained and inbreeding is avoided. At the same time, attempts are made to provide a suitable habitat in the wild, so that captive-bred animals can eventually be reintroduced to the wild; it is important to involve local people in such projects to increase the level of acceptance and the chances of success.

Methods of assisted reproduction, such as IVF, embryo transfer and surrogacy, are used in the conservation of endangered mammals. 'Frozen zoos' maintain collections of sperm, eggs, embryos and tissue samples of endangered species in cold storage.

CONTINUED

Botanic gardens and seed banks help to conserve threatened plant species by breeding them for reintroduction into an appropriate habitat. Seed banks provide suitable conditions to keep different types of seeds alive for as long as possible. Samples of the seeds are grown into adult plants every now and then, so that fresh seed can be collected.

Many countries have protected areas called national parks, which often cover large areas. National parks are set up to conserve rare and endangered species and to maintain their habitats; often legislation is passed to ensure their protection. Within national parks, activities such as agriculture, building, mining and other industries are forbidden or strictly regulated; access may be limited but not forbidden, as one aim of most such parks is to educate people about the importance of conservation.

Marine parks have been created in many parts of the world to protect the biodiversity of endangered ecosystems such as coral reefs; these parks usually prohibit fishing. One benefit of marine parks is that populations of fish in the area have increased. Other smaller conservation areas may be created to protect particular species and habitats.

Alien species are those that have been introduced or have invaded ecosystems where they did not exist before; alien or invasive species need to be controlled because they pose threats to native species. Alien species may be effective predators and/or competitors with native species.

Non-governmental organisations, such as the Convention on International Trade in Endangered Species of Wild Fauna and Flora (CITES) and the International Union for Conservation of Nature (IUCN), play important roles in local and global conservation.

EXAM-STYLE QUESTIONS

1   Some students investigated what size of quadrat they should use to assess the abundance of plant species in an old field ecosystem. They used quadrats of side 10, 25, 50, 75 and 100 cm and recorded how many plant species were present. They repeated their investigation five times and calculated mean numbers of species per quadrat.

Their results are in the graph.

COMMAND WORD

Assess: make an informed judgement.

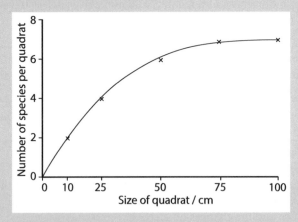

a   Calculate the area of each quadrat that the students used.   [2]
b   Explain why the students took five results for each quadrat.   [2]

CONTINUED

   c Based on their results, the students decided to use the 50 cm quadrat to study the old field. Why did they choose the 50 cm quadrat? **[2]**

   d Explain how the students would use the 50 cm quadrat to estimate the abundance of the different plant species in the field. **[3]**

[Total: 9]

2 Five 0.25 m² quadrats were placed randomly in an area of grassland in the UK. The percentage of each quadrat occupied by each species of plant was estimated to the nearest 5% and recorded in the table.

Species	Percentage cover of each plant species in each quadrat to the nearest 5%					Mean percentage cover
	1	**2**	**3**	**4**	**5**	
Timothy grass	60	30	35	70	25	
Yorkshire fog grass	25	70	30	15	40	
plantain	0	5	0	5	0	2
meadow buttercup	0	0	15	0	10	5
dock	5	10	5	0	5	5
cowslip	0	0	0	5	0	1
white clover	15	0	25	25	10	15
bare ground	0	15	15	5	20	11

   a Calculate the mean percentage cover for the first two species in the table. **[1]**

   b Explain why the percentage cover for all the species in each quadrat adds up to more than 100%. **[1]**

   c Suggest why the percentage cover was recorded to the nearest 5%. **[1]**

   d Could these results be used to obtain a valid estimate of the species frequency for each species? Explain your answer. **[4]**

   e State **four** factors that influence plant biodiversity in a field ecosystem. **[4]**

[Total: 11]

3 A sample of 39 ground beetles was captured from an area of waste ground measuring 100 × 25 metres. Each animal was marked and then released. A second sample of 35 was caught on the following day. Of these, 20 had been marked.

   a Use these results to estimate the number of ground beetles in the population. Show your working. **[2]**

   b State **three** assumptions that must be made in order to make this estimate. **[3]**

   c Describe a method that you could use to check that the mark–release–recapture method gives a valid estimate of the ground beetle population in the area of waste ground. **[4]**

[Total: 9]

CONTINUED

4   Light is an important abiotic factor that determines the distribution and abundance of plants. Some plants are adapted to grow in areas of low light intensity. They are known as shade plants. Some students investigated the abundance of dog's mercury, *Mercurialis perennis,* under forest trees in eight different locations. At each location, they used ten randomly positioned quadrats to measure the percentage cover of this shade plant.

Location	Light intensity at ground level / percentage of full sun	Mean percentage cover of *M. perennis*
A	90	10
B	50	65
C	30	90
D	20	80
E	80	34
F	88	20
G	93	10
H	100	0

a   Draw a scatter graph to see if there is a correlation between light intensity beneath the canopy and the abundance of *M. perennis.*   [2]

b   State a null hypothesis for this investigation.   [1]

c   Use the data in the table to calculate the Spearman's rank correlation, r_s. Show all your working.   [4]

d   What can you conclude from your calculation? You will need to consult Table P2.8 in Chapter P2 to help you answer this question.   [4]

[Total: 11]

5   Stoneflies, *Plecoptera* spp., lay eggs in freshwater streams and rivers. The eggs hatch into nymphs which live in the water for several years before changing to adults. Stonefly nymphs are known as good indicators of pollution since they are very sensitive to a decrease in the oxygen concentration of the water.

CONTINUED

A biologist wanted to find out whether stonefly nymphs would be suitable as an indicator of water hardness. She collected samples from 12 streams and obtained values of calcium carbonate concentration from the local water authority. The number of stonefly nymphs and the concentration of calcium carbonate for each of the 12 streams are given in the table.

Stream	Number of stonefly nymphs	Concentration of calcium carbonate / arbitrary units
1	42	17
2	40	20
3	30	22
4	7	28
5	12	42
6	10	55
7	8	55
8	7	75
9	3	80
10	7	90
11	5	145
12	2	145

a Draw a scatter graph to see if there is a correlation between the number of stonefly nymphs and the hardness of the water.   [2]

b State a null hypothesis for this investigation.   [1]

c Use the data in the table to calculate the Spearman's rank correlation, r_s. Show your working.   [4]

d What can you conclude from your calculation? You will need to consult Table P2.8 in Chapter P2 to help you answer this question.   [4]

[Total: 11]

6 Woodlice are small terrestrial crustaceans that feed on organic matter in leaf litter and in the soil. While carrying out an ecological survey in woodland, a student noticed that there seemed to be more woodlice in areas where there was plenty of leaf litter and other organic matter. He also noticed that there appeared to be more leaf litter towards the middle of the wood than at the edge. To find out if there is a relationship between the number of woodlice and the organic content of the soil, he used a line transect. At each point along the transect he:

- took a sample of soil
- counted the number of woodlice in three separate samples of leaf litter from the surface of the soil.

He took the samples of soil to a laboratory to find out their percentage organic content. His results are shown in the table.

Distance along transect / m	Percentage organic matter in the soil	Number of woodlice in sample			
		1	2	3	mean
1	5.42	2	0	0	0.6
4	10.02	3	4	0	2.3
8	15.56	3	2	2	2.3
16	8.25	0	1	3	1.3
20	9.62	5	7	6	6.0
24	11.73	9	9	9	9.0
28	10.67	8	14	15	12.3
32	9.36	14	16	3	11.6
36	11.35	12	17	6	11.6
40	15.11	17	9	7	11.0
44	20.87	20	2	9	10.3
48	20.30	20	1	12	11.0

a i Explain why the student has taken three samples of woodlice at each point along the transect. [2]

ii Suggest **three** further pieces of information you would need if you were to repeat the student's investigation. [3]

b Draw a scatter graph to see if there is any relationship between the number of woodlice and the mass of organic matter in the soil. [2]

c State the null hypothesis for this investigation. [1]

d Carry out the Spearman's rank correlation test on the data that you have used to draw the scatter graph. [4]

e What conclusions can you make? You will need to consult Table P2.8 in Chapter P2 to help you answer this question. [4]

[Total: 16]

7 Researchers investigated aspects of the anatomy of the Melina tree, *Gmelina arborea,* which has been introduced into wet and dry forests in Costa Rica. The researchers wanted to know if the diameter of the trees at head height was correlated with the overall height of the trees. The table shows the data for seven trees from each type of forest.

Tree number	Wet forest		Dry forest	
	diameter / cm	height / m	diameter / cm	height / m
1	38.0	25.5	31.9	20.8
2	31.5	22.0	29.8	19.5
3	33.2	18.5	32.5	24.7
4	32.0	23.5	30.5	24.0
5	30.7	18.0	33.2	27.1
6	25.0	19.0	19.7	19.5
7	28.5	22.5	22.5	23.3

The researchers calculated the Pearson's correlation coefficient for the two areas as:

Type of forest	Pearson's correlation coefficient
wet forest	0.47
dry forest	0.42

The coefficient at $p = 0.05$ for samples of this size is 0.75.

a Explain what conclusions the researchers should make from these results. **[4]**

b Explain why the researchers chose to calculate the Pearson's correlation coefficient and not the Spearman's rank correlation coefficient. **[2]**

c The researchers next measured the diameters of trees of the same heights in the two forests to see if their growth in width was influenced by the rainfall in the two forests.

  i State the independent and dependent variables in the investigation. **[2]**

  ii Describe the method that the researchers would follow to gain results. **[5]**

  iii State how the researchers would find out if the difference between the two populations of trees is significant. **[1]**

[Total: 14]

8 Sharks are an important part of the biodiversity of marine ecosystems. Many species are endangered as a result of overfishing. In 2004, the great white shark, *Carcharodon carcharias,* was added to Appendix II of CITES. Two other sharks, the porbeagle, *Lamna nasus*, and the scalloped hammerhead shark, *Sphyrna lewini*, were added to Appendix III in 2013.

a Explain what is meant by the term *biodiversity*. **[3]**

b i The IUCN lists the scalloped hammerhead shark as an endangered species. Explain what is meant by the term *endangered*. **[1]**

  ii Explain how the addition of species to the CITES lists provides protection for endangered species, such as sharks. **[3]**

c List **four** practical reasons why humans should maintain biodiversity. **[4]**

[Total: 11]

9 The numbers of elephants in Hwange National Park in Zimbabwe were counted each year between 1980 and 2001. In the 1980s, some of the elephants were culled. This practice stopped in 1986. The graph shows the changes in the numbers of elephants ($\pm SE$, see the section on standard error in Chapter P2), the bars indicate the numbers of elephants that were culled.

CONTINUED

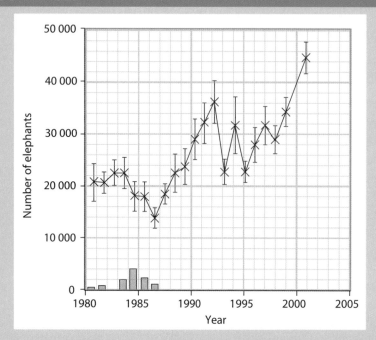

a   Explain the importance of showing the standard error (*SE*) on the graph.   **[2]**

b   Describe the changes in the numbers of elephants between 1980 and 2001.   **[4]**

c   Elephants feed by browsing on woody vegetation and other plants. They strip bark from trees and push over some trees, keeping patches of grassland open, but leaving much woodland.

   Explain how both high and low densities of elephants could result in reduced species diversity in national parks in Africa.   **[4]**

d   Explain the reasons for culling animals, such as elephants, in national parks, other than to prevent loss of biodiversity.   **[4]**

   [Total: 14]

10 a   There are many seed banks in different parts of the world. Explain the reasons for depositing samples of seeds in cold storage.   **[6]**

b   Explain what is meant by the term *frozen zoo*.   **[3]**

c   Przewalski's horse, *Equus ferus przewalskii,* is a species of horse that became extinct in the wild in the 1980s. Zoos throughout the world already held large numbers of this species. A captive breeding programme was so successful that these horses have been returned to the Dzungarian Gobi Strictly Protected Area in Mongolia.

   i   Explain how captive breeding of animals, such as Przewalski's horse, can help to conserve an endangered species.   **[3]**

   ii   Explain how genetic diversity is maintained during a captive breeding programme.   **[3]**

   iii   Suggest how the success of a scheme to reintroduce a species of mammal, such as Przewalski's horse, may be assessed.   **[3]**

   [Total: 18]

SELF-EVALUATION CHECKLIST

After studying this chapter, complete a table like this:

I can	See section...	Needs more work	Almost there	Ready to move on
discuss the meaning of the term *species* and explain how species are classified	18.1			
outline the characteristic features of the three domains and of the four kingdoms of eukaryotic organisms	18.1			
outline how viruses are classified	18.1			
explain the importance of biodiversity in terms of ecosystems, habitats, species and the genetic diversity within each species	18.2			
investigate ecosystems using techniques for assessing the occurrence, abundance and distribution of species	18.2			
calculate Simpson's index of diversity and use it to compare the biodiversity of different areas	18.2			
use statistical methods to analyse the relationships between the distribution and abundance of species and abiotic or biotic factors	18.2			
discuss the reasons for maintaining biodiversity and outline the ways in which biodiversity is conserved	18.3, 18.4			
describe methods of assisted reproduction used in the conservation of endangered mammal species	18.4			
explain why it is necessary to control invasive alien species	18.5			
discuss the roles of the International Union for Conservation of Nature (IUCN) and the Convention on International Trade in Endangered Species of Wild Fauna and Flora (CITES) in global conservation	18.6			

> Chapter 19

Genetic technology

LEARNING INTENTIONS

In this chapter you will learn how to:

- explain the principles of genetic technology
- describe the tools and techniques available to the genetic engineer
- describe and explain the polymerase chain reaction (PCR) and gel electrophoresis
- describe the uses of PCR and gel electrophoresis
- explain the use of microarrays
- outline the uses of databases that hold information about gene sequences, genomes and proteins
- describe some examples of the uses of genetic technology in medicine
- describe some uses of genetically modified organisms (GMOs) in agriculture
- discuss the social and ethical implications of gene technology in medicine and food production.

BEFORE YOU START

You studied the structure and function of DNA in Chapter 6. To understand much of this chapter, you need a good knowledge of DNA and how it differs from RNA and protein.

Make a large annotated diagram to show:

* the features of DNA

* the differences between DNA and mRNA

* how proteins differ from DNA.

Annotate your diagram to show how the structure of DNA makes it suitable for information storage and retrieval and for passing on from one generation to the next.

FIGHTING CRIME WITH DNA

Police are called to a domestic dispute. Neighbours say that there was a very loud disturbance in the night followed by the slamming of doors and the sound of a car leaving the street in a hurry.

When they arrive at the house, police officers find that it is empty, but there are signs of a struggle. In the kitchen, they find blood on the floor and a knife with blood on the blade and on the handle. Scene-of-crime officers are called and the knife is collected as evidence and handed on for forensic analysis.

A forensic scientist removes a small sample of blood and uses it to collect the DNA for analysis (Figure 19.1). Just a tiny quantity of blood from this knife is enough to help to identify the victim and perhaps the perpetrator of the crime (if a crime has been committed).

The DNA is extracted from white blood cells. To extract the DNA, the forensic scientist first treats the cells with a reagent that causes them to break open. A crude sample of DNA is captured on magnetic beads, leaving most of the cell debris and protein behind in solution. Any remaining protein in the sample is digested using a protease and then washed away to leave pure, intact DNA. Finally, the pure DNA is then washed off the beads into a small volume of solvent.

It is likely that the sample of DNA will be too small to analyse, so the quantity is increased by using DNA polymerase to replicate key regions of the DNA. This results in multiple copies of key regions of DNA that can be used to form a genetic profile. The profiles of the people who left their blood on the knife are compared with profiles held in the police DNA database to see if there is a match. If the profile is in the DNA database, the chances of

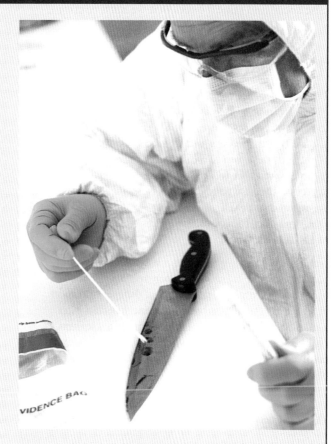

Figure 19.1: A forensic scientist takes a sample of blood from a knife removed from the scene of a crime.

a positive match are very high. If not, then the hunt for victim and suspects needs to continue using traditional policing methods.

Question for discussion

It is quite likely that your DNA is unique. Discuss the reasons for this.

The structure of DNA, and the way in which it codes for protein synthesis, was worked out during the 1950s and 1960s. Since then, this knowledge has developed so much that scientists can change the DNA in a cell, and thereby change the proteins which that cell synthesises. Not only that, but we can sequence the nucleotides in DNA and compare nucleotide sequences in different organisms. It is also possible to carry out genetic tests to see if people are carriers of genetic diseases and, in a few cases, use gene therapy or gene editing to treat those who have these diseases. Gene technologies have brought huge benefits to many people, but they may have consequences that we cannot foresee. These technologies raise social and ethical issues that we must confront.

19.1 Genetic engineering

The aim of genetic engineering is to remove a gene (or genes) from one organism and transfer it into another so that the gene is expressed. The DNA that has been altered by this process and which now contains lengths of nucleotides from two different organisms is called recombinant DNA (rDNA). The organism which now expresses the new gene or genes is known as a transgenic organism or a genetically modified organism (GMO); the DNA may be from another species or from an organism of the same species.

Genetic engineering provides a way of overcoming barriers to gene transfer between species. Genes are often taken from an organism in a different domain or kingdom, such as a bacterial gene inserted into a plant or a human gene inserted into a bacterium. Unlike selective breeding, where whole sets of genes are involved, genetic engineering often results in the transfer of a single gene.

An overview of gene transfer

There are many different ways in which a GMO may be produced, but these steps are essential.

1 The gene that is required is identified. It may be cut from a chromosome, made from mRNA by reverse transcription or synthesised from nucleotides.

2 Multiple copies of the gene are made using the technique called the polymerase chain reaction (PCR).

3 The gene is inserted into a vector which delivers the gene to the cells of the organism. Examples of vectors are plasmids, viruses and liposomes.

4 The vector takes the gene into the cells.

5 The cells that have the new gene are identified, often by using marker genes, and cloned.

To perform these steps, the genetic engineer needs a 'tool kit' consisting of:

- enzymes, such as restriction endonucleases, DNA ligases and reverse transcriptase
- vectors, including plasmids and viruses
- genes coding for easily identifiable substances that can be used as markers.

KEY WORDS

genetic engineering: any procedure in which the genetic information in an organism is changed by altering the base sequence of a gene or by introducing a gene from another organism; the organism is then said to be a genetically modified organism (GMO)

recombinant DNA (rDNA): DNA made by artificially joining together pieces of DNA from two or more different species

transgenic organism: any organism that contains DNA from another source, such as from another individual of the same species or from a different species

genetically modified organism (GMO): any organism that has had its DNA changed in a way that does not occur naturally or by selective breeding

vector: a means of delivering genes into a cell used in gene technology; e.g. plasmids and viruses

Question

1 Explain how selective breeding differs from genetic engineering.

19.2 Tools for the gene technologist

Restriction enzymes

Restriction endonucleases are a class of enzymes from bacteria. These enzymes recognise and cut the DNA of viruses which attack the bacteria. Such viruses are known as **bacteriophages** (often called **phages**; see Figure 18.14). Bacteria make these enzymes to cut up the phage DNA into smaller pieces. The cuts are made at specific places along the sugar–phosphate backbone of the phage DNA. The enzymes are known as endonucleases because they cut *within* DNA molecules rather than removing nucleotides from the ends. The role of these enzymes in bacteria is to *restrict* a viral infection, hence the name restriction endonuclease or **restriction enzyme**.

Each restriction enzyme binds to a specific target site on DNA and cuts at that site. Bacterial DNA is protected from such an attack either by chemical alteration to the bases in DNA or by not having the target sites. These target sites, or restriction sites, are specific sequences of four to six bases. For example, the restriction enzyme called BamHI always cuts DNA where there is a GGATCC sequence on the 5′ to 3′ strand and its complementary sequence, CCTAGG, on the 3′ to 5′ strand. This sequence reads the same in both directions: it is a palindrome. Many, but not all, restriction sites are palindromic. Restriction enzymes either cut straight across the sugar–phosphate backbone to give blunt ends or they cut in a staggered fashion to give 'sticky ends' (Figure 19.2).

Sticky ends are short lengths of unpaired bases. They form hydrogen bonds with complementary sequences of bases on other pieces of DNA cut with the same restriction enzyme. When long pieces of DNA are cut with a restriction enzyme, a mixture of pieces of DNA of different lengths is formed. Finding the specific piece of DNA required involves separating the lengths of DNA using gel electrophoresis and **gene probes**. A gene probe is a length of single-stranded DNA with a known base sequence. It is used to bind with lengths of DNA which have a complementary base sequence. These techniques are described in Section 19.5, Analysing and storing genetic information. Multiple copies of the required piece

of DNA can be made using the PCR, which is described in Section 19.4, Separating and amplifying DNA.

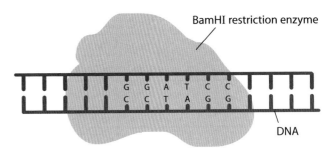

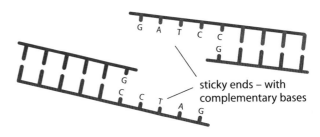

Figure 19.2: The restriction enzyme, BamHI, makes staggered cuts in DNA to give sticky ends. Note that the sticky ends are complementary to the base sequences –CTAG and –GATC.

Restriction enzymes are named by an abbreviation which indicates their origin (Table 19.1). Roman numbers are added to distinguish different enzymes from the same source. For example, EcoRI comes from *Escherichia coli* (strain RY13), and was the first to be identified from this source.

KEY WORDS

restriction endonuclease (restriction enzyme): an enzyme, originally derived from bacteria, that cuts DNA molecules; each type of restriction enzyme cuts only at a particular sequence of bases

bacteriophage (phage): a type of virus that infects bacteria; phages have double-stranded DNA as their genetic material

gene probe: a length of DNA that has a complementary base sequence to another piece of DNA that you are trying to detect

Restriction endonuclease	Restriction site	Site of cut across DNA	Source of enzyme
EcoRI	5′ –G AATTC– 3′ 3′ –CTTAA G– 5′	–G | AATTC– –CTTAA | G–	Escherichia coli
BamHI	5′ –G GATCC– 3′ 3′ –CCTAG G– 5′	–G | GATCC– –CCTAG | G–	Bacillus amyloliquefaciens
HindIII	5′ –A AGCTT– 3′ 3′ –TTCGA A– 5′	–A | AGCTT– –TTCGA | A–	Haemophilus influenzae
HaeIII	5′ –GG CC– 3′ 3′ –CC GG– 5′	–GG | CC– –CC | GG–	Haemophilus aegyptius

Table 19.1: Four restriction endonucleases, their restriction sites and the bacteria in which they were first discovered.

Question

2　a　Explain the term *sticky end*.

　　b　Four different lengths of DNA, **A** to **D**, were cut with the restriction enzyme EcoRI. These fragments had the following numbers of restriction sites for this enzyme: **A** – 5, **B** – 7, **C** – 0 and **D** – 3. State the number of fragments that will be formed from each length of DNA after incubation with EcoRI.

　　c　Describe the features of the restriction sites shown in Table 19.1.

　　d　Use the information in Table 19.1 to explain the advantages of using restriction endonucleases in genetic engineering.

Reverse transcriptase

Using chromosomal DNA can be a problem because each gene in eukaryotic organisms is composed of sequences of bases (called exons) that code for sequences of amino acids. In between are sequences of bases (introns) that do not. Once RNA is formed by transcription, it is cut into fragments and the lengths corresponding to the exons are joined together to form mRNA, which leaves the nucleus. To avoid using DNA with both exons and introns, mRNA from the cytoplasm is used as the template for making DNA. This only became possible with the discovery of reverse transcriptase, the enzyme found in viruses that have RNA as their genetic material (see Table 18.2). Reverse transcriptase uses single-stranded mRNA as a template and free DNA nucleotides to form single-stranded DNA. The process is complete when DNA polymerase is used to synthesise another polynucleotide to form double-stranded complementary DNA, often abbreviated to cDNA (Figure 19.3).

Synthesising DNA

It is possible to use the genetic code (see Chapter 6, Section 6.4, The genetic code) to synthesise DNA from nucleotides rather than cut it out of chromosomal DNA or make it by reverse transcription. Genes and even complete **genomes** can be made directly from DNA nucleotides without the need for template DNA. Scientists can do this by choosing codons for the amino acid sequence that they need. The sequence of nucleotides is held in a computer that directs the synthesis of short fragments of DNA in DNA synthesiser machines. These fragments are then joined together to make a longer sequence of nucleotides that can be inserted into plasmids for use in genetic engineering. This method is used to generate completely new genes that are used, for example, in the synthesis of vaccines. They have even been used to produce the genomes of synthetic bacteria consisting of a million base pairs.

KEY WORD

genome: the complete set of genes or genetic material present in a cell or an organism; the genome of a eukaryote includes the DNA in the nucleus and in the mitochondria; the genomes of plants include chloroplast DNA

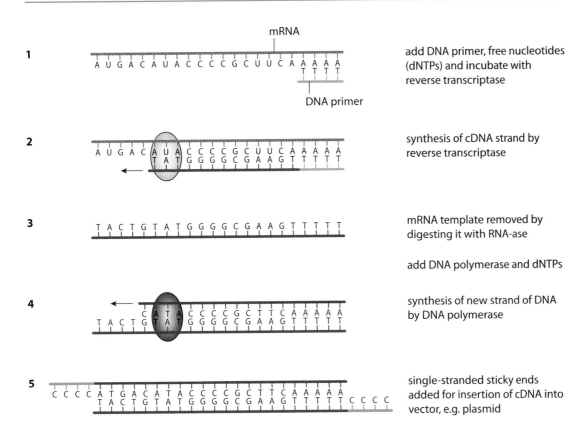

Figure 19.3: Reverse transcription from mRNA to form cDNA. dNTPs are deoxyribonucleotide triphosphates, i.e. dATP, dTTP, dGTP and dCTP.

Vectors

Inserting a gene into a plasmid vector

The next step in genetic engineering is to put a length of DNA that may contain one or more genes into a recipient cell. Vectors are used to do this. One type of vector is a plasmid (Figure 19.4). These are small, circular pieces of double-stranded DNA. Plasmids occur naturally in bacteria and often contain genes for antibiotic resistance. They can be exchanged between individual bacteria – even between individuals of different species. If a genetic engineer inserts a piece of DNA into a plasmid, then the plasmid can be used to take the DNA into a bacterial cell.

Note that the term *vector* is also used for animals that transmit pathogens (disease vector). Vectors transport something from one place to another.

Plasmids are obtained by treating bacteria with enzymes to break down their cell walls. The 'naked' bacteria are then spun at high speed in a centrifuge, so that the relatively large circular DNA are separated from the much smaller plasmids.

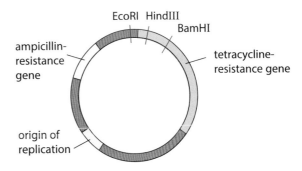

Figure 19.4: Plasmids are circular pieces of double-stranded DNA, usually drawn as shown here. This is plasmid pBR322, which was used in the production of human insulin by GM bacteria.

The circular DNA of the plasmid is cut open using a restriction enzyme (Figure 19.5). The same enzyme as the one used to cut out the gene should be used, so that the sticky ends are complementary (Figure 19.2). If a restriction enzyme is used that gives blunt ends, then sticky ends need to be attached to both the gene and the plasmid DNA.

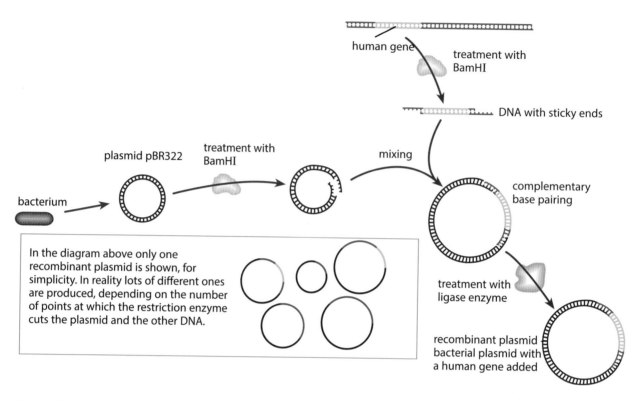

Figure 19.5: Inserting a human gene into the plasmid pBR322.

The opened plasmids and the lengths of DNA with the human gene are mixed together. Some of the sticky ends on the plasmids pair up with sticky ends on the DNA. Many simply reform plasmids without incorporating the DNA. The enzyme DNA ligase links together the sugar–phosphate backbones of the DNA and the plasmid (Chapter 6, Section 6.3, DNA replication). The enzyme does this by catalysing the formation of phosphodiester bonds. This forms a closed circle of double-stranded DNA containing the new gene. A recombinant plasmid has now been formed.

Bacterial plasmids can be modified to produce good vectors. Plasmids can also be made artificially. For example, the pUC group of plasmids have:

- a low molecular mass, so they are readily taken up by bacteria

- an origin of replication so they can be copied

- several single target sites for different restriction enzymes in a short length of DNA called a polylinker

- one or more marker genes, allowing identification of cells that have taken up the plasmid.

Plasmids are not the only type of vector. Viruses can also be used and so can liposomes, which are tiny spheres of lipid containing the DNA. There is more about these other vectors in Section 19.6, Genetic technology and medicine.

Getting the plasmids into bacteria

The next step in the process is to get bacteria to take up the plasmids. First, the bacteria and plasmids are put into a solution with a high concentration of calcium ions, then the mixture is cooled and given a heat shock. This increases the chances of plasmids passing through the cell surface membrane of the bacteria. A small proportion of the bacteria, perhaps 1%, take up plasmids with the gene and are said to be transformed. The rest either take up plasmids that have closed without incorporating a gene or do not take up any plasmids at all.

Identifying bacteria with recombinant DNA

It is important to identify which bacteria have been successfully transformed so that they can be used to make the protein coded by the gene. In the past, this was done by spreading the bacteria on agar plates which each contained an antibiotic. However, this technique has fallen out of favour and has largely been replaced by simpler methods of identifying transformed bacteria using genetic markers

DNA polymerase in bacteria copies the plasmids; the bacteria then divide by binary fission so that each daughter cell has several copies of the plasmid. Producing many copies of the recombinant plasmid is known as gene cloning. This is one way to produce multiple copies of a gene for use in genetic engineering or for research. The bacteria may also transcribe the new gene and use the mRNA in translation to form a protein, known as a recombinant protein (Figure 19.6).

Questions

3   Distinguish between rDNA and cDNA.

4   Summarise the advantages of using plasmids as vectors in genetic engineering.

5   Make a diagram to show how a piece of DNA is cut by restriction enzymes and then inserted into a plasmid. Show both strands of DNA in your diagram.

Recombinant human insulin

One form of diabetes mellitus is caused by the inability of the pancreas to produce insulin (Chapter 14, Section 14.4, The control of blood glucose). Before insulin from GM bacteria became available, people with this form of diabetes were treated with insulin extracted from the pancreases of pigs or cattle. In the 1970s biotechnology companies began to work on the idea of inserting the gene for human insulin into a bacterium and then using this bacterium to make insulin. They tried several different approaches, finally succeeding in the early 1980s. Recombinant human insulin became available in 1983. The procedure for producing recombinant insulin is shown in Figure 19.6.

There were problems in locating and isolating the gene coding for human insulin from the rest of the DNA in a human cell. So, instead of cutting out the gene from the DNA in the relevant chromosome, researchers extracted mRNA for insulin from pancreatic β cells. These are the only cells to express the insulin gene and they contain large quantities of the mRNA for insulin. The mRNA was used as the template for reverse transcriptase to make single-stranded DNA. The single-stranded DNA molecules were then used as the template for DNA polymerase to make double-stranded DNA (Figure 19.3). The genetic engineers then had insulin genes that they could insert into plasmids to transform the bacterium *Escherichia coli*.

Recombinant human insulin is now made in genetically modified yeast or animal cells rather than in bacteria. This is because eukaryotic cells have Golgi bodies where the two polypeptides of insulin can be assembled and folded correctly. The main advantage of this recombinant insulin is that there is now a reliable supply available to meet the increasing demand. Supplies are not dependent on factors such as the availability of pancreases from the meat trade. The insulin is also *human* insulin, not animal insulin. The two are not exactly identical.

Genetic engineers have changed the nucleotide sequence of the insulin gene to give molecules with slightly different amino acid sequences. These insulin analogues have different properties. For example, some may act faster and be useful for taking immediately after a meal (see Figure 19.7). Some may act more slowly over a period of between 8 and 24 hours and be useful to maintain a near constant blood concentration of insulin that does not decrease too far. Many diabetics take both these forms of recombinant insulin at the same time.

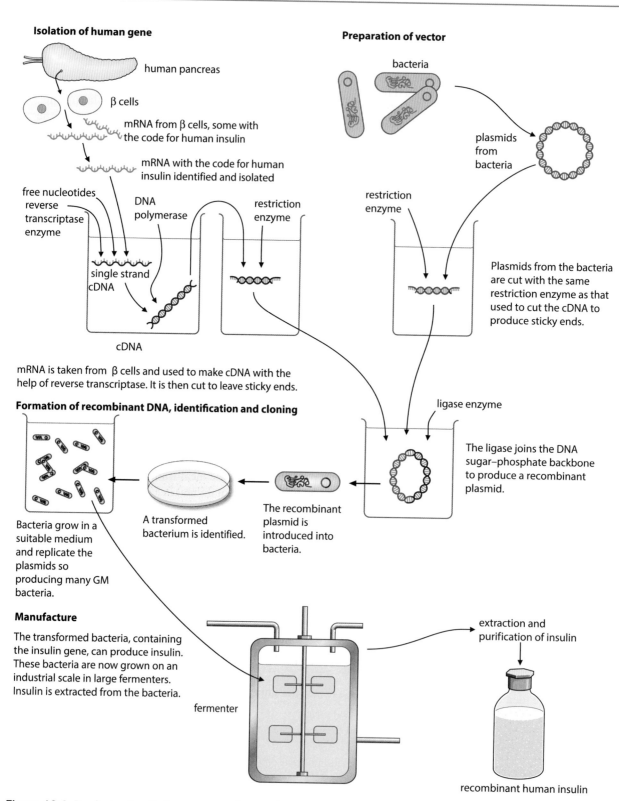

Isolation of human gene

human pancreas

β cells

mRNA from β cells, some with the code for human insulin

mRNA with the code for human insulin identified and isolated

free nucleotides
reverse transcriptase enzyme

DNA polymerase

restriction enzyme

single strand cDNA

cDNA

mRNA is taken from β cells and used to make cDNA with the help of reverse transcriptase. It is then cut to leave sticky ends.

Preparation of vector

bacteria

plasmids from bacteria

restriction enzyme

Plasmids from the bacteria are cut with the same restriction enzyme as that used to cut the cDNA to produce sticky ends.

Formation of recombinant DNA, identification and cloning

Bacteria grow in a suitable medium and replicate the plasmids so producing many GM bacteria.

A transformed bacterium is identified.

The recombinant plasmid is introduced into bacteria.

ligase enzyme

The ligase joins the DNA sugar–phosphate backbone to produce a recombinant plasmid.

Manufacture

The transformed bacteria, containing the insulin gene, can produce insulin. These bacteria are now grown on an industrial scale in large fermenters. Insulin is extracted from the bacteria.

fermenter

extraction and purification of insulin

recombinant human insulin

Figure 19.6: Producing insulin from genetically modified bacteria.

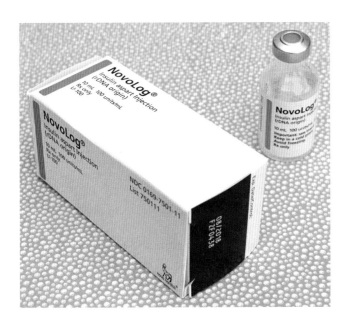

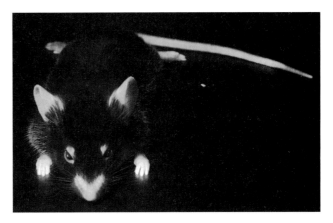

Figure 19.8: A transgenic mouse expressing a gene for a fluorescent protein.

Figure 19.7: Insulin aspart is a type of recombinant insulin made by genetically engineered yeast and sold under the brand name Novolog® among others. It is often taken just before eating and has its maximum effect after about two hours and lasts for four hours.

Genetic markers

Because of the risk of creating pathogenic antibiotic-resistant bacteria, there is now much less use of antibiotic-resistance genes as markers to show which bacteria have been transformed. One method to identify bacteria that have been transformed uses enzymes that produce fluorescent substances. For example, enzymes obtained from jellyfish make a protein called GFP (green fluorescent protein) that fluoresces bright green in ultraviolet light. The gene for the enzyme is inserted into the plasmids, so all that needs to be done to identify the bacteria that have taken up the plasmid is to shine ultraviolet light onto them. The ones that glow green are the genetically modified ones. The same marker gene can be used in a range of organisms (Figure 19.8).

Another marker is the enzyme β-glucuronidase (known as GUS for short), which originates from *E. coli*. Any transformed cell that contains this enzyme, when incubated with some specific colourless or non-fluorescence substrates, can transform them into coloured or fluorescent products. This is especially useful in detecting the activity of inserted genes in plants, such as the sundew in Figure 19.9.

Figure 19.9: Sundews are carnivorous plants that use sticky hairs to catch insects. On the left is a leaf of a transgenic sundew plant which is expressing the gene for GUS. The leaf has been placed in a solution of a colourless substance and the enzyme GUS has converted it into this dark blue colour. This indicates that the plant has been genetically modified successfully. On the right is a normal sundew leaf.

Question

6 Would all the bacteria that fluoresce definitely have taken up the gene that it is hoped was inserted into them? Explain your answer.

Promoters

Bacteria contain many different genes, which make many different proteins. But not all these genes are switched on at once. The bacteria make only the proteins that are required in the conditions in which they are growing. For example, as you saw in Chapter 16 (Section 14.4, The control of blood glucose), *E. coli* bacteria make the enzyme β-galactosidase only when they are growing in a medium containing lactose and there is no glucose available.

The expression of genes, such as those in the *lac* operon, is controlled by a **promoter**. This is the region of DNA to which RNA polymerase binds as it starts transcription. An appropriate promoter has to be inserted into a bacterium if the gene is going to be expressed. When bacteria were first transformed to produce insulin, the insulin gene was inserted next to the β-galactosidase gene so that they shared the same promoter (see the diagram of the *lac* operon in Figure 16.14). The promoter switched on the insulin gene when the bacterium needed to metabolise lactose. So, when bacteria were grown in a medium containing lactose but no glucose, they synthesised both β-galactosidase and human insulin.

The promoter allows RNA polymerase to bind to DNA and also ensures that it recognises which of the two DNA strands is the template strand. Within the sequence of nucleotides in the promoter region is the transcription start point: the first nucleotide of the gene to be transcribed. In this way, the promoter can be said to control the expression of a gene and can ensure a high level of gene expression. Remember that, in eukaryotes, proteins known as transcription factors are also required to bind to the promoter region or to RNA polymerase before transcription can begin (Chapter 16, Section 16.8, Control of gene expression).

Question

7 Rearrange the statements below to produce a flow diagram showing the steps involved in producing bacteria capable of synthesising a recombinant human protein, such as insulin or factor VIII.

A Insert the plasmid into a host bacterium.

B Isolate mRNA for the gene required.

C Use ligase to seal the sugar–phosphate backbone of the recombinant plasmid.

D Use DNA polymerase to produce double-stranded cDNA.

E Clone the modified bacteria and harvest the recombinant protein.

F Use reverse transcriptase to produce single-stranded cDNA.

G Use a restriction enzyme to cut plasmids.

H Use an enzyme to add short length of single-stranded DNA to form sticky ends.

I Form recombinant plasmids by complementary base pairing.

J Mix the double-stranded DNA with plasmids.

19.3 Gene editing

Until 2012, genetic technology relied on relatively poor methods of editing DNA. For example, a modified virus could be used to insert DNA into the human genome, but genetic engineers had no control over where in a cell's genome the DNA is inserted. It might be inserted in the middle of another gene, with unpredictable consequences.

A technique called Crispr/Cas9 has changed that. Crispr/Cas9 has been developed from a mechanism used by some bacteria to defend themselves against bacteriophages. This defence mechanism was first discovered in 1987, but the details of how it could be used for **gene editing** did not become available until 2012. Since then, it has been used successfully in many

---

KEY WORDS

promoter: a length of DNA that includes the binding site for RNA polymerase where transcription of a gene or genes begins; in eukaryotes, promoters also have sites for binding of transcription factors

gene editing: a form of genetic engineering in which the genome of an organism can be changed by deleting, inserting or replacing a length of DNA using a method such as the Crispr/Cas9 system

laboratories worldwide to edit DNA in a range of organisms, including human cells.

Crispr (pronounced 'Crisper') is a group of base sequences that code for short lengths of RNA that direct a nuclease enzyme known as Cas9 towards specific base sequences. The Crispr-associated (Cas) enzyme is an endonuclease that cuts DNA at a point that is determined by these RNA molecules, known as guide RNA (gRNA). Part of each gRNA has a sequence of 20 bases that can locate and bind to a strand of DNA with the complementary base sequence. The enzyme Cas9 has two active sites to cut DNA across both strands (Figure 19.10).

The Crispr/Cas9 system has been developed so that gRNA can be made with base sequences that are complementary to any base sequence of DNA. This gives the genetic engineer a way to edit DNA at specific places anywhere within an organism's genome (Figures 19.10 and 19.11). After the DNA is cut by Cas9, natural DNA repair mechanisms can repair the break by:

- adding one or more nucleotides that change the base sequence

- inserting a short length of prepared double-stranded DNA with a specific base sequence.

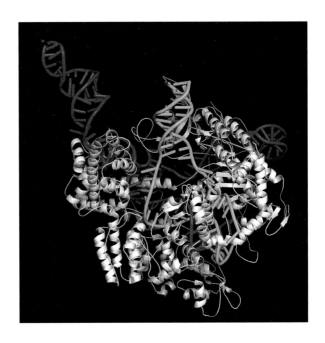

Figure 19.11: The Crispr/Cas9 system makes it possible to insert DNA at a precisely determined point in a chromosome. The Cas9 nuclease protein (white) uses a gRNA sequence (red) to cut DNA (green) at a sequence that is complementary to the gRNA.

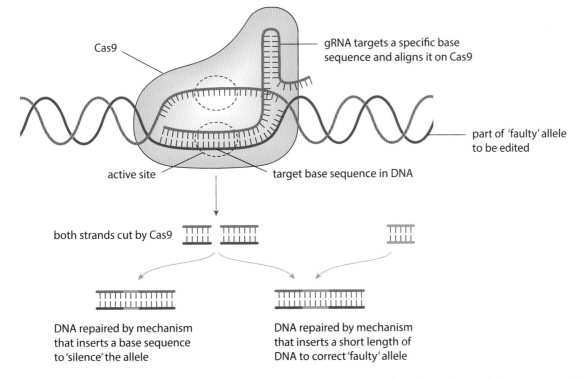

Figure 19.10: Gene editing using the Crispr/Cas9 system. Crispr is short for Clustered Regularly Interspaced Short Palindromic Repeats.

Crispr/Cas9 technology is used to remove DNA, for example removing a 'faulty' allele or removing part of the faulty allele so that, instead of producing a misfunctioning protein, it does not code for anything that functions. Gene editing can also be used to replace a faulty allele with a functioning one or replace part of a faulty allele so that it then codes for the functioning protein. Scientists have a 'tool kit' that can 'cut and paste' genes or parts of genes with much greater precision than was possible when using vectors (see Section 19.6).

Crispr/Cas9

Crispr/Cas9 is short for Clustered Regularly Interspaced Short Palindromic Repeats plus Crispr-associated protein 9. The Crispr base sequences are found naturally within the genomes of prokaryotic organisms – both bacteria and archaea. These sequences have come from DNA fragments in phages that infected the prokaryote. The sequences are used to detect and destroy DNA from similar phages that attack the prokaryote. They do this by producing gRNA that directs the nuclease enzyme Cas9 to break the sugar–phosphate backbone of phage DNA. This stops the virus from 'taking over' the prokaryote. Crisp/Cas9 has a similar function to restriction enzymes: it provides protection against viruses. However, Cas proteins can integrate parts of the viral DNA by inserting them into the Crispr sequences. This means that bacteria retain a 'memory' of past infections because the Crispr base sequences are derived from these infections. The Crispr base sequences are passed on when the bacteria reproduce.

In 2012 Dr Emmanuelle Charpentier and Dr Jennifer Doudna proposed the use of Crispr/Cas9 as a tool for genome editing (Figure 19.12). They showed that if the guide RNA is changed then Cas9 will cut DNA at a site complementary to the gRNA sequence. Cas9 therefore becomes a custom-made endonuclease with a 20-base-pair recognition site instead of the much shorter restriction sites used by restriction endonucleases (Table 19.1).

The potential uses of Crispr/Cas9 are almost endless. For example, it is possible to sequence the genome of individual people. This means that it is possible to prepare customised drugs to treat cancers. There is also the possibility of editing the genomes of insect vectors to prevent the transmission of diseases such as malaria and to provide bacteria used in industry with protection against viruses. Genetic engineering can now edit or correct the genome of any cell and organism in ways that are easy, fast, cheap and highly accurate.

Figure 19.12: Dr Emmanuelle Charpentier and Dr Jennifer Doudna, who showed the potential of gene editing using Crispr/Cas9, pose in front of a children's painting of DNA in a park in Oviedo, Spain, in 2015.

Tens of thousands of such gRNA sequences have already been created and are available to the research community. Crispr/Cas9 can also be used to target multiple genes simultaneously, which is another advantage that sets it apart from other gene-editing tools.

In 2014 a group of Chinese scientists used Crispr/Cas9 to edit the genome of a human embryo. In 2018 a group in Shenzen in China released information stating that they had used the system to delete part of the gene coding for the cell surface receptor known as CCR5. HIV gains entry to cells through binding to this receptor. The group carried out the procedure on early embryos formed in IVF. The intention of the group was to make the children resistant to HIV. However, many people think that this type of intervention crosses an ethical boundary because the modified DNA enters all the cells of the body and can be passed on to future generations.

Question

8 a State the base sequence of gRNA that is required to edit a section of DNA with the base sequence:
AAATTTCGCTCAGCCTTCCC

b Explain the advantage of using Crispr/Cas9 over using restriction enzymes.

c Describe how Crispr/Cas9 can be used to correct a genetic fault.

19.4 Separating and amplifying DNA

Polymerase chain reaction

The **polymerase chain reaction** (generally known as **PCR**) is used in almost every application of gene technology to amplify lengths of DNA. Virtually unlimited quantities of a length of DNA can be produced from the smallest quantity of DNA (even one molecule). Figure 19.13 shows the stages involved in one cycle of PCR. It is a fast and easy method for the rapid production of a very large number of copies of a particular fragment of DNA.

> **KEY WORD**
>
> **polymerase chain reaction (PCR):** an automated process that amplifies selected regions of DNA using alternate stages of polynucleotide separation (denaturation of DNA) and DNA synthesis catalysed by DNA polymerase

The following are added to each tube in the PCR machine:

- a sample of DNA, part of which is going to be amplified

- two different short lengths of single-stranded DNA to act as primers for the DNA polymerase

- free deoxynucleotide triphosphate molecules (dNTPs); these provide the energy for the formation of phosphodiester bonds

- a buffer solution, at pH 7 to 8

- a solution of a thermostable (heat-stable) DNA polymerase.

The PCR machine is switched on and left to work. Each stage requires a different temperature. PCR machines automatically change the temperature of the mixtures. The tubes are very small (they hold about 0.05 cm³) and have very thin walls, so when the temperature in the machine changes, the temperature inside the tubes changes very quickly (Figure 19.14).

- **Stage 1 (denaturation):** First, the DNA is denatured by heating it to about 95 °C. This breaks the hydrogen bonds between base pairs, and separates the double-stranded DNA molecules into their two strands, leaving bases exposed.

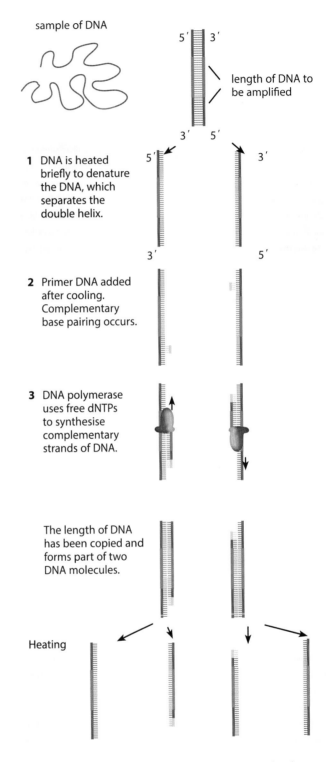

sample of DNA

length of DNA to be amplified

1   DNA is heated briefly to denature the DNA, which separates the double helix.

2   Primer DNA added after cooling. Complementary base pairing occurs.

3   DNA polymerase uses free dNTPs to synthesise complementary strands of DNA.

The length of DNA has been copied and forms part of two DNA molecules.

Heating

Heating denatures the DNA, which starts a new cycle of copying following steps 1 to 3. Repeating the cycle 10 to 12 times copies the length of DNA many times.

Figure 19.13: The three stages in one cycle of the PCR. The only region of the DNA in the sample to be amplified is that between the two primers.

Figure 19.14: Loading a PCR machine (thermocycler) with the reagents needed to amplify small samples of DNA. The machine automatically changes the temperature of the mixtures in each tube. After 30 cycles in this machine there are 2 billion copies (2^{30}) of the original DNA.

- **Stage 2 (annealing):** The primers bind to the base sequences on either side of the length of DNA which is being amplified. They do this by forming hydrogen bonds. Primers are required because DNA polymerase cannot begin synthesising DNA without an existing strand on which to build. Primers are often about 20 base pairs long and have base sequences complementary to the base sequences either side of the part of the length of DNA that is to be copied. The primers have different base sequences – one binds to the 'upward' strand and the other binds to the 'downward' strand, as shown in Figure 19.13. Attaching the primers requires a temperature of about 60 °C.

- **Stage 3 (extension):** The enzyme DNA polymerase then uses the dNTPs to build new strands of DNA against the exposed ones. The synthesis of new DNA strands using DNA polymerase (known as extension) requires a temperature of around 72 °C. The DNA polymerases used for this process come from microorganisms that have evolved to live in hot environments.

At the end of the first cycle after DNA has been copied, the mixture is heated again to begin the second cycle. Heating separates the two strands in each DNA molecule. Primers bind themselves to the start of each strand of unpaired nucleotides and DNA polymerase makes complementary copies. After this second cycle there are now four molecules of double-stranded DNA.

Taq polymerase was the first heat-stable DNA polymerase to be used in PCR. It was isolated from the thermophilic bacterium *Thermus aquaticus*, which is found in hot springs in Yellowstone Park in the USA (see Figure 3.9). It is valuable for PCR for two reasons. First, it is not destroyed by the denaturation stage, so it does not have to be replaced during each cycle. Second, its high optimum temperature means that the temperature for the extension stage does not have to be dropped below that of the annealing process, so efficiency is maximised. There are now many different thermostable DNA polymerases available for PCR.

Question

9 a Explain the difference between a primer and a probe.

   b Suggest why the primers used in PCR do not anneal together.

   c State the **four** types of free nucleotides (dNTPs) that are added to reaction vessels at the start of the PCR process.

   d Explain why only certain DNA polymerases, such as *Taq* polymerase, are used in PCR.

   e State what happens to DNA during one cycle in PCR.

You can see that theoretically this could go on forever, making more and more copies of what might originally have been just a tiny number of DNA molecules. A single DNA molecule can be used to produce literally billions of copies of itself in just a few hours. PCR has made it possible to get enough DNA from a tiny sample – for example, a microscopic portion of a drop of blood left at a crime scene.

PCR is now routinely used in forensic science to amplify DNA from the smallest tissue samples left at the scene of a crime. Many crimes have been solved with the help of PCR together with analysis of DNA using gel electrophoresis.

Question

10 a How many molecules of DNA are produced from one double-stranded starting molecule, after eight cycles of PCR?

    b Explain why it is not possible to use PCR as shown in Figure 19.13 to increase the number of RNA molecules in the same way as it is used to increase the number of DNA molecules.

Gel electrophoresis

Gel electrophoresis is a technique that is used to separate different molecules (Figure 19.15). It is used extensively in the analysis of DNA by separating fragments of DNA. This technique involves placing a mixture of molecules into wells cut into a gel and applying an electric field. The movement of charged molecules within the gel in response to the electric field depends on a number of factors. The most important are:

- net (overall) charge – negatively charged molecules, such as DNA, move towards the anode (+) and positively charged molecules move towards the cathode (–); highly charged molecules move faster than those with less overall charge

- size – smaller molecules move through the gel faster than larger molecules

- composition of the gel – the size of the 'pores' within the gel determines the speed with which fragments of DNA move.

Figure 19.15: Analysing genetic diversity in corals. DNA isolated from coral polyps was amplified by PCR and loaded on to a gel to be separated by electrophoresis.

DNA fragments carry a small charge thanks to the negatively charged phosphate groups along the sugar–phosphate backbone. In DNA electrophoresis, these fragments move through the gel towards the anode. The smaller the fragments, the faster they move. The distance travelled by a length of DNA is inversely proportional to its length: the shorter it is, the further it travels though the gel.

KEY WORD

gel electrophoresis: the separation of charged molecules (e.g. DNA) by differential movement through a gel in an electric field; the degree of movement is dependent on the mass of the fragments of DNA

Two types of gel are used. Polyacrylamide gel is used for separating small fragments of DNA that differ by as little as one nucleotide in length, and agarose gel is used for separating fragments that are between 100 base pairs and 50 000 base pairs in length

Procedure

1 The gel is prepared by dissolving a powder in hot water. While still fluid it is poured into an electrophoresis tank. A 'comb' is placed at one end. After the gel solidifies, the comb is removed, leaving the wells where samples are loaded.

2 When the gel is set, buffer solution is poured into the tank so that it covers the gel. This gives a constant pH.

3 A micropipette is used to transfer samples of DNA to all of the wells (Figures 19.15 and 19.16). The samples of DNA contain a tracking dye which is used to show how far the material in the samples has travelled across the gel. This serves the same function as the solvent front in chromatography (see Figure 13.6).

4 Often a reference sample with DNA fragments of known lengths is placed into a well at one side or at both sides of the gel. This DNA 'ladder' is used to determine the lengths of the fragments of DNA in the samples (Figures 19.17 and 19.18).

5 A battery pack is connected to the electrodes. The negative electrode is at the same end as the wells loaded with DNA (Figure 19.17).

6 The tracking dye shows how far material in the samples has moved across the gel. When the dye has moved across most of the gel, the battery must be disconnected.

7 The buffer solution is poured away and a suitable stain is added to the gel. The stain is rinsed away to reveal bands across the gel showing the positions of the DNA fragments. Alternatively, probes may be labelled with a fluorescent stain. Some stains are only visible when the gels are viewed in ultraviolet light. The lengths of DNA fragments can be determined by comparing them with the DNA 'ladder' at the side of the gel.

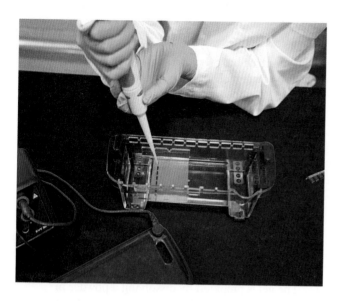

Figure 19.16: Using a micropipette to load the wells in agarose gel with samples of DNA mixed with a blue tracking dye.

DNA in the nuclei of eukaryotes has short nucleotide sequences that are repeated, often many times. These lengths of DNA with repeated sequences are found at particular locations on chromosomes. The DNA at each location has different number of repeats. For example, on a pair of homologous chromosomes the base sequence ACA may be repeated 65 times on one chromosome and 118 times at the same location on the other chromosome. Each location may have many variants, each with a different number of repeats of the base sequence. These variants are inherited in the same way as alleles of genes (Chapter 16). The discovery of these repeated sequences led to methods of genetic profiling (often called genetic fingerprinting).

Among the first of these repeated sequences to be used were minisatellites, which have base sequences of between 10 to 100 base pairs in length that are repeated between 5 and 50 times. These minisatellites can be cut from DNA by restriction endonucleases and the lengths of the fragments determined by gel electrophoresis. The greater the number of repeats, the longer the fragment of DNA. Minisatellites

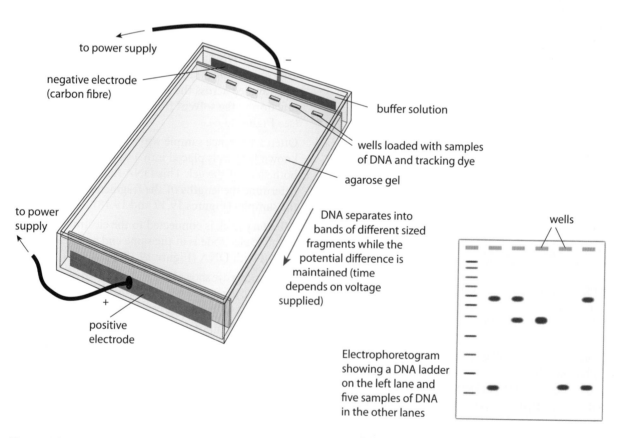

to power supply

negative electrode (carbon fibre)

buffer solution

wells loaded with samples of DNA and tracking dye

agarose gel

to power supply

DNA separates into bands of different sized fragments while the potential difference is maintained (time depends on voltage supplied)

positive electrode

wells

Electrophoretogram showing a DNA ladder on the left lane and five samples of DNA in the other lanes

Figure 19.17: An electrophoresis tank containing a gel with DNA samples in the wells. The tank is filled with a buffer solution and is connected to the power supply. The samples of DNA will move towards the anode (positive electrode).

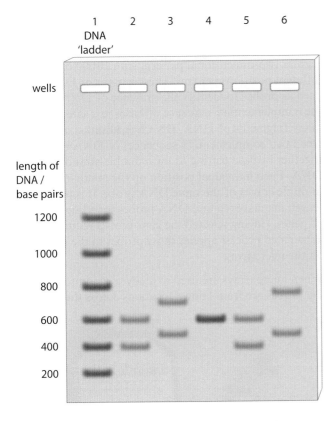

wells

length of
DNA /
base pairs

1200

1000

800

600

400

200

Figure 19.18: A drawing of a gel stained to show the products of PCR of a selected VNTR from five people. Each person has one or two variants of this particular VNTR each with lengths between 400 and 800 base pairs. The DNA in lane 4 is more darkly stained because the person is homozygous for a variant with 600 base pairs so there is twice as much DNA present than in the bands in lanes 2, 3, 5 and 6.

are also known as Variable Number Tandem Repeats (VNTRs) and they were used in the first form of genetic fingerprinting to give the ladder-like bands on gels.

Short tandem repeats (STRs), also known as microsatellites, have largely replaced minisatellites in genetic profiling. STRs are repeated sequences of nucleotides which are much shorter than minisatellites. STRs are composed of 2 to 5 nucleotides which are repeated 10 to 30 times. One STR has the base sequence CACACA repeated between 5 and 20 times. As with minisatellites, the number of repeats in any one STR is variable.

Minisatellites and microsatellites are found on the 22 autosomal chromosomes as well as both X and Y sex chromosomes. In DNA profiling, the lengths of the different variants of selected STRs are determined. Many of the STRs used in genetic profiling are in regions of non-coding DNA between structural genes. The Federal Bureau of Intelligence (FBI) in the USA uses 20 of these STRs (including some on the X and Y chromosomes) in its DNA database.

Questions

11   The genetic researcher Nancy Wexler discovered the position of the gene responsible for Huntington's disease (see Chapter 16) by studying all the descendants of Mary Soto who died from the disease in the early 1800s. Many of these descendants live in fishing villages around Lake Maracaibo in Venezuela. Figure 19.19 is a pedigree diagram showing the inheritance of Huntington's disease in three generations of a family.

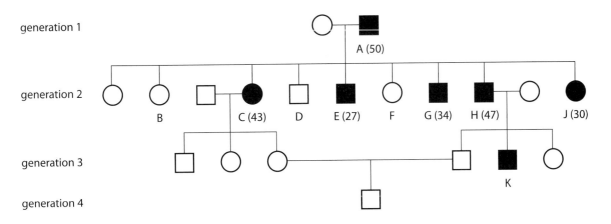

Figure 19.19: A pedigree diagram for a family with Huntington's disease. The numbers in brackets indicate the ages when members of the family first developed symptoms of the disease.

Blood samples were collected from some members of the family. The DNA was extracted and, after treatment with PCR, separated by electrophoresis. Figure 19.20 shows the electrophoretogram.

a   Explain why PCR was used in the analysis of the DNA of this family.

b   Explain why fragments of DNA of different lengths can be separated by gel electrophoresis.

c   Explain why **D** has one band of DNA while all the others in Figure 19.20 have two bands.

d   Looking at Chapter 16 and Figures 19.19 and 19.20, describe the conclusions that can be made from the data in the electrophoretogram.

e   Discuss the advice that could be given by a genetic counsellor to the people in generations 3 and 4 in the family.

12   Suggest why the FBI uses STRs from the X and Y chromosomes in its database.

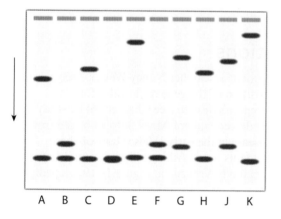

Figure 19.20: An electrophoretogram of samples of DNA from selected members of the family shown in Figure 19.19. The arrow shows the direction of movement of DNA from the wells.

19.5 Analysing and storing genetic information

Microarrays

Microarrays are a valuable tool. They are used to identify the genes present in an organism's genome and to find out which genes are expressed within cells. They have allowed researchers to study very large numbers of genes in a short period of time, increasing the information available.

A microarray is based on a small piece of glass or plastic usually $2\,cm^2$ (Figure 19.21). Short lengths of single-stranded DNA are attached to this support in a regular two-dimensional pattern, with 10 000 or more different positions per cm^2. These lengths of DNA are used as probes to identify the presence of DNA with the complementary sequence of bases in a sample of many fragments of DNA. **DNA hybridisation** occurs when two complementary sequences of DNA bind together by base pairing to form double-stranded DNA. Each individual position on the microarray has multiple copies of the same DNA probe. It is possible to search databases to find DNA probes for a huge range of genes. Having selected the gene probes required, an automated process applies those probes to the positions on the microarray.

When microarrays are used to analyse genomic DNA, the probes are from known locations across the

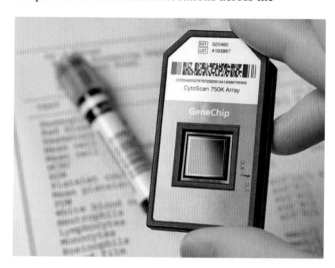

Figure 19.21: A microarray, also known as a DNA chip.

KEY WORDS

microarray (also known as gene or DNA chips): slides that are printed with thousands of tiny spots in defined positions, with each spot containing a known DNA sequence; the DNA molecules attached to each slide act as probes to detect lengths of DNA or RNA with complementary sequences

DNA hybridisation: binding together of two molecules of single-stranded DNA by complementary base pairing

chromosomes of the organism involved. The probes are 500 or more base pairs in length. A single microarray can hold probes from the entire human genome.

Microarrays can be used to compare the genes present in two different species. DNA is collected from each species and cut up into fragments. It is then denatured to give lengths of single-stranded DNA. The DNA is labelled with fluorescent tags so that, for example, DNA from species **A** may be labelled with green tags and DNA from species **B** labelled with red tags. The labelled DNA samples are mixed together and allowed to hybridise with the probes on the microarray. Any DNA that does not bind to probes on the microarray is washed away. The microarray is then inspected using ultraviolet light, which causes the tags to fluoresce. The fluorescence indicates that hybridisation has taken place because the DNA fragments are complementary to the probes on the microarray. Green and red fluorescent spots indicate where DNA from one species only has hybridised with the probes. Where DNA from both species hybridise with a probe, a yellow colour is seen. Yellow spots indicate that the two species have DNA with exactly the same base sequence. This suggests that they have the same genes (Figure 19.22). If there is no colour (or, in the case of Figure 19.22, a blue colour) for a particular position on the microarray, it means that no DNA has hybridised with the probe and that a particular gene is not present in either species.

The microarray is then scanned so that the data can be read by a computer. Data stored by the computer indicate which genes are present in both species, which genes are only found in one of the species and which genes are not present in either species.

Microarrays also make it possible to detect which genes are being expressed at any specific time in each cell in the body. For example, the genes that are expressed in a cancer cell are different from those active in non-cancerous cells. Microarrays are used to compare which genes are active by identifying the genes that are being transcribed into mRNA (Figure 19.23). The mRNA from the two types of cell is collected and reverse transcriptase is used to convert mRNA to cDNA (see Figure 19.3). As the quantity of mRNA in a cell at one time is quite small, the quantity of cDNA may need to be increased by PCR. The cDNA is labelled with fluorescent tags, denatured to give single-stranded DNA and allowed to hybridise with probes on the microarray. Spots on the microarray that fluoresce indicate the genes that were being transcribed in the cell. The intensity of light emitted by each spot indicates the level of activity of each gene. A high intensity indicates that

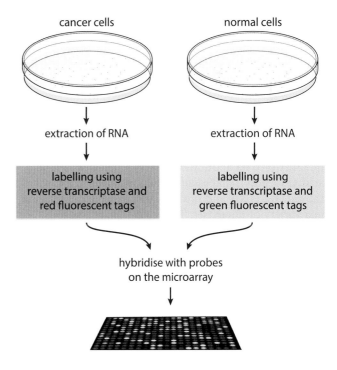

Figure 19.23: How to use a microarray to compare the mRNA molecules present in cancerous and non-cancerous cells. The results identify which genes in the cancerous cells that are not normally expressed are being transcribed.

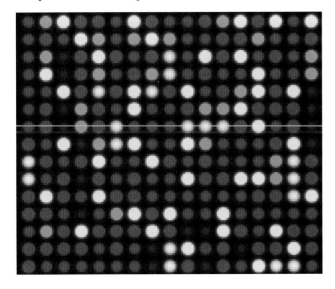

Figure 19.22: A DNA microarray as viewed with a laser scanner. The colours are analysed to show which genes or alleles are present (see text for explanation of the colours).

many mRNA molecules were present in the sample; a low intensity indicates that there were very few. The results therefore show not only which genes are active but also their level of activity. Microarrays have been used to investigate mutations of the genes believed to be involved in breast cancer.

Question

13 The latest estimate of the number of genes in the human genome is between 19 000 and 22 000. Before the invention of microarrays, it was very time-consuming to find out which genes were expressed in any particular cell.

a Explain how it is possible to find out which genes are active in a cell at a particular time in its development.

b Why is it not possible to use the same technique to find out which genes are active in red blood cells?

Digital biology handles big data

Research into the genes that are present in different organisms and the genes that are expressed at any one time in an organism's life generates huge quantities of data. As you have seen, one DNA chip may give 10 000 pieces of information about the presence and absence of genes in genomes or the activity of genes within cells.

DNA sequencing is a fully automated process and the nucleotide (base) sequences of whole genomes and many individual genes are known. There are also a vast quantity of data about the primary structures (amino acid sequences), shapes and functions of proteins. All the data on DNA and proteins are stored in digital form in a variety of databases. The collection, processing and analysis of biological information and data using computer software is known as **bioinformatics**.

> KEY WORD
>
> **bioinformatics:** the collection, processing and analysis of biological information and data using computer software

The quantity of data held in databases is vast and is growing at an exponential rate. The information needs to be in a form that can be shared between scientists. Software developers play an important role in developing systems to store, search, retrieve and analyse data. Computer technology facilitates the collection and analysis of this mass of information and allows access to it via the internet.

The database Ensembl holds data on the genomes of eukaryotic organisms. Among others, it holds the human genome and the genomes of zebra fish and mice that are used a great deal in research. UniProt (universal protein resource) holds information on the primary sequences of proteins and the functions of many proteins, such as enzymes. The Protein Data Bank holds information on the amino acid sequences of proteins and details of their structures (Figure 19.24). Some databases hold very specific information; for example, the database of mutations of the gene *F9* which codes for blood-clotting factor IX is held by University College, London.

Associated with databases are the tools for selection and retrieval of information. Without good search and retrieval tools, all the information stored would be of little value. The search tool BLAST (Basic Local Alignment Search Tool) is an algorithm for comparing primary biological sequence information, such as the primary sequences of different proteins or the nucleotide sequences of genes. Researchers use BLAST to find similarities between sequences that they are studying and those already saved in databases.

When a genome has been sequenced, comparisons can be made with other known genomes. For example, the human genome can be compared to the genomes of the fruit fly, *Drosophila*, the nematode worm, *Caenorhabditis*, or the malarial parasite, *Plasmodium*. Sequences can be matched and degrees of similarity calculated. Similarly, comparisons can be made between amino acid sequences of proteins or structures of proteins. Close similarities indicate recent common ancestry.

Human genes, such as those that are concerned with development, may be found in other organisms such as *Drosophila*. This makes *Drosophila* a useful model for investigating the way in which such genes have their effect. Microarrays can be used to find out when and where genes are expressed during the development of a fruit fly. Researchers can then access information about these genes and the proteins that they code for. For example, they can search databases for identical or similar base sequences in other organisms, compare primary structures of proteins and visualise the 3D structure of the proteins.

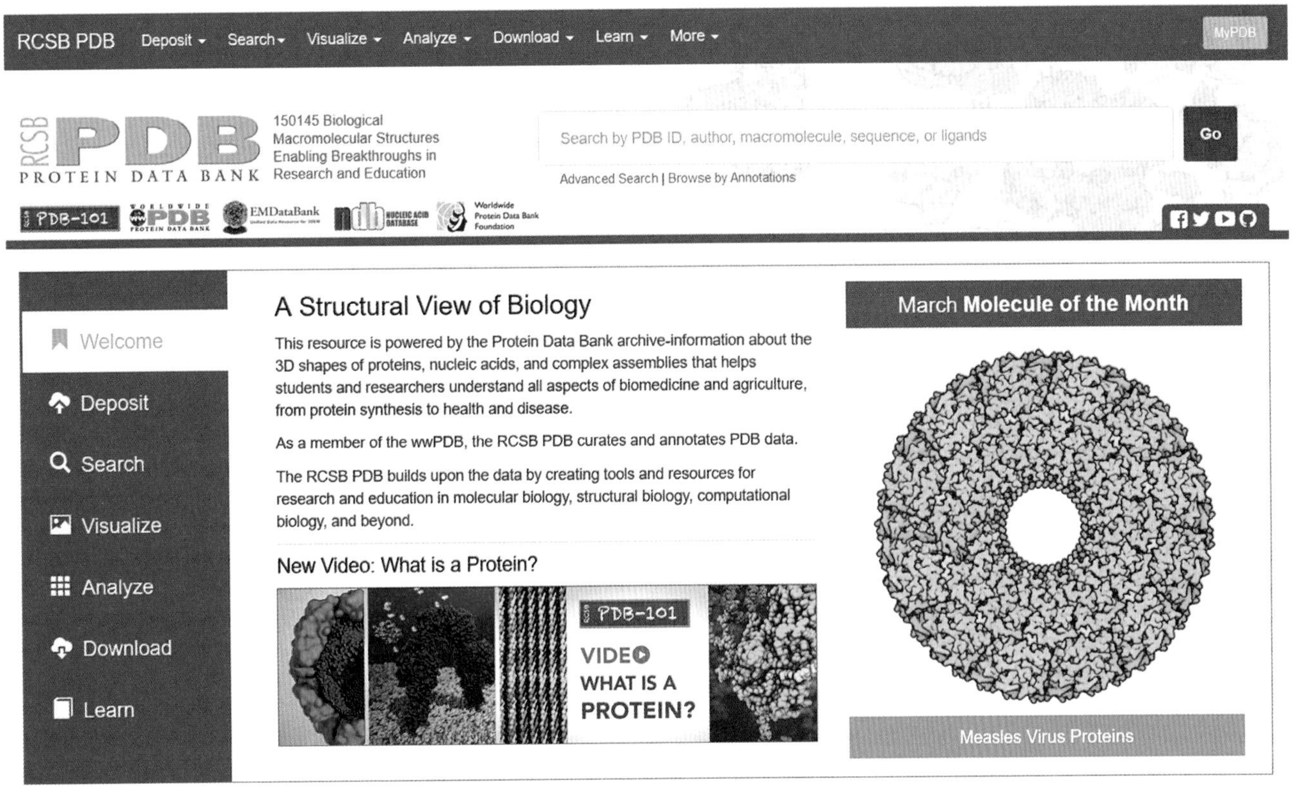

Figure 19.24: The home page of the RCSB Protein Data Bank (www.rcsb.org) which, as of 2019, holds over 150 000 entries. One of the features of the RCSB PDB is the Molecule of the Month.

The nematode *Caenorhabditis elegans* was the first multicellular organism to have its genome fully sequenced. It has fewer than 1000 cells in its body, of which about 300 are nerve cells. It is conveniently transparent, allowing the developmental fate of each of its cells to be mapped. Because of its simplicity, it is used as a model organism for studying the genetics of organ development, the development of neurones into a nervous system and many other areas of biology such as cell death, ageing and behaviour.

All the information we have about the genome of *Plasmodium* is now available in databases. This information is being used to find new methods to control the parasite. For example, being able to read gene sequences is providing valuable information in the development of vaccines for malaria.

The information held in sequences of nucleotide bases is vast and ever growing. Once a complete genome or part of a genome is sequenced, a major focus of research is to identify the genes. This can be done by searching for start and stop codons and also by comparing sequences against the sequences of bases in mRNA from the same organism. The mRNAs represent genes that are transcribed. Detecting mRNA at different times during an organism's development gives data on gene expression that also needs to be stored and analysed.

Some databases provide information that people beyond the research community can use. For example, the CFTR2 database holds information on all 412 variants (as of March 2019) so far identified of the *CFTR* gene. The database makes it possible to search for details of these variants; this means health professionals have up-to-date information on the mutations than can cause cystic fibrosis.

19.6 Genetic technology and medicine

Genetic technology allows products specific to humans to be made by recombinant DNA techniques, such as various types of recombinant human insulin.

The advantages of using bacteria, yeasts and cultures of mammalian cells to produce these proteins include:

- these cells have simple nutritional requirements

- large volumes of product are produced

- the production facilities do not require much space

- the processes can be carried out almost anywhere in the world

- proteins do not have to be extracted from animal sources or by collecting blood from many donors so there are few practical or ethical problems.

Besides insulin, two other human proteins are produced by similar techniques:

- factor VIII – a blood-clotting protein

- adenosine deaminase, which catalyses the breakdown of deoxyadenosine, particularly in T-lymphocytes.

Factor VIII is a protein required for blood clotting. Genetically modified hamster cells are used by several companies to produce recombinant factor VIII. The human gene *F8* codes for factor VIII. *F8* has been inserted into hamster kidney and ovary cells which are then cultured in fermenters. The cells constantly produce factor VIII which is extracted and purified before being used to treat people with haemophilia (Chapter 16, Section 16.4, Monohybrid inheritance and genetic diagrams). These people need regular injections of factor VIII which, before the availability of recombinant factor VIII, came from donated blood. Using donated blood carried risks of infection – for example, from HIV (Chapter 10, Section 10.1, Infectious diseases). Recombinant factor VIII avoids such problems.

Haemophilia is caused by a mutation of *F8* on the X chromosome. Mutations of the gene *ADA* on chromosome 20 lead to a deficiency of adenosine deaminase (ADA). This is one cause of the disease known as severe combined immunodeficiency (SCID). The enzyme catalyses the deamination of adenosine and deoxyadenosine as part of the metabolism of DNA in cells. Deoxyadenosine is toxic to T-lymphocytes,

so children born without functioning ADA have a weakened immune system. Children with SCID can be treated by receiving regular injections of ADA. The enzyme is extracted from cattle, but is also made by genetically modified bacteria (*Escherichia coli*) and in cell cultures derived from insect larvae. Enzyme replacement therapy using ADA has been used successfully to treat people with SCID for more than 20 years. Although other treatments exist, they may not always be successful so this is a long-term alternative.

What is genetic screening?

Genetic screening is the analysis of a person's DNA to check for the presence of one or more alleles that are associated with disease. Samples of DNA can be taken for testing from embryos, newborn babies, children and adults. Some screening can be carried out before a baby is born (Figures 19.25 and 19.26).

If a person from a family with Huntington's disease begins to develop symptoms of the disease, he or she is likely to be advised to have a genetic test to confirm the diagnosis. Other people in the family who do not show any symptoms may also be offered the opportunity to have the genetic test (Figures 19.19 and 19.20). When people who are free of symptoms of a disease are tested like this, it is known as genetic screening. The test is the same whether a person has symptoms or not. It involves PCR to amplify the gene *HTT* and electrophoresis to determine the lengths of the two alleles and to count the number of CAG repeats.

Cystic fibrosis (CF) is one of the most common serious genetic disorders in people of Northern European origin. The disorder affects about one in 2000 live born infants. Cystic fibrosis is caused by a recessive allele of the gene that codes for a transporter protein called cystic fibrosis transmembrane conductance regulator (CFTR). This protein is a transmembrane channel protein that controls the movement of chloride ions down an electrochemical gradient into or out of

---

KEY WORDS

genetic screening: testing an embryo, fetus or adult to find out whether a particular allele is present

cystic fibrosis (CF): a genetic disease caused by recessive alleles of the *CFTR* (cystic fibrosis transmembrane regulator) gene

---

cells. The transport of chloride ions helps control the movement of water in tissues, which is necessary where mucus is produced in places such as the digestive and gas exchange systems (Chapter 9).

The cells in the airways that have the highest concentrations of CFTR are the recently discovered pulmonary ionocytes. Although very few in number, these cells are responsible for most of the movement of chloride ions. The mucus made by goblet cells and mucous glands in the airways is thick and very sticky and does not flow easily. In people who do not have CF, ionocytes pump out chloride ions to give a relatively high concentration of these ions outside cells. The chloride ions decrease the water potential below that of the cytoplasm of the cells so that water moves out of the cells through aquaporins by osmosis. Water mixes with the mucus, making it thin enough for easy removal by the sweeping movements of cilia.

There are many alleles of the gene *CFTR*. Many of these alleles code for faulty versions of this membrane protein. People who have two copies of these alleles may have non-functional CFTR and have the disease CF. Much less water moves out of the cells, so the mucus on their surfaces stays thick and sticky. The cilia cannot remove it all and coughing does not move it either.

Because the faulty *CFTR* alleles are recessive, someone with one faulty allele and one normal allele is able to make enough of the CFTR protein to remain healthy. Such a person is a symptomless carrier of the disease. Each time two heterozygous people have a child, there is a one in four chance that their child will have the disease. This makes it important to screen people who have a history of the disease in their families.

The genetic test for CF involves sequencing the two alleles of the *CFTR* gene that are located on chromosome 7. The current test detects many of the most common mutations. If a couple find that they are both heterozygous for faulty alleles of *CFTR,* then a genetic counsellor may suggest that they undergo IVF treatment and have an embryo biopsy carried out on the embryos so that the implanted embryos are those that will develop into people free of CF.

Mutations of the genes *BRCA-1* (pronounced 'brak-uh one') and *BRCA-2* are involved in the development of breast cancer. The genes *BRCA-1* and *BRCA-2* code for proteins that inhibit the development of tumours. These proteins, known as BRCA1 and BRCA2, play a central role in DNA repair. They move to the site of any DNA damage and attract other proteins to initiate repair of the damage. When either BRCA1 or BRCA2 is absent as the result of a mutation, these DNA repair mechanisms fail. BRCA1 also activates p53, a key protein involved in activating cell death if DNA damage is not repaired. If the damage is not repaired, the cell may become cancerous.

There are more than 1500 known mutations of the two *BRCA* genes. Inherited *BRCA* gene mutations are responsible for about 5−10% of breast cancers and about 15% of ovarian cancers.

An adult woman with a family history of breast cancer may choose to be screened for the mutant alleles of *BRCA-1* and *BRCA-2*, which considerably increase an individual's chance of developing breast cancer. Should the results be positive, the woman may well have frequent tests for the first signs of cancer or decide to have treatment with a drug such as Tamoxifen, which blocks the action of oestrogen on breast tissue. Some women decide to have their breasts removed before any cancer appears.

The genetic test involves sequencing the regions of chromosomes 7 and 13 where the *BRCA* genes are located.

Prenatal diagnosis

Prenatal diagnosis for certain conditions has been available for many years. This has given parents the choice of terminating a pregnancy if the fetus is found to have a serious inherited disease. Recent developments in gene technology now allow parents to request genetic screening for a great variety of conditions. The tests that parents request will most likely be conditions in their family or those that are common in their ethnic group.

Amniocentesis is used to obtain a sample of amniotic fluid at 15−16 weeks of pregnancy. Various tests can be carried out on this sample to check the health of the fetus. Most amniocentesis samples are taken to look for chromosomal mutations.

Ultrasound scanning is used to visualise the fetus and to locate the position of the placenta, fetus and umbilical cord. A suitable point for the insertion of the hypodermic syringe needle is chosen and this is marked on the abdominal skin surface. Generally, this position is away from the fetus, umbilical cord and placenta.

Chorionic villus sampling (CVS) can be carried out between 10 and 13 weeks of pregnancy. It allows parents to get an earlier warning of any genetic abnormalities in the fetus than is possible with amniocentesis. A small sample of part of the placenta called the chorion is removed by a needle. The needle is narrow (less than 0.8 mm in diameter). The procedure is monitored by ultrasound scanning (Figure 19.25).

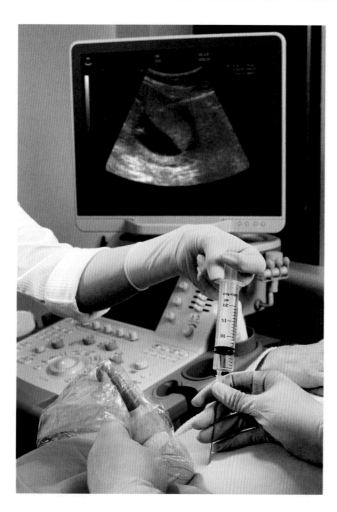

Figure 19.25: In chorionic villus sampling, an ultrasound scanner is used to guide the needle to the placenta to remove a small sample of the fetal chorionic villi which are embedded in the placenta. A small sample of the fetal blood is removed for analysis.

The typical miscarriage rate for all women is about 2–3% at 10–12 weeks of pregnancy. Like amniocentesis, CVS has a small increased risk of miscarriage. It has been estimated that the miscarriage rate is increased by about 1–2%. This is a slightly greater risk than for amniocentesis but, before 15 weeks, chorionic villus sampling is probably less risky than amniocentesis.

Non-invasive prenatal genetic screening is an alternative to amniocentesis and CVS. Fragments of DNA of cells from the placenta that have the same genotype as the fetus find their way into the maternal circulation. These fragments are isolated from blood samples and

tested. These tests can indicate whether the fetus has any genetic abnormalities, such as changes in the number of chromosomes, changes in chromosome structure and gene mutations (Figure 19.26).

Prenatal diagnosis linked with programmes of genetic screening have proved very successful in countries such as Cyprus at reducing the number of children born with thalassaemia, a disease similar to sickle cell anaemia. This is because some parents who discover that their child may be born with the severe form of the disease decide to have an abortion.

Questions

14 A couple find that they are both heterozygous for a mutant allele of *CFTR*. They are recommended to have IVF treatment and embryo biopsy. State the genotype of the embryo that is likely to be implanted.

15 Suggest how genetic screening can reduce the numbers of children born with severe genetic disorders.

What is gene therapy?

Gene technology and rapidly increasing knowledge of the positions of particular genes on human chromosomes have given scientists the opportunity to identify many genes that are responsible for genetic disorders such as the deficiency of adenosine deaminase (ADA-SCID) and some inherited eye diseases. When techniques of genetic engineering were developed in the 1980s, it was envisaged that it would not be long before gene technology could 'cure' many genetic diseases by inserting into cells the 'normal' alleles of the genes involved. This process is called **gene therapy**. But gene therapy has proved to be far more difficult than was originally thought. The problems lie in getting normal alleles of the genes into a person's cells and then making them work properly when they get there.

> ### KEY WORD
>
> **gene therapy:** treatment of a genetic disorder by inserting genetically corrected cells into the body or introducing functioning genes directly into affected cells

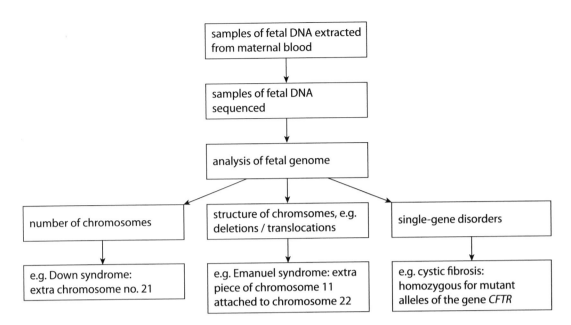

Figure 19.26: Fetal DNA can be sequenced to check for a variety of inherited disorders, involving changes in chromosome number and structure and those caused by gene mutations.

Gene therapy for SCID

The first successful gene therapy was performed in 1990 on a four-year-old girl from Cleveland, Ohio. She had the disease ADA-SCID, which meant that her immune system did not function correctly and she was therefore very susceptible to infectious diseases. Children with ADA-SCID were often isolated inside plastic 'bubbles' to protect them from infections.

Some of the child's T-lymphocytes were removed and normal alleles of the *ADA* gene were introduced into them, using a virus as a vector. The cells were then replaced. This was not a permanent cure. Regular transfusions (every three to five months) were necessary to keep the immune system functioning properly.

Two years later, gene therapy using stem cells harvested from bone marrow was successful. Unfortunately, in 2000, four children in France who had received gene therapy for a different form of SCID developed leukaemia as a result of the retrovirus used as a vector. Retroviruses insert their genes into the host's genome randomly. This means that they may insert their genes within another gene or into the regulatory sequence of a patient's gene, which may then activate a nearby gene causing cancer.

The adeno-associated virus (AAV) is now used as a vector for inserting the gene into stem cells in bone marrow. This virus does not insert its genes into the host genome and so they are not passed on to daughter cells when a cell divides. Gene therapy of stem cells is more successful than it was in the 1990s since there is no need for regular transfusion of T-lymphocytes.

Gene therapy for Leber congenital amaurosis

A rare form of inherited blindness called Leber congenital amaurosis (LCA) causes cells in the retina to die off from an early age. This condition has been reversed using gene therapy. The recessive allele causes impaired vision from birth leading to complete blindness in early adulthood. The dominant allele of the gene, *RPE65*, codes for a protein that regenerates visual pigment in rod and cone cells in the retina after they have been exposed to light. This allele has been inserted into the cells of people who are homozygous recessive for this gene.

The eye is considered to be a good organ for developing gene therapies because it is small and easy to target. Genes can be delivered precisely to the retina, the layer of light-sensitive cells at the back of the eye. The progress of the treatment can be monitored easily. Also there is little activity of immune cells inside the eye, so there is a low risk of harmful immune responses to wthe vector.

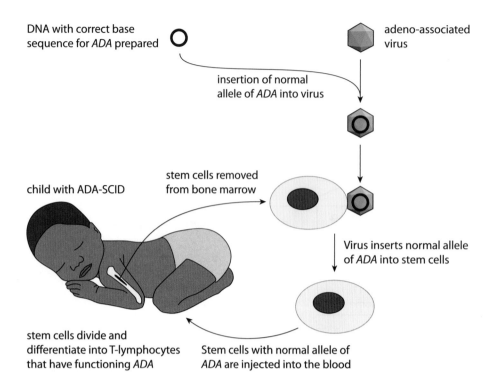

Figure 19.27: The procedure for carrying out gene therapy for SCID.

Questions

16 Gene therapy for diseases such as ADA-SCID and LCA is possible because they are caused by recessive alleles. Explain how it might be possible to treat or cure Huntington's disease which is caused by a dominant allele.

17 Summarise the challenges posed by gene therapy that have had to be overcome by researchers.

18 Outline the different uses of recombinant DNA in the treatment of genetic diseases.

Social and ethical considerations of genetic screening and gene therapy

Genetic screening

There are social benefits of genetic screening. If people at risk of developing diseases such as breast cancer can be identified before they develop symptoms, they can be offered preventative treatments. They can also be offered advice about changes in lifestyle to reduce the risk of developing the condition. Genetic screening also has economic benefits for society because money that health services would otherwise spend on long-term treatments is saved. Many people take the view that, where the technology exists to identify people at risk of genetic disease, it should be applied so that they can be treated and helped. However, this is controversial.

Genetic screening raises ethical issues. These issues involve the principles that determine people's behaviour and the decisions that they make over their personal and professional lives. Consider genetic screening for Huntington's disease.

Huntington's disease is a late-onset disease – symptoms do not usually appear until middle age, by which time people have usually already had children (see Chapter 16 and Question 11). There is no cure for this disease and the treatments available can only alleviate the symptoms. People in families with Huntington's have a dilemma: should they have the genetic test to find out whether or not they have the dominant allele for the disease? This also poses ethical dilemmas: would you rather be told that you are at high risk of developing this disease, even though nothing can be done about it, or live with the uncertainty of not knowing? Is it a good idea to have this information before you start a family? Decisions are made even more difficult by the possibility that a person with the dominant allele for Huntington's may live their whole life completely free of the disorder as it sometimes does not develop.

In 1989 the first 'designer baby' was created. Officially known as pre-implantation genetic diagnosis (PGD), the technique involved mixing the father's sperm with the mother's eggs (oocytes) in a dish – that is, a normal IVF procedure. It was the next step that was new. At the eight-cell stage, one of the cells from the tiny embryo was removed. The DNA in the cell was analysed and used to predict whether or not the embryo would have a genetic disease for which both parents were carriers. An embryo not carrying the allele that would cause the disease was chosen for implantation, and embryos that did have this allele were discarded.

Since then, many babies have been born using this technique. It has been used to avoid pregnancies in which the baby would have had haemophilia, Huntington's disease and other genetic diseases. In 2004 it was first used in the UK to produce a baby that was a tissue match with an elder sibling. The purpose was to use cells from the umbilical cord as a transplant into the sick elder child.

Many people have ethical objections to PGD and prenatal testing because they believe it has been abused. Some parents have decided to terminate pregnancies simply because the child is not the sex that they want. They have also used PGD to select the sex of the embryo that they choose to implant. This is called sex pre-selection, and many people think is totally unethical. On a practical level, this practice may unbalance the sex ratio in the population. Some people also disagree with termination of pregnancy in any circumstances, regardless of what may be revealed by screening.

There are also those who believe that the resources spent on providing expensive genetic technology for the rich could otherwise be spent on providing basic health care for the poor.

Gene therapy

Gene therapy is one of the gene technologies that has so far cost huge amounts of money in research but has produced very few successful treatments or cures for diseases. As you have seen, there are several successful gene therapies, but others have yet to proceed beyond the stage of medical trials.

As far as anyone can predict, the children who have been treated successfully for ADA-SCID can expect to lead a normal life and have a normal lifespan. People given gene therapy of LCA have had their sight restored. However, some gene therapies are considered to be dangerous because they have led to unfortunate side effects. For example, the immune system may be stimulated to respond to the vector (e.g. a virus) or a protein that is coded for by the gene inserted.

Gene therapy has brought limited benefits to society because only a tiny minority of people have benefited. Some people argue that changing the genes we inherit is unethical and is a first step on the road to changing genes to 'improve' humans. Eugenics is the idea that the human population can be 'improved' by selecting or encouraging some people to have children and discouraging others. Eugenics was a fashionable theory in the early part of the 20th century. However, it was applied in horrific circumstances and totally discredited in Nazi Germany in the 1930s and 1940s.

There are also practical problems with gene therapy.

- Gene therapies may be temporary because the cells that are genetically modified have a sort lifespan, such as those lining the airways that are targeted in treating CF.

- It has proved difficult to direct vectors to the specific cells where the allele is to be expressed. If the allele is inserted into the genome of the cell, it is not always expressed.

- Only recessive conditions, such as haemophilia and LCA, can be treated. It is not yet possible to switch off a dominant allele such as the one that causes Huntington's disease.

The problems about directing genes into appropriate places in the genome may soon be solved by the use of Crispr/Cas9 technology, discussed earlier. However, this raises many ethical problems.

It is possible that, once gene therapies for monogenic conditions become accepted, there will be similar therapies for the more complex diseases, such as heart disease, dementias and cancers, that are influenced by environmental factors as much as by genes. The types of gene therapy described so far are examples of somatic cell gene therapy. The solution to the problem of delivering genes to all the cells that require them could be overcome by germ-line therapy. This means placing the gene or genes concerned into an egg or into a zygote. The gene would then be in every cell of the body and may be passed on to future generations. At present, germ-line gene therapy is not legal in any country, although it may have been carried out in China.

RNA interference (iRNA) is a new alternative to the methods of gene therapy described above. Small molecules of RNA are taken up by cells and combine with the mRNA of a gene that needs to be 'silenced'. Results of a clinical trial of a drug which uses this technique were published in 2019. The drug silenced a gene that codes for an enzyme in the pathway that produces haem in the liver. iRNA has none of the ethical issues associated with the techniques that involve changing genomic DNA.

Question

19 What are the limits to gene therapy? Discuss the social and ethical issues surrounding this technology. Decide which procedures are ethical and which are not.

19.7 Genetic technology and agriculture

Genetically modified plants

Most genetically modified (GM) plants are crop plants modified to be resistant to herbicides (e.g. glufosinate and glyphosate) or insect pests. Herbicide resistance allows farmers to spray herbicides to kill weeds while a crop such as maize is growing (Figure 19.28). Weeds would otherwise compete with the crop for space, light, water and nutrients from the soil. Pest resistance reduces losses to insect pests such as the cotton boll weevil. These modifications reduce some costs for farmers and increase crop yields.

Herbicide-resistant crops

Growing a herbicide-resistant crop allows crop plants to make full use of the resources available so yields increase.

The herbicide glyphosate inhibits an enzyme involved in the synthesis of three amino acids: phenylalanine, tyrosine and tryptophan. These amino acids are needed to produce proteins essential for growth. Glyphosate is absorbed by a plant's leaves and is then transported to the growing tips. Without the production of proteins in the growth areas, the plant dies.

Figure 19.28: Part of a field of herbicide-resistant maize, *Zea mays*. The crop has been sprayed with a herbicide which kills the weeds but leaves the maize plants unaffected.

Various microorganisms have versions of the enzyme involved in the synthesis of phenylalanine, tyrosine and tryptophan that are not affected by glyphosate. The gene that was transferred into crop plants came from a strain of the bacterium *Agrobacterium*.

There are concerns that cultivating crops that are resistant to herbicides may have detrimental effects on the environment. These include the following.

- GM plants are likely to become an agricultural weed when they grow in fields of other crops.

- Pollen will transfer the resistance gene to wild relatives of the crop plant, producing hybrid offspring that are invasive weeds.

- Herbicide-resistant weeds will evolve because so much of the same herbicide is used.

Herbicide-resistant mutant plants of various species have been found growing near fields where glyphosate has been used extensively. However, the herbicide is widely used as a general weedkiller as well as on glyphosate-resistant crops. Gene technology is not necessarily responsible for this evolution of resistance, which may arise in areas where no GM crops are grown.

Insect-resistant crops

Another important agricultural development is that of GM plants that are protected against attack by insect pests. Maize is protected against the corn borer. This pest eats the leaves of the plants and then burrows into the stalk, eating its way upwards until the plant cannot support the cobs where the grains are forming. Cotton, *Gossypium hirsutum*, is protected against pests such as the boll worm (Figures 19.29 and 19.30). In both plants, yield is improved by genetic modification.

Figure 19.30: The cotton boll worm, *Helicoverpa armigera*, is a major insect pest of cotton plants. Caterpillars of this pest species feed on cotton bolls.

Figure 19.29: Cotton plants are grown for the fibres that develop inside the fruits, known as bolls. In this photograph, a cotton boll is about to open just before the crop is harvested.

Bt toxin is lethal to insects that eat it but harmless to other animals. A gene for this toxin has been taken from a bacterium, *Bacillus thuringiensis*. Different strains of *B. thuringiensis* produce different toxins that can be used against different insect species. Crop plants that contain the Bt toxin gene from *B. thuringiensis* produce their own insecticides. However, insect populations can evolve resistance to toxins.

Large numbers of crop plants containing the genes for Bt toxin may accelerate the evolution of resistance to it. The most likely detrimental effects on the environment of growing insect-resistant crops are:

- the evolution of resistance by the insect pests

- a damaging effect on other species of insect

- the transfer of the added gene to other species of plant.

On the positive side, less pesticide is used. This reduces the risk of spray carrying to other areas and affecting non-target species of insect. Remember also that only insects that actually eat the crop are affected by Bt toxin.

Questions

20 Several crop species have been genetically modified to express poisons based on a toxic compound from the bacterium *B. thuringiensis* (Bt). GM varieties of soya, oil seed rape, cotton, maize and tobacco are all grown in countries such as the United States, China and Brazil.

> ### KEY WORD
>
> **Bt toxin:** insecticidal toxin produced by the bacterium *Bacillus thuringiensis*; the gene for Bt toxin is transferred to crop plants to make them resistant to insect pests

a Explain the advantages of growing Bt varieties of these crop plants.

b Outline how crop plants, such as those listed above, are genetically modified to improve productivity.

21 Outline the potential risks of growing GM crop varieties and suggest steps that can be taken to minimise them.

Genetically modified animals

GM animals for food production are much rarer than crop plants. An example is the GM Atlantic salmon, developed in the USA and Canada (Figure 19.31). A growth-hormone regulating gene from a Pacific Chinook salmon and a promoter from another species of fish, an ocean pout, were injected into a fertilised egg of an Atlantic salmon. By producing growth hormone throughout the year, the modified salmon are able to grow all year, instead of just in spring and summer. As a result, modified fish reach market size in about 18 months, compared with the three years needed by an unmodified fish. It is proposed to rear only sterile females and to farm them in land-based tanks. The characteristics of the GM salmon reduce their ability to compete with wild salmon in a natural environment. This has led the US Food and Drug Administration (FDA) to declare that they are highly unlikely to have any significant effects on the environment and are 'as safe as food as conventional Atlantic salmon'.

In 2013 Canada approved the production of GM salmon eggs at a facility on Prince Edward Island for onward shipping to a larger facility in Panama where the adult fish are raised. In 2016 Canadian authorities permitted the sale of GM salmon. As recently as March 2019 the Food and Drug Administration gave permission for salmon eggs to be imported from Canada to be raised in Indiana for sale in the USA. This comes nearly 20 years after work on genetically modifying salmon began.

Ethical and social implications of using GMOs in food production

The justification made by the big companies that have invested heavily in GM crops is that agriculture needs to increase yields if we are to grow enough food for the world population. Productive land will have to be even more productive if lots of low-lying land currently used to grow crops is lost to rising sea levels. A reason for investing in herbicide-resistant and insect-resistant crops is to reduce the very heavy losses that occur before and after harvest.

Many people, however, are sceptical of these claims and are concerned about the environmental impact of GM crops. Some of the concerns about GM crops are as follows.

- The modified crop plants may become agricultural weeds or invade natural habitats.

- The introduced gene(s) may be transferred by pollen to wild relatives whose hybrid offspring may become more invasive.

Figure 19.31: A GM salmon and non-GM salmon of the same age. Note that the GM fish do not grow larger than non-GM salmon but attain their maximum size more quickly.

- The introduced gene(s) may be transferred by pollen to unmodified plants growing on farms that grow organic crops.

- The modified plants may be a direct hazard to humans, domestic animals or other beneficial animals, by being toxic or by causing allergic reactions.

- The herbicide that can now be used on the crop will leave toxic residues in the crop which may harm consumers.

- GM seeds are expensive and their cost may remove any advantage of growing a resistant crop.

- Growers mostly need to buy seed each season, keeping costs high. In contrast, seed from this year's crop of traditional (non-GM) varieties can be kept to sow for next year's crop.

- In parts of the world where a lot of GM crops are grown, there is a danger of losing traditional varieties. This is important because these varieties have desirable background genes for particular places and they may have characteristics that could be useful in a world where the climate is changing. This requires a programme of growing and harvesting traditional varieties and setting up a seed bank to preserve them (Chapter 18, Section 18.4, Protecting endangered species).

Despite these concerns, there are now millions of hectares of GM crops and trees growing across the world. In the USA in 2011, half the cotton crop and more than half the maize and soya crops were GM. Significant areas of China, Brazil and India are used for these crops, and farmers in developing countries are adopting the products of gene technology with enthusiasm. The exception is Europe, with its careful and strict controls. Europe also has well-organised groups of protesters. Although large quantities of GM crops are grown in the USA, there have been campaigns waged against the introduction of GM salmon, named 'Frankenfish' by some people.

But are there any damaging effects on human societies of genetic technology? Have any of the theoretical hazards had an actual effect on human societies?

There is little evidence of genes 'escaping' into the wild. No 'superweed' has appeared to reduce crop growth. There are very few examples of foods produced from GMOs unexpectedly turning out to be allergenic. Unless the known effects of GM crops become much greater than have so far been measured, the effect on human societies may be said to be small but positive. There are, though, possible effects that cannot yet be measured, such as the future consequences of any loss of biodiversity from growing GM crops.

REFLECTION

List the different ways in which genetic technology can be used to alter the genomes of plants, animals (including humans) and microorganisms. Summarise the benefits and hazards associated with each of these genetic technologies described in this chapter.

- Use a suitable way to present the benefits and hazards of using genetic technologies.

- How did you go about choosing a suitable way to present the information in this activity? Did you find it helpful to talk to others and, if so, what help did they give you?

Final reflection

Discuss with a friend which, if any, parts of Chapter 19 you need to:

- read through again to make sure you really understand

- seek more guidance on, even after going over it again.

SUMMARY

Genetic technology involves using a variety of techniques to investigate the sequence of nucleotides in DNA and alter an organism's DNA. Genetic engineering involves extracting DNA from one organism and placing it into the DNA of another to form recombinant DNA (rDNA). Gene(s) must be inserted in such a way that they will be expressed in the genetically modified organism (GMO).

Restriction endonucleases are enzymes that cut across DNA at specific sites, known as restriction sites. Restriction enzymes can make staggered cuts in DNA that give rise to short lengths of unpaired bases known as sticky ends or straight cuts to give blunt ends. Pieces of DNA with sticky ends that are complementary to each other are able to join together by forming hydrogen bonds. The enzyme DNA ligase joins together the sugar–phosphate backbones of pieces of DNA by catalysing the formation of phosphodiester bonds.

In genetic engineering, vectors are used to carry pieces of DNA into cells: typical examples are plasmids, viruses and liposomes.

Plasmids are small circles of double-stranded DNA; they are useful for genetic engineering because they can be cut with restriction enzymes and have promoters and gene markers (e.g. genes for antibiotics, GFP or GUS) inserted into them alongside the gene(s) to transform the host cell.

A promoter must be inserted alongside the gene because organisms will not transcribe and express a gene unless there is a binding site for RNA polymerase.

Cells that have taken up plasmids with the desired gene can be identified by detecting fluorescence (GFP) or appropriate staining (GUS).

Lengths of DNA for genetic modification can be synthesised directly from mRNA by using the enzyme reverse transcriptase. Specific lengths of DNA can also be synthesised from nucleotides using knowledge of the genetic code.

Gene editing is a form of genetic engineering in which DNA can be inserted into a genome using the Crispr/Cas9 system.

Electrophoresis is used to separate fragments of DNA of different lengths; the material to be tested is placed in wells in agarose gel and a voltage applied across the gel.

The polymerase chain reaction (PCR) is a method of making very large numbers of copies of DNA from very small quantities (even one molecule). In PCR, DNA is denatured by heat to separate the strands; a short length of DNA known as a primer attaches to one end of each strand so that DNA polymerase can start synthesising a complementary strand using free nucleotides (as in replication). The double-stranded copies of DNA are separated again and the process repeated many times to 'bulk up' the DNA. Heat-stable DNA polymerases are used in PCR; the first was *Taq* polymerase that is found in a thermophilic bacterium, *Thermus aquaticus*.

A gene probe is a length of single-stranded DNA, which has a known base sequence and is used to hybridise with lengths of DNA which have the complementary sequence; probes are labelled in some way to make them 'visible' (e.g. with radioactive phosphorus). PCR and gene probes are used in forensic investigations to look for matches between the DNA left at crime scenes and the DNA of suspects.

Microarrays contain many thousands of gene probes and are used in two ways: to analyse the presence or absence of genes in different genomes and detect the presence of mRNA from cells to detect the genes that are being expressed at any one time.

Databases hold huge amounts of information on DNA and proteins. Bioinformatics deals with the storage and analysis of biological data; more specifically, nucleotide sequences and amino acid sequences of proteins.

Information in databases is available to researchers. They can compare genes from different organisms, can search details of the various mutant alleles that cause genetic diseases and compare the shapes of proteins.

CONTINUED

Many recombinant human proteins are now produced by GMOs, such as bacteria and yeasts. This makes available drugs, such as recombinant adenosine deaminase (ADA) to treat SCID and recombinant factor VIII to treat haemophilia. This production also secures the supply of others that were previously available from other sources, such as insulin.

Genetic screening involves testing people to find out if they carry any faulty alleles for genes that can cause disease; there are genetic tests for many genetic diseases including breast cancer associated with *BRCA-1* and *BRCA-2*, Huntington's disease and cystic fibrosis. Genetic counsellors may help people, who find that they or their unborn children have a disease-causing allele, to make a decision about how to act on this information.

Gene therapy involves the addition of genes to human or animal cells that can cure, or reduce the symptoms of genetic diseases, such as SCID and some inherited eye diseases. Successful gene therapy involves selecting a suitable vector, such as viruses or liposomes, or inserting DNA directly into cells.

Genetic engineering is used to improve the quality and yield of crop plants and livestock. Crops, such as maize and cotton, have been genetically modified for herbicide resistance and insect resistance to decrease losses and increase production.

Genetic technology can provide benefits in, for example, agriculture and medicine, but has the associated risk of the escape of the gene concerned into organisms other than the intended host. The risk is seen to be particularly high for genetically modified crops that are released into the environment to grow.

The social implications of genetic technology are the beneficial effects of the this technology on human societies. Ethics are sets of standards by which a particular group of people agree to regulate their behaviour, distinguishing an acceptable from an unacceptable activity. Each group must decide, first, whether research into gene technology is acceptable, and then whether or not it is acceptable to adopt the successful technologies.

EXAM-STYLE QUESTIONS

1 a The table shows enzymes that are used in gene technology. Copy and complete the table to show the role of each enzyme.

Enzyme	Role
DNA ligase	
DNA polymerase	
restriction enzyme	
reverse transcriptase	
Cas9	

[5]

b Explain why it is easier to devise a gene therapy for a condition caused by a recessive allele than for one caused by a dominant allele. [3]

c Explain the advantages and disadvantages of genetic screening. [7]

[Total: 15]

CONTINUED

2 The Crispr/Cas9 system is a gene-editing technique that has been used extensively since being introduced in 2012.

The diagram shows how Cas9 functions.

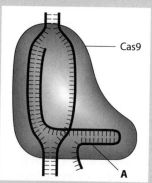

a i Name the molecule labelled **A and** explain its role in gene editing. [3]

ii Explain how Crispr/Cas9 can be used to correct the function of a faulty allele. [3]

b In 2016 it was reported that scientists had removed the protein PD-1 from T-lymphocytes in a human patient.

i Outline the importance of T-lymphocytes. [2]

ii Explain how Crispr/Cas9 can be used to remove a protein from specialised cells, such as T-lymphocytes. [5]

c i Explain why Crispr/Cas9 is likely to be used to treat people with blood disorders rather than disorders of the nervous and muscular systems. [3]

ii Suggest the advantages of using gene editing using Crisp/Cas9 over other methods of gene technology, such as gene therapy using viruses. [3]

[Total: 19]

3 The graph shows the changes in temperature in a PCR machine during two cycles.

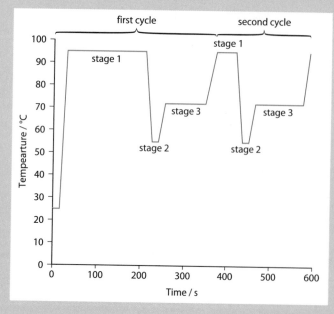

CONTINUED

a   Name the enzyme that carries out the synthesis of DNA during PCR.   [1]

b   Explain why

   i   a high temperature is required for stage 1   [2]

   ii   enzymes do not need to be added for each cycle   [2]

   iii   a buffer solution with magnesium ions is used in PCR.   [2]

c   i   Describe what happens in stages 2 and 3.   [3]

   ii   Suggest why stage 1 of the first cycle is longer than stage 1 of the second and all subsequent cycles.   [2]

d   Explain why one pair of primers is not suitable to use for amplifying all samples of DNA when using PCR.   [2]

e   Explain why single-stranded DNA produced after stage 1 do not recombine to form double-stranded DNA.   [2]

f   Explain how PCR differs from DNA replication during the cell cycle.   [4]

[Total: 20]

4   A gene construct is one or more genes together with regulatory base sequences which are inserted into a vector to produce recombinant DNA. Gene constructs often contain a marker gene, such as enhanced green fluorescent protein (*GFP*).

a   i   Explain why marker genes, such as enhanced *GFP*, are included in gene constructs.   [3]

   ii   Explain the advantage of using an enzyme as a marker gene.   [1]

    AqauAdvantage® salmon are genetically modified female Atlantic salmon, *Salmo salar*. These fish have a single copy of opAFP-GHc2, which is a gene construct prepared from a structural gene from chinook salmon, *Oncorhynchus tshawytscha*, that codes for a growth hormone and a promoter from ocean pout, *Zoarces americanus*.

b   i   Outline **one** method in which the gene that codes for growth hormone may have been obtained from *O. tshawytscha*.   [2]

   ii   Explain why it is necessary to include a promoter in the construct.   [3]

   iii   Suggest how the components of the gene construct were assembled.   [3]

   iv   Outline how the gene construct is inserted into cells of *S. salar*.   [3]

c   The GM salmon are all triploid ($3n$). Suggest the advantages of making the salmon triploid.   [3]

d   These GM salmon are grown in facilities in Panama, but for many years they were not approved for human consumption by the Food and Drug Administration in the USA.

   Suggest why it has proved difficult for GM salmon to receive approval for human consumption.   [4]

[Total: 22]

5 Aphids are economically important pests of many crop plants worldwide. Aphids have piercing mouthparts as shown in the drawing. They insert their mouthparts into phloem tissue and feed on the sap.

Peach potato aphids, *Myzus persicae*, not only reduce the yield of crops by their feeding, but also transmit more than 100 different plant viruses.

a State the term given to an organism that transmits pathogens. **[1]**

There are varieties of *M. persicae* that are resistant to many insecticides. The insecticide pirimicarb acts by binding to acetylcholinesterase (AChE) at synapses in insects. The gene *Ace* codes for acetylcholinesterase which consists of over 500 amino acids. Sequencing of the DNA of this gene found that resistant aphids had a change to a single amino acid in AChE as shown in the diagram.

AChE from pirimicarb-susceptible aphids	glu glu gly tyr tyr ser ile phe tyr tyr leu
AChE from pirimicarb-resistant aphids	glu glu gly tyr tyr phe ile phe tyr tyr leu

b **i** Explain how it is possible to predict the primary structure of a protein from a gene sequence. **[2]**

  ii Researchers are likely to find a function for a protein from knowledge of its primary structure alone. Explain how this is possible. **[3]**

  iii Explain how a change to a single amino acid in AChE can give resistance to an insecticide such as pirimicarb. **[3]**

c Other aphid species that showed resistance to pirimicarb had the same change in the primary structure of acetylcholinesterase.

Explain how resistance to pirimicarb may have arisen and evolved in a population of *M. persicae*. **[6]**

[Total: 15]

6 Soya plants have been genetically engineered to be resistant to certain insect pests. The *cry* gene from the bacterium *Bacillus thuringiensis* that codes for a toxin is inserted into soya plants using the bacterium *Agrobacterium tumefaciens* as outlined in the steps of the flow chart.

CONTINUED

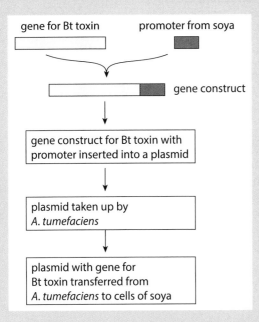

a   Explain why a promoter is attached to the gene for Bt toxin as shown in
    the flow chart.   [2]

b   The enzyme DNA ligase is used in the steps shown in the flow chart.

    Explain the role of DNA ligase in producing genetically engineered soya. [2]

c   Outline how the cells of cotton plants use the *cry* gene to make the toxic
    protein.   [5]

d   Before becoming widely available to farmers, genetically modified (GM)
    soya is grown in extensive field trials. Suggest two reasons why field trials
    are necessary.   [3]

e   Large areas of land in North and South America and in China are devoted
    to growing GM crops, such as herbicide-resistant maize and pest-resistant
    cotton.

    Outline the arguments made for the introduction of these GM crops.   [5]

                                                                    [Total: 17]

7   BRCA1 and BRCA2 are proteins each composed of a single polypeptide.
    These two proteins are involved in the control of the cell cycle and in the
    repair of DNA.

    Mutations to the genes *BRCA-1* and *BRCA-2* can cause changes to the proteins
    so that the cell cycle is not controlled correctly.

    DNA sequencing has detected many mutations within both genes. Some of
    these are known to lead to cancer. Many are known to be harmless, but the
    effects of others are unknown.

    BRCA1 is composed of 1863 amino acids. One of the many mutations that
    occur in *BRCA-1* leads to a change in the amino acid at position 871 in the
    primary structure of the protein as shown in the table.

CONTINUED

| codon in the coding strand of normal gene | CCA | amino acid in position 871 of normal BRCA1 | proline |
| codon in the coding strand of mutant variant | CAA | amino acid in position 871 of mutant BRCA1 | glutamine |

a **i** State the type of gene mutation that is shown in the table. [1]

ii The amino acid proline has a non-polar R group (side chain) and glutamine has a polar R group.

Suggest the effect that this mutation may have on the structure of BRCA1. [3]

b Mutations to *BRCA-1* are inherited as autosomal dominant disorders. Explain how the inheritance of this disorder differs from the inheritance pattern for an autosomal recessive disorder, such as cystic fibrosis. [3]

c Some mutations in *BRCA-1* are much more common in certain groups of people. A deletion of two nucleotides from the gene results in molecules of BRCA1 that are only 38 amino acids in length. This mutation is more common in Ashkenazi Jews than in other ethnic groups.

i Explain why the protein BRCA1 is only 38 amino acids in length in people with this mutation. [2]

ii Explain why particular mutations of *BRCA-1* are more likely to occur in certain ethnic groups. [3]

iii Some countries have genetic screening programmes for breast cancer. Suggest the implications of the higher frequency of some mutations in certain ethnic groups for these screening programmes. [3]

[Total: 15]

SELF-EVALUATION CHECKLIST

After studying this chapter, complete a table like this:

I can	See section...	Needs more work	Almost there	Ready to move on
explain the principles of genetic technology	19.1			
describe the tools and techniques available to the genetic engineer	19.2, 19.3			
describe and explain PCR and gel electrophoresis	19.4			
describe the uses of PCR and gel electrophoresis	19.4			
explain the use of microarrays	19.5			
outline the uses of databases that hold information about gene sequences, genomes and proteins	19.5			
describe examples of the uses of genetic technology in medicine	19.6			
describe some uses of GMOs in agriculture	19.7			
discuss the social and ethical implications of gene technology in medicine and food production	19.6, 19.7			

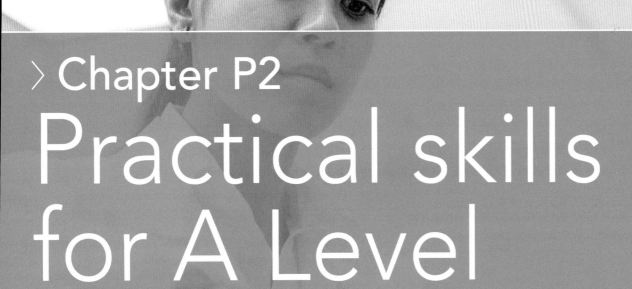

> # Chapter P2
> # Practical skills
> # for A Level

CONTINUED

- calculate standard error, and use it to draw error bars on graphs and to interpret apparent differences between two sets of data
- state a null hypothesis for a statistical test
- use a *t*-test to find the probability that differences between two sets of data are due to chance
- use Pearson's linear correlation to find out if two sets of data have a linear relationship
- use Spearman's rank correlation to find out if two sets of data are correlated
- justify the choice of statistical test used.

The information in this section is taken from the Cambridge International syllabus (9700) for examination from 2022. You should always refer to the appropriate syllabus document for the year of your examination to confirm the details and for more information. The syllabus document is available on the Cambridge International website at www.cambridgeinternational.org.

P2.1 Practical skills

Each time you carry out an experiment or analyse data collected through experiment, you will use a variety of skills. In this chapter you will look at the different components of the skills in detail, and consider what you must be able to do in order to demonstrate these skills most effectively.

Some of the skills are the same as those that were covered at AS Level. However, the questions are usually a little more demanding at A Level.

P2.2 Planning an investigation

As you progress through your A Level biology course, you should develop the ability to plan your own experiments, rather than simply following instructions on a worksheet provided by someone else. In your practical examination you are likely to be asked to plan an experiment that investigates the effect of one factor (the independent variable) on another (the dependent variable).

Sometimes, the context and the type of experiment will be familiar – you will be able to remember a similar experiment that you have done yourself. But sometimes it will be completely new. You will have to use your experience in other experiments to think about the best way to design the particular one you have been asked to plan.

It is very important to read the instructions in the question extremely carefully. For example, the question might tell you what apparatus you should use in your experimental design. If you do not use that apparatus in your plan – even if you do not think it the best apparatus for that particular investigation –it is unlikely that you are answering the question appropriately.

P2.3 Constructing a hypothesis

You could be asked to make a **prediction** about what will happen to the dependent variable when you change the independent variable. A prediction is a 'guess' on your part about what you think will happen. For example, you might be asked to plan an experiment to investigate the relationship between temperature and the rate of respiration of yeast. Your prediction might be:

> As temperature increases, the rate of respiration of yeast will increase up to a maximum temperature, above which it will fall.

You could be asked to construct a **hypothesis**. A hypothesis is very similar to a prediction, but it should

KEY WORDS

prediction: a statement about what you think might happen; a prediction could just be guesswork, but a good one is based on prior knowledge and an underlying hypothesis

hypothesis: a tentative statement providing an explanation or prediction, based on a body of prior knowledge and testable by experiment

always be based on prior knowledge. A good hypothesis can be tested by experiment. In this case, the prediction above could also be considered to be a hypothesis – it meets the criteria of being based on your knowledge of how enzyme activity is affected by temperature and it can be tested by experiment.

Note that you cannot 'prove' that a hypothesis is correct just by doing one experiment. Your results may support your hypothesis, but they cannot prove it. You would need to do many more experiments before you can be sure that your hypothesis really is correct in all situations.

But you can disprove a hypothesis more easily. If you found that the rate of respiration did not increase as temperature increases, then this suggests that the hypothesis is incorrect. Nevertheless, it would be a good idea to do the experiment two or three times more, to make sure that the results can be repeated.

Sometimes, you could be asked to sketch a graph of your predicted results, if your hypothesis is supported. A sketch graph relating to the prediction and hypothesis is shown in Figure P2.1.

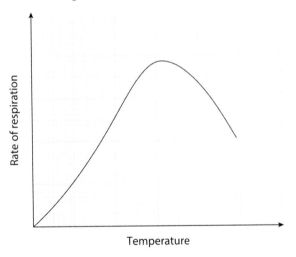

Figure P2.1: Using a sketch graph to show the predicted results for the yeast experiment.

Using the right apparatus

Imagine the question has asked you to plan your experiment using the apparatus shown in Figure P2.2.

As the yeast respires, it produces carbon dioxide gas. This collects above the liquid in the syringe, increasing the pressure and causing the meniscus to move down the capillary tubing.

You may have done an experiment to investigate the relationship between temperature and rate of respiration of yeast, using a respirometer (as described in Chapter 12, Practical Activity 12.1). And you would be right if you think that this would be a much better way of doing this investigation. But if the question asks you to plan using the syringe apparatus, that is what you must do.

Question

1   Describe how you could use the apparatus in Figure P2.2 to measure the rate of respiration of yeast.

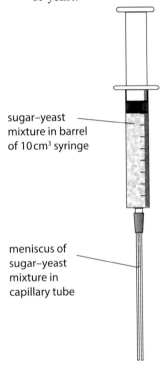

sugar–yeast mixture in barrel of 10 cm³ syringe

meniscus of sugar–yeast mixture in capillary tube

Figure P2.2: Apparatus for measuring the rate of respiration of yeast.

P2.4 Identifying variables

It is usually a good idea to make a clear statement about the independent and dependent variables as part of your plan.

You also need to think about the standardised variables – the ones that you will keep constant as you change the independent variable. It is very important to include only variables that really might have an effect on your results – the key variables – and not just give a long list including unimportant ones.

Question

2 Which of these variables should be standardised (kept constant) when investigating the effect of temperature on the rate of respiration of yeast?

a the concentration of sugar solution

b the initial volume of the sugar–yeast mixture inside the syringe

c the length of the capillary tubing

d the diameter of the capillary tubing

e the type of sugar (e.g. glucose, sucrose)

f the light intensity

g the pH of the sugar–yeast mixture

Changing the independent variable

You should be prepared to describe how you will change the independent variable. In this experiment, this means changing the temperature, and you should already know how to do this using a water bath. You should describe how you would do it, and how you would measure the different values of temperature.

There are many other possible independent variables that a question could involve. For example, the independent variable could be pH, in which case you would use buffer solutions. It could be concentration. By now, you should be familiar with using a stock solution to make up solutions with lower concentrations, using the serial dilution technique described in Chapter P1, Figure P1.2. But at A Level, you could also be asked how to make up the initial stock solution with a particular concentration.

For example, you may need to describe how to make up a 1% sugar solution. This means a solution containing 1 g of sugar for every 100 g of water. Remember that 1 cm³ of water has a mass of 1 g. So, to make up a 1% sugar solution, you would:

1 use a top pan balance to measure out 1 g of sugar

2 place it into a 100 cm³ volumetric flask (a kind of flask that enables the volume to be measured very accurately)

3 add a small amount of distilled water and dissolve the sugar thoroughly

4 add distilled water to make up to exactly 100 cm³.

You could also be asked to make up a 1 mol dm⁻³ solution. This means a solution containing 1 mole of the solute in 1 dm³ of solution. A mole is the relative molecular mass of a substance in grams. To work this out, you need to know the molecular formula of the substance, and the relative atomic masses of each atom in the formula. You would be given these in the question. For example, for sucrose:

- molecular formula of sucrose is $C_{12}H_{22}O_{11}$

- relative atomic masses are: carbon 12, hydrogen 1, oxygen 16.

So the relative molecular mass of sucrose is:

$$(12 \times 12) + (22 \times 1) + (11 \times 16) = 144 + 22 + 176$$
$$= 342$$

To make a 1 mol dm⁻³ sucrose solution:

1 use a top pan balance to measure out 342 g of sucrose

2 put the sugar into a 1 dm³ volumetric flask

3 add a small amount of distilled water and shake until the sugar has completely dissolved

4 add more distilled water until the meniscus of the liquid is exactly on the 1 dm³ mark (Figure P2.3).

You also need to think about a suitable range and interval of the independent variable. This is described in Chapter P1 (Section P1.3, Variables and making measurements). Read the question carefully, as it may give you some clues about this. If not, use your biological knowledge to help you make your decision.

Question

3 The molecular formula of glucose is $C_6H_{12}O_6$.

a Describe how you would make up 100 cm³ of a 1% solution of glucose.

b Describe how you would make up 250 cm³ of a 1% solution of glucose.

c Describe how you would make up a 1 mol dm⁻³ solution of glucose.

d Describe how you would use the 1 mol dm⁻³ solution to make up a 0.5 mol dm⁻³ solution.

e Imagine you are carrying out an investigation into the effect of glucose concentration on the rate of respiration in yeast. Suggest a suitable range and interval for your independent variable.

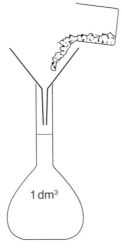

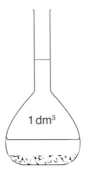

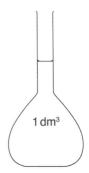

1 Add 342 g of sucrose to a beaker. Take the mass of the beaker into account or tare the beaker to zero.

2 Pour the sucrose into a volumetric flask. Wash any sugar crystals left behind into the flask.

3 Add water and shake the flask until all the sucrose is dissolved.

4 Top up the solution with water until the meniscus reaches the line.

Figure P2.3: Making up a 1 mol dm⁻³ sucrose solution.

Measuring the dependent variable

Now go back to the yeast respiration rate experiment and the apparatus shown in Figure P2.2.

The dependent variable is the rate of respiration of the yeast. This can be measured by recording the rate of movement of the meniscus. Remember that, if you are investigating rate, then time must come into your measurements. You would need to record the position of the meniscus at time 0, and then perhaps continue to do this at regular time intervals for, say, ten minutes. Alternatively, you could just record the position at time 0 and again at ten minutes. You would need to do this at each temperature that you have decided to test.

Whatever the experiment that you are describing, take care to describe exactly how you would measure the dependent variable. Say what measuring instruments you would use, and what you would do to make sure that your measurements are made accurately. Say exactly what you would measure and when you would measure it.

Identifying different types of variable

Often, the data about the dependent variable that you collect in your experiment (your results) are numerical. These are called quantitative data.

These quantitative data may be **continuous** or **discrete**. If the variable is continuous, then each measurement, count or reading can be any value between two extremes. Your results will not necessarily be whole numbers. The results for the yeast respiration rate experiment will be a quantitative and continuous variable.

> **KEY WORDS**
>
> **continuous data:** a set of data in which any individual reading can have any value between the two extremes
>
> **discrete data:** a set of data in which each measurement can only belong to one of a limited number of values

If the variable is discrete, then each measurement, count or reading is only one of a set number of possible values. For example, you might be asked to count the number of prickles on each leaf in a sample of holly leaves. The number of prickles will always be a whole number – you cannot have half a prickle on a leaf.

Sometimes, the data you collect about the dependent variable are not numerical. These are called qualitative data. Qualitative data can be ordinal or nominal. Ordinal variables are those that – although you do not have actual numerical values for them – can be organised into an order or sequence. For example, you might do a series of Benedict's tests on a set of glucose solutions of unknown concentration and decide on the relative depth of colour of each one. You can sort these into an order – from the one that is least brick-red to the one that is darkest brick-red – but you can't assign an actual numeric value for the colour of any of them.

Nominal variables are completely discrete, and you cannot put them into order. Each observation fits into a particular, clearly defined category. For example, in a sample of dead leaves taken from a forest floor, you might record the species of tree from which each leaf comes. Each leaf comes from one species – there are no 'overlaps' between categories, and there is no way of ordering or ranking them.

Standardising the other key variables

You will be expected to describe how to standardise each of the other key variables in your plan. This is described in Chapter P1 (Section P1.3, Variables and making measurements).

> **KEY WORDS**
>
> **ordinal data:** a set of data in which, although the values are not numerical, the individual results can be arranged in a sequence
>
> **nominal data:** a set of data in which the individual results cannot be arranged in a sequence; instead, each is assigned to a distinct category
>
> **control experiment:** an experiment in which the factor whose effect is being investigated (the independent variable) is absent; it is used as a standard of comparison

You might also need to think about doing a **control experiment** as part of your investigation. The purpose of a control is to check that it is the factor you are investigating that is affecting the dependent variable, and not some other factor. For example, in the yeast respiration experiment, it would be a good idea to set up at least one syringe with sugar solution but no yeast. This would be a check that it is something that the yeast is doing that is causing the change in position of the meniscus.

P2.5 Describing the sequence of steps

When you are describing your planned experiment, make sure that you describe a logical sequence of steps that you would follow. It is always worth jotting these down roughly first, to make sure that the steps follow one another in a sensible order, and that everything is fully explained. You might like to draw labelled or annotated diagrams to explain some of the steps – it is sometimes quicker and easier to do it that way. Diagrams are very often the best way to describe how you would assemble the apparatus.

P2.6 Risk assessment

An extremely important part of planning any experiment is to think about the potential hazards involved. In biology experiments, there are often no significant risks. If that is the case, you should say so. Do not invent a risk when there is none. But always mention risk, even if it is just to say that you do not think there is any.

If you do identify any significant risks, you should explain how you would minimise them. For example, in the yeast experiment, you might decide to use temperatures up to 80 °C. This is hot enough to burn the skin, so you would need to take precautions when handling the apparatus in a water bath at that temperature. You should lift the apparatus in and out using tongs or use heatproof and waterproof gloves.

P2.7 Recording and displaying results

You may be asked to construct a results table that you could use to fill in your results. This is described in Chapter P1 (Section P1.4, Recording quantitative results).

You may also want to describe how you would use the data to plot a graph, explaining what you would put on each axis and the type of graph you would draw.

Using the data to reach a conclusion

You may be asked how you would use your collected results to reach a conclusion. Usually, the conclusion will be whether or not the results support your hypothesis or prediction. (Remember that they will never prove it.) This is described in Chapter P1 (Section P1.6, Making conclusions).

P2.8 Analysis, conclusions and evaluation

Some questions will provide you with sets of data. You could be asked how to process the data (e.g., by doing calculations) in order to be able to use them to make a conclusion. You could be asked to assess the reliability of the investigation. This should be familiar from your AS work, but there is one big step up at this stage – you need to be able to use statistics to assess the variability of the data, or the significance of your results.

Note that you do not have to learn *any* of the formulae for the statistical tests. They will *always* be provided for you in the question. The only exception is when calculating the number of degrees of freedom in the chi-squared and *t*-tests, where you will not be given the formula.

Mean, median and mode

A large lemon tree has several hundred fruits on it. Imagine that you have measured the masses of 40 lemons from this tree. These are the results,

recorded to the nearest gram and arranged in order of increasing mass.

> 57, 60, 67, 72, 72, 76, 78, 79, 81, 83, 84, 86, 87, 88, 88, 90, 92, 92, 93, 94, 95, 97, 98, 99, 100, 101, 101, 103, 105, 106, 107, 109, 111, 113, 119, 120, 125, 128, 132, 135

To calculate the mean, add up all the readings and divide by the total number of readings.

$$\text{mean} = \frac{\text{sum of individual values}}{\text{total number of values}} = \frac{3823}{40} = 96$$

When you do this calculation, your calculator will read 95.575. However, you should not record this value. You need to consider the appropriate number of decimal places to use. Here, the masses of the lemons were recorded to the nearest whole number, so you can record the mean either to the nearest whole number, which is 96, or to one more decimal place, which is 95.6.

To find the median and mode, you need to plot your results as a frequency histogram (Figure P2.4).

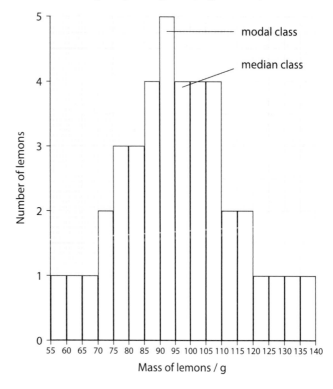

Figure P2.4: Lemon mass data plotted as a histogram.

The **modal class** is the most common class in the set of results. For these results, the modal class is 90–94 g.

The **median** is the middle value of all the values in the data set. The median value is half way between the smallest mass (57 g) and the largest (135 g), which is 96 g. You can also identify the median class, which is the middle class on the graph, in this case 95–99 g.

Range

You have already met the term *range*, in the context of the range of the independent variable. It means exactly the same thing when applied to the results – it is the spread between the smallest number and the largest. For the fruit masses, the range is from 57 g to 135 g.

Normal distribution

Many sets of data produce a symmetrical pattern when they are plotted as a frequency diagram. This is called a **normal distribution** (Figure P2.5a).

The data in a frequency diagram can also be plotted as a line graph (Figure P2.5b). If the data show a normal distribution, then this curve is completely symmetrical.

Question

4   In a perfect normal distribution curve, what will be the relationship between the mean, median and mode?

Standard deviation

A useful statistic to know about data that have an approximately normal distribution is how far they spread out on either side of the mean value. This is called the **standard deviation**. The larger the standard deviation, the wider the variation from the mean (Figure P2.6).

> ### KEY WORDS
>
> **mode (modal class):** the most common value, or class, in the set of results
>
> **median:** the middle value of all the values in the data set
>
> **normal distribution:** a set of data in which a graph shows a symmetrical distribution around the central value
>
> **standard deviation:** a calculated value that indicates how widely a set of data spreads out from the mean value

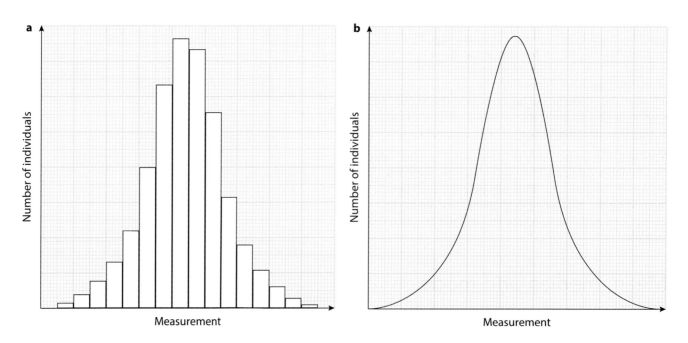

Figure P2.5: Normal distribution curves shown as **a** a frequency diagram and **b** a line graph.

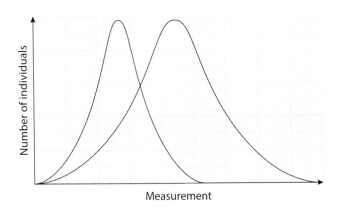

Figure P2.6: Normal distribution curves with very small (on the left) and much larger standard deviations.

A student measured the lengths of 21 petals from flowers of a population of a species of plant growing in woodland. These were the results:

Petal lengths in woodland population / mm

3.1	3.2	2.7	3.1	3.0	3.2	3.3
3.1	3.1	3.3	3.3	3.2	3.2	3.3
3.2	2.9	3.4	2.9	3.0	2.9	3.2

You may have a calculator that can do all the hard work for you – you just key in the individual values and it will calculate the standard deviation. However, you do need to know how to do the calculation yourself. The best way is to set your data out in a table, and work through it step by step.

1 List the measurement for each petal in the first column of a table like Table P2.1 overleaf.

2 Calculate the mean for the petal length by adding all the measurements and dividing this total by the number of measurements.

3 Calculate the difference from the mean for each observation. This is $(x - \bar{x})$.

4 Calculate the squares of each of these differences from the mean. This is $(x - \bar{x})^2$.

5 Calculate the sum of the squares. This is $\Sigma(x - \bar{x})^2$.

6 Divide the sum of the squares by $n - 1$.

7 Find the square root of this. The result is the standard deviation, s, for that data set.

Table P2.1 shows the calculation of the standard deviation for petals from plants in the woodland.

IMPORTANT

The formula for calculating standard deviation is:

$$s = \sqrt{\frac{\Sigma(x - \bar{x})^2}{n - 1}}$$

where:

$\bar{x}$ is the mean

Σ stands for 'sum of'

x refers to the individual values in a set of data

n is the total number of observations (individual values, readings or measurements) in one set of data

s is standard deviation

$\sqrt{}$ is the symbol for square root.

Question

5 The student measured the petal length from a second population of the same species of plant, this time growing in a garden. These are the results:

Petal lengths in garden population / mm

2.8	3.1	2.9	3.2	2.9	2.7	3.0
2.8	2.9	3.0	3.2	3.1	3.0	3.2
3.0	3.1	3.3	3.2	2.9		

Show that the standard deviation for this set of data is 0.16.

Standard error

The 21 petals measured were just a sample of all the thousands of petals on the plants in the wood and in the garden. If you took another sample, would you get the same value for the mean petal length? You cannot be certain without actually doing this, but there is a calculation that you can do to give a good idea of how close your mean value is to the true mean value for all of the petals in the wood. The calculation works out the **standard error (SE)** for your data.

KEY WORD

standard error (SE): a calculation that indicates how close the calculated mean value is likely to be to the true mean value

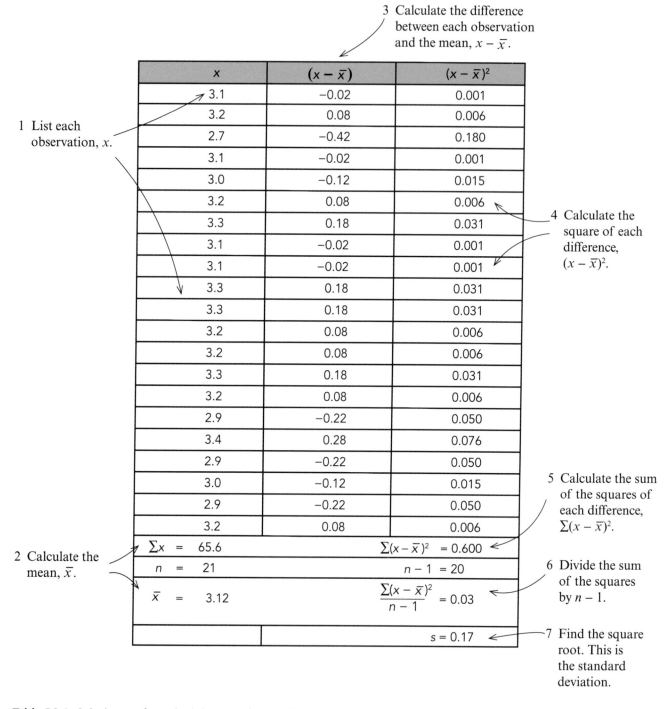

3 Calculate the difference between each observation and the mean, $x - \bar{x}$.

1 List each observation, x.

x	$(x - \bar{x})$	$(x - \bar{x})^2$
3.1	−0.02	0.001
3.2	0.08	0.006
2.7	−0.42	0.180
3.1	−0.02	0.001
3.0	−0.12	0.015
3.2	0.08	0.006
3.3	0.18	0.031
3.1	−0.02	0.001
3.1	−0.02	0.001
3.3	0.18	0.031
3.3	0.18	0.031
3.2	0.08	0.006
3.2	0.08	0.006
3.3	0.18	0.031
3.2	0.08	0.006
2.9	−0.22	0.050
3.4	0.28	0.076
2.9	−0.22	0.050
3.0	−0.12	0.015
2.9	−0.22	0.050
3.2	0.08	0.006

$\Sigma x = 65.6$ $\Sigma(x - \bar{x})^2 = 0.600$

$n = 21$ $n - 1 = 20$

$\bar{x} = 3.12$ $\dfrac{\Sigma(x - \bar{x})^2}{n - 1} = 0.03$

$s = 0.17$

4 Calculate the square of each difference, $(x - \bar{x})^2$.

5 Calculate the sum of the squares of each difference, $\Sigma(x - \bar{x})^2$.

2 Calculate the mean, $\bar{x}$.

6 Divide the sum of the squares by $n - 1$.

7 Find the square root. This is the standard deviation.

Table P2.1: Calculation of standard deviation for petal length in a sample of plants from woodland. All lengths are in mm.

Once you have worked out the standard deviation, s, then the standard error is very easy to calculate.

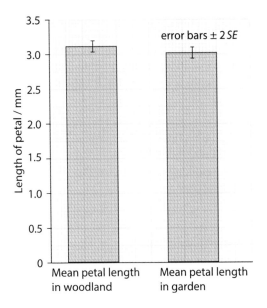

> **IMPORTANT**
>
> The formula for calculating standard error is:
>
> $$SE = \frac{s}{\sqrt{n}}$$
>
> where: SE = standard error
>
> s = standard deviation
>
> n = the sample size (in this case, the number of petals in the sample).

So, for the petals in woodland:

$$SE = \frac{0.17}{\sqrt{21}} = \frac{0.17}{4.58} = 0.04$$

What does this value tell you?

The standard error tells you how certain you can be that your mean value is the true mean for the population that you have sampled.

You can be 95% certain that, if you took a second sample from the same population, the mean for that second sample would lie within $\pm 2 \times$ your value of SE from the mean for your first sample. This is known as the **95 per cent confidence interval**. (Confidence interval is sometimes abbreviated to CI.)

In other words, you can be 95% certain that the mean petal length of a second sample would lie within 2×0.04 mm of your mean value for the first sample.

Question

6   Show that the standard error for the lengths of the sample of petals taken from the garden (Question 5) is also 0.04. Show each step in your working.

Error bars

The standard error can be shown on a graph. Figure P2.7 shows the means for the two groups of petals, plotted on a bar chart.

The bars drawn through the tops of the plotted bars are called **error bars**. If you draw an error bar that extends two standard errors above the mean and two standard

Figure P2.7: Mean petal lengths of plants in woodland and garden.

errors below it, then you can be 95% certain that the true value of the mean lies within this range. You can also add error bars to line graphs, where your individual points represent mean values.

You can use these error bars to help you to decide whether or not there is a significant difference between the petal length in the woodland and the garden. If the error bars overlap, then the difference between the two groups is definitely not significant. If the error bars do not overlap, you still cannot be sure that the difference is significant – but at least you know it is possible that it is.

> **KEY WORDS**
>
> **95 per cent confidence interval:** a range of values calculated as the mean $\pm 2 \times$ standard error; you can be 95% certain that the true mean lies within this range
>
> **error bar:** a line drawn through a point or the top of bar on a graph, extending two standard errors above and below the mean value indicated by the point or bar; you can be 95% certain that the true value lies within the range indicated by the error bar

Questions

7 Calculate the standard deviation, s, for the fruit mass data in the section 'Mean, median and mode' (displayed in Figure P2.4). Use the formula:

$$s = \sqrt{\frac{\Sigma(x - \bar{x})^2}{n-1}}$$

Show each step in your working.

8 Calculate the standard error, SE, for this set of data. Use the formula:

$$SE = \frac{s}{\sqrt{n}}$$

Show each step in your working.

9 A sample of lemon fruits was taken from a different population of lemon trees. The mean mass of this sample of fruits was 84 g. The standard error was 0.52.

a Draw a bar chart to show the means of the fruit masses for these two populations. Draw error bars on your bar chart, and add a key to explain what the error bars represent.

b Are the differences between the masses of the fruits in the two different populations significant? Explain your answer.

The *t*-test

The *t*-test is used to assess whether or not the means of two sets of data with roughly normal distributions are significantly different from one another.

For this example, you will use data from another investigation.

The corolla (petal) length of two populations of gentian were measured.

Corolla lengths of population A / mm:

13, 16, 15, 12, 18, 13, 13, 16, 19, 15, 18, 15, 15, 17, 15

Corolla lengths of population B / mm:

16, 14, 16, 18, 13, 17, 19, 20, 17, 15, 16, 16, 19, 21, 18

If you want to use the *t*-test to determine whether the mean values for these two populations are significantly different, you first construct a **null hypothesis**. This states what you would expect if the two means are *not* significantly different, and any difference that you see could be due to chance. In this case, the null hypothesis would be:

There is no difference between the means of corolla length for population A and population B.

> **IMPORTANT**
>
> The formula for the *t*-test is:
>
> $$t = \frac{|\bar{x}_1 - \bar{x}_2|}{\sqrt{\dfrac{s_1^2}{n_1} + \dfrac{s_2^2}{n_2}}}$$
>
> where: $\bar{x}_1$ is the mean of sample 1
>
> $\bar{x}_2$ is the mean of sample 2
>
> s_1 is the standard deviation of sample 1
>
> s_2 is the standard deviation of sample 2
>
> n_1 is the number of individual measurements in sample 1
>
> n_2 is the number of individual measurements in sample 2.

1 For each set of data, calculate the mean.

2 Calculate the differences from the mean of all observations in each data set. This is $x - \bar{x}$

3 Calculate the squares of these. This is $(x - \bar{x})^2$

4 Calculate the sum of the squares. This is $\Sigma(x - \bar{x})^2$

5 Divide this by $n_1 - 1$ for the first set and $n_2 - 1$ for the second set.

6 Take the square root of this. The result is the standard deviation for each set of data.

For population A, $s_1 = 2.06$

For population B, $s_2 = 2.20$

7 Square the standard deviation and divide by the number of observations in that sample, for both samples.

> **KEY WORDS**
>
> **t-test:** a statistical procedure used to determine whether the means of two samples differ significantly
>
> **null hypothesis:** a statement saying that there is no association or difference between two sets of data

8   Add these values together for the two samples and take the square root of this.

9   Divide the difference in the two sample means with the value from step 8. This is t and, in this case, is 2.14.

10   Calculate the total degrees of freedom for all the data (v). $v = (n_1 - 1) + (n_2 - 1) = 28$

11   Refer to the table of t values for 28 degrees of freedom and a value of $t = 2.14$ (Table P2.2).

The probabilities that you look up in the t-test table are probabilities that the null hypothesis is correct and there is no significant difference between the samples. The probability you find is the probability that any difference between the samples is just due to chance.

You may remember that this idea is also used in the χ^2 test (Chapter 16, Section 16.6, The chi-squared (χ^2) test). In both the χ^2 test and the t-test, you usually take a probability of 0.05 as being the critical one. This is sometimes called the 5% confidence level.

Degrees of freedom	Value of t			
1	6.31	12.7	63.7	63.6
2	2.92	4.30	9.93	31.6
3	2.35	3.18	5.84	12.9
4	2.13	2.78	4.60	8.61
5	2.02	2.57	4.03	6.87
6	1.94	2.45	3.71	5.96
7	1.90	2.37	3.50	5.41
8	1.86	2.31	3.36	5.04
9	1.83	2.26	3.25	4.78
10	1.81	2.23	3.17	4.59
11	1.80	2.20	3.11	4.44
12	1.78	2.18	3.06	4.32
13	1.77	2.16	3.01	4.22
14	1.76	2.15	2.98	4.14
15	1.75	2.13	2.95	4.07
16	1.75	2.12	2.92	4.02
17	1.74	2.11	2.90	3.97
18	1.73	2.10	2.88	3.92
19	1.73	2.09	2.86	3.88
20	1.73	2.09	2.85	3.85
22	1.72	2.07	2.82	3.79
24	1.71	2.06	2.80	3.75
26	1.71	2.06	2.78	3.71
28	1.70	2.05	2.76	3.67
30	1.70	2.04	2.75	3.65
>30	1.64	1.96	2.58	3.29
Probability that chance could have produced this value of t	0.10	0.05	0.01	0.001
Confidence level	10%	5%	1%	0.1%

Table P2.2: Values of t.

If your *t*-test value represents a probability of 0.05 or more, then you can assume that the differences between the two sets of data are due only to chance. The differences between them are not significant.

If the probability is less than 0.05, then this is strong evidence that something more than chance is causing the difference between the two sets of data. You can say that the difference is significant.

If the total number of observations (both samples added together) is below 30, error due to chance is significant and the table of *t* makes an adjustment to critical values to take this into account, which is why you need to calculate the value of degrees of freedom. However, above 30 observations, the number of observations makes little or no difference to critical values of *t*.

For the data sets of corolla length, the value of *t* is 2.14. This is above the critical value of *t* at the 5% confidence level for 28 degrees of freedom, which is 2.05. Looking at the table, your value of *t* lies between 2.05 and 2.76, so the probability of chance producing the difference between the means is between 5% and 1% – in other words, it is less than 5%. You can therefore say that the two means are significantly different. You can reject the null hypothesis.

The χ^2 test

You have already met the χ^2 test, in Chapter 16 (Section 16.6, The chi-squared (χ^2) test). This statistical test is used to determine whether any differences between a set of observed values are significantly different from the expected values. It is most likely to be used in genetics or ecology.

Pearson's linear correlation

Sometimes, you want to see if there is a relationship between two variables – are they correlated? For example, imagine you have measured the numbers of species **P** and species **Q** in ten different 1 m² quadrats. Table P2.3 shows what you found. Are the numbers of these two species related to each other?

The first thing to do is to plot a scatter graph of your data. This is shown in Figure P2.8. Note that it does not matter which set of values goes on the *x*-axis or the *y*-axis.

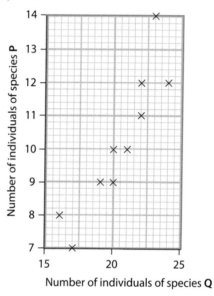

Figure P2.8: Scatter graph of the data in Table P2.3.

Quadrat	Number of individuals of species P	Number of individuals of species Q
1	10	21
2	9	20
3	11	22
4	7	17
5	8	16
6	14	23
7	10	20
8	12	24
9	12	22
10	9	19

Table P2.3: Numbers of species P and species Q in ten quadrats.

Looking at this graph, you can see that the data look as though they might lie approximately on a straight line. It looks as though there might be a linear correlation between them.

To find out whether this is so, you can carry out Pearson's linear correlation test. This test can only be used if the data are interval data and are normally distributed, which is the case for these data. You can see

that because they do not appear to be skewed in any one direction, and there are no obvious outliers.

Table P2.4 shows you the steps to follow in order to calculate the value of r, using the data in Table P2.3.

The value of r, 0.81, is the correlation coefficient. This value should always work out somewhere between -1 and $+1$. (If it doesn't, check your calculation!)

1 Calculate $x \times y$ for each set of values.

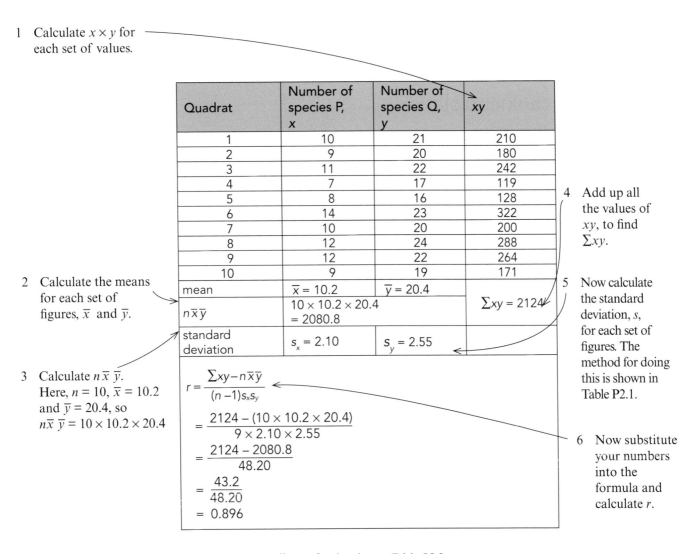

2 Calculate the means for each set of figures, $\bar{x}$ and $\bar{y}$.

3 Calculate $n\bar{x}\,\bar{y}$.
Here, $n = 10$, $\bar{x} = 10.2$ and $\bar{y} = 20.4$, so
$n\bar{x}\,\bar{y} = 10 \times 10.2 \times 20.4$

Quadrat	Number of species P, x	Number of species Q, y	xy
1	10	21	210
2	9	20	180
3	11	22	242
4	7	17	119
5	8	16	128
6	14	23	322
7	10	20	200
8	12	24	288
9	12	22	264
10	9	19	171
mean	$\bar{x} = 10.2$	$\bar{y} = 20.4$	
$n\bar{x}\bar{y}$	$10 \times 10.2 \times 20.4$ $= 2080.8$		$\Sigma xy = 2124$
standard deviation	$s_x = 2.10$	$s_y = 2.55$	

4 Add up all the values of xy, to find Σxy.

5 Now calculate the standard deviation, s, for each set of figures. The method for doing this is shown in Table P2.1.

$$r = \frac{\Sigma xy - n\bar{x}\,\bar{y}}{(n-1)s_x s_y}$$

$$= \frac{2124 - (10 \times 10.2 \times 20.4)}{9 \times 2.10 \times 2.55}$$

$$= \frac{2124 - 2080.8}{48.20}$$

$$= \frac{43.2}{48.20}$$

$$= 0.896$$

6 Now substitute your numbers into the formula and calculate r.

Table P2.4: Calculating Pearson's correlation coefficient for the data in Table P2.3.

> **IMPORTANT**
>
> The formula for calculating Pearson's linear correlation coefficient is:
>
> $$r = \frac{\sum xy - n\bar{x}\bar{y}}{(n-1)s_x s_y}$$
>
> where: r is the correlation coefficient
>
> x is the number of species **P** in a quadrat
>
> y is the number of species **Q** in the same quadrat
>
> n is the number of readings (in this case, 10)
>
> $\bar{x}$ is the mean number of species **P**
>
> $\bar{y}$ is the mean number of species **Q**
>
> s_x is the standard deviation for the numbers of **P**
>
> s_y is the standard deviation for the numbers of **Q**.

Spearman's rank correlation

Spearman's rank correlation is used to find out if there is a correlation between two sets of variables, when they are *not* normally distributed.

As with Pearson's linear correlation test, the first thing to do is to plot your data as a scatter graph, and see if they look as though there may be a correlation. Note that, for this test, the correlation need not be a straight line – the correlation need not be linear.

Let's say that you have counted the numbers of species **R** and species **S** in ten quadrats. Table P2.5 shows your results, and Figure P2.9 shows these data plotted as a scatter graph.

Quadrat	Number of species **R**	Number of species **S**
1	38	24
2	2	5
3	22	8
4	50	31
5	28	27
6	8	4
7	42	36
8	13	6
9	20	11
10	43	30

Table P2.5: Numbers of species **R** and species **S** found in ten quadrats.

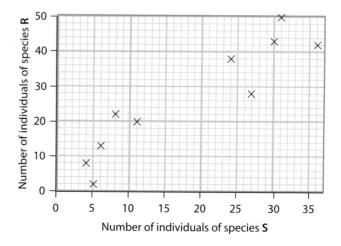

Figure P2.9: Scatter graph of the data in Table P2.5.

Now rank each set of data. For example, for the number of species **R**, Quadrat 4 has the largest number, so that is ranked as number 1. This is shown in Table P2.6.

Once you have ranked both sets of results, you need to calculate the differences in rank, D, by subtracting the rank of species **S** from the rank of species **R**. Then square each of these values. Add them together to find $\sum D^2$. This is shown in Table P2.7.

Substituting into the formula shown in the box on the next page, you can calculate Spearman's rank correlation coefficient for the distribution of species **R** and species **S**.

Quadrat	Number of species R	Rank for species R	Number of species S	Rank for species S
1	38	7	24	6
2	2	1	5	2
3	22	5	8	4
4	50	10	31	9
5	28	6	27	7
6	8	2	4	1
7	42	8	36	10
8	13	3	6	3
9	20	4	11	5
10	43	9	30	8

Table P2.6: Ranked data from Table P2.5.

Quadrat	Rank for species R	Rank for species S	Difference in rank, D	D^2
1	7	6	1	1
2	1	2	−1	1
3	5	4	1	1
4	10	9	1	1
5	6	7	−1	1
6	2	1	1	1
7	8	10	−2	4
8	3	3	0	0
9	4	5	−1	1
10	9	8	1	1
				$\Sigma D^2 = 12$

Table P2.7: Calculating ΣD^2 for the data in Table P2.5.

IMPORTANT

The formula for calculating Spearman's rank correlation coefficient is:

$$r_s = 1 - \left(\frac{6 \times \Sigma D^2}{n^3 - n} \right)$$

where: r_s is Spearman's rank coefficient

ΣD^2 is the sum of the differences between the ranks of the two samples

n is the number of samples.

$$r_s = 1 - \left| \frac{(6 \times 12)}{(10^3 - 10)} \right|$$

$$= \frac{1 - 72}{1000 - 10}$$

$$= \frac{1 - 72}{990}$$

$$= 1 - 0.072$$

$$= 0.923$$

$$= 0.93 \text{ (to 2 decimal places)}$$

This number is the correlation coefficient. The closer the value is to 1, the more likely it is that there is a genuine correlation between the two sets of data.

Your value is very close to 1, so it certainly looks as though there is strong correlation. However, as with the t-test and the χ^2 test, you need to look up this value in a table, and compare it against a critical value. As in most statistical tests used in biology, we often use a probability of 0.05 as the baseline; if your value indicates a probability of 0.05 or less, then you can say that there is a significant correlation between your two samples. In other words, the null hypothesis (that there is no correlation between the two samples) is not supported.

Table P2.8 shows these critical values for samples with different numbers of readings.

Notice that, the smaller the number of the readings you have taken, the larger your value of r_s needs to be in order to say that there is a significant correlation. This makes logical sense – if you have taken only five readings, then you would really need them all to be

n	5	6	7	8	9	10	11	12	14	16
Critical value of r_s	1.00	0.89	0.79	0.74	0.70	0.65	0.62	0.59	0.54	0.50

Table P2.8: Critical values of r_s at the 0.05 probability level.

ranked identically to be able to say they are correlated. If you have taken 16 readings, then you could accept a smaller value of r_s.

Remember that showing there is a correlation between two variables does not indicate a causal relationship – in other words, you cannot say that the numbers of species **R** have an effect on the numbers of species **S**, or vice versa. There could well be other variables that are causing the numbers of both of them to vary.

For the data, there are ten quadrats, so $n = 10$. The critical value is therefore 0.65. Your value is much greater than this, so you can accept that there is a significant correlation between the numbers of species **R** and the numbers of species **S**.

Question

10 The scatter graphs in Figure P2.10 show values for x plotted against values for y.

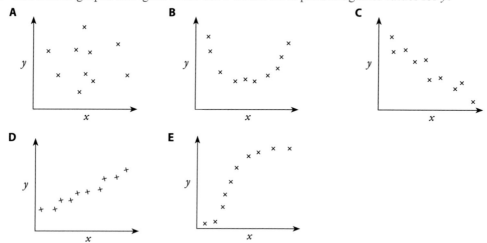

Figure P2.10

State the letter of any graph or graphs that:

a indicate there could be a positive correlation

b indicate that there is probably no correlation

c indicate that there is a linear correlation

d indicate that Spearman's rank correlation could be used

e indicate that Pearson's linear correlation test could be used.

Table P2.9 summarises the circumstances in which you would use each of the statistical tests that help you to decide whether or not there is a relationship between two sets of data.

Test	When to use it	Criteria for using the test	Examples of use	How to interpret the value you calculate
t-test	You want to know if two sets of continuous data are significantly different from one another.	• You have two sets of continuous, quantitative data. • You have more than ten readings for each set of data. • Both sets of data come from populations that are normally distributed. • The standard deviations of the two sets of data are very similar.	Are the surface areas of the leaves on the north-facing side of a tree significantly different from the surface areas on the south-facing side? Are the reaction times of students who have drunk a caffeine-containing drink significantly different from students who have drunk water?	Use a *t*-test table to look up your value of *t*. If this value is greater than the *t* value for a probability of 0.05 (the critical value), then you can say that your two populations are significantly different.

Test	When to use it	Criteria for using the test	Examples of use	How to interpret the value you calculate
χ^2 test	You want to know if your observed results differ significantly from your expected results.	You have two or more sets of quantitative data, which belong to two or more discontinuous categories (i.e. they are nominal data).	Are the numbers of offspring of different phenotypes obtained in a genetic cross significantly different from the expected numbers?	Use a χ^2 table to look up your value of χ^2. If this value is greater than the χ^2 value for a probability of 0.05, then you can say that your observed results differ significantly from your expected results.
Pearson's linear correlation	You want to know if there is a linear correlation between two paired sets of data.	• You have two sets of continuous data. • You have at least five pairs of data, but preferably ten or more. • A scatter graph suggests there might be a linear relationship between them. • Both sets of data have an approximately normal distribution.	Is there a linear correlation between the rate of an enzymic reaction and the concentration of an inhibitor? Is there a linear correlation between the numbers of limpets and the numbers of dog whelks on a sea shore?	A value close to +1 indicates a positive linear correlation. A value close to -1 indicates a negative linear correlation. A value close to 0 indicates no correlation.
Spearman's rank correlation	You want to know if there is a correlation (not necessarily linear) between two paired sets of data.	• You have quantitative data that can be ranked. • The samples for each set of data have been made randomly. • You have at least 5 pairs of data, but preferably between 10 and 30. • A scatter graph suggests there might be a relationship between the two sets of data (not necessarily linear). Note: you cannot use this test if the scatter graph is U-shaped (i.e. the correlation is positive for some values and negative for others). • The sets of data do not have a normal distribution.	Is there a correlation between the surface area of a fruit and the time it takes to fall to the ground? Is there a correlation between the numbers of limpets and the numbers of dog whelks on a sea shore?	Use a correlation coefficient table to look up your value of r_s. If your value of r_s is greater than the r_s value for a probability of 0.05, you can say there is a significant correlation between your two values.

Table P2.9: Summary of statistical tests.

P2.9 Evaluating evidence

It is important to be able to assess how much confidence you can have in the data that you have collected in an experiment, and therefore how much confidence you can have in any conclusions you have drawn. Statistical tests are a big help in deciding this. But you also need to think about the experiment itself and any sources of error that might have affected your results.

Sources of error were discussed in Chapter P1 (Section P1.9, Identifying sources of error and suggesting improvements). Errors stem from three main sources: uncertainty in measurements because of limitations of measuring instruments, difficulty in standardising important variables, and limitations of the technique for measuring the dependent variable.

Many questions will ask you to analyse data that you have not collected yourself, so you will have only the information provided in the question and your own experience of carrying out experiments to help you to decide how much confidence you can have in the reliability of the data. Important things to think about include the following questions.

- How well were the key variables standardised?

- Was the range and interval of the independent variable adequate?

- Do any of the results appear to be anomalous? If so, what could have caused these anomalous readings?

- Have the provided readings been replicated sufficiently?

Another aspect of the experiment that needs to be considered is its validity. A valid experiment really does test the hypothesis or question that is being investigated.

A key feature to consider is whether the experimenters really were measuring the dependent variable that they intended to measure. For example, if you were doing a transpiration experiment using a potometer, were you really measuring the rate of loss of water vapour from the shoot's leaves? The measurement you were making was actually the rate of uptake of water by the shoot from the potometer. You should be able to explain why you think (or do not think) that this measurement can be relied upon to give you valid data about the rate of transpiration.

It is important to be able to bring all of this information together, and to be able to make an informed judgement about the overall validity of the investigation and how much it can be trusted for testing the hypothesis. As at AS Level, you should be able to suggest improvements to the experiment that would increase your confidence in the results and your conclusions.

P2.10 Conclusions and discussion

The construction of a simple conclusion was described in Chapter P1 (Section P1.6, Making conclusions). At A Level, you will often be making conclusions from data that you have not collected yourself, which is a bit more difficult. The more experience you have of doing real practical work, the better equipped you will be to understand how to make conclusions from data provided to you.

Your conclusion should begin with a simple statement about whether or not the hypothesis that was being tested is supported. This would also be the point at which you could mention the results of any statistical tests, and how they have helped you to make your conclusion.

You may also be asked to discuss the data and your conclusion in more depth. You should be prepared to give a description of the data, pointing out key features. This might involve looking for trends or patterns in the data, and identifying points on a graph where there is a marked change in gradient, for example (Chapter P1, Section P1.7, Describing data).

You could be asked to use the data to make further predictions, perhaps suggesting another hypothesis that could be tested. For example, for the petal length investigation earlier in this chapter, you could start to think about *why* the petal length in the woodland is greater than in the garden. A new hypothesis could be: *petals grow longer in lower light intensity*.

As well as describing the data, you could be asked to use your scientific knowledge to attempt to explain them. It is important to remember that the data in an A Level question could relate to anything from either the first or second year of your course.

REFLECTION

Biology experiments have a reputation for often not producing the 'right' results. Discuss with a partner whether or not you think this reputation is appropriate. Use your own experience to support your viewpoint. If you agree with the statement, why do you think this is so? If you or a friend also studies physics or chemistry, you could also discuss whether biology differs from those subjects in this respect.

Be ready to share your ideas with others.

Final reflection

Discuss with a friend which, in any, parts of Chapter P2 you need to:

• read through again to make sure you really understand

• seek more guidance on, even after going over it again.

SUMMARY

You should also look again at the summary for Chapter P1.
A hypothesis about the relationship between two variables predicts how one variable affects the other. It should be testable and falsifiable by experiment.
To make up a 1% (mass/volume) solution, dissolve 1 g of the solute in a small amount of water, then make up to a total volume of $1\,dm^3$. To make up a $1\,mol\,dm^{-3}$ solution, dissolve 1 mole of the solute in a small amount of water, then make up to a total volume of $1\,dm^3$.
The mean of a set of data is calculated by adding up all the individual values and dividing by the total number of readings. The median is the middle value in the set of results. The mode is the most common value in the set of results. The interquartile range is the range into which the middle 50% of the data fall. Standard deviation is a measure of how much the data are spread on either side of the mean.
Standard error is a measure of the likelihood of the mean of your sample being the true mean of the whole population. There is a 95% probability that the true mean lies within ±2 standard errors of the mean you have calculated. This can be shown by drawing error bars on a bar chart, where the error bar extends two standard errors above and below the plotted value.
If the error bars for two sets of data overlap, then there is no significant difference between the two sets of data. If the error bars do not overlap, it is possible that there is a significant difference between them, but this is not necessarily so.
The t-test is used to determine whether or not two sets of quantitative data, each with an approximately normal distribution, are significantly different from one another.
The χ^2 test is used to determine whether or not observed results differ significantly from expected results.
The Pearson's linear correlation test is used to determine whether or not there is a linear correlation between two sets of quantitative data.
Spearman's rank correlation test is used to determine whether or not there is a correlation between two paired sets of data that can be ranked.
When discussing an experiment, you need also to consider possible sources of error and validity of the experiment, and be able to suggest ways in which the experiment's reliability could be improved. You should be able to reach a conclusion about the data and use of statistical tests, and perhaps make suggestions for further experimental work.

EXAM-STYLE QUESTIONS

1   A student measured the length of eight randomly selected bean pods and the total mass of the seeds inside them. The table shows her results.

Pod	Length/mm	Mass of seeds/g
1	134	35
2	71	18
3	121	30
4	83	21
5	99	23
6	107	29
7	82	17
8	119	34

a   Draw a scatter graph of these results.   [3]

b   Describe the relationship that is suggested by your scatter graph.   [1]

c   Use Pearson's linear correlation test to analyse these results.

Use the formula:

$$r = \frac{\sum xy - n\bar{x}\bar{y}}{(n-1)s_x s_y}$$

where:

r is the correlation coefficient

x is the number of species $\mathbf{P}$ in a quadrat

y is the number of species $\mathbf{Q}$ in the same quadrat

n is the number of readings (in this case, 10)

$\bar{x}$ is the mean number of species $\mathbf{P}$

$\bar{y}$ is the mean number of species $\mathbf{Q}$

s_x is the standard deviation for the numbers of $\mathbf{P}$

s_y is the standard deviation for the numbers of $\mathbf{Q}$.

Show all of your working, and explain what your calculated value of r suggests about the relationship between the length of a bean pod and the mass of the seeds.   [8]

[Total: 12]

CONTINUED

2 The table shows the numbers of two species, **F** and **G**, found in eight randomly placed 10×10 m quadrats.

Quadrat	Number of species F	Number of species G
1	34	8
2	8	22
3	47	8
4	19	21
5	6	38
6	41	3
7	22	15
8	38	10

a Draw a scatter graph of these results. [3]

b Describe the relationship that is suggested by your scatter graph. [1]

c Explain why it is better to use Spearman's rank correlation, rather than Pearson's linear correlation test, to find out if there is a correlation between the numbers of species **F** and species **G**. [1]

d Use Spearman's rank correlation to analyse these results.

Use the formula:

$$r_s = 1 - \left(\frac{6 \times \sum D^2}{n^3 - n} \right)$$

where:

r_s is Spearman's rank coefficient

$\sum D^2$ is the sum of the differences between the ranks of the two samples

n is the number of samples.

(***Note:*** *If two values are equal, then you must give them equal rank.*)

Show all of your working, and explain what your calculated value indicates. [7]

[Total: 12]

3 A student noticed that the leaves on a plant growing close to a wall had two sorts of leaves. The leaves next to the wall were in the shade and looked different from the leaves on the side away from the wall that were exposed to the sun. The length of the internodes on the stem also looked different.

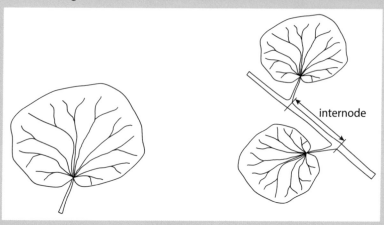

The figure on the left shows the leaf shape. The figure on the right shows an internode.

The student decided to investigate the differences by measuring some features of 30 leaves and internodes from each side of the plant.

Feature	Shaded leaves	Exposed leaves
mean internode length / mm	23 ± 4	15 ± 3
mean surface area of leaves / mm²	2750 ± 12	1800 ± 15
mean mass of leaves / mg	50 ± 8	60 ± 10
mean leaf surface area : leaf mass ratio	55 ± 9	30 ± 6
rate of water loss / mg mm⁻² h⁻¹	50 ± 11	65 ± 12

   a i   State the independent variable being investigated.   [1]

      ii Outline the procedures the student could use to obtain these results.

                                                                           [max 8]

   b The student carried out *t*-tests for the leaf surface area : leaf mass ratio and for internode length.

      The leaf surface area : leaf mass ratio gave the value $t = 12.6$.

      The formula for the *t*-test is:

$$t = \frac{|\bar{x}_1 - \bar{x}_2|}{\sqrt{\left(\frac{s_1^2}{n_1} + \frac{s_2^2}{n_2}\right)}}$$

CONTINUED

i   Copy and complete the calculation to find the value of t for the internode length.

$$t = \dfrac{-}{\sqrt{\dfrac{4^2}{30} + -}}$$

$$t = \dfrac{}{0.9}$$

$$t =$$

The table shows the critical values at $p = <0.05$ for the t-test.   [3]

Degrees of freedom	18	20	21	22	23	24	25	26	27	28	29	30	40	60	∞
Critical value	2.10	2.09	2.08	2.07	2.06	2.06	2.06	2.06	2.05	2.05	2.04	2.04	2.02	2.00	1.96

The number of degrees of freedom is 58.

ii   State how the number of degrees of freedom was calculated.   [1]

iii   State and explain the meaning of these results.   [2]

[Total: 15]

Cambridge International AS & A Level Biology (9700/51), Question 1, November 2010

4   The figure shows one type of potometer used by a student to investigate transpiration.

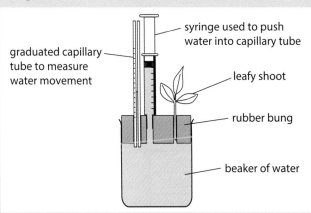

graduated capillary tube to measure water movement

syringe used to push water into capillary tube

leafy shoot

rubber bung

beaker of water

a   i   Suggest a hypothesis the student could test about the transpiration of a mesophyte (a plant adapted to a moist environment) and a xerophyte (a plant adapted to a dry environment).   [1]

ii   Outline a procedure involving the potometer that the student could use to test this hypothesis.   [8]

iii   The capillary tube measures the distance moved by the water. Explain how the actual volume of water lost can be calculated.   [2]

b Sketch a graph to predict the expected results of the investigation. **[2]**

COMMAND WORD

Sketch: make a simple drawing showing the key features.

The student then measured the surface area of the leaves by tracing the outline on a grid and counting the number of squares covered by the leaves. This area was doubled.

Mesophyte:

surface area of leaves $= 36\,cm^2$

water loss in 30 minutes $= 0.018\,cm^3$

c i Calculate the rate of water loss in $cm^3\,m^{-2}\,min^{-1}$. Show all the steps in your calculation. **[3]**

ii State a statistical test that the student could use to find out if the difference in water loss between the two types of leaf is significant. State a reason for your choice. **[2]**

In a further investigation, the student measured the loss in mass of each type of leaf. The figure shows the experimental set-up.

The table shows the results of this investigation.

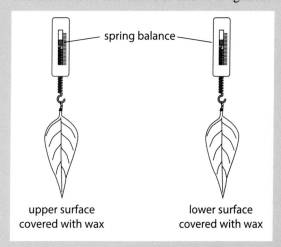

upper surface covered with wax

lower surface covered with wax

Day	Loss in mass / g per day			
	Upper side covered		Lower side covered	
	Mesophyte	Xerophyte	Mesophyte	Xerophyte
1	4.25	0.55	1.15	0.05
2	3.20	0.35	1.00	0.05
3	1.55	0.20	0.75	0.00
4	0.50	0.10	0.95	0.05
5	0.05	0.04	1.00	0.00
Total loss in mass / g	9.55	1.24	4.85	0.15

d State **three** conclusions that can be drawn from these results. **[3]**

[Total: 21]

Cambridge International AS & A Level Biology (9700/52), Question 1, June 2010

SELF-EVALUATION CHECKLIST

After studying this chapter, complete a table like this:

I can	See section...	Needs more work	Almost there	Ready to move on
define a problem in a given context, including stating a prediction and constructing an hypothesis	P2.3			
plan an investigation to test a hypothesis or to investigate a problem, identifying the independent variable and the dependent variable, and listing key variables to standardise	P2.4			
describe how the independent variable would be altered, how the dependent variable would be measured, and how the key variables would be standardised	P2.4			
describe how any control experiments would be used	P2.4			
describe a logical sequence of steps for the investigation, including identification of any risks and how they can be minimised	P2.5, P2.6			
describe how to make up solutions in per cent (mass per volume) and in $mol\,dm^{-3}$	P2.4			
assess validity of results by identifying anomalous results, looking at the spread of results and using standard deviation, standard error or 95% confidence intervals (CI)	P2.7, P2.8			
calculate standard error, and use it to draw error bars on graphs and to interpret apparent differences between two sets of data	P2.8			
state a null hypothesis for a statistical test	P2.8			
use a t-test to find the probability that differences between two sets of data are due to chance	P2.8			
use Pearson's linear correlation to find out if two sets of data have a linear relationship	P2.8			
use Spearman's rank correlation to find out if two sets of data are correlated	P2.8			
justify the choice of statistical test used	P2.8			

> Appendix 1

Amino acid R groups

The general structure for an amino acid is shown in Figure 2.16a. In the list below, only the R groups are shown; the rest of the amino acid molecule is represented by a block.

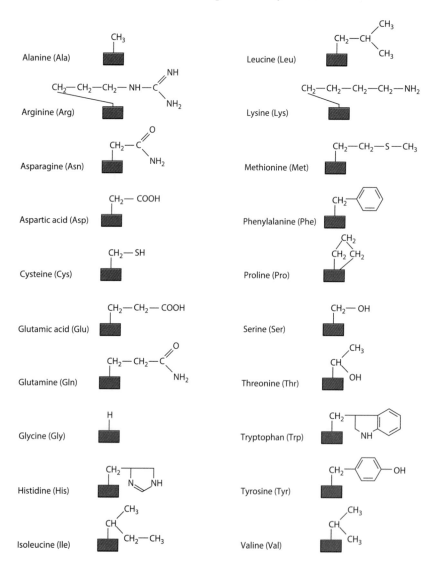

> Appendix 2

DNA and RNA triplet codes

Table A2.1 shows all the possible triplets of bases in a DNA molecule and what each codes for. The three-letter abbreviation for each amino acid is, in most cases, the first three letters of its full name (Appendix 1).

First position	Second position				Third position
	A	G	T	C	
A	Phe	Ser	Tyr	Cys	A
	Phe	Ser	Tyr	Cys	G
	Leu	Ser	STOP	STOP	T
	Leu	Ser	STOP	Trp	C
G	Leu	Pro	His	Arg	A
	Leu	Pro	His	Arg	G
	Leu	Pro	Gln	Arg	T
	Leu	Pro	Gln	Arg	C
T	Ile	Thr	Asn	Ser	A
	Ile	Thr	Asn	Ser	G
	Ile	Thr	Lys	Arg	T
	Met	Thr	Lys	Arg	C
C	Val	Ala	Asp	Gly	A
	Val	Ala	Asp	Gly	G
	Val	Ala	Glu	Gly	T
	Val	Ala	Glu	Gly	C

Table A2.1: DNA triplet codes.

Table A2.2 shows all the possible codons of bases in a messenger RNA (mRNA) molecule and what each codes for.

First position	Second position				Third position
	U	C	A	G	
U	Phe	Ser	Tyr	Cys	U
	Phe	Ser	Tyr	Cys	C
	Leu	Ser	STOP	STOP	A
	Leu	Ser	STOP	Trp	G
C	Leu	Pro	His	Arg	U
	Leu	Pro	His	Arg	C
	Leu	Pro	Gln	Arg	A
	Leu	Pro	Gln	Arg	G
A	Ile	Thr	Asn	Ser	U
	Ile	Thr	Asn	Ser	C
	Ile	Thr	Lys	Arg	A
	Met	Thr	Lys	Arg	G
G	Val	Ala	Asp	Gly	U
	Val	Ala	Asp	Gly	C
	Val	Ala	Glu	Gly	A
	Val	Ala	Glu	Gly	G

Table A2.2: RNA codon codes.

› Glossary

Command words

Below are the Cambridge International definitions for command words which may be used in exams. The italic text provides some additional explanation on the meaning of these words, written by the authors of this coursebook.

The information in this section is taken from the Cambridge International syllabus (9700) for examination from 2022. You should always refer to the appropriate syllabus document for the year of your examination to confirm the details and for more information. The syllabus document is available on the Cambridge International website www.cambridgeinternational.org.

assess: make an informed judgement

calculate: work out from given facts, figures or information – *it is usually a good idea to show all of the steps in your working*

comment: give an informed opinion – *you will often need to use your biological knowledge and understanding to make a range of statements about the topic*

compare: identify / comment on similarities and/or differences – *you can often use a table for this; if writing sentences, then use comparative words*

contrast: identify / comment on differences – *you can often use a table for this; if writing sentences, then use comparative words*

define: give the precise meaning – *that is, provide a short but complete description of what the term means*

describe: state the points of a topic / give characteristics and main features – *for example, use words to say clearly what is shown by a graph, or give a step-by-step account of something*

discuss: write about issue(s) or topic(s) in a structured way; *it is often a good idea to state points on both sides of an argument, e.g. reasons for and against a particular viewpoint, or how a set of results could be interpreted to support or reject a hypothesis*

explain: set out purposes or reasons / make the relationships between things evident / provide why and/ or how and support with relevant evidence – *note that you will often need to use your knowledge of biology to say why or how something happens*

give: produce an answer from a given source or recall/ memory – *for example, using information provided in the question, or from knowledge you have learnt during your course*

identify: name / select / recognise – *for example, labelling a structure on a diagram or micrograph*

outline: set out the main points – *that is, give a brief account, picking out the most important points and omitting detail*

predict: suggest what may happen based on available information

sketch: make a simple drawing showing the key features

state: express in clear terms – *that is, give a short, precise answer*

suggest: apply knowledge and understanding to situations where there is a range of valid responses, in order to make proposals / put forward considerations – *that is, use information provided, and your biological knowledge, to put forward possible answers; there is often more than one possible correct answer*

Key words

95 per cent confidence interval: a range of values calculated as the mean $\pm 2 \times$ standard error; you can be 95% certain that the true mean lies within this range

α-helix: a helical structure formed by a polypeptide chain, held in place by hydrogen bonds; an α-helix is an example of secondary structure in a protein

abiotic factor: an environmental factor that is caused by non-living components (e.g. soil pH, light intensity)

abscisic acid (ABA): an inhibitory plant growth regulator that causes closure of stomata in dry conditions

absorption spectrum: a graph showing the absorbance of different wavelengths of light by a photosynthetic pigment

accuracy: how close a reading is to the 'true' value

acetylcholine (ACh): a molecule made up of coenzyme A and a 2C acetyl group, important in the link reaction; a type of neurotransmitter released by cholinergic synapses

acetylcholinesterase: an enzyme in the synaptic cleft and on the postsynaptic membrane that hydrolyses ACh to acetate and choline

actin: the protein that makes up the thin filaments in striated muscle

action potential: a brief change in the potential difference from −70 mV to +30 mV across the cell surface membranes of neurones and muscle cells caused by the inward movement of sodium ions

action spectrum: a graph showing the effect of different wavelengths of light on a process, e.g. the rate of photosynthesis

activation energy: the energy that must be provided to make a reaction take place; enzymes reduce the activation energy required for a substrate to change into a product

active immunity: immunity gained when an antigen enters the body, an immune response occurs and antibodies are produced by plasma cells

active site: an area on an enzyme molecule where the substrate can bind

active transport: the movement of molecules or ions through transport proteins across a cell membrane, against their concentration gradient, using energy from ATP

adenylyl cyclise: enzyme that catalyses formation of the second messenger cyclic AMP

ADP (adenosine diphosphate): the molecule that is converted to ATP by addition of phosphate (a reaction known as phosphorylation) during cell respiration; the enzyme responsible is ATP synthase; the reaction requires energy

aerenchyma: plant tissue containing air spaces

afferent arteriole: arteriole leading to glomerular capillaries

AIDS: acquired immunodeficiency syndrome

aleurone layer: a layer of tissue around the endosperm that synthesises amylase during germination

alien species: a species that has been moved into a new ecosystem where it was previously unknown; also known as invasive species

allele: a variety of a gene

allopatric speciation: the development of new species following geographical isolation

all-or-none law: neurones and muscle cells only transmit impulses if the initial stimulus is sufficient to increase the membrane potential above a threshold potential

alveolus (plural alveoli): a small air sac in the lungs composed of a single layer of squamous epithelium and some elastic fibres; each alveolus is surrounded by capillaries that transport blood from the pulmonary artery to the pulmonary vein

anabolic reaction: a chemical reaction in which small molecules are built up into larger ones

anaerobic: without oxygen

Animalia: kingdom of eukaryotic organisms which are multicellular and heterotrophic and have a nervous system

antibiotic: a substance derived from a living organism that is capable of killing or inhibiting the growth of a microorganism

antibiotic resistance: the ability of bacteria or fungi to grow in the presence of an antibiotic that would normally slow their growth or kill them; antibiotic resistance arises by mutation and becomes widespread when antibiotics are overused

antibody: a glycoprotein (immunoglobulin) made by specialised lymphocytes in response to the presence of a specific antigen; each type of antibody molecule has a shape that is complementary to its specific antigen

anticodon: sequence of three unpaired bases on a tRNA molecule that binds with a codon on mRNA

antidiuretic hormone (ADH): hormone secreted from the pituitary gland that increases water reabsorption in the kidneys and therefore reduces water loss in urine

antigen: a substance that is foreign to the body and stimulates an immune response (e.g. any large molecule such as a protein)

antigen presentation: the process of preparing antigens and exposing them on the surface of host cells (e.g. macrophages) for recognition by T-lymphocytes

apoplast pathway: the non-living system of interconnected cell walls extending throughout a plant, used as a transport pathway for the movement of water and mineral ions

Archaea: the domain of prokaryotic organisms that resemble bacteria but share some features with eukaryotes

arteriole: small artery

artery: vessel with thick, strong walls that carries high-pressure blood away from the heart

artificial active immunity: immunity gained by putting antigens into the body, either by injection or by mouth

artificial insemination (AI): injection of semen collected from a male into the uterus

artificial passive immunity: the immunity gained by injecting antibodies

artificial selection: the selection by humans of organisms with desired traits to survive and reproduce; also known as selective breeding

asexual reproduction: the production of new individuals of a species by a single parent organism

assisted reproduction: any technique that is involved in treating infertility or protecting a female mammal of an endangered species from the health risks of pregnancy

ATP (adenosine triphosphate): the molecule that is the universal energy currency in all living cells; the purpose of respiration is to make ATP

ATP synthase: the enzyme that catalyses the phosphorylation of ADP to produce ATP

atrial systole: the stage of the cardiac cycle when the muscle in the walls of the atria contracts

atrioventricular node: a patch of tissue in the septum of the heart which transmits the wave of excitation from the walls of the atria and transmits it to the Purkyne tissue

atrioventricular valve: a valve between the atria and ventricles that closes when the ventricles contract and stops backflow of blood into the atria

atrium (plural: atria): one of the chambers of the heart that receives low-pressure blood from the veins

autosomal linkage: the presence of two genes on the same autosome, (any chromosome other than a sex chromosome) so that they tend to be inherited together and do not assort independently

auxin: a plant growth regulator (plant hormone) that stimulates cell elongation

β-galactosidase: an enzyme that catalyses the hydrolysis of lactose to glucose and galactose

β-pleated sheet: a loose, sheet-like structure formed by hydrogen bonding between parallel polypeptide chains; a β-pleated sheet is an example of secondary structure in a protein

B-lymphocyte (B cell): a type of lymphocyte that gives rise to plasma cells and secretes antibodies

Bacteria: the domain that contains all prokaryotic organisms except those classified as Archaea

bacteria (singular: bacterium): a group of single-celled prokaryotic microorganisms; they have a number of characteristics, such as the ability to form spores, which distinguish them from the other group of prokaryotes known as Archaea

bacteriophage (phage): a type of virus that infects bacteria; phages have double-stranded DNA as their genetic material

bar chart: a graph in which the categories on the x-axis are discontinuous – i.e., entirely separate from one another; the bars are drawn with spaces between them

behavioural separation: the separation of two populations because they have different behaviours which prevent them breeding together

Benedict's test: a test for the presence of reducing sugars; the unknown substance is heated with Benedict's reagent, and a change from a clear blue solution to the production of a yellow, red or brown precipitate indicates the presence of reducing sugars such as glucose

bicuspid valve: the atrioventricular valve on the left side of the heart

biodiversity: the variety of ecosystems and species in an area and the genetic diversity within each species

bioinformatics: the collection, processing and analysis of biological information and data using computer software

biological classification: the organisation of living and extinct organisms into systematic groups based on similarities and differences between species

biological species: a group of organisms with similar morphology and physiology, which can breed together to produce fertile offspring and are reproductively isolated from other species

biosensor: a device that uses a biological material such as an enzyme to measure the concentration of a chemical compound

biotic factor: an environmental factor that is caused by living organisms (e.g. predation, competition)

biuret test: a test for the presence of amine groups and thus for the presence of protein; biuret reagent is added to the unknown substance, and a change from pale blue to purple indicates the presence of protein

bivalent: two homologous chromosomes lying alongside each other during meiosis I

Bohr shift: the decrease in affinity of haemoglobin for oxygen that occurs when carbon dioxide is present

bottleneck (evolutionary): a period when the numbers of a species fall to a very low level, resulting in the loss of a large number of alleles and therefore a reduction in the gene pool of the species

Bowman's capsule: the cup-shaped part of a nephron that surrounds a glomerulus and collects filtrate from the blood

bronchiole: a microscopic branch of a bronchus that leads to the alveoli

bronchus (plural: bronchi): a major branch of the trachea that extends into the lungs

Bt toxin: insecticidal toxin produced by the bacterium *Bacillus thuringiensis*; the gene for Bt toxin is transferred to crop plants to make them resistant to insect pests

buffer solution: a solution that has a known pH, which can be added to a reacting mixture to maintain the pH at that level

Calvin cycle: a cycle of reactions in the light-dependent stage of photosynthesis in which carbon dioxide is reduced to form carbohydrate

cancers: a group of diseases that result from a breakdown in the usual control mechanisms that regulate cell division; certain cells divide uncontrollably and form tumours, from which cells may break away and form secondary tumours in other areas of the body (metastasis)

capillary: the smallest blood vessel, whose role is to deliver oxygen and nutrients to body tissues, and to remove their waste products

carbaminohaemoglobin: a compound formed when carbon dioxide binds with haemoglobin

carbonic anhydrase: an enzyme found in the cytoplasm of red blood cells that catalyses the reaction between carbon dioxide and water to form carbonic acid

carcinogen: a substance or environmental factor that can cause cancer

cardiac cycle: the sequence of events taking place during one heartbeat

cardiac muscle: the type of muscle that makes up the walls of the heart

carrier: an individual that possesses a particular allele as a single copy whose effect is masked by a dominant allele, so that the associated characteristic (such as a hereditary disease) is not displayed but may be passed to offspring

carrier protein: a membrane protein which changes shape to allow the passage into or out of the cell of specific ions or molecules by facilitated diffusion or active transport

cartilage: a type of skeletal tissue that is strong and flexible and supports the larynx, trachea and bronchi in the gas exchange system; cartilage is also found at joints between bones and in the external ear

cell: the basic unit of all living organisms; it is surrounded by a cell surface membrane and contains genetic material (DNA) and cytoplasm containing organelles

cell cycle: the sequence of events that takes place from one cell division until the next; it is made up of interphase, mitosis and cytokinesis

cell signalling: the molecular mechanisms by which cells detect and respond to external stimuli, including communication between cells

cell surface membrane: a very thin membrane (about 7 nm diameter) surrounding all cells; it is partially permeable and controls the exchange of materials between the cell and its environment

cell wall: a wall surrounding prokaryote, plant and fungal cells; the wall contains a strengthening material which protects the cell from mechanical damage, supports it and prevents it from bursting by osmosis if the cell is surrounded by a solution with a higher water potential

cellulose: a polysaccharide made from beta-glucose subunits; used as a strengthening material in plant cell walls

centriole: one of two small, cylindrical structures, made from microtubules, found just outside the nucleus in animal cells, in a region known as the centrosome; they are also found at the bases of cilia and flagella

centrosome: the main microtubule organising centre (MTOC) in animal cells

channel protein: a membrane protein of fixed shape which has a water-filled pore through which selected hydrophilic ions or molecules can pass; *see* facilitated diffusion

chemiosmosis: the synthesis of ATP using energy released by the movement of hydrogen ions down their concentration gradient, across a membrane in a mitochondrion or chloroplast

chemoreceptor: a receptor cell that responds to chemical stimuli; chemoreceptors are found in taste buds on the tongue, in the nose and in blood vessels where they detect changes in oxygen and carbon dioxide concentrations

chiasma (plural: chiasmata): a position at which non-sister chromatids of homologous chromosomes cross over each other

chi-squared (χ^2) test: a statistical test that can be used to determine whether differences between observed and expected results are significant

chloride shift: the movement of chloride ions into red blood cells from blood plasma, to balance the movement of hydrogencarbonate ions into the plasma from the red blood cells

chlorophyll: a green pigment responsible that absorbs energy from light, used in photosynthesis

chloroplast: the organelle, bounded by an envelope (i.e., two membranes), in which photosynthesis takes place in eukaryotes

cholesterol: a small, lipid-related molecule with a hydrophilic head and a hydrophobic tail which is an essential constituent of membranes; it is particularly common in animal cells and gives flexibility and stability to the membrane as well as reducing fluidity

cholinergic synapse: a synapse at which the transmitter substance is ACh

chromatid: one of two identical parts of a chromosome, held together by a centromere, formed during interphase by the replication of the DNA strand

chromatin: the material of which chromosomes are made, consisting of DNA, proteins and small amounts of RNA; visible as patches or fibres within the nucleus when stained

chromatography: a technique that can separate substances in a mixture according to their solubility in a solvent

chromosome: in the nucleus of the cells of eukaryotes, a structure made of tightly coiled chromatin (DNA, proteins and RNA) visible during cell division; the term circular DNA is now commonly used for the circular strand of DNA present in a prokaryotic cell

chromosome mutation: a random and unpredictable change in the structure or number of chromosomes in a cell

cilia (singular: **cilium**): whip-like structures projecting from the surface of many animal cells and the cells of many unicellular organisms; they beat, causing locomotion or the movement of fluid across the cell surface

ciliated epithelium: an epithelium that consists mainly of ciliated cells; may also contain goblet cells

circulatory system: a system that carries fluids around an organism's body

clonal expansion: the increase in number of specific clones of lymphocytes by mitosis during an immune response

clonal selection: individual lymphocytes have cell surface receptors specific to one antigen; this specificity is determined as lymphocytes mature and before any antigens enter the body (during an immune response the only lymphocytes to respond are those with receptors specific to antigens on the surface of the invading pathogen)

closed blood system: a circulatory system made up of vessels containing blood

codominant: codominant alleles each affect phenotype when both of them are present

codon: sequence of three bases on an mRNA molecule that codes for a specific amino acid or for a stop signal

coenzyme A (CoA): a molecule that supplies acetyl groups required for the link reaction

collagen: the main structural protein of animals; known as 'white fibres', the fundamental unit of the fibre consists of three helical polypeptide chains wound around each other, forming a 'triple helix' with high tensile strength

collecting duct: tube in the medulla of the kidney that carries urine from the distal convoluted tubules of many nephrons to the renal pelvis

collenchyma: a modified form of parenchyma in which the corners of the cells have extra cellulose thickening, providing extra support, as in the midrib of leaves and at the corners of square stems; in three dimensions the tissue occurs in strands (as in celery petioles)

colorimeter: an instrument that measures the colour of a solution by measuring the absorption of different wavelengths of light

community: all of the living organisms, of all species, that are found in a particular ecosystem at a particular time

companion cell: a cell with an unthickened cellulose wall and dense cytoplasm that is found in close association with a phloem sieve element to which it is directly linked via many plasmodesmata; the companion cell and the sieve element form a functional unit

competition: the need for a resource by two organisms, when that resource is in short supply

competitive inhibition: when a substance reduces the rate of activity of an enzyme by competing with the substrate molecules for the enzyme's active site; increasing substrate concentration reduces the degree of inhibition; increasing inhibitor concentration increases the degree of inhibition

complementary base pairing: the hydrogen bonding of A with T or U and of C with G in nucleic acids

condensation reaction: a chemical reaction involving the joining together of two molecules by removal of a water molecule

continuous data: a set of data in which any individual reading can have any value between the two extremes

continuous variable: a variable which can have any value within a range

continuous variation: differences between individuals of a species in which each one can lie at any point in the range between the highest and lowest values

control: a standard of comparison in an experiment; it is used to compare the results of changing the independent variable with a sample in which the independent variable is not present, or is unchanged

control experiment: an experiment in which the factor whose effect is being investigated (the independent variable) is absent; it is used as a standard of comparison

coronary arteries: arteries that branch from the aorta and spread over the walls of the heart, supplying the cardiac muscle with nutrients and oxygen

corrective action: a response or series of responses that return a physiological factor to the set point so maintaining a constant environment for the cells within the body

cristae (singular: **crista**): folds of the inner membrane of the mitochondrial envelope on which are found stalked particles of ATP synthase and electron transport chains associated with aerobic respiration

crossing over: the exchange of alleles between non-sister chromatids of homologous chromosomes during meiosis I

cuticle: a layer covering, and secreted by, the epidermis; in plants it is made of a fatty substance called cutin, which helps to provide protection against water loss and infection

cyclic AMP (c-AMP): a second messenger in cell–signalling pathways

cyclic photophosphorylation: the production of ATP using energy from light, involving only photosystem I

cystic fibrosis: a genetic disease caused by a recessive allele of the *CFTR* (cystic fibrosis transmembrane regulator) gene

cytokine: any signalling molecule released by cells to influence the growth and/or differentiation of the same or another cell

cytoplasm: the contents of a cell, excluding the nucleus

deamination: the breakdown of excess amino acids in the liver, by the removal of the amine group; ammonia and, eventually, urea are formed from the amine group

decarboxylation: the removal of carbon dioxide from a substance

dehydrogenation: the removal of hydrogen from a substance

dependent variable: the variable (factor) that is affected by changes in the independent variable; this is the variable that you record as a measurement

depolarisation: the reversal of the resting potential across the cell surface membrane of a neurone or muscle cell, so that the inside becomes positively charged compared with the outside

diastole: the stage of the cardiac cycle when the muscle in the walls of the heart relaxes

dicotyledon: flowering plants can be classified as monocotyledons or dicotyledons; the seeds of dicotyledonous plants contain an embryo with two cotyledons (seed leaves) in their seeds and the adult plant typically has leaves with a blade (lamina) and a stalk (petiole)

diffusion: the net movement of molecules or ions from a region of higher concentration to a region of lower concentration down a concentration gradient, as a result of the random movements of particles

dihybrid inheritance: the inheritance of two genes

dinucleotide: two nucleotides joined together by a phosphodiester bond

diploid: containing two complete sets of chromosomes; can be signified by the symbol $2n$

directional selection: natural selection that causes a gradual change in allele frequency over many generations

disaccharide: a sugar molecule consisting of two monosaccharides joined together by a glycosidic bond

discontinuous variable: a variable in which the different categories are separate from one another

discontinuous variation: differences between individuals of a species in which each one belongs to one of a small number of distinct categories, with no intermediates

discrete data: a set of data in which each measurement can only belong to one of a limited number of values

disease carrier (or simply **carrier**): person infected with a pathogen who shows no symptoms, but can be the source of infection in other people (not carrier of an inherited disease)

disease eradication: the complete breakage of the transmission cycle of a pathogen so that there are no more cases of the disease caused by the pathogen anywhere in the world

disease transmission: the transfer of a pathogen from a person infected with that pathogen to an uninfected person; transmission may occur by direct contact, through the air or water or by animal vectors, such as insects

disease vector: an organism which carries a pathogen from one person to another or from an animal to a human

disruptive selection: natural selection that maintains relatively high frequencies of two different sets of alleles; individuals with intermediate features and allele sets are not selected for

dissociation curve: a graph showing the percentage saturation of a pigment (such as haemoglobin) with oxygen, plotted against the partial pressure of oxygen

distal convoluted tubule: part of the nephron that leads from the loop of Henle to the collecting duct

DNA hybridisation: binding together of two molecules of single-stranded DNA by complementary base pairing

DNA ligase: an enzyme that catalyses the joining together of two nucleotides with covalent phosphodiester bonds during DNA replication; used when inserting DNA into a plasmid

DNA polymerase: an enzyme that copies DNA; it runs along the separated DNA strands lining up one complementary nucleotide at a time ready for joining by DNA ligase

domain: the highest taxonomic rank

dominant: a dominant allele has the same effect on phenotype, whether or not another allele is present

double circulation: a circulatory system in which the blood passes through the heart twice on one complete circuit of the body

ecological separation: the separation of two populations because they live in different environments in the same area and so cannot breed together

ecological species: a population of individuals of the same species living in the same area at the same time

ecosystem: a relatively self-contained, interacting community of organisms, and the environment in which they live and with which they interact

effector: a tissue or organ that carries out an action in response to a stimulus; muscles and glands are effectors

efferent arteriole: arteriole leading away from glomerular capillaries

elastic arteries: relatively large arteries, which have a lot of elastic tissue and little muscle tissue in their walls

elastic fibres: bundles of the fibrous protein elastin which can stretch and recoil like elastic bands; they can stretch up to twice their length before breaking

electrochemical gradient: a gradient across a cell surface membrane that involves both a difference in concentrations of ions and a potential difference

electron transport chain: a chain of adjacently arranged carrier molecules in the inner mitochondrial membrane, along which electrons pass by redox reactions

embryo transfer: embryos are removed from the uterus of a female mammal of an endangered species shortly after fertilisation and transferred to surrogate females to bring to full term

endemic: of disease, a disease that is always in a population; of species, a species that is only found in a certain area and nowhere else

endocrine gland: an organ that secretes hormones directly into the blood; endocrine glands are also known as ductless glands

endocrine system: consists of all the endocrine glands in the body together with the hormones that they secrete

endocytosis: the bulk movement of liquids (pinocytosis) or solids (phagocytosis) into a cell, by the infolding of the cell surface membrane to form vesicles containing the substance; endocytosis is an active process requiring ATP

endodermis: the layer of cells surrounding the vascular tissue of plants; it is most clearly visible in roots

endoplasmic reticulum (ER): a network of flattened sacs running through the cytoplasm of eukaryotic cells; molecules, particularly proteins, can be transported through the cell inside the sacs separate from the rest of the cytoplasm; ER is continuous with the outer membrane of the nuclear envelope

endosperm: a tissue in some seeds, such as barley, that is a store of starch and other nutrients

endothelium: a tissue that lines the inner surface of blood vessels

environmental factor: a feature of the environment of an organism that affects its survival

enzyme: a protein produced by a living organism that acts as a catalyst in a specific reaction by reducing activation energy

epidermis: the outer layer of cells covering the body of a plant or animal; in plants it is usually one cell thick and may be covered with a cuticle which provides additional protection against loss of water and disease

epistasis: the interaction of two genes at different loci; one gene may affect the expression of the other

epithelium: a tissue that forms the lining of the respiratory passages and the alimentary canal

error bar: a line drawn through a point or the top of bar on a graph, extending two standard errors above and below the mean value indicated by the point or bar; you can be 95% certain that the true value lies within the range indicated by the error bar

ester bond / ester linkage: a chemical bond, represented as –COO–, formed when an acid reacts with an alcohol

ethanol fermentation: anaerobic respiration in which pyruvate is converted to ethanol

Eukarya: the domain that contains all eukaryotic organisms: protoctists, fungi, plants and animals

eukaryote: an organism whose cells contain a nucleus and other membrane-bound organelles

evolution: a process leading to the formation of new species from pre-existing species over time

excretion: the removal of toxic or waste products of metabolism from the body

exocytosis: the bulk movement of liquids or solids out of a cell, by the fusion of vesicles containing the substance with the cell surface membrane; exocytosis is an active process requiring ATP

expansions: proteins in the cell walls of plants that loosen the attachment of microfibrils of cellulose during elongation growth

eyepiece graticule: small scale that is placed in a microscope eyepiece

F_1 generation: the offspring resulting from the cross between individuals with a homozygous recessive and a homozygous dominant genotype

F_2 generation: the offspring resulting from a cross between two F_1 individuals

facilitated diffusion: the diffusion of a substance through a transport protein (channel protein or carrier protein) in a cell membrane; the protein provides hydrophilic areas that allow the molecule or ion to pass through the membrane, which would otherwise be less permeable to it

fertilisation: the fusing of the nuclei of two gametes, to form a zygote

fibrous protein: a protein whose molecules have a relatively long, thin structure that is generally insoluble and metabolically inactive, and whose function is usually structural, e.g. keratin and collagen

fitness: the ability of an organism to survive and reproduce

flagella (singular: flagellum): whip-like structures projecting from the surface of some animal cells and the cells of many unicellular organisms; they beat, causing locomotion or the movement of fluid across the cell surface; they are identical in structure to cilia, but longer

fluid mosaic model: the currently accepted model of membrane structure, proposed by Singer and Nicolson in 1972, in which protein molecules are free to move about in a fluid bilayer of phospholipid molecules

founder effect: the reduction in a gene pool compared with the main populations of a species, resulting from only two or three individuals (with only a selection of the alleles in the gene pool) starting off a new population

frozen zoo: a facility where genetic materials taken from animals are stored at very low temperatures (–196 °C); sperm, eggs, embryos and tissue samples are examples of these genetic materials

Fungi: kingdom of eukaryotic organisms which do not photosynthesise and have cell walls but without cellulose

gamete: a sex cell; during sexual reproduction, two gametes fuse together to form a zygote; gametes are usually haploid

gas exchange surface: any part of an organism that allows the movement of gases between the surroundings and the body; gas exchange occurs across the body surface of some organisms that have large surface area : volume ratios; organisms with small ratios have specialised gas exchange surfaces, such as the lungs of mammals and the gills of fish

gel electrophoresis: the separation of charged molecules (e.g. DNA) by differential movement through a gel in an electric field; the degree of movement is dependent on the mass of the fragments of DNA

gene: a length of DNA that codes for a particular protein or polypeptide

gene editing: a form of genetic engineering in which the genome of an organism can be changed by deleting, inserting or replacing a length of DNA using a method such as the Crispr/Cas9 system

gene mutation: a change in the base sequence in part of a DNA molecule

gene pool: the complete range of DNA base sequences in all the organisms in a species or population

gene probe: a length of DNA that has a complementary base sequence to another piece of DNA that you are trying to detect

gene therapy: treatment of a genetic disorder by inserting genetically corrected cells into the body or introducing functioning genes directly into affected cells

genetic diagram: a standard format in which the results of a genetic cross are predicted and explained

genetic diversity: all the alleles of all the genes in the genome of a species

genetic drift: the gradual change in allele frequencies in a small population, where some alleles are lost or favoured just by chance and not by natural selection

genetic engineering: any procedure in which the genetic information in an organism is changed by altering the base sequence of a gene or by introducing a gene from another organism; the organism is then said to be a genetically modified organism (GMO)

genetic screening: testing an embryo, fetus or adult to find out whether a particular allele is present

genetic variation: differences between the DNA base sequences of individuals within a species

genetically isolated: no longer able to breed together; there is no exchange of genes

genetically modified organism (GMO): any organism that has had its DNA changed in a way that does not occur naturally or by selective breeding

genome: the complete set of genes or genetic material present in a cell or an organism; the genome of a eukaryote includes the DNA in the nucleus and in the mitochondria; the genomes of plants include chloroplast DNA

genotype: the alleles possessed by an organism

geographical isolation: separation by a geographical barrier, such as a stretch of water or a mountain range

gibberellin: a plant growth regulator (plant hormone) that stimulates seed germination and regulates plant height (stem growth); a lack of gibberellin causes dwarfness

globular protein: a protein whose molecules are folded into a relatively spherical shape, often has physiological roles and is often water-soluble and metabolically active, e.g. insulin, haemoglobin and enzymes

glomerulus (plural: glomeruli): a group of capillaries within the 'cup' of a Bowman's capsule in the cortex of the kidney

glucagon: a small peptide hormone secreted by the α cells in the islets of Langerhans in the pancreas to bring about an increase in the concentration of glucose in the blood

gluconeogenesis: the formation of glucose in the liver from non-carbohydrate sources such as amino acids, pyruvate, lactate and glycerol

glycerate-3-phosphate (GP): a three-carbon compound which is formed when RuBP combines with carbon dioxide

glycogen: a polysaccharide made of many glucose molecules linked together, that acts as a glucose store in liver and muscle cells

glycogenesis: synthesis of glycogen by addition of glucose monomers

glycogenolysis: the breakdown of glycogen by removal of glucose monomers

glycolysis: the splitting (lysis) of glucose; the first stage in respiration

glycosidic bond: a C–O–C link between two sugar molecules, formed by a condensation reaction; it is a covalent bond

goblet cell: a cell shaped like a drinking goblet that secretes mucus; goblet cells are found in epithelia lining parts of the gas exchange system and other organ systems, e.g. reproductive and digestive

Golgi body (Golgi apparatus, Golgi complex): an organelle found in eukaryotic cells; the Golgi apparatus consists of a stack of flattened sacs, constantly forming at one end and breaking up into Golgi vesicles at the other end

Golgi vesicles: carry their contents to other parts of the cell, often to the cell surface membrane for secretion; the Golgi apparatus chemically modifies the molecules it transports, e.g. sugars may be added to proteins to make glycoproteins

grana: (singular: **granum**) stacks of membranes inside a chloroplast

guard cell: a sausage-shaped epidermal cell found with another, in a pair bounding a stoma and controlling its opening or closure

habitat: the place where an organism, a population or a community lives

haemoglobin: the red pigment found in red blood cells, whose molecules contain four iron atoms within a globular protein made up of four polypeptides; it combines reversibly with oxygen

haploid: containing one complete set of chromosomes; can be signified by the symbol n

herd immunity: vaccinating a large proportion of the population; provides protection for those not immunised as transmission of a pathogen is reduced

heterozygous: having two different alleles of a gene

hierarchical classification: the arrangement of organisms into groups of different rank. The lowest rank is the species; similar species are grouped together into the next rank, which is the genus; this continues to the highest rank, which is the domain where many species are grouped together

histogram: a graph in which the categories on the x-axis are continuous; the bars are drawn with no gaps between them

HIV: human immunodeficiency virus

homeostasis: the maintenance of a relatively constant environment for the cells within the body

homologous chromosomes: two chromosomes that carry the same genes in the same positions

homozygous: having two identical alleles of a gene

hormone: a substance secreted by an endocrine gland that is carried in blood plasma to another part of the body where it has an effect

hybridoma: a cell formed by the fusion of a plasma cell and a cancer cell; it can both secrete antibodies and divide to form other cells like itself

hybrid vigour: an increased ability to survive and grow well, as a result of outbreeding and therefore increased heterozygosity

hydrogen bond: a relatively weak bond formed by the attraction between a group with a small positive charge on a hydrogen atom ($H^{\partial+}$) and another group carrying a small negative charge ($^{\partial-}$), e.g. between two $-O^{\delta-}H^{\delta+}$ groups

hydrolysis: a chemical reaction in which a chemical bond is broken by the addition of a water molecule; commonly used to break down complex molecules into simpler molecules

hypothesis: a tentative statement providing an explanation or prediction, based on a body of prior knowledge and testable by experiment

immobilised enzymes: enzymes that have been fixed to a surface or trapped inside beads of agar gel

immune response: the complex series of responses of the body to the entry of a foreign antigen; it involves the activity of lymphocytes and phagocytes

immune system: the body's internal defence system

immunological memory: the ability of the immune system to mount a larger and more rapid response to an antigen that has already been encountered before

***in vitro* fertilisation (IVF):** the fertilisation of an egg that occurs outside the body of a female (e.g. in a Petri dish)

inbreeding: breeding between organisms with similar genotypes, or that are closely related

inbreeding depression: a loss of the ability to survive and grow well, due to breeding between close relatives; this increases the chance of harmful recessive alleles coming together in an individual and being expressed

incipient plasmolysis: the point at which plasmolysis is about to occur when a plant cell or a prokaryote cell is losing water; at this point the protoplast is exerting no pressure on the cell wall

independent assortment: the production of different combinations of alleles in daughter cells, as a result of the random alignment of bivalents on the equator of the spindle during metaphase I of meiosis

independent variable: the variable (factor) that you purposefully change in an experiment

induced-fit hypothesis: a hypothesis for enzyme action; the substrate is a complementary shape to the active site of the enzyme, but not an exact fit – the enzyme or sometimes the substrate can change shape slightly to ensure a perfect fit, but it is still described as showing specificity

inducible enzyme: an enzyme that is synthesised only when its substrate is present

infectious disease: a disease caused by an organism such as a protoctist, bacterium or virus

insulin: a small peptide hormone secreted by the β cells in the islets of Langerhans in the pancreas to bring about a decrease in the concentration of glucose in the blood

interquartile range: the range of values not including the top quartile and the bottom quartile

interval: the spacing between the different values of the independent variable

islet of Langerhans: a group of cells in the pancreas which secrete insulin and glucagon

K_m: *see* **Michaelis–Menten constant**

kinetochore: a protein structure found at the centromere of a chromatid to which microtubules attach during nuclear division

kingdom: the taxonomic rank below domain

Krebs cycle: a cycle of reactions in aerobic respiration in the matrix of a mitochondrion in which hydrogens pass to hydrogen carriers for subsequent ATP synthesis and some ATP is synthesised directly; also known as the citric acid cycle

***lac* operon:** an operon found in some bacteria that controls the production of β-galactosidase and two other structural proteins

lactate fermentation: anaerobic respiration in which pyruvate is converted to lactate

lagging strand: during DNA replication, the parent strand that runs in the 5′ to 3′ direction is copied to produce the lagging strand

lamellae: membranes found within a chloroplast

leading strand: during DNA replication, the parent strand that runs in the 3′ to 5′ direction is copied to produce the leading strand

ligand: a biological molecule which binds specifically to another molecule, such as a cell surface membrane receptor, during cell signalling

light-dependent stage: the first series of reactions that take place in photosynthesis; it requires energy absorbed from light

light-independent stage: the final series of reactions that take place in photosynthesis; it does not require light but does need substances that are produced in the light-dependent stage

lignin: a hard material made by plants and used to strengthen the cell walls of certain types of cell, particularly xylem vessel elements and sclerenchyma cells; it is the main material in wood

limiting factor: the requirement for a process to take place that is in the shortest supply; an increase in this factor will allow the process to take place more rapidly

linkage: *see* autosomal linkage; *see* sex-linked gene

link reaction: decarboxylation and dehydrogenation of pyruvate, resulting in the formation of acetyl coenzyme A, linking glycolysis with the Krebs cycle

lock-and-key hypothesis: a hypothesis for enzyme action; the substrate is a complementary shape to the active site of the enzyme, and fits exactly into the site; the enzyme shows specificity for the substrate

locus: the position of a gene on a chromosome

loop of Henle: the part of the nephron between the proximal and distal convoluted tubules

lymphocyte: a white blood cell with a nucleus that almost fills the cell, which responds to antigens and helps to destroy the antigens or the structure that is carrying them

lysosome: a spherical organelle found in eukaryotic cells; it contains digestive (hydrolytic) enzymes and has a variety of destructive functions, such as removal of old cell organelles

macromolecule: *see also* polymer; a large molecule such as a polysaccharide, protein or nucleic acid

macrophage: phagocytic cell found in tissues throughout the body; they act as antigen-presenting cells (APCs)

magnification: the number of times larger an image of an object is than the real size of the object; magnification = image size ÷ actual (real) size of the object

mark–release–recapture: a method of estimating the numbers of individuals in a population of mobile animals

median: the middle value of all the values in the data set

meiosis: nuclear division that results in the production of four daughter cells with half the chromosome number of the parent cell and with reshuffled alleles; in animals and plants it results in the formation of gametes

memory B cell: long-lived, activated B-lymphocyte that is specific to one antigen; memory cells are activated to differentiate (develop) into plasma cells during secondary immune responses to the specific antigen

mesophyll: the region of a leaf between the upper and lower epidermis; in dicotyledonous plants the mesophyll has an upper palisade layer and a lower mesophyll layer; the palisade mesophyll cells are column-shaped and form the main photosynthetic layer, whereas the spongy mesophyll has large air spaces between the cells for gas exchange

Michaelis–Menten constant (K_m): the substrate concentration at which an enzyme works at half its maximum rate (½Vmax), used as a measure of the efficiency of an enzyme; the lower the value of K_m, the more efficient the enzyme

microarray (also known as **gene** or **DNA chips**): slides that are printed with thousands of tiny spots in defined positions, with each spot containing a known DNA sequence; the DNA molecules attached to each slide act as probes to detect lengths of DNA or RNA with complementary sequences

micrograph: a picture taken with the aid of a microscope; a photomicrograph (or light micrograph) is taken using a light microscope; an electron micrograph is taken using an electron microscope

microtubules: tiny tubes made of a protein called tubulin and found in most eukaryotic cells; microtubules have a large variety of functions, including cell support and determining cell shape; the 'spindle' on which chromosomes separate during nuclear division is made of microtubules

microvilli: (singular: **microvillus**) small, finger-like extensions of a cell which increase the surface area of the cell for more efficient absorption or secretion

mitochondrion: (plural: **mitochondria**) the organelle in eukaryotes in which aerobic respiration takes place

mitosis: the division of a nucleus into two so that the two daughter cells have exactly the same number and type of chromosomes as the parent cell

mode (**modal class**): the most common value, or class, in the set of results

monoclonal antibody: an antibody made by a single clone of hybridoma cells; all the antibody molecules made by the clone have identical variable regions so are specific to one antigen

monocyte: the largest type of white blood cell; it has a bean-shaped nucleus; monocytes can leave the blood and develop into a type of phagocytic cell called a macrophage

monohybrid inheritance: inheritance of one gene

monomer: a relatively simple molecule which is used as a basic building block for the synthesis of a polymer; many monomers are joined together to make the polymer, usually by condensation reactions; common examples of monomers are monosaccharides, amino acids and nucleotides

monosaccharide: a molecule consisting of a single sugar unit and with the general formula $(CH_2O)_n$

morphological: relating to structural features

morphological species: a group of organisms that share many physical features that distinguish them from other species

motor neurone: a neurone whose cell body is in the brain, spinal cord or a ganglion (a swelling on a nerve), and that transmits nerve impulses to an effector such as a muscle or gland

mucin: any glycoprotein that forms part of the mucus secreted by goblet cells and mucous cells

multiple alleles: the existence of three or more alleles of a gene, as, e.g., in the determination of A,B,O blood groups

muscular arteries: arteries that are closer to the final destination of the blood inside them than elastic arteries, with more smooth muscle in their walls which allows them to constrict and dilate

murein: *see* peptidoglycan

mutation: a random change in the base sequence (structure) of DNA (a gene mutation), or in the structure and/or number of chromosomes (a chromosome mutation)

myelin: insulating material that surrounds the axons of many neurones; myelin is made of layers of cell surface membranes formed by Schwann cells so that they are very rich in phospholipids and therefore impermeable to water and ions in tissue fluid

myofibril: one of many cylindrical bundles of thick (myosin) and thin (actin) filaments inside a muscle fibre

myogenic: a word used to describe muscle tissue that contracts and relaxes even when there is no stimulation from a nerve

myosin: the protein that makes up the thick filaments in striated muscle; the globular heads of each molecule break down ATP (they act as an ATP-ase)

NAD (nicotinamide adenine dinucleotide): a hydrogen carrier used in respiration

NADP: a coenzyme that transfers hydrogen from one substance to another, in the reactions of photosynthesis

natural active immunity: immunity gained by being infected by a pathogen

natural passive immunity: the immunity gained by a fetus when maternal antibodies cross the placenta or the immunity gained by an infant from breast milk

natural selection: the process by which individuals with a particular set of alleles are more likely to survive and reproduce than those with other alleles; over time and many generations, the advantageous alleles become more frequent in the population

negative feedback: a process in which a change in some parameter (e.g. blood glucose concentration) brings about processes which return it towards normal

nephron: the structural and functional unit of the kidney composed of Bowman's capsule and a tubule divided into three regions: proximal convoluted tubule, loop of Henle and distal convoluted tubule

nerve impulse: (usually shortened to impulse) a wave of electrical depolarisation that is transmitted along neurones

neuromuscular junction: a synapse between a motor neurone and a muscle

neurone: a nerve cell; a cell which is specialised for the conduction of nerve impulses

neurotransmitter: a chemical released at synapses to transmit impulses between neurones or between a motor neurone and a muscle fibre

neutrophil: one type of phagocytic white blood cell; it has a lobed nucleus and granular cytoplasm

niche: the role of an organism in an ecosystem

node of Ranvier: a very short gap between Schwann cells where myelinated axons are not covered in myelin so are exposed to tissue fluid

nominal data: a set of data in which the individual results cannot be arranged in a sequence; instead, each is assigned to a distinct category

non-competitive inhibition: when a substance reduces the rate of activity of an enzyme, but increasing the concentration of the substrate does not reduce the degree of inhibition; many non-competitive inhibitors bind to areas of the enzyme molecule other than the active site itself

non-cyclic photophosphorylation: the production ATP using energy from light, involving both photosystem I and photosystem II; this process also produces reduced NADP

non-self: refers to any substance or cell that is recognised by the immune system as being foreign and will stimulate an immune response

noradrenaline: a type of neurotransmitter, which is also released by cells in the adrenal glands as a hormone

normal distribution: a set of data in which a graph shows a symmetrical distribution around the central value

nuclear envelope: the two membranes, situated close together, that surround the nucleus; the envelope is perforated with nuclear pores

nuclear pores: pores found in the nuclear envelope which control the exchange of materials, e.g. mRNA, between the nucleus and the cytoplasm

nucleolus: a small structure, one or more of which is found inside the nucleus; the nucleolus is usually visible as a densely stained body; its function is to manufacture ribosomes using the information in its own DNA

nucleotide: a molecule consisting of a nitrogen-containing base, a pentose sugar and a phosphate group

nucleus: (plural: nuclei) a relatively large organelle found in eukaryotic cells, but absent from prokaryotic cells; the nucleus contains the cell's DNA and therefore controls the activities of the cell; it is surrounded by two membranes which together form the nuclear envelope

null hypothesis: a statement saying that there is no association or difference between two sets of data

operon: a functional unit of transcription; a cluster of genes that are controlled by the same promoter

opportunistic infection: an infection caused by pathogens that take advantage of a host with a weakened immune system, as may happen in someone with an HIV infection

ordinal data: a set of data in which, although the values are not numerical, the individual results can be arranged in a sequence

organelle: a functionally and structurally distinct part of a cell, e.g. a ribosome or mitochondrion

osmoreceptor: type of receptor that detects changes in the water potential of blood

osmoregulation: the control of the water potential of blood and tissue fluid by controlling the water content and/or the concentration of ions, particularly sodium ions

osmosis: the net diffusion of water molecules from a region of higher water potential to a region of lower water potential, through a partially permeable membrane

outbreeding: breeding between individuals that are not closely related

oxidation: the addition of oxygen, or the removal of hydrogen or electrons from a substance

oxidative phosphorylation: the synthesis of ATP from ADP and P_i using energy from oxidation reactions in aerobic respiration (compare photophosphorylation)

oxygen-evolving complex: an enzyme found in photosystem II that catalyses the breakdown of water, using energy from light

parenchyma: a basic plant tissue typically used as packing tissue between more specialised structures; it is metabolically active and may have a variety of functions such as food storage and support; parenchyma cells also play an important role in the movement of water and food products in the xylem and phloem

parental type: offspring that show the same combinations of characteristics as their parents

partial pressure: a measure of the concentration of a gas

passive immunity: the temporary immunity gained without there being an immune response

pathogen: an organism that causes disease

Pearson's linear correlation: a statistical test used to determine if there is a linear correlation between two variables that are normally distributed

peptide bond: a C–N link between two amino acid molecules, formed by a condensation reaction; the covalent bond joining neighbouring amino acids together in proteins

peptidoglycan: a polysaccharide combined with amino acids; it is also known as murein; it makes the bacterial cell wall more rigid

percentage saturation: the degree to which the haemoglobin in the blood is combined with oxygen, calculated as a percentage of the maximum amount with which it can combine

phagocyte: a type of cell that ingests (eats) and destroys pathogens or damaged body cells by the process of phagocytosis; some phagocytes are white blood cells

phagocytosis: *see* endocytosis

phenotype: the observable features of an organism; it is affected by genes and also by environment

phenotypic variation: differences between the observable characteristics of individuals within a species

phloem: a tissue containing tubes called sieve tubes and other types of cell, responsible for the transport through the plant of organic solutes (assimilates) such as sucrose

phosphodiester bond: a bond joining two nucleotides together; there are two ester bonds, one from the shared phosphate group to each of the sugars either side of it

phospholipid: a lipid to which phosphate is added; the molecule is made up of a glycerol molecule, two fatty acids and a phosphate group; a double layer (a bilayer) of phospholipids forms the basic structure of all cell membranes

phosphorylase kinase: an enzyme that is part of the enzyme cascade that acts in response to glucagon; the enzyme activates glycogen phosphorylase by adding a phosphate group

phosphorylation: the addition of a phosphate group to a molecule

photoactivation: the emission of an electron from a molecule as a result of the absorption of energy from light

photolysis: splitting a water molecule, using energy from light: $H_2O \rightarrow 2H^+ + 2e^- + O_2$

photophosphorylation: producing ATP using energy that originated as light

photosynthesis: the production of organic substances from inorganic ones, using energy from light

photosynthetic pigments: coloured substances that absorb light of particular wavelengths, supplying energy to drive the reactions in the light-dependent stage of photosynthesis

photosystem: a cluster of light-harvesting pigments surrounding a reaction centre

physiological: relating to metabolic and other processes in a living organism

pinocytosis: *see* endocytosis

plant growth regulator (**plant hormone**): any chemical produced in plants that influences their growth and development (e.g. auxins, gibberellins, cytokinins and ABA)

Plantae: kingdom of eukaryotic organisms which are multicellular, have cell walls that contain cellulose and can photosynthesise

plasma: the liquid component of blood, in which the blood cells float; it carries a very large range of different substances in solution

plasma proteins: a range of several different proteins dissolved in the blood plasma, each with their own function; many of them are made in the liver

plasmid: a small circular piece of DNA in a bacterium (not its main 'chromosome'); plasmids often contain genes that confer resistance to antibiotics

plasmodesma: (plural: **plasmodesmata**) a pore-like structure found in plant cell walls; plasmodesmata of neighbouring plant cells line up to form tube-like pores through the cell walls, allowing the controlled passage of materials from one cell to the other; the pores contain ER and are lined with the cell surface membrane

plasma cell: short-lived, activated B-lymphocyte produced during clonal expansion; plasma cells produce and release antibody molecules

plasmolysis: the loss of water from a plant or prokaryote cell to the point where the protoplast shrinks away from the cell wall

podocyte: one of the cells that makes up the lining of Bowman's capsule surrounding the glomerular capillaries

polygenes: a number of different genes at different loci that all contribute to a particular aspect of phenotype

polymer: a giant molecule made from many similar repeating subunits joined together in a chain; the subunits are much smaller and simpler molecules known as monomers; examples of biological polymers are polysaccharides, proteins and nucleic acids

polymerase chain reaction (PCR): an automated process that amplifies selected regions of DNA using alternate stages of polynucleotide separation (denaturation of DNA) and DNA synthesis catalysed by DNA polymerase

polymorphism: the continued existence of two or more different phenotypes in a species

polynucleotide: a chain of nucleotides joined together by phosphodiester bonds

polypeptide: a long chain of amino acids formed by condensation reactions between the individual amino acids; proteins are made of one or more polypeptide chains; *see* peptide bond

polysaccharide: a polymer whose subunits are monosaccharides joined together by glycosidic bonds

population: all of the organisms of the same species present in the same place and at the same time that can interbreed with one another

positive feedback: a process in which a change in some parameter such as a physiological factor brings about processes that move its level even further in the direction of the initial change

postsynaptic neurone: the neurone on the opposite side of a synapse to the neurone in which the action potential arrives

potential difference: the difference in electrical potential between two points; in the nervous system, between the inside and the outside of a cell surface membrane such as the membrane that encloses an axon

precision: how close two or more measurements of the same value are to each other

prediction: a statement about what you think might happen; a prediction could just be guesswork, but a good one is based on prior knowledge and an underlying hypothesis

presynaptic neurone: a neurone ending at a synapse from which neurotransmitter is released when an action potential arrives

primary immune response: the first immune response to a specific antigen

primary structure: the sequence of amino acids in a polypeptide or protein

prokaryote: an organism whose cells do not contain a nucleus or any other membrane-bound organelles

promoter: a length of DNA that includes the binding site for RNA polymerase where transcription of a gene or genes begins; in eukaryotes, promoters also have sites for binding of transcription factors

protein kinase A: enzyme that is activated by c-AMP and once activated adds phosphate groups to other proteins, including phosphorylase kinase, to activate them

Protoctista: kingdom of eukaryotic organisms which are single-celled or made up of groups of similar cells

protoctist: a member of the Protoctista kingdom

protoplasm: all the living material inside a cell (cytoplasm plus nucleus)

protoplast: the living contents of a plant cell, including the cell surface membrane but excluding the cell wall

proximal convoluted tubule: part of the nephron that leads from Bowman's capsule to the loop of Henle

pulmonary circulation: the part of the circulatory system that carries blood from the heart to the gas exchange surface and then back to the heart

Punnett square: part of a genetic diagram in which the genotypes of the offspring are worked out from the genotypes of the gametes

Purkyne tissue: a bundle of fibres that conduct the wave of excitation down through the septum of the heart to the base (apex) of the ventricles

quadrat: a square frame which is used to mark out an area for sampling populations of organisms

quaternary structure: the three-dimensional arrangement of two or more polypeptides, or of a polypeptide and a non-protein component such as haem, in a protein molecule

random error: a source of uncertainty in your results that gives incorrect values that can be of different magnitudes and err in different direction; random errors can affect trends shown by results

random sampling: method of investigating the abundance and/or distribution of populations which is determined by chance and shows no bias on the part of the person carrying out the sampling

range: the spread between the lowest and highest values of the independent variable

reaction centre: the part of a photosystem towards which energy from light is funnelled; it contains a pair of chlorophyll *a* molecules, which absorb the energy and emit electrons

receptor: a cell or tissue that is sensitive to a specific stimulus and communicates with a control centre by generating nerve impulses or sending a chemical messenger

receptor potential: a change in the normal resting potential across the membrane of a receptor cell, caused by a stimulus

receptor protein: a protein on a postsynaptic membrane that is a ligand-gated channel protein opening in response to binding of a neurotransmitter

recessive: a recessive allele only affects phenotype if no dominant allele is present

recombinant: offspring that show different combinations of characteristics from their parents

recombinant DNA (rDNA): DNA made by artificially joining together pieces of DNA from two or more different species

redox indicator: a substance that changes colour when it is oxidised or reduced

redox reaction: a chemical reaction in which one substance is reduced and another is oxidised reduction: the removal of oxygen, or the addition of hydrogen or electrons to a substance

reduction division: nuclear division that results in a reduction in chromosome number; the first division of meiosis is a reduction division

refractory period: a period of time during which a neurone is recovering from an action potential, and during which another action potential cannot be generated

regulatory gene: a gene that codes for a protein that helps to control the expression of other genes

replicates: two or more trials of the same experiment, using the same materials and apparatus

repolarisation: returning the potential difference across the cell surface membrane of a neurone or muscle cell to normal following the depolarisation of an action potential

repressible enzyme: an enzyme that is normally produced, and whose synthesis is prevented by the presence of an effector

reproductive isolation: the inability of two groups of organisms to breed with one another; two populations of the same species may be geographically separated, or two different species are unable to breed to produce fertile offspring

resolution: the ability to distinguish between two objects very close together; the higher the resolution of an image, the greater the detail that can be seen

respiration: the enzymatic release of energy from organic compounds in living cells

respiratory quotient (RQ): the ratio of the volume of carbon dioxide produced to the volume of oxygen used

respirometer: a piece of apparatus that can be used to measure the rate of oxygen uptake by respiring organisms

resting potential: the difference in electrical potential that is maintained across the cell surface membrane of a neurone when it is not transmitting an action potential; it is normally about $-70\,mV$ inside and is partly maintained by sodium–potassium pumps

restriction endonuclease (restriction enzyme): an enzyme, originally derived from bacteria, that cuts DNA molecules; each type of restriction enzyme cuts only at a particular sequence of bases

R_f value: a number that indicates how far a substance travels during chromatography, calculated by dividing the distance travelled by the substance by the distance travelled by the solvent; R_f values can be used to identify the substance

ribosome: a tiny organelle found in large numbers in all cells; prokaryotic ribosomes are smaller (20 nm diameter) than eukaryotic ribosomes (25 nm diameter)

ribulose bisphosphate (RuBP): a five-carbon phosphorylated sugar which is the first compound to combine with carbon dioxide during the light-independent stage of photosynthesis

ring immunity: vaccinating all those people in contact with a person infected with a specific disease to prevent transmission in the immediate area

rubisco: the enzyme that catlalyses the combinbation of RuBP with carbon dioxide

saltatory conduction: movement of an action potential along a myelinated axon, in which the action potential 'jumps' from one node of Ranvier to the next

sarcolemma: the cell surface membrane of a muscle fibre

sarcomere: the part of a myofibril between two Z discs

sarcoplasm: the cytoplasm of muscle cells

sarcoplasmic reticulum (SR): the endoplasmic reticulum of muscle fibre

sclerenchyma: a plant tissue consisting of thick-walled cells with a purely mechanical function (strength and support); the cell walls have usually become impregnated with lignin and the mature cells are dead with no visible contents; many sclerenchyma cells take the form of fibres

secondary immune response: the second and any subsequent immune responses to a specific antigen

secondary structure: the structure of a protein molecule resulting from the regular coiling or folding of the chain of amino acids (an α-helix or β-pleated sheet)

seed bank: facility where seeds are dried and kept in cold storage to conserve plant biodiversity

selection pressure: an environmental factor that affects the chance of survival of an organism; organisms with one phenotype are more likely to survive and reproduce than those with a different phenotype

selective breeding: *see* **artificial selection**

selective reabsorption: movement of certain substances from the filtrate in nephrons back into the blood

self: refers to substances produced by the body that the immune system does not recognise as foreign, so they do not stimulate an immune response

semi-conservative replication: the method by which a DNA molecule is copied to form two identical molecules, each containing one strand from the original molecule and one newly synthesised strand

semilunar valve: a half-moon shaped valve, such as the ones in the veins and between the ventricles and arteries

sensory neurone: a neurone that transmits nerve impulses from a receptor to the central nervous system

septum: the layer of tissue that separates the left and right sides of the heart

set point: the ideal value of a physiological factor that the body controls in homeostasis

sex chromosomes: the chromosomes that determine sex; in humans, these are the X and Y chromosomes

sex-linked gene: a gene found on a region of a sex chromosome that is not present on the other sex chromosome; in humans, most sex-linked genes are found on the X chromosome

sexual reproduction: reproduction involving the fusion of gametes (fertilisation) to produce a zygote

sickle cell anaemia: a genetic disease caused by a faulty gene coding for haemoglobin, in which haemoglobin tends to precipitate when oxygen concentrations are low

sieve element or sieve tube element: a cell found in phloem tissue, with non-thickened cellulose walls, very little cytoplasm, no nucleus and end walls perforated to form sieve plates, through which sap containing sucrose is transported

sieve tube: tube formed by sieve elements lined up end to end

Simpson's index of diversity (*D*): used to calculate the biodiversity of a habitat; the range of values is 0 (low biodiversity) to 1 (high biodiversity)

sink: a site in a plant which receives food from another part of the plant, the source

sinoatrial node (SAN): a patch of cardiac muscle in the right atrium of the heart which contracts and relaxes in a rhythm that sets the pattern for the rest of the heart muscle

sliding filament model: the mechanism of muscle contraction; within each sarcomere the movement of thin filaments closer together by the action of myosin heads in the thick filaments shortens the overall length of each muscle fibre

smooth muscle: a type of muscle that can contract steadily over long periods of time

sodium–potassium pump (Na^+–K^+ pump): a membrane protein (or proteins) that moves sodium ions out of a cell and potassium ions into it, using ATP

source: a site in a plant which provides food for another part of the plant, the sink

Spearman's rank correlation: a statistical test to determine if there is a correlation between two variables when one or both of them are not normally distributed

speciation: the production of new species

species: *see* biological species

species diversity: all the species in an ecosystem

squamous epithelium: one or more layers of thin, flat cells forming the linings of blood vessels and alveoli

stabilising selection: natural selection that tends to keep allele frequencies relatively constant over many generations

stage micrometer: very small, accurately drawn scale of known dimensions, engraved on a microscope slide

standard deviation: a calculated value that indicates how widely a set of data spreads out from the mean value

standard error: a calculation that indicates how close the calculated mean value is likely to be to the true mean value

standardised variables: all variables (factors) that are kept constant in an experiment, which otherwise might affect the dependent variable

stem cell: a relatively unspecialised cell that retains the ability to divide an unlimited number of times, and which has the potential to become a specialised cell (such as a blood cell or muscle cell)

stimulus: (plural: **stimuli**) a change in the external or internal environment that is detected by a receptor and which may cause a response

stoma: (plural: **stomata**) a pore in the epidermis of a leaf, bounded by two guard cells and needed for efficient gas exchange

striated muscle: type of muscle tissue in skeletal muscles; the muscle fibres have regular striations that can be seen under the light microscope

stroma: the background material in a chloroplast in which the light-independent stage of photosynthesis takes place

structural gene: a gene that codes for a protein that has a function within a cell

substrate-linked reaction: in the context of ATP formation, the transfer of phosphate from a substrate molecule directly to ADP to produce ATP, using energy provided directly by another chemical reaction

surrogacy: a female becomes pregnant with an embryo from another female and carries it to full term; embryos can be conceived naturally, by AI or by IVF

sympatric speciation: the development of new species without any geographical separation

symplast pathway: the living system of interconnected protoplasts extending throughout a plant, used as a transport pathway for the movement of water and solutes; individual protoplasts are connected via plasmodesmata

synapse: a point at which two neurones meet but do not touch; the synapse is made up of the end of the presynaptic neurone, the synaptic cleft and the end of the postsynaptic neurone

synaptic cleft: a very small gap between two neurones at a synapse; nerve impulses are transmitted across synaptic clefts by neurotransmitters

systematic error: a source of uncertainty in your results that gives incorrect values that are always the same magnitude and always err in the same direction; systematic errors do not affect trends shown by results

systematic sampling: a non-random method of investigating the abundance and/or distribution of populations in which the position of sampling points are determined by the person carrying out the sampling (e.g. at every 2 m)

systemic circulation: the part of the circulatory system that carries blood from the heart to all of the body except the gas exchange surface, and then back to the heart

T-helper cell: type of T-lymphocyte that secretes cytokines to coordinate activity during immune responses

T-killer cell: type of T-lymphocyte that attaches to cells, releasing toxic substances to kill infected cells and cancer cells

T-lymphocyte (T cell): a lymphocyte that does not secrete antibodies; T helper lymphocytes stimulate the immune system to respond during an infection, and killer T lymphocytes destroy human cells that are infected with pathogens such as bacteria and viruses

taxon: (plural: **taxa**) a taxonomic group of any rank, such as a particular species (e.g. *Giraffa camelopardalis*), a family (e.g. Elephantidae), a class (e.g. Mammalia) or a kingdom (e.g. Plantae)

taxonomic rank: one of the groups used in the hierarchical classification system for organisms, e.g. species, genus, family, order, class, phylum, kingdom and domain

taxonomy: the study and practice of naming and classifying species and groups of species within the hierarchical classification scheme

telomere: repetitive sequence of DNA at the end of a chromosome that protects genes from the chromosome shortening that happens at each cell division

tertiary structure: the compact structure of a protein molecule resulting from the three-dimensional coiling of the already-folded chain of amino acids

test cross: a genetic cross in which an organism showing a characteristic caused by a dominant allele is crossed with an organism showing the dominant characteristic is crossed with a homozygous recessive organism; the phenotypes of the offspring can indicate whether the original organism is homozygous or heterozygous

threshold potential: the critical potential difference across the cell surface membrane of a sensory receptor or neurone which must be reached before an action potential is initiated

thylakoid: a flattened, membrane-bound, fluid-filled sac which is the site of the light-dependent reactions of photosynthesis in a chloroplast

thylakoid membranes: the membranes inside a chloroplast that enclose fluid-filled sacs; the light-dependent stage of photosynthesis takes place in these membranes

thylakoid spaces: fluid-filled sacs enclosed by the thylakoid membranes

tissue fluid: the almost colourless fluid that fills the spaces between body cells; it forms from the fluid that leaks from blood capillaries

tonoplast: the partially permeable membrane that surrounds plant vacuoles

trachea (windpipe): the tube-like structure that extends from the larynx to the bronchi; it allows movement of air into and out of the lungs

transcription: copying the genetic information in a molecule of DNA into a complementary strand of mRNA; a single strand of the DNA is used as a template (this is called the template or transcribed strand) – the enzyme responsible is RNA polymerase

transcription factor: a molecule that affects whether or not a gene is transcribed

transduction: occurs during cell signalling and is the process of converting a signal from one method of transmission to another

transect: a line marked by a tape measure along which samples are taken, either by noting the species at equal distances (line transect) or placing quadrats at regular intervals (belt transect)

transgenic organism: any organism that contains DNA from another source, such as from another individual of the same species or from a different species

translation: a stage in protein synthesis during which a sequence of nucleotides in a molecule of messenger RNA (mRNA) is converted (translated) into a corresponding sequence of amino acids in a polypeptide chain; it takes place at ribosomes

transmission cycle: the passage of a pathogen from one host to another is continually repeated as the pathogen infects new hosts

transpiration: the loss of water vapour from a plant to its environment; it mostly takes place through the stomata in the leaves

transverse system tubule (or T-system tubule or T-tubule): infolding of the sarcolemma that goes deep into a muscle fibre and conducts impulses to the SR

tricuspid valve: the atrioventricular valve on the right side of the heart

triglyceride: a type of lipid formed when three fatty acid molecules combine with glycerol, an alcohol with three hydroxyl ($-OH$) groups

triose phosphate (TP): a three-carbon phosphorylated sugar, the first carbohydrate to be formed during the light-independent stage of photosynthesis

tropomyosin: a fibrous protein that is part of the thin filaments in myofibrils in striated muscle; tropomyosin blocks the attachment site on the thin filament for myosin heads so preventing the formation of cross-bridges

troponin: a calcium-binding protein that is part of the thin filaments in myofibrils in striated muscle

t-test: a statistical procedure used to determine whether the means of two samples differ significantly

ultrafiltration: filtration on a molecular scale separating small molecules from larger molecules, such as proteins (e.g. the filtration that occurs as blood flows through capillaries, especially those in glomeruli in the kidney)

urea: a nitrogenous excretory product produced in the liver from the deamination of amino acids

V_{max}: the theoretical maximum rate of an enzyme-controlled reaction, obtained when all the active sites of the enzyme are occupied

vaccination: giving a vaccine containing antigens for a disease, either by injection or by mouth; vaccination confers artificial active immunity without the development of symptoms of the disease

vaccine: a preparation containing antigens to stimulate active immunity against one or several diseases

vacuole: an organelle found in eukaryotic cells; a large, permanent central vacuole is a typical feature of plant cells, where it has a variety of functions, including storage of biochemicals such as salts, sugars and waste products; temporary vacuoles, such as phagocytic vacuoles (also known as phagocytic vesicles), may form in animal cells; *see* endocytosis

variable region: region of an antibody molecule composed of parts of the light and heavy polypeptide chains that form the antigen-binding site; the amino acid sequences of the variable site form a specific shape that is complementary to a particular antigen

vascular: a term referring to tubes or vessels (from the Latin 'vascul', meaning vessel)

vascular bundle: a strand of vascular tissue running longitudinally in a plant; within the bundle, the arrangement of tissues like xylem, phloem and sclerenchyma varies in different plants and organs

vascular system: a system of fluid-filled tubes, vessels or spaces, most commonly used for long-distance transport in living organisms; examples are the blood vascular system in animals and the vascular system of xylem and phloem in plants

vasoconstriction: the narrowing of a muscular artery or arteriole, caused by the contraction of the smooth muscle in its walls

vasodilation: the widening of a muscular artery or arteriole, caused by the relaxation of the smooth muscle in its walls

vascular tissue: a tissue in plants consisting mainly of xylem and phloem but also containing sclerenchyma and parenchyma cells

vector: a means of delivering genes into a cell, used in gene technology; e.g. plasmids and viruses; *see also* disease vector

vein: vessel with relatively thin walls that carries low-pressure blood back to the heart

ventricle: one of the chambers of the heart that receives blood from the atria and then pushes it into the arteries

ventricular systole: the stage of the cardiac cycle when the muscle in the walls of the ventricles contracts

venule: small vein

virus: a very small (20–300 nm) infectious particle which can replicate only inside living cells; it consists of a molecule of DNA or RNA (the genome) surrounded by a protein coat; an outer lipid envelope may also be present

voltage-gated calcium ion channel protein: a channel protein in presynaptic membranes that responds to depolarisation by opening to allow diffusion of calcium ions down their electrochemical gradient

voltage-gated channel protein: a channel protein through a cell membrane that opens or closes in response to changes in electrical potential across the membrane

water potential: a measure of the tendency of water to move from one place to another; water moves from a solution with higher water potential to one with lower water potential; water potential is decreased by the addition of solute, and increased by the application of pressure; symbol for water potential is ψ or ψ_w

xerophyte: a plant adapted to survive in conditions where water is in short supply

xylem: a tissue containing tubes called vessels and other types of cell, responsible for the transport of water through a plant and for support

xylem vessel: a dead, empty tube with lignified walls, through which water is transported in plants; it is formed by xylem vessel elements lined up end to end

xylem vessel element: a dead, lignified cell found in xylem specialised for transporting water and support; the ends of the cells break down and join with neighbouring elements to form long tubes called xylem vessels

zygote: a cell formed by the fusion of the nuclei of two gametes; most zygotes are diploid

$\rangle$ Index

α-helix, 59
abiotic factors, 469
abscisic acid (ABA), 375, 415
absorption spectrum, 334–5
abundance, estimation, 512–13
abundance scale, 513
accuracy, 297
acetyl coenzyme A, 315
acetylcholine (ACh), 403–5
acetylcholinesterase, 404
actin, 407, 410,411
action potentials, 392, 395–401
    plants, 413–15
    stimulus for, 399–402
action spectra, 336
activation energy, 77–78
active immunity, 277–278
active site, 76–79 81–86
active transport, 113–14
adenine, 144–148
adeno-associated virus (AAV), 567.568
adenosine deaminase, 564,566
ADP (adenosine diphosphate), 26, 114
adrenaline, 368
aerenchyma, 322
aerobic respiration, 313–316 318
African bush elephants, 498, 523
ageing, 124, 133
AIDS (acquired immune deficiency syndrome),
    238–239 , 245–9
airways, examination, 224
albinism, 451
albumin, 202
alchemists, 124
alcohols, 54
algae, fuel production, 331
alien species, 530
all-or-none law, 401
alleles, 430 432–437, 439–440
allopatric speciation, 483–4, 486
AlphaZero, 44
alternative splicing, 152
alveoli, 225–31
amino acids, 45–46, 57–60 63–4 76–7, 82, 99–101
    150–156 322, 339
ammonia, 348, 351

amniocentesis, 565–6
AMP (adenosine monophosphate), 312–13
amylase, 80, 417, 456
amylase/starch experiment, 80
amylopectin, 50, 51
amylose, 50
anaerobic respiration, 314 320, 322–3
anaphase, 128, 129, 131, 430–432
animal cells, 5–8, 18–19, 24, 27–8
Animalia, 498, 501,504
anole lizards, 475, 486–7
Anopheles mosquitoes, 241–2
anthocyanins, 31
anti-cancer drugs, 523
antibiotic resistance, 254–65 472–3, 547,551
antibiotic sensitivity testing, 255–6
antibiotics, 251, 253–6
antibodies, 268–279
    functions, 275
    monoclonal, 281–2
    structure, 273–4
anticodon, 153–4
antidiuretic hormone (ADH), 359, 360
antigen presentation, 275
antigen–antibody binding, 274–5
antigens, 268–271 273–282
antiretroviral therapy, 248
antitoxins, 274–8
aorta, 194–7 200–213
apoplast pathway, 30, 174, 177–9 184–5
aquaporins, 360–3, 374
Archaea, 32, 499–500
arteries, 194–7, 199–200, 204, 210–12
arterioles, 195–201
artificial heart, 193
artificial insemination, 526
artificial intelligence, 44–5
artificial selection, 478–81
asexual reproduction, 131
assisted reproduction, 526
ATP (adenosine triphosphate), 25–6, 48 113–14, 145,
    312–322, 332,337–9 413
    structure, 312
    synthesis, 313,315–18, 337
ATP synthase, 316–18
atrial systole, 211–12

atrioventricular node (AVN), 215
atrioventricular valve, 210–13
atrium (atria), 210, 212–14
autolysis, 25
autosomal linkage, 445, 447
auxins, 415–16
axon, 389–406

β-galactosidase (lactase), 453–5
β-glucuronidase (GUS), 551
β-lactamase (penicillinase), 85, 254, 472
B-lymphocytes (B cells), 132, 270–2
β-pleated sheet, 58–9
Bacillus thuringiensis, 244, 271
bacteria, 32–3
   characteristic features, 500
   gene control, 453–4
   sites of action of antibiotics, 253
   structure, 32–3
bacterial plasmids, 547–8
bacteriophages, 545,552
bar charts, 300
BCG vaccine, 252, 280
bee orchids, 464
behavioural separation, 485–6
Benedict's test, 49–50, 78, 294
bicuspid valve, 210–11
biochemistry, 45
biodiversity, 507–20
   assessment, 509–12
   loss, 520–2
   reasons for maintaining, 521–4
bioinformatics, 562
biological classification, 497–8
biological drawings, 10, 164–70, 230–1, 304–5
biological species, 497
biological washing powders, 81–2
biosensor, 369–70
biotic factors, 469
biuret test, 65
bivalent, 430–36
black bear, 348
BLAST, 562
blood, 202–9
blood glucose, 349, 364–70
   measurement, 369–71
blood groups, 268, 283, 437, 465–6
blood pressure, 196, 198–200, 356
blood vessels, 195–199
blubber, 56
bobcat, North American, 522
Bohr shift, 206–7

Bombardier beetle, 75
bone marrow, 268–71,
bone marrow stem cells, 134
botanic gardens, 527–28
bottleneck effect, 476
Bowman's capsule, 352–56
Braun–Blanquet scale, 512
BRCA-1/BRCA-2 genes, 565
breast cancer, 282, 565
breathing, 228–9
bronchi, 226, 227
bronchioles, 226, 227, 228
bronchoscopy, 224
Bt toxin, 571
budding, 131
buffer solutions, 296
building blocks of life, 45

Caenorhabditis elegans, 563
Calvin cycle, 332, 339
cancers, 134–6
cane toads, 530
capillaries, 198–9, 201–03
capsid, 35
carbaminohaemoglobin, 208
carbohydrates, 46–53,
   synthesis, 339
carbon, 45
carbon dioxide 207–209
   photosynthesis, 332–37 340–2
   transport, 207, 208
carbonic anhydrase, 84, 85, 207–08
carcinogens, 134, 136
cardiac cycle, 211–145
cardiac muscle, 209, 210, 214
carotene, 334–5
carrier, 441
carrier proteins, 107–8, 113
cartilage, 226
Casparian strip, 178–9
cat species, extinctions, 520–1
catalase, 76–83
cattle, selective breeding, 480–2
cell biology, 4
cell cycle, 126–7
cell division, 124–5
cell membranes, 3, 20
   bacteria, 33
   molecules, 101–2
   movement of substances across, 104–15
   structure, 98–101
cell signalling, 102–4, 364

cell surface antigens, 268
cell surface receptor, 103
cell walls, 7–8, 30, 33
cell–cell recognition, 102
cells
    animal, 5–7
    plant, 5–10
cellulose, 30, 46, 52–3
centrioles, 7, 27–8, 130
centromeres, 126, 130
centrosomes, 27, 130
CFTR gene, 564–5
CFTR2 database, 563
channel proteins, 107–8, 118, 375, 395
Chargaff, Erwin, 146–7
Charpentier, Dr Emmanuelle, 554
cheetahs, 476, 525
chemiosmosis, 313, 317
chemoreceptors, 399–401
chi-squared (χ^2) test, 449–51, 594, 599
chiasma, 430–2
chloride shift, 208
chlorophyll, 332, 334–6
chloroplasts, 2, 6, 8, 26, 29–30, 333–6
chloroquine, 243
cholera, 239–41
cholesterol, 101
cholinergic synapses, 403
chorionic villus sampling, 565–6
chromatid, 125–6, 128, 130
chromatin, 7, 22, 126
chromatography, 335–6
chromosome mutations, 153
chromosomes, 7, 22
    human, 125, 429
    length, 126
    structure, 125–6
chymotrypsin, 85
cichlid fish, 485–6
cilia, 28–9, 228
ciliated epithelium, 227, 228, 229
circulatory system, 194–5
CITES (Convention on International Trade in
    Endangered Species), 531–2
classification, 497–505
clonal expansion, 271
clonal selection, 271
co-transporter, 184, 185, 357
coat colour, 428, 436, 437–8, 441,470–2
cocoa, 529
codominant alleles, 437

codon, 152–4
coenzyme A (CoA), 315
coevolution, 464
cohesion–tension, 177
collagen, 63–5
collecting duct, 352–55, 358–9, 361–63
collenchyma, 166
colorimeter, 79–80, 295
colostrum, 278
colour changes, observing/measuring, 295
community, 507
companion cells, 180, 181, 184
competition, 469, 521–2
competitive inhibition, 85–6
complementary base pairing, 147
conclusions, 301, 600
condensation reaction, 46, 48–9
confidence interval, 591
conservation organisations,
    international, 531–2
continuous variation, 465–8
controls, 297
coordination, in plants, 413–17
coral reefs, 508, 530
corals, 504, 557
coronary arteries, 210
corrective action, 350
correlation, 518–21
cotton, 571, 573
covalent bonds, 52
coyote, 522
creatine, 351
Crick, Francis, 145–6,
Crispr/Cas9, 552–4
cristae, 25
crops
    genetically modified, 570–3
    selective breeding, 478–9
    wild sources, 523–4
crossing over, 430–1, 433–4, 447–8
cuticle, 173
cyanobacteria, 499–500
cyclic AMP (cAMP), 361, 367
cyclic phosphorylation, 337
cysteine, 151
cystic fibrosis, 563, 564–5
cytokines, 276
cytokinesis, 127, 128, 129, 432
cytoplasm, 7
cytosine, 144, 146, 148
cytoskeleton, 102

Darwin, Charles, 496
data
    analysis, 301–3, 587–600
    describing, 301
    displaying, 299–300
databases, 562–3
deamination, 351
decarboxylation, 315
Deep Blue, 44
degrees of freedom, 450
dehydrogenation, 315
deletions, 155–6
DELLA protein, 456
dendrites, 390
dependent variable, 294, 303, 585
depolarisation, 396–7
diabetes mellitus, 368, 549
diastole, 212–13
dichlorophenolindophenol (DCPIP), 325, 343
dicotyledons, 164, 172, 178
diester, 145
diffusion, 104–8, 194, 228–9
    demonstration of, 105
    facilitated, 107–8
digestion, 114
digital biology, 562–3
dihybrid inheritance, 441–4
dihybrid test cross, 443
dinucleotides, 145, 146
diploid cells, 429
dipole, 53
direct observation treatment short course
        (DOTS), 251
directional selection, 471–2
disaccharides, 48–9
discontinuous variation, 465–9
discrete data, 585
discussion, 600
disease carriers, 238
disease defences, 267–8
disease resistance, 479
disease transmission, 238, 241
disease vectors, 241, 554
disruptive selection, 472
dissociation curve, 205
distal convoluted tubule, 352, 353, 359–60
disulfide bonds, 60, 61
DNA chip (microarray), 560–2
DNA (deoxyribonucleic acid), 7, 22, 125–6
    circular, 33
    complementary, 546, 547
    crime investigation, 543

mitochondrial (mtDNA), 486–7
    packaging ratio, 126
    recombinant (rDNA), 544, 549
    replication, 126–7, 149–50
    separating and amplifying, 555–6
    structure, 144–9
    synthesising, 546
    triplets, 152–3
DNA hybridisation, 560
DNA ligase, 149
DNA polymerase, 149, 547, 549, 556
dog species, extinctions, 520–1
domains, 498–9
dominant alleles, 437–9
double circulation, 194
Doudna, Dr Jennifer, 554
drawings, 10, 165–70, 230–1, 304–5
Drosophila melanogaster, 433, 445–8, 562
drug resistance, TB, 251
Durrell Wildlife Conservation Trust, 525

Ebola virus, 280
ecological separation, 485
ecosystems, 507–8
    environmental services, 524
effector, 350
elastic arteries, 197
elastic fibres, 228, 229
elastin, 228
electrochemical gradients, 374, 404
electromagnetic spectrum, 14–15
electron microscopy, 4, 14–17
electron transport chain, 316–18
elephants, 498, 523, 525
embryo transfer, 526–7
emulsion test, 56
end product inhibition, 87
endangered species, 524–7
    extinctions, 521
    protection, 524–9
endemic disease, 238
endemic species, 484, 507
endocrine glands, 388
endocrine system, 350, 388
endocytosis, 25, 114–15, 269–70
endodermis, 167
endoplasmic reticulum, 22–3
endosymbiont theory, 26
endothelium, 196
energy currency, 313
energy needs, 312
Ensembl, 562

environmental factors, 469
enzyme–product complex, 76–7
enzyme–substrate complex, 77, 78
enzymes, 75–88
    comparing affinities, 84–5
    definition, 75
    factors affecting action, 81–4
    immobilised, 87–8
    inducible, 455
    inhibitors, 85–7
    intracellular and extracellular, 76
    investigations, 79–81
    in membranes, 102
    mode of action, 76–8
    repressible, 455
    V_{max}, 84
epidemics, 239, 240
epidermal strips, 112
epidermis, 166
epistasis, 445
error bars, 591
errors, sources, 303–4, 600
Escherichia coli, 255–6, 454, 545–6, 549, 564
ester bonds, 54–5
ethanol fermentation, 320–2
ethical issues, 143, 522, 554, 568–70, 572–3
ethylene glycol, 86
eucalyptus trees, 162
eugenics, 569
Euglena, 331
Eukarya, 498
eukaryotes, 4, 34, 498
    characteristic features, 500
    gene expression, 455–6
evidence, evaluation, 600
evolution, 482–6
evolutionary bottleneck, 476
evolutionary relationships, 486–7
excretion, 351–2
exercise physiology, 231–2
exocytosis, 25, 114, 115
exons, 546
expansins, 416
experiments, 292
    conclusions/discussions, 301, 600
    description, 586
    evaluating evidence, 600
    planning, 582
    results, 298–9, 587
    risk assessment, 586
    variables, 292–7, 583–6
extinctions, 521

extremophiles, 499
eyepiece graticule, 11, 166

F_2 and F_2 generations, 439
F8 gene, 452
factor VIII, 452, 564
FAD (flavin adenine dinuceotide), 315, 316, 317, 320
fatty acids, 54
fertilisation, 429
    random, 435
fitness, 470
flagella, 28–9, 33, 34
fluid mosaic model, 99–101
fly orchid, 464
forensic science, 543
founder effect, 475–6
frame-shift mutations, 155–6
Franklin, Rosalind, 146–7
'frozen zoo', 527
fructose, 48
fuels, from algae, 331
fungi, 501–2

G protein, 103
Galapagos Islands, 496, 525
gametes, 428–32, 437
gas exchange, 224–31
    plants, 371–5
gel electrophoresis, 557–60
gene bank, 479
gene editing, 143, 552–4
gene expression, 453–6, 552
    detection, 561–2
    eukaryotes, 455–6
    prokaryotes, 453–5
gene mutations, 153–6, 465
gene pool, 475
gene probe, 545
gene therapy, 566–8, 569–70
gene transfer, 544
genes, 22, 125, 126, 150, 436
genetic code, 150–1
genetic diagrams, 437–9, 443–4
genetic diversity, 509
genetic drift, 474–5
genetic engineering, 544
genetic information, analysis and storage, 560–3
genetic isolation, 482–6
genetic markers, 551
genetic screening, 564–6, 568–9
genetic technology, 564
genetic variation, 433–5, 465–9

genetically modified organisms (GMOs), 544
   animals, 572
   ethical and social issues, 572–3
   plants, 570–2
genetics, 435–7
genome, 546
genome sequencing, 562–3
genotype, 436–7
geographical isolation, 483–4
giant panda, 526
gibberellin, 415–17, 453, 456
Gila monster, 487–8
globin, 62
glomerular filtrate, 355, 356–60
glomerular filtration rate, 356
glomerulus, 352–5
glucagon, 103, 364, 366–7
gluconeogenesis, 367
glucose, 46–7
   blood, 349, 364–71
   forms of, 46–7
   measurement in urine, 368–9
   storage, 50
glucose oxidase, 368–9
GLUT transporters, 364–5, 367
glycerate-3-phosphate, 339–40
glycerol, 54–5
glycine, 57
glycogen, 50, 51, 365
glycogenesis, 365
glycogenolysis, 367
glycolipids, 24, 101–2
glycolysis, 314–15, 318
glycoproteins, 24, 101–2
glycosidic bonds, 48, 49
goblet cells, 24, 227, 229
golden lion tamarin, 525
Golgi apparatus, 7, 23–4, 115, 227
Golgi vesicles, 23, 24, 115
gradients, 302
grana, 6, 8, 29, 333
graphs, 299–300, 302
green fluorescent protein, 551
growth, 124–5
guanine, 144, 146, 148
guanine triphosphate (GTP), 103
guard cells, 371–5

habitat, 508
haem group, 61, 63
haemoglobin, 61, 62–3, 155, 203
   sickle cell anaemia, 155, 452

haemoglobin dissociation curve, 205–7
haemoglobinic acid, 207
haemophilia, 440–1, 452, 467, 564
hairy-cell leukaemia, 135
haploid cells, 429
Hardy–Weinberg principle, 476–8
Hawaiian islands, 483–4
HBB gene, 452
heart
   artificial, 193
   structure, 209–11
heartbeat, 212–15
herbicide-resistant crops, 570–1
herd immunity, 279
Herpestes auropunctatus, 530
heterozygous, 436, 438, 439, 480
hexose, 46
hibernation, 348
hibiscus plants, 483, 498
hierarchical classification, 498–9
histograms, 300
histones, 126
HIV/AIDS, 238, 245–9
Holstein cattle, 481
homeostasis, 201, 349–52
   in plants, 371–5
homologous chromosomes, 430, 434–5
homozygous, 436, 438, 439
Hooke, Robert, 3
hormones, 350, 388–9
Howea spp., 484–5
HTT gene, 452–3
human evolution, 486
Hunter syndrome, 143
Huntington's disease, 452–3, 559–60, 564, 568–9
hybrid vigour, 480
hybridoma, 281–2
Hydra, 131
hydrogen bonds, 52–3, 59, 61, 147
hydrogencarbonate ions, 208
hydrolysis, 46, 48, 49, 58, 313
hydrophobic interactions, 60–1, 66
hydroxyl groups, 50, 52, 55
hypothalamus, 360, 361
hypothesis, 582–3

IAA (indole 3-acetic acid), 415
immune response, 132, 268, 270–2
immune system, 267, 268–77
immunity, 277–8
immunoglobulins, 273
immunological memory, 273

in vitro fertilisation (IVF), 311–12, 527
inbreeding, 479
inbreeding depression, 479–80
incidence of disease, 239
incipient plasmolysis, 111, 112
independent assortment, 434–5
independent variable, 293–4, 583–4
induced-fit hypothesis, 76–7
industrial melanism, 473–4
infectious diseases, 238–52
infliximab, 282–3
insect-resistant crops, 571
insecticides, 244
insertion, 155–6
insulin, 364, 365, 366, 370–1
    recombinant human, 549–51, 564
intermediate (relay) neurones, 389–90
International Potato Center (CIP), 524
International Rice Research Institute (IRRI), 479, 529
International System of Units (SI units), 4
interphase, 126
interrupted belt transect, 516–17
introns, 152, 546
iodine test, 80
ion channels, 103
ionic bonds, 60, 61
ipilimumab, 282
island populations, 483–4
islet of Langerhans, 364
IUCN (International Union for Conservation
    of Nature), 531

Japanese knotweed, 530

Kaposi's sarcoma, 247
karyogram, 429
keratin, 62
keystone species, 522
kidneys, 114, 352–63
kinetochores, 130–1
kingdoms, 498, 501–2
kite diagram, 516–18
Krebs cycle, 26, 315–16, 318, 351
kwashiorkor, 202

lac operon, 454, 552
lactase, 87–8, 453–5
lactate fermentation, 320–1
lactose, 48
lactose-free dairy products, 87–8
lamellae, 333
latex, 31
Le gene, 453

leaves
    adaptations, 173, 174
    stomata, 170, 172, 371–5
    structure, 168, 172
    water movements, 170–4
Leber congenital amaurosis, 567
leukaemia, 135
ligands, 103–4
light, and photosynthesis, 337–8, 340–3
light microscope, 4–5, 9
lignin, 30, 167, 175
Lincoln Index, 513
line graphs, 299–300
line transect, 516
link reaction, 315, 316, 319
Linnaeus, 497
lipids, 53–6, 323
liposomes, 97
Little Cayman, 525
liver, 366
lock-and-key hypothesis, 76
locus, 433
loop of Henle, 352, 358–9
lung cancer, 134, 135, 224
lungs, 225
lymphocytes, 204, 267, 268, 270–7
lysosomes, 24–5, 269, 270
lysozyme, 60, 77, 78, 85

macromolecules, 45–6
macrophages, 204, 228, 268, 269
magnification, 11–14, 165–6
maize, 468–9, 479–80, 524, 570, 573
malaria, 237, 239, 241–5
maltose, 48
Margulis, Lynn, 2
marine reserves, 525
mark–release–recapture, 514
marram grass, 173, 174
mass flow, 175, 183
mean, 301, 587
measles, 267, 280
measurements, 4, 11–14, 297, 303
median, 587–8
medicines, wild sources, 523
meiosis, 430–2, 433–4
melanin, 451, 452
membrane transport, 357
memory B cells, 271, 273
meristems, 132
mesophyll cells, 168, 170, 371
metabolic reactions, control, 86–7

metaphase, 128, 129
methionine, 151
methylene blue, 343
micelle, 98
Michaelis–Menten constant, 85
microarrays, 560–2
microsatellites, 559
microscopy
electron microscope, 4, 14–17
light microscope, 4–5, 9
measurements and magnification, 11–14
microtubule organising centres (MTOCs), 26, 130
microtubules, 26–7, 128, 129, 130
microvilli, 21, 357, 358
milk production, 480–2
Millennium Seed Bank, 528
minisatellites, 558–9
mitochondria, 2, 7, 25–6, 115, 319–20
mitochondrial disease, 311–12
mitochondrial DNA (mtDNA), 486–7
Mitochondrial Eve, 486
mitosis, 126, 127–32
MMR vaccine, 279
mockingbirds, 495, 496
mode, 588
monoclonal antibodies (Mabs), 281–3
monocotyledon, 164
monocytes, 204, 268
monohybrid crosses, 437, 439–40
monohybrid inheritance, 437–9
monomers, 46
monosaccharides, 46–8
morphological features, 482
morphological species, 497
mortality rate, 239
mosquitoes, 241, 243
motor neurones, 389–90
MRSA (methicillin-resistant *Staphylococcus aureus*),
255, 473
mucin, 24, 227
mucus, 227, 229
multiple alleles, 437
muscle contraction, 406–13
muscular arteries, 197
mutations, 134, 136, 153–6, 465, 472
Mycobacterium bovis, 249
Mycobacterium tuberculosis, 249, 250, 251, 253, 254
myelin, 391–2, 398, 399
myelin sheath, 101
myofibrils, 407, 408, 409
myoglobin, 60
myosin, 407, 411

NAD (nicotinamide adenine dinucleotide),
314, 338
NADP (nicotinamide adenine dinucleotide phosphate),
332, 338
national parks, 524–5
natural selection, 469–74
negative feedback mechanisms, 349, 368
nephrons, 352–5, 363
nerve impulse, 389
nerve impulses, 392–402
nervous system, 389–406
neuromuscular junction, 405
neurones, 389–90
neurotransmitters, 402
neutrophils, 204, 268, 269
niche, 508
nitrogen fixation, 33
nodes of Ranvier, 391–2
non-competitive inhibition, 86
non-cyclic phosphorylation, 338
non-self, 267
normal distribution, 588–9
nose, 226
nuclear division, 127
nuclear envelope, 21–2, 128
nuclear pores, 22
nucleic acids, 144
nucleolus, 7, 22
nucleotides, 144, 146
nucleus, 3, 5, 21–2, 124–5
null hypothesis, 451

ocicats, 428
oedema, 201
Okazaki fragments, 149
oncogene, 136
operon, 454
oral rehydration therapy, 240
orangutans, 521
organelles, 3, 7, 21–6, 34
oryx, scimitar-horned, 526
osmoreceptors, 360
osmoregulation, 360
osmosis, 108–12
ouabain, 397
outbreeding, 480
oxidation, 314
oxidative phosphorylation, 316–19
oxygen transport, 206–8
oxygen uptake, 228–9, 318, 324–5
oxygen-evolving complex, 338
oxyhaemoglobin, 205

paclitaxel, 523
palisade mesophyll, 168, 170
pancreas, 364
pancreatic acinar cells, 115
pandemic, 239
parenchyma tissue, 166, 176
parental types, 448
partial pressure, 205
passage cells, 179
passive immunity, 277–8
pathogen, 238
Pearson's linear correlation, 518, 519–20,
    594–6, 599
Penfield, Wilder, 387
penicillin, 252–3
penicillin resistance, 254–5, 472–3
penicillinase, 85, 254, 472
pentoses, 144–5
peppered moth, 473–4
pepsin, 82
peptide bonds, 58, 65
peptidoglycan, 33
percentage saturation, 205
peroxidase, 368–9
pH
    control in experiments, 296
    and enzyme activity, 81–2, 349
phages, 545
phagocytes, 115, 204, 267, 268–9
phagocytic cells, 228
phagocytosis, 115, 269–70
phenotype, 436–7
phenotypic variation, 465, 509
phloem, 163–4, 166, 180–5
phloem sap, 182–3
phosphodiester bonds, 145, 152
phospholipids, 35, 56, 98–9, 101
phosphorylation, 314
photoactivation, 337
photolysis, 332, 338
photosynthesis, 8, 29, 312, 332–3
    action spectra, 336
    equation, 332
    investigations, 342–3
    light-dependent stage, 332, 337–8
    light-independent stage, 332, 339
    limiting factors, 340–3
photosynthetic pigments, 334–6
photosystems, 334, 338
physiological features, 482
pili, 33
pinocytosis, 115

plant cells
    compared to animal cells, 5–8
    division, 128
    ultrastructure, 19–20
plant hormones, 415–17
plant transport, 162–85
    assimilates, 180–5
    need for, 163
    water, 170–80
Plantae, 502–3
plants
    control and coordination, 413–18
    height, 466
    homeostasis, 371–5
    vascular tissue, 163–4, 167, 168, 178
plasma, 200–1
plasma cells, 271, 273
plasma proteins, 200, 202
plasmids, 33, 254, 544, 547–9
plasmodesmata, 6, 8, 174, 175, 177–8, 181
Plasmodium spp., 239, 241
plasmolysis, 111–12
podocytes, 355–6
polar molecules, 53, 101
polio, 266
polygenes, 467
polymerase chain reaction (PCR), 555–6
polymers, 46
polymorphism, 472
polynucleotides, 144, 145, 148
polypeptides, 58
polysaccharides, 50–3
pooter, 510
population, 496
population size, estimation, 513–14
positive feedback, 350
potassium ions, 373–4, 375
potato, 524
potential difference, 114, 393, 396
pre-implantation genetic diagnosis (PGD), 569
precision, 297
prediction, 582
prenatal diagnosis, 565–6
prevalence of diseases, 239
primary immune response, 272, 274
probability, 450
prokaryotes, 4, 32–3
    domains, 499–500
    gene expression, 453–5
promoters, 454, 552
prophase, 128
proteases, 82

Protein Data Bank, 562, 563
protein kinase A, 367
protein synthesis, 151–4
protein-folding problem, 44–5
proteins, 57–65
   fibrous, 62, 63–5
   globular, 62–3
   primary structure, 58
   quaternary structure, 62
   secondary structure, 58–60
   tertiary structure, 60–2
   testing for, 65
   transport, 102
protoctists, 331, 332, 499–501
proton pumps, 184–5, 373, 374
protoplasm, 7
protoplast, 111
proximal convoluted tubule, 352, 353, 356–8
pulmonary capillaries, 230
pulmonary circulation, 194, 200
pulmonary ionocytes, 456
Punnett square, 438, 442
purines, 148, 351–2
Purkyne tissue, 215
pyrimidines, 148
pyruvate, 315, 320

quadrats, 510–12
qualitative data, 586
quantitative data, 298–9, 585–6
quinine, 243

R groups, 57, 62
rabbits, 469–72
random error, 303
random fertilisation, 435
random sampling, 511
range, 293, 588
reabsorption, 355–63
reaction centre, 334
receptor, 349
receptor cells, 399–401
receptor potential, 400–2
receptor protein, 403
recombinant human insulin, 549–50, 564
recombinant offspring, 448
red blood cells, 63, 110, 203, 207, 242
Red Cross, 280
red lionfish, 530
redox indicators, 325
redox reaction, 317
reduction, 314
reduction division, 432

reflex arc, 392, 393
refractory period, 397
regulatory gene, 453
renal artery, 352, 353
renal pelvis, 352
renal vein, 352, 353
rennin experiment, 292, 294, 297
replicates, 297
repolarisation, 396
reproductive isolation, 483
respiration, 312
   aerobic, 194, 313–19
   anaerobic, 320–2
   measuring rate of, 325
respiratory quotient (RQ), 323–5
respiratory substrates, 322–3
respirometer, 324–5
resting potential, 393–5
restriction endonucleases, 545–6
results, 298–9, 587
reverse transcriptase, 546, 547
ribonuclease, 58
ribosomes, 22, 23, 26, 33, 320
ribulose bisphosphate (RuBP), 339
rice, 523–4
   adaptation to flooding, 321–2
   selective breeding, 479
ring immunity, 280
risk assessment, 586
rituximab, 283
RNA interference (iRNA), 570
RNA polymerase, 151, 152, 552
RNA (ribonucleic acid)
   guide (gRNA), 553
   messenger (mRNA), 22, 151–2, 563
   ribosomal (rRNA), 22, 23
   structure, 149
   transfer (tRNA), 22, 152, 153, 154
Roll Back Malaria, 237
root hairs, 177
root tip squash, 132
roots
   structure, 167
   water movement, 177–9
rough endoplasmic reticulum, 23
Royal Botanic Gardens, Kew, 528
rubber, 46
rubisco, 339

S phase, 126–7
S (Svedberg) units, 23
S-shaped curve, 206

Sacks, Oliver, 387
salmon, GM, 572
saltatory conduction, 398
sampling, 511–13
San Diego Zoo, 527
sarcolemma, 406, 407, 408, 411
sarcoplasm, 406
sarcoplasmic reticulum, 407, 408
scanning electron microscope (SEM), 16
scatter graphs, 518, 598
Schwann cells, 391–2
sclerenchyma, 167, 176
sea otters, 522–3
second messengers, 103–4
secondary immune response, 272, 274
seed banks, 527–9
seed germination, 415–16, 456
selection pressures, 470–1
selective breeding, 478–82
selective reabsorption, 355, 356–60
self, 267
semi-conservative replication, 150
semilunar valves, 199, 212
sensory neurones, 389, 390, 392–3
septum (heart), 211
serial dilution, 293
set point, 350
severe combined immunodeficiency disease (SCID), 567, 568
sex chromosomes, 440–1
sex linkage, 440–1
sexual reproduction, 428
short tandem repeats (STRs), 559
sickle cell anaemia, 63, 155, 452, 467
sieve tubes, 180, 181, 183
signalling receptors, 102
Simpson's index of diversity, 514–15
sink, 180
sinoatrial node (SAN), 214
slide preparation, 9
smallpox, 238, 266, 280
smooth endoplasmic reticulum, 23
smooth muscle, 196, 228, 406
sodium–potassium pumps, 113–14, 357–8, 393–5, 397
soil water, 179–80
solutions, making up, 584–5
source, 180
Spearman's rank correlation, 519–20, 596–9
speciation, 482–6
species, 482, 496–7
species diversity, 508–13
species richness, 508

spindle, 128, 129, 130–1
spongy mesophyll, 168, 170
squamous epithelium, 196
stabilising selection, 471
standard deviation, 588–90
standard error, 589, 591
standardised variables, 295–6, 303
starch, 50–1
statistical tests, 587–9
staurosporine, 97
stem cells, 133–4
stem elongation, 453
stems
    structure, 167, 174–5
    water movements, 175–6
stimuli, 350
stomata, 170, 172, 371–5
striated muscle
    contraction, 410–13
    structure, 406–10
stroma, 333
structural genes, 453
suberin, 178–9
substitution, 155
substrate-linked reaction, 313
sucrose, 48, 49, 183–5
sugars, 46–50
    testing for, 49–50
sundews, 551
surface area:volume ratio, 106
surrogacy, 527
Svalbard Global Seed Vault, 528
sympatric speciation, 484–6
symplast pathway, 174, 177–8
synaesthesia, 387
synapses, 402–6
synaptic cleft, 402
syncytium, 406
systematic sampling, 511, 515–18
systemic circulation, 194, 200

T-helper cell, 275
T-killer cell, 275
T-lymphocytes (T cells), 132, 270, 275–7
t-test, 592–4, 598
Taq polymerase, 523, 556
taste buds, 400–1
taxon, 497
taxonomic rank, 498
taxonomy, 498
telomeres, 126, 127, 132–3
telophase, 128, 129

temperature
    control in experiments, 295–6
    and enzyme activity, 81
    human body, 350
    and photosynthesis, 341–3
tendons, 65
test cross, 439–40
threshold potential, 396
thylakoids, 29, 30, 333
thymine, 144, 146, 148
tissue fluid, 200–1, 349, 361
tobacco mosaic virus, 505–6
tonoplast, 6, 8, 111
totipotent stem cells, 133
tourism, 525
trachea, 225–7, 228, 229, 230
transcription, 151–2
transcription factors, 455–6, 552
transduction, 103
transects, 515
transgenic organisms, 544, 551
translation, 152–4, 154
transmission cycle, 238
transmission electron microscopy (TEM), 16
transpiration, 170–3
transport proteins, 102, 107–8
transverse system (T-system) tubule, 407, 408
trastuzumab, 282
tricuspid valve, 210
triglycerides, 55–6
triose phosphate, 314, 339–40
triploid, 433
tropomyosin, 410, 412
troponin, 410, 412
trypsin, 82
tuatara lizard, 488
tuberculosis (TB), 238, 249–52, 280
tubulin, 26
tumours, 134–5
TYR gene, 451–2
tyrosinase, 451–2

ultrafiltration, 354–5
ultrasound, prenatal, 565
UniProt, 562
units of measurement, 4
uracil, 144, 151
urea, 202, 348, 351–2, 357
ureters, 353
urine, 354–5
    measurement of glucose, 368–9
    reabsorption of water, 361–2
vaccinations, 238, 240, 244, 252, 266, 277, 279–81

vacuoles, 7, 8, 30–1, 115
Variable Number Tandem Repeats (VNTRs), 559
variable regions, 273
variables, 292–7, 583–6
variation, 465–9
vascular bundles, 166, 167, 168
vasoconstriction, 198
vasodilation, 198
vectors (of genes), 254, 544, 547–9
vectors (of disease), 241, 243, 554
veins, 199
venae cavae, 210, 211, 212
ventricles, 210
ventricular systole, 212
venules, 199
Venus fly trap, 413–14
Vibrio cholerae, 239–41
viruses, 34–5, 505–6
Visking tubing, 105
voltage-gated calcium ion channel protein, 403–4
voltage-gated channel protein, 395, 396

water, 52–3, 66–7
    control of body content, 360–3
    molecular structure, 52–3, 66
    photolysis, 332, 338
    properties of, 66–7
    transport in plants, 170–80
water hyacinth, 530
water potential, 109–10
    blood, 356, 357, 360
    measurement, 110
    plants, 112–13, 170–1, 373–4
    tissue fluid, 349
Watson, James, 145–6, 150
Wexler, Nancy, 559
wheat, 478–9
white blood cells, 115, 204, 267
World Health Organization (WHO), 238, 242, 244, 251, 252, 266, 279–81

X chromosomes, 440–1
xerophytes, 173, 174
XET, 416
xylem, 163–4, 168, 174–7, 180–5

Y chromosomes, 440–1
yeast cells, 325
Yellowstone National Park, 81, 524–5

Z-scheme, 338
zidovudine, 248
zoos, 525–6
zygote, 133, 428

› Acknowledgements

The authors and publishers acknowledge the following sources of copyright material and are grateful for the permissions granted. While every effort has been made, it has not always been possible to identify the sources of all the material used, or to trace all copyright holders. If any omissions are brought to our notice, we will be happy to include the appropriate acknowledgements on reprinting.

Thanks to the following for permission to reproduce images:

Cover Coldimages/Getty Images; **Unit 1** Steve Gschmeissner/SPL; Nancy R. Schiff/GI; Print Collector/GI; Dr Gopal Murti/SPL/GI; ISM/Phototake; Biomedical Imaging Unit, University of Southampton (x2); Power and Syred/SPL; CasarsaGuru/GI; Medimage/SPL; Biomedical Imaging Unit, used with the permission of University of Southampton; Biophoto Associates; Don Fawcett/SPL; NIBSC/SPL; Pasieka/GI; Dennis Kunkel Microscopy/SPL; Dr Gopal Murti/SPL; Bill Longcore/SPL; Dr Torsten Wittmann/SPL/GI; Biophoto Associates; NIBSC/GI; Dr Kari Lounatmaa/GI; Luismmolina/GI; Smith Collection/Gado/GI; Dr David Furnless, Keele University/GI; Steve Gschmeissner/SPL; **Unit 2** Chris Frost/GI; Alfred Pasieka/SPL/GI; Dr Jeremy Burgess/SPL; Biophoto Associates/SPL; Tom Mchugh/SPL; Dr Arthur Lesk/SPL; Omikron/SPL; Omikron/SPL; Steve Gschmeissner/SPL; J. Gross, Biozentrum/SPL; **Unit 3** Wolfgang Baumeister/SPL; EdwardSnow/GI; Div. of Computer Research & Technology, National Institute of Health/SPL; Richard Fosbery; Simon Fraser/SPL; **Unit 4** SPL/GI; David Mccarthy/SPL; Don W. Fawcett/SPL; J.C. Revy, ISM/SPL; Don W. Fawcett/SPL; **Unit 5** Sciepro/GI; Will Brown/ Chemical Heritage Foundation/SPL; Biophoto Associates; Arturo Londono, ISM/SPL; Eric Grave/SPL; Kage Mikrofotografie Gbr/SPL; Eric Grave/SPL; Adrian davies/Alamy; SPL; James Steveson/SPL; SPL; Eye of Science/SPL; SPL; **Unit 6** Stocktrek Images/Superstock; Kimberly White/GI; Donaldson Collection/GI; SPL/GI; Universal History Archive/GI; **Unit 7** Moment/GI; Dea/Random/GI; © CSIRO Australia, from article 'Gilding the gumtree - scientists stike gold in leaves', October 2013; Biodisc, Visuals Unlimited/SPL; Dr Keith Wheeler/SPL; Biophoto Associates/SPL; Power and Syred/SPL; Sinclair Stammers/SPL; Power and Syred/SPL; Power and Syred/SPL; Geoff Jones; Dr Keith Wheeler/SPL; Dr Keith Wheeler; Biophoto Associates/SPL; Steve Gschmeissner/GI; Biophoto Associates/SPL; Dr Jeremy Burgess/SPL; Dr Keith Wheeler/SPL; Biophoto Associates/SPL; Bill Brooks/Alamy; **Unit 8** Spanteldotru/GI; Dpa picture alliance/Alamy; CNRI/SPL; Steve Gschmeissner/SPL; Ed Reschke/GI; Dennis Kunkel Microscopy/SPL; Steve Allen/SPL; Steve Gschmeissner/SPL/GI; Steve Gschmeissner/SPL; SPL/GI; CNRI/SPL; National Geographic Image Collection/Alamy; **Unit 9** John Greim/GI; RGB Ventures/Alamy; BSIP/GI; John Adds; Biophoto Associates/SPL; Eddy Gray/SPL; Jose Calvo/SPL; Biomedical Imaging Unit, University of Southampton; CNRI/SPL/GI; Jose Calvo/SPL; Microscape/SPL; Vincent Starr Photography/GI; **Unit 10** David Scharf/SPL; RGB Ventures/Alamy; Eye of Science/SPL; Dpa picture alliance/Alamy; Cecil H. Fox/SPL; Omikron/SPL; AusAID/Alamy; Eye of Science/SPL; Cordelia Molloy/SPL; Kwangshin Kim/SPL; AFP/GI; Steve Turner/Alamy; John Durham/SPL; Dennis Kunkel Microscopy/SPL; **Unit 11** Eye of Science/SPL; Xinhua/Alamy; Biophoto associates/SPL; Biophoto associates; Steve Gschmeissner/SPL; Dr Tim Evans/SPL/GI; Karen Kasmauski/GI; Hank Morgan/SPL; Omikron/SPL; **P1** Caiaimage/Sam Edwards/GI; Geoff Jones; Dr Keith Wheeler/SPL; Visuals Unlimited/SPL; **Unit 12** Steve Gschmeissner/SPL; Professors P.M. Motta, S. Makabe & T. Naguro/SPL; Don W. Fawcett/SPL; Geoff Jones; **Unit 13** Frank Krahmer/GI; David Maung/Bloomberg via GI; Biophoto associates; Martyn F. Chillmaid/SPL; **Unit 14** Steve Gschmeissner/SPL/GI; John Hyde; Richard Fosbery; Kage Mikrofotografie Gbr/SPL; Image Source/GI; Dennis Kunkel Microscopy/SPL; Steve Gschmeissner/SPL; Sciepro/SPL; Biomedical Imaging Unit, used with the permission of University of Southampton; Lothar Drechsel/GI; Jim Varney/SPL; Power and Syred/SPL; Biophoto Associates/SPL; Kage Mikrofotografie Ggr/SPL; Dr. Fred Hossler, Visuals Unlimited/SPL; **Unit 15** Alfred Pasieka/SPL; William Taufic/GI; Alvin Telser/SPL; Biophoto Associates; Dr Donald Fawcett and R. Coggeshall, Visuals Unlimited/SPL; Thomas Deerinck, NCMIR/SPL; Ed Reschke/GI; Innerspace Imaging/SPL; Biophoto Associates/SPL; Margot Fosbery; Maximilian Weinzierl/Alamy; Thierry Berrod, Mona Lisa Production/SPL; Dr Rosalind King/SPL; **Unit 16** Equinox Graphics/SPL; Mary Jones; Biophoto Associates; Image from "The Use of Grasshopper Chromosomes to Demonstrate Meiosis" in Tuatara: Journal of the Biological Society of Victoria University of Wellington, 18 (1), 1970, by J. M. Martin; Friedrich Stark/Alamy; **Unit 17** All Canada Photos/GI; Richard Becker/Alamy; Hulton Deutsch/GI; Nature